Creating a Learning Society

KENNETH J. ARROW LECTURE SERIES

KENNETH J. ARROW LECTURE SERIES

Kenneth J. Arrow's work has shaped the course of economics for the past sixty years so deeply that, in a sense, every modern economist is his student. His ideas, style of research, and breadth of vision have been a model for generations of the boldest, most creative, and most innovative economists. His work has yielded such seminal theorems as general equilibrium, social choice, and endogenous growth, proving that simple ideas have profound effects. The Kenneth J. Arrow Lecture Series highlights economists, from Nobel laureates to groundbreaking younger scholars, whose work builds on Arrow's scholarship as well as his innovative spirit. The books in the series are an expansion of the lectures that are held in Arrow's honor at Columbia University.

JOSEPH E. STIGLITZ AND BRUCE C. GREENWALD

CREATING A LEARNING SOCIETY

A New Approach to Growth, Development, and Social Progress

Columbia University Press
New York

Columbia University Press
Publishers Since 1893
New York   Chichester, West Sussex
cup.columbia.edu

Library of Congress Cataloging-in-Publication Data
Stiglitz, Joseph E. Creating a learning society :
a new approach to growth, development, and social progress /
Joseph E. Stiglitz and Bruce C. Greenwald; with commentary and contributions
from Philippe Aghion, Kenneth J. Arrow, Robert M. Solow, and Michael Wood Ford.
pages cm. — (Kenneth Arrow Lecture)
Includes bibliographical references and index.
ISBN 978-0-231-15214-3 (cloth : alk. paper) —
ISBN 978-0-231-52554-1 (ebook)
1. Social learning. 2. Information society.
3. Progress. I. Greenwald, Bruce C.
II. Title. III. Series.

HQ783.S694 2014
303.3'2—dc23
2013047698

Columbia University Press books are printed on permanent
and durable acid-free paper.

This book is printed on paper with recycled content.
Printed in the United States of America

c 10 9 8 7 6 5 4 3 2 1

Cover design: Noah Arlow

Contents

Preface

THIS VOLUME is the result of the first in a series of lectures to honor one of Columbia University's most outstanding graduates, Kenneth J. Arrow, who received his Ph.D. from Columbia in 1951. His thesis, later published as *Individual Choice and Social Values*, was a landmark in economics, philosophy, and political science. In the more than sixty years that followed, Ken went on to become a giant in economics, political science, organization theory, and operations research.

Columbia University has had a long line of distinguished graduates and faculty—including six Nobel Prizes in the past thirteen years. The faculty list for economics includes Milton Friedman, who taught at Columbia for ten years; Arthur Burns, who served on President Eisenhower's Council of Economic Advisers from 1953 to 1956 and as chair of the Federal Reserve Board from 1970 to 1978; and Wesley Mitchell, who along with Burns played a central role in founding the National Bureau of Economic Research, one of the nation's most important think tanks, which focused in its earlier years on enhancing understanding of economic fluctuations. There are a host of other greats, known more to those within the economics profession than those outside, including Harold Hotelling, Albert Hart, and John Bates Clark (whose namesake medal is awarded every year to the economist under forty who has made the most significant contribution to economics; Arrow was the fifth recipient of the honor.)

With all of these potential luminaries, our decision to honor Kenneth Arrow was easy: No individual has done more to change how we think about economics—and about society beyond economics—during the past six decades. In a sense, virtually all theorists—and most policymakers—of our generation are students of Arrow (and, it might be added, our students can be considered their "grandstudents"). Ideas that he first put forward a half-century ago have permeated our thinking.

A lecture series like this provides the opportunity to approach issues a little bit more expansively than one is able to in journal articles. When we initiated the series, we had hoped that it would open up a lively discussion about a variety of areas within economics, political science, and philosophy. The Committee of Global Thought spans multiple disciplines, and Arrow is one of the few scholars of recent decades whose work has cut across fields, having profound implications on each. One of the reasons why it is a particular pleasure to have Ken Arrow as the honoree of this lecture series is that we hoped to focus every year on one aspect of Ken's work. Since Ken has written about so many different areas, this would make the lecture series broad, engaging people from throughout the university community.

The lecture series has lived up to our hopes. In the first lecture, in late 2008, Bruce Greenwald and I focused on one aspect of Arrow's contribution to our understanding of growth: how technological progress is related to what we do. It was, in a sense, the founding paper in what has since blossomed into a huge literature on endogenous growth, where the pace of innovation is the central object of study.

The second lecture took up Arrow's seminal thesis, in which he asked a question of greater generality than had ever been posed—and academia has struggled to come to terms with the disturbing answer that he provided. Nearly two hundred years earlier, the great French mathematician Nicolas de Condorcet had shown that a democracy, making a choice among three alternatives by a majority vote, might not be able to reach a determinate answer. Alternative A might be preferred over B by a majority, B over C by a majority, and C over A by a majority. Under a set of plausible hypotheses, Arrow showed that this problem could arise with any voting mechanism (with the obvious exception of giving all decision-making power to a single individual).

The implications of this—and the conditions in which this seeming paradox might not hold—were discussed in the Second Annual Arrow Lecture, delivered at Columbia University on December 11, 2009, by two distinguished Nobel Prize winners who have devoted considerable intellectual energies to understanding the Arrow Impossibility Theorem, Eric Maskin and Amartya Sen.

In 2010, we turned to his contributions to financial markets, with a lecture by Jose Scheinkman, then of Princeton University and now of Columbia (with discussions from Patrick Bolton of Columbia University and Sanford Grossman).

The 2011 lecture focused on Arrow's contributions to the environment, and climate change in particular, with a lecture by Sir Partha Dasgupta, and discussions by Geoffrey Heal and Scott Barrett, both of Columbia University. In 2012, Amy Finkelstein of MIT, along with discussant and MIT colleague Jonathon Gruber, continued Ken Arrow's pathbreaking work in the economics of health, a paper written forty-seven years earlier, whose influence continues today, and which was also a pathbreaking paper in the broader area of the theory of moral hazard.

In 2013, we returned once again to climate change, with a lecture by Christian Gollier of the Toulouse School of Economics entitled "Pricing the Planet's Future: The Economics of Discounting in an Uncertain World," with discussions by Bernard Salanié of Columbia, Stiglitz, and Arrow.

What made each of these occasions so exciting—and moving—was Arrow's participation and his reactions to these lectures inspired by his own work.

What also made these occasions moving was that the speakers had not only a strong intellectual bond with Arrow but also close personal ties—sometimes as students, often as colleagues. No one that we have approached to give the Arrow Lecture has ever turned us down—everyone, as busy as they are, went to great lengths to rearrange their schedules so they could have this opportunity to show their respect and honor for one of the century's great economists. Each delivered a lecture worthy of the person they were honoring.

The inaugural lecture of the series, on November 12, 2008, was an especially important event, because it brought together Ken Arrow and Robert Solow, two of the economists who were responsible for creating a new field of economics—growth theory—perhaps the most important area in the decades immediately after World War II. The events gave them an opportunity to reflect on what has happened to the subject in the half-century since their seminal contributions. Philippe Aghion of Harvard supplemented his comments on the lecture by offering his observations on industrial policy (one of the main topics of the talk) in the paper published here, "The Case for Industrial Policy."

The original lecture has been extended (partly at the suggestion of Solow and Arrow) into a fuller treatment of the subject. In the original lecture, Bruce Greenwald and I had focused our attention on showing how Arrow's insights into learning necessitated rethinking one of the most fundamental tenets of modern economics, the virtues of free trade. We showed that there was an infant-economy argument for protection. Solow and Arrow observed that our analysis showing the desirability of government intervention into the market applied equally forcefully to a closed economy, without trade. We publish here their comments on our original lecture. The research that we did subsequently, and report here, shows how right they were.

This volume begins with introductory remarks by Bruce Greenwald and me, our personal tribute to Ken, showing our affection and respect.

Joseph E. Stiglitz,
University Professor and Co-Chair of
the Committee on Global Thought,
Columbia University

Acknowledgments

Acknowledgments for the Series

The Kenneth J. Arrow Lecture Series has been made possible through the efforts of Columbia University's Committee on Global Thought (which I chaired at the time the series was inaugurated, and which is now co-chaired by Saskia Sassen) and by the Program in Economic Research (PER) of the Department of Economics at Columbia University (chaired by Michael Woodford) with the support and encouragement of the Columbia University Press.

We are especially indebted to Robin Stephenson, Gilia Smith, and Sasha de Vogel of the Committee on Global Thought and Myles Thompson and Bridget Flannery-McCoy of the Press for guiding this book to publication.

We are grateful for the support of the Kaufman Foundation, who funded the Inaugural Lecture.

Acknowledgements for the First Arrow Lecture

While this lecture represents a continuation of my extraordinarily fruitful collaboration with Bruce Greenwald, extending now for more than three decades, my work on the topics covered here goes back to my days as a graduate student, with a half-century of accumulated debts. I need to begin by especially thanking two of my teachers, who were present at the lecture at which the earlier version of these ideas was presented, Kenneth Arrow and Robert Solow. At the time I was a graduate student, growth theory was all the rage, and *endogenous* growth theory—explaining the rate of technological progress—absorbed much of our attention. I was fortunate to be able to spend time not only at MIT but also at the University of Chicago and Cambridge University. At MIT, I should acknowledge the influence of Evsey Domar, Paul Samuelson, and Franco Modigliani; at Cambridge, of Nicholas Kaldor, James Meade, James Mirrlees, David Champernowne, and Frank Hahn. Hirofumi Uzawa brought a group of us together from throughout the United States for a summer at the University of Chicago to discuss these issues—including George Akerlof, Eytan Sheshinki, and Karl Shell. While at Cambridge, I began my collaborations with Tony Atkinson and Partha Dasgupta, and the ideas developed with them permeate this book. Other coauthors whose ideas are discussed extensively below and who have influenced my thinking on the topics discussed here include Karla Hoff, Raaj Sah, Barry Nalebuff, Carl Shapiro, Richard Arnott, Avi Braverman, Andrew Charlton, Mario Cimoli, Michael Cragg, Domenico Delli Gatti, Giovanni Dosi, Avinash Dixit, Shahe Emran, David Ellerman, Jean-Paul Fitoussi, Drew Fudenberg, Jason Furman, Mauro Gallegati, Richard Gilbert, Sandy Grossman, Geoff Heal, Thomas Hellman, Claude Henry, Arjun Jayadev, Kevin Murdoch, David Newbery, Akbar Noman, Jose Antonio Ocampo, Michael Salinger, Marilou Uy, Alec Levinson, and Andy Weiss.

And then there are the host of others with whom I have had discussions on the topics included here, who have helped shape my thinking, and whose influence can be felt in the pages below. These include Alice Amsden, Amar Bhide, Hans Binswanger, Bob Evenson, Ha-Joon Chang, Paul David, Gene Grossman, Glen Loury, Peter Howitt, Justin Lin, Mort Kamien, Edwin Mansfield, Richard Nelson, Takashi Omari, Edmund Phelps, Hamid Rashid, Jerome Reichman, Rob Porter, Dani Rodrik, Paul Romer, Nancy Schwartz, Michael Spence, Robert Wade, Michael Whinston, and Sidney Winters.

We need to extend a special thanks to the participants in the lecture, and especially the commentators, including Philippe Aghion, Kenneth Arrow, Robert Solow, and Michael Woodford.

For this volume, the authors wish to express their gratitude to Julia Cunico, Kevin Findlan, Laura Morrison, Hannah Assadi, and most importantly, to Ava Seave and Anya Schiffrin.

I should also acknowledge the team of research assistants who helped prepare the book. Special thanks goes to Laurence Wilse-Samson and Eamon Kircher-Allen for their much appreciated assistance in preparing this manuscript. Sandesh Dhungana, An Li, Erin Kogan, and Feiran Zhang also provided valuable input.

Joseph Stiglitz, 2012

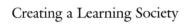

Creating a Learning Society

Introduction

JOSEPH E. STIGLITZ AND BRUCE C. GREENWALD

IT WAS a real pleasure for us to deliver the First Annual Kenneth J. Arrow Lecture at Columbia University—to honor our teacher, someone who has had a lifelong influence on our thinking, as he has had on an entire generation of economists.

There is, in fact, a sense in which everyone in our generation was a student of Kenneth Arrow—even those who were not fortunate enough to take his class. His ideas influenced us, as did his style of research and his breadth of vision. He is a true model of a scientist. He could provide the definitive proof of the Pareto optimality of the competitive equilibrium (the first fundamental theorem of welfare economics), then go on to explain why the assumptions were wrong—and then go on to develop models incorporating more realistic assumptions, overturning the earlier conclusions about the efficiency of the market.

Both Arrow and Robert Solow, another of our teachers that our lecture honored, performed just those kinds of analytical feats in a series of papers that inspired this volume. The first was a paper that Solow wrote in 1956, which showed that an increase in the savings rate would *not* lead to an increase in the long-run growth rate—that was determined by the rate of productivity growth. Then, in 1957 he decomposed the sources of economic growth and argued that most of economic growth was related not to increases in factors of production—like labor and capital—but rather to increases in productivity. Before that, economists focused on savings and capital accumulation, but not on the role of technological progress, as the source of the enormous increases in our standard of living over the past two hundred years.

In 1962 Ken Arrow published two important papers attempting to explain technological progress. One focused on research and development (1962b) and the other on learning by doing (1962a). This latter paper observed that, in the process of producing and investing, one learns. As we produce and invest, we get better at what we do. If one builds more ships, one becomes more efficient at building ships. Productivity increases. This was one of the earliest papers on what has come to be called endogenous growth theory, where the pace of innovation is determined within the model.

Each of the Arrow lectures is intended to build off one of Arrow's pathbreaking contributions. For our lecture, we took his work on innovation, in particular his remarkable 1962 paper on learning by doing. That paper itself is in part a commentary on an earlier important Arrow paper. Two hundred and forty years ago Adam Smith talked about the efficiency of the competitive market economy. He argued that competitive equilibrium was efficient, that the pursuit of self-interest would lead, as if by an invisible hand, to the well-being of society. It took a long time for economists to determine in what sense that was true (what economists now refer to as Pareto optimality) and the circumstances under which it was true. The critical works proving the conditions under which competitive equilibrium was in fact Pareto efficient were Arrow's (1951b) and, contemporaneously, Gerard Debreu's (1952; also Arrow and Debreu 1954).

Arrow had assumed in that paper that technology was fixed, that is, that there was no innovation.[1] His paper on learning by doing challenged that assumption. For a modern economy, innovation is clearly central. In that paper, as well as in his other 1962 paper on R & D (1962b), Arrow explained why the production of knowledge is very different from the production of conventional goods.

When technology is endogenous, markets are not, in general, efficient. But this immediately raises a further question: How should government intervene in the market to enhance efficiency and societal welfare? Remarkably, in the fifty years since Arrow's 1962 paper, that question has been addressed only in a piecemeal way (e.g., in discussions about intellectual property and patent policy).

In our lecture, we investigated the implications of learning by doing for the long-standing presumption in favor of free trade. It made for a good lecture topic, which gave way to a day of useful discussions and interesting reactions, many of which are included at the end of this volume. But as we prepared our lecture for publication—since the Arrow lectures' inception, a book series was planned to accompany them—and we took to heart the comments made by Arrow and Solow, it became clear to us that to do justice to the issues we had raised required more than a short lecture. Arrow's work had opened the door to a large body of fresh analysis on how to create a learning economy and society—and how government can and should intervene to improve societal well-being.

That we chose Arrow's learning perspective as the foundation for our lecture—and the subsequent elaboration that resulted in this volume—is neither coincidence nor contrivance. Rather, Arrow's work proved the perfect starting point for the same reason that the lecture series was named after him: The contributions he made to the field are still so important that half a century later they are often the ineluctable jumping-off point for present-day work.

Like other great economists of his generation (including Solow), Arrow has ultimately been interested in improving the practice of economic policy. Clarifying economic thinking, while valuable in itself, really accrues value in the course of being applied to particular situations where policy decisions are being made, in some cases being made badly, almost always in ways that can be improved upon. In approaching the question of free trade from Arrow's learning perspective, not only do we honor his legacy and challenge the conventional views, but also hopefully we make a contribution to a key set of policy issues: how to increase the pace by which living standards increase, especially in developing countries.

The fact that markets on their own are not efficient when innovation is endogenous raised the question which is at the heart of our lecture and the book to which it gave rise: What should be the role of policy in promoting economic efficiency? Advocates of unfettered markets often respond to this question by championing the market's ability to innovate. But there is remarkably little systematic inquiry into whether markets generate the optimal level and form of innovation. Our lecture was intended to fill this gap, with specific applications to trade policy.

There was at the time we delivered our lecture already a long-standing exception to the presumption in favor of free trade in the idea that it might be appropriate to protect infant industries.[2] Thus, if a particular industry grew with protection, and got stronger as it grew because it benefited from economies of scale, one might think there was an argument to protect that industry. There is a second exception to the principle of free trade associated with price manipulation. If a country has a large industry in the world economy, then it can manipulate the terms of trade (that is, international prices) to its benefit. These two exceptions are related, and under careful scrutiny the second argument enhances our understanding of the limits of the first: if one does not alter the terms of trade, it does not matter where the protected industry develops. Nigeria might, say, protect its auto industry until it was strong enough to compete in global markets. But if that industry can efficiently develop in England—and as long as the import prices reflect the productivity gains—Nigerians will benefit by buying and importing those cars just as much as people in England do.[3]

In fact, the terms-of-trade argument has always been a fairly weak argument. The argument that countries, even the United States, can move the terms of trade is difficult to make in practice. Thus, the standard theories do not provide very persuasive reasons for trade interventions. Nevertheless, there seems to be a persistent pattern of *successful* economies practicing trade restrictions.

In thinking about this problem, we applied Arrow's lessons in a way that brought us to a different conclusion, which forms the heart of this lecture and book. Our analysis shows that these successes are not based on the infant-industry argument for protection, where there are benefits *within* an industry to learning by doing. Instead, there is an infant *economy* argument for trade interventions. The intuition is remarkably simple: We explain why innovation is likely to be more centered in the industrial sector rather than the agricultural or craft sector. The industrial sector is not only better at learning, but also generates more externalities—more learning benefits—to the rest of the economy. An economy that starts out without a strong urban industrial sector—one that is importing those goods—is unlikely to develop improvements in productivity, even within that sector. There is little learning, little innovation. Trade barriers are necessary to enable that economy to develop those industrial enterprises even though it might seem inefficient to do so in the beginning, because it runs counter to the country's current comparative advantage.

So far, the argument runs parallel to that of the standard infant-industry argument. But here is where the difference arises: enterprises in protected industries will generate productivity growth not only in their sector, but also across different individual products within that sector—and also across to agriculture and other sectors of the economy. It is the externalities generated by the sector that provide the real rationale for intervention.

The classic example of this is, of course, the Agricultural Extension Service in the United States, where principles of industrial research got applied to farms in an extraordinarily efficient manner. As much as anything, it accounts for the remarkable growth in agricultural productivity in the United States.

That was the basic idea that we proposed in our lecture. It calls for a kind of protection that is not industry specific. The classic complaint about infant-industry arguments—that trying to pick successful industries is a doomed effort—does not apply. This is an argument for a broad set of tariff barriers (or exchange rate interventions), within which one hopes that the best industries will survive and prosper.

A Guide to This Volume

In the years following the first lecture, our ideas took on new life. As we worked the ideas of our lecture into different papers and continued our research on related topics, it became clear to us that we had more than a slim conference volume's worth of material. Our lecture on "creating a learning society" was growing into a full-fledged body of theory that required historical context, examples of general and specific applications, and discussions of political economy. With that realization, this book began to take shape. The result is something far more expansive than the original lecture, though the core intellectual inspirations for the book are the same as those that guided us in 2008.

In the first few chapters of this book, we lay out our basic theses: that most of the increases in standards of living are, as Solow suggested, a result of increases in productivity—learning how to do things better. And if it is true that productivity is the result of learning and that productivity increases (learning) are endogenous, then a focal point of policy ought to be increasing learning within the economy; that is, increasing the ability and the incentives to learn, and learning how to learn, and then closing the knowledge gaps that separate the most productive firms in the economy from the rest. Therefore, *creating a learning society should be one of the major objectives of economic policy.* If a learning society is created, a more productive economy will emerge and standards of living will increase. By contrast, we show that many of the policies focusing on static (allocative) efficiency may in fact impede learning and that alternative policies may lead to higher long-term living standards. Thus, the theory that we develop provides one of the most compelling and fully articulated critiques of the Washington consensus policies that dominated development thinking in the quarter century before the Great Recession. The theory also provides the basis of a new theory of the firm—a new answer to the question posed more than 75 years ago by Ronald Coase: What determines the boundaries of firms, what goes on inside the firm? It also provides a new approach to thinking about both static and dynamic comparative advantage.

Part One also gives the reader a view of the historical, empirical, and theoretical background and justification for our learning-society perspective. We describe key aspects of creating a learning society: the processes and determinants of learning and some of their broad implications for economic architecture—the design of the economic system and its subcomponents (most importantly, firms)—and policy. We explain the implications of "localization of knowledge" (both technologically and spatially), extend the concept of learning by doing to learning to learn by learning, explain why geographically concentrated large enterprises, traditionally in the industrial sector but more recently in the modern services sector, have been at the center of growth—with high rates of productivity increases and large spillovers to other sectors of the economy. We explain, too, the link between macro-stability and long-run productivity growth—a new rationale for why *real* macro-stability is so important.

Having analyzed the basic determinants of learning, we address two critical questions: Is there likely to be more or less learning in economies that are more competitive (with more firms)? And is the market likely to be efficient in the level and pattern of innovation and learning? In asking the latter question, we note that the level of competition (concentration) is itself *endogenous* — though it can be affected by government policies. As we have already noted, Arrow's earlier work provided more than a little hint that the outcomes of market processes would not be efficient, though he did not directly challenge Schumpeterian views which championed the innovative virtues of the market. The picture that emerges from our analysis is complex: Joseph Schumpeter was overly optimistic about monopolies — he thought that they would be only temporary and that competition to be the dominant firm drove innovation. We show that monopolies may be far more persistent than he (and latter-day Schumpeterians) thought and that the fight to be the dominant firm may be far less effective in stimulating innovation than he thought. Still, Schumpeter was right that more competitive markets, with many small firms, are likely to be *less* innovative.

The central message that emerges is that there is an important role for government to play in shaping an innovative economy and in promoting learning. Parts Two and Three of the book explore in more detail how the government can best do this.

Part Two provides the key analytical results, moving from simple models to more complex. The two key chapters are 7 and 11. Chapter 7 looks at a two-good (agriculture and manufacturing) closed economy (no trade) model and explains how policies promoting the industrial (manufacturing) sector (such as subsidies) lead to higher rates of growth and welfare. The short-run (allocative) distortions are more than offset by the long-term learning benefits. Simple formulae describing the optimal subsidy are derived. In this simple setting, we can compare the rate of innovation if there is competition with that when the industrial sector is dominated by a single firm. Innovation will be higher with monopoly, but whether welfare will be higher is ambiguous and depends on learning elasticities and discount rates.

Chapter 11 extends the analysis to an open economy, establishing the infant-economy argument for protection. Because the industrial sector not only has a greater capacity for learning but also more learning spillovers, encouraging that sector through protection or industrial policies can lead to higher growth and societal welfare. The force of the argument for protection is much weaker in developed economies. In economies like the United States, Europe, and Japan, there is already a dense infrastructure that has the scale to develop ideas and innovations, though there may still be cross-sector or cross-industry learning externalities that might warrant government intervention.

The theory has a wide range of implications. To illustrate: Our analysis suggests that it is desirable for large groups of countries to work together to facilitate trade amongst each other, while erecting certain barriers to trade from the outside. Competition and incentives matter. Having broad collections of countries, like the European Union, competing behind broad barriers, has considerable attraction. The protection enables the development of the "learning" (industrial) sector; the size provides scope for competition. (Our earlier remark explains why the degree of protection should be reduced over time.)

The structure of trade policy in the successful developing economies, like Japan, Europe after the Second World War, or other economies in Asia, has been very much of this sort. They have not focused on particular industries and protected them; they have tended to have broad protection across a range of industries, and they have actually encouraged competition behind those barriers.

The question of how this affects financial markets also arises—a question that Arrow's and Solow's work is particularly well positioned to help answer. When a country exports capital, the owners of that capital are, in effect, importing capital services from overseas. Just as imports of manufactured and industrial goods fail to carry with them the learning that is associated with those sectors, imports of financial services fail to carry with them the important learning that is associated with that sector. If there are powerful arguments for broad barriers to imported industrial goods, those apply equally to restrictions on capital exports overseas and the import of financial services. In short this theory provides a new rationale for why capital and financial market liberalization may lead to lower rates of growth. Similar arguments also apply, we show, to labor exports overseas.

Chapters 8, 9, and 10 extend the basic analysis of a two-period, two-good model into a multiperiod, multigood model. For example, these chapters derive more general formulae for optimal interventions; show that there may be multiple equilibriums, in one of which societal welfare is higher than another; explain that the composition of output can affect the long-run pace of innovation (an insight which obviously cannot be derived in the highly aggregative models used in macro-growth theory); and demonstrate that it may be desirable for a country to intervene in the exchange rate, setting it at such a low rate that it runs a *perpetual* surplus, with the benefits of learning outweighing the foregone consumption and investment.

From these analytics, the book moves (in part Three) to a broader policy discussion, beginning with trade and industrial policy, moving on to macro, financial, and investment policies, and to intellectual property. We explain why the political economy objection to specific infant-industry protection—that, for instance, the special interests that benefit from such protection work to keep it in place long after the economic justification for such protection has gone—have much less force in the context of the *infant-economy argument for protection*. We show that political economy concerns affect not whether there should be industrial and trade policies, but which policies and how they are best designed. We show too that intellectual property laws, if not well-designed, may actually impede learning and that "stronger" intellectual property regimes may be associated with a slower pace of innovation.

This part ends by moving beyond creating a learning *economy* to creating a learning *society*, and beyond the standard economic model, with its assumptions of rational individuals with predetermined preferences, incorporating insights from recent advances in behavioral economics, including the notion that preferences and beliefs are, at least in part, socially determined. We ask, for instance, whether there are policies that can help create a learning "mindset."

We hope this selection of insights has provided enough tempting morsels to persuade the reader to delve deeper into what follows. As we attempted to exposit our ideas, we faced a major dilemma: Mathematics is the language of modern economics. It can help ensure that putative conclusions follow from the assumptions. It can help test the robustness of the results: Do changes in assumptions lead to markedly different conclusions? But it can also obscure: the complexity of the analysis can also hide the role of particular assumptions. Arrow and Solow taught us the value of simple models—that we should strive to find the simplest and most general model to explore and explain the particular issue at hand. We hope the exposition here lives up to the high standards that they set.

But even the simplest analysis in this area can be relatively complex. And testing the robustness of the results requires exploring multiple variants of the basic model. The most complex calculations are concentrated in the appendices and in chapters 8, 9, and 10. Still, to make persuasively particular points (for instance, concerning the persistence of monopolies or that innovation in more competitive markets may be lower than in monopolies), we felt compelled to present some of the analytics within the body of the main text. We have written the book, however, so that the interested reader can skip over those analytic sections with little loss of continuity.

As our growing manuscript for this book grew beyond the bounds of the lecture, we still wished to preserve some of the valuable contributions from that day in 2008 when it was first presented. Both Solow and Arrow themselves were present and gave their own commentaries. Michael Woodford and Philippe Aghion also participated in discussions on the lecture topic, and Aghion delivered an entire lecture, "Rethinking Industrial Policy," that was complementary to our own. These commentaries and Aghion's lecture enriched our lecture at the time we delivered it and influenced our subsequent development of this book in important ways. We thus thought it desirable to retain these invaluable contributions in this volume. The main chapters of this book are followed by adapted transcripts of the commentaries from the lecture day. Aghion's lecture is included in its totality as an afterword.

In deciding to include these additional materials, we hope the reader enjoys getting a flavor of the day's proceedings. We feel the commentaries give a window into how our teachers and colleagues shaped our own thinking. Aghion's lecture adds depth and additional perspectives to our analyses.

This lecture also provides us with an opportunity to honor another of our teachers, Robert Solow, the father of modern growth theory. Solow and Arrow taught us how simple ideas can have profound effects. Bringing in insights from the economics of knowledge and learning fundamentally changes one's view about how to think about policies designed to promote growth. The infant-economy argument, inspired by Ken Arrow's paper on learning by doing, is, we believe, in the broad tradition of Ken Arrow and Bob Solow, in extending economic insights to new areas. We hope that the insights it provides will help poorer countries employ novel and effective policies to promote their economic growth and development.

PART ONE

Creating a Learning Society

*A New Approach to Growth, Development,
and Social Progress: Basic Concepts*

CHAPTER ONE

The Learning Revolution

FROM ROMAN times, when the first data on per-capita output are available, until 1800, average human standards of living increased only imperceptibly if at all (see, e.g., Maddison 2001). Consumption for the great majority of human beings consisted predominantly of food, and food was largely limited to staples—rice, wheat, and other grains. Housing entailed barnlike living conditions with no privacy, and climate control consisted only of necessary heat in winter. Clothing was utilitarian and rarely involved more than single outfits with the seasonal addition of overclothes. Medical care was almost nonexistent. Travel was rare, largely local, difficult, and uncomfortable. Recreation was self-generated and primitive. Only a small aristocratic minority enjoyed what we would consider today an appropriate human standard of living—varieties of fresh food, including meat; private, well-warmed accommodations; multiple sets of clothing for varied occasions; rudimentary personal and medical care; and opportunities for travel and sophisticated entertainment.

Beginning in 1800 and accelerating markedly after the mid-to-late nineteenth century, that privileged standard of living began to diffuse throughout Europe, North America, and Australia. The impact of this change is apparent even in critical contemporary commentaries. The Communist Manifesto is in many ways a paean to the potential of the newly apparent economic progress—the benefits of which had not yet been widely shared.

In the twentieth century, elite standards of living became pervasive in Europe, North America, Australia, and many parts of Asia; a trend which continues in much of Asia today.

The significance of these transformations can be seen in another way: until the beginning of the nineteenth century, most individuals spent most of their time meeting the basic necessities of life—food, shelter, clothing. Today, for most of those in the advanced industrial countries—and for an increasing number in the emerging markets— satisfying these basic necessities of life takes but a few hours of work a week. Individuals can choose how to spend the "extra" time available: to work, to earn enough to consume more (whether higher quality "necessities" or luxuries) or to enjoy more leisure.[1,2]

What was the source of these societal transformations? Was it capital accumulation or technological progress? Although economists, such as Schumpeter (1943), had identified the major source of these transformative developments as technological progress, it was not until Robert Solow (1957) that there was a way of quantifying the relative importance of capital accumulation versus technical progress. Changes in capital intensity could account for at most a third of changes in output per worker. The remainder was attributable largely to various forms of technical progress.[3]

Subsequent literature suggested that the quantification was perhaps less robust than seemed initially the case, partly because the measurement of key inputs (capital, human capital) was more difficult and problematic than had at first been realized, partly because the underlying model, entailing a constant returns to scale aggregate production function and full competition, seemed more questionable.[4] Some of the difficulties of parsing out the sources of growth was that they were intertwined—new machines (investment) were required to implement new technologies.[5] Still, there is no doubt that there have been enormous increases in productivity and that advances in technology as well as "learning to do things better" have played a critical role in these increases in productivity. For our purposes, that is all that matters.[6]

Not only is the pace of learning (innovation) the most important determinant of increases in standards of living, the pace itself is almost surely partially, if not largely, endogenous. The speed of progress has differed markedly both over time and across countries, and while we may not be able to explain all of this variation, it is clear that government policies have played a role. Learning is affected by the economic and social environment and the structure of the economy, as well as public and private investments in research and education. The fact that there are high correlations in productivity increases across industries, firms, and functions within firms suggests that there may be common factors (environmental factors, public investments) that have systemic effects or that there may be important spillovers from one learner/innovator to others. But the fact that there are large, persistent differences across countries and firms—at the microeconomic level, large discrepancies between best, average, and worst practices—implies that knowledge does not necessarily move smoothly either across borders or over firm boundaries.

All of this highlights that one of the objectives of economic policy should be to create economic policies and structures that enhance both learning and learning spillovers; creating a learning society is more likely to increase standards of living than is making small, one time improvements in economic efficiency or sacrificing consumption today to deepen capital.[7]

And this is even more so for developing countries. Much of the difference in per capita income between these countries and the more advanced is attributable to differences in knowledge. Policies that transformed their economies and societies into "learning societies" would enable them to close the gap in knowledge, with marked increases in incomes.[8] Development entails learning how to learn (Stiglitz 1987c).

Solow, in his seminal paper on the economics of growth (1956), had, for simplicity, modeled the rate of technological progress as fixed and exogenous, unaffected by the decisions of firms. This left unexplained the most important source of increases in living standards—and thus provided little guidance on how economic policy might increase that pace. Thus, Solow's 1957 paper showed that what his 1956 paper focused on, capital accumulation, was relatively unimportant; what was important was what his 1956 paper took as simply *given*. Not surprisingly, soon after Solow's pioneering work, there developed a large literature in growth theory attempting to "endogenize" technological change—starting at least as early as the 1960s,[9] with further progress being made during the 1980s.[10]

The best work tried, of course, to base the analysis of aggregate (macro) behavior on micro-foundations. There is, by now, a large literature on the microeconomics of technological progress,[11] but many of the insights of that literature have not been incorporated into the macroeconomic growth models, which often take a simplistic view, ignoring, for instance, sectoral differences in the pace of innovation, the multitude of ways in which progress occurs, and the interrelationships among them and alternative policies. To deal with the complexities posed by endogenous growth, and the challenge of deriving long-run steady-state growth, much of the literature has focused on parameterizations that turn out to be very, very special. While some of the literature has recognized that when innovation is endogenous, markets are not likely to be fully competitive, the interplay between market structure and innovation is typically not at the center of discussion. Is even the kind of competition that Schumpeter envisaged really viable? Some of the literature makes assumptions that virtually prejudge the conclusions: If trade is assumed to enhance learning (and more effectively than a corresponding amount of domestic production), then trade barriers have an adverse effect on economic growth. As we show, alternative (and we would argue more plausible) assumptions about the innovative process suggest that some trade restrictions may be desirable.

If our contention that the success of modern economies is due to innovation and learning is correct, then understanding the processes of learning and innovation, and how policy can affect its pace, should be at the center of economic analysis.[12] We can think of an economy's "innovation system" broadly as running from basic research—typically financed by government, occasionally by a government sanctioned monopoly (like Bell Labs), and typically produced by research universities and government research laboratories—to applied research, sometimes building on these basic ideas, at other times refining and developing "prior art." Ideas have to be disseminated and put into practice: much of the increase in productivity occurs as firms learn from each other or as technology improves through practice. More of our analysis ought to focus on how such learning occurs.

Kenneth Arrow was a pioneer in examining the economics of these "learning processes"—the factors which promote or retard them, their likely response to normal market incentives, and their relationship to the broader macro- and microeconomic environment—notably in his papers on the economics of R & D and learning-by-doing (1962a,1962b). He called attention to the fact that while some knowledge was produced as a result of the deliberate allocation of resources to research and development, much of technical progress was a by-product of production or investment.

One of the advances in modern economies has been improvements in the processes by which they learn—they have learned how to learn. There is not a single breakthrough that led to enhanced learning capacities, but rather a series of organizational innovations.[13]

Consistent with this, subsequent work, including that of Nordhaus (1969a, 1969b), identified the greater part of such progress as arising from the continuous accumulation of small improvements in production processes rather than from dramatic technological breakthroughs, though some, perhaps many, of these small improvements may be based on or related to transformative changes. For example, computerization and electrification were big changes, but their full effects were brought about in small steps.[14] So too, the separation between capital accumulation and "learning" is not a clean one: It is often through new investments that new ideas are discovered and new research is "embodied."[15] If the pace of investment determines the pace of learning, then of course it is impossible to neatly separate out what part of the increase in productivity is a result of capital accumulation and what part is a result of improvements in technology, because the two are inextricably intertwined.

The highly aggregate models that have been at the center of modern growth and development theory miss another key point: In the standard paradigm, except for market distortions (and the elimination of such market distortions is the passion of most economists), firms are always assumed to be on the production possibilities curve (in the jargon of traditional economics.) Productivity increases, in this standard model, result from moving the production possibilities curve out, as a result either of more accumulation of human or physical capital or of R & D. Indeed, much of the literature treated knowledge essentially as another form of capital—"knowledge capital"—ignoring its distinctive properties, which will be the focus of discussion in later chapters, especially chapter 5. But in reality, most firms operate well below their production possibilities curve. There are large gaps between "best practices" and "average practices." Countries differ in the size of these gaps. Closing these gaps can, at least for a while, provide an important impetus to societal increases in productivity. And for the typical firm, even as it closes yesterday's gap, new gaps open up. Most firms are forever "catching up."

The most successful economies are those that have succeeded in not only moving out their production possibilities curve more rapidly, but also ensuring that the gap between "average" and "best" practices is small. There is more diffusion of knowledge, more learning; and it is these achievements in learning that largely account for the ever-rising standards of living in these successful economies.

In short, *the transformation to "learning societies" which occurred around 1800 for Western economies, and more recently for those in Asia, appears to have had a greater impact on human well-being than improvements in allocative efficiency or resource accumulation.* If this is so, understanding how to create a learning society should be one of the central preoccupations of economists and other social scientists. Success in this endeavor can have a far greater impact on increasing long-term living standards than ascertaining how to increase resource accumulation or reduce short-term allocative inefficiencies.

This book seeks to present the simplest framework for understanding some of the critical determinants of the rate of progress—disaggregated enough for sectoral policies to make a difference, aggregated enough to retain our focus on the determinants of the economy's overall rate of progress

Central to our enquiry are two basic questions: Do markets, by themselves, result in an efficient level and pattern of learning and innovation? And if not, what are desirable interventions by government?

Market Inefficiency

The answer to the first question is simple and straightforward: *There is no presumption that markets are efficient in the production and dissemination of knowledge and learning. Quite the contrary, there is a presumption that markets are not efficient.*

Modern notions of the efficiency of markets date back to the work of Adam Smith (1776) and his invisible hand: the notion that the pursuit of self-interest would lead, as if by an invisible hand, to the well-being of society. It would take 175 years before Arrow (1951b) and Debreu (1959) would establish the sense in which that was true (markets are "Pareto efficient"; that is, no one could be made better off without making anyone worse off) and the conditions under which it was true. Arrow provided *sufficient conditions* for the Pareto efficiency of markets (see Arrow 1951b; Debreu 1959). Subsequent work showed that those conditions were also essentially necessary. For instance, his proof of the efficiency of markets required that information was exogenous (that is, it needn't be perfect, but beliefs couldn't change as a result of what individuals observed or did); it was subsequently shown that whenever markets were incomplete or information was endogenous and asymmetric (that is, essentially *always)* markets were not (constrained) Pareto efficient.[16]

For the purposes of this book, though, the central assumptions in the proof of the efficiency of the market economy were that markets were perfectly competitive and that the state of technology was fixed, exogenous. Arrow and Debreu, in their proof of the efficiency of the market economy, assumed away innovation. In doing so, they left unanswered the question of whether a market economy was efficient in innovation. Given that many advocates of markets assumed that their innovativeness was their central virtue, this was obviously a central lacuna. Indeed, earlier Schumpeter (1943) had gone so far as to argue that one of the distortions on which many economists had focused attention—monopoly—could actually be a virtue in an innovation economy: it provided the rents which supported R & D, and so long as there was competition *for the market*, one should not worry about competition *in the market*. But neither Schumpeter, nor others arguing for the virtues of markets on the basis of their innovativeness, was able to show that markets were efficient in innovation.

The reason that they did not do so is that they could not do so: the discussion below, building on the work of Arrow and others, shows that there is a presumption that markets on their own are efficient neither in the level nor the pattern of innovation. Arrow recognized that market failures in the production and dissemination of knowledge (whether as a result of the allocation of resources to R & D or as a result of learning) were pervasive.[17] Thus, following Arrow's lead in understanding the economics of learning processes—and the pervasive market failures in learning processes—is critical to formulating effective economic policies.

Analyzing the nature of these inefficiencies—and their implications for public policy—requires the construction of a general equilibrium model in which R & D or learning and market structures are both endogenous. The market inefficiencies are multiple and complex. We will explain, for instance, why some sectors may be more amenable to learning than others; why some sectors may generate more externalities (spillovers to other sectors) than others. We will see that sectors in which learning is important are often imperfectly competitive, so that not only may production—and learning—be constrained below its optimal level because firms fail to take into account the spillovers that their learning has for other sectors; but production—and learning—may be constrained as a result of the exercise of market power. We will explain why Schumpeter's view that such market power was of positive value (it helped finance research that otherwise would not have received funds) and that abuses would be limited because of the discipline of "Schumpeterian" competition (competition to be the dominant firm through innovation) needs to be qualified. His view on monopoly was too panglossian.

Further inefficiencies in the innovation process are introduced as a result of capital market imperfections and imperfections in risk markets. The Arrow-Debreu analysis establishing the efficiency of markets required not only unreasonable assumptions about the nature of competition and innovation, but also that there be a complete set of risk markets and perfect capital markets. The imperfections in these markets, especially as they relate to innovation, are not just a happenstance, but an inherent feature of innovation, as we explain in chapter 6.

The Role of Government in Promoting a Learning Society

If learning, and R & D more generally, is at the center of the success of an economy, and if there is no presumption that markets are efficient in making decisions which affect the pace of learning (or R & D), then longstanding presumptions against government intervention are simply wrong. The financial crisis has called attention to the role of government in crisis prevention. Widespread environmental problems have called attention to the role of government in preventing pollution and potentially catastrophic climate change. These are examples of government's role in preventing *negative* externalities. The production of knowledge entails *positive* externalities. The private sector produces too much of goods that give rise to negative externalities, which is why government must either impose charges when firms generate pollution, or otherwise regulate pollution-generating activities. By contrast, the private sector typically produces too little of goods that give rise to positive externalities. Again, to correct this market distortion requires some form of government intervention.

These interventions, though, are more complex than those that are necessary to correct the negative externalities; there are limited and well-identified environmental externalities and a well-developed set of tools for addressing these market failures. So too there is widespread understanding of the externalities that can be generated by underregulated financial markets and, especially in the aftermath of the financial crisis, even an understanding of what good regulation entails.[18] But learning touches every aspect of a modern dynamic economy, and even more so of an emerging market struggling to become an advanced industrial country. If there are market failures in learning, then the market failures are pervasive in the economy. They are diffuse. More pervasive government interventions are required to correct them.

Many of these advances on which our dynamic economy is based rest on government-funded research, and without that support, the pace of innovation—and the pace of increases in standards of living—would have been far lower. And many of the advances attributable to the private sector are shaped by our legal framework, including those governing intellectual property. Critics on both the left and right assert, though, that this legal framework may be far from ideal, some suggesting that innovation is impeded as a result of insufficient protection of property rights, others that progress is hampered because of a poorly designed intellectual property regime, more focused on increasing the rents of, say, the pharmaceutical industry than advancing standards of living. Whatever one's views on these questions, there is a consensus that public policy is central and unavoidable. Government has a responsibility in "creating a learning society." If we are to understand what that responsibility is—and how it can best be fulfilled—we have to understand why it is that markets on their own don't "work" and how innovation actually occurs in our society.

The analysis presented here thus changes the presumption about the desirability of government intervention: now there is a presumption of market failure and a presumption for government to take actions to correct these market failures.

This book, then, is an attempt to study the economics of "learning societies," focusing especially on the role of government in promoting growth through the creation or strengthening of a learning society. This book lays out simple models in which learning spillovers are well identified. The models generate policy prescriptions which differ markedly from standard policy recommendations focusing on enhancing allocative efficiency. It is not just a difference in emphasis between classical economic policy prescriptions—based on notions of static allocative efficiency and the idea that growth in productivity arises chiefly from resource accumulation (physical, human, and scientific capital)—and those that we stress for creating dynamic learning environments. Rather, our concern is that some of these classical policy prescriptions, though well-intentioned, may actually lead to a reduction in the rate of progress of societies and a deterioration in long-run societal well-being. In the attempt to improve the static efficiency of the economy, learning may be impeded. Our analysis supports numerous policies that have been proscribed by economists wedded to the neoclassical model and suggests new measures that will help create a more dynamic learning economy. In that sense, our work is similar to that of Schumpeter (1943), who criticized conventional economists for overemphasizing competition. But while Schumpeter was correct in his critique of neoclassical economics, he never formulated a coherent analytic normative or positive theory. The result is that some of his normative stances were misguided. For instance, he was overly optimistic (as we shall see) about the potential for what has come to be called "Schumpeterian competition" to ensure, by itself, a dynamic economy and overly sanguine about the virtues of (temporary) monopolies.

This reassessment of policy is especially important for developing countries and emerging markets. As we noted earlier, what separates developed from less-developed countries is not just a gap in resources but a gap in knowledge. Thus, a central focus of development policy should be closing that gap—and that means enhancing learning. This is, for instance, one of the central objectives of modern industrial policies, which seek to promote particular industries and particular technologies with greater learning capabilities and greater spillovers to other sectors. (While industrial policies were originally targeted toward supporting the industrial sector, today the term is used much more broadly, to embrace any set of policies designed to encourage particular sectors or technologies. Policies promoting the agricultural sector, the research sector, or the service sector would thus be included under the term *industrial policy*.)[19] Policies that in any way impede learning—including those that seek to circumscribe the use of industrial policies—may, over the long run, lower well-being.[20] This is but one example of many places where we argue that traditional developmental policy stances, such as those associated with the Washington consensus, are misguided: Well designed trade restrictions, subsidies, and exchange rate interventions can play an important role in promoting learning. We argue, furthermore, that removing domestic content restrictions on foreign direct investment, as called for by trade and investment agreements, may impede learning.

One of the clearest points of departure between our focus and that of more traditional development economics concerns the role of institutions. Much of the standard literature has emphasized the role of institutions that protect *property rights*. As knowledge has become more important, there is an increasing emphasis on intellectual property rights and the institutions that protect them. By contrast, we take a broader view: Intellectual property rights is one institution that incentivizes innovation. But there are others that are as or more important. We ask what the institutions are that promote a learning society. We also argue for an intellectual property rights regime that is markedly different from the regulations incorporated into the TRIPS agreement of the WTO. Indeed, we argue that poorly designed "strong" intellectual property regimes actually impede learning and innovation.

There are, in fact, many examples where the approach we take leads to policy recommendations that are contrary to those of the Washington consensus: We argue against measures on financial market liberalization that have typically been included in agreements signed under bilateral trade agreements and under the Financial Services Agreement of the WTO. We provide an explanation for why trade and capital market liberalization have often failed to promote growth in the way that was hoped and suggest how these measures should be modified, once one takes a learning perspective.

Much of this book centers around the question of how to best promote learning, including how to balance optimally the dynamic gains from faster learning with the short-run (static) costs associated with interventions, and how best to design interventions. But much of the debate around government intervention has centered on political economy concerns. These should not, and cannot, be ignored. We will argue that these have more to do with the form of government intervention than they do with *whether* there should be government intervention.

The Theory of Comparative Advantage Redefined

Perhaps the most important way in which our book differs from classical prescriptions is that we argue that there is an *infant economy argument for protection*. Growth and standards of living can be raised by *defying* a country's seeming comparative advantage and imposing trade restrictions that encourage industrialization. But our book also provides a different perspective on what is meant by comparative advantage. The traditional theory of comparative advantage (as developed by Heckscher and Ohlin[21]), based on the notion that knowledge was fully available, focused on relative factor endowments. Portugal exported wine because it was endowed with weather more suitable for growing wine, England cloth. Countries that had an abundance of unskilled labor exported unskilled labor intensive goods.

Krugman's (1979) research building on the Dixit-Stiglitz model of product differentiation made it clear that something besides factor endowments mattered. He observed that most trade today is between countries that have similar factor endowments. And he observed that they often traded similar products. Germany exports cars to the United States and the United States exports cars to Germany and other countries. But in the Krugman-Dixit-Stiglitz model, there is no explanation of why Germany is exporting the kinds of cars that it does. There are multiple equilibriums: the United States could have wound up exporting the cars that Germany did and vice versa. Our analysis suggests that, to a large extent, these patterns are not just the outcome of fortune, the toss of a coin, but are related to the more fundamental endowments— the state of knowledge and learning capabilities.

Justin Lin (2012) has distinguished between industrial policies that defy comparative advantage, which he argues are likely to be unsuccessful, and those that are consistent with comparative advantage, which can be an important component of successful development. While there is considerable insight in this distinction, the key question is, what are a country's *endowments*, which determine its comparative advantage? This is equivalent to asking, what are the relevant *state* variables, those that describe the state of the economy today? And what is the "ecology" against which the country's endowments are to be compared, i.e., what are the *relevant* endowments of other countries?

It has become conventional wisdom to emphasize that what matters is not static comparative advantage but dynamic comparative advantage. Korea did not have a comparative advantage in producing semiconductors when it embarked on its transition. Its static comparative advantage was in the production of rice. Had it followed its static comparative advantage (as many neoclassical economists had recommended) then that might still be its comparative advantage; it might be the best rice grower in the world, but it would still be poor. But a country's dynamic comparative advantage is endogenous, a result of what it does. There seems to be a circularity here. The central question is, What should a country do today to create its dynamic comparative advantage?

Ascertaining a country's static comparative advantage is difficult; ascertaining its dynamic comparative advantage is even harder. As we noted, standard comparative advantage focused on *factor* endowments (capital-labor ratios). But with capital highly mobile, capital endowments should matter little for determining even static comparative advantage. Still, capital, or more accurately, the knowledge of the various factors that affect returns and that is required to use capital efficiently, doesn't move perfectly across borders; neither does knowledge about how effective a particular enterprise is in using various inputs to produce and market outputs. That means that the resident of country j may demand a higher return for investing in country i than they would demand for investing in their own country. There is, in practice, far less than perfect capital mobility.

The "state" variables that determine comparative advantage relate to those "factors" that are not mobile, which, in varying degrees, include knowledge, labor, and institutions.

Multinationals can, however, convey knowledge across borders. Highly skilled people move too. Migration has resulted in large movements in unskilled labor, but, in most cases, not enough to change endowments of the home or host country significantly. Even institutions can sometimes effectively move across borders, as when parties to a contract may agree that disputes will be adjudicated in London and under British law. Still, there are numerous aspects of tacit knowledge, about how individuals and organizations interact with each other, and norms of behavior that affect economic performance and, most particularly from our perspective, how (and whether) they learn and adapt. Such tacit knowledge does not typically move easily across borders. (Indeed, as we argue below, it does not even move easily among or within firms. There are natural barriers to the flow of knowledge, including incentives on the part of market participants to take actions that would impede the flow of knowledge.)

The most important "endowment," from our perspective, is a society's learning capacities (which in turn is affected by the knowledge that it has; its knowledge about learning itself; and its knowledge about its own learning capacities), which may be specific to learning about some things rather than others. The spirit of this book is that a country's policies have to be shaped to take advantage of its comparative advantage in knowledge and learning abilities, including its ability to learn and to learn to learn, in relation to its competitors, and to help develop those capacities and capabilities further. Even if it has the capacity to learn how to make computer chips, if a country's learning capacity is less than its competitors, it will fall behind in the race. But each country makes, effectively, decisions regarding what it will learn about. There are natural nonconvexities in learning, benefits to specialization. If a country decides to learn about producing chips, it is less likely that it will learn about some other things. There will be some spillovers to closely related technologies—perhaps to, say, nanotechnology. The areas to which there are spillovers may not lie nearby in conventional product space. There may, for instance, be similarities in production technologies (as in the case of just-in-time production or the assembly line). That is why the evolution of comparative advantage may be so hard to predict.

But while standard economic analysis may provide guidance to a country about its current (static) comparative advantage (e.g., given current technology, for a country with an abundance of unskilled labor, what are the unskilled-labor intensive goods), guidance about its comparative advantage defined in this way (dynamic learning capacities) is much more difficult. In part this additional difficulty is because this advantage depends on judgments by other countries about their dynamic comparative advantage and their willingness to invest resources to enhance those advantages. Whether ex ante the United States, Japan, or Korea initially had a dynamic comparative advantage in producing chips, once Korea had invested enough in learning about certain kinds of chip production, it would be difficult for another country to displace it. Another country would have to leapfrog—and whether it could do so depends not only on the other country's capabilities and its willingness to invest to enhance those capabilities, but also on Korea's responses to these competitive threats.[22]

Looking at what other countries at similar levels of per capita income did in the past or what countries with slightly higher levels of per capita income are doing today (as Lin suggests) may be helpful, but only to a limited extent. The world today (both in terms of global geo-economics and geo-politics, and technology) is different than it was in the past. Competing in textiles today requires different skills and knowledge than in even the recent past; a lagging country wanting to enter a market may (or may not) be able to displace a country that currently has a comparative advantage in some product; that country may (or may not) be in the process of attempting to establish a comparative advantage in some other area.

In short, the learning perspective redefines the theory of dynamic comparative advantage and does so in ways which make formulating development strategies more complicated—but more interesting. Less-developed countries today cannot simply imitate patterns of development that were pursued by earlier developers. That this is so should be evident by now. Those countries in the early to mid-twentieth century that followed the heavy industrialization strategy that was the basis of the success of the United States and Germany in the nineteenth century failed. African countries that try to follow blindly the export-led strategies of East Asia may find them far less successful than they were when they were employed in East Asia in the latter third of the twentieth century. While development economists are likely to praise East Asia's export-led growth strategy, it was not growth in exports per se that led to their success; it was growth in particular kinds of exports that were associated with high levels of learning. Other countries pursuing export-led growth strategies but exporting goods for which there are not such learning benefits may find themselves sorely disappointed.

This discussion highlights the important ways in which the learning perspective redefines basic concepts, like comparative advantage, policies, and economic strategies. The learning perspective also leads to rethinking other long-standing notions. We have already noted that our theory calls into question the usefulness of the concept of an aggregate production function, especially one predicated on the assumption that all firms (say, within the country) have the same knowledge and are equally capable of converting inputs into outputs. In chapter 2 we reconsider the concept of the production possibilities schedule, and in chapter 4 we consider the question, posed some 75 years ago by Ronald Coase, of the boundary of the firm—what activities go inside the firm and what goods and services are purchased in the market.

CHAPTER TWO

On the Importance of Learning

THE CENTRAL thesis advanced in chapter 1 was that what distinguishes the modern era of the last two hundred years from the millennia that preceded is *learning*—we have learned how to increase productivity, the outputs that can be produced with any inputs. There are two aspects of learning that we can distinguish: an improvement in best practices, reflected in increases in productivity of firms that marshal all available knowledge and technology, and improvements in the productivity of firms as they catch up to best practices. In fact, the distinction may be somewhat artificial; there may be no firm that has employed best practices in every aspect of its activities. One firm may be catching up with another in some dimension, but the second firm may be catching up with the first in others. In developing countries, almost all firms may be catching up with global best practices; but the real difference between developing and developed countries is the larger fraction of firms that are significantly below global best practices and the larger gap between their productivity and that of the best-performing firms.

While we are concerned in this book with both aspects of learning, it is especially the learning associated with catching up that we believe has been given short shrift in the economics literature, and which is central to improvements in standards of living, especially in developing countries. But as we noted in chapter 1, the two are closely related; because of the improvements in best practices by the most innovative firms, most other firms are always engaged in a process of catching up.

While the evidence of Solow and the work that followed demonstrated (what to many seems obvious) the importance of learning for increases in standards of living, to further explicate the role of learning, the first three sections of this chapter marshal other macro- and microeconomic evidence. In particular, we stress the pervasive gap between best practices and the productivity of most firms. We argue that this gap is far more important than the traditional allocative inefficiencies upon which most of economics has focused and is related to learning— or more accurately, the lack of learning.

The final section provides a theoretical context within which to think about the sources of sustained increases in standards of living, employing the familiar distinction of movements of the production possibilities curve and movements toward the production possibilities curve. Using this framework, we explain why it is that we ascribe such importance to learning.

Macroeconomic Perspectives

There are several empirical arguments that can be brought to bear to support our conclusion concerning the importance of learning. The first is a simple argument: In theory, leading-edge technology is globally available. Thus, with sufficient capital and trained labor (or sufficient mobility for capital and trained labor), all countries should enjoy comparable standards of living. The only difference would be the rents associated with *ownership* of intellectual property rights and factor supplies. Yet there is an enormous divergence in economic performance and standards of living across national economies, far greater than can be explained by differences in factor supplies.[1] And this includes many low-performing economies with high levels of capital intensity (especially among formerly socialist economies) and highly trained labor forces. Table 2.1 presents a comparison of formerly socialist countries with similar nonsocialist economies in the immediate aftermath of the collapse of the state-controlled model of economic activity.

TABLE 2.1
Quality of Life Comparisons, 1992–1994 (U.S. $)

	Formerly Centralized			Noncentralized		
Region	Country	Per Capita GDP	Life Expectancy	Country	Per Capita GDP	Life Expectancy
Baltic	Lithuania, Latvia, Estonia	7,800	70.4	Finland	16,150	76.2
Middle Europe	Czech Republic	7,350	73.5	Austria	17,500	76.9
Agricultural Europe	Poland	4,920	73.1	Spain	13,125	77.9
China	China	2,500	68.1	Taiwan	12,070	75.5
Southeast Asia		870	55.3	Thailand	5,970	68.4
Korea	North Korea	920	70.1	South Korea	11,270	70.9
Unweighted Average		*4,060*	*68.4*		*12,681*	*74.3*

Source: Greenwald and Khan (2009). p. 30.

In most of these cases, at the time communism was imposed after World War II, the subsequently socialist economies enjoyed higher levels of economic development than those of the "comparator." Czechoslovakia was more highly industrialized than Austria. Finland was perhaps the poorest of the Baltic countries. Spain, a large Catholic agricultural country, was poorer than Poland. Taiwan, occupied by the Japanese for many years, was a relatively backward part of China. Vietnam and Cambodia were at least as well-off as Thailand. And North Korea was more heavily industrialized than South Korea. Over the intervening 40 years from the late 1940s to the late 1980s, the socialist economies focused strongly on the traditional growth prescriptions of capital accumulation and education. They had high savings and investment rates—far higher in many cases than those in the West—and even invested heavily in education, especially the kinds of technical education that might seem most directly relevant to production (and even some forms of innovation). Yet by the end of that period, they had levels of economic output less than one-half of that of the comparison economies (and often far less than one-half).

On one side of the line, economies developed based on steady improvements in economic performance over time. On the other side, economies largely failed to "learn," even if they did better in accumulating factors of production and even, in some cases, if they did better at developing advanced products, like the Sputnik. These countries (and the firms within them) not only failed to make productivity-enhancing innovations, they failed to learn from the innovations and best practices that were going on in the other parts of the world.

It should be clear that the differences that emerged were beyond those that could be explained simply by static inefficiencies (e.g., those associated with distorted incentive systems and the misallocation of resources). If that had been the key problem, then the move from Communism to a market economy would have quickly closed the gap; moving to market prices and incentive structures should have eliminated these static inefficiencies. In fact, in most countries of the former Soviet Union, output actually fell (see Stiglitz 2000c). This is not to say that, for instance, distorted incentive structures played no role. When China moved from collective farming to the individual responsibility system, there was a large increase in productivity; but even then, productivity remained markedly below that of other countries. The magnitude of the gaps and their evolution over time (both before and after the end of Communism) suggest that they cannot simply be attributed to static inefficiencies.

The same argument is, of course, true for changes over time. The same changes are available globally—especially for the many aspects of technology not protected by intellectual property—yet there are large differences in changes in productivity, differences not accounted for by differences in changes in other factor inputs.[2] This is again illustrated by the economies in transition. Indeed, nothing could illustrate more the significance of learning and learning capacities than the experience of those (and other) economies since the transition. Movements to higher standards of economic performance after the transition have been far from uniform. Some countries adapted quickly and well. From 1975 to 1980, reported annual per capita income growth in China was 4.1 percent. From 1980 to 1985, after altering the conditions under which businesses could operate and learn, growth accelerated to 8.4 percent, and since 1985 has been about 10 percent per year.

This rapid turnaround could not be attributable either to education or to capital accumulation.[3] A reformed education system would take at least 8 years before it could produce more highly trained graduates (since older classes would be inadequately prepared by their prereform training), and these graduates would transform the total labor force only slowly over time.[4] As for capital accumulation, even if the fraction of GDP devoted to investment were to have increased by 25 percent, at a real return of 5 percent, the acceleration in growth would have been just 1.25 percent; if the real return were even 10 percent, the acceleration of growth would have been just 2.5 percent. Clearly what changed was the effectiveness with which capital and labor were being employed using technologies that were preexistent and widely available globally.

Of course, improved incentives[5] in, say, agriculture and the reduction of sectoral misallocation of resources played some role in China's growth. Improvements in productivity resulting from the removal of a static inefficiency result, as we discuss more thoroughly later, in a one-time (or short-lived) increase in productivity were important. But while that was true (to a large extent) in agriculture,[6] it is striking that the most important sources of growth were in manufacturing, where one could visibly see improvements in productivity, quality, and practices, and these improvements were persistent.

Other formerly socialist countries experienced much slower convergence to high performance levels of per capita income.[7] In general the

Baltic countries and many of those in Eastern Europe "learned" far more slowly than their Asian counterparts (at least as reflected in rates of increase in aggregate productivity[8]), China and Vietnam. When they did eventually start to grow more rapidly, it was often through a real estate bubble: global financial practices—good and bad—seem among the easiest to move across borders.

India had a similar experience of accelerating growth after commercial reforms in the 1980s. It was these reforms, not the later trade liberalizations, from which one dates the rapid changes in India's growth (see Rodrik and Subramanian 2005).

Other countries, both formerly socialist and in Latin America, Africa, and parts of Asia, have yet to experience such high rates of growth. This has been true despite their frequent embrace of accepted market principles, their access to global technology, high rates of savings, sound macroeconomic policies, and well-developed educational systems. What has failed in these countries is, to a large extent, their ability to adapt existing global technology and deploy resources effectively *within each sector*. They remain mired well inside their *theoretical* production possibility frontiers.

Microeconomic Perspectives

Even in highly developed economies, like the United States or Japan, there is substantial evidence (see, e.g., Baily and Solow 2001) that most firms operate well below their theoretical capabilities (the "best practices" within the industry), implying a large scope in productivity increases from movements to the production possibility frontier by each firm.[9] Although, clearly, unrealized potential gains would eventually be exhausted without leading-edge research and development, for practical purposes, "learning" to exploit existing opportunities and the diffusion of existing technology contribute more to rates of productivity growth *at any particular moment* than leading-edge technological improvements.

One of the most striking aspects of firm-level studies of productivity is the existence of large and persistent productivity differences across firms, both at the level of overall output and at the level of the individual processes that generate overall output. At the firm level, differences in productivity of two-to-one or more between leading

TABLE 2.2

Data—Life Insurance Companies (General Expense as Percentage of Premiums)

Year	Connecticut Mutual	Phoenix Mutual	Northwestern Mutual
1988	20.9	16.7 (17.6)	6.8
1989	19.8	15.7	6.9
1990	20.2	14.9	7.4
1991	20.9	15.6 (18.2)	6.3

firms in an industry and the industry average were first documented systematically by Baily et al. (1992) and have been confirmed by most subsequent studies.[10]

An example for mutual life insurance underwriters is presented in table 2.2. Northwestern Mutual, the acknowledged industry leader, was able to process life insurance premiums at a cost of about 40 percent of that of an average performer, like Phoenix Mutual, and less than a third of that of a relative laggard like Connecticut Mutual. Correcting for differences in operations, like product mix and organizational form (e.g., using proprietary sales agents versus independent agents), actually increased Northwestern's measured performance advantage. For example, Northwestern Mutual sold a higher proportion of term-life policies (as opposed to whole-life policies) than its competitors, and term-life policies with lower premiums per policy typically required a higher administrative effort per premium dollar than whole-life policies.

Just as strikingly, another feature of table 2.2 appears to be broadly representative of within-industry performance differences: There is only limited convergence in productivity levels between leading companies and their less efficient competitors. (An equilibrium model explaining why that might be so is presented in the appendix.)

Baily et al. (1992) and others (see, e.g., Dwyer 1998) typically find that rates of convergence for productivity levels across firms within an industry are very slow indeed. Leading firms with successful learning environments appear to increase productivity at rates which are comparable to those of their less efficient competitors despite being necessarily nearer the industry production possibility frontier. These firms seem more capable of learning.[11]

Of course, to remove redundancy leading-edge firms are also likely to be operating well below what might be feasible, even with reasonable levels of investment, say, in engineering or new technology. This highlights a point of general relevance: the distinction between learning involved in moving toward the leading-edge technology and learning by those at the frontier may be less than is commonly thought. Moreover, even advances in leading-edge technology are typically the result of small improvements—not big innovations of the kind covered by the patent system. They are the result of learning—learning from doing and learning from others, figuring out what ideas and practices in other industries, for instance, are relevant to, or can be adapted to, the industry or enterprise in question.

The inescapable conclusion from this firm-level data is that most firms operate well within their industry production possibility frontier. But if firms operate inside their production possibility frontiers, then it follows that economies as a whole operate below their levels of optimal output. The potential for learning-driven output growth is clearly apparent in the microeconomic data.

Evidence from Episodes of Rapid Productivity Increases

The existence of this unexploited potential productivity is confirmed under some special historical circumstances where there was a sudden necessity to increase output. For example, a labor agreement in the U.K. engineering industry in the 1980s provided for a workweek reduction from five to four days at proportionately reduced wages. The idea was that employment would increase so that the available work would be spread among more union members. In response, process changes at the firms, forced to accommodate new working schedules, led to further significant reductions in employment despite increasing industry output.[12]

Another firm-level example of unexploited productive capacity can be seen on the occasion of a strike at the New York Telephone and New England Telephone companies in 1989. The firms had 80,000 workers prestrike; of these, 57,000 went on strike. During the first week of the strike, 22,000 of the 23,000 managers were assigned to cover for the missing union members. Their learning curve was so sharp that during the second week of the strike, half of these workers (11,000) were able to be reassigned to their original jobs and all the prior management work continued to be performed. The only normal work not being done during this second week was residential phone installations that involved rewiring the network and some new plant construction. Both functions could have been completely covered by hiring an additional 3,000 workers (using prestrike industry productivity norms). Under the special pressures of the strike, 26,000 workers fulfilled the role of 80,000 prestrike workers, a threefold increase in productivity. The evidence again argues for a substantial gap between where economies typically operate and the true frontier of potential production.

The fact that it is possible to increase productivity quickly—without dramatic changes in technology or inputs—provides further evidence for the potential role of learning.[13] If firms were indeed achieving their full productive potential, then further improvements in performance should be relatively slow, steady, and positive. Changes in the quality of a firm's labor force take place only slowly; most employees do not turn over during the course of a year, and new employees tend to have qualifications similar to existing ones. Capital additions during any particular year also tend to occur at a relatively stable rate and change the existing stock of capital only marginally. Finally, dramatic technological breakthroughs are rare, and firms most often adopt proven technologies rather than transformative leading-edge new ones.

In practice, however, productivity growth at the firm level tends to be highly episodic. The question is, why are such opportunities recurrently available? A firm on or near its production possibility frontier should not be able to achieve such sharp short-term improvements in operations (usually without significant investment or employee turnover), and it shouldn't be able to achieve such cost reductions repeatedly. All of this strongly suggests that productivity shifts at the firm level often, or even typically, consist far more of movements *toward* the production possibility frontier than of movement in the frontier itself.[14]

Macroeconomic Episodes

At the macroeconomic or sector level, there is also strong evidence of the disproportionate importance of "learning" environments. The most compelling example of this was the performance of the United States economy during World War II. Notwithstanding the massive shifts in production to war material and of manpower to the armed forces, output of consumption goods actually increased between 1941, by which time mass unemployment had largely disappeared, and 1945.

Another major example is suggested by the performance of the U.S. manufacturing sector between the 1970s and early 1980s on the one hand and the late 1980s and 1990s on the other. Between these two periods, the annual rate of growth of U.S. manufacturing productivity rose by 2.0 percent from 0.9 percent to 2.9 percent. The improvement coincided with a marked rise in U.S. real interest rates (normally associated with *less* investment in technology) and government deficits, a decline in U.S. research and development spending, and no detectable improvement in the performance of U.S. education (as measured by standardized tests). At the same time, it cannot be attributed to the availability of new technology. Such technology would have been equally available to other G7 economies. Over the period in question, the U.S. improvement in annual manufacturing productivity growth was 1.9 percent higher than that of the other G7 countries. The improvement was thus a U.S., not a global, phenomenon. What seems to have changed in U.S. manufacturing was an intensified focus on improved operations management through the rigorous implementation of procedures like benchmarking, total quality management, and reengineering—in our language, an intensified focus on learning. America seemed to have learned how to learn.[15]

Table 2.3 illustrates that something similar took place in the U.S. economy as a whole during subsequent years. After decades of productivity growth at rates well below those in Europe and Japan, U.S. productivity growth performance outstripped that of all these rivals in the years between 1995 and 2001. And again the relative changes involved were not related to changes in either capital accumulation (U.S. investment rates were little changed[16]), educational improvements, or formal R & D spending. They appear to have been rooted in improved learning in the United States.[17]

Alternative Theories of Growth

So far, we have presented convincing evidence that economies and firms operate well below the production possibilities frontier—what they could have produced, given the current state of knowledge, the best practices that are available within the economy—and that much of

TABLE 2.3
Productivity Growth Total, 1996–2001

Country	Change in Output per Worker (%)	Change in Hours per Worker (%)	Change in Output per Hour (%)
United States	11.4	−2.2	13.6
Canada	9.6	2.2*	7.4
Japan	6.4	−2.1	8.5
Germany	1.0	−8.5**	9.5
United Kingdom	7.2	−1.0	8.2
Italy	6.3	−0.3	6.6
France	5.2	−4.0	9.2

Sources: European Community Statistical Annual; U.S. Department of Commerce; U.S. Department of Labor; Canadian Government Statistics.

*Hours paid.

**Hours paid, major statistical revision in 2000.

the growth in productivity can be related to moving toward the frontier. While this is especially true in developing countries, it is even true in advanced industrial countries, highlighted by the marked differences among firms within the same industry in the same country.

We have suggested, moreover, that much of what occurs in this process of moving to the frontier can be described as "learning," catching up to best practices.

A standard analysis breaks down increases in productivity (output per worker, say) into two parts: How do we move economies to the frontier, and how do we move the frontier out? By the same token, policy analysis focuses on why the economy might be below the production possibilities curve (looking for reasons other than learning, with a focus on static inefficiencies), and why it might not be moving the frontier out in the optimal way. Such an analysis begins with the presumption that well-functioning economies operate at or near this frontier—as opposed to the presumption suggested in the first part of the chapter that even in a well-functioning economy, most or, indeed, even all firms operate well within the frontier of what is possible. In traditional approaches, learning plays little or no role, and, if it occurs, it is simply *exogenous*, that is, goes on independent of anything we do, how we structure the economy, how we restructure firms, and so forth. All firms have access to and make full use of all relevant knowledge.

In the traditional perspective, moreover, the only reason that firms would not operate at the frontier is if the government imposed distortionary taxes or regulations or did not prevent monopolies.[18] (There are a few other instances in which markets might "fail" to produce efficient outcomes, such as pollution, where one firm's pollution damaged another firm, but these too typically were given short shrift, particularly because they are easy to resolve, at least in principle, simply by imposing optimal corrective taxation [abstracting from the difficulties of politics]. Externalities mattered not so much for producers as for consumers, who might live a shorter life as a result.[19]) A first task of policymakers, then, is to eliminate these sources of *allocative efficiency.*

However, dating back to the work of Harberger (1954), there has been a strong sense that the loss in welfare arising from these distortions is small. Hence these interventions, while beneficial, have impacts which are an order of magnitude smaller than the effects of movements in the frontier as well as those arising from macroeconomic disturbances, the periodic recessions and depressions that have plagued capitalism since its beginning and which leave large amounts of resources idle (so the economy is operating well below the production possibilities curve).[20]

Moreover, a movement toward the frontier results in a *one-time* increase in GDP, not a persistently higher level of growth. Even small increases in such growth rates—in the pace at which the frontier moves out—can, in the long run, lead to far larger increases in long-term GDP than the elimination of allocative inefficiencies.

Moving the Frontier out by Investments in Capital and People

In the standard theory, then, sustained increases in standards of living, at least within developed countries, are largely associated with investments in capital and people that move the frontier outward. Within the United States, for instance, public discourse about the challenges of slow growth and the loss of international competitiveness have focused on increasing the amount and quality of physical and human capital. Concretely, discussions have centered on the quality of education (viewed as the major impediment to increases in human capital) and low levels of savings (the household savings rate reached near zero in the years before the 2008 crisis).

But Solow's brilliant 1956 paper laid to rest the view that higher savings and investment rates (including investments in human capital) would lead to sustained higher growth rates. He showed that a higher savings rate would lead to higher levels of per capita income but not permanently higher growth rates. The growth benefits might last longer, but the costs were more apparent than those associated with improving allocative efficiency. While the latter were typically described as (potential) Pareto improvements—in which *everyone,* now and in the future, could be made better off—the former entailed sacrificing current consumption for higher future consumption.

Hence, in the absence of a market failure, there is no presumption that individuals will save too little—that growth will be too low *even in the short run.* Whether increasing growth was socially desirable depended on intertemporal judgments—weighing the higher standards of living of future generations against the lower standard of living of the current generation. When, because of technological progress, future generations are likely to be much better off than the current generation in any case, it was not always convincing to ask further sacrifices of today's workers.[21]

Conceptually, even with a low savings rate, there were two other ways of increasing GDP, the production that occurred within a country, within the standard paradigm. One was to import capital, though the benefits of the increased domestic output might accrue largely to the suppliers of capital. Within developing countries, there was much discussion of what they could do to attract more investment, from taking actions which ensured that the citizens of the country would receive ever less of the benefits of growth (e.g., as a result of tax holidays and land and other grants), to eliminating artificial impediments to the movement of foreign firms into the country. In some cases, so enthusiastic did governments become in recruiting investment that they "gave the company store away"; that is, while GDP went up—the value of what was produced inside the country increased—GNP, the income of the citizens, decreased. It is the latter (correctly measured) that matters, of course, and in many cases once the environmental and health effects were taken into account, the benefits to those living in the country were even more negative.[22]

In these circumstances, it is not surprising that foreign direct investment in some areas can generate enormous opposition. Later in this book, we will explain why this neoclassical analysis leaves out one of the most important potential benefits—those associated with learning—but that these learning benefits won't necessarily come on their own:

policies have to be designed to maximize them. And some international agreements are designed to limit the benefits that can accrue to developing countries. In some arenas, the *net* learning benefits may even be negative; that is, *from the perspective of learning*, given the constraints imposed by these international agreements, the country might be better off without (at least some of its) foreign direct investment. (See chapters 13 and 14.)

There is a second way to improve the outward movement of the production possibilities curve with a given rate of savings, and that is to improve the allocation of capital—how it is deployed. In the standard neoclassical economy (which is serving as a foil to the learning economy that we analyze here), capital goods are allocated efficiently, or at least would be in the absence of government distortions. One could not obtain more growth from the given level of savings. Of course, in the aftermath of the 2008 crisis (and the myriad of bubbles that preceded it in the short history of capitalism; see Kindleberger and Aliber [2005]), no one could claim that financial markets are efficient in either allocating capital or managing risk. We and others have treated these market failures extensively elsewhere (see, e.g., Stiglitz 2010b), and they are not, for the most part, the subject of this book, except to the extent that the policies that gave rise to these instabilities directly and indirectly may inhibit learning, thereby imposing lasting costs on society.

In short, we have argued that prospects for sustained increases in growth rates under the traditional neoclassical perspective are limited. There is a once-and-for-all gain as a result of eliminating static inefficiencies. If these are eliminated quickly, there is a rapid increase in growth while they are being eliminated, but then growth slows down to the rate at which the production possibilities schedule moves outward. Even the "growth" perspective focusing on increased savings has limited growth benefits, and these have to be offset by the significant costs associated with sacrifices in current consumption. Traditional analyses provide an uncompelling case for government intervention to increase the savings rate, and therefore even growth in the short run.

The one argument for government intervention that we have raised (beyond the direct role of government in enhancing societal learning, which is the focus of this book) is itself beyond the neoclassical model; it is that markets by themselves may be associated with inefficiencies in the allocation of capital and excessive instability. But even here, we argue that the standard analysis does not fully capture what is going on. Chapter 4 explains why instability is adverse to learning. There is thus a further long-run benefit to government policies directed at stabilizing the economy—not only do such policies result in fuller and more efficient utilization of resources, they may lead to systematically higher rates of productivity increase.

Reexamining Conceptual Foundations

Our analysis calls into question not only the traditional frame for parsing the sources of economic growth, but even the underlying notion of a production possibilities schedule. If we assume that it represents the maximum level of output of, say, one product, given the output of others, *given the state of knowledge of each firm,* then it subsumes the knowledge of each market participant. It begs the key questions of why differences in knowledge persist, what can be done to reduce the gaps, or what limits the scale of production of, say, the more efficient firms.

Many years ago, Nicholas Kaldor similarly argued against the notion of a production possibilities schedule for a firm—and, by implication, for an economy, on a somewhat similar basis. He suggested that a firm typically had knowledge of its own production processes and knowledge of some nearby deviations. To be sure, there might be markedly different capital-labor ratios for which technologies *could* be developed, but such technologies did not exist and could only be brought into existence by investments in engineering (see Atkinson and Stiglitz 1969).

By the same token, the traditional approach encourages tautologies, such as treating differences in the knowledge of workers which might affect their productivity as differences in human capital. By definition, then, outward movements of the production possibilities curve as a result of learning are transformed into outward movements of the curve as a result of the accumulation of human capital. One might argue that this is a distinction without a difference; but there is a difference: Here (as we shall emphasize shortly), we want to understand the learning process. Are there, for instance, ways of organizing the work experience that accelerate the learning process? Is there something that can be done to enhance the learning capacities of individuals? What are the trade-offs? What does a firm, or a society, have to give up if it is to become more dynamic?

Concluding Comments

It follows from the analysis of this chapter that it is possible for countries to increase their rate of growth, if not permanently, at least for an extended period of time, well beyond that associated with a one-time improvement in allocative efficiency, or even beyond that associated with an increase in the savings rate.[23] (In some of the models we construct later, we are able to show that countries can permanently increase their rate of growth.) The way they can do this is to create a learning society. For developed countries, this means ensuring that all firms learn quickly to improve their productivity, as best practices themselves improve, so that the gap between average and best practices is reduced;[24] distorting resource allocations toward sectors with more learning and more learning spillovers; and investing more in R & D and in learning to learn. For developing countries, it means doing all of this, but with an eye mostly on closing the gap between their firms and best practices in the advanced industrial countries. Some resource allocations have more potential for doing so than others; the learning generated in some sectors and with some technologies has a greater potential of generating spillovers to others and enhancing societal learning capacities.

As we have emphasized, the fact that as firms move toward the frontier, the frontier itself has moved out means, of course, that the gap between best practices and average practices is never eliminated: learning is a perpetual process. And as we have suggested at a number of points, there may be less to the distinction between the two types of learning—moving the frontier out and moving closer to the frontier—for there is typically room for improvement in even the industry leader, and it may have something to learn from other firms both in its industry and in others.

This book focuses on learning as the basis of sustained growth and development, either to catch up with the best practices or to improve upon them. This chapter has presented micro- and macro-evidence supporting in particular the proposition that the productivity of firms and economies is well below what it might be, given the extant state of knowledge, and has highlighted the importance of learning in closing that gap. The appendix to this chapter constructs an equilibrium model in which it is optimal for some firms always to remain at some distance from best practices. There is always a knowledge gap. The next chapter takes a closer look at how learning takes place and the determinants of the pace of learning, the critical ingredients in creating a learning society.

APPENDIX

Equilibrium Knowledge Gaps

It is easy to construct simple models in which knowledge gaps persist; they are part of an equilibrium. There are costs of closing the knowledge gap which are sufficiently great that the lagging firms decide never to do so. We assume that there are two types of firms, those on the frontier and those that lag, and that the rate of growth of productivity is a function of the firm's investment in productivity enhancement, i (measured as a share of, say, its output), and the relative gap that exists between it and the best-practice firms, G:

$$g = H(G, i). \tag{A.1}$$

The rate of increase in productivity of the firm(s) on the frontier is given by[25]

$$g = H(0, i). \tag{A.1a}$$

A full analysis would entail each firm beginning with a given level of technology (initial values of productivity, defining then the initial productivity gaps). Given its beliefs about the actions (investments in productivity enhancement) of other firms, each firm chooses an optimal path of investments in productivity enhancement ($i[t]$) which maximizes the present discounted value of its profits. An equilibrium is one where beliefs about others' actions are consistent with their actual optimal policies.

We simplify by focusing on steady states. We denote the frontier firm with a subscript f, and the laggard firms with a subscript l. The present discounted value of profits is given by $\prod(G, i)$. Then an equilibrium knowledge gap is a set of $\{i_f^*, i_l^*, g^*, G^*\}$ such that all firms are maximizing profits, and at the given gap, G^*, the rate of productivity enhancement of the frontier firm and the laggard firms are identical. The gap between the two types of firms persists. That is:

$$\Pi_i^f (G^*, i_f^*) = 0 \qquad\qquad\qquad (A.2)$$

$$\Pi_i^l (G^*, i_l^*) = 0 \qquad\qquad\qquad (A.3)$$

$$g^* = H(G^*, i_l^*) \qquad\qquad\qquad (A.4)$$

$$g^* = H(0, i_f^*). \qquad\qquad\qquad (A.5)$$

A frontier firm could, of course, always decide to join the laggard firms, saving in the interim considerable investments in productivity enhancement; but a laggard firm could only become a frontier firm by spending considerably more than it is current doing to close the knowledge gap. Hence, $\Pi^f(G^*, i_f^*) \gg \Pi^l(G^*, i_l^*)$, and the differences are its knowledge rents.[26]

CHAPTER THREE

A Learning Economy

A "LEARNING society" perspective takes a very different view of growth and development strategies from the standard neoclassical approach in several respects. It begins, as the last chapter explained, by focusing on the knowledge embedded in individuals, firms, and in society more generally—and how that knowledge changes, is transmitted, and is put to use. It recognizes that the state of knowledge of each individual in the economy can be (and typically is) markedly different. Knowledge, like information, is *asymmetric*. Each individual knows things that others don't. From the perspective of the individual, an advance in his or her knowledge is simply knowing something that he or she had not previously known. Indeed, in perhaps most cases, the knowledge that an individual obtains is already known (in some sense) by someone else; in a few cases, the knowledge that an individual obtains may not be known by anyone else, at least in a form which is easily recognizable. While the consequences of information asymmetry have been extensively explored over the past forty years,[1] the consequences of differential knowledge have not.[2]

Creating a dynamic learning society has many dimensions: individuals have to have a mindset and skills to learn. There has to be some motivation for learning. Knowledge is created by individuals, typically working within organizations, and transmitted to others within the organization. It is then transmitted from one organization and individual to another. But the extent, ease, and rapidity of transmission of knowledge is itself one of the central features of a learning society: for the new knowledge spurs new thinking; it is the catalyst as well as the input out of which new ideas and creativity emerge.

Some societies are better at learning than others—both in ensuring that the gap between best and average practices is smaller and in the pace with which the knowledge frontier moves out.

This chapter explores some of the elements that make for a learning society, asking how we can create an economic architecture that facilitates learning. Conventional discussions, especially among certain policy circles, focus too narrowly, for instance, in providing better incentives through greater appropriation of returns through stronger intellectual property rights (IPR). Not only is this view too narrow—as we explain later in this chapter, nonpecuniary intrinsic incentives may play a more important role in motivating learning than IPR—but it may be misguided, with stronger IPR encouraging secrecy and impeding the transmission of knowledge. As we show in appendix A to chapter 5, the result may be that innovators take more out of the pool of opportunities than they contribute, resulting in a smaller pool of opportunities and a slower pace of innovation. This book will explain how many other aspects of the legal, institutional, and policy framework affect learning—including not just education and labor market policies, but also trade and industrial policies.

The first three parts of the chapter discuss *what is to be learned, the process of learning*, and *the determinants of learning*. We provide a taxonomy of the basic ingredients to a learning society. The next parts of the chapter look in depth at two of the major determinants of a learning society—spillovers and motivation. After then discussing some of the important impediments to creating a learning society, the final section of the chapter analyzes some of the key trade-offs in the design of a learning society.

Much of learning occurs within firms. The next chapter uses the ideas developed in this chapter to examine more closely what enables some firms to learn better than others and to explain why policies that

help promote the industrial sector are likely to be particularly conducive to creating a dynamic learning society.

1. What Is to Be Learned

Most of this book focuses on learning how to use inputs better to produce outputs: how to increase productivity, getting more output per
unit labor, capital, energy, or other resource inputs. The data discussed
in the last chapter showed the dramatic differences in productivity
across societies and firms.

New Products: Learning How to Better Meet Consumer Needs

When we think of societal learning (and a society's learning capacities), we need to think broadly, not just in terms of particular production processes, upon which much of our discussion so far has focused.
Societies also have to learn what products are best suited for their environment, an environment which is always changing, as both as preferences and market conditions change. Sometimes, it is best to think of
the outputs as certain "services" that are enjoyed by consumers, and
innovation consists of new products that provide these services in better and less expensive ways.

Learning about Comparative Advantages

Some individuals in society are more capable than others, or at least
better suited for particular jobs. Part of the role of the education system is to identify these absolute and comparative advantages. But some
education systems perform these "learning" tasks better than others
(see, e.g., Stiglitz 1975b).

Learning to Manage Organizations and Societies

One of the most important aspects of learning is learning to "organize,"
to manage collectivities of individuals. Large organizations can do
things that small organizations can't, but managing large organizations
requires knowledge that is different from that associated with managing
small organizations. One of the main advances of the twentieth century

was figuring out how to manage large research projects—divide tasks into components that could be undertaken by different groups, with pieces that could be subsequently put together.

In each arena of our society, there has been learning that has enabled our complex society to function. Keeping accounts is necessary for the functioning of a modern firm and a modern society. Thus, learning about accounting is essential; and keeping accounts for large organizations or in a modern large economy requires ever more complex systems. (The accounting scandals show that there has perhaps been more "learning" about how to circumvent or take advantage of existing accounting rules than there has been on the design of rules and conventions that are immune to such circumvention and that provide the information that is needed or desirable in an effective way.)

Our complex society could not function without regulations, either. But again, there is considerable scope for learning—learning, for instance, how to regulate in ways which control externalities without imposing undue costs. The failure of banking regulations—both to ensure that financial markets perform the societal functions that they are supposed to perform and that they not impose the enormous adverse externalities that they did in the crisis of 2008—shows that there is still much to be learned.[3] This is part of a broader theme: learning how to make markets act like markets are supposed to behave.

Firms and societies have to learn how to *compete*. They have to learn how to export as well.

In short, everything we do—as individuals, as organizations, as societies—requires learning. Things can be done better; we can be more successful in accomplishing our ends—in ways which require less resources and less time.

Learning Capacities and Learning to Learn[4]

Not only do firms (and societies) differ in their ability to transform inputs into output (i.e., they differ in their *knowledge*), they also differ in their ability to learn. Some individuals, firms, and countries are quicker at picking up changes that have occurred elsewhere, discovering knowledge that might be relevant, and adapting technology to their circumstances.

But just as *knowledge* itself is endogenous, so is the ability to *learn*. Some economic activities (conducted in certain ways) not only facilitate learning, they may facilitate *learning to learn*.

Paul MacCready's attempt to design a human-powered flight vehicle illustrates a recent instance of "learning to learn." He realized that key to designing such a vehicle was learning to learn. Previous attempts involved large investments based on often well-conceived theories, but when the vehicle crashed, there was no opportunity to make refinements. He focused on how to build a plane that could be rebuilt in hours. That enabled him to *learn*, to correct mistakes at reasonably low costs, and in short order, he was then able to construct the desired device.[5]

Learning abilities can, of course, be specific or general, and there may be trade-offs between the two: Some individuals may have an ability to learn quite generally, while others have developed more focused capacities. We can direct our efforts at enhancing specific learning abilities—that may serve an economy well if it is pursuing a narrow niche; or efforts can be directed at more general learning abilities, which may serve it well in periods of rapid transition and great uncertainty.

Learning for Development

Within developing countries, skills that are of especial relevance but particularly scarce are those associated with entrepreneurship.[6] One of the attributes of good entrepreneurs is their ability to learn and adapt. Some societies do a better job at learning who is better at this kind of learning, of selecting potential entrepreneurs.

So too, developing countries have to learn what products they are best capable of producing and are best suited to their conditions (see Hoff [1997] and Hausmann and Rodrik [2003]; later in the chapter, we discuss these issues further).

One of the key problems facing many developing countries is that they are exposed to high levels of volatility, and they have weak institutions for coping with this. Learning to manage risks is thus also important for successful development.[7]

2. The Process of Learning

Some learning is a result of explicit allocation of resources to research and development, but much learning is a by-product of production and investment.

Learning by Doing

We learn by doing. We learn how to produce more efficiently by producing—and as we produce, we observe how we can do it more efficiently. There is ample empirical evidence supporting this hypothesis at the micro-level, both before and after Arrow's classic work.[8] Much of the formal analytics of this book is predicated on the assumption that much learning occurs by doing.[9] While this assumption greatly simplifies the analysis, it is a straightforward matter to extend the model, and at a few points, we show how this can be done.

How much we learn by doing is affected by how we do what we do. If we consciously experiment on the job, looking for alternative ways of doing what we are doing, we are likely to learn more than if we passively wait for a *eureka* moment, when we have a brilliant insight about an alternative way of doing what we have been doing.

Arrow's model itself linked learning with investment. Many advances in technology are embodied in new capital goods (Solow 1962b). The more "machines" that are made, the better the machines and the higher productivity. But interestingly, much of the cited evidence on learning by doing relates learning more directly to production, to, for instance, the number of airplanes constructed.

But investments can promote learning and productivity improvements in other ways as well. Technological knowledge is embodied in machines, and a machine constructed for one purpose can often be adapted for quite another. It is not an accident that the Ohio Valley (stretching up to Michigan) gave rise to innovations in bicycles, airplanes, and cars. While the products were distinct, the development of these products shared some of the same technological know-how. This illustrates the principle that it may be difficult to identify ex ante what are "nearby" products, products such that advances in learning in one affect the other. (We will return to these themes later.)

New machines can also be a catalyst for learning. Computerization provides an important example. In the process of computerization, firms had to rethink their business operations, to codify much of what they had done without thinking. Through that process, they came to learn, to think about how much of what they did could be done better.

So can new production methods be a catalyst for learning. Just-in-time production not only served the function of reducing inventory costs. But following the motto "you only find out who is swimming naked when the tide goes out,"[10] just-in-time production exposed problems in the production process, forcing firms to address them. In a sense, it forced learning.

It follows from the fact that we learn by doing, that what we do and how we do it affects what we learn and the evolution of our economy and society. When a society focuses on learning how to save labor, reducing the labor input per unit output, it increases its capacities for this type of learning; conversely, if it chooses to focus on learning how to reduce the environmental footprint of products and production, its learning capacities in that direction can be enhanced.[11]

Learning to Learn by Learning

Just as we learn by doing, we learn to learn partly by learning. Hence, there may be a virtuous cycle: Countries that have managed to advance technology, providing more opportunities (and a greater necessity) for learning, may simultaneously enhance the ability to learn.[12]

Learning from Others

We also learn from others, both in formal education and, even more importantly, in everyday contact with others. Knowledge is embodied in people and is transmitted by contact among people. This is especially relevant for what is called *tacit knowledge*, understandings that are hard to codify, to articulate as simple prescriptions that can easily be conveyed through textbooks or classroom learning. Workers move from firm to firm and thus convey some of the learning that has occurred in one firm to those in others.

Equally importantly, what we learn from others (or from achievements of others) can be a *catalyst* for our own learning: it may lead us to ask new questions or to see things in a slightly different way, and the result of this may be new insights, new learning.

Knowledge is also embodied in firms that supply inputs to multiple firms. What they learn in dealing with one firm in one industry may be relevant for another firm. There can be backward, forward, and horizontal linkages (Hirschman 1958).

The structure of the economy (including policies and regulations) affects the extent to which learning from others occurs. An economy with more mobility and openness is likely to be one in which there is more such learning. Some labor contracts are designed both to reduce mobility and to reduce the scope for ideas to be transmitted through mobility. Universities have traditionally been structured to maximize the extent to which there can be learning from others. More recently, however, the intrusion of IPR through the Bayh-Dole Act (which enables universities to appropriate some of the returns to research which goes on within them) may have provided increased incentives for secrecy and for less openness. On the other hand, the Internet has provided a technology which has facilitated learning from others.

More openness and mobility affects the flow of information through society, but it may have adverse effects on incentives to learn. This is another example of a kind of trade-off that is pervasive in the analysis of learning economies. In later chapters, we will show that the market solution—for instance, the level of mobility that results as part of a Nash equilibrium in which each firm tries to recruit workers from others but imposes restraints on others from recruiting from itself[13]—is not in general efficient.

One of the objectives of industrial policies (broadly construed, as described earlier in this book) is to facilitate learning from others. This is especially true in agriculture, particularly in developing countries, where "model farms" have sometimes been used to help disseminate best practices. One of the objectives of colleges and universities has traditionally been to facilitate learning from each other.

Learning by Trade

Trade, of course, facilitates interactions and thus learning. Advocates of free trade suggest that expanding trade is important because it facilitates learning. Successful exporters *have* to learn what it is that customers want; they have to learn about what competitors are supplying and figure out how to outperform. Domestic producers exposed to foreign competition from imports *have* to learn how to compete—how to produce products that are at least as good as those by foreign competition. More broadly, opening up to the rest of the world catalyzes learning and provides contacts from whom one can learn.

Later, we will explain why some trade restrictions may actually enhance societal learning. In making this argument, we are not arguing for autarky; we are not even denying that there are learning benefits from trade. What we are saying is that there are also learning benefits from domestic production and that the free trade literature has essentially ignored these benefits. We are also arguing that in assessing the learning benefits from trade, one has to be more precise in the analysis: (1) What are the sectors/products/technologies being traded? (2) What are the learning spillovers from abroad to the domestic agents? (3) What are the learning spillovers from those domestic agents to the rest of the economy? (4) What is the counterfactual learning: if the product had not been imported, or imported to the same extent, what is the level of learning that would have occurred? With what spillovers? Could the government have shaped the domestic production (e.g., the choice of technology) in a way which enhanced learning, more effectively than it can shape learning that is brought about through trade?

In the simple models presented in later chapters, we provide unambiguous answers to these questions, showing that there are contexts in which trade restrictions can help promote learning and hence raise long-run living standards to a far higher level than would have been achieved through free trade.

Technology and Learning Processes

Changes in technology affect what and how we learn (and what and how we *should* learn). One might caricature the "old" learning model as one in which the teacher pours knowledge, viewed as relevant at the time the kid is going to school, into the brain of the child, which he will then draw upon the rest of his life to solve problems. This model was never fully appropriate: at least the better schools prided themselves in also providing analytic skills critical for problem solving.

More recent years have seen a shift in focus to lifelong learning, with the recognition that what one is going to need to know in twenty years can't be adequately anticipated today. But the Internet and the vast store of knowledge instantaneously accessible there has changed matters further. Why store in the brain information that can be accessed in a moment? Some suggest that all that one needs to store in the brain is knowledge relevant to accessing information quickly, but that is clearly wrong. There is a plethora of information that flows over the Internet, and one must constantly make judgments about the quality (veracity) and relevance of the information. One must put the information received into context and be able to use it in conjunction with other information.

By the same token, much of what goes on in the workplace is constantly changing, and employers do not expect employees to come to them equipped to be a fully productive member of the workforce. The expectation is that there will have to be on-the-job training—and this on-the-job training will be ongoing. Hence, we can think of our lifetime education system as consisting of two parts, a formal part ("schools") and an informal part ("jobs and elsewhere"). The two are complementary as much as they are substitutes: if the first does its job well, it increases the returns to expenditures by the second. But unfortunately, there is little coordination between the two, at least in most countries, and hence formal schooling is often of limited relevance to on-the-job learning in many sectors.

What should be clear is that changes in production and knowledge technologies have altered the way we do and should learn, and a well-functioning learning society adapts itself to these changes.[14]

In the previous section, we discussed the learning associated with trade. But that too can be affected by technology. If a country produces a complex product (like an automobile), for which it imports most of the parts but makes some of the parts locally, there is *some* learning associated with the manufacturing of these local parts. But when the technology becomes highly complex, all of the components may be made and assembled abroad; even the technology for assessing whether the object is working effectively may be imported from abroad. There may be learning associated with how to use the technology but little learning relevant to production. The extent of spillovers may be lower, and thus the learning benefits of trade may be reduced.

3. The Determinants of Learning

A central thesis of this book is not just that learning provides the key explanation for the remarkable increases in standards of living in the past, but that the rate and direction of learning is endogenous, differs across countries and over time, and can be affected by the decisions of individuals, firms, and governments. The central policy issue of this book is how to enhance learning—how to create a learning economy and society.

With our previous discussion of the objectives and processes of learning as background, this section provides a taxonomy of the major determinants of learning: (1) learning capabilities; (2) access to knowledge; (3) the catalysts for learning; (4) creating a creative mindset—the right cognitive frames; (5) contacts—people with whom one interacts—which can catalyze learning, help create the right cognitive frame, and provide crucial inputs into the learning process; and (6) the context for learning.

Learning occurs at all levels within a society—individuals learn, but so do enterprises, and even governments. More generally, there may be "social learning," changes in societal beliefs that lead, in turn, through the political system, to different public actions.[15]

The analysis of these determinants provides the crucial ingredients for the design of a *learning architecture*: designing structures (e.g., firms, institutions, and frameworks in which they interact), policies, and societies more generally that promote learning and innovation. While some firms—the most innovative ones—have worried about how to design themselves in ways that promote learning within themselves,[16] surprisingly—given the importance ascribed to innovation in modern capitalism—the subject of how to design the overall economy to promote innovation has been given short shrift.[17] The objective of this book is to fill this lacuna.

Learning Capabilities

The most important determinant of individuals' learning is their capabilities, their ability to learn, and perhaps the most important determinant of that is education. As we emphasized earlier, individuals have to learn how to learn. Well-designed education systems (not those focusing on rote learning) are concerned precisely with learning to learn. As we have noted, modern education and labor market policies focus on "lifelong learning," enhancing the ability to adapt to an ever-changing marketplace. This facilitates individuals moving from one firm to another, with large private and social benefits to the ensuing flexibility. Since much, if not most, economically relevant learning occurs on the job, not in formal schooling, one should see formal education and on-the-job training as complements, with the former designed to enhance the productivity of the latter.

Much of traditional economics focuses on education's role in increasing human capital, the stock of knowledge embodied in individuals. It is typically measured by years of schooling. Our emphasis is quite different. Years spent on rote learning might (or might not) increase the stock of (even relevant) knowledge and, in that sense, increase productivity, at least temporarily, until that knowledge becomes obsolete. But such schooling would not necessarily increase the ability to learn—increasing capacities for lifelong learning—and could actually impede it, especially if, as part of such education, there is an attempt to inculcate ideas that are antithetical to science.[18]

Earlier, we emphasized trade-offs between static efficiency and dynamic gains. This is also true in education. In the short run, we might be able to impart more knowledge through an education system that demanded frequent testing of what students have learned and that focused less on enhancing analytic skills and cognitive abilities; but the learning capacities and creativity of those emerging from such an education system might be less.

AGE STRUCTURE   Among the determinants of a society's (or firm's) ability to learn is its age structure—and possibly the age profile of its management structure. As the old saw has it, you can't teach an old dog new tricks. *On average*, younger individuals are more capable of (and open to) learning. In a sense, they have no choice: they have to learn the skills and knowledge that will enable them to succeed.

They also are likely to have greater incentives for learning. They are not invested in old ideas and ways of doing things; indeed, they even can have incentives to create new ways of doing things in which they excel.[19] They have a lifetime to benefit from such learning, and such learning gives them a competitive advantage over those who are older.[20]

One of the concerns facing Western societies (including Japan) is their changing demographics, in which the proportion of young people in the workforce will diminish markedly. The effects of this can be partially offset in economic systems in which there is a rapid pace of turnover of firms—with new firms, dominated by younger individuals, playing a vital role.[21]

Access to Knowledge

All knowledge builds on preexisting knowledge. As Isaac Newton described his own path-breaking work, "If I have seen further, it is by standing on the shoulders of giants."[22] That is especially true in our fast-moving innovation economy, where producing a complex product requires solving dozens, perhaps even hundreds, of problems. That is why access to knowledge is key to learning and to the further advancement of knowledge. We have noted the special importance of this in the process of development, given the recognition that what separates developing from developed countries is more a gap in knowledge even than a gap in resources.

Many aspects of the design of the economic system affect access to knowledge. The open-source movement is motivated by a commitment to access. As we noted, universities and modern science too work hard to maintain a culture of openness which ensures access to knowledge.

Later (chapter 15), we will discuss the ambivalent role played by intellectual property: while it may provide greater incentives for undertaking research, it simultaneously restricts access to and use of knowledge. While one of the key provisions of patent law is that to obtain a patent, one has to disclose information so that others can build upon it (a provision designed partially to ameliorate the adverse effects of the patent system on access to knowledge), many, especially in software, have criticized and tried to circumvent these disclosure requirements. And there is some evidence that the disclosures made as part of patent applications are often of a pro forma nature and do not adequately reveal what has been learned.[23] Complex products make use of multiple patents, and if even one seemingly small patent holder refuses to grant use of the patent (a "holdup"), there can be large costs in inventing around the patent, and innovation can be substantially impeded.[24]

Many in the developing world believe that the intellectual property regime adopted as part of the Uruguay Round trade negotiations impeded development because it impeded access to knowledge. Subsequently, in 2004, the World Intellectual Property Organization (WIPO) called for a *developmentally oriented intellectual property regime*, one in which access to knowledge for developing countries would be pivotal.[25]

Catalysts

Learning requires individuals and organizations to have the capabilities to learn, but individuals and organizations have to be spurred to learn. In a learning society, individuals are exposed to many *catalysts*. We use the term *catalyst* deliberately. As we have noted, much knowledge (innovation) builds on other innovations. But sometimes, one idea can incite new ideas—even if the new ideas do not "use" the old idea or build on it directly. In that sense, they are like a catalyst—a chemical that facilitates a reaction but is not itself used (or used up) in the process.

We learned from the discovery of rayon that it was possible to create (at affordable prices) synthetic fibers. Simply knowing this—even without knowing the precise way that rayon was constructed—can be an important spur to further learning and research. But we learn even more—we can be stimulated even more—from the disclosure of information that is contained in a patent application, even if, because of the patent, we cannot use (without paying for it) the patented product itself.

Advances in technology are among the most important catalysts to learning: We can learn more if there is more to learn. Policies, including government expenditures, that result in faster movements outward of leading-edge technologies mean that there is more for others to learn— if we do not impose impediments to their learning (e.g., through intellectual property).

Contacts

Earlier, we described the learning process, and central to the learning process is people learning from other people. These interactions both provide the knowledge input that is the basis of learning and provide the catalyst which enhances innovation.

Knowledge, in this sense, is like a (good) disease: it can spread upon contact. But some kinds of contact are more likely to lead to the transmission of knowledge than others. Some of the people who might possibly come into contact with the knowledge are "susceptible"; i.e., they are more likely to learn, to use the knowledge, and perhaps even to develop it further. And some types of economic structures can facilitate individuals coming into contact with each other—while other structures can impede contact. Universities and research institutes try to create an interactive environment to enhance the range and depth of contacts.[26] Economic systems that encourage mobility may increase the extent of contacts that bring with them learning and catalyze learning. Structured interaction can be even better—that is, organizational architectures that help bring individuals who might stimulate each other into contact. Some firms have policies of regularly shifting their employees, partly because in doing so, it facilitates the spread of ideas across the firm and promotes learning within the firm.

Traditionally interactions were largely affected by geographical proximity, and this helps explain the development of learning clusters— locales at which learning, especially in particular areas, occurs at a more rapid pace than elsewhere. The strength of these local interactions provides one of the main sources of agglomeration economies—why it makes sense for certain activities to congregate together in particular places. The "localization" of contacts and the ability to communicate provides one of the explanations for why knowledge moves more freely within a country than across national boundaries. Differences in language are a barrier to the movement of ideas; sharing a common education system can, by contrast, facilitate the movement of ideas.[27]

One of the benefits of globalization is that it has expanded individuals' exposure to new ideas.[28,29] Contacts, of course, don't have to be face-to-face; the Internet has vastly expanded the ability of individuals to communicate with each other, improving both access to knowledge and the possible range of contacts.[30]

Cognitive Frames

Individuals and firms have to adopt a cognitive frame, a mindset, that is conducive to learning. That entails the belief that change is possible and important—and can be shaped and advanced by deliberate activities.[31] Part of the reason for the relative stagnation in living standards that persisted for thousands of years before the industrial and learning revolutions was that there was not this cognitive frame.[32] And of course, the absence (or slow pace) of change meant that these beliefs were self-reinforcing. In a world with little change, there are few catalysts to learning, and little effort is spent on creating change and adapting to it. And because people were so bad at adapting to change, because they had not learned how to learn and did not have the institutional structures that helped them bear the costs of change, there was often large resistance to change (e.g., the Luddite movement of the nineteenth century).[33]

In the West, the Enlightenment—with its belief in science and rationality, careful experimentation, and close inference—was pivotal in creating the learning mindset. It represented a marked departure from a mindset that saw truth as being revealed from on high. It is curious that while those in developing countries are striving to embrace the scientific method, in the United States, the country which has led the world in the development of technology, large swaths of the population cast aspersions on the results of modern science, most notably evolutionary theory and climate change.[34] Policy makers trying to promote learning and the advancement of science and technology often seem to face the task of relitigating the Enlightenment.

How a learning mindset is created is a complex matter.[35] Fundamental beliefs, such as those that we have been discussing (such as that change is desirable and can be created) are, to a large extent, social constructions. We believe what we believe partly because those that we talk to believe similarly. This can result in societal rigidities—it is hard for any individual to change his mindset on his own, or for any single individual to bring about a change in the collective mindset. But such changes are essential for development—for the transformation of countries from stagnation to growth, to becoming a learning economy.

At the same time, beliefs have to confront reality. A large gap between beliefs and reality provides a strong impetus for a change in beliefs. But ideas matter and have a life of their own. The spread of the Enlightenment and the scientific method was partly based on their ability to provide convincing interpretations of observations that seemed otherwise inexplicable, to make predictions that could not have otherwise been made, but it was partly based, too, on the power of the ideas themselves.[36]

While we may not fully understand the spread of the "learning mindset," what is clear is that education is pivotal. A well-designed education system can help create the right cognitive frame, but there are also education systems that can "inoculate" individuals against the Enlightenment and the development of a learning mentality.

Context: General Observations on a Learning Environment

Learning occurs in a context. Most learning occurs within a firm. Some environments (e.g., the culture of some firms or societies) are more conducive to learning than others. They can help create learning capabilities and a learning mindset and establish networks of contacts that provide strong catalysts for learning. Some environments can stifle learning, failing to develop learning capabilities, inhibiting the flow of knowledge, making it difficult to put to use learning that occurs, and because much learning, as we noted, is a result of "doing," this inhibits further learning.

The extent of learning can be affected both by the macro-economy and by the structure of the firms in which individuals work. Later in this chapter, we'll discuss two key aspects of the learning environment, spillovers and motivations, and we'll discuss in greater detail some of the other more salient aspects of the learning environment in the next chapter. (Later chapters, especially in part 3, will discuss still other aspects of a learning environment, touching on social protection, labor legislation, and laws affecting finance and investment.) We note that both the macro-environment and the system of social protection—as well as the level of inequality and other attributes of the economic system—can affect learning. For instance, individuals who are preoccupied with survival or who face high levels of stress typically cannot learn as well as those who have a modicum of security. The prevalence of stress and anxiety is likely to be greater in societies in which there is a low level of trust.[37]

Here, we note that there may be multiple societal equilibria. More dynamic societies with larger change create a greater demand for learning; they reward those with learning capabilities more and incentivize individuals to acquire those skills and mindsets. Societies with little change put little value in these skills and thus fail to incentivize individuals to acquire them. The result is that there is little change. (Assume, for example, that some individuals are better in bureaucratic skills, others at innovation. There is one societal equilibrium which can be thought of as "bureaucratic," where those who are better in bureaucratic skills thrive, and individuals within this society learn to better manage bureaucratic processes. Other societies become more innovative. In such societies, those with more innovative abilities prosper, relative to those who are better at managing bureaucratic processes, and individuals develop the learning capacities that enable them to prosper in such societies.)[38]

In the appendix, we illustrate these ideas with a formal model.

4. A Closer Look at Learning Spillovers

We emphasized earlier that there are important positive externalities from learning. Such spillovers are pervasive and large, and they are larger in some industries than in others. Obviously, markets will not take into account these externalities—a critical market failure which is at the heart of the analysis of this book.

Localized Learning

There are many aspects of learning spillovers. As Atkinson and Stiglitz (1969) noted, learning is localized: it affects production processes that are similar to those for which there has been learning more than it affects production processes that are markedly different. Improvements in a capital-intensive process of making textiles may have little impact on hand-loom technology. But the learning is not limited to a single process and related processes for a particular product. Innovations in one sector may benefit seemingly unrelated sectors, because the production of any good involves many stages, and some of the stages may involve processes that are similar to those used in another seemingly distinct sector. Sectors that are, in one way or another, more similar may, of course, benefit more. Indeed, the spillovers may be greater to other products using analogous technologies than to firms using dissimilar technologies within the same industry.

The spillovers involve more than learning about technology. There are especially important spillovers in methods of production. Inventory control and cash management techniques affect virtually every firm in an economy. Just-in-time production or assembly lines are examples of production processes that affect many industries.[39]

There are, by the same token, "institutional" spillovers. The development of a financial sector suited to serve, say, the manufacturing industry may have enormous benefits to other sectors of the economy. Many of these spillovers can be economy-wide. Similarly, improvements in the education system, necessary for an effective industrial sector, too can have benefits for the service sector or the agricultural sector; indeed, the benefits are likely to be economy-wide.

The spillovers involve not just technologies but people. Improvements in skills in one sector have spillover benefits to other sectors in which analogous skills are employed.

The theory of localized learning suggests that spillovers may flow more naturally not only from one technology to other similar technologies, but from one product to certain other products. This may because of institutional factors—people flow more frequently from firms producing one product to those producing another—or because of technological factors, related to the similarities in certain aspects of the production processes. Hidalgo and colleagues (2007) characterize the product space, attempting to identify where there are the most significant spillovers, e.g., which sectors entail similar "capabilities." Presumably, if two products entail similar capabilities, learning that enhances a particular capability in one sector will have spillover benefits to related sectors for which that same capability is relevant.[40] Capabilities, in this sense, can include not only worker skills but organizational learning and institutional developments. They map out industries that seem related, i.e., where the development of one industry is associated with the development of another, but this describes the spillover that exist under current institutional arrangements. It does not describe the spillovers that might occur under alternative institutional arrangements, e.g., with a more active industrial policy.

GEOGRAPHICAL AND CULTURAL LOCALIZATION[41] There is another aspect of localization: geographic and cultural. Learning is geographically localized, in part, because knowledge relevant to one locale is less so to another. It is also localized because information flows are localized. When people are spread apart geographically, there is a less dense set of contacts, and because of language and cultural differences, communication may be less effective. Transportation networks, too, facilitate interactions, say, within a country rather than across national boundaries. Because learning itself is a complex process, one may be able to learn more easily from those who speak the same language and are attuned to how one thinks and perceives the world—and so there may be larger learning spillovers.

Thus, learning spillovers may be larger to countries (regions, locales) that are *similar* in some fundamental ways. This is obviously the case in agriculture, where agriculture improvements suitable for one locale may not be for another, where soil types and rainfall and other aspects of climate may be markedly different.

Geographical localization is one of the reasons that knowledge flows less freely across borders than it does within borders—something which should be apparent from the large disparities in productivities across countries and which is central to the analysis of later chapters.

While geographical localization means that some learning that is relevant in one locale will be *less* relevant in another, most changes in technology and many changes in institutional learning, however, *could* confer benefits across borders. The extent to which that is the case may depend on the level of skills (human capital) and the institutional arrangements.

In chapter 4, we will note another aspect of "localization," the fact that knowledge or learning flows more easily within a firm than across firm boundaries. Multinational firms have facilitated the movement of knowledge across national boundaries—but often have been effective in restricting the flow of knowledge within firm boundaries, limiting, as a result, the benefits of foreign direct investment (FDI). Chapter 14 discusses government policies which can enhance the learning benefits that can be reaped from FDI.

LOCALIZED LEARNING TO LEARN   Not only is knowledge (learning) localized, so too may be learning how to learn. Countries (firms) are likely to learn about this learning more easily from neighbors. It is not an accident, in this view, that Japan's neighbors were the first to learn how to learn—they observed, and imitated, what Japan had done. This knowledge of learning how to learn then diffused around Asia. Korea was attentive to the policies that Japan had pursued that had allowed it to close the knowledge gap between it and the more advanced industrial countries. (Some of these policies will be the subject of subsequent discussion.)

There is another aspect of localized learning to learn. Learning involves specialized skills, and improvements in learning in one area may be at the expense of learning to learn in other areas. Western firms have learned how to save labor—even when there is a high unemployment rate, so there is a high social costs to such labor-saving innovation. But they have not done well in learning how to protect the environment and reduce their resource footprint.

LOCALIZED LEARNING, CONVENTIONAL ECONOMIC THEORY, AND WHY HISTORY MATTERS   The fact that much learning occurs within a firm (or a country) and does not easily or costlessly move across (firm or country) boundaries has profound implications for conventional economic theory. It means that firms (countries) necessarily have different production functions. To assume that they have the same knowledge is as silly as assuming that they have the same factor endowments. Indeed, much of the modern theory of trade is predicated on the imperfect mobility of factors of production but the perfect mobility of knowledge (that is, it is *assumed* that production functions are the same); but the movement of knowledge across boundaries (whether of firms or countries) is even more difficult than the movement of factors. Indeed, it is imperfections of information that represent the most important impediment to the movement of capital: if information flowed perfectly, it is arguable that so too would capital.

If, of course, at least some learning/knowledge never moved, then we could still approach the problem of resource allocation using conventional frameworks. Given the state of knowledge of each enterprise, we would allocate factors to ensure marginal returns are the same for each use. But a central message of this book is that that approach is misguided: we can affect the flow of knowledge; we can affect learning; these are affected by economic policies, institutions, the design of economic structures, and resource allocations (both sectoral allocations and choices of technologies).

The fact that learning is specific to a particular technology (a particular technique) means that, in a sense, the set of techniques available at any point of time is likely to consist of techniques presently used or used in the past. Of course, there are a range of techniques which, with additional investments, could be developed. But it means that, for practical purposes, the distinction between movements along an isoquant and "technical" change may be less important than is usually assumed.

It means too that history matters—in a way that is not the case in the standard model. Figure 3.1. shows an isoquant of a firm, entailing two techniques of production, a capital-intensive technique labeled A and a labor-intensive technique labeled B. The notion of localized technical change means that an improvement in A may leave B unaffected, and vice versa. Thus, common formulations of technological change, which see it as shifting the production function in some smooth way (reducing the input requirements for *all* technologies), are fundamentally misguided.[42]

Assume that initially, the economy is in a steady-state growth path in which it uses B, with capital expanding at the rate of the labor force. Assume, further, that this technology is one which gives rise to little learning—per capita income stagnates.

Then the country faces a plague, which wipes out a large fraction of the labor force. Given the increased labor scarcity, wages rise and the economy shifts to the capital-intensive technology A. But there is

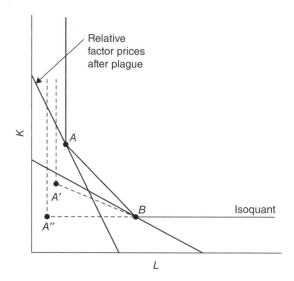

Figure 3.1 Localized technical progress: History matters

Improvements in the capital-intensive technology leave the other technology unaffected. Eventually, the capital-intensive technology dominates the other technology. (Before the plague, with the abundance of labor, the economy uses technology B, in which there is little learning. The change in relative prices induces a switch to technology A. As A is used, it improves, moving to A′ and A″.)

considerable "learning by doing" associated with A. Productivity per worker increases markedly, so that A moves from A to A′ to A″[43]—to the point where eventually technique A dominates technique B. But that means that even as the economy recovers from the plague, and the capital-labor ratio diminishes, A continues to be used. The history of the economy is qualitatively and quantitatively different from what it would have been had there been no plague. In the long run, output per head and the rate of growth in output per head are higher than what they otherwise would have been.[44]

LOCALIZED LEARNING AND LEARNING STRATEGIES But if history matters, it means that planning and strategy are important. One has to plan present activity with a view to its long-run consequences.

This is perhaps especially true of developing countries, which (at least historically) received their technology from the advanced countries.

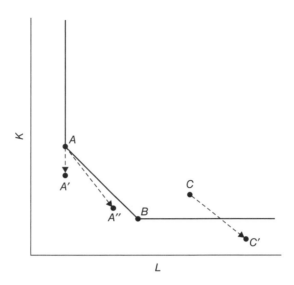

Figure 3.2 Localized learning

Developing countries have a choice of relying on technology made available by advanced countries, trying to adapt that technology to their circumstances, or taking a technology which may currently be inferior but has greater potential for being developed into a labor-using, capital-saving technology. (They can use technology A, moving it toward A′ and A″; or choose the inferior technology C, in the hope that they can move it to C′, which, given their factor endowments, would be preferable.)

Those technologies were developed to reflect their circumstances (for instance, the scarcity of labor in their countries.) But the economic circumstances of developing countries are markedly different: they would have preferred developed countries to have developed labor-intensive technologies that made little use of capital. They thus have a strategic choice: they can continue to borrow technology from the advanced industrial countries (in figure 3.2., the capital-intensive technology is expected to improve from A to A′), they can try to take that technology and reduce the capital requirements and increase the labor requirements (moving technology A to A″), or they can try to improve a technology which is now inferior, but for which the potential for their economy is better (moving C to C′). Because so much learning is related to "doing," it may even pay them to use the inferior technology C—knowing that in doing so, they will develop a technology more appropriate to their circumstances.[45]

There are other elements of strategy: Though one can learn more easily "locally," i.e., about products and processes that are similar to those that one currently employs, there is *less to learn*. Thus, we spoke earlier of the large knowledge gap between developing countries and developed. They have more to learn. *If* they can learn how to learn about these more advanced technologies, because there is more to learn, there may be more learning—higher rates of productivity growth. At a given set of learning capabilities, the relationship between productivity increases may be complex, e.g., exhibiting an initial phase of increasing returns with respect to the size of the gap (one can learn very little if there is virtually no gap), a phase of diminishing returns and, finally, if the gap is too large, even decreased learning.

The fact that there is more to learn from more distant technologies but weaker learning capabilities poses a difficult strategic choice: Should one follow a strategy of incrementalism (small changes) or of a "big leap"?

The appendix to chapter 2 described "equilibrium knowledge gaps." There are large costs associated with overcoming knowledge gaps, and if the knowledge gap is too large, it may not be optimal to do so; that is, it pays a firm (country) to remain a laggard, absorbing knowledge (with a lag) as it filters down from those in technological leadership.

There is one further factor that may be relevant to a big leap: conventions, institutional arrangements, and mindsets are forced to change, thus facilitating the process of change. Rigidities in these represent a major impediment to learning and are the focus of the next section of this chapter.

5. Impediments to Learning

Earlier, we referred to the importance of the Enlightenment in helping create a learning society. But even within an enlightened society, there are barriers to learning at the individual, organizational, and societal level. Understanding these barriers—and doing what can be done to remove them—is central to creating a learning society.[46]

Biased Perceptions

Learning involves seeing what works and doesn't work—learning from experience. In science, we learn through controlled experiments. In real-life situations, it is often difficult if not impossible for individuals to conduct controlled experiments.⁴⁷ We attempt to make inferences from our experiences about what works and what doesn't. But the inferences we make are themselves affected by our beliefs. What information we process, the way we process it, and the weight we give to various observations are all affected by our prior beliefs. The tendency to see the world through lenses that are shaped by our prior beliefs—to discount information which is inconsistent with those beliefs and to see information that is consistent with those beliefs as particularly salient— is called confirmatory bias (see Hoff and Stiglitz [2010] and the references cited there). The result is that we can live in a world which Hoff and Stiglitz describe as an "equilibrium fiction." The world—as we see it—confirms our prior conceptions.

The notion that a belief system can be a fiction—even an equilibrium fiction—does not mean that it is necessarily bad. Long ago, Frank Knight (1921) argued that entrepreneurs systematically overestimate returns to innovation, or (to use more modern terminology) exhibit irrational exuberance. This irrational exuberance can be a major spur to innovative activity, offsetting in part the underinvestment that results from firms paying too little attention to the externalities to which their innovative activity gives rise. The irrational exuberance of the dot com bubble left in its wake a host of thriving enterprises (such as Google) that might not have otherwise obtained financing. The excessive investment in fiber optics played a key role in spurring India's technology boom, as the cost of interconnectivity fell dramatically (see Stiglitz 2006a).

At the same time, shorter term bursts of irrationality—fictions that come to be believed and are seemingly validated by the selective framing of evidence⁴⁸—play a key role in the booms and busts (both in credit and equity markets) that have marked capitalism from the beginning.⁴⁹

Belief Systems as Social Constructs

Belief systems themselves are to a large extent social constructs: What each individual believes is affected by what others believe. It is not just belief systems that are social constructs. The prisms through which we see the world are largely socially determined. (This is sometimes referred to as *preconfirmatory bias*.)⁵⁰ Sociologists and anthropologists (such as Mary Douglas [1986]) have long argued for the need to incorporate belief systems into our understanding of how societies (including economies) perform. Firms are, of course, mini-societies, and understanding their behavior requires an understanding of the belief systems of the firm, a key ingredient in what is commonly called corporate culture.

Countries don't exist in isolation, and not everyone within a country shares the same belief systems. Belief systems within a country are affected by those outside and especially so by those that are nearby and similar and with whom the members of the country are closely linked. So too for a firm. And if the linkages of members of a firm with members of other firms is more dense, the belief systems of outsiders has a greater impact; it is harder for those within a firm to have a belief system that it markedly at variance with those outside. With globalization, those in one country encounter, and have to come to terms with, other belief systems.

Cognitive Frames and Learning

Here, our interest is in how these ideas relate to creating a learning society. First, our cognitive frames affect *whether* we learn. We argued earlier that there is a "learning" cognitive frame and that we have to learn to learn. In some societies (in some firms), there is an attempt to constantly assess whether what is being observed is consistent with prior beliefs and models, and when it is not, to change beliefs and models. Other societies (firms) are far more conservative. More weight is given to inherited truths, and such societies resist evidence that contradicts those truths. (Some of our earlier discussion provides a partial explanation of the differences; societies with more educated individuals have a greater capacity to learn and are more likely to learn.[51])

Second, because what one individual believes is affected by what others believe, it is hard for belief systems to change. No individual or firm on its own can change societal cognitive frames; the result is that cognitive frames are a major source of institutional and societal rigidities. If a society is trapped into a belief system in which particular categories of individuals (women, individuals ascribed as lower caste or assigned to a particular ethnic group) are viewed as less productive, they will be treated in that way, there will be less investment in, say, their education, and their behavior may reflect that treatment (thus partially validating the differential treatment). Even if there were some isolated individuals who understood the notions we have just presented, including that of an equilibrium fiction and what gives rise to it, it would be hard for them to move the society to a different (say, nondiscriminatory or pro-learning) equilibrium. So too for a firm: Though the head of a firm may have disproportionate influence, what she can do is circumscribed by the beliefs of others within the firm, who almost inevitably are closely linked to those outside the firm, and the (head of the) firm will have at most a limited ability to change their beliefs.

These cognitive impediments to learning and change are reinforced by economic interests: Change always has winners and losers, and losers have an incentive to mount a challenge to the change. They have an incentive to see the world through a lens which sees the change in a less positive light.[52]

Third, cognitive frames affect not only the extent of our learning but *what* we learn. As we argued before, those with a strong ideological commitment to a particular view will resist information that seems to contradict it—they will either totally ignore it or, if they can't ignore it, discount it.[53] (By *ideologies*, we refer to beliefs that may be far narrower than those to which the term is usually ascribed, e.g., about whether markets work well—the ideology of market fundamentalism. An ideology can refer to a notion such as that race matters, or even a more specific notion, such as that consumer purchases are driven by packaging or by the color of the product.) The world is a complex place, and we can almost always put a spin onto what we observe to make it consistent with prior beliefs—and this means that we can, at least for a long while, not learn from what is occurring.

In spite of these impediments to change and learning, change and learning do occur. The dynamics of change are themselves complex, affected by changes in the outside world (including changes in technology and advances in science) and by economic interests. But unlike naïve Marxians, we do not believe that economic interests alone drive change. Change is often affected by the evolution of ideas, and particularly of overarching beliefs.[54] Once the Enlightenment notion that "all men are created equal" was accepted (however that idea came to be accepted, whatever the drivers), it was no surprise that it evolved in directions that brought within its ambit women and slaves. Given these beliefs, it would be hard to preserve the slavery system, in spite of the economic interests in preserving slavery—and even though motivated interests may have played a role in the creation and spread of the racial "construct" in the first place.[55]

The uber-ideology of the Enlightenment—the questioning of authority and the belief in meritocracy, the notion that change is possible and desirable, the respect extended to science and technology—have created preconditions that are favorable to the creation of a learning society and to learning institutions (firms) within our society.

Finally, not only is it possible for belief systems to change, belief systems are malleable[56]—though not perfectly, and not instantaneously. Thus, over time *we can help create a learning society*. We can do this partly by understanding the limitations in our perceptions—how our perceptions and learning are shaped (e.g., by ideologies, by confirmatory and preconfirmatory biases). We can do it partly by creating a learning culture—a culture that respects and reflects science and the values of the Enlightenment, including the questioning of authority. We can do it partly by rewarding successful learning.[57] Both the public policies described below and the policies pursued by individual firms can, if appropriately designed, assist in creating a learning society. By the same token, the *wrong* policies can impede the creation of a learning society.

Impediments to the Transmission of Knowledge

There are other, both natural and "manmade" impediments to the creation of a learning society, most notably with respect to the transmission of knowledge. Knowledge does not diffuse on its own; it has to be transmitted and received, and there are barriers at both ends.

The previous section described some of the impediments to learning, to extracting information out of the cacophony of signals with which the individual is bombarded. There are also barriers on the "sending" side. It is plausible that a market economy engages in excessive secrecy (relative to the social optimum). This, of course, has been the contention of the open-source movement. Collaborative research in the open-source movement is still economically viable, both because there are still economic returns (e.g., because of the tacit knowledge that is created by the learning/innovation process itself and from the advantages that come from being first in the market) and because there are important noneconomic returns to and incentives for innovation, which we will discuss briefly below.

But these impediments are augmented by legal frameworks (including prosecutorial norms and decisions) that have been increasingly adopted. For instance, intellectual property regimes can not only create an impediment to the transmission of knowledge, but encourage a culture of secrecy and a lack of openness. And while the disclosure requirements of patent laws have as their intent the dissemination of information upon which further innovation and learning can occur, in practice these requirements have been ineffectively enforced, and some firms (e.g., in software) actively promote weakening them. We will discuss these issues further in chapter 15.

It is worth noting that the "ideology" that emphasizes the comparative efficiency of the private sector in all matters, including research, and that stresses the importance of monetary incentives in promoting private sector activities, has in large measure led to these policies, the effect of which may in fact be counterproductive. This is itself an example of what may be an equilibrium fiction: Those who believe this believe that the "evidence" supports that belief. To them, any observed deficiencies in the performance of the economy must accordingly be traced to some government intervention. It was not the market's irrationality that led to the housing and credit bubble, but rather government's encouragement of home ownership among the poor. If the private sector appears less innovative than it should (or less innovative in one place than in another), it is because of government regulations that stifle innovation.[58]

The proclivity for secrecy by private firms may be only one of the reasons that the state has played a central role in creating an innovative economy and a learning society (see Mazzucato [2013]). Innovation is very risky and often entails large investments—even large firms are risk averse; capital markets are imperfect—especially when it comes to investments like R & D that are risky and can't be collateralized; and the most important innovations have large societal spillovers. Hence, as we explain in chapters 5 and 6, there is a strong presumption that there will be underinvestment in research, and especially in the kind of basic research from which all else flows.

6. Motivating Learning

Because learning requires effort and resources, individuals and firms have to be incentivized to do research and to learn. But it is important to realize that it is not just monetary (pecuniary) rewards that are important. Indeed, much of the most important advances are motivated by curiosity, or by a desire for recognition by one's peers (see David 2004a, 2004b; David and Dasgupta 1994), or by the excitement of solving a difficult problem that no one else may have even posed, let alone solved. (In fact, it should be apparent that the first sentence of this paragraph is itself a reflection of a prevailing way of framing the issue by economists: Many individuals, particularly, those who are successful scientists, *do not* necessarily have to be motivated to learn. The pleasure of learning is its own reward.)

There is a large literature suggesting that such intrinsic rewards can be a far stronger motivator than extrinsic rewards, like money (see, e.g., Stiglitz [2001a, 2012b] and the references cited there). Most of the most important discoveries (such as the decoding of DNA) were motivated not so much by financial rewards as by these other factors.[59] And to the extent that extrinsic rewards do play a role, it is more from peer recognition than from monetary returns.

Appropriability

For those who believe that the major issue in motivating learning is financial rewards, the question of the appropriability of returns becomes central: Only a fraction of the social returns to innovation can be captured by the innovator. There are learning spillovers, externalities. This suggests that, to the extent that learning depends on financial returns, there will be underinvestment in learning. (Later, we will explain that there are many circumstances in which the returns to innovation may well exceed the social returns; much innovation in a market economy can be thought of as rent seeking, and some of the returns to innovation represent rents that otherwise would have accrued to others. This implies that there may be too many resources allocated to such activities.)

Spillovers occur even in the presence of a patent system. Many advances cannot be patented (many advances in mathematics, for example), and the benefits of much of what is learned in the process of research cannot be appropriated. Indeed, the disclosure requirements of a patent are intended to enhance these societal benefits.

An idea like just-in-time production, replaceable parts, or assembly lines spreads quickly throughout the economy and can't be protected by intellectual property laws. Firms may engage in experiments, e.g., about what products will be well-received by consumers, but successful experiments may quickly be imitated, so the benefits of such learning may not be appropriated by those engaging in the experiment.[60]

Consider an "experiment" to discover whether conditions in a country are particularly suitable for growing a particular kind of coffee. If the experiment fails, those who conduct the experiment lose money. Because learning what grows well in a particular climate with a particular soil is information that is not patentable, if the experiment succeeds, there may be quick entry. The country benefits, but the "innovator" can't capture much of the returns. As a result, there will be underinvestment in this kind of experimentation.

A similar argument holds for why private markets will lend too little to new entrepreneurs. There is a learning process in the discovery of who is a good entrepreneur. A bank that lends money to a young entrepreneur who proves her mettle may find that the entrepreneur can easily be poached away by a competitive bank. Assume in the initial period that it cannot be ascertained who is a good entrepreneur and will repay her loan and who is a bad one and will not. The bank loses money on the bad entrepreneurs, but may not be able to be adequately compensated by "excess" returns from the good entrepreneurs. Because of the threat of poaching, the interest rate that the bank can charge a good entrepreneur (after the entrepreneur has demonstrated her success) will be limited to the competitive rate. But Stiglitz-Weiss adverse selection and adverse incentive effects limit the interest rate that can be charged in the initial period, which implies that there will be limited lending to new entrepreneurs.[61]

Market responses to the appropriability problem can impede learning—it leads to more extensive patenting and greater secrecy. As we explain later, the former can result in a patent thicket, imposing significant barriers to the use of knowledge. The latter can lead to impediments in the transmission of knowledge and undermine the open architecture that has traditionally been so important in the advancement of knowledge.

7. Trade-offs

Previous sections have described a number of factors that can contribute to creating a learning society. But there are a number of subtle and complicated trade-offs.

Trade-offs Between the Efficient Utilization of Knowledge and Incentives to Produce Knowledge

One trade-off centers around the benefits arising from the free flow of knowledge and the attenuation of (financial) incentives to learn: With the free flow of knowledge, it becomes more difficult for someone investing in knowledge to appropriate the returns. The issues are the same as those at the root of the Grossman-Stiglitz (1976, 1980) critique of the efficient markets hypothesis: If knowledge were perfectly transmitted, there would be no incentive to expend resources on gathering and producing knowledge. There would be underinvestment in knowledge creation (and in the case of developing countries, gathering knowledge from others). One of the costs of relying on the private finance of knowledge production is that it *must* entail the imperfect transmission of knowledge. And indeed, this is one of the advantages of public support for the creation of knowledge.

There can then emerge a number of complex and subtle trade-offs, at the level of the individual, the firm, and the economy: Not sharing knowledge will typically mean not receiving knowledge, or at least not as much knowledge. Knowledge is often "traded" not through market mechanisms, but in a process better described as gift exchange.[62] In an academic community—out of which the most important advances occur—there are tacit understandings about the culture of exchange. An individual who did not share would be cut off from her colleagues, and the likelihood that (at least in most fields) she could make a significant breakthrough would be limited, since every innovation is based on dozens, or hundreds, of smaller ideas and concepts.

An organization might want to keep knowledge that it produces "private" so that it could appropriate more of the returns, but it wants knowledge to be shared fully within the organization, so that anyone in the organization can build on it. But here too there are trade-offs: The more individuals in the organization that have the knowledge, the more likely that the information will leak out.

We noted earlier that the free mobility of people, ideas, and products helps disseminate ideas and can be a catalyst for learning. But again, such mobility may make it more difficult to appropriate the returns to investments in innovation. That is why many firms impose mobility restrictions in contracts with employees: It may lead to short-run inefficiencies in the allocation of labor, but these may be partially offset by long-run dynamic benefits—or at least firms insisting on these contracts believe it enhances their long-run profits.[63] (The appendix to chapter 4 explains why it is likely that the market equilibrium may result in insufficient mobility.)

Intertemporal Trade-offs: Static Inefficiencies Versus Dynamic Gains

The earlier discussion of the process of learning highlights the importance of intertemporal trade-offs in the process of learning. Learning is an investment. We normally have to sacrifice current consumption—the additional experimentation from which we may be able to learn more comes with a cost. Even if (as in the simpler models presented later in this book) learning followed automatically from production, we can learn more—lower future production costs—by producing more today than we would have produced from the perspective of short-run static efficiency.

Investments in "technology capital" or "knowledge capital" are, in this respect, much like investments in human and physical capital, with one important difference, to which we have already alluded: Because of the importance of knowledge spillovers, there is a presumption that there will be underinvestment in learning (in technology capital), while there is no such presumption concerning human and physical capital. More precisely, as we will explain in later chapters, social and private returns are not likely to be well aligned.

As in the case of the savings rate, there is thus (often)[64] a short-run versus long-run trade-off. But in the case of the savings decision, there is no general theoretical presumption that government intervention is desirable—future generations are normally expected to be better off, so asking the current generation to make still further sacrifices so that future generations could be still better off is problematic. Moreover, even with such sacrifices, the increase in the growth rate is only temporary. In the case of learning, there is a presumption (shown more fully in chapter 6) that the market allocation is inefficient and that government intervention can enhance societal well-being; and intervention can lead to a permanently higher growth rate. *It may be desirable to distort resource allocations in the short run, to operate below the production possibilities curve, or to force consumption patterns that do not maximize short-run "utility,"[65] in order to achieve dynamic benefits—higher growth rates.* This trade-off is at the heart of the analysis of this book.

Indeed, if there were not such a trade-off, one could view growth and efficiency policies as complementary. The neoclassical (Washington Consensus) policies move the economy to the production possibilities curve as quickly as possible, and then the growth policies move the production possibilities curve out as rapidly as possible. If the first policy is successful, then the benefits of the second policy—say, an increase in the growth rate of potential output (the rate at which the production possibilities curve moves out) by a given delta (denoted by Δg)—are even greater, since the level of output which is multiplied by Δg (the change in growth rate) is greater.

Much of modern growth policy analysis is based on this kind of dichotomy. Growth theory is based on the "supply" side, assuming that the economy is on its production possibilities curve—i.e., resources are fully used and allocated efficiently. This book will explain why that approach is misleading, if not just wrong.

Our "learning society" perspective even sees the reason that the economy might perform below its production possibilities schedule differently,[66] and accordingly, it sees the short-run versus long-run trade-offs differently. As chapter 2 explained, even well-functioning economies operate well within the output limits set by a traditionally defined production possibility frontier. The gap arises not so much from market distortions (associated, say, with taxes), but from disparities in knowledge and practice that exist even *within a country*. For most firms, as we noted in the last chapter, there is a significant gap between their productivity and "best practices." Current output can be expanded, therefore, without significant creation of new technology through the better use and wider deployment of existing technologies. If those who use less-efficient technologies can only "learn" best practices, there will be large increases in output. Output can be expanded by the more-effective deployment of labor within a firm, if only firms learn how better to use their workers—not just the reallocation of labor across firms caused by labor market rigidities. Typically small detailed changes in production processes can lead to large increases in productivity, without significant improvements in the quality of labor emerging from formal school systems. To assume that knowledge flows freely within and across firms (or across national boundaries) is as unrealistic as to assume that production could occur without inputs. Knowledge is as important a constraint on output as conventional inputs.

But policies that focus on static inefficiencies and their removal may, at the same time, reduce incentives for learning, or even impede learning. There can be, as a result, a trade-off between static inefficiency and dynamic efficiency. For instance, as we have repeatedly noted, intellectual property regimes (or other impediments to the free flow of knowledge) mean that knowledge is not being efficiently used (see chapter 15). Such impediments contribute to static inefficiency. But they *may* lead to enhanced incentives to research—to dynamic efficiency. But as chapter 15 also explains, poorly designed intellectual property regimes can be a lose-lose situation—less efficient use of knowledge today, less innovation and less growth in the future. Earlier in this chapter we noted another example of such a trade-off—creating a less competitive banking sector may introduce a static inefficiency, but at the same time, it reduces the chance of a good entrepreneur being poached away, and hence may lead to more lending to new entrepreneurs, enhancing the dynamic efficiency of the economy.

In each of these instances, of course, there may be policies which change the nature of the trade-off, that is, induce as much learning with a lower loss of static efficiency.

There are many other trade-offs in the construction of a learning society. Learning abilities can, for instance, be specific or general, and there may be trade-offs between the two: We can direct our efforts at enhancing specific learning abilities, which may serve an economy well if it is pursuing a narrow niche; or efforts can be directed at more general learning abilities, which may serve it well in periods of rapid transition and great uncertainty.[67]

Concluding Comments

This chapter has focused on several of the critical determinants of learning, in the hope that by understanding better the factors that affect learning, we can be more successful in creating a learning society—in the case of a developing country, one which more quickly closes the gap between itself and the more advanced countries; in the case of a developed country, one which moves out the frontier of knowledge at a faster pace; in the case of all economies, one which reduces the gap between average and best practices. It should be obvious that the conditions (the institutions, the legal frameworks, the contractual arrangements, etc.) which facilitate learning for different economies facing different circumstances may differ markedly. In particular, those which are appropriate for an economy trying to catch up may differ markedly from those appropriate for one at the frontier—trying to move that frontier out further. (Later chapters will illustrate this.)

There are several questions to which we have so far given short shrift. Much of the learning in our society occurs within firms. What are the determinants of the learning that goes on within a firm? Are firms in some sectors better at learning? Is there a tendency for firms in some sectors to provide greater externalities to the rest of the economy? Are there macroeconomic conditions that facilitate learning? And what policies can help bring about those macroeconomic conditions? We turn to these questions in the next chapter.

APPENDIX

Multiple-Equilibria and Evolutionary Processes

The presence of pervasive externalities in the learning process means that it is easy to construct models in which the economy may be trapped in a low-level equilibrium (low rate of productivity growth). In the following subsections, we describe two simple models generating such results.[68]

Innovators and Inventors

Assume that the skills and personalities that are required to invent (to think up a new idea) are markedly different from those required to innovate—to bring a new idea to market, to translate inventions into commercial successes. Innovators, like Henry Ford, have to raise capital, organize production processes, and market the products. Inventors only reap a reward from their inventions if they can find an innovator willing to undertake the risk of trying to market the invention—and indeed, until the idea has been put to the test, it may not be possible to ascertain whether it is a "good" invention or not. But just as inventors need innovators, innovators require inventions. Without inventions to develop and market, they have nothing to do.

A major cost of innovation is the cost of finding a good invention. Each innovator, of course, has different comparative advantages, different kinds of inventions for which they are particularly suited, that is, for which the costs of bringing the innovation to fruition is relatively low or the likelihood of success is relatively high. The greater the number of innovators, the greater the return to inventive activity, since the greater the likelihood that some innovator will find an invention that is well suited to his talents and to be to his liking. And the greater the number of inventors, the greater the return to being an innovator, since again, the greater the likelihood that the innovator will find an invention for which he is well suited.[69] Of course, the greater the return to innovation, the greater the number of innovators; and the greater the return to invention, the large the number of inventors. Figure 3.3. plots the number of innovators as an increasing function of the number

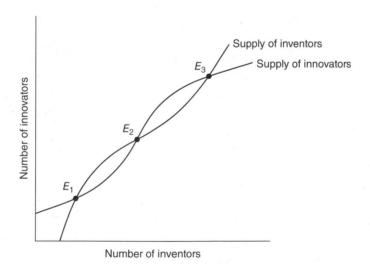

Figure 3.3 Multiple equilibria

The number of innovators is an increasing function of the number of inventors, and the number of inventors is an increasing function of the number of innovators. There can be a stable equilibrium at E_1 or E_3.

of inventors and the number of inventors as an increasing function of the number of innovators. There can be (and in the example drawn, there are) multiple equilibria: The economy can be trapped in a low-level equilibrium, in which there is little inventive or innovative activity occurring, or it can be in a high-level equilibrium, in which there is a great deal of invention and innovation going on.

Our earlier discussion highlighted other factors that can reinforce the high- (or low-) level equilibrium. In the high-level equilibrium, institutional innovations, like venture capital firms, can emerge, which help provide finance. In the low-level equilibrium, such institutions do not exist.

Bureaucracy and Innovation

In a modern mixed economy, the successful introduction of an innovation entails more than just satisfying a market test. There are often a variety of regulatory and legal hurdles that must be overcome. The number and nature of such hurdles may differ in different societies.

Just as the characteristics which make for successful innovators and inventors may differ, so to for those that make for a successful bureaucrat. For purposes of this section, we ignore the distinction between innovation and invention, but focus on the distinction between "inventors/innovators" and bureaucrats. To caricature the differences, one prefers change, the other prefers orderly rules and procedures. One focuses on developing his own vision, the other centers on building consensus among different views. Thomas Edison and Steve Jobs may have been good innovators/inventors, but might have been far less successful as bureaucrats.

Rules and procedures often hinder change, and change makes the implementation of rules and procedures more difficult, for they have to be constantly adapted to the changing circumstances. There is thus a natural conflict between the two. But bureaucrats also perform important social functions, e.g., in regulating externalities.

On the horizontal axis of figure 3.4, we plot the number of bureaucrats in a society; on the vertical, the number of innovators/inventors. The "supply" of innovators/inventors is a negative function of the number of bureaucrats, B,

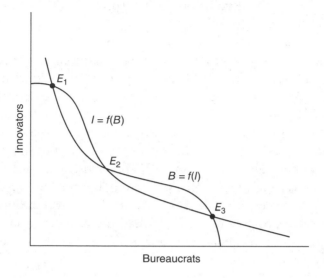

Figure 3.4 Multiple equilibria

The number of bureaucrats may be inversely related to the number of innovators and inventors and vice versa, leading to the possibility of either a high-innovation society or a low-innovation society.

$$I = F(B), \qquad F' < 0;$$

and the supply of bureaucrats is a negative function of the number of innovators,

$$B = f(I), \qquad f' < 0.$$

Equilibrium requires

$$I^* = F(B^*), \text{ and } B^* = f(I^*).$$

The figure makes it clear that there can exist multiple equilibria—a low-innovation equilibrium with many bureaucrats and few innovators/inventors and a high-innovation equilibrium with few bureaucrats and many innovators/inventors. The latter is a "learning" society.[70]

An Evolutionary Interpretation

The above analysis highlights that there may be multiple equilibria to a society. The equilibrium to which the economy converges may depend on history. Figure 3.5 depicts the dynamics. We characterize the relative returns to being a bureaucrat versus an innovator/inventor as depending on the ratio of bureaucrats to innovators. When that ratio is high at time t, bureaucrats prosper (relatively) so that number will be high at time $t + 1$. In the figure, the relationship between the ratio at $t + 1$ and at t is S-shaped, and crosses the 45-degree line three times, each of which is an equilibrium, but the lower and higher intersections represent stable equilibrium. If the ratio of bureaucrats to inventors/innovators is below b^*, then the economy converges to the high-innovation equilibrium; if it is above b^*, it converges to the low-innovation equilibrium.

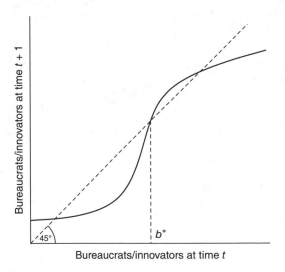

Figure 3.5 Evolutionary dynamics

The economy can converge to either a high-learning society or a low-learning society. If the initial ratio of bureaucrats to innovators is below b^*, the economy converges to the high-innovation equilibrium; if it is above b^*, it converges to the low-innovation equilibrium.

Government Intervention: Moving Toward a Learning Society

There are a variety of policies that can affect the equilibrium to which the economy converges. The most direct would entail supporting research and innovation to increase the number of innovators, so $b < b^*$, which would lead to convergence to the high-innovation equilibrium. Alternatively, the government could change tax and expenditure policies, so that, for instance, the returns to innovation are increased, increasing the critical threshold b^*.[71]

CHAPTER FOUR

Creating a Learning Firm and a Learning Environment

THE PREVIOUS chapter described many of the ingredients of a "learning society": what is to be learned, how learning occurs, and the central determinants of learning, including the role played by learning spillovers and appropriability. Among our central objectives was to describe some of the components of an economic architecture (including all the attendant institutions and laws, such as intellectual property rights) which would best facilitate learning.

This chapter focuses on two critical aspects of this learning architecture: creating a learning firm and a learning macro-environment.

1. The Learning Firm

A subproblem within the systemic problem of creating a learning economy is the design of the component institutions (e.g., corporations). This is especially important because so much learning occurs within organizations and because so much knowledge resides within firms. Chapter 2 described the marked differences in productivity across firms.

Somehow, knowledge that resides in the more productive firms does not seamlessly get transmitted and absorbed by the less productive.

Learning and the Boundaries of Firms

Within any institution, there may be incentives to develop knowledge and to hoard or to transmit it. The issue of the architecture of a learning firm is parallel to that of the architecture of a learning economy. In some ways, the two cannot be separated. Traditional discussions of the boundary of firms (Coase 1937) focused on transactions costs, but equally important is the structure of learning. It may be easier to transmit information (knowledge) within a firm than across enterprises, partly because the "exchange" of knowledge is not well-mediated by prices and contracts[1]. If so, and if learning is at the heart of a successful economy, it would suggest that firms might be larger than they would be in a world in which learning is less important.[2]

While firms seek to maximize the flow of information/knowledge within themselves, realizing that knowledge is power (or at least money), they seek to limit the transmission of knowledge to others, for instance, requiring employees to sign nondisclosure agreements. Thus, firms go to great lengths to maintain secrecy. While for the advancement of society, it is desirable that knowledge, once created, be transmitted as broadly and efficiently as possible, profit-maximizing firms have traditionally sought to limit to the extent possible the transmission of knowledge.

The Design of a "Learning" and "Innovative" Firm

There is a large literature—too large to reference here—that describes how to "create" a learning firm. We describe below some of the significant advantages that large firms have in financing research and bearing the associated risk. But large enterprises often develop bureaucratic structures to manage resource allocations, and while they prevent waste and even bad projects from being undertaken—reining in the excessive optimism that is often associated with the entrepreneurial spirit—those same processes may at the same time stifle innovation. So too, bureaucratic structures may reinforce the excessive loss aversion to which behavioral economists have called attention (see Kahneman 2011). And even if knowledge is *supposed* to flow freely within an organization, individuals realize that "knowledge is power" and attempt to hoard it, to impede its free flow. Innovative firms create organizational designs and incentive structures that attempt to address each of these problems.[3]

It is worth noting that a key aspect of this large literature on innovative firms is a notion that parallels one of the main themes of this book, on learning-by-doing—what is referred to as "learning by experience." (See, for instance, Morgan McCall's [2004] discussion of "Leadership development through experience" and the references cited there.)

Most of this book, though, is not concerned with how to design a firm to maximize learning, but rather how government policy can affect the structure of the economy to maximize societal learning. Accordingly, in the discussion below, we mostly abstract from microeconomic structures, focusing on broader policies: on the principles which should guide government intervention and on alternative instruments.

Why Industrial Firms Are the Source of Innovation

In the analysis in the ensuing chapters, a key assumption is that the industrial sector is the source of innovation. The justifications for such an assumption are rooted in the nature of industrial activity. Innovation activity takes place in firms that (relative to firms in other sectors) are (1) large, (2) long-lived, (3) stable, and (4) densely concentrated geographically. Agricultural and craft production, by contrast, typically takes place on a highly decentralized basis among many small, short-lived, unstable firms.

In the following paragraphs we describe in more detail why these attributes are conducive to learning, some of the reasons for the comparative advantage of the industrial sector in learning, and why that sector is more likely to give rise to learning externalities.[4]

(1) LARGE ENTERPRISES Since particular innovations are far more valuable to large organizations that can apply them to many units of output than to smaller ones with lower levels of output (see Arrow 1962b), there is far greater incentive to engage in R & D in large enterprises; because enterprises are larger in the industrial sector than in the agricultural/craft sector, there is likely to be more innovation in the industrial sector. The result will be higher investments in innovation in the former sector than the latter. This can be looked at another way:

Large firms can internalize more of the externalities that are generated by learning.[5] Moreover, innovation is highly uncertain, and firms and individuals are risk averse. Large enterprises are likely to be less risk averse, and thus better able to bear the risks of innovation. Moreover, because of information imperfections, capital markets are imperfect, especially so for investments in R & D, which typically cannot be collateralized. Capital constraints are less likely to be binding on large enterprises.

(This does not necessarily mean, however, that within the industrial sector the largest firms are the most innovative. The difficulties of developing appropriate incentives for the reward of innovation may militate against large enterprises. There is an ongoing debate over whether large or small enterprises are most conducive to innovation. Large firms may have the resources to finance innovation, typically lacking in smaller enterprises, but there is an impressive record of large firms not recognizing the value of pathbreaking innovations, including Microsoft being too wedded to the keyboard, and Xerox not recognizing the importance of a user-friendly interface in its bid to bring its earlier computing innovations to consumers.)[6]

(2) STABILITY AND CONTINUITY The accumulation of knowledge on which productivity growth is based is necessarily cumulative. This, in turn, greatly depends on a stable organization for preserving and disseminating the knowledge involved and on continuity in jobs and personnel to support these processes. In large organizations, with the resources to provide redundant capacity where needed, the required degree of stability and continuity is much more likely to be present than in small, dispersed organizations, where the loss of single individuals may completely compromise the process of knowledge accumulation. As a result, steady productivity improvement will be much more likely to arise from industrial than agricultural and craft production.

There is another way of seeing why stability and continuity contribute to learning. As we noted earlier, the benefits of learning extend into the future. Long-lived firms can value these distant benefits more. Also, because industrial firms are typically longer lived and more stable than firms in other sectors, they can access capital at lower interest rates. They are likely to be less capital constrained, to act in a less risk-averse manner, and to discount future benefits less.[7]

(3) HUMAN CAPITAL ACCUMULATION Opportunities and incentives for accumulating general human capital are likely to be far greater in large, complex, long-lived, stable industrial enterprises with a wide range of interdependent activities than in small, dispersed, narrowly focused agricultural or craft enterprises. There is a greater likelihood of benefits from the cross-fertilization of ideas.

Long-lived stable firms have a greater incentive to promote increased human capital that leads to greater firm productivity and a greater ability to adapt to changing circumstances. As we noted in the previous paragraph, they also have a greater capacity to finance these investments and an enhanced ability and willingness to bear the risks. The resulting human capital accumulation is a critical element in both developing the innovations on which productivity growth depends and in disseminating them as workers move within and between enterprises and across sectors.

(4) CONCENTRATION AND DIFFUSION OF KNOWLEDGE ACROSS FIRMS Diffusion of knowledge among densely collocated, large-scale industrial enterprises (often producing differentiated products) is likely to be far more rapid than diffusion of knowledge among dispersed, small-scale agricultural or craft enterprises. The fact that they are producing different products enhances the likelihood that they will make different discoveries. The fact that they are producing similar products enhances the likelihood that a discovery relevant to one product will be relevant to another.

Recall that earlier we emphasized the importance of the diffusion of knowledge and stressed the key role that geographical proximity plays. More recent discussions of the role of clusters have reemphasized the importance of geographical proximity (see Porter 1990). Geographical proximity promotes cross-firm mobility, an important catalyst to learning and an important way in which learning gets transmitted. (Firms try to restrict the mobility of their workers out—it reduces the return to their investments in human capital and may reduce their competitive advantage over other firms, as the firm's knowledge is shared with others; at the same time, they try to encourage the mobility of other workers to their firm. In the appendix, we analyze a standard competitive market with labor mobility, but in which firms can take actions which reduce mobility out of their firm. We show that the market equilibrium is not efficient.)[8]

(5) CROSS-BORDER KNOWLEDGE FLOWS While learning is facilitated by geographical proximity, especially developing countries (where many firms are operating far below "best practices") can learn from advances in other countries. While agricultural conditions may differ markedly from one country to another, the potential for cross-border learning may be greater in the industrial sector. The existence of large, stable enterprises with the incentives and capacities to engage in cross-border learning enhances the role of that sector in societal learning. Indeed, it is widely recognized that success in the industrial sector requires not just knowledge, but also the ability to acquire knowledge that is common across borders.

Why There May Be Significant Spillovers from the Industrial Sector to the Rest of the Economy

Learning by one firm or subsector spills over to other firms and subsectors within the industrial sector, through, for instance, the movement of skilled people and advances in technology and capital goods that have cross-sector relevance. But the benefits spill over more broadly, even to the agricultural sector. In the following paragraphs we describe some of the ways that this occurs, especially as a result of the tax revenues that a growing industrial sector can generate. Large-scale, densely concentrated activities are by these very attributes far easier to tax than small-scale, dispersed activities.

(1) THE ABILITY TO SUPPORT PUBLIC RESEARCH AND DEVELOPMENT One of the important uses to which tax revenues can be put is to support publicly sponsored R & D. This factor may be especially important in the support of agricultural research, like that undertaken by the Agricultural Extension Service in the United States. These activities directly contribute to agricultural productivity growth but could not be supported without a taxable base of industrial activity. And the private sector, on its own, would not have undertaken this research, let alone the widespread dissemination which was so critical to the growth of agricultural productivity.

(2) PUBLIC SUPPORT FOR HUMAN CAPITAL ACCUMULATION Another important use of these funds is investment in human capital. Our earlier discussion focused on investments in human capital by the firm.

These investments are, to a large extent, complementary to investments in human capital that occur within the formal education system. Just as in the case of R & D, private capital market failures mean that public support in the form of free primary and secondary education is a critical component of general human capital accumulation and yields high social returns. Moreover, the high returns to education in the industrial sector lead to a greater demand for an educated labor force. And again, as workers migrate across sectors, ultimately higher productivity growth in the agricultural and craft sector will be engendered as well. Moreover, eventually public education gets extended to all parts of the economy, not just urban areas.

(3) THE DEVELOPMENT OF A ROBUST FINANCIAL SECTOR   In chapter 3, we noted that the spillovers from one sector to another may take many forms. Much of the discussion focuses on technological spillovers. But there are important spillovers from the institutional developments that are necessary to make an industrial economy function. The previous paragraph stressed the benefits to the rest of the economy from the development of a general publicly supported education system. The heavy investment of a modern industrial economy requires finance. It is not surprising, then, that an industrial environment should be characterized by a more highly developed financial sector than that found in an agricultural/craft environment. Once developed, a strong financial sector facilitates capital deployment throughout the economy, even in the rural sector.[9]

The above discussion highlights both why learning (innovation) may occur more rapidly within the industrial sector, and also why the learning and innovation (broadly understood, to include institutional innovations) developed there have spillovers, not only within the industrial sector, but to the rest of the economy. These spillovers involve knowledge, human capital, and institutional development. For instance, improvements in financial institutions and education have systemic benefits. While knowledge moves more freely within a country than across countries, it moves more freely across borders in the industrial sector, but some of the knowledge thus transmitted—including learning to learn—may be of value to other sectors.

There are still other channels through which spillovers occur. For instance, industrial mechanization improved agricultural productivity.

There are, in short, multiple channels through which the technological and institutional innovations of the industrial sector get translated into higher productivity growth for the economy as a whole.

Geographical Localization

The analysis in later chapters makes three critical assumptions: (i) the industrial sector is more successful in learning; (ii) spillovers are concentrated within national boundaries; and (iii) the learning spillovers across sectors within a country are significant—more significant than the cross-border spillovers. We have discussed at length the rationale for the first and third assumptions.

The second assumption rests on four factors: (1) geographic proximity, (2) international restrictions of the movement of labor (and associated movements in knowledge and human capital), (3) language and cultural barriers, and (4) historical patterns of social interactions, which are strongly affected by national boundaries and which get reflected not just in language and culture but also in transportation systems, social networks, and institutional arrangements. Individuals are the main carrier of learning,[10] and the factors listed above imply that, by and large, labor mobility is easier within a country than between countries. Moreover, as we noted earlier, learning is local, and much of the knowledge which is relevant in one country may be less relevant to others.

The results of our analysis in later chapters, however, require only that transmission of knowledge to the agricultural and craft sector be stronger within a country than between countries. Indeed, our results are strengthened if there is some element of transmission across countries within the industrial sector, so long as that transmission increases with the size of the industrial sector in the developing country. For then, for the developing country, there is a further reason for promoting the industrial sector: It is the "window to the world," the channel through which more advanced knowledge gets transmitted to the developing country for both industry and agriculture. A manufacturer of textiles, for instance, absorbs information about textile production from other countries (perhaps because he buys machines from other countries). But some of that knowledge may be relevant for the agricultural or other sectors of the economy.[11]

2. Macro-conditions for Creating a Learning Society

Most of this book is concerned with microeconomic policies. But creating a learning society requires creating an economic environment that is conducive to learning. For this, the macroeconomic environment is central. As we suggested earlier in this chapter, economic stability appears to play an important role in creating a successful "learning" environment: Stability and continuity are important to the learning process.

Evidence for this comes from the experience of developed economies during recessions. Productivity growth is normally low during contractions and there is no offsetting gain during subsequent expansions.[12] The productivity loss during the dislocation associated with the recession appears to be permanent.[13]

There are several reasons why stability is important for *societal* learning.[14] The first is that much information is embodied within existing institutions, in complex webs of interactions. Key institutions — firms — often die in the face of high levels of instability. They are not simply brought back to life when the economy recovers. There are important hysteresis effects. New institutions may be created, but much of the knowledge that was embedded in the old institutions (especially knowledge that is typically referred to as "tacit") has to be re-created.

Contrary to the popular impression, it is not just the worst firms that die. For instance, during the East Asian crisis, the Korean firms that died differed little from those that survived — except that they were more encumbered with debt. Their main mistake was committed by the financial officers (who undertook excessive debt) and was predicated on (ex post) excessive confidence in macroeconomic stability. In short, though the evolutionary process showed itself to be enormously destructive (with 50 percent of all firms facing bankruptcy), it was not very creative.[15]

Moreover, managerial attention is limited. When firms are focusing on survival, they have less attention to devote to "learning," except learning how to survive.

Third, high levels of macro-instability lead firms to act in a more risk-averse manner. When firms go into recessions, among the first things to be cut are investments in R & D, and this is even true among firms that are relatively dependent on innovation. Part of the reason is that learning is future oriented. One has to make sacrifices today and undertake risks today for future benefits. But in the presence of instability, there is a risk that there will be no future—and hence less reason to make the requisite investments today. Instability weakens future-oriented incentives.

Fourth, learning requires resources, including access to capital. Instability may make capital less accessible and more costly.[16] In downturns, capital is likely to be rationed, and investments in R & D are often sacrificed (Greenwald, Salinger, and Stiglitz 1990).[17] Because investments in research cannot be collateralized and because they are particularly risky, they may be particularly hard hit in economic downturns.

Deep downturns have even more adverse effects, since in that case, not only are the balance sheets of firms hit, but so are those of financial institutions. Hence, there can be system-wide constraints on credit availability, even for working capital, forcing firms to cut back even more on their investments, including and especially investments in innovation.[18] Similarly, cutbacks in production mean that there will be less learning-by-doing.

Thus, finally, instability affects the average level of output (that is, the average "output gap"—the difference between what the country could have produced and what it actually produces—is larger) and the structure of output. Capital-intensive industries, with larger learning potentials and more learning spillovers, may be disadvantaged relative to other sectors with less learning and less learning spillovers.

Thus, our view is markedly different from that which sees recessions as having a purging effect on the economy—the idea that the silver lining in the cloud of a recession is the shake out that results. In that view, firms cut out fat, fire unnecessary workers, and restructure the firm to make it leaner and meaner. Firms that are less efficient, that have been surviving off previously earned capital, can no longer do so. The Darwinian struggle for the survival of the fittest means that those firms that are less fit don't make it through a serious downturn, and thus recessions speed the process of natural selection. Schumpeter trumpeted these virtues. He wrote, on recessions:

> They are but temporary. They are the means to reconstruct each time the economic system on a more efficient plan. But they inflict losses while they last, drive firms into the bankruptcy court, throw people out of employment, before the ground is clear and the way paved for new achievement of the kind which has created modern civilization and made the greatness of this country.
>
> —SCHUMPETER 1934, 113

Schumpeter's views were much more in line with those of Andrew Mellon, secretary of treasury under President Hoover, who famously said:

> Liquidate labor, liquidate stocks, liquidate farmers, liquidate real estate . . . it will purge the rottenness out of the system. High costs of living and high living will come down. People will work harder, live a more moral life. Values will be adjusted, and enterprising people will pick up from less competent people.

Indeed, Schumpeter seems to have believed that, net, depressions were good for the economy, more in the nature of "a good cold douche" (Heilbroner 1980, 311).

While there may be some virtues in the process of "creative destruction" that is associated with innovation, the destruction that occurs in the process of cyclical fluctuations is not offset by any creation, and the anticipation of future volatility dampens investment in learning and R & D. The long-term benefits from the purging effect—the incentive to reduce slack posed by a recession—are outweighed by the costs associated with cutbacks in R & D. Part of the reason for this is that because of the learning spillovers upon which we focus here, in general, private firms underestimate the benefits of R & D; and because, especially in a recession, the social costs of unemployment are high, firms underestimate the social costs of "purging" and thus take it too far (Stiglitz 1994b). In short, volatility is bad for the long-term growth of the economy.

Policy Implications

This has important implications for policy: Policies which *expose* countries to a high level of instability or which increase the economy's instability (e.g., by weakening automatic stabilizers) have an adverse effect on learning. Examples of policies that have exposed countries to greater risk include financial and capital market liberalization and deregulation.[19]

By the same token, policies that focus on price stability, at the expense of *real* stability, may be counterproductive (see Stiglitz et al. 2006). Inflation targeting, with its focus on price stability attained by interest rate adjustments, may be "doubly" bad: Responding to inflation by increasing interest rates—even when the cause of the inflation is an exogenous supply shock—is an example of a pro-cyclical policy. And the increases in interest rates have a disproportionate effect on certain sectors, those that are most interest sensitive and which rely most on bank financing. Small businesses, in particular, bear the burden. We have already noted that firms that die in a downturn don't come back to life when the economy recovers. There is a loss of informational capital. So too, firms that may be killed when interest rates are raised dramatically don't come back to life when they are subsequently lowered. This is especially important in developing countries, where there may be a dearth of entrepreneurship. If, as some claim, much of the learning and innovation in society occurs within small and young enterprises, then these policies increase the burden on these key "learning" sectors. But whether that is the case or not, these policies exacerbate the already adverse effects on learning and investments in R & D arising from the cyclical volatility in the "shadow" cost of capital.

APPENDIX

On the Inefficiency of Market Mobility

In this appendix, we explore briefly the question of whether the level of interfirm mobility that emerges in the market is likely to be efficient. We assume each firm's profits are a function of its labor turnover. It loses when workers leave, but benefits from hiring trained workers from other firms. It takes the level of training of other firms, t_{-i} as given, as well as the level of mobility inducements (e.g., wages and sign-up bonuses) and constraints (e.g., restrictions imposed in the contract) of other firms and their level of investment in their workers (m_{-i}, L_{-i}). It chooses its level of training, mobility inducements, and mobility constraints to maximize its profits (minimize its labor costs) given its labor force. New workers bring with them some benefits (e.g., knowledge), as well as costs (e.g., to train them). The net benefit we denote by B, which is a function of the knowledge they bring with them and the firm's expenditure on training, as well as the flow into and out of the firm. The flow of workers out of the firm is given by $q(m_{-i}, L_i)$, and the acceptances are given by $a(m_i, L_{-i})$. Hence, the firm maximizes

$$B_i(t_i, m_i, L_i; t_{-i}, m_{-i}, L_{-i})$$

with respect to $\{t_i, m_i, L_i\}$ subject to the constraint that

$$q(m_{-i}, L_i) = a(m_i, L_{-i}),$$

yielding first-order conditions for $\{t_i, m_i, L_i\}$ in terms of $\{t_{-i}, m_{-i}, L_{-i}\}$. The (symmetric) Nash equilibrium occurs where $\{t_i, m_i, L_i\} = \{t_{-i}, m_{-i}, L_{-i}\}$.

Social welfare, however, is markedly different. Social welfare is maximized when the following problem is solved.

$$\max_{\{t_i, m_i, L_i\}} B_i(t_i, m_i, L_i; t_i, m_i, L_i)$$

$$\text{s.t. } q(m_i, L_i) = a(m_i, L_i).$$

That is, it takes into account all of the externalities—the fact that increasing training costs in one firm benefits other firms ($\partial B_i / \partial t_{-i} > 0$), that an increase in mobility constraints by one firm increases the required mobility inducements by other firms to offset the effects, if it is to hire the requisite number of workers; or that an increase in mobility inducements by one firm imposes costs on other firms. Because of these "mobility externalities," one should expect firms to train too little. It is a more complicated matter to ascertain whether there is too much or too little mobility. In our model, mobility has a social benefit—knowledge/learning is conveyed from one firm to another. But firms pay no attention to this social benefit; on the contrary, they may view this as a private cost, as rival firms gain from the spread of knowledge. Hence, it has an incentive to try to "lock up" knowledge by reducing mobility. This suggests that firms will try to discourage mobility, e.g., by imposing *excessive* mobility constraints.[20] (These results are consistent with, and in effect strengthen, well-established results on the inefficiency of labor turnover in models in which there are no learning benefits from mobility.)[21]

CHAPTER FIVE

Market Structure, Welfare, and Learning

ADVOCATES OF free market economies often stress the virtues of a market economy in promoting innovation. Remarkably, in spite of the constant praise of the market system's "innovativeness," there appear to be no general theorems on the efficiency of markets with respect to the pace and direction of innovation.

Joseph Schumpeter (1912, 1943), who argued for the centrality of innovation, cast aspersions on standard economic theory and its policy prescriptions, which had lauded the virtues of competition and castigated monopolies as the "supreme evil."[1] To Schumpeter, not only was the heart of capitalism innovation, but innovation required some degree of monopoly power.[2] If competition were perfect, and knowledge flowed freely, innovators would not be able to appropriate any returns to their innovations, and without innovations, economies would stagnate. Moreover, competitive firms would have difficulty raising the finance that investments in innovation require. Monopolies could generate the profits necessary to fund research—especially important in an era when financial markets were less developed and venture capital firms did not exist. Borrowing to finance speculative research was limited because, if the research project failed, there was nothing for the lender to seize.[3] In real estate, at least there is some collateral.

Schumpeter clearly took a more benign view of monopolies than did the rest of the economics profession. Indeed, he looked with some jaundice at the conventional economists' single-minded preoccupation with the dangers of monopolies and their hagiography of competitive markets. Schumpeter thus countenanced monopoly: He saw the monopolist's constraints on output as a small price in static inefficiency to pay for the speedier innovation associated with monopoly.[4]

Writing after a period in which the capitalist economies' performance was less than stellar—the Great Depression, in which large fractions of the capital and human resources had been left idle, at great human suffering, for an extended period of time—Schumpeter could still look at the great sweep of history. Such fluctuations had happened repeatedly, and even taking the loss in output during such episodes into account, he noted the huge increases in living standards which capitalism had brought about and which it was likely to continue to bring about.[5] He was even optimistic about the elimination of poverty: With little evidence of an increase in inequality,[6] as average incomes were increased, it was likely that those at the bottom would see new-found prosperity.

Schumpeter did think competition was important, but the kind of competition that he thought was central was markedly different from that modeled in standard competitive theory, in the models growing out of the work of Walras, later to be refined by Arrow and Debreu. In those models, there were a large number of firms in each market, so many that each took the price it received for its goods as given. Schumpeter replaced the notion of competition in the market with competition *for the market*, argued for the benefits of the kind of creative destruction that arose out of the innovative process, and suggested that the monopoly power thus created would only be temporary. One monopolist succeeds another, and the threat of competition induces the incumbent monopolist to engage in a high level of innovation.

This and the next chapter address several related questions: (a) Does more *market* competition (that is, more competition *within a market at a particular point of time*) result in more innovation? (b) Was Schumpeter correct in his analysis of Schumpeterian competition, i.e., that competition *for* the market would sustain a high level of innovation? (c) Are markets efficient in the level and nature of the innovation and learning?

This chapter focuses on the link between competition and innovation, a link which is controversial and remains unsettled. The traditional view is that competition provides a spur to innovation, while monopolies are lethargic (see Leibenstein 1966). But Schumpeter viewed traditional economists' view as a fetish. As we explained in the last chapter, large enterprises have distinct advantages in learning and innovation.

The first three sections of this chapter explain whether and the circumstances under which the level of innovation with monopoly is greater than that in more competitive environments, even apart from imperfections in risk and capital markets. Section 1 examines the question using a standard learning model, in which the level of production affects next-period productivity. Section 2 uses a variant of the standard Bertrand price-competition model to establish a set of conditions under which market structure makes no difference to the set of research projects undertaken. The third section examines the effect of competition in a standard innovation (patent) race, in which the winner takes all, showing the conditions under which innovation is higher under monopoly than under duopoly, but explaining how further entry into the market can lead to further innovation.

The first three sections take the level of competition (the number of firms in the market) as exogenous. But market structure is endogenous. A full analysis thus needs to examine simultaneously market structure and the level of innovation.[7] Of course, government policy can play an important role in determining the level of industrial concentration, which is why it is important to know whether policies which lead to more entry lead to a faster or slower pace of innovation.

Schumpeter, of course, had a theory of market structure. He believed that at any one moment of time, the market would be dominated by a single firm but that there would be a succession of monopolists. The final section of this chapter explains the flaws in Schumpeter's analysis, showing why the monopoly power that Schumpeter seemed to extol may be more persistent than he thought and why Schumpeterian competition may not suffice to lead to a dynamic, learning economy, or at least leads to an economy which is not as dynamic as it could or should be.

This chapter primarily provides *descriptive analytics*. It simply compares (under certain idealized assumptions) the level of innovation under different institutional arrangements. It does not ask whether there is too much innovation under monopoly or too little under competition. That is the subject to which we turn in the next chapter.

1. Market Structure and Innovation

Arrow (1962b) noted that market structure (i.e., whether there was a monopoly or competition) affected incentives to innovate. Consider a cost-reducing innovation. The benefit is proportional to the amount produced. But because the amount produced in a monopoly (or, more generally, in imperfectly competitive markets) will be less than in a competitive market, the level of innovation is less than it would be in the first-best situation, where the government decides on the level of both output and innovation, and finances the research through a lump sum tax. But the level of innovation may still be higher than in a competitive market because, in a competitive market, the scale of production of each firm will be small—smaller than that of the monopolist. Thus, each firm's incentives to innovate will be limited. This reasoning applies for market structures that lie between these extremes. While total output under duopoly will be more than in monopoly and less (except in the extreme case of Bertrand competition with two firms with the same cost function) than in competitive equilibrium, the output of each duopolist is smaller than the output of each monopolist. Thus, the bias toward underinvestment in R & D that Arrow noted for monopoly is exacerbated in these more competitive structures. Monopoly has a second advantage: With monopoly, there is (within the sector) full appropriation of the benefits of the research. With more competition, sectoral output may be higher (the distortions arising from production restriction lessened), and so the *social* returns to innovation will be larger; but there will be greater learning externalities, and there will be a greater discrepancy between social and private returns to investments in innovation.

In the simple two-period model below, we are able to show that under plausible conditions, with no learning spillovers across firms, consumers may be better off with monopoly than with duopoly. Remarkably, we show that output under monopoly may well be higher even *in the second period*; that the level of innovation under monopoly is higher even when aggregate output in the first period is higher under duopoly; and that as a result, it is possible that consumers are better off under monopoly. While, in the two-period model, the welfare comparison is somewhat delicate (depending on discount rates, the sensitivity of costs of production to R & D investments, etc.), there is some presumption that *eventually* consumer welfare will be higher under monopoly than under duopoly (or other more competitive structures).

These results hold even with a high degree of spillovers. The essential insight is that even though total output with duopoly at the same cost structure would be considerably higher, each firm produces less, and hence has less incentive to innovate. Hence, costs are higher under duopoly than under monopoly. And if the difference in costs is large enough, the innovation benefit of monopoly more than offsets the losses from the monopolist's greater exploitation of its market power. In that sense, Schumpeter's insight that less competition may lead to a higher level of welfare is correct.

A Simple Model of Innovation

For simplicity, we assume symmetry. We let p denote price and C_i denote the output of the ith firm. We assume the output of the goods produced by different firms are perfect substitutes, so that

$$p = p(C), \tag{1}$$

where C is total (sectoral) output; $C = C_m$ under monopoly, but $C = C_1 + C_2$ under duopoly.

MONOPOLY EQUILIBRIUM   The monopolist maximizes

$$p(C_m)C_m - c(I_m)C_m - I_m, \tag{2}$$

where c is the marginal cost of production, a function of the investment in cost-reducing innovation, I:

$$c = c(I), \, c(0) = c_0, \, c' < 0, \, c'' > 0. \tag{3}$$

We assume a linear demand curve,[8]

$$p = a - bC, \tag{4}$$

so that the first-order conditions are

$$C_m = (a - c)/2b, \text{ and} \tag{5}$$

$$\theta_m \chi = 1, \tag{6}$$

where

$$\theta = cC/I,$$

the ratio of expenditures on (variable) costs to expenditures on innovation (I); and

$$\chi = - d(\ln c)/d(\ln I),$$

the elasticity of cost reduction with respect to investments in innovation.[9]

While this analysis focuses on cost-reducing innovations, many product innovations can be recast into this formulation: Many new products can be thought of as delivering certain basic services in a more efficient way.

DUOPOLY EQUILIBRIUM Consider now what happens if there are two firms in the industry. If there are no spillovers within the industry (that is, learning by one firm does not affect the knowledge of the other), the first duopolist maximizes (with respect to C_1 and I_1)

$$p(C_1 + C_2)C_1 - c(I_1)C_1 - I_1,$$

$$\{C_1, I_1\},$$

taking C_2 as given. This yields the first-order conditions in the symmetric equilibrium:[10]

$$C_i = (a - c)/3b, \tag{7}$$

and

$$\theta_i \chi = 1. \tag{8}$$

COMPARISON OF INNOVATION WITH MONOPOLY AND DUOPOLY Substituting (3) into (4) and (5) into (6), we obtain

$$c(a - c)/I = 2b/\chi, \tag{9a}$$

and

$$c(a - c)/I = 3b/\chi, \tag{9b}$$

respectively.

It is easy to show that

$$-d \ln[c(a - c)/I]/d(\ln I) = \{\chi(a - 2c)/(a - c)\} + 1, \tag{10}$$

which is positive so long as $c < a/2$. This means that[11]

$$I_i < I_m.$$

PROPOSITION 1. *Under Cournot equilibrium, the pace of innovation with duopoly is less than with monopoly.*[12]

COMPARISON OF WELFARE UNDER MONOPOLY AND DUO-
POLY The calculation of whether welfare is higher under duopoly than under monopoly is more delicate, because while innovation is lower, so is the distortion. Define

$$\Psi(I) = c(a - c)/I, \tag{11a}$$

$$k = b/\chi, \tag{11b}$$

and

$$\gamma = (\ln 4/3)/(\ln 3/2). \tag{11c}$$

Then the monopoly and duopoly equilibrium can be described by the same pair of equations:

$$C = (\lambda^\gamma/2)[a - c(I)]/b, \tag{12a}$$

$$\Psi(I) = 2\lambda k, \tag{12b}$$

where $\lambda = 1$ for monopoly and $\lambda = 3/2$ for duopoly. Second-period consumer welfare (consumption) is increased as we move from monopoly to duopoly if, as we increase λ from 1 to 3/2, C is increased. Assuming χ is a constant,

$$d(\ln C)/d(\ln \lambda) = \gamma - [\chi c/(a - c)]/\{\chi(a - 2c)/(a - c) + 1\}. \tag{13}$$

If χ is small, there is little benefit from innovation, and the effect of the reduced distortion dominates: $d(\ln C)/d(\ln \lambda) > 0$. However, if χ is large, then consumption is increased.

PROPOSITION 2. *If innovation is sufficiently responsive to increased investment (i.e. χ is large enough), second-period welfare is unambiguously higher under monopoly than under duopoly.*[13]

An overall welfare comparison requires comparing the lower level of consumption the first period (before the innovation occurs) under monopoly $[2(a - c_0)/3b > (a - c_0)/2b]$, with the higher level of profits and the higher level of second-period consumption. It is easy to see that if χ is high enough and the rate at which future utility is discounted low enough, then monopoly generates a higher level of social welfare.

This analysis, however, underestimates the benefits of monopoly, because the higher levels of innovation, year after year, bring down the costs. Thus, eventually, output and consumption will be higher under monopoly than under duopoly. In those cases where there is a short-run sacrifice, the question is whether the discount rate is sufficiently high that that sacrifice outweighs the long-term gain from monopoly.

PROPOSITION 3. *Provided* c < a/2, *for sufficiently low discount rates, welfare is higher under monopoly than under duopoly.*[14]

It also understates another potential benefit of monopoly *in early periods*. With learning by doing (where future costs of production are lowered by higher levels of production today), the monopolist will have an incentive to produce more in the first period. Thus, it is even possible (with a small enough discount factor and a large enough learning elasticity) that output will be higher with monopoly than with duopoly *both* periods.

PERFECT SPILLOVERS Consider now the other polar case, where there are perfect spillovers. Then the duopolist maximizes

$$p(C_1 + C_2)C_1 - c(I_1 + I_2)C_1 - I_1, \tag{14}$$

taking $\{C_2, I_2\}$ as given, yielding the same first-order conditions for C_i, but now

$$\theta_i^s \chi/2 = 1, \tag{8'}$$

where we use the superscript s to denote values in the case of full spillovers.

In the case of a linear demand curve, we can again substitute (9a) into (8′) to obtain

$$c(a - c)/I^s = 3b/\chi,$$

where $I^s = I_1 + I_2$, total investment in research. We obtain exactly the same equations as before, except now, each of the firms does half the research. The consequences of having perfect spillovers is simply to increase the profits of producers. Output and the total level of innovation remain the same. Hence, the result that innovation (and welfare) is higher under monopoly than under duopoly remains valid.

Similar results hold if the elasticity of demand is constant.[15]

EXTENSIONS It is easy to use the same techniques to show that a Cournot oligopoly with $n + 1$ firms will have a higher level of innovation than a Cournot oligopoly with n firms and that if the elasticity of the research curve is large enough and the discount rate is small enough, welfare is higher.

The firms in the model presented thus far are short sighted, i.e., focus only on the next period. They don't take into account how more investment in R & D today lowers costs in all future periods and provides a higher base off of which future research will be based. It should be obvious, however, that a future-oriented monopolist—producing more than the duopolist—will engage in more research than the duopolist (and a fortiori more than the representative firm in the n-firm oligopoly ($n > 2$). Thus, with future-oriented firms, investment with monopoly will be even larger relative to that with oligopoly, and the conditions under which welfare is higher (i.e., the values of discount rates and learning elasticities) will be weaker.

SOME GENERAL OBSERVATIONS The basic insight of this section is simple.[16] As the number of firms increases, total output increases, but the output of each firm decreases. Each firm's investment in R & D depends only on its own production, not industry production. Therefore, the level of innovation will be lower. It follows that if innovation is important enough—i.e., if it is sensitive enough to increased investment and if the future is valued enough—then welfare will monotonically decrease as competition increases.

The results of this section need, however, to be taken with considerable caution. We have modeled a duopoly using the standard Cournot-Nash equilibrium concepts, while the advocates of competition (rightly, we think) suggest that that approach does not fully capture the spirit of competition in the marketplace. A monopolist is more likely to rest on its laurels, enjoying its monopoly rents. Schumpeter envisaged a different form of competition—what has subsequently come to be called Schumpeterian competition. The fourth section of this chapter analyzes the effectiveness of this form of competition in spurring innovation. But first, we analyze the effect of competition on innovation in the context of somewhat different models of market interaction, based on Bertrand competition, obtaining two rather surprising results: First, the level of competition may have little effect; second, in the context of patent races, its effects may even be negative (in agreement with the result of this section).

2. The Intensity of Competition and the Efficiency of Innovation

In this section, we alter our analysis in two ways: First, we focus on research "projects". And second, we assume market participants interact through price competition. When the number of firms is fixed (that is, entry is *not* an issue), Bertrand (fierce price) competition leads to the Sah-Stiglitz (1987) *invariance theorem*: *the number of research projects undertaken—and the effort with which each is undertaken—is invariant to the number of firms.*

The reason is simple and is seen most simply in the context of a model in which there is a well-defined innovation that will lower the marginal cost of production to c^* from c_0. If each firm takes the projects of all other firms (and the intensity with which they are executed) as given, then any project which it undertakes has a return if and only if no other project succeeds. If the firm's project succeeds, and no other project succeeds, the return is $\Pi(c^*, c)$, where $\Pi(c^*, c)$ is the level of profits given that other firms have a fixed marginal cost of c and the firm faces a cost of c^*. If the project succeeds, and some other project succeeds, then the return is zero. By the same token, if the firm undertakes more than one project and only this project succeeds, its return is $\Pi(c^*, c)$, while if any other project succeeds, the return *to this project* is zero. Hence, a set of projects is an equilibrium if (and only if) the expected return for each project is positive, and there does not exist another project for which the expected return is nonnegative. But the expected return is just $\Pi(c^*, c)$ times the probability that the project is successful and no other project undertaken is successful. But that probability (under the assumption that there are no economies or diseconomies of scope, i.e., the project's probability of success does not depend on the other projects undertaken) does not depend at all on who undertakes the research. Thus, if there is an equilibrium set of projects under one market structure (i.e., with n firms), there is an equilibrium—with the same set of projects and hence the same pace of innovation—under any other market structure, i.e., with n' firms, so long as n and n' are greater than one, i.e., so long as there is Bertrand competition.

By the same token, assume that by exerting more effort, c^* could be lowered and that there is a cost to effort. So long as all firms face the same marginal cost of effort (and again, there are no economies or diseconomies of scale/scope), then if there exists a set of projects, each associated with an equilibrium level of effort, under one market structure, there exists an identical innovation equilibrium with any other nonmonopoly market structure. (The same is not true, however, if effort levels affect the probability of success, for then, if any firm undertakes multiple projects, it takes into account the effect of an increased probability of success for one project on the reduced expected return to other projects.)

But while the equilibrium under Bertrand competition may, under these circumstances, be invariant to the market structure, the number of projects undertaken (and the effort exerted in each project) will not be socially optimal. To see this, note that for a small innovation, the innovator will charge the price c, and the firm's profits will be $D(c)(c - c^*)$, where $D(c)$ is the demand for the product at the price c. But social optimality requires that the firm charge the price c^*, and the social value of the innovation is

$$S(c^*, c) = \int_{c^*}^{c} D^{-1}(p)\, dp > \Pi(c^*, c)$$

(by the amount of the consumer surplus), so that there will be more "socially profitable" innovations than privately profitable innovations. In other words, *the pace of innovation will be slower under market competition, even fierce Bertrand competition.*[17]

When competition is less intense (i.e., with Cournot competition), then in general profits will be higher than they would have been with Bertrand competition in those states of nature where two projects are successful. (In Bertrand competition, it will be recalled, profits are zero in this situation.) But the less-intense competition when only one project is successful will mean that the successful innovator's incremental profits will be smaller with Cournot than with Bertrand competition. For instance, for a small innovation, with two firms, industry output will be smaller than under Bertrand competition—where output is close to the competitive level—and in Cournot competition, the successful firm gets only slightly more than half of the industry output. Hence, the value of an incremental cost reduction is considerably smaller. Hence, if the probability of success of the various projects is highly correlated (so it is likely that there are two successful projects), then more projects may be undertaken. But if the probability of success of various projects is not highly correlated and is low, then the expected return to a slightly greater cost reduction is lower with Cournot competition than Bertrand, so fewer projects will be undertaken and there will be less effort at cost reductions.[18]

Of course, in the limiting case of a monopolist (or collusion among the existing firms), industry output will be smaller than with, say, duopoly, but the output of the monopolist will be higher than that of either duopolist. Thus, the value of the innovation will be higher with monopoly, and hence there will be more innovation. (This result should be contrasted with Arrow's 1962b result suggesting that innovation with monopoly will be less; it is less than the socially efficient level with competition, but not less than the market level with competition.[19])

The same kind of analysis leads to the result that the level of risk taking will be affected by the nature of competition and will typically be different in markets than in the socially optimal allocation. For instance, under Bertrand competition, firms only obtain a return when they succeed and no one else does, so there are large incentives to undertake projects with low (negative) correlations. The same is true in the socially optimal allocation. One wants to avoid largely duplicative research projects. But in the Cournot equilibrium, there is much less sensitivity of the returns to the success or failure of competitors, as we have noted. Undertaking highly correlated research projects still yields a return—and indeed, may lead to a lower level of risk.[20]

3. Why More Competition in Patent Races May Not Spur a Faster Rate of Innovation

Even if a monopolist were not challenged by potential entrants, it would engage in research, to lower the firm's costs and to provide products that are more valuable to its customers, from whom it can make more profits. The question on which this chapter has focused is whether competition leads to higher levels of innovation than would occur under monopoly and whether more competition accelerates the level of innovation. We have seen that the answer is ambiguous at best. The complexity is further illustrated in the case of patent races. Assume that there is a probability distribution of arrival of an innovation, $F(T, I)$. Assume that the benefits that are appropriable are given, normalized at unity, so that the net value of the innovation is

$$V = \int e^{-rT} dF(T, I) - I. \tag{15}$$

The monopolist maximizes this with respect to I.

Now assume that there are n firms in the race. The firm only gets the return if it is first, i.e., if it makes the discovery at time T and no one else has done so previously. Focusing on the symmetric equilibrium,[21] where all other firms are investing I^*, the firm chooses I to maximize

$$V = \int e^{-rT} [1 - F(T, I^*)]^{n-1} [dF(T, I)] - I, \tag{16}$$

i.e.,

$$\int e^{-rT}[1 - F(T, I^*)]^{n-1}[dF_I(T, I)] = 1. \tag{17}$$

The fixed point of (17), i.e., the values of I such that

$$\int e^{-rT}[1 - F(T, I^*)]^{n-1}[dF_I(T, I^*)] = 1, \tag{18}$$

represents the equilibrium I for a given n. Thus, we solve (18) for

$$I^* = I^*(n). \tag{19}$$

We wish to know whether the innovation will occur earlier (i.e., is the pace of innovation higher) when n is larger. The probability distribution of arrival of the innovation is

$$G(T, n) \equiv 1 - [1 - F(I^*(n), T)]^n. \tag{20}$$

We can ask, for instance, whether $G(T, n')$ stochastically dominates (first order) $G(T, n)$, for $n' > n$, i.e., is it unambiguously clear that the innovation will occur earlier; or we can ask a simpler question: Is the expected time of arrival of the innovation, ET $dG(T, n)$, shorter?

If I^* were unchanged, the answer would be easy: Having more researchers unambiguously leads to faster outcomes. But having more researchers means that it is more likely that someone will beat any particular researcher to the discovery. And that means that the incentive to engage in research is lowered. The effect on the probability distribution of discovery then depends on the strength of the investment response and the effect of the investment on the probability distribution of arrival, i.e.,

$$dG(T, n)/dn = n(1 - F)^{n-1}F_I(dI^*/dn) - [\ln(1 - F)](1 - F)^n$$

$$= (1 - F)^{n-1}[nF_I(dI^*/dn) - (1 - F)\ln(1 - F)]. \tag{21}$$

The first term is negative, the second term is positive, and so the effects (at any T) are ambiguous. In the appendix, we analyze a specific example, in which we show that more competitors may indeed slow down the pace of innovation. In that example, the adverse effects on investment of each competitor outweigh the benefits of more competitors.

4. Schumpeterian Competition and Endogenous Market Structure

The question traditionally posed—whether competition, oligopoly, or monopoly is better for innovation—only partially answers the question about the efficiency of markets. Market structures themselves are endogenous and, hence, we must simultaneously analyze market structure and innovation and assess the efficiency of the resulting market equilibrium.[22] Similarly, when we discuss government interventions, we need to ask not just what is the effect of a particular intervention on, say, innovation and welfare, *given* a market structure, but also what are the effects, recognizing that market structure may also change and that such changes in turn may have further effects on innovation and welfare. The discussion in the previous section showed that more competitive structures did not *necessarily* lead to more innovation.

Schumpeter provided a theory of the simultaneous determination of market structure and innovation. Implicitly, he suggested, there would be only one firm in a market at a time, or at least only one dominant firm. Keen competition to be the dominant firm—to capture monopoly rents—spurred research. The dominant firm couldn't rest on its laurels, for unless it continued to innovate, it would be quickly replaced by another. But try as firms might, their monopoly power was inevitably only temporary. There was competition *for* the market, rather than competition in the market, and the contention (or hope) was that this competition would suffice to ensure efficiency, as well as a high level of innovation, and that the benefits of innovation would be widely shared.

As appealing as Schumpeter's ideas might seem—as widely accepted by economists focusing on innovation as they were—it has turned out that they did not withstand scrutiny. In the following paragraphs, we look at each of the major contentions.

The Domination of the Market at Each Moment of Time by a Single Enterprise

Schumpeter seemed to claim that the "natural" market structure *at each moment* was a monopoly. The analysis of the previous section actually provides some support for this view.[23]

Consider, for instance, a Nash-Cournot model and assume that the monopolist has a high discount rate—sufficiently high that it ignores the benefit of future learning. And assume that one of the firms has infinitesimally lower marginal costs than the other. It follows that it will produce more. But that means that it will learn more. And that means that in the following period, its level of production will be relatively greater, compared to that of its rival. Over time, one of the firms has an increasing competitive advantage over the other, until the firm that began with just an infinitesimal advantage becomes dominant—it becomes the monopolist.

Of course, if the firms are less myopic, then the firm with the competitive advantage realizes that it will be growing relative to the other, and that implies that it has an incentive to expand production now even more, relative to its rival. It would appear that convergence to the monopoly equilibrium would be even faster.

With Bertrand competition, divergence is still more rapid, for the firm with the slight competitive advantage grabs the entire market; it learns, and its rival does not.

There is a knife-edge equilibrium, in which (with symmetry) one might have *n* identical firms cohabiting the market. It should be clear that learning would be lower in such a world than if there were a single firm. (This is an insight of the previous subsection.) But here, we wish to emphasize the fragility of that equilibrium. For if one of the firms should, for any reason, get a cost advantage relative to its rivals, it would expand production and learning relative to its rival(s), with cumulative effects over time.[24]

The Temporary Nature of Monopoly Power

While Schumpeter was correct that at each moment of time markets would be dominated by a single firm, monopolies can be far less temporary than Schumpeter thought; while in some cases the threat of entry can be an important impetus to innovation, in other cases, to maintain their monopoly power, firms devote considerable resources to creating socially unproductive entry barriers. In doing so, incumbents can discourage the overall pace of innovation. Microsoft has become the poster child of how an incumbent can discourage innovation. Modern monopolists have become highly innovative—in creating new forms of entry barriers and in extracting rents out of their monopoly power.

By controlling the "platform" (PC operating system), Microsoft could use anticompetitive practices to leverage and extend its market power in the operating system to other areas, and in so doing undermine, and in some cases drive out, potential innovative competitors: Netscape in the browser market, Real Networks in the multimedia market. By bundling, for instance, Internet Explorer into the operating system, it was charging in effect a zero price—and it is hard for entrants to compete against a zero price. It was clear that a zero price did not maximize Microsoft's short-run profits, but it seemingly believed that (if it could get away with it) such predatory behavior was consistent with long-run profit maximization. (Indeed, it turned out that even after it was found guilty of anticompetitive practices and some of these practices were enjoined, Netscape did not revive. Effective competition was brought about only by Mozilla's open-source Firefox.[25])

Not surprisingly, efforts at entry deterrence can be welfare decreasing (Stiglitz 1981). In particular, they can discourage innovation. A potential innovator knows that a dominant firm like Microsoft can engage in predatory and other behavior that will result in the innovative firm not capturing much of the benefits of its innovation.

Analytics

Dasgupta and Stiglitz (1980b) established a general result showing that monopolists have an incentive to preserve their monopoly power—to do more research than competitors and thus to preempt them (see also Gilbert and Newbery 1982). They model the innovation game as a patent race, where the first innovator owns the new technology with costs $c^* < c_0$, the costs associated with the old technology.

Consider a Stackleberg equilibrium, where the (potential) entrant takes the level of R & D of the incumbent as given, and given that chooses the optimal level of research. The incumbent firm knows this and so chooses its level of research, given the reaction function of the entrant(s).

Assume that there are a large number of symmetric potential entrants. Free entry ensures that, if there is entry, there are zero profits. Thus, if V_e^d is the present discounted value of profits for the entrant in the duopoly, as of the date of discovery, and the date of discovery T is a function of the investment in research (I_d), then

$$V_e^d \, e^{-rT(Id)} = I_d. \tag{22}$$

The race drives profits to zero. This reflects intense "competition for the market." We let I_d^* be the solution to the above equation. But if the monopolist wins the patent race (e.g., as a result of going slightly faster than I_d^*), it controls the entire market, and

$$V_m > V_e^d + V_m^d, \qquad (23)$$

where V_m^d represents the incumbent's profits after entry (that is, in the duopoly that emerges after entry). Since no competitor will choose a level of R & D in excess of I_d^*, by spending even marginally in excess of I_d^*, the monopolist can guarantee the patent for itself. The present value of profits of the monopolist, if it does this, is

$$V_m e^{-rT} + \Pi_m (1 - e^{-rT})/r - I, \qquad (24)$$

where Π_m is the monopolist's flow of profits under the old technology. Using (23), we can show that (24) is greater than

$$(V_e^d + V_m^d) e^{-rT} + \Pi_m (1 - e^{-rT})/r - I = V_m^d e^{-rT} + \Pi_m (1 - e^{-rT})/r, \quad (25)$$

(using (22)), the present discounted value of profits if it does not pre-empt. Therefore, the monopolist will always forestall entry by competitors by spending in excess of I_d (perhaps only marginally so).

The reason the monopolist will always preempt potential competitors is intuitively clear. If any other firm were to win the patent, the industry would be characterized by a duopoly structure. However, the existing monopolist can always ensure that it remains a monopolist by spending a little more on R & D than any potential competitor would find profitable. It is always in the monopolist's interest to do so, because by remaining a monopolist it can earn a flow of profit in excess of the sum of the two firms' profits under duopoly.

The argument is, of course, reinforced if the existing monopolist is more efficient than its competitors in R & D activity or in ancillary services (e.g., in distribution). The implication is that even if there is competition in R & D activity, there are strong tendencies for a monopolized industry to remain a monopoly. The fact that the monopolist is threatened by potential competitors *at most* spurs the monopolist to spend more on R & D than it would otherwise. But (at least in this model), the industry remains a monopoly.

The results are in many ways far more general than this model suggests. There can, for instance, be uncertainty in the research process, both about time and the eventual cost of production; but if there is any research project which is worthwhile for an entrant to undertake, it is profitable for the incumbent to preempt.

Why Contestability Doesn't Suffice to Ensure Innovation, Efficiency, or Zero Profits

The notion that all that is needed for markets to be efficient is that there be competition for the market (potential competition), rather than competition in the market, is obviously very appealing and applies to all natural monopolies, not just those that arise out of the fixed costs associated with innovation. Were it true, it would mean that government wouldn't even have to worry about regulating natural monopolies. Potential competition would provide the necessary market discipline. Potential competition would ensure that the monopolist not exploit its market power by charging a price in excess of average cost. In the context of an innovation economy, it would mean that the monopolist would be forced by potential competition both to innovate and *not* to exploit its (temporary) monopoly power by earning excess profits.

This idea gained currency at the time that the AT&T monopoly began to be attacked in the 1970s. The defenders of monopoly argued that potential competition would ensure that profits would be driven down to zero. Markets where potential competition was sufficiently strong to do this were called *contestable*.[26]

It turns out, however, that these notions of *contestability* are not robust. Even if there are arbitrarily small sunk costs, even very strong potential competition may not result in zero profits. This can be seen in a simple example, where there are small sunk costs ε and fixed marginal costs c. Assume the entrant is just as efficient as the incumbent and that after entry, the two engage in Bertrand competition (i.e., each takes the price of the other as given). Then *after* entry, the price will be c: there will be no profits. But that means that the entrant will lose its sunk costs. But knowing this, the entrant will not enter. The incumbent can charge the monopoly price with impunity.

What matters is not, of course, the level of competition *now*, but that after entry. And if there is keen competition after entry, then potential entrants will be deterred from entering. Ironically, the stronger competition is in markets *after entry*, the less likely that there will be entry and the more likely that a monopoly will be sustained (Stiglitz 1987c; Farrell 1986).

Since R & D expenditures (or investments in learning) are by their very nature sunk costs, and in the sectors with which we are concerned, where R & D or learning is important, they are significant, it should be clear that the contestability notion is of little relevance; potential competition does not suffice either to ensure efficiency or zero profits (see, in particular, Dasgupta and Stiglitz 1988b).

Entry Deterrence

The analysis of the previous section argued that potential competition does not ensure effective competition or efficiency—prices may remain sustained at well above marginal costs, and potential competition will not force the incumbent to engage in the efficient level of research. But matters may be even worse, for firms may undertake costly actions to deter entry (Stiglitz 1981, 1987c). They may, for instance, hold excess capacity, so that potential entrants will know that there can be a strong competitive response to entry. Or they may invest in high levels of cost reduction to preempt rivals from entering—levels that are greater than the most efficient or socially optimum.

Why Patent Races May Provide Only a Limited Spur to Innovation

In the context of innovation—patent races—entry deterrence may be even easier, for this analysis is essentially static. Patent races, however, are dynamic. The first firm to patent gets a big prize; the losers get nothing—or at least very little. (The knowledge that they acquired may have considerable value, enabling them to compete more effectively in some other race. For purposes of simplicity, we will ignore this in the subsequent discussion.)

One of the problems of contests in general is that if there is some firm (individual) that is viewed as likely to win, others will drop out of the competition. Why put up the effort if the chances of winning are low? But if this happens, contests may be much less effective in spurring effort than is generally assumed. Nalebuff and Stiglitz (1983b) studied equilibrium behavior in contests (with possibly many contestants). They show that contests have to be carefully designed to avoid this pitfall. For instance, one way of ensuring that all participants exert effort is to punish the loser (the one in the last place), rather than rewarding the winner. But in the context of innovation races, we can only tell who is the winner—the person who makes the discovery.

Thus, in a patent race, the optimal strategy of the incumbent is simply to get far enough ahead of the rivals that they are discouraged from entering—and having done that, it can rest on its laurels. Patent races may provide only limited spurs to innovation (Fudenberg, Gilbert, Tirole, and Stiglitz 1983).

Matters may not be as bad as this analysis suggests, since there are often multiple dimensions to (product) innovations. One innovator may succeed in getting a product that is better in one dimension, another in another. What matters is that one is not dominated in all dimensions. Those who fail in every dimension are the "losers," and market competition may drive them out of business. Thus, the force of competition may serve to encourage high levels of research by punishing the laggards, consistent with the Nalebuff-Stiglitz analysis.

Some Caveats on the Ability of a Dominant Firm to Perpetuate Dominance

There are three caveats to these conclusions suggesting that a firm, once it becomes dominant, will remain so. The first concerns diseconomies of management: The monopolist, which has to manage the task of production as well as innovation, may become less nimble in its research. If the entrant has, as a result, a cost advantage, then it may not pay the incumbent to preempt its rival. This is especially so if there are multiple avenues to be pursued. If the firm attempts too many diverse research projects, performance will deteriorate.

Second, the rival may be irrationally enthusiastic about its abilities, and this may lead it to engage in an excessive level of research.[27] Given this irrational exuberance, the level of R & D that the incumbent would have to undertake to preempt the rival may be very high—so high that the incumbent may decide not to preempt.

This is especially so because there is a great deal of uncertainty about the outcome of R & D. The entrant may engage in a sufficiently low level of R & D that the incumbent thinks that there is a low probability of the entrant being successful enough to become a major player. (It may in fact share some of the same overconfidence in its *relative* abilities.) Given this low probability, it simply doesn't pay to engage in even more R & D to drive the entrant out. But even at the low level of research, there is a chance that the entrant will be successful—and the incumbent will not be—so that the entrant displaces the incumbent as the dominant player.

Finally, as we have emphasized earlier, there may be multiple technologies for producing the same goods or services. While the incumbent may have a comparative advantage in the current technology, there may be an alternative technology, related to a technology employed elsewhere in the economy; and firms employing that technology may have a comparative advantage *in lowering costs associated with that technology.*

In other words, it may not pay the incumbent to explore every possible technology and preempt potential entrants in each of these areas; so long as that is the case, stochastically, one of the other researchers will, eventually, succeed in developing an alternative technology. Indeed, there may again be managerial limitations that force the incumbent to focus its attention on one, or a limited number, of technologies, leaving space for the arrival of a new dominant firm based on an alternative technology.

In any of these cases, there can be entry, and the new entrants can even displace the existing firm. But the lesson of this chapter is still relevant: Monopolies can persist for a long time. While they persist, markets are distorted, and the threat of competition does not in general induce the optimal amount of research and learning.

5. Agency Issues and X-Inefficiency

The standard theory of monopoly holds that monopolists are efficient in their production decisions; the only distortion arises from restrictions on the level of production. In this context, we have assumed that if there is a monopoly, the monopolist chooses the level of innovation to maximize its profits. But there is a wealth of evidence and some theory that without the discipline of competition, monopolies in fact often become inefficient and lethargic. (See Leibenstein [1966], who refers to the loss of efficiency from what is called today agency problems as X-inefficiency and suggests that it may be far more important than the allocative efficiency that economists have traditionally focused upon.[28]) Thus, the real reason that more competition may lead to more innovation is not captured well in the models that we have been analyzing.

In the presence of imperfect information, it is hard to design good incentive structures to motivate managers. If things turn out badly, is it because the manager didn't work hard enough, or because there was an adverse turn of circumstances? If the firm fails to make the innovation that it sought to achieve, was it because it turns out that the problem was harder than was at first realized, or because the researchers didn't exert sufficient effort? In these circumstances, Nalebuff and Stiglitz (1983a, 1983b) have shown that well-designed compensation schemes may base pay on relative performance and that more generally contests, where compensation is based on rank ordering, may be desirable. Patent races in effect do this; the first to make the discovery gets the prize.

While competition can thus be a spur for innovation (more than would seem to be the case in the standard models examined elsewhere in this book), compensation systems based on relative performance have their own problems. They can, for instance, give rise to fads. If all banks decide to lend to Latin America, it may be risky for any bank (bank manager) to deviate. If the fad proves right, she will be punished, but if the fad turns out wrong, she will suffer little, for her performance will differ little from that of everyone else. Similar reasoning applies to decisions concerning innovation.

6. Concluding Comments

One purpose of this chapter has been to show that the relationship between competition, innovation, and welfare in quite standard models of market interaction is far different than has been widely presumed. Indeed, in the basic model, there is a presumption that more competition leads to less innovation (a presumption which will be reinforced in the next chapter).

There are other factors that affect the relationship between competition and innovation beyond those on which this chapter has focused. For instance, larger firms may have a greater ability to bear the risks associated with innovation and get access to (or generate) the funds necessary to finance it; this provides still further reasons that more-competitive markets with smaller firms may be less innovative.[29]

With more firms, there are likely to be more "knowledge spillovers"; that is, more of the benefits of one firm's research are likely to accrue to others, which implies a larger disparity between private and social returns.

This chapter thus provides some support to Schumpeter's view that markets dominated by a single firm may be more innovative than more competitive markets.

But Schumpeter was too sanguine about Schumpeterian competition. He overestimated the force of competition "for the market" as a spur to innovation and underestimated the ability and incentive of the incumbent monopolist to deter entry and to maintain its monopoly position.[30]

The next chapter (and especially, the appendices to that chapter) will elaborate on the theme struck here that the relationship between the level of competition (both *for* the market and *in* the market) and innovation is complex. When, for instance, the research is stochastic, with uncertain and uncorrelated returns, then the more firms (the more research projects) the greater the likelihood of success *if the effort of each enterprise were fixed*. But whether competition *spurs* innovation or dampens it (given that the chance of becoming the dominant firm is diminished) is ambiguous. While section 5 explained how competition can enable the design of better incentive structures, more competitive patent races (races with more entrants) may not lead to more innovation. A well-designed contest with just two contestants may, in some circumstances, be optimal (see Nalebuff and Stiglitz 1983b). There may be an inverted U-shaped relationship.[31] But, by contrast, in the appendix to this chapter, we show that in a particular parameterization of the patent race, there may be a U-shaped relationship between competition and innovation.

The result derived here that, in standard models, the level of innovation *may* be higher with monopoly than with duopoly, or than with more competitive market structures more generally, runs at odds with a strong presumption that competition is good for innovation. But the failure of monopoly lies, I suspect, outside the bounds of this (and other) standard models. Perhaps most importantly, the standard theory of monopoly holds that monopolists are efficient in their production decisions; the only distortion arises from restrictions on the level of production. In this context, we have assumed that if there is a monopoly, the monopolist chooses the level of innovation to maximize its profits.

Monopolies, unconstrained by competitive threats, still have an incentive to innovate. The (expected) present discounted value of profits is increased as a result of cost reducing innovations, or as a result of the creation of products that consumers value more. Our analysis noted the limited impact of the pressure of competition *in standard models*.

But section 5 of this chapter explained how lack of competition may lead to monopolies becoming inefficient and lethargic. Thus, the real reason that more competition may lead to more innovation is not captured well in the models that we have been analyzing. The failure of monopoly is related to problems associated with agency costs and the design of good incentive structures.

Policy Implications

We have not explored the policy implications of our analysis. But we should be clear: It is *not* that monopoly should be condoned because of the beneficial effects on innovation (as Schumpeter seems to have suggested). There is enough experience (e.g., with Microsoft) to suggest that a dominant firm may not only be less innovative (perhaps because of internal problems of bureaucracy that more than offset the advantages of scale, perhaps because of the issues of X-inefficiency referred to earlier), but may actually take actions that suppress the innovation of others.[32]

What our analysis does suggest is that for a fuller understanding of the innovative process, we will need to go beyond the standard models and, at the very least, incorporate agency issues into the analysis.

Competition, Innovation, and Endogenous Market Structures

Market structure itself must, of course, be viewed as endogenous and affected by, say, the technology of technological progress. If so, the right question is not so much the effect of market structure on innovation but under what circumstances the market structure that emerges endogenously leads to efficient allocation of resources to innovation.

There are other contexts in which the endogenous market structure (the number of firms) has been studied.[33] They share with the problem at hand two central features: (a) the importance of fixed costs (which serves to limit the number of firms); and (b) there is some value to having more than one firm, e.g., diseconomies of scale or scope, the value of product variety, or, here, of diversification of research strategies. The general result of such analyses is that markets are not, in general, (constrained) Pareto optimal. This reinforces the presumption that markets with innovation will not be Pareto optimal.

Overall, the picture that emerges is complex (again, the next chapter will explore these complexities further). Even in the best of circumstances, the level of innovation in the market is distorted. There is no presumption that Schumpeterian competition leads to a socially optimal level of innovation; indeed, this chapter explains why there is some presumption that there will be too little innovation (a result that is reinforced by the next chapter, especially in appendix C).

Still, when the market endogenously arrives at a market structure dominated by a single firm, it *may* be the case that innovation is higher than would have been the case if there were two firms. Even welfare *may* be higher with monopoly than with competition.

We should emphasize, however, that these are *n*th-best results. We could achieve higher levels of innovation and higher levels of welfare by curbing monopoly and by government actions that induce more innovation.

Before turning to a detailed analysis of how the government might improve societal welfare by helping creating a truly creative learning economy in parts 2 and 3 of this book, we investigate in the next chapter in more detail the various reasons that and ways in which the market economy misallocates its scarce innovative resources. This analysis will, furthermore, help clarify the ambiguous relationship between competition in the market and competition for the market and the pace of innovation.

APPENDIX A

Impact of the Number of Firms on the Pace of Innovation in a Patent Race

In the text, we explained why an increase in the number of firms may result in a low rate of innovation, as each firm invests less in research. While patent races have been extensively studied,[34] with somewhat ambiguous results on the relationship between the number of competitors and the pace of innovation, the parametric model of this section provides neat results showing the effects of competition on the pace of innovation. What makes the analysis both complicated and tricky is that the arrival date of an innovation (winning the patent race) is stochastic and that the participants in the patent race are in effect choosing probability distributions, given the probability distributions chosen by their rivals. We simplify by focusing on a context in which there is only one relevant parameter.

We assume the innovation, without further investment, will arrive at time $T = 2$, but that with additional investment, there is a probability that it will arrive at $T = 1$. The incremental profit to the firm (if it is the only firm to make the early discovery) is $\pi = 1$. To achieve a probability of arrival at time $T = 1$ of α requires an investment of $\alpha^2/2\gamma$. Thus, a monopolist maximizes with respect to α

$$\alpha - \alpha^2/2\gamma, \tag{A.1}$$

implying

$$\alpha^* = \gamma. \tag{A.2}$$

Now assume there are two firms. Assume the second firm sets $\alpha = \alpha^{d*}$. Then the first firm maximizes

$$\alpha(1 - \alpha^{d*}) - \alpha^2/2\gamma, $$

implying

$$(1 - \alpha^{d*}) = \alpha/\gamma, \tag{A.3}$$

or

$$\alpha^{d*} = \gamma/(1 - \alpha^{*d}) \tag{A.4}$$

In the symmetric equilibrium $\alpha^{*d} = 1 + \gamma$.

We now ask, when is $\alpha^{d*} > \alpha^*$, γ and, more relevant, when is

$$1 - (1 - \alpha^{d*})^2 > \alpha^*, \tag{A.5}$$

so that the probability of arrival of the innovation at date 1 is higher with duopoly than monopoly? By direct substitution, we ask, when is

$$1 - \alpha^* = 1 - \gamma > [1/(1 + \gamma)]^2 = (1 - \alpha^{d*})^2, \qquad (A.6)$$

i.e., when is

$$\gamma - \gamma^2 - \gamma^3 > 0? \qquad (A.7)$$

Thus, innovation is higher (faster) with duopoly if and only if $\gamma < (\sqrt{5} - 1)/2 \approx .618$. Otherwise, if the opposite holds, then innovation is higher (faster) with monopoly.

In the case of a patent race with n firms, the corresponding value of α, denoted α_n, is the solution to

$$(1 - \alpha_n^*)^{n-1} = \alpha_n^*/\gamma, \qquad (A.8)$$

or

$$(n - 1) \ln(1 - \alpha_n^*) - \ln \alpha_n^* = -\ln \gamma.$$

From this we can calculate for $n > 1$ (treating n as a continuous variable).

$$da_n^*/dn = [\alpha_n^*(1 - \alpha_n^*) \ln(1 - \alpha_n^*)]/[\alpha_n^* (n - 1) \\ + (1 - \alpha_n^*)] < 0. \qquad (A.9)$$

What we are really interested in is the probability of early arrival:

$$A \equiv 1 - (1 - \alpha_n^*)^n. \qquad (A.10)$$

We wish to ascertain the sign of

$$dA/dn = (1 - \alpha_n^*)^n \{n[\alpha_n^* \ln(1 - \alpha_n^*)]/[\alpha_n^*(n - 1) \\ + (1 - \alpha_n^*)] - \ln(1 - \alpha_n^*)\} \qquad (A.11)$$

$$= \{(1 - \alpha_n^*)^n \ln(1 - \alpha_n^*)/[\alpha_n^*(n - 1) \\ + (1 - \alpha_n^*)]\}\{n\alpha_n^* - [\alpha_n(n - 1) + (1 - \alpha_n^*)]\}$$

$$= \{(1 - \alpha_n^*)^n \ln(1 - \alpha_n^*)/[\alpha_n^*(n-1) + (1 - \alpha_n^*)]\}$$
$$(2\alpha_n^* - 1) > 0, \text{ so long as } \alpha_n^* < \tfrac{1}{2}.$$

This result, in conjunction with the earlier comparing monopoly and duopoly, implies that for small γ (less than .618), innovation is higher the larger the number of research enterprises.

On the other hand, we can show that

$$d\alpha_n^*/d\gamma = [\alpha_n^*(1 - \alpha_n^*)]/[\alpha_n^*(n-1) + (1 - \alpha_n^*)]\gamma > 0. \qquad (A.12)$$

At $\{n = 2, \gamma = 1\}$, it is easy to show that $\alpha^{d*} = .5$, which means that for all $\{n > 2, \gamma < 1\}$, $\alpha_n^* < .5$. This means that for $1 > \gamma > .618$, there is an U-shaped relationship between the pace of innovation and the number of firms, with a local peak at $n = 1$, a minimum at $n = 2$. Substituting (A.8) into (A.10) we obtain

$$A = 1 - (\alpha_n^*/\gamma)^{n/n-1} \qquad (A.13)$$

which, as n approaches infinity, approaches $1 - \alpha_n^*/\gamma$. Moreover α_n^* must approach 0. (Assume it were bound away from zero. Then as n approaches infinity, the LHS of (A.8) would approach zero, which would be less than the RHS.) But that implies that A approaches 1, which is greater than the value of A when $n = 1$.

$A(n)$ can thus take on one of two forms, illustrated in figure 5.1. For $\gamma < .618$, A increases monotonically with n, while for $1 > \gamma > .618$, $A(2) < A(1) < 1$, and there exists an n^* such that $A(n) > A(1)$ for $n > n^*$. In other words, with *enough* competition, the innovation will arrive earlier than with monopoly.

It should be clear that what has driven this analysis is the elasticity of investment in innovation with respect to competition (n), and the elasticity of innovation with respect to investment in innovation. Our parametric model has enabled us to derive simple relationships describing innovation and investment as a function of n. In more general models, the relationships can be expected to be complex, and as a result, we cannot expect simple monotonic or U-shaped relationships.

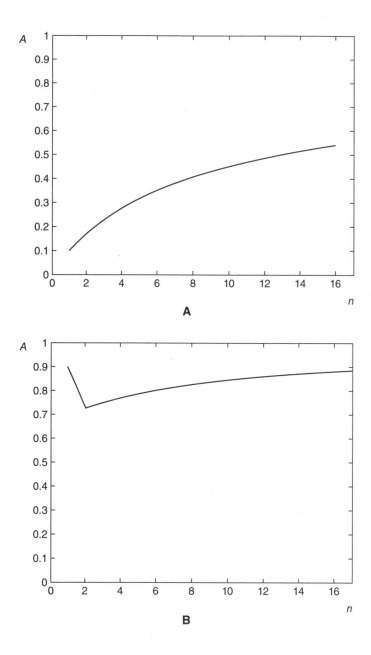

A

B

Figure 5.1 Probability of early discovery as a function of the number of firms

A. When γ is low (an increase in R & D investment increases the probability of early arrival only a little), the adverse effects on investment in R & D of more competition have little effect and the probability of arrival increases monotonically with *n*. B. When γ is high, more competition initially decreases innovation, then increases it.

CHAPTER SIX

The Welfare Economics of Schumpeterian Competition

SCHUMPETER AND his latter-day followers were clearly more optimistic about the effectiveness of "Schumpeterian" competition—that competition for the market could replace competition in the market to ensure economic efficiency—than the analysis of chapter 5 would suggest. We have seen that dominant market power can persist and that the threat of competition may lead to neither high levels of innovation or low levels of profits.

As we remarked at the beginning of the last chapter, there are no general proofs of the efficiency of the market economy in producing innovation. And as we commented in chapter 1, the dominant paradigm—the competitive equilibrium model—does not even address the issue. The central theorem of welfare economics (usually called the *fundamental theorem of welfare economics*, formalizing Adam Smith's notion that competitive market economies lead to [Pareto] efficiency through the invisible hand, and due to Arrow [1951] and Debreu [1959]) *assumed* that technology was fixed, or at least *exogenous*, unaffected by anything that market participants might do. The followers of neither the Arrow-Debreu or the Schumpeterian traditions have succeeded in remedying the obvious lacuna in their analyses: The former have not shown that competitive markets with innovation are Pareto efficient, and the latter have not been able to show that Schumpeterian competition would ensure economic efficiency *even in the production of innovations*. The reason that they failed is simple: There is, in fact, *no presumption that markets where innovation is endogenous are efficient.*

Until the development of the modern theory of the economics of information, the presumption in conventional economics was that markets, by themselves, result in efficiency (with well-known exceptions, such as those associated with pollution). Schumpeterian competition *seemed* to create a similar presumption for dynamic economies, in which the center of attention is on innovation.

As a result of our research on the economics of information over the past four decades, even as we began our research into the economics of learning, we were less sanguine about the outcome of these market processes. In our earlier work, we had established that markets in which information was endogenous (or risk markets were not perfect) were generally not efficient.[1] Knowledge (say, about new technology) can be viewed as a special kind of information, sharing the same essential properties (to be discussed below). Not surprisingly, then, the *economics* of information and the economics of knowledge were very similar.[2] Given the similarities between "information" and "knowledge," it was clear that economies in which knowledge (including knowledge about technology) was endogenous would also be inefficient. Moreover, the fact that R & D was risky, and the risks could not be insured against, strengthened presumption *against* unfettered markets.

The market failures that we describe take on many forms: the structure of the economy, the allocation of resources to R & D—not only the total amounts, but the allocation to various sectors and projects and the directions in which research is pursued—the levels of output (both in total and across sectors), the choice of technique, and how much information and knowledge gets disseminated. This chapter thus describes the numerous ways in which markets fail to allocate resources efficiently toward innovation and, more broadly, fail in creating (on their own) as dynamic a "learning" society as they might. It serves as a prelude to the rest of the book, where we describe how government actions can help create a learning economy. In the ensuing chapters, we will be able to pursue only a few of these distortions, explaining how government actions might partially correct them and help create a learning economy. But underlying all these market failures is a simple point: where there is learning (i.e., nearly always), there are marked divergences between social and private returns.

This chapter is divided into five sections. The first examines the distinctive properties of knowledge—why the production of knowledge is different from the production of steel and why, as a result, while there is some presumption that markets make the "correct" decisions about the level of production of steel (or would, in the absence of learning and other externalities), the same is not true for the production of knowledge. The second section delves further into several of the key market failures—why social and private returns to learning and R & D are likely to differ markedly.

In the third section, we ask whether innovation is always welfare enhancing. At a broad level, we know the answer. Many of the financial innovations directed at circumventing regulations intended to enhance macroeconomic stability contributed to the instability of the economy and played an important role in the 2008 crisis. We focus, however, on a narrower but long-standing question: Is it possible that the market focuses excessively on saving labor, contributing to higher levels of unemployment and more inequality? We show that the answer is yes: There is a systematic bias in the market toward excessive labor-saving (labor-augmenting) innovations and even toward skill-biased technological progress. In appendix B, we formulate a dynamic model in which we show that the convergence of the economy to the long-run steady state is oscillatory—the model naturally gives rise to wage and employment cycles, with high wages inducing labor-saving innovations that contribute to higher unemployment, which brings wages down. We suggest that under some conditions, the dynamic process may even be unstable.

The fourth section looks at the innovation process in broader, evolutionary terms. Though the results of our analysis differ markedly from that of the standard neoclassical analysis, the tools of analysis we use in most of this book are standard. But looking at the issues of innovation through the lens of evolutionary processes leaves us no more sanguine about the efficiency of market processes.

In the final section, we make some more general observations about innovation and the nature of our society.

We end the chapter with four important appendices. Appendix B is described above. Appendix A analyzes the conditions under which a labor-augmenting innovation lowers the demand for labor—in which case there will be excessive investments in labor-augmenting innovations.

Appendix C shows that in a model of sequential innovation (with each monopolist being succeeded by another)—a model of Schumpeterian creative destruction—there is some presumption that there will be under-investment in innovation, because each innovator ignores the benefits conferred on successors. (This is in addition to the underinvestment that results from a failure, in the case of "large" innovations, to take into account increases in consumer surplus.) There are, in this sense, externalities (spillovers), not only from one innovator today to other firms today, but to innovators in other periods. This appendix illustrates, moreover, many of the complexities associated with both the descriptive and the normative analysis of the economics of innovation. Results are highly sensitive to specifications concerning the innovation process (e.g., whether the arrival of innovations can be described by a Poisson model); competition (both ex ante, i.e., for innovation, and ex post, i.e., in the product market after the innovations have occurred, whether there is Bertrand or Cournot competition); and the potential for entry deterrence. The analysis of this chapter reinforces that of the previous, in showing that more competition in innovation may lead to less innovation; our analysis undermines the longstanding presumption for an inverted U-shaped relationship between competition and innovation. More generally, it strengthens the presumption that the level and direction of innovation in an unfettered market economy will not be optimal.

Appendix D notes that the level of innovation is a function not just of investments in R & D by the firm, but of the size of the pool of ideas that the innovator can draw upon. Innovative activity can add to or subtract from the pool of ideas that are available to others. How much is added to the pool of ideas depends on the intellectual property regime. We establish the important result that while tighter intellectual property rights (IPR) may lead to more innovative activity *given a particular size of the knowledge pool*, stronger IPR has an adverse effect on the size of the knowledge pool from which others can draw. The net effect is that stronger IPR can, under plausible conditions, lead to a lower level of innovation. By the same token, an increase in the number of firms engaged in research—more competition—has ambiguous effects on the pace of innovation.

Before beginning the analysis, some further introductory remarks are in order. In comparing innovation under different market structures with that under the "socially optimal" arrangements, it is important to note two critical distinctions: First, while we saw that monopoly results in a lower level of output in the monopolized sector, and hence the benefit from innovation is lower than in the social optimum, the level of innovation, *given the level of output*, may still be optimal. We often speak of "constrained optimality." For example, given that the government cannot eliminate the monopoly, is the level of innovation "optimal"? The analysis below (elaborated further in part 2 of this book) shows that, in general, markets are not even constrained optimal.

Second, societies with the highest levels of innovation (whether from learning by doing or from investment in research and development) may not have the highest levels of societal welfare, since there is a trade-off between current consumption (well-being) and future consumption. Indeed, later we shall note some instances where there is too much innovation, and especially too many resources may be allocated to innovation in a particular sector or in a particular direction. In chapter 5, we described how different market structures or institutional arrangements affect the pace of innovation, but one should not confuse such an analysis with an analysis of which kinds of market structures or institutional arrangements enhance societal welfare. We will, however, show that, in general, there are welfare-enhancing interventions in the market.

Still, it is important to note that, while *ex ante* societal welfare may not be enhanced if there are *excessive* investments in innovation, in the long run citizens in those countries which have engaged in these excessive investments are better off. They benefit from the sacrifices in consumption made by their forebears.

1. Distinctive Properties of Knowledge

Knowledge is different from conventional goods in three ways that result in markets normally not being competitive (and, of course, if markets are not competitive, they normally won't be efficient), and, even if competitive, normally not being efficient.

Knowledge as a Public Good and Learning Externalities

Most importantly, knowledge is a Samuelsonian (1954) *public good* (Stiglitz 1987b, 1999a)—the marginal cost of another person or firm enjoying the benefit of knowledge (beyond the cost of transmission) is zero; usage is nonrivalrous.[3] Moreover, it is typically difficult, if not impossible, to exclude others from enjoying the benefits of the knowledge produced. These were the spillovers that we emphasized in chapter 3, and these spillovers (externalities) play a central role in the analysis of this book.

Markets are not efficient in the production and distribution of public goods—including the production and dissemination of knowledge. So long as there are spillovers, there will be underproduction—the firm won't take into account the benefits that accrue to others.[4] Even when an innovator becomes rich as a result of an innovation, what the innovator appropriates is often but a fraction of what the innovation has added to GDP. This is especially obvious in the case of those who have made the most important discoveries—those who have made major contributions to the advances of basic science and technology receive rewards that are substantially below their social contributions. Think of Alan Turing, James Watson and Francis Crick, Timothy Berners-Lee, or even the discoverers of the laser/maser and the transistor.[5] It is fortunate that most of these were not motivated by material rewards—a hint that the obsession with such rewards by the advocates of stronger intellectual property protection may be misguided (as we argued in chapter 3).

But externalities are more pervasive than these examples illustrate, and most innovations cannot be protected even by the most stringent intellectual property protection laws. Some knowledge has spillovers to particular industries, or to particular processes in particular industries, while the benefits of other knowledge can be more widespread, as we noted in our earlier discussions. The assembly line and then just-in-time production transformed production processes across wide swaths of the economy. The discovery of rayon showed that artificial fibers could be created and provided impetus for others to find alternative fibers not covered by the patent. Individuals who learn about better ways of doing business transmit that knowledge when they move from one firm to another. (See chapter 3 for a more extensive discussion of the nature of innovation spillovers.)

There are two properties of public goods—nonrivalrous consumption and nonexcludability—and intellectual property aims to partially address the second. It attempts to "solve" the excludability problem, simply by not allowing others to use the knowledge for a limited period of time without the consent of the producer of the knowledge (the owner of the patent). In doing so, it attempts to reduce the extent of spillovers. But attempts to "capture" the returns to knowledge by restricting its dissemination introduce another distortion—in the efficient utilization of knowledge.

OPTIMAL RESOURCE ALLOCATIONS WITH LEARNING AND LEARNING EXTERNALITIES: BASIC INTUITION It is easy to describe the efficient resource allocations without learning: In each period, the marginal benefit of producing one more unit of a good must equal its marginal cost.

$$\text{The value of the marginal product} = \text{marginal cost today.} \quad (1)$$

In the case of a good produced by labor alone, the marginal rate of substitution between the good and leisure (which should be the same for all persons) should equal the marginal rate of transformation, that is, the marginal product of labor.

With learning, producing or investing more today has future benefits—lower future production costs—and this needs to be taken into account. This can easily be done:

$$\text{The value of the marginal product} + \textit{total} \text{ future cost savings}$$
$$= \text{marginal cost today.} \quad (2)$$

The competitive equilibrium with learning will entail a higher level of production, because of the benefits from learning. But with learning externalities, the social benefits of learning (the total future cost savings) are far greater than the benefits of learning that accrue to the firm.

$$\text{Social value of learning} \gg \text{private value of learning.}$$

Hence, the level of production will be smaller than is socially optimal. In fact, with very small firms, the value of the learning to each firm from its own production is very small, even if the value of learning to society as a whole (to all firms in the industry) may be large and even if the value of learning arising from *total* production, even to a single firm, is significant. The result is that the competitive equilibrium with learning and that without learning will differ little. It should be clear, then, that there will be too little production, and thus too little learning.

Imperfections of Competition

The second distinctive property of knowledge follows from the first: innovation is marked by returns to scale. In certain limiting cases, where there are no offsetting diseconomies of scale, it will be characterized by a natural monopoly. In other cases, there may be an oligopoly. In all cases where R & D is important, competition is likely to be limited.

The acquisition of knowledge (R & D) can be viewed as a fixed cost. Consider a simple model where there are constant (marginal) costs of production. Those costs can be lowered by investing more in research; but the knowledge, once acquired, can be used no matter what the scale of production. If costs of production of one unit are lowered by a dollar, total costs are lowered by $1,000 if the firm produces 1,000 units, and by $1 million if the firm produces a million units. Larger firms have an incentive to "learn" more—the value of any cost reduction is proportionately greater—and to engage in more R & D, giving them a competitive advantage over smaller firms. Over time, their cost advantages increase, to the point that they come to dominate the economy. We obtain a natural monopoly, so long as marginal costs are constant.

These results hold even if there are spillovers, so long as spillovers are imperfect. For as long as that is the case, the firm engaging in learning (R & D) will have a cost advantage over rivals that engage in less learning (R & D). In practice, there are likely to be some but imperfect spillovers, so that markets where innovation is important are likely to be marked by large externalities *and* high levels of imperfections of competition.[6] Thus, both the level of production and the level of innovation will be distorted.

The only way that there can be effective competition in the situation just described (constant marginal costs of production) is that there be *full* spillovers to others in the same industry; but if that is the case, then each firm will free ride off the research efforts of others and, if the number of firms is large, there will be no incentive to engage in R & D. If knowledge (learning) is a by-product of production or investment, each will have insufficient incentives to produce or invest. Either way, the economy will not be efficient.

Competition can, of course, be sustained if there is some offsetting force for decreasing returns (e.g., diseconomies of scale arising from, say, limits to managerial span of control). Though we can obtain an equilibrium with many firms if the diseconomies of scale are large enough to outweigh the economies of scale in learning, even then market equilibrium may well be characterized by a limited number of firms, with a consequent restriction in the level of production. And so long as there are a limited number of firms, market equilibrium will be inefficient. But there is a dilemma, the nature of which will be made clearer in this chapter: With more firms, the distortions in production will be reduced, but this leads to slower innovation.

Not only are there likely to be multiple market failures, but imperfections in one arena are likely to lead to failures in others. As Arrow (1962a) pointed out fifty years ago, the production of knowledge is often a joint product with the production of goods (there is learning-by-doing), which means that the production of goods themselves will not in general be (intertemporally) efficient.

LEARNING EXTERNALITIES AND MARKET STRUCTURE In the analysis that follows, we make two important distinctions. The first concerns the structure of the product market. As we have noted, endogenous learning makes some market structures infeasible: In the absence of *full* within-industry spillovers, a natural monopoly may exist. With full spillovers, there can be many firms in the industry; there will be competition, but no firm will take into account the learning benefit its production confers on others.

It is possible that the market might best be described as monopolistically competitive, with only one firm in each "industry" but spillovers to other industries. In this case, we will see two distortions: underproduction as a result of the exercise of monopoly power and underproduction as a result of failing to take into account the learning benefits that accrue to others.

The second distinction that plays an important role in the analysis below concerns the nature of spillovers.[7] In the discussion in the following chapters, we use a general formulation that has as limiting cases no and perfect spillovers.

Table 6.1 outlines the three cases. Much of our attention will focus on the cases with perfect competition and full spillovers, or monopolistic competition and no spillovers.[8] As we have explained, the only case which is consistent with competitive markets (in the absence of some other source of strong decreasing returns to scale) is full spillovers.

TABLE 6.1
Spillovers and Market Structures

	No Cross-Firm Spillovers	Full Cross-Firm Spillovers
Perfect Competition	X (not feasible)	Underinvestment in learning
Monopolistic Competition	Restricted output	Both market distortions

THE CASE OF MONOPOLY/MONOPOLISTIC COMPETITION
Monopoly (or more accurately, monopolistic competition, where there is a single firm producing any commodity, but there are many producers producing different products vying for the consumers' dollars) provides a limiting case. When competition is restricted, market allocations are not efficient. But now there are two inefficiencies: In addition to the static inefficiencies associated with the exercise of monopoly power, there may be dynamic inefficiencies.

As a first approximation, these inefficiencies are reflected in the condition for optimum production:

$$\text{Marginal revenue product} + \text{future cost savings } \textit{to the firm} \qquad (3)$$
$$= \text{marginal cost today.}$$

Equation (3) should be contrasted with (1) and (2): the monopolistically competitive firms underestimate the static benefit of production, ignore learning benefits to other firms, and, because production may be lower, assign a lower value even to firm cost savings (than would be the case at the social optimum). Products in which firms have more monopoly power will have less production, and the lower production will lead to less learning. Productivity growth in these sectors may, accordingly, be slower.[9] In addition to the static consequence of the loss of consumer surplus from underproduction, there is a dynamic cost: The lower learning and higher costs in subsequent periods associated with monopoly today result in lower output in future periods.

Of course, labor not used in the monopolized sector gets displaced to other sectors, but if those sectors are sectors with less learning, the overall rate of growth of the economy is reduced. Moreover, monopoly power will result in lower real wages; lower real wages will normally result in lower equilibrium labor supply; and hence less learning.

One of the important methodological implications of the analysis is that not only must one simultaneously consider market structure and innovation (both are endogenous), but the analysis must be conducted within a general equilibrium framework. In a partial equilibrium context, one might conclude—as Schumpeter did—that monopoly is better than competition because it internalizes the benefits of learning, without noting adverse general equilibrium effects, arising from impacts on the *pattern* of production and overall labor supply.

Understanding the structure of learning and knowledge dissemination is essential to understanding efficient production. We are concerned with societal learning, not just sectoral or firm learning. For example, some sectors may have stronger learning curves; that is, the elasticity of learning may be larger for a firm. But what matters is not just the ability of a firm or sector to learn but also the benefits that sector (firm) transmits to other sectors (firms) and the extent to which it does not appropriate for itself the benefits of the learning. If learning in one sector generates more externalities to other sectors than do others, production in that sector should be increased (relative to what it would be in the market equilibrium that ignored these learning externalities) at the expense of others. The dynamic (future) benefits need to be offset against the static (short-run) costs.

Imperfect Risk and Capital Markets

The third distinctive property of knowledge production leading to pervasive market failure in innovation—one which interacts with the previous two—arises from the fact that R & D is inherently risky, and risk markets with innovation are inherently imperfect. The outcomes of research and learning cannot typically be fully foreseen: Research is an exploration into the unknown. As research proceeds, new ideas are developed and new (and unanticipated) products may emerge.

One cannot buy insurance against the risk that a research venture will prove fruitless or that there will be little learning as one gains experience. Part of this is explained by theories of asymmetric information. There are inherent problems of moral hazard and adverse selection. The researcher is more likely to know more about the likelihood of success or failure of a research venture than any outsiders. Insurance markets where information asymmetries are large often don't exist, and even when they exist, the insurance offered is limited. (And as we have repeatedly noted, even when competitive markets do exist, they are typically not Pareto efficient.)

There are, in addition, fundamental conceptual issues: One cannot buy insurance (an Arrow-Debreu state contingent security) against an event (the discovery of nuclear power) prior to the conceptualization of that event. Nor can one have an insurance market for the "explosion" of a nuclear reactor before the development of nuclear power, and one cannot have an insurance market on nuclear power replacing fossil fuels before the development of the understandings of modern physics on which nuclear power was based.

The absence of adequate risk markets presents a barrier to entry: Large, well-capitalized firms are better able to bear the risks associated especially with large-scale investments in research. This reinforces the conclusion reached earlier that markets where R & D is important are likely to be marked by significant imperfections of competition.

The absence of imperfect risk markets compounds the problems posed by imperfect capital markets. The modern theory of information asymmetries has helped explain why capital markets are often highly imperfect: why, for instance, they may be marked by credit rationing. Capital market imperfections can be particularly adverse for learning. Because R & D investments (or, more generally, "learning investments"[10]) typically cannot be collateralized, unlike investments in buildings, machines, or inventories, it is more likely that there will be credit and equity rationing, leading to underinvestment in these areas, compared to others.[11] (Moreover, as we have noted, there are other fundamental reasons for capital market imperfections: a borrower with a good idea worries that telling a potential lender about the idea will lead to his stealing the idea, or in some other way taking advantage of that knowledge to advantage himself, at the expense of the borrower.)

Because of imperfections in capital and risk markets, firms act in a risk-averse manner, particularly in the presence of bankruptcy costs (Greenwald and Stiglitz 1993), and this discourages investment in riskier innovation. (It also explains why, as we argued in chapter 4, cyclical fluctuations are so bad for innovation: in economic downturns, investments in R & D are among the categories of expenditures that suffer the most.)

Given the pervasive market failures that we have already identified—the public good nature of knowledge, the pervasiveness of externalities/knowledge spillovers, the limitations of competition, the imperfections of risk and capital markets—there is no reason to be sanguine that markets are efficient in the level or direction of innovation. In fact, matters are worse: there are a number of other market failures that are intimately associated with innovation. Moreover, the various market failures are interlinked; one market failure can reinforce another. We explore these issues in the next section.

2. Further Reasons Why Markets for Innovation Are Inefficient

Markets fail to produce efficient outcomes whenever private rewards and social returns differ. This occurs when there are externalities or imperfect competition, imperfect risk markets, imperfect capital markets, or information asymmetries—and these "imperfections" are inherent and important in the innovation process itself. The previous section emphasized, for instance, that there are inevitably important spillovers, competition is necessarily imperfect, and innovation investments are risky, often requiring large up-front investments, so the absence of perfect capital and risk markets is consequential. This section highlights further limitations: private rewards differ—and sometimes exceed—social returns, and there are large coordination failures.

Private Rewards and Social Returns

Our earlier discussion highlighted that firms (individuals) appropriate less than the full value of their societal contributions from learning and R & D; there are important spillovers. This by itself might suggest that there is a presumption of too little learning or investment in R & D. But there are some circumstances in which private rewards may exceed the social returns, with the consequence that there may be excessive investment in R & D, and the problem may be exacerbated by (inappropriately designed) intellectual property regimes. In the paragraphs below, we illustrate several important instances in which this is likely to occur, especially in the context of a poorly designed patent system.

ME-TOO INVENTIONS An obvious example is "me-too" innovations,[12] where researchers try to develop a product essentially identical to one already on the market. The object of the research is to find a way around the patent and to grab a share of the patent holder's profits (rents). While me-too innovations are particularly pronounced in pharmaceuticals, they arise in other sectors as well. This illustrates a general aspect of the returns to innovation: *The rents captured by a monopolist are not directly related to the increase in consumer welfare (surplus) associated with the innovation.* Some of the rents are rents *diverted* from other firms.[13] Firm *i*'s profits from an innovation are *not* a good measure of the social contribution of its innovation, as they would be in a competitive market, where the price of the product was given and equal to the marginal cost of production, and the increase in profits would simply measure the reduction in societal resources required to produce the firm's output.

THE COMMON POOL PROBLEM   Patent races (a winner-takes-all system) give rise to several distortions. The first to patent gets all the returns (in a game with n symmetric competitors, the expected return is $1/n$ of the returns to obtaining the patent). Assume the social returns increase with the number of researchers: $S = S(n)$, and that each firm captures a pro-rata share of the social returns. If each researcher spends I, entry occurs until

$$S(n^*)/n^* = I.\text{[14]} \tag{4}$$

But the socially efficient level of entry is given by

$$\max S(n) - nI, \tag{5}$$

that is,

$$S'(n^0) = I. \tag{6}$$

So long as there are diminishing returns,

$$S' < S/n, \tag{7}$$

the marginal return to entry is less than the average return, and thus

$$n^* > n^0. \tag{8}$$

In other words, there will be excessive entry.

In appendix D, we examine a more general model, in which innovations can both contribute to and take from the pool of publicly available ideas that can be drawn upon to innovate. This reinforces the conclusions reached in chapter 5 concerning the ambiguous effects of the number of firms on the level of innovation, though the most important lesson of the model—and the focus of our analysis—concerns intellectual property rights: Stronger intellectual property rights may have an adverse effect on innovation.

SOCIAL AND PRIVATE RETURNS TO WINNING A RACE The discussion of the previous section illustrates the general proposition that the private return to innovation and learning may exceed the social return. In an innovation process, the social return is only that the innovation is available earlier than it otherwise would have been. Myriad Genetics obtained a patent on the BRAC genes (which are critical in assessing the likelihood of getting breast cancer). The gene would have been discovered shortly later, as part of the more systematic attempt to decode the human genome. Thus, while Myriad has made large profits, its social returns were small. Indeed, arguably, because it has exercised its monopoly power, charging high prices for the tests to detect the presence of the gene and preventing follow-on research, including the development of superior tests, the social return has been negative—and depending on how one assesses the value of lives lost as a result of women who could not afford the test at Myriad's monopoly price, perhaps very negative. Had Myriad not entered the fray, the test would have been available at a very low, competitive price (see Stiglitz 2006; Azvolinsky 2012; Goozner 2010).

MONOPOLY RENTS AND THE ENCLOSURE OF THE COMMONS Another reason that social returns may differ from private returns is that the profits of the winner of the patent typically include not just monopoly rents but, in some cases, a return to the privatization of knowledge that was previously in the public domain.[15] Moreover, because success in getting a patent converts what would be a public good into a private good, while success in challenging a patent converts what would have been a private good into a public good—that is, the opposition to the granting of a patent is itself a public good—there will be excesses in the granting of patents.

HOLDUPS "Holdup" patents provide another instance in which social returns are almost surely markedly lower than private returns, and they reflect another major source of distortion in market-driven innovation, related to bargaining problems. Modern inventions often require a number of ingredients (ideas), each of which can be patented separately. Thus, putting the product together requires agreement among a large number of patent holders. Some patents are less important than others. For example, the inventor can invent around the patent, though at some cost. There can be asymmetries of information. In the presence of such asymmetries, bargaining often leads to inefficient outcomes. Efficiency clearly requires the full utilization of the available knowledge, but as each side attempts to show its determination and to disguise the costs of a lack of agreement, bargaining sometimes breaks down. Firms are then forced to invent around the patent, which not only entails diverting scarce research dollars into duplicative research but may also result in costly delays in bringing the product to market.[16] Beyond this, there are often large wastes of resources in litigation expenses.

Holdup patents are used by patent trolls to extract rents out of successful innovators, claiming that they have infringed on their patents. Given the high costs of inventing around the patent or litigating, patent trolls can often extract handsome sums, reducing, by the same amount, the returns obtained by the "true" innovator. Thus, the returns on their "innovations" exceed the social returns, while those of the "true" innovators are less than their social contributions.[17]

Coordination Failures

We champion the virtue of private markets in solving the complex coordination problems that are required for our large, interdependent economy to function. Prices play the central role in that coordination. Successful innovation, too, requires coordination, but prices don't (and can't) play the role that is usually hypothesized in the "normal" context of a market economy in the absence of innovation. In fact, matters are worse: Secrecy that is central to much of the market production of knowledge (part of the attempt to increase the degree of appropriability and to enhance the likelihood one will win the patent race) means that coordination is difficult.

There are many dimensions to socially desirable coordination. If research is uncertain, but additional research enterprises are imperfectly correlated with research enterprises already being undertaken (say, in producing a new product or reducing the cost of production of an existing product), then there is a gross social return to additional entry. We can easily describe optimum entry, where the marginal social value of an additional entrant equals the extra cost. But if no one knows who else is undertaking research, it is hard to achieve this. Moreover, the social optimum entails an optimal diversification of research projects, but again, with secrecy concerning what other researchers are doing, it is unlikely that this optimum will be obtained. There is likely to be excessively duplicative research.[18]

Moreover, the value of invention A may depend on the existence of a complementary invention B. Unless A knows that there is a high likelihood that B will be produced, A will have limited incentives, and similarly for B. Sometimes this coordination problem can be internalized: a large firm undertakes (or at least coordinates) the various parts of the research project. Indeed, the development of firms with these capabilities is one of the major advances of the twentieth century. Still, competencies and skills differ, and knowledge about competencies and skills is limited, so that a firm may not be able to bring under one roof (or, more broadly coordinate) those most likely to succeed in each of the parts of the research enterprise. If it turns out different "ingredients" are patented by different parties, a bargaining problem, with the associated inefficiencies and potentials for holdups, may well arise.[19]

Interactions among Market Failures

There are important interactions between traditional market failures, like imperfect competition, and those associated with learning. Problems of appropriability of returns, imperfections of capital markets, and the absence of good risk markets result in barriers to the entry of new firms (entrepreneurs) and the exploration of new products—including products or processes that might be particularly appropriate for a developing country. As we have explained, they give an advantage to large enterprises.

So too, there will be underinvestment in areas where market prices do not fully reflect scarcity or societal costs—most importantly, in the environment. Because, for instance, the global costs of global warming are not reflected in our price system, there will be little incentive for innovations that reduce carbon emissions. (Later, we will explain how markets also pay insufficient attention to the social costs of unemployment to which their innovations give rise.)

Theory of the Second Best—and the Financing of Innovation[20]

As we have seen, to Schumpeter, the fact that there is a distortion associated with monopolies/imperfect competition in innovation economies was not, by itself, of too much concern. After all, the fixed costs of financing R & D or learning had to be paid for somehow. Indeed, that was an implicit aspect of the argument that contestable markets (that is, markets where potential competition is so fierce that price is driven down to average costs) were efficient. Even if price equaled average cost (i.e., there were zero profits) rather than marginal costs, so that compared to the standard first-best resource allocation, there was a distortion, the fixed costs had to be financed *somehow*; and however the fixed costs were financed would impose a cost to society.

We can thus ask the question, What is the optimal way of financing the public good of research? Having it financed by a monopoly is *not* in general optimal. First, as we noted earlier, even with potential competition, monopoly profit—after paying for the cost of innovation—is not driven down to zero. Second, the incentive of monopolies is to increase profits in any way (legally) that they can, and that includes expending resources to reduce the elasticity of demand, which allows them to raise their price. Innovation too is directed wrongly—it is directed at strengthening and extending monopoly power and the profits derived from monopoly power; and those objectives are at odds with innovation directed at enhancing societal welfare.

Third, relying on patents and the monopoly profits to which they give rise to finance research results in an underutilization of knowledge. As we have noted, research is a fixed cost, and there is no marginal cost to the use of an idea, so that knowledge should be freely provided. But that would imply that the producer of information (knowledge) would receive no returns. Thus, it is inevitable that, in the absence of government finance, there be underproduction of knowledge (relative to the first best) and underutilization of the knowledge that is produced. The patent system (in principle) attempts to balance out the dynamic gains with the short-run costs of the underutilization of knowledge and imperfections of market competition, but it does so most imperfectly.[21]

On the other hand, when the government finances research and disseminates it freely, there is still a static distortion (from the distortionary imposition of taxes), but no distortion in the dissemination and use of knowledge. But a patent system can be viewed as financing the research by a tax on the buyers of the product with the innovation. Standard tax analysis would suggest that this "monopoly tax" is not the ideal way of raising the revenue. Such a tax does not minimize the distortions (dead-weight loss) associated with raising the requisite revenue. Also, the "monopoly tax" is a benefit tax, and while in certain circumstances one can argue for such a tax regime (those who benefit from the product pay for its development), in other cases, it is hard to justify. Someone suffering from a life-threatening disease is already unfortunate enough; to ask the patient, in addition, to pay an R & D tax to finance the development of the patient's own medicines is not consistent either with most ethical principles or with social welfare maximization.

3. Socially Unproductive Innovation: Is Innovation Always Welfare Enhancing?

This and the previous chapters have explained why it is that the allocation of resources to innovation is not likely to be socially optimal. There is no presumption that markets are efficient, either in the amount of research or direction of research and learning. We have emphasized, in particular, the failure of market participants to take into account externalities—the benefits that their learning has for others.

Historically, there have often been instances in which significant groups within societies have resisted innovation, most notably, the Luddites in the beginning of the nineteenth century, who saw modern machines as leading to unemployment and impoverishment. While increases in productivity *in principle*, could make everyone better off—the production possibilities curve moves out—in practice there are always winners and losers. Innovations that reduce the demand for unskilled workers decrease their wages, even if it increases the wages of skilled workers. The statement that such skill-biased innovation could be welfare enhancing is usually taken to mean that the gains of the skilled workers are more than sufficient to compensate the losses of the unskilled workers. But while the skilled workers *could* compensate the unskilled workers, such compensation seldom occurs. Thus, there are winners and losers. And if, as has been happening in the United States and many other advanced industrial countries, the losers are those at the bottom of the income distribution, then innovation can contribute to growing inequality. In this situation, whether societal welfare is increased depends on how one weighs the benefits to the relatively rich against the losses to the relatively poor.[22]

More recently, however, we (with several coauthors—Delli Gatti et al. 2012, 2013) have shown that with market imperfections and societal rigidities, all (or at least most) groups in society can be worse off. In the 1920s, productivity increases in agriculture were so large that (especially given the inelasticity of demand for agricultural goods) incomes in that sector declined. With perfect mobility, the surplus agricultural workers would have moved into the urban sector. But there are significant costs to the mobility of labor, and with wages in agriculture declining and the value of rural assets (like houses) declining as well, many in that sector couldn't afford to move to the city and obtain the skills that would make them productive there. Worse still, neither they nor the banks that provided credit anticipated these events. Hence, as incomes in the rural sector collapsed, those in that sector were left with a legacy of debt burdens and banks faced massive losses. The result was a marked decline in demand for urban goods—so great that incomes in the urban sector itself fell. Innovation may have helped precipitate the Great Depression.

We have argued, by the same token, that improvements in productivity in manufacturing, leading to decreased employment and wages in that sector, have contributed to the current economic slowdown. Innovation requires economic restructuring, and markets often do not manage such restructurings well. But as firms make decisions that affect the pace and direction of innovation, they do not take these general equilibrium effects into account. Each small firm takes the course of wages and unemployment, for instance, as given; but collectively, as they make their innovation decisions, they affect the evolution of wages and unemployment. *Unfettered and undirected markets may result in patterns of learning and innovation that result in more inequality and higher unemployment than is socially desirable. There are other patterns that would enhance societal well-being.*

These results should not come as a surprise, for they reflect the general proposition enunciated earlier that there are marked discrepancies between private rewards and social returns, especially when it comes to innovation or when there are imperfections of information and incomplete markets—that is, always (Greenwald and Stiglitz 1986). (Nowhere was that more evident than in the financial sector, where much of the innovation was directed at circumventing regulations that were designed to enhance the stability and efficiency of the financial system. The result was that, as Paul Volcker pointed out,[23] it was hard to identify innovations that had increased the productivity of the overall economy. The innovations had led not to better risk management and resource allocations, but rather to more risk and a massive misallocation of capital.[24])

In this section, I construct a simple model examining the factor bias of technological change (i.e., the extent to which it is labor- or capital-augmenting, or skilled- or unskilled-biased) to show that the market solution is not Pareto efficient. In the particular model examined here, we establish that there is excessive labor-saving technological change and that the equilibrium unemployment rate that emerges is too high.[25]

Analytics: Innovation and Excessive Unemployment

To see these results more clearly, we focus here on some simple models where there are a large number of identical firms, each of which faces a decision about the direction of innovation—whether to focus on making, say, labor or capital more productive, or skilled or unskilled labor more productive. This can come about as a result of either devoting efforts at learning or investing resources in R & D.

We assume a simple aggregate production function with constant returns to scale of the form

$$Q = F(\mu^{t+1}K, \lambda^{t+1}L), \tag{9}$$

where μK and λL are the effective capital and labor supply. If we set μ^t and $\lambda^t = 1$, then μ^{t+1} and λ^{t+1} measure the level of capital- and labor-augmenting technological progress, respectively. In the following discussion, without ambiguity, we drop the superscript on λ and μ. Q is output, K is the capital stock, and L is the labor supply.

Because of constant returns to scale, we can write

$$Q/\lambda L = f(\mu k/\lambda) = f(\kappa),$$

where $k = K/L$, the ratio of capital to labor (henceforth referred to as the capital-labor ratio) ratio, assumed for the moment as given, f is output per unit of effective labor, and $\kappa \equiv \mu k/\lambda$, the ratio of *effective* capital to effective labor (henceforth referred to as the effective capital-labor ratio).

We make use of the well-established concept of the *innovation possibilities curve*, postulating that there is a trade-off between μ and λ, as depicted in figure 6.1:

$$\mu = Z(\lambda), \; Z' < 0, \; Z'' < 0. \tag{10}$$

If the rate of labor augmenting technological progress is to increase, capital augmenting progress must decrease; and as λ increases, the sacrifice in μ becomes greater.

Each firm takes the next period's wages and cost of capital as given, and maximizes the next period's profits:[26]

$$\max Q - WL - RK, \tag{11}$$

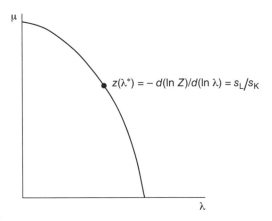

Figure 6.1 Determination of factor bias of technological change

There is a trade-off between capital-augmenting technological progress, μ, and labor-augmenting technological progress, λ. Market equilibrium is the point where the elasticity of the curve $z(\lambda) \equiv d(\ln Z)/d(\ln \lambda)$ equals the relative shares, $wL\lambda/r\mu K = s_L/s_K$.

where W is the wage per worker and R is the cost of a unit of capital, yielding

$$WL = -RK \, d(\ln Z)/d(\ln \lambda) \tag{12}$$

or

$$z(\lambda) \equiv -d(\ln Z)/d(\ln \lambda) = s_L/s_K, \tag{13}$$

where s_L and s_K are the share of labor and capital, respectively, in national income. *Optimization entails setting the (absolute value of the) elasticity of the innovation curve equal to the relative shares.* But the relative shares themselves are a function of λ:

$$\begin{aligned} s_K = 1 - s_L = f'[Z(\lambda)K/\lambda L]\mu K/Q \\ = f'(Z(\lambda)k/\lambda)(Z(\lambda)k/\lambda)/f(Z(\lambda)k/\lambda) = s_K(\lambda; k), \end{aligned} \tag{14}$$

where $f = Q/\lambda L$, output per unit of effective labor, assuming, for the moment, that next period's capital stock is unaffected by the choice along the innovation frontier. The equilibrium "direction" of innovation is given by the solution to[27]

$$z(\lambda^*) = s_L(\lambda^*)/[1 - s_L(\lambda^*)], \tag{15}$$

where, for the moment, k, the capital-labor ratio, is assumed fixed. Thus, (15) can be solved for the equilibrium factor bias $\{Z(\lambda^*), \lambda^*\}$.

Figure 6.2 graphically depicts the solution to (15). Straightforward calculations show that z is an increasing function of λ (under our assumptions concerning Z). An increase in λ lowers the effective capital-labor ratio. When the elasticity of substitution is less than unity, this means that the share of labor decreases, so there is a unique value of λ for which the elasticity of the innovation curve equals the relative shares, illustrated in figure 6.2A. When the elasticity of substitution is greater than unity, the share of labor increases as λ increases, so there may be multiple values of λ for which the elasticity of the innovation curve equals relative shares.

SHORT-RUN EQUILIBRIUM Now assume that, as in Shapiro and Stiglitz (1984), as the level of unemployment decreases, the wage

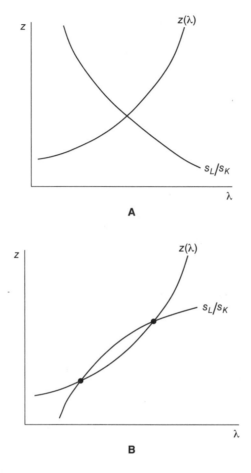

Figure 6.2 Determination of factor bias of technological change

A. Elasticity of substitution less than unity. There is a unique value of λ for which the elasticity of the innovation curve equals the relative shares. B. Elasticity of substitution greater than unity. There may be multiple values of λ for which the elasticity of the innovation curve equals relative shares.

that firms must pay increases (in their model, to avoid shirking;[28] in other models, similar results obtain as a result of a bargaining process). Then an increase in productivity of labor and a corresponding decrease in the productivity of capital (along the innovation frontier) may shift the demand curve for labor up or down, depending on the elasticity of substitution. The marginal return to an effective labor unit is

$$W/\lambda = f(\kappa) - \kappa f'(\kappa) \equiv g(\kappa), \qquad (16)$$

where

$$\kappa = Z(\lambda)K/\lambda L^D, \qquad (17)$$

the ratio of "effective" capital to "effective" *employed* labor. Hence,

$$L^d = ZK/\lambda g^{-1}(W/\lambda). \qquad (18)$$

An increase in λ shifts the demand curve for labor. Figure 6.3 shows how a shift in the demand curve for labor affects the equilibrium unemployment.

PROPOSITION 1. *If the demand for laborers decreases as a result of a change in technology (innovation is labor saving, in the sense that at any wage, the demand for workers decreases[29]) then unemployment increases.*

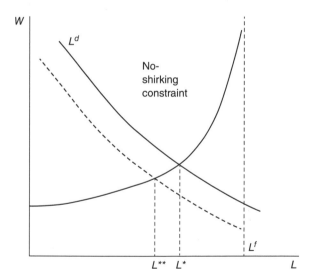

Figure 6.3 Effect of labor-augmenting innovation in Shapiro-Stiglitz model

If the demand curve for labor shifts down, then labor-augmenting technological progress leads to more unemployment. The market does not take into account the social costs of this induced unemployment. (L^f represents full employment. $L^f - L^*$ is the number of unemployed in initial equilibrium.)

There is, in this sense, a negative externality associated with the innovation. If changes in technology shift the demand curve for labor up, then there is a positive externality associated with the innovation. In general, the direction of innovation will not be optimal.

In the appendix, we show that if the elasticity of substitution is less than unity, then (at the equilibrium wage), the increase in productivity of each worker leads to a reduced demand for workers.

SOCIAL WELFARE MAXIMIZATION   Assuming that costless redistributions are possible, social welfare is maximized by maximizing national output with respect to λ, taking into account the effect of λ on the unemployment rate:

$$\max F(\mu K, \lambda(1 - U)L), \tag{19}$$

where U is the unemployment rate, i.e.,

$$d(\ln Q)/d(\ln \lambda) = \{F_1 \lambda Z'K + F_2[(1 - U)\lambda L] - w\lambda L \, dU/d(\ln \lambda)\}/Q \tag{20}$$

$$= [r\mu K \, d(\ln \mu)/d(\ln \lambda) + (1 - U)L\lambda w - w\lambda L \, dU/d(\ln \lambda)]/Q$$

$$= s_k \, d(\ln \mu)/d(\ln \lambda) + (1 - s_k)\{1 + d[\ln (1 - U)]/d(\ln \lambda)\}.$$

At the private sector optimization, this is < or > 0 as $dU/d(\ln \lambda) >$ or < 0. In other words, *there is excessive labor-augmenting innovation if the effect of innovation is to increase the unemployment rate*, i.e., if $\sigma < 1$.

Empirical estimates suggest that the elasticity of substitution is less than unity. There is thus a presumption that (in the short run, with fixed K and L) innovation focuses excessively on increasing the productivity of labor. The market does not take into account the effects of labor-saving innovation in increasing unemployment.

By the same token, if social welfare is concerned with the distribution of income (inequality), the market will also lead to excessively labor-augmenting innovation, if the elasticity of substitution is less than unity. If redistributions were costless, lump sum transfers could undo the distributive effects. But redistributions are not costless, so there is a social cost of such innovations.

SKILL-BIASED INNOVATION The same kind of analysis applies if we extend the model to innovation that is skill-biased. Assume, for instance, that

$$Q = F(\lambda_s L_s, \lambda_u L_u),$$

where L_s is the input of skilled labor, L_u that of unskilled labor, and λ_s and λ_u are the levels of skill-augmenting and unskilled-augmenting technological progress, with an innovation frontier

$$\lambda_u = Z(\lambda_s).$$

As before, the market allocation will pay no attention to distributive and unemployment effects of the choices it makes.

For instance, if employers can distinguish who is skilled and unskilled, there will be a different no-shirking curve (as in the Shapiro-Stiglitz model) for each group. A change in the skill bias of techno-logical change will typically shift the demand curve for one group of workers up and the other down, leading to a reduction of one type of unemployment and an increase in the other. If monitoring is, say, more difficult for unskilled workers than for skilled workers, unskilled worker unemployment may be more important. (In the limit, if the performance of skilled workers was perfectly observable, then there would be no efficiency-wage unemployment of skilled workers, only of unskilled workers.) Efficiency may require that innovation be designed to shift the demand curve for unskilled labor upward. It follows, then, from the same logic as used earlier, that if the elasticity of substitution between skilled and unskilled workers is less than unity, then the mar-ket equilibrium will be associated with excessively skill-biased techno-logical progress.

In appendix B, we observe that if the elasticity of substitution is greater than unity, then the long-run equilibrium may be unstable. An increase in the share of capital leads to a bias toward further capital-augmenting technological progress, further increasing the share of capi-tal. The same logic applies as well to innovations augmenting the pro-ductivity of skilled and unskilled workers. In the case of a low elasticity of substitution, if productivity of the highly skilled workers increases relative to unskilled, the share of skilled workers goes down, and this then leads to reduced incentives for such innovation. But if the elasticity of substitution is large, then the share of income going to skilled workers increases, and the bias increases. The implication is that the ratio of income (wages) of skilled and unskilled workers increases (without bound), with increasing incentives for more skill-biased innovation.

There are peculiar long-run implications of such an analysis. The share of skilled labor would increase toward unity. It also means that the return to converting an unskilled worker into a skilled worker increases (again without bound). An increasingly large fraction of the labor force would thus become "educated." If there are increasing costs associated with converting the marginal unskilled worker into a skilled worker, at each date there will be a residual of unskilled workers, suffering from increasing relative deprivation.

But again, there may be an equilibrating force, as skilled-labor-augmenting technological progress becomes increasingly difficult, especially relative to, say, capital or unskilled-biased technological change.

Implications and Interpretations

In the standard neoclassical model, factor supplies (including the [given] relative productivities of different factors) determine the distribution of income. In the Solow (1956) growth model, however, growth itself does not in any way depend on the distribution of income. Moreover, there is always full employment. If there is unemployment, there is only one reason: wage rigidities. Conventional discourse attributes wage rigidities either to what the government does (minimum wages) or what it does not do (circumscribing unions.) Eliminating such rigidities increases efficiency and eliminates unemployment. With a high elasticity of substitution, a relatively small change in the wage will return the economy to full employment, so that not even workers will suffer much. (Though firms choose the technology to employ, factor prices always adjust so that the technology they choose is such that factors are fully employed.)

Here, the distribution of income matters a great deal: it determines the pattern of innovation. And wage rigidities are a consequence of market forces—given imperfections of information, it pays firms to pay wages above the market clearing level. This model provides a far better interpretation of the pattern of unemployment than that which attributes unemployment either to minimum wages or unions, for we see high levels of unemployment both in nonunionized sectors and at skill levels far above those for which the minimum wage is relevant.

But these high wages provide firms with an incentive to reduce the demand for labor by innovation, leading to a still higher (equilibrium) level of unemployment. The market on its own is inefficient, both in the level of unemployment (Shapiro and Stiglitz 1984) and, importantly, in the pattern of innovation. Moreover, if the elasticity of substitution (ex post) is low, then to achieve full or even significantly *fuller* employment in the short run may require a large reduction in wages. Indeed, it may not even be possible to achieve full employment. The short-run effect of lowering wages on employment may be nil.

The efficiency wage model is the simplest within which to explore market distortions in the pattern of innovation, but similar results emerge in other models with (endogenous) market imperfections. Economic historians, such as Salter (1966) and Habakkuk (1962) have emphasized the role of "labor scarcity" as an inducement to labor-saving innovation. (Such explanations seem to have particular relevance in particular historical periods, e.g., in the period of the rapid expansion of the United States in the nineteenth century.) Standard economic theory has had a hard time understanding what labor scarcity might mean, other than a high price (or share) of labor.[30] But in models with costly information and highly differentiated labor, there is a natural interpretation: It may take time and resources to recruit a new worker to replace a worker that leaves. Labor-augmenting technological progress reduces not only the direct labor costs, but these indirect turnover (search and recruitment) costs. But in economies with costly search, a decision by a firm to engage in more labor-augmenting technological progress—and thus in less recruitment—imposes externalities on other market participants, both on workers (who must now search longer to find a job) and on other firms (who now may face lower recruitment costs). Again, there is no presumption that the market equilibrium factor bias will be efficient; indeed, there is a presumption that it will not be (see Greenwald and Stiglitz 1988; Arnott and Stiglitz 1985).

More generally, we note that from the perspective of the firm, what matters is not just the wage or interest rate, as it might show up in the system of national income accounts, but the *effective* total labor and capital costs, which can differ markedly from the recorded labor and capital shares, for several reasons. First, because of taxes and fringe benefits, the cost of labor to the firm may exceed the wage that workers receive by a considerable margin. Second, if there is credit rationing, the "shadow" cost of capital may well exceed the interest rate charged; and if firms can't instantaneously hire workers of the particular type in which they are interested (there is, in this sense, a labor scarcity), then the shadow cost of labor will exceed the wage. Even a relatively small gap in time in being able to fill a position may be costly. By the same token, if machines are not fully reliable and cannot be easily replaced, a breakdown of a machine can be costly. Third, workers have to be managed. Strikes are costly. All of this requires scarce managerial time. When a firm assesses whether to save on labor or capital, all of these costs are relevant.

POLICY IMPLICATIONS There are several important policy implications. First, policies which increase the national savings rate can be an effective way of increasing employment in the medium term. (This is especially true in the model presented in the appendix, where there is zero ex post elasticity of substitution.)

Second, wage subsidies reduce the cost of labor, and it is the high cost of labor that induces firms to shift the direction of technological development toward excessive labor-saving and capital-using technologies. By the same token, when the Fed lowers the cost of capital dramatically (as it attempted to do after the Great Recession), it encourages labor-saving innovation. Thus, we observe the curious phenomenon of firms replacing unskilled labor (with presumably a low shadow price, given the high unemployment rate among unskilled workers) such as checkout clerks with machines, e.g., automatic tellers. While there are almost surely positive social benefits from the induced employment resulting from the increased aggregate demand from such investments, those benefits have to be set against the social costs of higher unemployment in the medium term as a result of the labor-saving innovation induced by the lower cost of capital. A full analysis of the intertemporal tradeoffs would take us beyond the confines of this discussion.

Third, increasing the price paid by firms for environmental impacts (e.g., carbon emissions) shifts innovation away from labor-saving (-augmenting) innovation, again with positive effects on the distribution of income and employment.

TOWARD A MORE GENERAL THEORY By bringing together a plausible theory of wage determination with the theory of induced innovation, we have provided a general theory of growth and employment which makes sense of discussions of technological unemployment or job shortages—concepts that have no meaning in Solow's formulation. In this theory the distribution of income matters; it affects technology and the dynamics of the economy, and these in turn affect the distribution of income at later dates.[31]

Recent discussions of persistent unemployment and growing inequality have centered around labor-saving innovations and in particular on skill-biased innovation (Autor and Dorn 2013). Critics of such innovation are sometimes referred to as modern-day Luddites, and defenders of the market have claimed that one should not interfere with market processes; in the long run, they argue, everyone will be better off. Our analysis has suggested that such views may be Panglossian. Not only within their life span may workers *not* be better off—the benefits of the improvements may not trickle down—but additionally, the changes in factor demands may actually lead them to be worse off even in the longer run.[32]

We have shown not only that innovations may fail to improve the welfare of all groups in society—they may not result in Pareto improvement—but also that the outcome of market processes may lead to patterns of innovation that are not even output maximizing—they would not be Pareto efficient even if redistributions could be made costlessly. Indeed, there is a presumption that unfettered markets will not be efficient in the choice of factor bias and will lead to excessively high levels of unemployment.

4. Evolutionary Processes

The central message of this chapter is that in an innovation economy, there are marked discrepancies between social returns and private rewards, so that there is no presumption that markets yield efficient outcomes. To the contrary, the presumption is that they do not and that there is a role for government to "correct" the market failure.

The fact that private and social profitability may differ markedly also helps explain why naïve arguments about the positive benefits of evolutionary processes are wrong. These arguments are often invoked by those who believe in the market but understand that the standard (Arrow-Debreu competitive) analysis fails to establish the efficiency of markets.

The recent crisis has cast further doubt on the validity of these perspectives.[33] For instance, financial institutions that had understood better the nature of risk and undertaken more prudent actions (e.g., not undertaken excessive leverage) did not survive. Investors observed their seemingly lower returns and demanded that management be replaced. This is not just a hypothetical possibility; it actually occurred. To be sure, those who argued for greater prudence can say, "I told you so." But firms (and their management) that were wiped out in the "creative destruction" of the process of irrational optimism and deficient risk analysis are not easily brought back to life.

The critique of the standard argument of evolutionary selection is that it makes *both* type I and type II errors. Firms and individuals that did well, and survived at least for a long time, were not necessarily those that contributed the most to societal well-being or even had attributes that suited them for long-run survival; rather, they were the firms that were well suited to take advantage of the irrational exuberance and the potential for exploiting the poor and market irrationalities that the era of deregulation had opened up. And those firms that were eliminated were not necessarily those that should have been.[34,35]

Reward structures have allowed those who led the economy to the abyss to walk away with billions—less than they would have had if their flawed analyses had been right, but far more than they deserve, given the costs that they have imposed on the rest of society. With their wealth accumulation, they can exercise undue influence on the allocation of societal resources for years to come.[36]

Four critical insights help explain why evolutionary processes may not be efficient. The first, and most basic, is this: A necessary condition for evolutionary selection processes to work well is that profits are a good measure of social contribution. If that were the case, the firms that survived—had high profits—would be the ones that were making the most important social contributions; the firms that were making losses would be those making a negative social contribution, using up more resources than the value they created. But a central message of this book is that, particularly in the arena of innovation, profits may be a particularly bad measure of social contribution. More generally, evolutionary processes fail to produce efficient outcomes precisely in the same circumstances in which markets traditionally "fail," i.e., fail to produce efficient outcomes.

Second, markets are myopic. They ascertain how well firms are doing today—though because of accounting problems, so evident in the scandals that marked the beginning of this century, they perform this task very imperfectly (see Stiglitz 2003). They have a hard time ascertaining who will do better over the long term.

Moreover, even if a firm might do well over the long term, capital-market imperfections may mean that it will not be able to get the funds to survive now, if it is losing money. Thus, firms that may be more "flexible" and adaptable for changing circumstances might do well in the long run but not survive in the heat of the short-run competition. There may be firms that are better suited to the current circumstances. They may compete sufficiently intensely that the more adaptable firm has losses and can't survive.

But matters are even worse. Firms that are irrational can exert a negative externality on others—and cause them not to survive. The standard argument in economics is that if a firm is irrational (say, has irrational exuberance about the future of housing prices), it will pay the price—it will *eventually* lose on its speculation. But in its irrational exuberance, it can bid capital away from more rational firms, forcing them to pay a return beyond a level which they can sustain. This is not so much true if there is a single such irrationally exuberant firm, but will be especially true if there are many such firms—as was the case prior to the breaking of the bubble in 2006/2007.

The final important idea is the irreversibility of death. We have stressed that firms embody institutional knowledge—knowledge that is more than (and different from) the knowledge that is embedded in each of the individuals who is part of the organization. When an institution dies, much of the embedded knowledge disappears with it. And once a firm dies, when circumstances change—including circumstances under which it would have flourished—it does not come back to life. A new firm bearing some resemblance to the old might be created, but that entails large investments, sunk costs which might not be undertaken unless the expected returns are quite high.

Schumpeter stressed the importance of *creative destruction*. Firms with deep pockets and irrational exuberance may enter and drive out incumbents who are more rational and who are, in fact, better suited for long-run survival. That the former firms eventually die too is little comfort for those who disappear. This and previous financial crises illustrate that the externalities arising from such irrationalities may be economy-wide: the credit bubble imposed large costs, as we noted, on the rest of society.

5. Broader Considerations: Innovation and the Nature of Society

Innovation shapes and is shaped by our society. Decentralized market processes typically pay little attention—for good or for evil—to these consequences. We have already noted two aspects: the effects on unemployment and the distribution of income.

The analysis so far has embedded innovation in a market economy in which, while there may be limited competition in the product market, there is a perfectly competitive labor market. But mobility is limited, and labor markets are often far from competitive. Employers—who manage the innovative process—may have an incentive to manage it in a way that enhances their bargaining process vis-à-vis workers, for that will lead to lower wages. Labor-augmenting innovations, which increase unemployment, do so. So do innovations which make workers more substitutable for each other. The pattern of innovation that has occurred in recent years, leading to lower wages for most workers, may not be just an accident of nature, nor may it even be the result of normal competitive market forces working themselves out; it may be the result of employers deliberately shaping the innovative process in ways which enhance their well-being at the expense of workers.[37]

Workers and management care not just about wages but about "control." Management, for instance, might like to reduce the scope for "agency" problems, where workers shirk or take actions which are not in the company's interests.[38] They may seek to reduce the scope for discretion. Innovations that increase the ability of management to monitor and control (the assembly line, just-in-time inventory systems) may be viewed as desirable by management, even when they are viewed adversely by workers.[39] There may be broader consequences to society of such changes in the workplace.

Of course, as firms engage in labor-saving (-augmenting) innovations, they "learn to learn"; they become better at this form of innovation.[40] This reinforces the process of labor-augmenting (-saving) innovation.

On the other side of the ledger, consumers, workers, and management may all get direct pleasure out of living in a more dynamic economy and society, and from the enjoyment of new experiences that results. These benefits too may not be adequately reflected in market prices and incentives.[41]

6. Concluding Comments

This chapter explains why the production of knowledge—or learning more generally—is different from the production of steel or other conventional commodities. While research over the past forty years has called into question the presumption that markets are efficient, in the case of a learning economy, the presumption is clear: It is unlikely that markets are actually efficient. In an innovation economy, Adam Smith's invisible hand is invisible because it's simply not there.

This chapter provided a list of key attributes of learning and innovation (characterized by fixed, sunk costs, being a public good, spillovers, etc.)—attributes which differ from ordinary commodities. This list explains the pervasiveness and importance of market failures associated with learning, why the level, direction, and form of investments in learning in unfettered markets are not likely to be optimal. The existence of spillovers, for instance, means that those engaged in learning cannot appropriate for themselves the full social benefits of the learning, both today and in the future. (Appendices C and D highlight some of the important intertemporal spillovers. Learning today, for instance, provides a higher base off from which future learning starts; future firms will face lower costs, and future consumers will pay lower prices and enjoy higher levels of consumer surplus. Those engaged in learning and research today will fail to take into account these benefits.) Learning also may require forgoing output today, or bearing risk today, in the hope of higher output in the future; but risk and capital markets are imperfect, especially in relation to investments in learning, and for intrinsic reasons related to information imperfections. Even when firms can appropriate future benefits that derive from their research and learning today, they may discount those benefits with a high discount factor, resulting in suboptimal levels of learning and research. Our list of determinants of learning also includes key societal attributes, like stability, which themselves are the result of public policy; markets by themselves do not necessarily result in the optimal level of macroeconomic stability.[42]

In short, if technological progress is endogenous, there is a raft of market failures: Markets are not likely to be perfectly competitive; benefits of research or learning are likely to spill over to others, both today and into the future; firms engaged in research will appropriate only a portion of the societal benefits arising from their research; but attempts to strengthen appropriation will introduce further distortions in the economy.

While the *sources* of market failure are multiple and complex, so are the consequences. Both the level of R & D, the portfolio of R & D research projects, and the direction of research are distorted. Because, as we have noted, production is linked to learning, the level and pattern of production is distorted, relative to the first best. Because labor contracts too affect labor mobility and the extent and manner in which learning occurs, these too are distorted (relative to what they would be in a society that sought to maximize learning). The central thesis of this book is that every aspect of the market economy (and more broadly of our society) needs to be reexamined from the perspective of learning and innovation. In part 3 of this book, we look more closely at several key policy issues.

Do Markets Engage in Too Little Research and Learning?

One of the central questions in the economics of innovation and learning is: Do markets on their own engage in too little research and learning? The central insight that knowledge is a public good suggests that the answer is yes. And indeed, the case that markets invest too little in basic research seems compelling—with the obvious implication that there is an important role for government. But what about more applied research? Most of the market failures (e.g., those arising from imperfections of competition and the inability to appropriate all the benefits of R & D) suggest that there is in fact underinvestment in research and learning, certainly relative to what would be the case in a first-best world, and even (as we show more clearly in part 2) relative to a second-best world, in which there are a variety of constraints on the kinds of interventions that government can undertake.[43] But our discussion has also made it clear that matters are more complicated; in some cases, private returns can exceed social returns, in which case there can be excessive research—and especially excessive research in certain areas.

In markets with imperfect competition, one of the objectives of research is rent seeking—obtaining the monopoly rents derived from patents or simply the first-mover advantage. The fact that investments in innovations are driven by rent seeking shows that rent seeking need not *only* have adverse effects on the economy. It can be channeled toward more constructive purposes.[44] But rent seeking here, as elsewhere, can also result in distortions to the economy, as firms direct research to seize part of the profits of rivals, in me-too inventions.

There are other forces offsetting the tendency for market economies to underinvest in learning and research. Frank Knight (1921) long ago noted the tendency of entrepreneurs to be irrationally overconfident—one might say irrationally exuberant. They systematically believe that the returns on their innovative activities will be greater than they will be, that the probability of failure is smaller. Entrepreneurs *have* to have confidence in themselves and in their relative ability. But if this is so, it means that the level of investment (including investments in R & D and learning), especially in certain "exciting" areas, may be excessive—excessive given the *private* returns, though not necessarily from the perspective of social returns. Indeed, this irrational exuberance serves to partially counterbalance the underinvestment arising from the market failures upon which we have focused in this chapter.

(Some of this seeming irrationality can, in fact, be explained in models with imperfect and asymmetric information, using models analogous to those that explain the winners' curse in auctions. It is those that have obtained the most favorable information that bid the highest; but then, in formulating their bid, they need to take into account that others have obtained information that is less favorable. So too for the decision to undertake any project, including a research project.)

Intellectual Property Rights

Much of the popular discussion of innovation focuses on the consequences of the imperfect appropriability of the social returns to innovation. Given that this is seen as the central problem, it is natural that attention is focused on government policies at improving appropriability, through strong intellectual property rights.

Our analysis has shown that this focus is incorrect in three respects. First, it focuses on only one of several market failures. Second, the attempt to correct this problem through strong patent protection can result, as we noted, not only in underutilization of knowledge but in overinvestment, especially in certain types of research. Markets may not only invest too much or too little in research, they may invest too much in some kinds of research (me-too patents in the drug industry or research that may lead to holdup patents) and too little in others (especially in basic research).

With patents, the pressure of competition under some circumstances can lead to excessive research under free entry—ideas are like fish in a fish pond, in which there is no charge imposed for fishing. Fishing occurs until the cost of the vessel equals the average catch. What one fishing vessel catches detracts from what others can catch, but each vessel ignores this externality. The zero-profit fishing equilibrium entails too many fish getting caught. Indeed, the myopic fishermen pay little attention to the dynamics of fishing, the effects of excessive fishing today on the size of the fisheries in the next period; they can even fish the fishery to exhaustion. Applied researchers use (and patent) ideas from the existing pool of ideas but do little to ensure that the pool of ideas to be drawn upon in the next period is replenished. In the United States, conservative ideologues, convinced that the private sector is the font of all advances, vote against supporting basic research that would replenish the pool of ideas. In appendix D, we show that stronger (and especially, poorly designed) intellectual property rights can lead to a smaller pool of knowledge, diminishing research opportunities, with the result that the pace of innovation in the long run is actually reduced. Though *given* a particular size pool of ideas, stronger intellectual property protection may lead to more investment in R & D, once account is taken of how IPR affects the flow of knowledge into and out of the pool, stronger IPR may even lead to a lower equilibrium level of investment in R & D.

Patterns of Research and Learning

As we have said, it is not just a matter of the *level* of R & D or learning. There may be too little risk taking of some kinds, too much of other; too much attention to correlation under some circumstances, too little in others.

Even more disturbing is that the *direction* of research is distorted. There is clearly too little research aimed at reducing environmental impacts (say, those associated with global warming)—not surprising, given the absence of a price associated with carbon emissions—and too little attention paid to the unemployment and distributive consequences of innovation.

Our analysis calls into question Schumpeter's euphoria about the virtues of a market in producing innovation. Schumpeter suggested (though never proved) that competition to be the dominant firm would lead to a high level (the "right" level, perhaps) of innovation. At the same time, he argued that monopoly power would be temporary and checked by potential competition. In chapter 5, we questioned those results: Monopoly power may persist, and the threat of competition, rather than leading to more innovation, may lead to costly entry deterrence. And the entry deterrence can be sufficiently successful that the monopolist can enjoy high profits.

While the high profits do provide a way to finance the up-front sunk costs associated with R & D, particularly important in the context of imperfect capital markets, this is not the best way to finance research, i.e., the way that is most equitable and least distortionary. Also, there are, as always, high costs associated with even temporary monopolies. In some cases, putting aside excess returns to the owners of the monopoly, more of the profits are invested in marketing and advertising than on research, with both marketing, advertising, and research directed more at further enhancing market power (reducing demand elasticities, increasing switching costs, disadvantaging rivals) than at enhancing consumer and societal welfare (see Stiglitz 2006a).

Moreover, Schumpeter, in his support for monopoly, ignores agency effects, what we have referred to as the lethargy that is often associated with monopolies.

Innovation and the Enhancement of Individual and Societal Well-being

Just as Schumpeter's faith that "Schumpeterian competition" would lead to overall economic efficiency appears misplaced, so too, Schumpeter's optimism that *all* (or most) citizens would benefit from dynamic capitalism appears unwarranted. Twenty-first-century capitalism illustrates that inequality can increase so much that most individuals can be worse off: In the United States, median household income has been falling and, as this book goes to press is lower (adjusted for inflation) than it was almost a quarter century ago. And this does not take into account the decreased sense of well-being from increased insecurity and environmental degradation. Those who are losing their homes and their life savings as a result of the "innovations" of America's financial system may take little comfort in the notion that *perhaps* their grandchildren will be better off. (The realization that, say, the median income of male full-time workers is lower today than it was forty years ago may also diminish confidence in trickle-down economics.)

Those who glorify the market's innovativeness, of course, pay little attention to the distributive and unemployment effects. They believe that the market (unfettered by government direction) will produce the highest level of innovation and that that will result in the highest level of societal welfare. The presumption is that there may be winners and losers, but society as a whole benefits, which means that the winners could more than compensate the losers. One naïve version of this holds that there are no losers, that somehow the benefits do trickle down to everyone. There is no empirical support for the strong version of trickle-down economics—it should be obvious that, repeatedly, large numbers of individuals have become worse off as a result of innovations that seemingly increased GDP. A weaker version holds that *eventually* everyone benefits from higher growth, and that would be true if at the same time there was not an increase in inequality. But in recent years, as we have noted, growth in the United States has been associated with marked increases in inequality, so large parts of the population, in some cases, a majority, over long periods of time, have seen their standards of living erode, and the increase in inequality may itself be, at least in part, a consequence of innovation, and the way that markets have directed innovative activity.[45] (Matters can be made better or worse by government policy; more recently, some countries seem to have taken the stance that for the country to compete, social programs have to be cut back, so those at the bottom and middle have suffered even more.)

Schumpeter was right that over the two hundred years prior to his writings, innovation had been so strong that almost all benefited. It does not follow that that will necessarily be true over the next hundred years.

It should be obvious that if market prices are distorted, then the market will pay insufficient attention to saving underpriced resources.

Because environmental resources are underpriced, innovation is excessively directed at saving labor and insufficiently directed at saving natural resources. Endogenous labor saving innovation almost surely has played a role in contributing to growing inequality in more advanced industrial countries. Government interventions in R & D that redirect innovation may make it more likely that more will benefit and fewer will lose.

This book is much about how the government either deliberatively or unintentionally directs this process of Schumpeterian creative destruction, by its own research programs (say, on basic research) and the terms on which it makes the results of that research program available; by the structure of the intellectual property laws (e.g., what has to be disclosed, what can be patented, the breadth and novelty standard, the nature of the remedy for violation); and through virtually every other aspect of the country's legal and economic framework, including the standards for competition law (when will firms be found in violation of such laws, and what is the enforcement). Each of these laws and policies affects the pattern and direction of innovation, so that all governments implicitly or explicitly have an innovation policy; they simply may not know it. The U.S. legal system led to a policy that almost surely encouraged financial innovations relative to the social optimum and that discouraged other kinds of innovation, such as those which would have helped protect the environment (more by what they did not do—ensuring that there were appropriate environmental prices in place—than by what they did do).

The presence of the pervasive market failures associated with learning and innovation that we have detailed in this and the previous chapter raises the question: What would constitute optimal, or at least better, resource allocations? More broadly, what government interventions would enhance societal well-being? Part II of this book provides an analysis of what optimal interventions might look like in the context of some highly stylized models, while part III discusses more broadly an array of policy interventions that may enhance societal well-being. Some of these interventions are "fine-tuned," calling for targeted subsidies to one sector or technology. But others are broader in scope and can (and we would argue should) be undertaken even by governments with limited capacities; we show that there is a presumption that developing countries should protect their industrial (including "modern" service and agricultural) sectors. Markets on their own will not create a learning society, or, even if they do, they will do so more slowly and less extensively than they should. Governments can help infant economies grow. In most of the countries that have been successful in making the transition from less developed to more developed, from a stagnant economy to a dynamic learning economy, governments have done so.

APPENDIX A

Conditions Under Which Innovation Lowers the Demand Curve for Labor

In the text we assumed that innovation will decrease the demand for labor at any given wage. In this appendix, we show the demand for labor will be decreased or increased as the elasticity of substitution is less than or greater than unity. Recall the definition of $g(k)$:

$$g(\kappa) \equiv f(\kappa) - \kappa f' = w = W/\lambda, \tag{A.1}$$

the marginal return to an effective unit of labor, where (as before)

$$\kappa = \mu K/\lambda L,$$

the ratio of effective capital to effective labor, and

$$f(\kappa) = F/\lambda L, \tag{A.2}$$

the output per effective labor, and where we have made use of the assumption of constant returns to scale. Then the demand for effective labor units is given by $g'^{-1}(W/\lambda)$. But this means that the demand for workers is

$$L^d = \mu K g'^{-1}(W/\lambda)/\lambda.$$

Then, taking the wage per worker and K as given, and differentiating (A.1), we obtain

$$-[\kappa^2 f''/(f - \kappa f')] \{[d(\ln \mu)/d(\ln \lambda) - 1] [d(\ln \lambda) - d(\ln L)]\} + d(\ln \lambda) = 0.$$

Using (13), using the definition of σ,[46] and simplifying, we obtain

$$d(\ln L^d)/d(\ln \lambda) = (\sigma - 1), \qquad (A.3)$$

which is < 0 or > 0 as σ < or > 1.

APPENDIX B

Long-Run Dynamics and Factor-Biased Technological Progress

In the text, we assumed that the capital stock was fixed. Over time, however, it increases. In this appendix, we describe the long-run equilibrium of the economy. We focus on the special case of fixed coefficients (in the short run—in the long run, the capital-labor ratio can change because of induced innovation). We also simplify by assuming a fixed savings rate. Both of these assumptions can be generalized. The assumption of fixed savings rate implies that

$$I = sQ = dK/dt, \qquad (A.4)$$

where s is the savings rate, I is investment, and K is (as before) the capital stock, so that

$$d(\ln K)/dt = sQ/K = sb, \qquad (A.5)$$

where $1/b$ is the capital output ratio, and

$$Q = Kb. \qquad (A.6)$$

We let

$$aL = Q. \qquad (A.7)$$

It follows that the rate of growth of employment is

$$d(\ln L)/dt = sb + d(\ln b)/dt - d(\ln a)/dt. \qquad (A.8)$$

In steady state, the rate of growth of employment equals the rate of growth of the labor force, n:

$$n = sb + d(\ln b)/dt - d(\ln a)/dt. \tag{A.9}$$

We again postulate a trade-off between labor-augmenting and capital-augmenting technological progress. In the text, we used a discrete time model. Here, we use a continuous time analog, where now μ and λ are the rates of capital- and labor-augmenting technological progress, i.e.,

$$\mu = d(\ln b)/dt \tag{A.10}$$

and

$$\lambda = d(\ln a)/dt. \tag{A.11}$$

We postulate an invention possibilities frontier as before, with

$$\mu = Z(\lambda). \tag{A.12}$$

Steady-State Equilibrium

In steady-state equilibrium, it can be shown that $d(\ln b)/dt = 0$, which in turn means that equilibrium λ^* is given by the solution to

$$0 = Z(\lambda^*). \tag{A.13}$$

This means that technology adjusts to ensure that, in the long run,

$$n + \lambda^* = sb^*. \tag{A.14}$$

From the discussion of the text, it should be clear that

$$z(\lambda^*) \equiv -d(\ln Z)/d(\ln \lambda) = s_L^*/(1 - s_L^*), \tag{A.15}$$

where

$$s_L = wL/Q = w/a. \tag{A.16}$$

Given λ^*, we can easily solve for s_L^* (from A.15). In steady state, not surprisingly, the share of labor is constant. We assume that the relationship between wage and productivity is a function of the unemployment rate; i.e., the wage per efficiency unit is[47]

$$w = am(U), \; m' < 0. \tag{A.17}$$

Given s_L^*, we can solve (A.16) for $(w/a)^*$, and given that, we can easily solve (A.17) for U^*, the equilibrium unemployment rate:

$$U^* = m^{-1}(s_L^*). \tag{A.18}$$

In steady state, the unemployment rate is constant. $d(\ln U)/dt = 0$. We can now solve for the equilibrium employment rate, $e = L/N$, where N is the total labor force (population). From the definition of U,

$$U^* = 1 - L/N = 1 - e^*. \tag{A.19}$$

In steady state, N grows at the rate n, a grows at the rate λ^*, K grows at the rate $n + \lambda^*$, b (the capital output ratio) is constant, the employment ratio is constant, and the share of labor is constant.

Dynamics

The dynamics of the economy are straightforward. In early models of growth with fixed coefficients, it was observed that if $sb > n$, the demand for labor grew at a rate faster than the labor force, and eventually the economy would face a problem of insufficient labor supply. Solow (1958) provided an answer: There are not fixed coefficients, so that b, the output capital ratio, would fall as the capital-labor ratio increased. Here we provide an alternative resolution. As the unemployment rate decreases, wages (per efficiency unit) increase, increasing the share of labor and inducing labor-saving and capital-using innovation. Again, b, the output capital ratio, falls. And it continues to fall until $sb = n$.

More formally, we can describe the dynamics by a pair of differential equations. First, note that

$$L = Q/a = (b/a)K, \tag{A.20}$$

and

$$e = (b/a)(K/N). \tag{A.21}$$

Hence,

$$d(\ln e)/dt = sb + z(\lambda(s_L)) - \lambda(s_L) - n. \tag{A.22}$$

The dynamics are described fully by (A.22) and

$$d(\ln b)/dt = z(\lambda(s_L)), \tag{A.23}$$

where

$$\lambda(s_L) \equiv z^{-1}[s_L/(1 - s_L)] = \lambda(m(1 - e)). \tag{A.24}$$

The phase diagram is depicted in figure 6.4.

$$d(\ln b)/dt = 0 \text{ when } e = e^*. \tag{A.25}$$

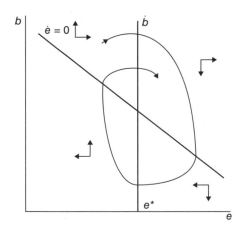

Figure 6.4 Dynamics of adjustment

Convergence to equilibrium may be cyclical.

$$d(\ln e)/dt = 0 \text{ when } b = [n - Z(\lambda(s_L^*)) + \lambda(s_L^*)]/s. \quad (A.26)$$

The $d(\ln e)/dt = 0$ curve is downward sloping.

An increase in the employment rate leads to an increase in wages, which leads to more labor-augmenting and less capital-augmenting progress, i.e., b falls, so $db/dt < 0$ to the right of the $db/dt = 0$ locus. Similarly, an increase in b leads to an increase in $d(\ln e)/dt$, i.e., $de/dt > 0$ above the $de/dt = 0$ locus. The economy oscillates into an equilibrium.[48]

While it is easy to show that in long-run steady state, equilibrium requires that technological progress be pure labor augmenting, and that there is such an equilibrium, it is possible that equilibrium [where $Z(\lambda^*) = 0$ and $z(\lambda^*) = s_L^*/(1 - s_L^*)$] is not stable. (In particular, in more general models, more complicated—and potentially unstable—dynamics arise when the elasticity of substitution is greater than unity. In that situation, a larger capital share leads to a factor bias toward capital-augmenting technological change, leading in turn to a still larger share of capital. If the share of wages increases above the equilibrium share, it continues to increase until it hits unity (and conversely, if the share of wages falls below the critical level). These results are a consequence of the strong assumption that the innovation frontier itself is invariant to the value of labor and capital augmentation previously achieved. That is, instead of (A.12), we could have written, say,

$$\mu = Z(\lambda, b), \quad (A.27)$$

so that as b gets increasingly large, it become increasingly hard to increase b further.[49] Similarly, if the economy has increasingly focused on labor-augmenting technical progress because of the increasing share of labor, further labor augmentation becomes more difficult. Thus, even at the high share of labor, there is a shift toward capital-augmenting technological progress.

APPENDIX C

Creative Destruction

Schumpeter talked about the creative destruction process, with one monopolist succeeding another—creating a new product or lowering costs of production, and in doing so, destroying the basis of the profits of its predecessor. The analysis of this chapter has suggested that Schumpeter was perhaps overly optimistic about the force of competition: The incumbent has the means and incentives to preempt and to forestall entry.[50]

But Schumpeter was right in noting important intertemporal linkages. Actions by firms at one date can have effects on firms at later or (if anticipated) at earlier dates. Innovation at time t provides the knowledge base that can be drawn upon by innovators at later dates.[51] (Appendix D to this chapter describes how firms contribute to and take out of the pool of knowledge.) Successors thus benefit from this knowledge. But at the same time, innovations at one time provide the "competitive baseline" for profits at subsequent periods: lower costs at t limit the price that the monopolist at $t + 1$ can charge.[52]

By the same token, part of the profits of the monopolist at time $t + 1$ may be a result of taking away profits that otherwise would have gone to the monopolist at time t, for instance, because the period of its monopoly is shortened. (As we noted, if the market structure at $t + 1$ is not a monopoly, it is still the case that some of the returns to innovation come from decreased profits of the other firms in the market.)

Because those at time t know that their profits will be reduced by successors, they may innovate less than they otherwise would. Firms at time t may invest too little, because they fail to take into account the benefits conferred on later dates; and their investments are further discouraged as they realize that some of their profits (which are typically less than the social benefits) will be stolen by their successor. But firms at time $t + 1$ may invest too much, because they fail to take into account the fact that some of their profits are "stolen" from others. But, of course, firms at each date are part of an infinite chain of innovators, and it is thus not apparent whether there is too much or too little investment in innovation.

Even this discussion oversimplifies the complexity of the possible interactions. An innovation at a later date may actually enhance the returns to an earlier innovation. This is the case, for instance, when there are complementary innovations. The social returns to innovation A are increased by an innovation B, and typically, innovation B will not fully capture these benefits which it confers on earlier innovations. Thus, rather than destroying the value of prior innovations, later innovations can have just the opposite effect. In this case, there will be underinvestment in follow-on research.

This appendix develops a sequence of models that explore some aspects of what is at issue, in an attempt to assess the efficiency of the Schumpeterian "creative destruction" process in, say, the speed of innovation, the size of the innovation steps, and the overall level of innovation. It complements and amplifies the important earlier work of Aghion and Howitt (1992), who identified two of the key market failures, externalities, already noted: a negative externality exerted by an innovator on previous firms, as a result of its stealing some (all) of their profits (what Aghion and Howitt call the business-stealing effect); and a positive externality on future innovators, who build off the base provided by current innovators and whose profits are thereby increased. This appendix also explores a third market failure related to the patent system (or any reward system based on the first to innovate) which was identified by Aghion and Howitt: In the rush to innovate and capture these innovation rents, the size of the innovation, and possibly even the pace of innovation, is smaller than it otherwise would be.

We identify several other market failures—firms focus on maximizing profits, while social welfare maximization takes into account consumer surplus;[53] firms may invest too much to accelerate the pace of innovation, beyond the optimal level, to capture the innovation rents (even when they are not stealing them from others already in the market); there is a contemporaneous cross-firm externality effect, as the research of each firm lowers the expected marginal returns to investment in competing innovative firms;[54] and an "innovation pool" effect, whereby the (expected) profits of the marginal entrant are related to the *average* (or expected) innovation rent, which can be considerably greater than the marginal return to having a new entrant.

There is also an entry-deterrence effect. Incumbents take actions that deter competitors from entering and that induce them, should they enter, to be less competitive. While some of these entry-deterring actions may offset other "biases," in other cases there may be significant social costs. Thus, in some circumstances, entry deterrence may lead the incumbent firm to do more research than it otherwise would, which would be socially desirable if, in the absence of the threat of entry, the incumbent engaged in excessively slow innovation. In other circumstances, however, the main effect of the threat of entry is for the incumbent to engage in a research strategy that is less efficient in producing innovations, but more efficient in deterring entry.

Thus, this analysis reinforces the conclusions of earlier studies of Schumpeterian competition that there is no presumption that the market equilibrium is efficient.

The analysis of this appendix is conducted in a much more partial equilibrium context than that of Aghion and Howitt and focuses on simpler market structures. As always, there are trade-offs: The closer focus on firm interactions not only uncovers new market failures not noted in their earlier work, but also shows that the balance of effects— the circumstances under which there will be under- or overinvestment in research—depends critically not only on the specification of the nature of the interactions among the competitors but also on the R & D process.[55,56] Moreover, earlier studies focusing on steady states employed tight parameterizations, known to have special properties.

Thus, an essential difference between this analysis and some of the earlier literature is that we assume that in any industry, several firms may coexist *after* the innovation—a situation that often, even typically, occurs (note Samsung and Apple, Xerox and a host of competitors) and, alternatively, that the incumbent dominant firm is also the innovator, which may be forced to do more research than it otherwise would by the threat of entry. Thus, we explore innovation when there is Bertrand or Cournot competition between the innovator and prior firms; and when the incumbent firm does and does not maintain its monopoly. The fact that the incumbent firm has the ability and incentive to maintain its dominant position, preempting rivals, has been established under a variety of quite general conditions (Dasgupta and Stiglitz 1980a; Fudenberg, Gilbert, Tirole, and Stiglitz 1983). These analyses suggest that it is worthwhile exploring the behavior of the *persistent monopolist* as one limiting case. The argument for persistence may be even stronger than these earlier studies suggested, because knowledge spillovers are essentially always imperfect, so that the incumbent firm has a distinct knowledge advantage.[57] The fact that one monopolist is followed by another is only a reflection of the stochastic nature of the equilibrium, even if the incumbent has a distinct advantage over rivals, others may engage in some research, and, stochastically, some of these rivals will succeed.[58] Typically, however, the firm that is dominant at t will dominate the next period. But even when a rival succeeds, it is typically not the case that the innovation is so large that it instantaneously eliminates the rival. The firms coexist, putting at the center of the discussion how they interact.

Not only may the incumbent and innovator coexist, when there are multiple potential innovators, more than one may be successful, and one firm's innovation may not exclude that of others. With non-exclusive innovations, the nature of ex post innovation becomes even more crucial. It is only with exclusive innovations that there is a real innovation race. But in innovation races, as is well known, there are marked discrepancies between private and social returns. The marginal social return is only the benefit of having the innovation slightly earlier than it otherwise would have occurred;[59] the private return entails the capturing of rents (including from existing producers and from other potential producers).

This analysis differs from the earlier literature in one other way. We explore a much simpler context, in which innovations simply lower the cost of production. Of course, new products can (e.g., in a Lancasterian framework) typically be viewed as lowering the costs of providing the "services" that individuals desire. In a sense, this biases the results; in effect, new and old products are perfect substitutes, which makes it all the more difficult for them to coexist in equilibrium. With differentiated competition (especially with heterogeneous populations), new products are more likely to coexist with old, so that anticipated sectoral interactions after innovation are critical in determining the returns to innovation. But even under the extreme assumptions posited here, sectoral interactions are crucial.

A central issue that we examine is the effect of an increase in competition. Though Schumpeter trumpeted the virtues of monopoly—or at least a sequence of monopolies—there has long been a presumption that there is an inverted U-shaped relationship between the number of firms and innovation. Competition spurs innovation. But competition to be the next monopolist may, in fact, lower the marginal expected returns to investments in R & D (or learning), and so it is possible that more competition may lower the speed of innovation. We show that there are, in fact, contexts in which there may be an inverted U-shaped relationship[60] and other contexts in which the more competitors, the lower the overall speed of innovation. (Recall that chapter 5 showed that there may even be a U-shaped relationship. With many firms undertaking at least slightly different research projects, the larger the number of firms, the higher the probability of at least one success—if the level of investment of each remains unchanged. But as more firms undertake research, the expected marginal return to innovation for each decreases, so that each diminishes his research effort. The net effect on innovation depends on how these two separate forces play out, and that depends both on the correlation of success and the sensitivity of research effort to returns. Our analysis has shown that the net effect is ambiguous. Earlier analyses giving "clean" results have made particular parametric assumptions.) Our analysis suggests, however, that with free entry, there are likely to be too many competitors.

This appendix is divided into nine sections. There are two aspects of the innovative process on which we focus—the size of the innovation and the pace of innovation.[61] In the first seven sections, we focus just on the size of the innovation, on the magnitude of cost reduction. We begin in the first section with a two-period model, in which we compare investments in R & D and the pace of innovation under a number of different institutional arrangements—that in which the incumbent is followed by a new monopolist; that in which the incumbent maintains its monopoly unfettered by potential competition; that in which the incumbent is forced to increase its pace of innovation to maintain its monopoly power; and the social welfare optimizing level of innovation. The next three sections explore in detail how the nature of ex ante and ex post competition and the stochastic innovation process affect marginal returns to and investments in innovation. In the fifth section, we focus on implications of the fact that the incumbent can take actions to deter entry and discourage competition from entrants should they enter. The sixth and seventh sections extend the analysis to an infinite-period model, first in the case of the market, comparing persistent and sequential monopolies. In the seventh section, we contrast the results with the social optimum. In the eighth section, we focus just on the speed of innovation, keeping the size of the innovation fixed. In the final section, we bring the two together.

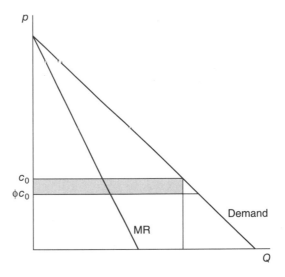

Figure 6.5 Successive monopolist, small innovations

With Bertrand competition, the innovator charges a price just below the costs of the incumbent, earning a profit equal to the shaded area.

1. Sequential and Persistent Monopolists

First, assume that Schumpeter was correct that there were a sequence of monopolists.[62] Each monopolist is precluded (by assumption) from getting the next innovation. The old monopolist, we refer to as the incumbent; the new as the entrant; and the market structure as sequential monopoly.

Figure 6.5 shows the demand and marginal revenue schedule of the monopolist. The original cost of production is c_0. The next monopolist lowers the cost of production per unit of output to ϕc_0, where ϕ is a function of the investment in innovation, I.

We refer to ϕ as the innovation function. We normally assume $\phi' < 0$ and $\phi'' > 0$. It is often convenient to take as our "control" variable the level of costs,

$$c_1 = \phi(I)c_0. \tag{A.28}$$

For simplicity, in some of the subsequent analysis we write:

$$c_1 = c_1(I), \, c_1' < 0, \, c_1'' > 0. \tag{A.28'}$$

The investment function,

$$I = \Psi(c_1, c_0), \qquad (A.29)$$

gives the investment required to obtain costs of c_1, when last period's cost is c_0.

$$\Psi(c_1; c_0) = \phi^{-1}(c_1/c_0). \qquad (A.30)$$

We denote by Ψ' the partial derivative of Ψ with respect to c_1.

1.1 *Sequential Monopoly Equilibrium with Small Innovations*

If ϕ is not too small (the innovation is not too large), then the monopolist will charge c_0 (i.e., with Bertrand competition, the monopolist just undercuts its rival), so its revenues net of production costs, R, will be

$$R(c_0, c_1) = (c_0 - c_1)Q(c_0) = c_0(1 - \phi)Q(c_0), \qquad (A.31)$$

(illustrated in figure 6.5 as the shaded area). Its profits (taking into account the cost of innovation) will be

$$\Pi = R - I, \qquad (A.32)$$

which will be maximized with respect to I at the point where

$$-\phi'Q(c_0)c_0 = 1. \qquad (A.33)$$

Using the envelope theorem, the marginal return to reducing costs, c_1, is just equal to $Q(c_0)$. And the marginal cost is Ψ'. Hence, we can also express the optimal investment in R & D by the equation

$$Q(c_0) = \Psi'(I), \qquad (A.34)$$

from which it follows that[63]

$$I - \Psi'^{-1}[Q(c_0)].\qquad (\text{A.35})$$

Using (A.33), we can solve for the pace of innovation:

$$I = hQ(c_0)c_1 = hQ(c_0)c_0\,\phi(I),\qquad (\text{A.36})$$

where $h = -d(\ln \phi)/d(\ln I)$, the elasticity of costs (productivity) with respect to investments in R & D. (If h is a constant, then (A.36) and (A.28) can be used directly to easily solve for c_1 as a function of c_0.)

Figure 6.6A shows costs and revenues as a function of c_1 (for a given c_0). Figure 6.6B illustrates the consequences of an alternative set of assumptions about the cost function, where there is a region of increasing returns.[64]

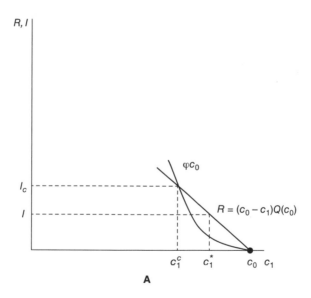

A

Figure 6.6 Small innovations

Net revenues and costs as a function of c_1, the marginal cost of production. A. Increasing costs associated with larger innovations. $\{I^*, c_1^*\}$ is the optimal investment, costs. It occurs at the point where the slopes of the revenue and cost curves are identical. B. Initially, there are increasing returns to innovation. $\{I_c, C^c\}$ is the contestable equilibrium where net profits are driven to zero, i.e. $R = I$.

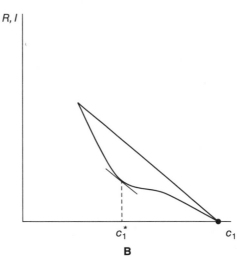

Figure 6.6 *(Continued)*

1.2 *Sequential Monopoly Equilibrium with Large Innovations*

If the price reduction is substantial, then the monopolist just sets price, p, as a markup over marginal costs (figure 6.7):

$$p = c_0\phi/(1 - 1/\eta) = c_1/(1 - 1/\eta). \tag{A.37}$$

where η is the elasticity of demand. This occurs when the profit-maximizing price lies below c_0, i.e., when

$$\phi < 1 - 1/\eta. \tag{A.38}$$

Let g be the percentage cost reduction, i.e., $g \equiv 1 - \phi$. Then a "large" innovation (for purposes of our analysis) is defined as one where

$$g > 1/\eta. \tag{A.38'}$$

We denote the critical-size innovation by g^*. Now revenues are given by

$$R = (p - \phi c_0)Q(p) \tag{A.39}$$
$$= c_0\phi Q[(c_0\phi)/(1 - 1/\eta)]/(\eta - 1).$$

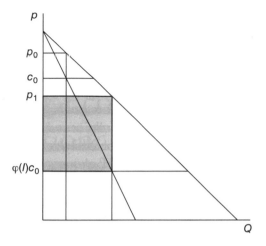

Figure 6.7 Large innovations

The shaded area gives the net revenues (after operating costs). The profit-maximizing price p_1 is less than c_0, the marginal costs of the incumbent.

Profits are again given by (A.32), and we obtain the equations describing the profit-maximizing value of I (or c_1) that are analogous to (A.34)

$$Q(p) = \Psi'(I). \qquad (A.40)$$

The only difference is that now, instead of $p = c_0$, we have (A.37).

1.3 *Multiple Local Optimum*

A careful look at the profit function (as a function of I) shows that that there may be multiple local optima, as illustrated in figure 6.8. For small I, we are in "regime 1" (small innovation), for which

$$\partial \Pi^2 / \partial I^2 = -\phi'' Q(c_0) c_0 < 0,$$

under the natural assumption that $\phi'' > 0$. Thus, for small I, profits are a concave function of I. For large I, we are in "regime 2" (large innovation), for which

$$\partial \Pi^2 / \partial I^2 = -\phi'' Q[c_0 \phi/(1 - 1/\eta)] c_0 + \phi'^2 Q[c_0 \phi/(1 - 1/\eta)] c_0 \eta/\phi.$$

Because as costs get lowered, output increases, the marginal benefit of research can actually increase, and profits can be a convex function of I, at least over an interval. At the switching point between the two regimes, I_s, where $c_0 = c_0\phi/(1 - 1/\eta)$, i.e., $\phi(I_s) = 1 - 1/\eta$, profits,[65] and the derivative of profits $(\phi'Q(p)c_0)$ are continuous. If output is highly elastic, and there are not sharply diminishing returns to research, however, then, as in figure 6.8, the marginal returns can increase beyond some point, and there can be two (or more) levels of I for which marginal returns to further investment in R & D equal marginal costs. Which yields higher profits requires a global analysis.[66] (Figures 6.8A and 6.8B provide an alternative diagrammatic expositions. The former shows revenues and costs of innovation as a function of c_1, second period's marginal cost of production. Figure 6.8B, provides an alternative diagrammatic exposition, plotting profits on the vertical axis against investment on the horizontal axis. Profits are concave for small innovations, but that is not in general the case for large innovations.)

One of the implications is that small changes in the economic environment (e.g., a shift in the demand curve) can lead to discontinuities in behavior, a sudden jump or fall in the level of investment in R & D and the pace of innovation.

1.4 *Persistent Myopic Monopolist*

In this and the following two subsections, we contrast the market equilibrium for the *sequential* monopolist with those of alternative market structures. Here we focus on a myopic persistent monopolist, i.e., the case where the incumbent makes the next innovation but, in deciding its investments in R & D, does not take into account the consequences for future profits. The profit-maximizing level of R & D is again given by (A.34) or (A.40). The only difference arises in the case of small innovations, where now price is not constrained by c_0. It is given by (A.37), which for small g is higher than c_0. That means that for large innovation, there is no difference in the level of R & D between sequential and persistent myopic monopoly; for small innovations, sequential monopoly innovation levels are higher. Denoting I^{sm} and c_1^{sm} the investment and (first-period) cost levels in sequential monopoly, and letting the superscript *pmm*

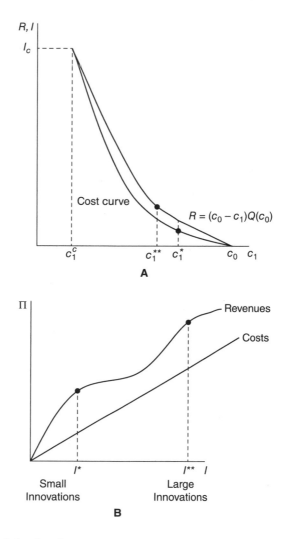

Figure 6.8 Multiple local optima

A. Marginal returns to further investments in innovation equals marginal costs at c_1^* and c_1^{**}. Which yields higher overall profits depends on a global analysis. In the figure, it pays the firm to engage in large innovation. B. Profits are a concave function of investment for small innovations, but there can be nonconcavities for large innovations, implying that there may be multiple local optima.

designate the corresponding values in the persistent myopic monopoly, we have

$$I^{sm} = I^{pmm} \text{ for } g \geq g^*; I^{sm} > I^{pmm} \text{ for } g < g^*. \qquad \text{(A.41a)}$$

$$c_1^{SM} = c_1^{pmm} \text{ for } g \geq g^*; c_1^{sm} < c_1^{pmm} \text{ for } g < g^*. \qquad \text{(A.41b)}$$

1.5 *Social Welfare Maximization*

The welfare-maximizing level of investment in R & D depends on the constraints facing the government: (a) Can it impose lump sum taxes and subsidies? (b) Can it restrain monopoly power? and (c) Can it provide R & D subsidies? Since R & D is a fixed cost, first best requires levying lump sum taxes to finance the research and charging a price equal to marginal cost. Let $V(p, Y)$ be the indirect utility function, giving utility as a function of prices, p, and net income (profits minus lump sum taxes), Y. Optimality requires that

$$V_p c_0 \phi' - V_Y = 0, \qquad \text{(A.42)}$$

or, using Roy's identity,[67]

$$Q(c_1)\phi' = 1. \qquad \text{(A.43)}$$

Because in the social welfare maximization problem, price equals today's marginal cost, output is higher, and the level of investment in R & D is therefore larger.

On the other hand, if the government cannot subsidize research and markets are contestable, then maximizing social welfare yields the contestable equilibrium, where profits are zero even though there is only a single firm in the market.[68]

Finally, if the government can subsidize research, financed by a lump sum tax (or a not too distortionary non–lump sum tax) but cannot change the market structure, then for $g < g^*$, the sequential monopoly equilibrium is efficient. In the other cases (i.e., the sequential monopoly for $g > g^*$ and the myopic persistent monopoly for all g), though, it is optimal for government to subsidize research. The marginal value of additional research is

$$V_p \phi' c_0 / (1 - 1/\eta) = -V_\Upsilon Q(p) \phi' c_0 / (1 - 1/\eta) > V_\Upsilon,$$

the marginal cost, so that it is desirable to subsidize research. This is even true in the contestability equilibrium, provided that it is possible to impose lump sum taxes.

In short, if we denote by superscripts *su*, the unconstrained social optimum; *ns*, the no-subsidy social optimum; and *sc*, the "constrained" social optimum, where research subsidies are allowed, but the government cannot constrain monopoly, then for large g,

$$I^{su} > I^{sc} > I^{ns}, c_1^{su} > c_1^{sc} > c_1^{ns}. \tag{A.44}$$

To anticipate one aspect of our later discussion of a multiperiod (infinite) model, we note the effect of each period's decision on profits and consumer welfare in future periods. For instance, for small innovations, using the envelope theorem,

$$\partial \Pi_t / \partial (\ln c_{t-1}) = c_0 (1 - \phi) Q(c_0)(1 - \eta) < 0.$$

Lowering costs at time $t-1$ increases profits at time t: there is an intertemporal spill-over. Similar results hold for large innovations.

2. Ex Post Competition

Bertrand competition has a number of distinct features. It entails fierce competition, in which the lowest-cost producer dominates the market—but charges a price set by the second-lowest-cost producer. When products are differentiated, there will be multiple producers in the market; an entrant only steals a fraction of the customers away from each of the incumbents.

In this section, we explore the simplest and longest-standing alternative to Bertrand competition—Cournot. With Cournot competition, so long as the innovation is not too large, the incumbent will continue to produce, and while price is higher than with Bertrand competition, less fierce ex post competition leads to less innovation. The returns to lowering costs are markedly smaller, since the sales of each company are smaller.

To make our analysis parallel to that of the first section, we assume that the incumbent, denoted by firm 0, cannot innovate, and there is a single entrant, denoted by subscript 1.

In the Cournot equilibrium, the entrant takes the level of output of the incumbent as given and chooses $\{I, Q_1\}$ to maximize profits:

$$\Pi_1 = [p(Q_1 + Q_0) - c_1] \, Q_1 - I.$$

Meanwhile, the incumbent takes Q_1 as given and chooses Q_0 to maximize

$$\Pi_0 = [p(Q_1 + Q_0) - c_0] \, Q_0.$$

The ex post equilibrium (given c_1) is the solution to

$$p(Q_0 + Q_1) = c_1/(1 - \alpha/\eta), \qquad \text{(A.45a)}$$

$$p(Q_0 + Q_1) = c_0/(1 - (1 - \alpha)/\eta), \qquad \text{(A.45b)}$$

where

$$\alpha = Q_1/(Q_0 + Q_1), \qquad \text{(A.46)}$$

the share of total output produced by the entrant. It follows that so long as the innovation is not too large —

$$g < 1/\eta \qquad \text{(A.47)}$$

— the incumbent continues to produce. (For $g \geq 1/\eta$, $\alpha = 0$).

The equilibrium condition for I is again given by

$$-c_1' Q_1 = 1. \qquad \text{(A.45c)}$$

The marginal return to an entrant's research — to lowering c_1 — is (again using the envelope theorem) Q_1.

The triplet of equations (A.45a), (A.45b), and (A.45c), together with the definition (A.46) give four equations in $\{Q_0, Q_1, c_1, \alpha\}$ defining the Nash-Cournot equilibrium. It is easy to show that there may exist more than one such equilibrium, as illustrated below.

In the obvious notation, for small innovations, since [using (A.45b)] $p_C > p_B$ (the price in the Cournot equilibrium is higher than in the Bertrand equilibrium), from which it follows that

$$Q_{1C} < Q_{1C} + Q_{0C} < Q_{1B} + Q_{0B} = Q_{1B}, \qquad \text{(A.48a)}$$

the marginal returns to innovation are less, which means that there will be less investment in innovation. Hence,

$$I_C < I_B, \text{ and } c_{1B} < c_{1C}. \qquad \text{(A.48b)}$$

The pace of innovation with Bertrand is faster than with Cournot.

This illustrates an important point: *changes in the economic environment (here, a move from Bertrand competition to Cournot competition) can have effects on average and marginal returns that are not only of different magnitudes, but even of different signs.* Profits of the entrant are unambiguously greater (provided $g < 1/\eta$; otherwise, they are the same) with Cournot, even though *marginal returns* to cost reductions are smaller.[69,70]

On the other hand, from (A.45a), price is lower (output is higher) under Cournot than under myopic monopoly, but the entrant only produces a fraction of that output. Hence, it is not apparent whether, in general, the level of innovation is higher. However, if $p'' \leq 0$, then it can be established that innovation with Cournot is lower than with myopic monopoly.[71]

We can see how this plays out by considering, for instance, the case of a linear demand function:

$$p = a - b(Q_1 + Q_0). \qquad \text{(A.49)}$$

The Cournot equilibrium is given by

$$Q_1 = [a + c_0 - 2c_1]/3b \qquad \text{(A.50a)}$$

and

$$Q_0 = [a + c_1 - 2c_0]/3b, \tag{A.50b}$$

so

$$Q = Q_0 + Q_1 = 2(a - \bar{c})/3b, \quad p = (a + 2\bar{c})/3, \tag{A.51}$$

where $\bar{c} = (c_0 + c_1)/2$.

With our linear demand function, the incumbent will continue to produce so long as

$$c_0 < (a + c_1)/2.$$

(Indeed, several previous "incumbents" will normally continue to produce. Here, we consider the case where innovations are small enough that the above condition is satisfied, but large enough that only one prior incumbent operates. The results are stronger for the more general case.)

Assume that the innovator lowers costs by a percentage g. Then, the entrant's output is given by

$$Q_1 = (a - c_0 + 2gc_0)/3b, \tag{A.50'}$$

which is less than the persistent myopic monopoly output so long as the incumbent continues to produce.[72] But this in turn means that the incentives to innovate will be lower.

The equilibrium is given by the pair of equations (A.50) and

$$-c'Q_1 = 1. \tag{A.45c}$$

(A.50a) is a linear equation between c_1 and Q_1 (for given c_0): the lower the cost of production, the higher is output. (See figure 6.9). Observing that $I = c^{-1}(c_1)$, (A.45c) can also be expressed as a downward-sloping curve between c_1 and Q_1:

$$dc_1/dQ_1 = c'''/c'' < 0.$$

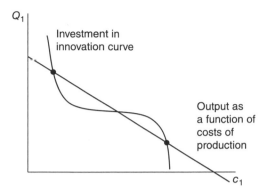

Q_1

Investment in
innovation curve

Output as
a function of
costs of
production

c_1

Figure 6.9 Cournot competition (symmetric equilibrium)

Output increases linearly as costs decline in the symmetric equilibrium (the straight line), but the larger the output, the larger the investments in research, and hence the lower costs. There may be multiple Nash-Cournot equilibria.

The higher output is, the more investment in innovation and the lower costs. Figure 6.9 shows a case where there are three possible equilibria: a low-innovation/low-output equilibrium and a high-innovation/high-output equilibrium.

2.1 *An Alternative Formulation*

In the formulation just presented, the Cournot duopolist makes its innovation decision assuming that the output of the rival will be unaffected by its own output *as it plans investments in innovation*. But there is an alternative formulation, viewing the innovative process as a two-stage game, in which, after the research is completed (in the production period), there is a Cournot equilibrium. The entrant knows, however, that the Cournot equilibrium will be affected by its costs, and, indeed, the entrant knows how the equilibrium will be affected.

Thus, for the first period (the research period), the entrant chooses a level of innovation that maximizes its profits, taking into account how profits depend on c_1:

$$\max \Pi_1 = R_1 - I = (a + c_0 - 2c_1)^2/9b - I, \qquad (A.52)$$

$$\{I\},$$

from which it follows that

$$\partial R_1/\partial c_1 = 4(a + c_0 - 2c_1)/9b = 4Q_1/3. \qquad (A.53)$$

The incumbent realizes that if it has lower costs, it will "crowd out" its rival. With rising marginal costs associated with cost reductions, there is a unique equilibrium.

The total return to innovation, for small innovations, is smaller than in the Bertrand equilibrium, while the marginal return is $4/3Q_1$, compared to the Bertrand equilibrium, where it equaled Q_1. But $Q_1^C < Q_1^B$, as we previously showed. Assume, for instance, that g is small. Then

$$Q_1^B = (a - c_0)/b \approx 3Q_1^C$$

The marginal return to innovation is 4/9 that under Bertrand competition, which means that there will be much less innovation. What this analysis shows is how sensitive results can be to the precise specification of firm interaction.

2.2 *Myopic Persistent Monopolist*

We now contrast these results with the incentives of a myopic persistent monopolist (one that only focuses on the increase in profits *next period*, i.e., not taking into account the benefits to future periods). Earlier, we noted that the myopic persistent monopolist would innovate more than in sequential monopoly with Bertrand competition, and it follows that this is true even more strongly with Cournot competition. How much more strongly can be seen in our linear demand model.

The marginal return to a myopic monopolist can be calculated in a straightforward way as[73]

$$(a - c_1)/2b,$$

which, for small g, is approximately half the return under Bertrand competition; monopoly significantly restricts output, and therefore marginal returns. But the myopic monopolist's marginal return to investment in R & D is still 9/8 times that in the Cournot equilibrium.[74]

2.3 R & D Subsidies

With Cournot equilibrium (with small innovations), *some* of the benefits of the innovation are translated into lower prices. Consumers benefit (in the way they did not, in the short run, in Bertrand competition). Thus, a subsidy to research has a larger consumer benefit—indeed, for small innovations, we observed that no R & D subsidy is desirable in Bertrand competition (in our two-period model—this result is not general).

The marginal social benefit can be derived from the indirect utility function. Assuming a linear demand function and small g, the marginal social benefit differs from the private return (as calculated in the previous section) for two reasons: There is a decline in price, with a marginal social value (for small g) of approximately $Q^C/3$, and the entrant does not take this into account;[75] but the entrant may take into account the effect of additional research on *the entrant's* next period's profitability, including the fact that it will grab a larger fraction of the industry profit. That will increase its marginal return to innovation by $1/3 \, Q_1^C$, (i.e., by $1/3$ of its own output), which for small g is approximately equal to $1/6 \, Q^C$ (i.e., by $1/6$ of total industry output). Thus, the marginal social return to cost reductions exceeds the private returns by (for small innovations) approximately $1/6 \, Q^C$. Some subsidy to R & D would be socially desirable.

(This describes the optimal intervention, *given* that the government cannot change the market structure. In a later section, we will describe the social optimum where the government can control production and R & D.)

3. Multiple Potential Innovators

Implicitly, in the model of the previous sections, the successor monopolist knew that it would be the successor and chose I accordingly. But, of course, the whole point of Schumpeterian competition was that there was competition to be the successor monopolist. There are several ways of modeling this, discussed in this and the next subsection. A critical distinction is whether the different firms are pursuing a cost-reducing innovation using the same technology, with an exclusionary patent, so that the firm that gets the patent *excludes* all other firms; or whether if several firms are successful, then all of them can participate in the market. (These are clearly two polar cases.)[76]

Here we assume that there are n potential entrants each period, but only one gets the right to produce. We begin our analysis by focusing on symmetric equilibria, where each invests the same amount, I, and, randomly, one gets the patent (effectively, making the discovery before the others).[77] But the convexities which are intrinsic in R & D may result in there being no symmetric equilibrium, a possibility we pursue in later sections.

The previous section made it clear that the equilibrium depended critically on the nature of ex post competition. Hence, while in the first three subsections, we discuss the innovation equilibrium assuming that ex post there is Bertrand competition, in the sections "Cournot Equilibrium: Nonexclusivity" and "Cournot Equilibrium: Free Entry," we analyze the equilibrium under Cournot competition.

3.1 *Bertrand Competition, Symmetric Equilibrium*

Each potential entrant's *expected* profit is $1/n$th that of the monopoly successor, so instead of (A.34), we obtain as the first-order condition for I:

$$Q(p) = \Psi'(I)/n, \qquad (A.54)$$

where, as before, $p = c_0$ for small innovations, and $c_1/(1 - 1/\eta)$ for large. In the case of small innovations, the returns to investments in innovation are reduced by a factor of n; in the case of large innovations, by a factor greater than n (since Q itself is a function of marginal costs, $c_0\phi$). This means that (in this model) *the greater the level of competition (the larger* n), *the lower the pace of innovation*. As we shall see, while the result is not general, this does demonstrate that there is no presumption that the greater the level of competition, the higher the level of innovation.

3.2 *Bertrand Equilibria, Multiple Potential Entrants: Contestability*

We noted in figures 6.6 and 6.8 that the (single) entrant made positive profits. If there are many potential entrants, all with the same innovation functions, then they will compete to become the next monopoly.

There will be competition *for* the market, rather than competition *in* the market. In this section, we assume that that competition actually works to drive the profits of the entrant down to zero.[78] (In later sections, we will explain why innovation markets are not, in general, contestable, e.g., why the incumbent can deter entry even as it earns positive profits.)

Zero profits for the entrant means that[79]

$$I = c_0(1 - \phi)Q(c_0). \tag{A.55}$$

I^c is the unique solution to[80]

$$I^c/(1 - \phi(I^c)) = c_0 Q(c_0). \tag{A.56}$$

(See figure 6.10; the contestable equilibrium occurs at the point where the revenue and innovation cost curves intersect.)

Note that the outcome does not depend on the number of potential competitors. It only depends on the "fierce" competition to be the successor monopolist. It is immediate that

$$I^c > I^{sm}, c_1^c < c_1^{sm}. \tag{A.57}$$

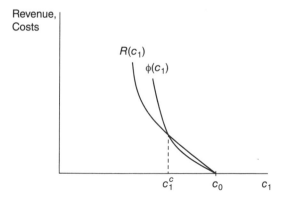

Figure 6.10 Contestability

The contestable equilibrium occurs at the point where the revenue and innovation cost curves intersect.

Contestability leads to more investment and more innovation than with sequential monopoly. Indeed, it should be clear that contestability can lead to *excessive* expenditures on research. Each competitor looks only at its (expected) average return *as a monopolist for a limited duration*, not at the marginal social return. As the discussion below will make clear, while the marginal social return is greater than the marginal private return (to a sequential monopolist), the average *private* return may well exceed the marginal social return.

3.3 *Asymmetric Bertrand Equilibria: Nonexclusivity*

To see, however, that the symmetric outcome cannot be an equilibrium under the assumption of nonexclusivity, consider the case with two potential entrants, where each takes the R & D of the other as given. Assume further that if there are two innovators, both can produce. Then, if each knows the level of investment of the other and takes that level of investment as given (irreversible, i.e., the first firm won't leave and won't reduce its research, no matter what the second firm does), then there can exist an equilibrium where the first firm makes a positive profit, but the second firm does not enter. Competition among innovators does not result in the contestability outcome.

This happens because the second firm assesses its profits not with the benchmark of $p = c_0$, but with that of the first entrant's costs of production, c_1^1. Thus, as figure 6.11A illustrates, the revenue of the second firm is zero for costs greater than c_1^1, and $Q(c_1^1)(c_1^1 - c_1^2)$ for costs less than c_1^1. If the second firm enters, it will enter at the point where marginal revenue equals marginal costs, i.e., undercutting its rival (implying that the first firm's actions could not have been part of a Nash equilibrium). It will enter if the lower shaded area of figure 6.11A is less than the upper shaded area.

Any c_1 such that

$$\max_{\{I_2\}} \; [c_1 - \phi(I_2)c_0]Q(c_1) \leq 0 \qquad (A.58)$$

deters entry. We denote the largest c_1 for which this is true by c_1^{d*}. c_1^{d*} is the highest cost for the first firm such that it does not pay the second

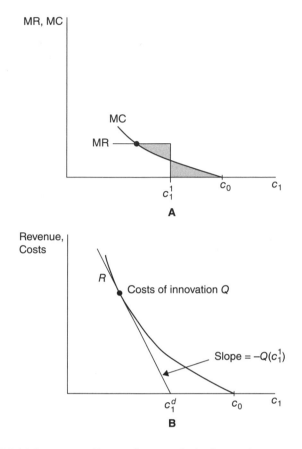

Figure 6.11 Multiple entrants; Bertrand; nonexclusive innovations

A. If there are two potential entrants, and the first entrant engages in R & D so that costs are c_1^1, then the second will engage in a faster pace of innovation, provided it pays the second to enter. B. By lowering costs enough, the first firm can deter the second firm from entering.

firm to enter. In figure 6.11B, we draw the total revenue curve *for the second entrant* and the total cost curve.[81] As figure 6.11B shows, even though at c_1^{d*} the first firm makes a profit (so it pays that firm to enter), it doesn't pay the second firm to enter. What matters is not profits today, but profits *after entry*.

Since the first firm knows this, it will choose the level of c_1 that maximizes profits given that it deters entry of the second firm. In other words, for a small innovation (where the threat of competition from the incumbent remains),

$$c_1 = \min \{c_1^{d*}, c_1^b\}, \tag{A.59}$$

where c_1^b is the Bertrand equilibrium described earlier, the solution to

$$-\phi'(I_1)Q(c_0)c_0 = 1. \tag{A.60}$$

3.4 *Cournot Equilibrium: Nonexclusivity*

With Cournot competition, profits after entry are markedly different than they are with Bertrand. Consider first the case of n innovators with small inventions, in which the incumbent continues to produce. Then the Cournot equilibrium will be described by the set of equations

$$p(Q_0 + Q_1) = c_i/(1 - \alpha_i/\eta), \tag{A.61}$$

$$p(Q_0 + Q_r) = c_0/(1 - (1 - \Sigma\alpha)/\eta), \tag{A.62}$$

where α_i is the share of output produced by the ith entrant. It is as if each firm perceives itself as facing a much more elastic demand curve — for small g, and just 2 entrants, a demand elasticity that is approximately 3 times that of the monopolist. While total output is higher, the output of each market participant is smaller, so that the marginal return to research is smaller.

In the case of the linear demand curves, we can describe the equilibrium simply:

$$Q = n(a - \bar{c}_1)/b(1 + n), \tag{A.63}$$

$$p = (a + n\bar{c}_1)/(1 + n), \tag{A.64}$$

$$Q_i = (a - \bar{c}_1)/(1 + n) + (\bar{c}_1 - c_i)/b, \tag{A.65}$$

$$\Pi_i = \{[(a - \bar{c}_1)/1 + n] + \bar{c}_1 - c_i\}^2/b - I_i, \tag{A.66}$$

where n is the number of firms ($n - 1$ the number of entrants) and

$$\bar{c}_1 = \Sigma j\, c_1^j / n,$$

and where c_1^j is the jth firm's (marginal) cost of production.

The ith firm maximizes with respect to $\{I_i, Q_i\}$

$$\Pi_i = (p - c_1^i)Q_i - I_i, \tag{A.67}$$

taking the level of output and investment in R & D of its rivals as given. I_i solves

$$-c_1^{i\prime} Q_i = 1. \tag{A.68}$$

Notice that since the output of *each* of the firms is smaller than under monopoly, the investment in R & D is lower. A set of $\{I_j, Q_j\}$ solving (A.63) and (A.68) is a Cournot-Nash innovation market equilibrium.

Consider the case of two innovating firms where the size of the innovation is sufficiently large to drive out the incumbent. Then by substituting (A.63) into (A.68), we can obtain a pair of equations in $\{I_1, I_2\}$:

$$-c_1^{\prime 1}[a - 2c_1^1 + c_1^2]/3b = 1 \tag{A.69a}$$

and

$$-c_1^{\prime 2}[a - 2c_1^2 + c_1^1)/3b = 1. \tag{A.69b}$$

Equation (A.69) gives rise to two symmetric reaction functions which are downward sloping.[82]

$$I^1 = F^1(I^2) \tag{A.70a}$$

and

$$I^2 = F^2(I^1). \tag{A.70b}$$

Figure 6.12 shows the Nash equilibria. (In figure 6.12A, the unique equilibrium is the symmetric equilibrium; in figure 6.12B, there exist asymmetric equilibria.)

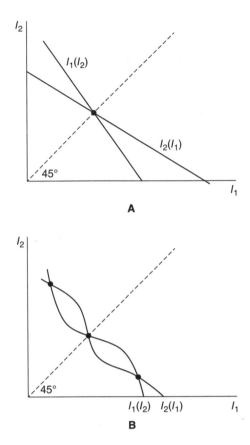

Figure 6.12 Multiple entrants; nonexclusive innovations; Cournot equilibrium

Given the level of investment of one firm, there is an optimal level of investment of the second firm. The interaction of the two reaction functions is the Cournot equilibrium. A. Unique symmetric equilibrium. B. There can be multiple equilibria.

Whether price goes up or down (whether consumer welfare is reduced or increased) when there are multiple entrants depends on whether the *competition effect* (from additional entry) outweighs *the innovation effect* (the adverse effect that arises because each firm anticipates selling less). That, in turn, depends on properties of the innovation function (how much does investment decrease as a result of a decrease in the marginal return to investment,[83] and by how much does innovation decrease with a decrease in investment).

3.5 *Cournot Equilibrium: Free Entry*

Next we focus on the symmetric equilibrium (assuming such an equilibrium exists). Entry occurs until (using A.66)

$$\Pi_i = \{[a - c_1^e(n)]/(1 + n)\}^2/b - I = 0, \qquad (A.71)$$

where (in the symmetric equilibrium) $c_1^e(n)$ is the equilibrium value of costs, c_1, when there are n entrants.[84] The equilibrium level of n, which we denote with n^e, is the solution to (A.71).[85]

Additional entry has a social benefit, in lowering prices, but diminishes aggregate profits. The marginal consumer benefit of additional entry is

$$V_p \, dp/dn = -Q \, dp/dn = Q[1/(1 + n)^2 - \partial c_1/\partial n]. \qquad (A.72)$$

Aggregate profits are $(p - c_1)Q(p) - nI$.

Ignoring distribution weights, we can write the change in the sum of the two (denoted by W) as

$$dW/dn = -Q \, dp/dn + \Pi_i + n(d \, \Pi_i)/dn \qquad (A.73)$$

$$= -Q \, dp/dn + nQ_i \, dp/dn + \Pi_i + n(\partial\Pi_i/\partial I_i)(\partial I_i/\partial n) \\ + n(p - c_1)(\partial Q_i/\partial n).$$

Since (in the symmetric equilibrium) $Q = nQ_i$, and $\partial\Pi_i/\partial I_i = 0$, (A.73) simplifies to

$$dW/dn = (p - c_1)Q_i[1 + d(\ln Q_i)/d(\ln n)] - I_i. \qquad (A.74)$$

"Normally" we expect

$$d(\ln Q)/d(\ln n) = d(\ln nQ_i)/d(\ln n) = 1 + d(\ln Q_i)/d(\ln n) > 0, \quad (A.75)$$

i.e., aggregate output increases with an increase in the number of firms. If investment in R & D per firm is not too large or the reduction in output of each firm is not too large, then welfare will be increased. But a *sufficient* condition for welfare to decrease is that aggregate output fall. Aggregate output can fall if, because the output of each firm falls, each invests less in R & D, and so c_1 increases.

Consider, for instance, our linear demand model. Then equilibrium investment in R & D is given by

$$-\phi'(a - c_1)/b(1 + n) = 1, \qquad (A.76)$$

which can be rewritten as

$$-\phi'(a - c_1) = b(1 + n). \qquad (A.77)$$

The right-hand side of (A.77) increases with n, while the left-hand side may increase or decrease in I, depending on properties of the innovation function ϕ. If ϕ' were constant, c_1 would have to fall as n increased. But if

$$-\phi''(a - c) + c_0\phi'^2 < 0, \qquad (A.78)$$

then the left-hand side of (A.74) would decrease with I, so that higher n means a lower I and a higher c_1. In particular, if ϕ'' is large enough (i.e., the marginal return to investment in R & D decreases fast enough), then an increase in n leads to a decrease in I_i and an increase in c_1 and, if this effect is large enough, to a decrease in aggregate Q and welfare. The marginal entrant has a negative effect on social welfare.

3.6 *Cournot Equilibrium: Exclusivity*

With exclusivity, only one of the potential innovators will be able to produce, and the Cournot equilibrium will be that described above in "Ex Post Competition," except the expected marginal (and average) return is diminished by a factor of $1/(n - 1)$, where $n - 1$ is the number of innovators. In this case, additional entry into innovation reduces the pace of innovation, without any gain in an increase in competitiveness of the product market (as in the previous subsection). Entry occurs until the expected average return is zero, entailing a slower pace of innovation and a higher level of aggregate (duplicative) research into innovation than in the case of a single entrant.

4. Stochastic Outcomes

The most important insight of the previous section was that competition among innovators may not have the sanguine effects usually associated with Schumpeterian competition and that the results depend critically on the nature of ex post competition.

In this section, we show that these results are sensitive to assumptions concerning the nature of the stochastic process producing innovation. As we noted earlier, while the Poisson process greatly simplifies the analysis, it is not plausible or general. For instance, in many research projects, the probability of success (of achieving the breakthrough) is (in any time interval) initially low, then increases. However, there is a time T beyond which, if success has not been achieved, the probability of success in each subsequent time interval decreases—one is pursuing a dead end. The Poisson model assumes a constant probability of success per unit time, with failure in previous periods having no implication for the likelihood of success in later periods.

4.1 *Bertrand Competition, Stochastic Research*

We simplify by assuming (as before) a fixed period of innovation and that there is a probability β of success, unaffected by the level of investment, but if the research project "succeeds," the marginal cost of production is $\phi(I)c_0$. The more investment in R & D, the lower the marginal cost of production. We assume two firms and that the success of the two different firms is uncorrelated. This implies that there is some social benefit from additional entry.

There are four possible outcomes: both firms succeed (probability β^2); neither succeeds (probability $[1 - \beta]^2$); firm 1 succeeds, while firm 2 fails; and vice versa (each with probability $\beta[1 - \beta]$). When both succeed, with Bertrand competition, the profit of the firm with the higher costs is zero, and the profit of the firm with the lower costs is $c_0 Q(\phi_i c_0)(\phi_i - \phi_j)$, where i is the higher cost firm and j the lower cost firm, provided the two costs are not too different (i.e., the price is set by the higher cost firm, and the lower cost firm gets the differential cost as its rent). Hence, for small innovations, the *marginal* return to increased investment in R & D is

$$-\beta\phi'c_0[\beta Q(\phi c_0) + (1-\beta)Q(c_0)] \quad \text{for } I_1 > I_2, \qquad (A.79)$$

$$-\beta\phi'c_0(1-\beta)Q(c_0) \quad \text{for } I_1 < I_2.$$

In other words, if the firm invests less than its rival, it only produces when the other firm fails in its research project. For $I_1 > I_2$, the marginal return is lowered by the fact that success is not guaranteed ($\beta < 1$), but increased by the fact that the output, against which costs are lower, has increased because of competitive pressures. But note that the first effect would be present for a monopolist (i.e., its marginal return would be $-\beta\phi'c_0 Q[\phi c_0]$).

There is a discontinuity in marginal returns at $I_2 = I_1$, i.e., at $c_1 = c_1(I_1)$. A careful look at the profit function, illustrated in figure 6.13, shows that if one firm chooses an investment level that leads to costs c_1, the other firm must have a cost level that is lower or greater than c_1: There cannot

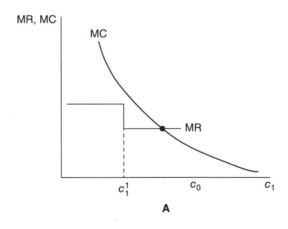

A

Figure 6.13 Bertrand competition; stochastic research

The only equilibria entail asymmetries—the second entrant either engages in more or less research than the first. A. The second entrant engages in less research. B. The second entrant engages in more research. C. There are two local optima that have to be compared. If the upper shaded area is larger than the lower one, the second entrant engages in more research.

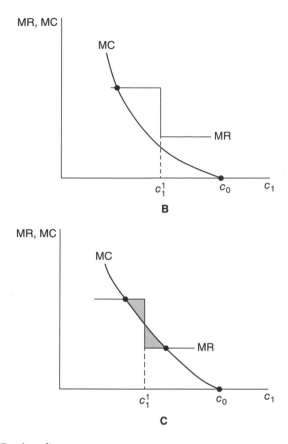

Figure 6.13 (Continued)

exist a symmetric equilibrium. If $c_2 > c_1$, then when both firms are successful, only the first firm produces, and conversely if the reverse inequality holds. The second firm does less research than the monopoly firm (the marginal return to research is reduced by a factor of β); the first firm does more than the monopoly firm (evident from equation (A.79)).

Hence, in this case, competition in innovation leads to faster innovation on two accounts: (a) one of the duopoly firms engages in more research, because the possibility that both firms are successful leads to a higher level of output *for the firm which is most successful*; and (b) there is a higher probability of success of at least one firm.

The increase in probability of success is

$$\Delta P = 1 - (1 - \beta)^2 - \beta = \beta(1 - \beta) > 0 \text{ so long as } 0 < \beta < 1. \quad \text{(A.80)}$$

ΔP is small if β is either very small or very large (but reaches a maximum at .5).[86]

Similar reasoning shows that *the larger the number of firms, the faster the pace of innovation.* (These arguments for why competition in the innovation market leads to more innovation are quite different from those in the contestability literature.)

4.2 *Random Cost Reductions*

But these results are, in a sense, "knife-edge." They depend critically on the result that, if one firm invests more in R & D, it becomes the low-cost provider, with probability 1. In practice, there is some randomness in cost reduction; i.e., with an investment of I^j, the cost of production next period is

$$c_0 \phi(I^j) + \varepsilon^j, \qquad (\text{A.81})$$

where, say, ε^j are independently and identically distributed, with $E(\varepsilon^j) = 0$.

Then, with two firms, the probability that any one firm will be the low-cost provider in a symmetric equilibrium (where all invest the same amount) is $1/2$, and the marginal return to increased investment is (approximately)

$$-\beta \phi' c_0 [\beta Q(\phi c_0)/2 + (1 - \beta)Q(c_0)]. \qquad (\text{A.82})$$

We now need to distinguish three situations: that where the rival is not successful, that where the rival is successful and has a higher cost, and that where the rival is successful and has a lower cost. In the latter case, the marginal return to cost reduction is zero. $1 - \beta$ is again the probability that the other firm has a higher cost because it is not successful. But if the other firm is successful but has higher costs (which occurs with probability $\beta/2$), the price is determined by the rival's marginal cost, which is (approximately) ϕc_0. But lowering one's own costs yields a return only in those states where one succeeds in having a lower cost than one's rival, i.e., in the symmetric equilibrium, only half the time. Hence, the marginal returns to innovation are reduced markedly.

Hence, compared to the monopoly, the marginal returns to investment in cost reduction are reduced provided

$$\beta Q(\phi c_0)/2 + (1 - \beta)Q(c_0) < Q(c_0), \qquad (A.83)$$

i.e., provided

$$Q(\phi c_0)/2 < Q(c_0). \qquad (A.84)$$

This will always be the case, so long as the magnitude of cost reduction $[1 - \phi]$ and the elasticity of demand are not too large, i.e., (using a Taylor series expansion), so long as $g < 1/\eta$, the same condition that we derived earlier (A.38) that the innovation be small.

Not surprisingly, if the variance of ε is small, while we smooth the kink in the profit function for, say, the second firm at the expected costs of the first firm, c_1, we don't eliminate the nonconvexity, so a symmetric equilibrium cannot exist. With a large enough variance of ε, however, there can be a symmetric equilibrium.[87]

Similar results hold for n firms, where now, the probability that the firm is the only successful firm is $(1 - \beta)^{n-1} < \beta(1 - \beta)$, and the probability that the firm is the lowest-cost provider among the successful firms is

$$\beta^2(1 - \beta)^{n-2}/2 + \beta^3(1 - \beta)^{n-3}/3 \ldots .$$

It follows that the marginal returns to investment in cost reduction decrease as n increases: More competition leads to a lower level of investment by each firm in cost reduction.

As n increases, there is a slightly higher probability of at least one successful project. (The probability with n firms is $1 - [1 - \beta]^n$.) Thus, letting $\phi(n)$ denote the (expected) cost reduction with n competing innovators given that an innovator is successful, the expected cost reduction is approximately $[1 - \phi(n)][1 - (1 - \beta)^n]$. We have shown that there is a presumption that as n increases, incentives for cost reduction are reduced; the magnitude of the reduction in costs is a function of the elasticity of ϕ'. With a high elasticity, a small change in incentives leads to a large decrease in investment, more than offsetting the effect on the increased probability of at least one success.

In short, it can be shown that as n increases, the pace of innovation may monotonically decrease. Alternatively, there can be (as is often asserted in the literature on Schumpeterian competition) an inverted U-shaped relationship, first increasing (with the benefit of the increased probability of success initially offsetting the disadvantage of reduced innovation incentives) and then decreasing.

4.3 *Potential Competition with Cournot*

Consider now the situation where there are two potential entrants; as in the previous subsection, success is not guaranteed. The interesting case is that where both entrants are successful and both firms produce. If they are successful on a large innovation, then the incumbent is driven out, but the two new firms share the market. By the above analysis, the marginal return to cost reductions is lower than it would be if either totally dominated the market. But matters are even worse in the case of a smaller innovation, where three firms will produce. Straightforward calculations show that the marginal returns to innovation (cost reductions) in these states of nature are markedly lower.

Incentives are different from what they would be if there were only one potential entrant only in the event that both firms succeed, which occurs (assuming the likelihood of success is independent) with probability β^2. (Note that if the likelihood of success of the two innovators is highly correlated, then the benefit of two researchers is decreased, and the likelihood of both succeeding is increased. Thus, if they are perfectly correlated, there is no increase in the likelihood of success, and, with probability 1, when there is success, the market will be characterized by duopoly.)

For simplicity, assuming that the innovation is large enough that the incumbent firm exits, then in the state where both succeed, the *decrease* in the marginal return to investing in cost reductions depends, as we noted in our earlier discussion, on how we formulate the game. If each firm takes the investment in R & D and output of rivals as given, then the change in the marginal return to innovation is equal to the difference in the output between the monopoly firm $(a - c_1)/2b$ and a duopoly $(a - c_1)/3b$, i.e., $(a - c_1)/6b$. In the case of the two-stage game, where the firms, in the first stage (investing in R & D), understand the consequences of changes in costs on their market share in the second, the reduction in marginal incentives is $2(a - c_1)/9$.

In short, an increase in competition in potential entry will result in markedly lower incentives to innovate. But, of course, with more firms engaged in research, it is more likely that one of the firms will be successful. Straightforward calculations verify that whether more (potential) competition leads to an increase or decrease in the (expected) pace of innovation depends on the responsiveness of the levels of investment in R & D to a lowering of incentives to innovate, in comparison to the improvement in the likelihood of success (given by (A.80)).

The change in the magnitude of cost reduction depends on the magnitude of the reduction in incentives, which in turn depends on the likelihood of the state in which both firms succeed occurring, β^2; and on the responsiveness of innovation to incentives, which in turn depends in part on the elasticity of ϕ'. If the elasticity is high, a large change in marginal incentives gives rise to a small change in investment in R & D and, if ϕ' is not too large, a small change in the pace of innovation. Then the effect of entry on ΔP dominates. But if innovation is highly responsive to marginal returns, the diminution in incentives has effects that exceed the benefits from the increase in P.

Thus, in a Cournot equilibrium, an increase in innovation competition can lead to a lower pace of innovation if (a) the likelihood of success of any innovation is very large, or the likelihood of one firm succeeding is highly correlated with that of another; and (b) the elasticity of ϕ' with respect to I is large, so that a relatively small change in incentives leads to a large change in investment in R & D.

4.4 *Entry*

The discussion in this section so far has assumed that the number of potential competitors is fixed at n, and we have analyzed the effect on the pace of innovation as n changes. But, of course, n should be viewed as endogenous.[88] As n increases, the expected profit of each firm diminishes, and there is thus a maximum value of n, n_{max}.[89] For $n > n_{max}$, some firms choose $I = 0$, in equilibrium; i.e., they choose not to compete.

If there are no barriers to entry, such that the research technology is freely available,[90] then of course n will increase so that n^*, the equilibrium number of active innovators, equals n_{max}. There is no presumption that the pace of innovation is maximized at n^*. In the case of highly correlated research outcomes, high probabilities of success in innovation, or a high elasticity of innovation, the presumption is that there will be excessive entry into innovation—in the sense that the level of innovation is lower than it would be with fewer innovators. The extent to which this is the case may be worse with Cournot competition than with the more intense Bertrand competition.

5. Strategic Behavior: Deterring Entry and Competitiveness

There are strong reasons to believe that the incumbent firm has the ability and incentives to continue its dominance of the market. Moreover, firms that engage in research can undertake actions which deter the entry of others.

5.1 *The Advantages of Incumbency and Deterrence*

Not all the knowledge that is gained as part of a cost reduction is available to others, even at the expiration of the patent. This may be particularly true of "learning by doing" (Arrow 1962a). Not only is production enhanced by experience, but so is research. The incumbent is likely to have a competitive advantage in R & D. Moreover, it has enhanced incentives for R & D: An entrant will typically have to share the market with the incumbent.[91] Moreover, if the incumbent deters entry, it can garner for itself the monopoly profits. Even without a competitive advantage in research, the incumbent has an incentive to deter entry.

In earlier sections, we explored the notion of the consequences of competition for entry. Even if there are many potential entrants, and even if there are significant profits, entry may not occur. As we have noted, a potential entrant looks not at profits as they are today, but as they would be after entry. If there is intense competition after entry, profits may be driven down so low that it does not pay to enter. In this peculiar sense, the threat of intense competition acts as an entry barrier (Stiglitz 1987a; Farrell 1986).

Consider, for the moment, a nonstochastic research process. Then, in Bertrand competition, any level of investment for which profits are greater than zero could not be an equilibrium, because another firm could enter with greater investment, yielding lower costs. (This was the contestability equilibrium discussed earlier.) But if the incumbent could engage in research (and had a research function at least as good as the best of the rivals), then (if the innovation step is not too large) it would pay the incumbent to invest slightly more than that amount, deterring entry.[92] The profit function is illustrated in figure 6.14. (In the absence of the threat of entry, the incumbent would have invested less than I^d, the entry-deterring level.)

But if there is randomness to research outcomes, if one firm (possibly the incumbent) engages in research at an intensity to generate positive profits, were a rival to engage in research at the same intensity, its expected revenues would be at most only half of that of the first firm's (if each is successful half the time, and only when the other is not successful), and it might accordingly not pay the second firm to enter.

Thus, for instance, the incumbent firm can deter any other firm from entering if it chooses an investment level I^0, such that

$$\pi^e(I^0) \equiv \max_{\{I^e\},} \pi^e(I^e, I^0) \le 0,$$

where π^e is the profits of the entrant, and I^e is the entrant's investment. We let $I^{e*}\{I^d\}$ be the profit-maximizing level of the entrant's investment, given the level of investment of the incumbent. The minimum

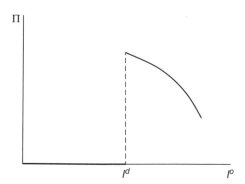

Figure 6.14 Entry deterrence

By investing in I^d, the incumbent deters entry. With less intensive ex post competition (e.g., that associated with Cournot), the entry-deterring level of investment is higher, and so the pace of innovation is higher.

value of I^0 for which $I^{e*}\{I^0\} = 0$ is denoted by I^d. Then I^0 is chosen to maximize

$$\pi^d(I),$$

subject to the constraint that that $I^0 \geq I^d$. π^d is the profits of the incumbent. The maximized value of π^d will, in general, be strictly positive.

We note that the profit functions themselves depend on the nature of ex post competition. Thus, if there is Cournot competition, profits of the entrant are higher, so entry is more desirable, and the entry-deterring level of innovation by the incumbent is higher. Hence, we obtain the somewhat paradoxical result that *with entry deterrence, less intense ex post competition may result in higher levels of innovation.* (This contrasts with the earlier result that when there *is* entry, Cournot equilibrium results in lower levels of innovation.)

5.2 *Limits on Entry Deterrence*

Entry does occur, and it often comes from new technologies, in which the incumbent does not have a comparative advantage.[93] Xerox was, for instance, faced with competition using a quite different technology from that which it had mastered. In these cases, the incumbent may not be able to fully deter entry, but it can still extend its market dominance by discouraging others' research.

In assessing the marginal return to further research, an entrant has to assess the likelihood that its technology will pay off—producing a competitive product at a lower cost of production. (In a more general model, producing a product that is sufficiently different from that of the incumbent that there is sufficient demand to compensate it for the cost of R & D.) The incumbent can discourage others' research—and sometimes even deter entry—by investing more in its own research, lowering the (expected) marginal returns to that of others.

If the incumbent succeeds in doing so, it acts as an unconstrained monopolist, earning, as we have noted, considerably higher profits than in the case of the constrained monopolist. It may be that at the optimum level of research for the unconstrained monopolist, entry is deterred. If not, the monopolist must compare the profits it earns if it undertakes enough further research to deter entry—resulting in a level of research that may even be higher than the social optimum—with the profits it earns (in expected value) with (potential) entry. Which is higher depends on the discount rate, the elasticity of the R & D function, the elasticity of the demand function, and the response of (potential) entrants to lower expected returns (i.e., on the elasticity of their R & D functions). It will be easier to discourage entry if success of rivals' research is highly correlated with that of the incumbent.

5.3 *Limiting the Impact of Entry*

In the last subsection, we showed that even if the incumbent can't preclude entry entirely, it can discourage entry. The incumbent can also limit the impact of entry by discouraging investment by entrants and therefore the competitive threat from entry. To see this even more forcefully—and to see why innovation markets may well not be contestable—we assume that the incumbent cannot "succeed" itself. We assume that there are a large number of potential entrants, but we model the "game" as a multistage game. In the first stage, one firm enters (say, chosen randomly from the pool of potential innovators), announces certain research plans, and takes certain actions ("commitments"). In the second, another firm can enter. In the third, the first firm can exit. In subsequent stages, other firms can enter and exit, plans are fully executed, the research results are realized, and production occurs.

The entrant, in the first stage, is aware of how other entrants will behave in subsequent stages. It will take actions that will attempt to ensure that subsequent entrants will not take actions that would induce him to leave. To see what this entails, we use a variant of the model employed in the section on stochastic outcomes. Assume the first mover has investment I_1. The expected profit of the second mover is

$$\max \Pi_2(I_1) \equiv \max \{0, \beta \max[\{\beta(c_1 - c_2)Q(c_1), 0\}$$
$$+ (1 - \beta)(c_0 - c_2)Q(c_0)] - I\} \equiv \Pi_2^*(I_1),$$

It is easy to show that as I_1 increases, the optimum value of I_2 decreases. Let $I_2^*(I_1)$ be the reaction function, and let I_1^{**} be the minimum value of I_1 such that $I_2^* = 0$; i.e., every other entrant is deterred. Then, the first entrant chooses I_1 to max Π_1 subject to the constraint that $I_1 \geq I_1^{**}$.

As we noted earlier, the first entrant can earn positive profits and still deter entry. The second entrant's profits are markedly lower than the first entrant's profits (assuming that the first entrant remains a monopoly).

But the first entrant does not have to invest this full amount to deter entry. All that it needs to do is "sink" enough costs to persuade the second entrant that it will not leave, should the second firm enter. Denoting by Π_1^d the (maximized) duopoly profits of the first firm, and by R_1^d and I_1^d the corresponding revenues and investment, respectively, the first firm will not leave so long as

$$ R_1^d - (I_1^d - I_1^s) \geq 0, $$

where I_1^s is the "sunk" research costs, spent in the first period, so $I_1^d - I_1^s$ is the incremental expenditures and $R_1^d - (I_1^d - I_1^s)$ is the net revenues from staying in the market. By sinking enough, it is clear that the first firm makes a credible commitment not to leave. In general, the first firm does not have to sink the entire amount I_1^{**} — entry deterrence does not require the acceleration of investment in R & D to the extent suggested by full contestability. Moreover, the "first" innovation firm can earn positive profits and still deter entry. A fortiori, the incumbent firm can still earn positive profits and deter entry.[94]

There are other instruments available for deterring and discouraging entry and for limiting the effectiveness of competition should there be entry. Assume that β_M, the success probability of the monopolist, can be increased by an increase in research expenditures. To delineate these "success probability" expenditures from cost-lowering research expenditures, we denote them by I_β. The monopolist (in the simple two-period model) in the absence of competition would choose I_β to maximize

$$ \beta(I_\beta)\Pi(\phi c_0) - I - I_\beta, $$

so

$$ \beta'(I_\beta)\Pi = 1. $$

But now, the expected profits of a potential new entrant are, letting the subscript 1 denote the incumbent (monopolist) and subscript 2 denote the (potential) entrant,

$$\max \Pi_2 \equiv \max \{0, \beta_2 \max[\{\beta_1(c_1 - c_2)Q(c_1), 0\}$$
$$+ (1 - \beta_1)(c_0 - c_2)Q(c_0)] - I\}$$

$$\equiv \Pi_2^* (I_1, \beta_1).$$

Define $I_1^{**}(\beta_1)$ as the minimum value of I_1 such that, with $\beta = \beta_1$, $\Pi_2^* = 0$. Provided $I_1 \geq I_1^{**}(\beta_1)$, there will be no entry. $\{I_1, \beta_1\}$ is chosen to maximize Π_1 subject to $I_1 \geq I_1^{**}(\beta_1)$.

There is no clear relationship between the social return to increasing β and the private return.

6. Monopoly Innovator

In this and the next three sections, we extend the monopoly to the context of an infinite-period model. This is essential, because each innovator is part of an infinite chain, affecting producers that precede and follow. A central objective of this appendix is to explore these intertemporal spillovers. Yet we should emphasize that in order to formulate such a model, we have to employ parameterizations which are very special—the special nature of which has been demonstrated in the discussion of the preceding sections. While the analysis is useful in exposing certain intertemporal externalities, some of the more precise results may be sensitive to the particular parameterizations employed.[95]

A monopoly innovator would maximize $\Sigma \Pi^t \delta^t$, where δ is the discount factor. We assume constant elasticity demand functions,[96]

$$Q = zp^{-\eta}, \tag{A.85}$$

with demand elasticity equal (in absolute value) to η and that the innovation function each period is the same (i.e., the costs of reducing costs by a given percentage from a baseline of a lower cost level are exactly the same as the costs of reducing costs by the same percentage from a baseline of a higher cost level).[97] This means that whatever policy is optimal at time t is optimal at $t + 1$. This means in turn that we can write the present discounted value (PDV) of profits as equal to[98]

$$V = kc_0^{1-\eta}\phi_1^{1-\eta}[1 + \delta(\phi_2^{1-\eta} + \delta(\phi_3^{1-\eta} + \delta(\phi_4^{1-\eta} \ldots] \\ - (I_1 + \delta I_2 + \delta^2 I_3 \ldots), \qquad (A.86)$$

where $k = z(\eta - 1)^{\eta-1}\eta^{-\eta}$.

In steady state,

$$V^* = kc_0^{1-\eta}\phi^{*1-\eta}/[1 - \delta\phi^{*1-\eta}] - I^*/(1 - \delta) \qquad (A.87)$$

$$= R^*/[1 - \delta\phi^{*1-\eta}] - I^*/(1 - \delta),$$

where R^* is the (optimized) level of net revenues (i.e., sales minus costs of production).

Maximizing V with respect to, say, I_1 yields.

$$\partial V_1/\partial I_1 = \partial\Pi_1/\partial I_1 + \delta\,\partial V_2/\partial I_1 = 0 \qquad (A.88)$$

where V_t is the PDV of profits as of time t. The monopolist realizes that lowering costs today increases profits not just today but in future periods and takes this into account. Hence, there will be a higher level of investment than there would be with the myopic monopolist described earlier.[99,100]

It immediately follows that

$$c^{ts} > c^{tmp} > c^{tp}, \qquad (A.89)$$

where c^{tp} are the marginal costs of production of the nonmyopic monopolist at time t. This result obviously does not depend on the particular parameterization we have employed.

6.1 *The Constrained Monopolist*

The above analysis assumed that the monopolist was unconstrained by competitive entry. The nature of the competitive constraints imposed on the monopolist depends on how knowledge diffuses and the intellectual property regimes. Assume, for instance, that at time $t + 1$, the monopolist's technology as of time t becomes freely available and there is Bertrand competition, as in the model of section 1.1. Then for small innovations, the PDV of monopoly profits is given by[101]

$$V = c_0^{1-\eta} z[(1 - \phi_1) + \delta\phi_1^{1-\eta}[(1 - \phi_2) + \delta\phi_2^{1-\eta}[(1 - \phi_3) + \ldots]$$
$$- (I_1 + \delta I_2 + \delta^2 I_3 \ldots), \qquad (A.90)$$

which, in steady state, implies that

$$V^* = c_0^{1-\eta} z(1 - \phi^*)/1 - \delta\phi^{*1-\eta} - I^*/(1 - \delta) \qquad (A.91)$$

$$= R^*/1 - \delta\phi^{*1-\eta} - I^*/(1 - \delta),$$

as before. Optimizing, say, with respect to I_1 yields an equation identical to that derived earlier, but now the marginal return to further spending on R & D is

$$\phi' c_0 Q(p^{mc}),$$

where p^{mc} is the price charged by the *constrained* monopolist, which is less than (for small innovations) that charged by the unconstrained monopolist. But this means, in turn, that the marginal return to investments in R & D is higher: The constrained monopolist has a higher level of innovation. Thus, letting c^{tmc} be the costs of the constrained monopolist at time t,

$$c^{ts} > c^{tmp} > c^{tp} > c^{tmc}.$$

Once again, we see that the effect of a change (here, moving from a unconstrained monopoly to a constrained monopoly) can lead to lower profits but increased marginal return to innovation.

6.2 *Contestability*

It is not apparent, however, whether the monopoly level of innovation is greater or less than the contestability level of innovation. At a very high discount rate, the monopolist acts effectively as if it were myopic. Then contestability leads to a higher level of innovation. But at a very low discount rate, the marginal value of more innovation becomes very large, so that the level of innovation with persistent monopoly is higher.

One might wonder: because contestability involves zero profits, how could the level of innovation be greater than that which generates zero profits? But remember, under contestability with a sequence of successive monopolists, each monopolist is constrained in the price it charges by competition from the incumbent. The monopolist that preempts its rivals is not so constrained.[102]

7. Socially Optimal Innovation

While the level of innovation under Schumpeterian competition (under the "contestability equilibrium") may be lower or higher than under a pure monopolist, there is some presumption that in either case, it is less than would occur under the social optimum. It is, in fact, easy to calculate the socially optimal level of innovation. Let W^t be the present discounted value of utility as of t, derived from the production of good i in a symmetric equilibrium with m products, so that each has $1/m$th of the labor force, which for convenience we normalize at m and assume to be fixed in supply. We assume a one-period utility function of the form

$$(1/m)\; \Sigma\; C_i^a/a, \qquad (A.92)$$

where $a = 1 - 1/\eta$, which gives rise to constant elasticity of demand functions, with elasticity equal to η.

The PDV of social welfare, W^t, is maximized by maximizing

$$aW^0 = H_0[((H(I_1)^a[(1 - I_1))^a + H_2^a \delta(1 - I_2)^a[1 + \ldots \quad (A.93)$$

$$= S^0 + \delta W^1,$$

where S^t is social welfare at time t; where we assume a fixed utility discount factor of δ; $H(I)$ is the output per unit of labor $= 1/[\phi(I)]$, when an amount of labor I is devoted to research; and where we renormalize W each period to the initial productivity of unity.[103,104] That is, innovation each period begins off the costs established in the previous period.

Because of our assumption of constant elasticity, optimal resource allocation at each date is identical, so[105],[106]

$$aW^* = [H(I^*)(1 - I^*)]^a/[1 - \delta H^a(I^*)]. \qquad \text{(A.94)}$$

I_0 (or, more generally, I_t) is chosen such that

$$\partial S_0/\partial I_0 + \delta\, \partial W^1/\partial I_0 = 0. \qquad \text{(A.95)}$$

The second term on the left-hand side represents the value of today's innovation on future welfare. If $\delta = 0$, there is no future value. Optimization with $\delta = 0$ is equivalent to maximizing short-run welfare, and it follows that for $\delta > 0$, I_0 is greater than the level of investment that maximizes one-period social welfare, which in turn is greater than or equal to the level of investment associated with our (one-period) monopolist (which pays no attention to the welfare of consumers).

We can easily characterize the optimal I^*. It is the solution to

$$h + [\delta H^a/(1 - \delta H^a)]ah = aI/(1 - I), \qquad \text{(A.96)}$$

where, it will be recalled, $h = d(\ln H)/d(\ln I)$ $[= -d(\ln \phi)/d(\ln I)]$.[107]

While both the monopolist and social welfare maximizer take into account the benefits of investments today in future productivity (lowering costs of production), the monopolist does not take into account the increase in consumer surplus. Even in the case of the constrained monopolist, where a lowering of c_1^t does not increase consumer surplus at time t (for small innovations), a lowering of c_1^t increases consumer surplus at time $t + 1$ and all subsequent dates.

This means that even if government can't eliminate the monopoly, societal welfare is increased if investments in R & D are subsidized.

8. An Alternative Formulation: Patent Races

There is a rather different set of models which focus not on the size of the innovation, but on the timing. More investment can lead to an earlier innovation. We assume the "step" is fixed, i.e., each innovation increases the output per unit labor by a factor H. We assume a deterministic model, but it is easy to extend the analysis to one in which innovations arrive by a Poisson process, where increased innovation in research increases the rate of arrival. For most of this section, we assume further that at the time the next step is made, knowledge about the previous step becomes de facto publicly available, so the previous price becomes the competitive benchmark. For simplicity, in this and the next section, we use a continuous time formulation.

8.1 *Sequential Monopoly*

Let T be the time of arrival of the next step, $T = T(I)$, $T' < 0$.[108] We will also use the inverse of T:

$$I = \tau(T), \tag{A.97}$$

giving the level of investment required to make the discovery at time T. $\tau' < 0$, $\tau'' > 0$.

Assume that the innovation steps are small. The discounted profits of the first innovator are given by (letting r be the interest rate)

$$\Pi = [e^{-rT1}(1 - \phi)Q(1)(1 - e^{-r(T2-T1)})/r] - I. \tag{A.98}$$

In other words, it doesn't get the profits until T_1, so they have to be discounted back to the time when the research starts, and the profits terminate when the next innovator brings its invention to the market. We normalize, assuming the initial cost of the product is unity and that the next innovator will enter the market at a given $\Delta \equiv T_2 - T_1$ after it succeeds. This model assumes that a particular innovator knows that it will be the successor; i.e., it is the monopoly successor. It knows that it won't be the *next* successor—it doesn't control T_2 (or more accurately Δ). Then T_1 is chosen to maximize Π. We denote by $R(T)$ the PDV of revenues. As figure 6.15 illustrates, $R(T)$ and τ are both convex functions, so there may be multiple local optima. We assume that the limit of $\tau(T)$ as T goes to zero is greater than $(1 - \phi)Q(1)(1 - e^{-r(T2-T1)})/r$ and the limit of $\tau(T)$ as T goes to infinity is strictly positive. Thus, the optimum entails a finite $T^* > 0$ and satisfies the first-order condition

$$-rT'e^{-rT1}(1 - \phi)Q(1)(1 - e^{-rT2})/r = 1. \tag{A.99}$$

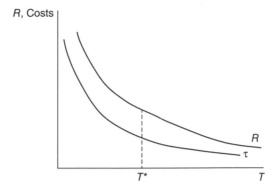

Figure 6.15 Optimal timing: Sequential monopoly

Both costs and PDV of revenues increase as research speed is increased. T^* is the point where (PDV of) Revenues – Costs are maximized.

With sequential monopoly, each monopolist knows that it will be succeeded by another. It has to form expectations about when it will be replaced. In the symmetric (time invariant) equilibrium, T^* is the solution to

$$-rT'e^{-rT^*}(1 - \phi)Q(1)(1 - e^{-rT^*})/r = 1,$$

or

$$I = -\varsigma \ln \lambda^*(1 - \phi)Q(1)(1 - \lambda)/r \qquad (A.100)$$

where $\varsigma \equiv d(\ln T)/d(\ln I)$ and where $\lambda = e^{-rT(I)} = \lambda(I)$. Under plausible assumptions, if, say, ς is a constant, it can be shown that there exists a unique solution to (A.100).

8.2 *Comparison with Persistent Monopolist*

In this model, later innovations reduce the value of earlier innovations, a negative externality which the (sequential) monopolists don't take into account. To see what this implies, let us denote the *gross* profits (i.e., not net of investments in innovation) associated with the tth innovation (i.e., the profits from the time of the tth innovation until the next innovation) by R^t. If each innovation reduces costs by a factor ϕ, then profits increase by a factor $\phi^{1-\eta}$.

The present discounted value of profits (for the succession of monopolists) is

$$V = \Sigma \ (\pi_t \lambda^t)(R^t - I_t), \qquad (A.101)$$

where

$$R^t = (1 - \phi_t)Q(c_0 \pi_t \phi_t)(1 - e^{-rT\{t+1,\, t\}})/r, \qquad (A.102)$$

where $\lambda^t = e^{-rT\{t,\, t-1\}}$, $T\{t, t-1\}$ is the length of time between innovation t and innovation $t + 1$,

$$\pi_t \lambda^t = \lambda^1 \lambda^2 \ldots \lambda^t.$$

and

$$\pi_t \phi_t = \phi_1 \ \phi_2 \ \phi_3 \ \phi_{4 \ldots \ldots} \phi_t$$

The steady-state values can be easily calculated as before. Indeed, exactly the same equation holds, replacing δ with λ:

$$\Pi^* = R^*/(1 - \lambda \phi^{*1-\eta}) - I^*/(1 - \lambda), \qquad (A.103)$$

where R^* is the present discounted value of revenue during the interval between innovations, Π^* is the present discounted revenue of monopoly profits, and where now ϕ has been fixed, and it is λ that is chosen. R^* is a slight modification of the earlier expression. For a small innovation,

$$R^* = \lambda c_0^{1-\eta} z[(1 - \phi)(1 - \lambda)/r] = \rho_s \chi. \qquad (A.104a)$$

For a large innovation, we can simply write,

$$R^* = \rho_L \chi, \qquad (A.104b)$$

where ρ_s is the *flow* of revenues for a small innovation, ρ_L for a large innovation, and

$$\chi = (1 - \lambda)/r \qquad (A.105)$$

is the PDV of those flows over the period between innovations. The PDV of the sum of all of the flows can then be simply written as

$$\chi \rho_i / (1 - \lambda \gamma), \qquad (\text{A.106})$$

where

$$\gamma = \phi^{1-\eta}. \qquad (\text{A.107})$$

In steady state, PDV of profits can thus be written as $[\rho_i (1 - \lambda) / r (1 - \lambda \gamma)] - I/(1 - \lambda)$

Choosing, say, I^1, to maximize the PDV of profits entails

$$-T'\lambda\rho(1 - 1/\gamma) - 1 - T'\lambda\rho/(1 - \lambda\gamma) = 0. \qquad (\text{A.108})$$

The first term is the gain from shortening the "high" cost initial period, the third term the benefit from moving forward in time all future profits. Equation (A.108) describes the optimal level of investment for a persistent monopolist, where ρ represents the flow of monopoly rents. It is clear from (A.108) that the higher ρ, the greater the benefit from accelerating research, and so the smaller T.

To contrast this with the optimization problem of the sequential monopolist, we rewrite the above equation as

$$-T'\lambda\rho(1 - \lambda) - 1 - T'\lambda\rho[(\lambda - 1/\gamma) + (1 - \lambda)/(1 - \lambda\gamma)]. \qquad (\text{A.109})$$

This equation highlights the two externalities noted by Aghion and Howitt (1992)(one of which was not present in the models of part 1): the business-stealing effect (always negative) and the benefits to future innovations (here, in moving them forward in time). In this model, it can be shown that the forward looking externality dominates.

But this does not give the full picture of the comparison of the persistent and sequential monopolist, for the returns to each during the period in which they are the monopolist are markedly different. The persistent monopolist earns a flow of returns (in, say, the first period) equal to $c_0 \phi Q[(c_0 \phi)/(1 - 1/\eta)]/(\eta - 1)$, while the sequential monopolist earns (for small innovations) a flow of returns equal to $c_0(1 - \phi)Q(c_0)$, which is unambiguously smaller. While there is some profit stealing, most of what occurs is "profit destruction." Hence, even when the business stealing effect exceeds the PDV of benefits to future producers, the sequential monopolist may innovate less than the persistent monopolist.

In addition, the monopolist (whether persistent or serial) also ignores the benefits to consumers of the succession of (earlier) lower prices, which is positive.

8.3 *Competitive Entry and Entry Deterrence*

The analysis of competitive entry and entry deterrence follows much along the lines of previous sections. Consider, for instance, the case with two firms and nonstochastic outcomes. Then if, say, the incumbent, has chosen a speed with success at T_M, an entrant who attempted to beat the incumbent to the patent would earn returns of $R(c_0)$ during the interval of time until the incumbent was successful and zero thereafter (assuming that the entrant's innovation does not preclude that of the incumbent, e.g., because of IPR). By shortening T_M, the profit function of the entrant is shifted down, and there exists a T^D, such that for $T \leq T^D$, there is no level of investment in R & D such that the entrant can make profits: there is full deterrence.

Markedly different results are obtained if the entrant's patent excludes that of the incumbent. For then, there is a discontinuity in the profit function depending on whether the entrant wins the patent race (has $T < T^M$, the time of discovery of the new process by the monopolist) or not. The profit function for the entrant is drawn in figure 6.16, where there is a discontinuity at T^M. The entrant chooses T just less than T^M. As T^M increases to, say, $T^{M'}$, the incumbent's profit function shifts down. In that case, the incumbent would have to accelerate its research markedly, to T^{Md}, to preempt its rival.[109]

Earlier analyses explain why it would always be profitable for the incumbent to preempt the rival, so long as its cost function for innovation is at least as good as that of the entrant—and that is the case here, so long as the incumbent's innovation function is at least as "good" as that of the entrant.

Earlier we explained why the incumbent (or the first entrant into a patent race) can deter competitors, even without investing as much as the above discussion would suggest. Fudenberg, Gilbert, Tirole, and Stiglitz (1983) have analyzed a patent race where the contestants can observe the "position" of rivals. In a patent race, those behind only need to know (believe) that those that are ahead could and would respond to any attempt to catch up and leapfrog by accelerating the pace of their

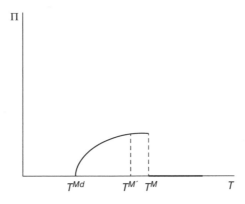

Figure 6.16 Deterrence

If the incumbent invests in research so that the innovation arrives at T^M, an entrant could make profits (with exclusivity) by beating the incumbent. Profits are depicted as diminishing the more the entrant accelerates research (i.e., the lower T), so profits are maximized by *just* beating the incumbent. If the incumbent increases research to reduce T^M, the entrant's maximum profits are reduced. There is a fast enough pace, T^{Md}, such that it would not pay rivals to enter.

research. Again, it's not the current research levels that matter, but the research levels that would then prevail. Hence, the incumbent need only establish a sufficient lead over potential rivals that should they enter, it could accelerate its research program to capture the patent.[110] In limiting cases, the incumbent can deter entry by accelerating its research program only a little.

8.4 Discouraging Investment in R & D

With stochastic research and differential research functions, it may not be possible to fully deter entry, but the incumbent can discourage entry and discourage research among those who do enter. Any discouragement of R & D by rivals extends the expected life of the monopolist's dominance and (except in the case of perfect substitutes with Bertrand competition) enhances the incumbent's post-entry profitability. As before, deterrence can sometimes be achieved with only limited alteration of the unconstrained monopolist's optimal research strategy.

9. Optimal Timing and Size of Innovation

In this section, we combine the insights of earlier sections, allowing firms to simultaneously choose the size of the step (ϕ) and the speed of innovation (T). Assume that by delaying innovation, one can lower the cost of any given innovation, i.e., the innovation function is of the form $H(I, T)$, where T is the time since the last innovation, with $H_T > 0$.

The long-run (persistent) monopolist now optimizes with respect to both T and I. It chooses the level of investment in R & D and the frequency of innovation. If there were no nonconvexities in the innovation process, innovations would be continuous. It is nonconvexities that give rise to "steps," i.e., episodic innovations. The monopolist realizes that if it hurries innovation, costs increase disproportionately.

The analysis for the sequential monopolist follows closely on the lines of the previous sections. There are some important interaction effects. Because the return to earlier innovation to the sequential monopolist is likely to be smaller than for the persistent monopolist, T will be longer (longer intervals between innovation), and the marginal benefits from undertaking larger steps will be greater. But there is no presumption that the second effect outweighs the first; the pace of innovation is likely to be slower, for all the reasons set forth in the previous section.

The more interesting question is posed by contestable markets, where there are multiple potential entrants. Take the standard contestability framework, where the first entrant cannot engage in entry deterrence for subsequent entrants, just as the incumbent can't. Assume, further, that the entry of a firm precludes the rivals from getting the patent (as opposed to the case where there are multiple processes by which costs could be reduced). That is, once one firm wins the race, the next round of the race starts from the new base. Prior research is, in effect, of no value.[111]

Assume, for the moment, that there is a single entrant, that believes that once it makes a discovery, there will be another innovation T^* later. Consider the set of zero profit $\{T^*, I\}$, i.e.,

$$\lambda(1 - \lambda)Q(1)[1 - 1/H(I, T)]/r = I. \qquad (A.110)$$

T^e is the smallest value of T for which there exists some I for which (A.110) is satisfied.[112] T^e is the contestable time of entry. Assume, to the contrary, that there were a steady-state contestable equilibrium with $T^* > T^e$. If an entrant were to choose $T < T^*$ and maximized profits, assuming future entry intervals were unchanged, it could earn positive profits, and thus it would be worthwhile for the entrant to break the equilibrium. The only value of T for which that is not true is T^e, for, by definition, there is no faster innovation which breaks even.[113]

Once the consequence of the "rush" for innovation is taken into account, *it is not even apparent that Schumpeterian competition leads to a high speed of innovation,* say, compared with a persistent monopolist, let alone the level of innovation which is welfare maximizing (to be discussed shortly). The average pace of innovation (improvements in productivity per unit of time) is approximately

$$H(I, T)/T.$$

The rush for innovation leads to an inefficient innovation process.[114]

A persistent, entry-deterring monopolist will choose $\{I^M, T^M\}$ to maximize the PDV of its profits:

$$\max_{\{I, T\}} \lambda^M (1 - \lambda^M) Q(1)[1 - 1/H(I, T)]/r - I, \qquad \text{(A.111)}$$

subject to the constraint that entry is deterred. In the case of *exclusivity*, if $T^M > T^e$, an entrant could enter, preempt the research project of the incumbent, and be profitable. Hence, in the case of exclusivity, the PDV of profits has to be maximized subject to $T \leq T^e$.

But the $\{I, T\}$ strategy that deters entry may still leave the incumbent with positive profits, because, unconstrained by entry, it can charge the monopoly price.

With a slightly different innovation process, where there are different technologies for cost reduction (covered, say, by different patents), the payoff function looks markedly different. Now, even when the entrant comes in at a date after that of the monopolist, it may make a profit, if it costs are lower; and even if it comes in at a date before that of the monopolist, its profits may be very limited, since it may be able to earn those profits only over the short span of time until the monopolist makes its innovation.

For instance, in the case of nonexclusivity, an entrant that came in slightly before T^M would only get a return of $c_{t-1}[1 - 1/H(I, T)]Q(c_{t-1})$ over the interval $\{T, T^M\}$ and would get a return of

$$c_{t-1} \max \{0, 1/H(I^M, T^M) - 1/H(I, T))Q[c_{t-1}/H(I^M, T^M)]\}$$

over the remaining interval of its "domination," so that beating the incumbent slightly would yield negligible profits—not enough to compensate for the cost of investment. Hence, the incumbent can deter entry with a value of T that is slower than T^e, if the entrant takes the incumbent's value of $\{I, T\}$ as given.

The monopolist can deter entry not only by moving earlier than it otherwise would, but also by reducing costs more aggressively. If the incumbent has a better technology for cost reduction, this may be a particularly effective means of entry deterrence.

This analysis assumes ex post Bertrand competition. As before, if ex post there is Cournot competition, then it is harder to deter entry, since typically the entrant will share the market with the incumbent and "steal" some of its profits. Hence, to deter entry, the incumbent may have to accelerate the research process even more than in the case of Bertrand competition.

9.1 *Social Welfare Optimization*

The expression for W^* is identical to that derived earlier, but now we must take into account the fact that the discount factor has to reflect the delay in introducing the next innovation and the fact that the length of the period over which the particular innovation remains dominant is endogenous. We can rewrite the present discounted value of utility as

$$aW^* = \max \{(1 - \lambda)[H(I, T)(1 - I)]^a/r(1 - \lambda H^a)\}. \quad \text{(A.112)}$$

The first-order condition with respect to T can be written

$$[rT\lambda/(1 - \lambda)] + \xi + [\lambda H^a/(1 - \lambda H^a)](a\xi - rT) = 0, \quad \text{(A.113)}$$

where $\xi \equiv d(\ln H)/d(\ln T) > 0$. It should be obvious that optimality requires $T > a\xi/r$. Optimal timing takes into account the fact that if we "hurry" innovation, we get smaller innovations.

Concluding Comments

It has long been recognized that when technological change is endogenous, competitive markets may well not be efficient. Schumpeter suggested that the true virtue of a market economy was its innovativeness. There was a hope that what came to be called Schumpeterian competition might have some optimality properties, i.e., that it would produce, in some sense, an "optimal" level of investment in R & D. Competition for the market could replace competition in the market, with a succession of monopolists.

Earlier work cast some doubts on those hopes, by showing both that an incumbent monopolist had the means and incentives to maintain its monopoly position and that the level of innovation necessary to do that might indeed be limited.

The purpose of this appendix has been to cast further doubt on these hopes, but in ways that have rather ambiguous implications and that demonstrate a sensitivity of results to particular formulations and parameterizations. We have shown the key role played both by the nature of ex post competition (e.g., Cournot versus Bertrand) and the innovation process: How correlated are the successes of different researchers? Does a patent granted to one innovator at time T preclude the innovations of others, which would not be the case, for instance, if different researchers are pursuing different innovation strategies?[115]

We have also suggested caution concerning the special properties of commonly used parameterizations, which often played a key role in analytic tractability. The Poisson process, which is assumed in much of the literature, has nice mathematical properties but is very special. We have explored alternative specifications, with sometimes markedly different results.

So too, the assumption that the market is characterized by a sequence of monopolies is special. Even with large innovations, there are substitutes to the innovator's product that limit its market power. The magnitude of the innovation rents depends, however, critically on the market power that an innovator can exercise. Moreover, under quite general conditions, the incumbent firm is at an advantage (over potential entrants) in extending his monopoly power.

While the analysis has been complex, there are a few general precepts that emerge. One is that a change in the economic environment (say, the level or nature of competition) may have markedly different effects on average and marginal returns to innovation. And what matters for determining investments in research is the *marginal return.*

Second, we have catalogued a long list of ways in which private and social returns to innovation (and to entry) may differ, reinforcing the conclusion that there is no presumption concerning the efficiency of the market economy. This is true even though we have ignored here the important knowledge spillovers from one sector to another or from one firm to another.[116]

A third is that marginal private incentives for cost-reducing innovations (upon which we have focused) are related to the level of output *of the firm.* Under Cournot competition, with more firms coexisting, each typically produces less, and so innovation is lower—lower than it would be with a monopoly innovator. Schumpeter is, in this respect, correct.

With uncertainty, the expected marginal return diminishes with one's chances of becoming one of the surviving or dominant firms. However, in the presence of Bertrand competition, which forces prices down if one succeeds in becoming the dominant firm, the chance that a rival will succeed in lowering costs, but to a level that is still higher than one's own marginal cost, may actually cause the expected marginal return to increase.

Our analysis has focused on analyzing innovation under a number of situations and market structures. We have analyzed market structures including persistent monopoly, sequential monopoly where there is a single potential entrant at any moment, and sequential monopoly with competition among innovators. And we have looked at market situations in which, after entry, there is Bertrand or Cournot competition. In the following paragraphs, we describe some of the contrasting results.

As noted in the earlier studies of Aghion and Howitt (1992), when there is a sequence of monopolists, each does not take into account the intertemporal spillovers—the benefits of larger or earlier innovations for the more distant future. This by itself leads to too little investment in innovation. But in the rush to become the next dominant firm, each firm does not take into account the diminution of profits of its predecessors[117] or, more generally, the extent to which its profits are at the expense of other firms,[118] both incumbents and entrants. The excessive speed that results can in some circumstances lead to overinvestment in *speed* (compared to the socially optimal level). The resulting shorter duration during which any firm dominates may, in turn, lead to a lower level of investment in cost reduction. Efficient research may entail bigger and less frequent steps in innovation.

The existence of "innovation rents" may, of course, attract entry, and there has long been a presumption that an increase in such potential competition may spur innovation. But this appendix has cast doubt on this presumption as well, explaining that an increase in the number of firms competing to become the next dominant firm may well decrease the overall pace of innovation. The lower chance of becoming the dominant firm reduces the incentives for each to invest in cost-reducing R & D, and this adverse effect on the innovative process *may* well exceed the benefits from the higher probability that at least one of the firms will succeed in its research endeavors—and this will almost surely be the case as the number of firms increases. While there may exist an inverted U-shaped relationship between competition and innovation, as is often posited in the literature, it is also possible that the level of innovation declines monotonically with the level of competition (or, as in chapter 5, a U-shaped relationship).

What matters for incentives is the effect of competition on the marginal returns, and that in turn depends on the nature of ex post competition. (Marginal returns are also affected by the extent of exclusivity, where one entrant precludes the entry and coexistence of other innovations.) But the incumbent (or the first entrant) knows that what it does has effects both on whether other firms enter the fray and, if they do, their level of investment in R & D. The incumbent may attempt to deter entry.

Our analysis thus casts further skepticism on theories suggesting that the threat of entry forces the incumbent to engage in more rapid research. The incumbent typically has a technological advantage in R & D, and it has the incentives, and often the ability, to deter entry— often with a limited investment in "entry deterrence." The social returns to such entry-deterring investments is typically lower than the private returns (the preservation of monopoly rents)—and often negative. We saw, for instance, how in some circumstances entry deterrence may accelerate the pace of innovation from the optimal speed.

But when R & D is stochastic and different research strategies are imperfectly correlated,[119] then it may be impossible to deter entry. Even then, of course, the incumbent can, and has the incentives to, take actions which discourage investment in R & D, ensuring that, should there be entry, the entrants are less of a competitive threat.

When ex post competition is very intense (Bertrand), then it is easier to deter entry, since profits after entry will be limited; when ex post competition is more limited (Cournot), then it may be harder to deter entry. This gives rise to the seemingly anomalous result that, when the incumbent seeks to deter entry, innovation is more stimulated by weaker ex post competition.

Moreover, with Cournot competition, the expected marginal returns to innovation decrease with the number of firms *in* the market. Particularly important is that as the number of firms increases, even though price and total output increase, the output of each firm decreases, so each has reduced incentives for innovation. Thus, again, there appears to be some ambiguity in the relationship between competition (now reflected both in the number of competitors, actual and potential, and in the intensity of competition) and the pace of innovation. Our analysis has identified some of the critical variables (such as key properties of the innovation function) that determine which of the various effects dominate, i.e., whether more competition leads to more innovation.

Free market entry into innovation continues until the expected return to further entry is negative. But the marginal entrant does not take into account the effect of its entry on the average or marginal profitability of others, and therefore on others' investments in innovation. It may well be the case that the marginal entrant so discourages investment in R & D by other innovators that the pace of innovation is reduced. There is, in effect, an externality *across firms engaged in the innovation process simultaneously*, whereby the increased returns from more research by one firm comes partly at the expense of profits that would otherwise have been earned by others.

Furthermore, there is a tendency, especially when competition is intense, to grab and patent ideas while they are not fully developed— and with a poorly constructed patent system, which allows such patents, the inhibition of follow-on research also results in an overall lower pace of innovation. Thus, an innovation, especially a patented innovation, has an *adverse* effect on innovation at subsequent dates (as opposed to the positive effect that has been focused on, the increase in the benchmark off of which future research is conducted). While we have not pursued the full implications in this appendix, we have noted the adverse consequences of the race to grab the market on the efficiency of the innovation process.

There are many other externalities and market failures associated with the innovation process that we have not explored here. Not all the benefits of the knowledge acquired through research or learning-by-doing by firm A are appropriated by that firm; there are cross-firm (and even cross-sector) externalities. Moreover, when a firm innovates, it draws upon the pool of publicly available ideas.[120] It may add to that pool, but especially when that innovation is protected by a patent, it may reduce the size of the pool, with adverse effects on others.[121]

The net result is that the overall level of innovation may be slower with sequential monopoly or with entry competition than with monopoly; persistent monopoly may do better than a sequence of monopolists. And this *may* even be true if innovation markets are contestable, i.e., potential competition is so strong that it drives down the returns of the entrant to zero. But in none of the situations is there a strong presumption that welfare is maximized, most notably because of the failure to take into account the increases in consumer surplus. Even though prices (in virtually all the models explored here) remain markedly above marginal costs, as costs of production fall over time, so do prices. *Eventually* consumers do reap the benefit from cost reductions. None of the firms in the models explored here take this increase in consumer welfare into account; by itself, this implies too little innovation.

APPENDIX D

Intellectual Property Rights, the Pool of Knowledge, and Innovation[122]

Advocates of stronger intellectual property rights argue that stronger intellectual property rights, *ceteris paribus*, leads to higher levels of investment in R & D, and therefore more innovation. But empirical research provides at best ambiguous support for a simple relationship between the strength of intellectual property rights and the level of innovation—or even higher levels of investment in R & D or learning.[123] The reason is that much is hidden in the assumption of ceteris paribus. There are many other ways of appropriating returns from research, and thus the *incremental* benefit from stronger IPR, at least in many industries, is less than it otherwise would be.[124]

What seems to be *more* important is the "opportunities," the potential for discoveries, related to the pool of knowledge to be exploited, i.e., the pool of ideas that awaits translation into processes and products that are valued in the market.[125] But the size of that pool is *endogenous*. As each individual or firm engages in research and learning, it both contributes to the pool and takes out from it. The "enclosure of the intangible commons of the mind"[126] that is associated with patenting, i.e., with the exercise of intellectual property rights, diminishes the size of the pool available to others. At the same time, each innovation that is not patented may contribute to the pool of ideas that others can build on. The strength and design of IPR thus affects the extent to which any innovation adds to or subtracts from the pool of ideas that are available, i.e., to the technological opportunities.[127]

A central theme of this book is that knowledge externalities are central to the analysis of creating a learning society. IPR, by affecting the extent to which each innovation contributes to or takes out of the knowledge pool, affects the extent of the externalities associated with investments in innovation. In this appendix, we construct the simplest possible general model to explore the resulting dynamics. We show that, in this quite general model, stronger intellectual property rights may well lead to a slower pace of innovation. This is in spite of the fact that *at any level of opportunities* it leads to more investments in R & D. The reason is that stronger IPR, by tilting the balance between additions to and subtractions from the pool of opportunities, *at any level of investment in R & D or learning*, leads to a diminution in the size of the knowledge pool. The effect on investments in R & D over the long run is ambiguous; that is, once the adverse effect on the size of the technological pool is taken into account, stronger IPR may in the long run actually lead to less investment. But with a small knowledge pool, even a given investment in R & D leads to less innovation. Thus, even if stronger IPR leads to more investment in R & D, taking account of the adverse effects on the knowledge pool, the adverse effect on innovation is so strong that the level of innovation may be reduced. Obviously, the magnitude of the adverse effects depends critically on the impact of stronger IPR on knowledge externalities (the positive externalities arising from additions to the knowledge pool and the negative externalities associated with subtractions from the knowledge pool) as well as the availability of alternative mechanisms for appropriating returns to innovation.

Beyond this introduction, this appendix is divided into four sections. We begin by examining an analogous problem, fishing from a renewable common resource pool, showing that changes in the legal or institutional environment which lead to more investment *at any given size of fishing stocks* can lead to steady states with a lower flow of fish catches. A distinctive aspect of the "commons" problem is that in the long run, the general equilibrium effect of a policy change can be of opposite sign to the short-run, partial equilibrium effect (in contrast to many other areas in economics, where, in a stable equilibrium, general equilibrium effects alter the magnitude but not the sign of the partial equilibrium effects).

The following section shows that analogous results hold in the context of a knowledge pool: Stronger intellectual property rights may lead to a lower level of innovation. The third section shows that entry (an increase in the number of firms) can lead to lower innovation, and, analogous to the fishing model, the marginal entrant in a world with free entry is likely to have a negative marginal effect on innovation. The final, concluding section argues that there are reforms in the design of intellectual property regimes which may result in a higher flow of innovations.

The Common Resources Problem

The problem of a large number of private firms drawing upon a common resource has been well studied in the environmental economics literature. (For an early treatment, see Dasgupta and Heal [1974].) In reduced form, there is, say, a population of fish, P, which reproduces at the rate $H(P)$, which depends on the size of the population, as depicted in figure 6.17. Below P_{min}, the population is not self-regenerating, i.e., $dP/dt < 0$, and the species becomes extinct. In the absence of fishing, the population reaches a self-sustaining asymptote of $\bar{P}$.[128] There is a maximum reproduction rate, $\dot{P}$, achieved at $\hat{P}$.

A fishing fleet consists of n symmetric firms, each of which invests i, a function of P and n, with the amount of fish caught being $Q(i(P, n), n, P) = Q(P, n)$, which we refer to as the fishing function.

It is easy to derive $Q(i(P, n), n, P)$. Each firm takes the level of investment of the $n - 1$ others as given, ignores the effects of its fishing on the size of the fishing stock, P,[129] and maximizes its profits:

$$\max_{\{i\},} pQ_j(i, i^{-j}, P) - c(i) \qquad \text{(A.114)}$$

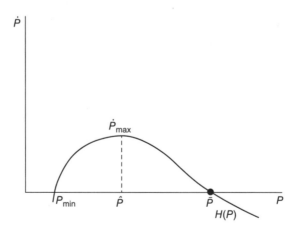

Figure 6.17 Rate of increase in fishing stocks as a function of fishing population (P)

Below a critical threshold level, the population is not viable. In the absence of fishing, there is a maximum sustainable population.

where p is the price of fish, $c(i)$ is the cost of an investment of i, and $Q_j(i, i^{-j}, P)$ is the level of fish caught by the jth firm when the other $n - 1$ firms invest i^{-j}.[130] The symmetric Nash equilibrium gives rise to the investment function described earlier, $i(P, n)$, and that in turn gives rise to the fishing function, $Q(P, n)$, depicted in figure 6.18 for a fixed n.

The long equilibrium size of the stock of fish is given by the solution(s) to

$$dP/dt = H(P) - Q(P, n) = 0, \qquad (A.115)$$

that is, the values of P for which

$$H(P) = Q(P, n). \qquad (A.116)$$

This can be seen diagrammatically by superimposing figures 6.17 and 6.18. We see in figure 6.19 that, for fixed n, there are three equilibria [i.e., three solutions to equation (A.116)]: $P = 0$; $P = P_1$, $P = P_2$, with the first and third stable. The equilibrium fish-catch is given by $H(P^*)$.

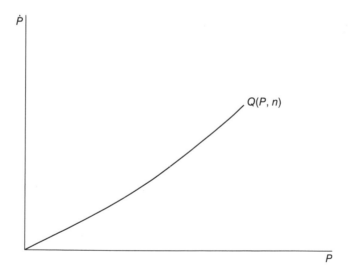

Figure 6.18 Equilibrium fish extraction as a function of fishing population

Symmetric Nash equilibrium of n profit-maximizing firms.

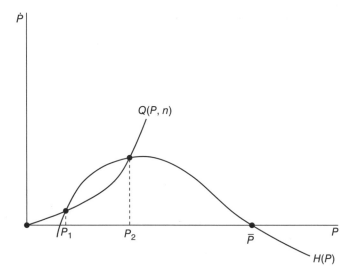

Figure 6.19 Equilibrium fishing stocks

Superimposing figures 6.17 and 6.18, we can ascertain values of P such that the rate of fish extraction equals the rate of reproduction. In the figure, there are three equilibria, two of which are stable: 0 and P_2.

Assume now that there is a change in the economic (legal or institutional) environment which leads firms, at any level of P, to invest more. The business community would celebrate the improved business environment and the increased income derived from fishing. But soon the fishing stocks would start to deplete, and the new stable equilibrium would shift from P_2 to $P_2' < P_2$, so that the flow of fish would actually be lower in the new equilibrium than in the old (see figure 6.20). This would be true whether or not investment is lower in the new equilibrium. That is, in the obvious notation, letting θ and θ' represent the two states of nature (the two different business environments), $i(P_2, n, \theta)$ may be > or < than $i(P_2', n, \theta')$.

There is an exception. It is possible that with an excessively large fish population, crowding actually interferes with reproduction, i.e., as we noted earlier, $H' < 0$ for $P > \hat{P}$. If $P_2 > \hat{P}$, then the upward shift in the fishing curve leads to a lower level of P but a higher sustainable flow of fish (figure 6.21).

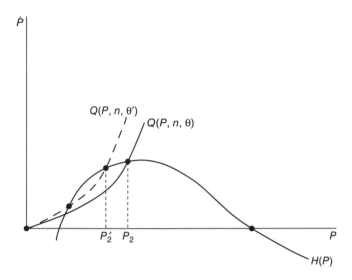

Figure 6.20 Effect of improved investment environment

At each P, there is more fish extraction, so the equilibrium P (and the equilibrium rate of fishing) is lowered.

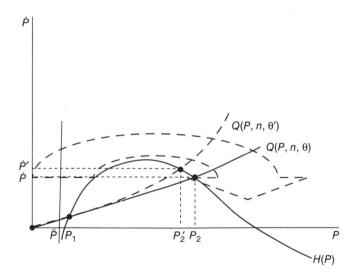

Figure 6.21 An exception

Beyond a critical level of P, increased P leads to lower rates of growth of the fish population. If P_2 occurs in this region, an improved investment environment may lead to a lower P but higher levels of catches.

Similar results hold for the effect of new entry. New entry leads to more competition and more fishing—normally thought of as positive for welfare. But here, if the initial equilibrium entails $P_2 < \hat{P}$, the upward shift in the Q curve leads to a lower level of equilibrium fish caught (and lower profits). While normally, we would expect that each individual enterprise would reduce its level of investment [$i(P, n') < i(P, n)$ for $n' > n$], we might have hoped that the effect of more firms outweighed the diminution of investment of each firm. But it is well known that there can be overfishing. Increased entry may reduce the size of the catch whether or not aggregate investment has increased or decreased [i.e., whether or not $n'i(P, n') < $ or $ > ni(P, n)$ or, indeed, whether or not $n'i(P_2', n') < $ or $ > ni(P_2, n)$]. (See figure 6.22.)

On the other hand if the equilibrium initially entails excessively large fish stocks—in the sense that the equilibrium value of P is greater than $\hat{P}$, then the new equilibrium that emerges entails a higher annual catch.

It is well known that in the case of common pools, the entry decision will not be efficient: firms enter so long as profits are positive, not taking into account the (adverse) effects that their entry has on the size of the catch of other firms. This has led to the presumption that there

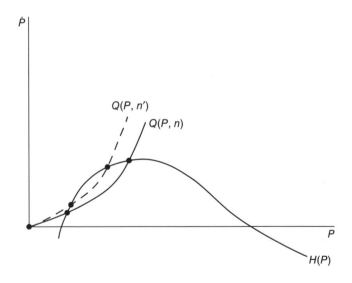

Figure 6.22 Increased competition

Increased competition has effects similar to an improved investment environment— leading to a lower equilibrium P and levels of fish extraction (if $P^* = P_2$ is less than $\dot{P}$).

is excessive entry. But entrants also fail to take into account the effect that their entry has on the size of the fishing stock, both directly (which is negative), and indirectly (because their entry discourages investment on the part of other firms). It is clear that if, at the free entry equilibrium, $P < (>) \hat{P}$, the flow of fish would be increased if entry were taxed (subsidized).[131]

It may be possible, however, to change the regulatory environment in ways which allow a higher sustained catch, and possibly with a lower level of expenditure on fishing. Let us denote the set of fishing regulations by ζ. There are some regulations which allow fish to be caught without as large an adverse effect on the growth of the fishing stock, e.g., regulations that ensure that small fish are not caught. We now write

$$dP/dt = H(P) - Q(P, n, \zeta)M(\zeta), \qquad (A.117)$$

with $M' < 0$. In other words, tighter regulations mean that the adverse effect of a given level of fishing is reduced, but $Q_3 < 0$, tighter regulations increase costs, and hence, at fixed P and n, lead to less fishing and a smaller catch. It follows that with tighter regulation, the equilibrium level of P, denoted P_2'', is increased. But that means that the flow of fish, H, has increased; tighter fishing regulations (in the sense defined) lead to an increased flow of fish, and this is true whether there is more or less investment in the fishing fleet. (That is, other things being equal, the increase in P results in a larger fishing fleet, but the increase in regulations leads to reduced investments—so the net effect is ambiguous.) (See figure 6.23.)

What is striking about these results, as we have noted, is that they reverse normal presumptions. Usually, general equilibrium responses diminish the magnitude of partial equilibrium responses but do not reverse the sign. Here (and in the analysis of the knowledge pool below) they do.

In the next section, we show that the same logic holds for innovation. Changes in the environment which lead to more investment *given a level of P*, the size of the "knowledge pool," may so diminish the equilibrium pool of knowledge (the set of technological opportunities) that the flow of innovations is reduced. This is true whether, at the new equilibrium level of P, there is more or less investment in R & D.

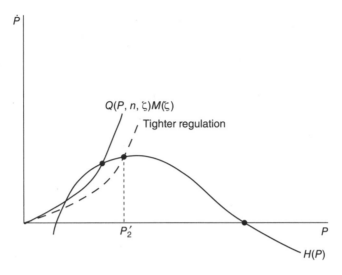

Figure 6.23 Better regulation

Better regulation can lead to a larger equilibrium fishing stock and a higher level of fishing catches (if $P^* = P_2$ is less than $\dot{P}$).

Knowledge Pools

In this section, we denote the set of technological opportunities, the knowledge pool, which can be drawn upon by innovators, by P. Each innovation both adds to the knowledge pool and, especially in the presence of strong IPR, subtracts from P, the set of ideas that can be drawn upon for subsequent innovations. (In the absence of IPR, in a technological sense, an innovation would not reduce the pool of technological opportunities. In another sense—in terms of the set of *profitable* opportunities that are available, given the technological opportunities—it does, given the first-mover and other advantages discussed elsewhere in the literature.[132] The analysis below is unaffected by which interpretation we give to the diminution in P.)

At the same time, government- and university-funded basic research adds to the pool of knowledge that can be drawn upon. We denote the level of public investment in basic research by K. We assume that the additions to knowledge, H, that flow from K depend upon the pool of knowledge that is in the public domain, P, i.e., we assume that $H(K, P)$, with

$$H_K > 0, \qquad H_P > 0.$$

An increase in investment in basic R & D leads to an increase in the flow of contributions to the knowledge pool, and the larger the knowledge pool, the larger the flow of contributions resulting from any level of investment in basic research.[133] (Figure 6.24 depicts $H(K, P)$ as a function of P. It looks much like figure 6.17, except we assume that the larger the pool of knowledge, the greater the increment in knowledge from any investment K. Figure 6.24 is drawn under the assumption that H approaches a constant. That is, at any moment of time, there is an upper bound to the pace of knowledge creation resulting from any given level of investment in basic research, K.[134] We also assume that there is a nonconvexity in the production process—at least for small P, the marginal return to an increase in P is increasing.[135])

Thus, we can write,

$$dP/dt = H - [\alpha(\xi) - \beta(\xi)]I(i, P; n), \qquad \text{(A.118)}$$

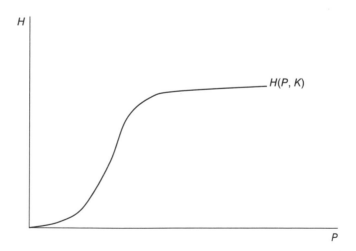

Figure 6.24 Increase in knowledge pool from basic research

As P increases, with fixed K (investments in basic research), H approaches a constant.

where I is the level of innovation;[136] $\alpha(\xi)I$ is the diminution in the available set of technological opportunities as a result of an innovation level of I, when the "tightness" of the IPR regime is ξ; $\beta(\xi)I$ is the addition to the available set of technological opportunities as a result of an innovation level of I, when the "tightness" of the IPR regime is ξ; and where $I(i, P; n)$ is the level of innovation, an increasing function of i, the level of investment in R & D (learning) of each of the fixed n firms (we focus on symmetric equilibria in which all firms engage in the same level of R & D), and P, the size of the technological pool:

$$I_i > 0, I_P > 0. \qquad (A.119a)$$

A tighter ("stronger") IPR regime means that, for others, access to the knowledge created by an innovation is smaller and that every innovation represents more of an enclosure of the knowledge commons (see, e.g., Boyle 2003), so that

$$\alpha'(\xi) > 0, \qquad \beta'(\xi) < 0. \qquad (A.119b)$$

For simplicity, we define $\gamma(\xi) = [\alpha(\xi) - \beta(\xi)]$, with $\gamma' > 0$.

The Steady State: Knowledge Inflows and Outflows

In steady state, $dP/dt = 0$, or

$$H(K, P) = \gamma(\xi)I(i, P; n). \qquad (A.120)$$

We can solve (A.120) for P as a function of K and i,[137] for any given ξ and n:

$$P = \phi(i, K; \xi, n), \qquad (A.121)$$

with[138]

$$\partial P/\partial i = -\gamma I_i/(\gamma I_P - H_p), \qquad (A.122a)$$

$$\partial P/\partial \xi = -\gamma'I/(\gamma I_P - H_p). \qquad (A.122b)$$

φ is the *steady-state locus*, giving the equilibrium level of P as a function of the level of investment in innovation of the representative firm, i, for a fixed level of $\{K, \xi, n\}$. P, as we have discussed, is the pool of technological opportunities available for commercial exploitation, which is why we expect the flow of innovations to be more sensitive to P than is the contribution of publicly funded basic research. In other words, we assume

ASSUMPTION A: $\qquad \gamma I_P > H_p.$

In that case, it follows that [using (A.119a) and (A.119b)]

$$\partial P / \partial i < 0, \qquad\qquad\qquad \text{(A.123a)}$$

$$\partial P / \partial \xi < 0. \qquad\qquad\qquad \text{(A.123b)}$$

Thus, we have established

LEMMA 1. *Under Assumption A, an increase in the strength of the IPR regime leads (in steady state, with a fixed level of investment in R & D, public and private) to a smaller pool of technological opportunities, and an increase in the steady-state level of investment leads to a smaller steady-state pool of technological opportunities.*

Profit-Maximizing R & D Investments

To determine the level of investment in R & D in the representative industry, we assume that there is a single firm in each industry[139] (so that we do not have to worry about interactions among the firms except through the knowledge pool P).[140] Each firm maximizes profit by choosing the level of investment in R & D, i, taking the set of technological opportunities as given. Let $R(I(i, P), \xi)$ be the flow of revenues for the representative firm associated with an innovation level of I, under an IPR regime of tightness ξ; then the flow of profits is

$$R(I(i, P), \xi) - i.$$

Profit is maximized at[141]

$$R_I I_i(i, P) = 1. \qquad\qquad\qquad \text{(A.124)}$$

(A.124) can be solved for i as a function of P and ξ:

$$i = \Psi(P, \xi),\qquad\qquad\qquad\text{(A.125)}$$

with

$$\partial i/\partial P = -[R_{II}I_p I_i(i, P) + R_I I_{iP}(i, P)]/D,\qquad\text{(A.126)}$$

where

$$D \equiv R_{II}(I_i(i, P))^2 + R_I I_{ii}(i, P).$$

D is unambiguously negative, by the second-order condition. The sign of the numerator is ambiguous. A larger pool increases the marginal return to investment, and normally, we would expect this effect to dominate, so that a larger P leads to more investment. But it is possible that there is sufficiently large decreasing profitability to an increased flow of innovations (i.e., R_{II} is sufficiently negative) that the normal presumption is reversed. We will refer to the case where $\partial i/\partial P > 0$ as the *normal* case.

It will be true if

$$d(\ln I_P)/d(\ln i) > -d(\ln R_I)/d(\ln i),\qquad\text{(A.127)}$$

which will be true if there is not rapidly diminishing marginal profitability to innovations.

Similarly,

$$\partial i/\partial\xi = -R_{I\xi}I_i/D > 0,$$

so long as

ASSUMPTION B: $R_{I\xi} > 0$.

In other words, stronger intellectual property rights increases the *marginal* return to an innovation. Thus, this model grants to the advocates of stronger IPR the notion that, *given the set of technological opportunities*, stronger intellectual property rights does lead to more investment. But to assess the overall effect, both on investment in R & D and innovation, we have to take into account the endogeneity of P.

Solving for the Steady State

We can solve for the equilibrium (steady-state) value of the knowledge pool by solving simultaneously (A.121) and (A.125), the steady-state equation (SS), giving P as a function of i, and the profit-maximizing equation (PM), giving the equilibrium value of i as a function of P. The steady-state values of i and P, $\{i^*, P^*\}$ thus solve, for given $\{n, \xi, K\}$,

$$P^* = \phi(i^*, K; \xi, n),$$

$$i^* = \Psi(P^*, \xi).$$

Because under assumption A, the SS curve is downward sloping and, in the "normal" case, the PM curve is upward sloping, there is a unique steady state (see figure 6.25A). (In the more general case, though, the PM curve can have an upward-sloping segment, in which case it is possible that multiple steady-state equilibria exist. See figure 6.25B. In the ensuing discussion, we will ignore this possibility.)

Once we have solved for the equilibrium value of P, P^*, the steady-state flow of innovations can easily be solved for, using (A.120):

$$I^* = H(K, P^*)/\gamma(\xi). \tag{A.128}$$

The Effect of Tighter IPR

Earlier calculations established that tightening IPR shifts the steady-state curve down [i.e., under assumption A, for a fixed value of i, the equilibrium P will be smaller—equation (A.123b)] and that a tighter intellectual property regime shifts the profit-maximizing locus to the right. In other words, *normally* a tightening of intellectual property rights leads to more investment in R & D, at a fixed opportunity set. It follows that that the steady-state level of the knowledge pool will be smaller. P^* is diminished as a result of a tighter intellectual property regime.

Under our assumptions that $H_P > 0$ and $\gamma'(\xi) > 0$, it follows directly from (A.128) that[142]

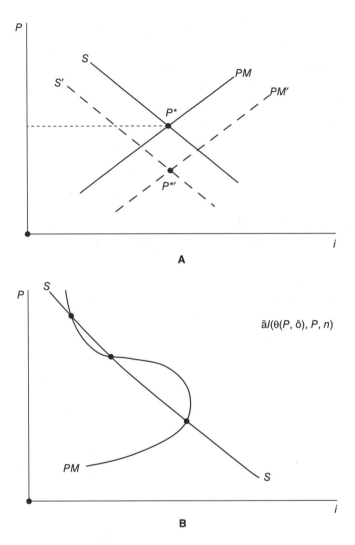

Figure 6.25 Equilibrium knowledge pool

Equilibrium is given by the intersection of the steady-state locus (*SS*) and the profit-maximizing locus (*PM*). A. Normally, there is a unique equilibrium. Tighter IPR leads to more investment at any level of P (a shift to the right in the *PM* curve) and a lower steady-state P at any given level of i (a shift down in the *SS* curve). Thus P^* shifts down. B. The *PM* locus may, however, not be upward sloping, in which case there can exist multiple steady-state equilibria.

PROPOSITION 1. *In the normal case, and under assumptions A and B, tighter intellectual property rights leads to less innovation.*

There is an alternative formulation where the analysis is more parallel to that of section 1. By substituting (A.125) into (A.120), we obtain

$$H(K, P) = \gamma(\xi)I(\Psi(P, \xi), P). \tag{A.129}$$

We can now calculate the total derivative with respect to t of the size of the innovation pool:

$$dP/d\xi = \gamma'(\xi)I + \gamma(\xi)I_i\Psi\xi/[H_P(K, P) - \gamma(\xi)(I_i\Psi_P + I_P)]. \tag{A.130}$$

Under assumption A, $\gamma I_P > H_p$. In the normal case, $\Psi_P > 0$. The result that

$$dP^*/d\xi < 0 \tag{A.131}$$

follows directly: Stronger intellectual property rights diminishes the size of the opportunities pool. It is then easy to show that the flow of innovation is diminished.

Notice that this result holds whether i increases in equilibrium or diminishes. Earlier, we showed that *given the set of technological opportunities*, i increases with the strength of IPR. But we also showed that i diminishes with P, and we have now shown that P diminishes with the strength of IPR. Thus, the net effect of the strength of IPR on investment in R & D remains ambiguous:

$$di/d\xi = \Psi\xi(P, \xi) + \Psi_P(P, \xi) \, dP/d\xi, \tag{A.132}$$

the sign of which is that of

$$R_{I\xi}I_i[H_P(K, P) - \gamma(\xi)(I_i\Psi P + I_P)] - [R_{II}I_pI_i(i, P)$$
$$+ R_I I_{iP}(i, P)][\gamma'(\xi)I + \gamma(\xi)I_i\phi\Psi_{P\xi}].$$

If investment in R & D is very sensitive to technological capabilities, especially relative to the sensitivity to IPR, then investment in R & D is likely to be decreased. For instance, if $R_{It} \approx 0$, then

$$di/d\xi \approx (\partial i/\partial P)|_{PM} \gamma'(\xi)I/[H_P(K, P) - \gamma(\xi)(I_i\Psi_P + I_P)] < 0,$$

(where $(\partial i/\partial P)\,|_{\mathrm{PM}}$ is the change in investment from an increase in P along the profit-maximizing curve), under our assumption that the contribution of public investments to the knowledge pool is not too sensitive to the size of the pool itself and our "normal" case that an increase in technological opportunities leads to an increase in the profit-maximizing level of investment in R & D.[143]

Diagrammatic Exposition

We can reframe the above analysis using the diagrammatic techniques used in the first section to analyze equilibrium fishing and fishing stocks. $H(K, P)$ is the flow of knowledge into the knowledge pool; $\gamma(\xi)I(\Psi(P, \xi), P)$ is the flow out. In equilibrium, the two are equal, as depicted in figure 6.26A. A tighter intellectual property regime represents an increase in the net outflow out of the pool at any given P and thus results in a lower level of P and a lower flow of innovations (figure 6.26B).

The Effect of Entry on Innovation

We can extend the model slightly to ask what happens if the number of firms, n, increases. The model is exactly the same, except now we assume the revenue flows to the jth firm in the representative industry from a given level of innovation for that firm, I^j, are diminishing in n: $R^j(I^j, n)$ with $R^j_n < 0$. The level of innovation for each firm, I^j, is a function of the number of other firms, their level of investment in R & D, and the opportunity set P:

$$I^j = I^j(i^j, -i^{-j}, n, P).$$

We assume for simplicity that all firms are identical. The Nash equilibrium investment in R & D is found by:

$$\max R^j(i^j, \xi, n, P, i^{-j}) - i^j,$$

$$\{i^j\}.$$

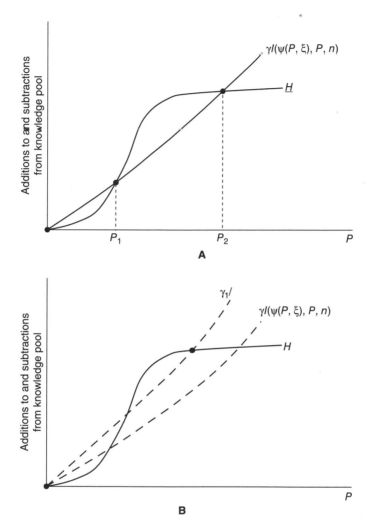

Figure 6.26 Tighter intellectual property rights

In equilibrium, the flow of knowledge (available to others) into the knowledge pool, *H*, equals the flow out. A. There may be multiple equilibria, but in the figure there is a unique steady state, P_2 (besides the no-innovation equilibrium $P = 0$). B. Tighter intellectual property rights shift the level of knowledge exploitation up (at each *P*), resulting in a lower level of the equilibrium knowledge pool and a small flow of innovations.

This generates the reaction function

$$i^j = z(i^{-j}, n, \xi, P),^{144}$$

which leads to the symmetric equilibrium where $i^j = i^{-j}$ (in the natural notation).

$$i^j = Z(P, \xi, n). \qquad (A.133)$$

Normally, we expect that an increase in the opportunity set, given the legal and economic environment and the number of firms, will increase the marginal return to investments in innovation, and hence

$$Z_P > 0. \qquad (A.133a)$$

On the other hand, more competition means that there is, say, a smaller probability of winning the patent race. Average and marginal returns to investment in R & D will be lowered, and so investment (by each firm) may be lowered (though aggregate investment, ni^j, may be increased). Hence, we assume

$$Z_n < 0. \qquad (A.133b)$$

The aggregate flow of innovations, I, is a function of Z, the level of investment of the representative firm, and n, the number of firms:

$$I = I(Z(P, \xi, n), P, n). \qquad (A.134)$$

The steady state is now described by

$$H(K, P) = \gamma(\xi)I(Z(P, \xi, n), P, n). \qquad (A.135)$$

We can solve (A.135) for P as a function of ξ, n, and K:

$$P = \Omega(\xi, n, K). \qquad (A.136)$$

As before, aggregate innovation is simply H/γ, so we can solve for the pace of innovation as a function of ξ, n, and K:

$$I = H(\Omega, K)/\gamma(\xi) = \Lambda(\xi, n, K). \qquad (A.137)$$

From (A.135)

$$dP/dn = \gamma(\partial I/\partial n)_{|P}/[H_P(K, P) - \gamma(\xi)(I_i Z_P + I_P)], \quad (A.138)$$

which implies that, in the normal case,

$$\text{sign } dP/dn = - \text{ sign } (\partial I/\partial n)_{|P}.$$

If that is so, it implies (since $I = H/\gamma$) that[145]

$$\text{sign } dI/dn = - \text{ sign } (\partial I/\partial n)_{|P}.$$

More precisely,

$$dI/dn = H_P(\partial I/\partial n)_{|P}/[H_P(K, P) - \gamma(\xi)(I_i Z_P + I_P)]. \quad (A.139)$$

The results parallel those of the previous section, where we showed that improved intellectual property rights led to more research, at any given size of knowledge pool, but this so drained the knowledge pool (the set of opportunities) that the full effect was to lower the equilibrium pace of innovation. The full effect of more competition is just the opposite of the "partial effect": More firms may lead, at any P, to more innovation, but this so drains the pool of opportunities that the steady-state flow of innovation is actually reduced (figure 6.27).

We now take a more careful look at (A.139) and, in particular, at the numerator. Normally, we expect that *at any size of technological pool*, more researchers will lead to more innovation:

$$\partial I/\partial n|_P = I_i Z_n + I_n > 0. \quad (A.140)$$

More researchers, taking the level of investment of each researcher as given, is likely to lead to more innovation (at a fixed P), i.e., $I_n > 0$; and more investment, by each researcher, will lead to more innovation, i.e., $I_i > 0$. But more competition (larger n) is likely to discourage each firm from investing in R & D ($Z_n < 0$).[146]

In our earlier discussion of (A.139), where we had assumed that more firms leads to more innovation, we had implicitly assumed

$$I_n/I_i > -Z_n.$$

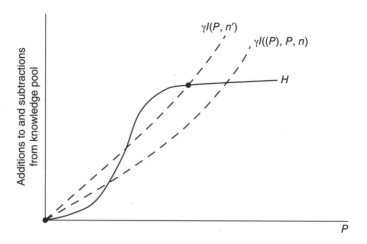

Figure 6.27 Increased researchers

An increase in the number of researchers has an analogous effect in reducing the equilibrium size of the knowledge pool and the equilibrium flow of innovations.

But that may not be so, and if $-Z_n > I_n/I_i$, then an increase in n leads to a smaller level of overall innovation, given P, but a larger level of *equilibrium* innovation, once we take into account the effect on the opportunity set.[147]

The literature has emphasized that (essentially at a fixed P) the effects of the number of firms on innovation are ambiguous, partly because the benefits of having more researchers may be small, beyond a small n (and especially so if research strategies are correlated), and the adverse effects on the investment of each may be large, because of a decrease in the marginal returns to investment (and especially so if the investment of each firm is highly sensitive to slight changes in marginal returns).[148]

By the same token, there may be significant externalities associated with the decision to enter: lower profitability associated with other firms contemporaneously engaged in research, a lower profitability associated with future firms engaged in research, because of the net drawdown in P, *but* a higher profitability associated with future firms engaged in research, because of the effects on other firms' R & D. In a sense, this is a classic problem of the second best. It should not come as a surprise that in such situations, the net welfare effects are ambiguous.

What our analysis has emphasized is that the partial equilibrium results (given P) may be reversed, once account is taken of the long-run effects on P.[149] More generally, the effect of an increase in n on innovation here is different from that in much of the conventional literature, which has emphasized the role that competition has in spurring competition. Here, we have emphasized the fact that even if that is the case, so that at a fixed opportunity set an increase in n increases innovation, under not implausible conditions related to the intellectual property regime, the long-run general equilibrium effects may be the opposite of the short-run partial equilibrium effects.

Concluding Remarks: Pro-Innovation Intellectual Property Regimes

There are reforms in the IPR regime that might lead to a greater pool of knowledge upon which innovators could draw and yet still incentivize research.[150] Provisions of the patent system that make it easier to "enclose the knowledge commons" (i.e., take out from the pool more than one contributes) are particularly harmful; disclosure requirements, rigorously enforced, can increase innovators' contributions to the knowledge pool, with only limited effects on incentives.

So too, an intellectual property regime that provides less scope for holdups, less scope for impediments imposed by patent thickets, etc. may lead to a higher equilibrium knowledge pool.

The "liability system,"[151] in which anyone can use an idea, upon the payment of an appropriately designed fee, leaves more knowledge in the pool to be used by others, but, of course, the price is a two-edged sword: The higher the price, the greater the incentives for innovation (at a fixed P); the lower the price, the larger the *effective P*. In an appropriately parameterized model, one could analyze the optimal price. The patent system can be thought of as associating an infinite price; the absence of a patent system, a zero price. In analyzing the optimal price, it should be observed that even at a zero price, firms have an incentive to innovate, because knowledge does not dissipate costlessly and instantaneously to others. In many sectors, in fact, there is little recourse to the patent system. Thus, it is possible that in some sectors, the optimal price is zero (i.e., all knowledge is freely available). The analysis of this appendix, highlighting the adverse effect of patents on innovation, suggests that in general, we should expect a price lower than the "infinite" price associated with the current system.

The effect of such changes can be shown diagrammatically in figure 6.28 as a downward shift in the net pace of knowledge extraction (more contributions to the knowledge pool, less enclosure of the knowledge commons) at any level of P.

The central message of this appendix is simple: We began by noting that some observers of innovation have claimed that a more important determinant of the levels of investment in R & D and the pace of innovation than the intellectual property regime is the "opportunity set," the knowledge pool from which applied researchers can draw. Knowledge, it has long been recognized, is a public good—a common resource from which all can draw (see, e.g., Stiglitz 1987). Intellectual property provides a way of appropriating the returns to investments in knowledge, but in doing so, effectively privatizes a public good. But every innovation draws upon prior knowledge, and the boundaries of "new" knowledge are inherently imprecise. Patents inevitably enclose what would otherwise have been in the public domain. In doing so, not only do they impede the efficient use of knowledge, but—because knowledge itself is the most important

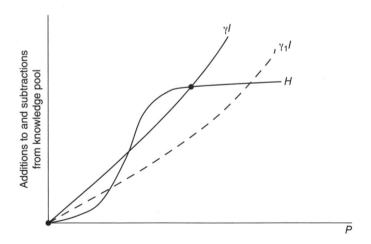

Figure 6.28 Better intellectual property regime

A better-designed intellectual property regime can lead to a larger knowledge pool and a higher rate of innovation.

input into the production of further knowledge (innovations)—they may even impede the flow of innovations.

We have provided a simple way of modeling additions to and subtractions from the technological opportunity set from which innovators can draw. We have shown that tighter intellectual property regimes, by reducing the newly available set of ideas from which others can draw and by increasing the extent of the enclosure of the knowledge commons, may lead to lower levels of innovation and even lower levels of investment in innovation, as a result of the diminution in the size of the knowledge pool. Advocates of stronger intellectual property rights, while noting the positive partial equilibrium effects, have ignored the even more important general equilibrium effects. The real lesson is that considerable care is needed in designing intellectual property regimes, with particular focus on the extent to which any particular regime increases or diminishes the technological opportunities upon which others can draw.

Analytics

CHAPTER SEVEN

Learning in a Closed Economy— the Basic Model

WHILE ONE of the major impetuses for our writing this book was to develop the *infant-economy argument for protection*—which claims, in part, that some degree of protection can facilitate learning—learning is important in all economies and societies, including "closed" economies. To understand fully the role of learning in an open economy, one has to understand how public policy can be used to enhance learning even in a closed economy.

When there is learning by doing, today's production has benefits for the future. We must ask whether firms will take that into account, and what the consequences are of not doing so. It should be obvious that in general (as we argued in part 1) there are learning externalities— knowledge accumulated by one firm can affect the knowledge of others— and firms obviously won't take that into account.

But even if learning is internal only to the firm, there is a market distortion. For then, as we noted in chapter 5, competition in sectors with learning is likely to be limited. But now in addition to the static inefficiencies associated with the exercise of monopoly power, there may be dynamic inefficiencies. These may be complex: Products in which firms have more monopoly power will have less production, and the lower production will lead to less learning.[1] In addition to the static consequence of the loss of consumer surplus from under-production, there is a dynamic cost: lower learning and so higher costs and prices in subsequent periods. Of course, labor not used in the monopolized sector gets displaced to others, but if those are sectors with less learning and weaker spillovers, the overall rate of growth of the economy is reduced. (This is typically the case, since, as we argued earlier, learning is more important in manufacturing than in agriculture,[2] and manufacturing is typically less competitive than agriculture.)

Moreover, as we noted in chapter 5, monopoly power will result in lower real wages; lower real wages will normally result in a lower equilibrium labor supply; and, if learning depends on production (i.e., increases with labor supply), there will be less learning (slower increases in productivity) even if the monopolized sectors did not have an advantage in learning.

We will thus typically see lower societal innovation with monopoly (than in the social optimum) *even in the absence of learning spillovers*—that is, even where the monopolist fully internalizes the benefits of learning—for two reasons: (1) The pattern of production will be distorted from what is optimal, that is, the pattern that would emerge from a careful balancing of static costs and dynamic gains; and (2) the lower real wages lead to lower production on average and hence less learning. With *some* spillovers, investments in learning are even more depressed relative to the optimum.

On the other hand, if learning is external to the firm—so much so that others in the industry benefit from its learning *as much as it does*—the industry can be competitive. Because of the externality, however, there will be underproduction of goods generating (positive) exter-nalities such as learning. And even if the pattern of production is not distorted (as it will not be if all sectors are symmetric), there will be less production in earlier periods; the private market will not take into account the learning benefits.

In short, whether learning is internal or external to the firm, the mar-ket equilibrium will not, in general, be Pareto efficient. Government has a role to play in correcting the market misallocations.

Optimal Resource Allocations with Learning: Basic Intuition

Understanding the structure of learning and knowledge dissemination is essential to understanding efficient production. We are concerned with societal learning, not just sectoral or firm learning. For example, some sectors may have stronger learning curves; that is, the elasticity of learning may be larger for some sectors or firms. But what matters is not just the ability of a firm or sector to learn but also the benefits that sector (firm) transmits to other sectors (firms) and the extent to which it does not appropriate for itself the benefits of the learning.

If learning in one sector generates more externalities to other sectors than do others, production in that sector should be increased (relative to what it would be in the market equilibrium that ignored these learning externalities) at the expense of others. The dynamic (future) benefits need to be offset against the static (short-run) costs.

Theory of the Second Best

Like much of the modern economics of the public sector, the nature of the optimal interventions depends on the instruments and powers of government. Throughout the book, we have emphasized that there are trade-offs between static inefficiencies and dynamic gains. Correcting a market failure (e.g., associated with a firm that generates a positive externality producing too little) is not costless. If production is encouraged through subsidies, the revenues to provide the subsidies have to be raised somehow. And if they can only be raised through distortionary taxation, then the cost of the intervention is greater than it would be if there were nondistortionary (lump sum) taxes.

So too, whether the government can abolish monopolies or undo their distortionary behavior has implications for the desirable levels of research and learning.

The economics of the second best is of particular relevance here: R & D and learning give rise to market imperfections, and all policies have to take into account the presence of these imperfections (sometimes referred to as "distortions") if they cannot undo them. Well-designed distortions in one market can partially offset distortions in others.

We use the word *distortions* with care: Common usage suggests that governments should simply do away with them. But as the term has come to be used, it simply refers to deviations from the way a classical model with, say, perfect information, might function. Information is inherently imperfect, and these imperfections can neither be assumed nor legislated away. Nor can the market power that naturally arises from the returns to scale inherent in research be legislated away. That is why simultaneously endogenizing market structure and innovation is so important. Similarly, the costs associated with R & D (or the "losses" associated with expanding production to "invest" in learning) cannot be ignored; they must be paid for. Monopoly rents are one way of doing so, but—as we argue here—a far from ideal way. There are ways to impose even distortionary taxes (i.e., taxes that give rise to a loss of consumer surplus) that increase societal well-being and the speed of innovation.

Outline of the Analysis

Part 2 consists of five chapters. The first four focus on a closed economy, the last on an open economy. This chapter considers a two-period, two-sector model, while the next considers a more general two-period, n-sector generalization with perfect competition. The following chapters look at an economy with monopolistic competition and at the long-term growth implications of learning.

Basic Model

To highlight the issues at hand, we assume that there are two types of goods—one industrial or manufacturing (M) and the other agricultural/craft (A). Both are produced using only labor as an input with technologies that at any point in time embody constant returns to scale. We define

$c_M(c_A) \equiv$ amount of labor per unit of industrial
(agricultural) output in the economy.

As a normalization, we assume that in the first period $c_M = c_A = 1$.

The production possibilities curve is a straight line with a negative slope of -1. (See figure 7.1.)

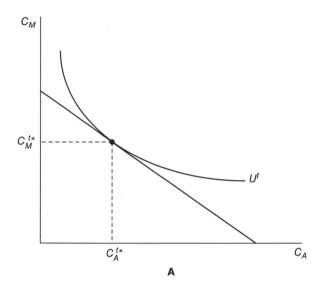

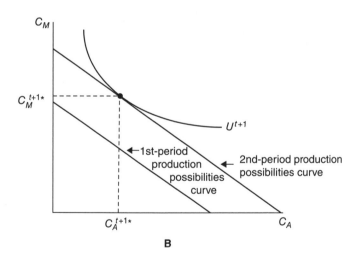

Figure 7.1 The competitive equilibrium

A. First-period equilibrium occurs at the tangency between the production possibilities schedule and the indifference curve, at C_A^{t*}, C_M^{t*}. B. Second-period equilibrium looks much like the first, except that the production possibilities schedule has shifted out. The equilibrium occurs at C_A^{t+1*}, C_M^{t+1*}.

We assume all individuals are identical and have homothetic utility functions[3] of the form (each period)

$$U = U(C_A, C_M) - v(L) = U[C_A\phi(C_M/C_A)] - v(L), \qquad (1)$$

where L is the amount of labor (v is the disutility of work), C_A is the level of consumption of the A goods, and C_M is the level of consumption of the M goods. Initially, we shall assume that the labor supply is fixed.

With full learning spillovers, each firm takes the state of technology next period as given—unaffected by what itself does—and hence the competitive equilibrium is represented by the tangency of the indifference curves to the production possibilities locus. We denote the competitive equilibrium levels of output by $\{C_M^*, C_A^*\}$.

Dynamic Development

We now introduce technological progress into this static equilibrium. Formally, we will assume first that productivity improvement affects the industrial and agricultural/craft sectors equally, i.e., there are perfect spillovers:

$$d(\ln c_M)/dt = -d(\ln c_A)/dt, \qquad (2)$$

so that

$$d[\ln(c_M/c_A)]/dt = 0.$$

Productivity increases spill over fully from one sector within the economy to the other. This has one important simplifying implication: Productivity growth does not affect the production costs of industrial goods relative to agricultural/craft goods. The production possibilities schedule for the second period is a straight line with a slope of minus one, just as it is the first period; but if there is learning, it has moved out.

The reasoning behind this assumption concerning spillovers follows from the discussion of chapter 4. Productivity growth results from (1) research and development efforts, which, while originally devoted to one sector, have benefits that inevitably spill over to other sectors; and (2) human capital improvements, which, while they arise in one sector, inevitably migrate with labor to other sectors of the economy; and (3) the accumulated knowledge of managers and engineers, which, although developed in one sector, also naturally migrate to other sectors.[4]

Next, we assume that the rate of technological progress, g, is determined by the output of the industrial sector:

$$g = -d(\ln c_M)/dt = d(\ln c_A)/dt = g(C_M), g' > 0, \text{with } g(0) = 0, \quad (3)$$

where C_M is the output (equal to consumption, in the absence of trade, as in this chapter) of the industrial sector. The greater the output of the industrial sector, the higher the growth rate. If there is no industrial production, there is no growth. This assumes that the forces driving productivity growth originate in the industrial sector of the economy and have an aggregate impact that is proportional to the total production of the industrial sector. Later, we will discuss briefly other formulations.

For most of the analysis, we will assume diminishing returns to learning, i.e., $g'' < 0$. But we note that learning processes may be subject to nonconvexities, so that there may exist a range of values (say for small C_M) over which $g'' > 0$.

In this chapter, we take a two-period discrete time formulation. Hence, we write

$$c_M^{t+1} = c_A^{t+1} = \psi(C_M^t), \quad (3')$$

where $\psi(C_M^t)$ represents the reduced labor input required to produce a unit of output the second period, when production of industrial goods the first period is C_M^t $\psi' < 0$.[5] (The superscript t refers to variables in the first period, $t+1$ to those in the second period.)

The second-period production possibilities locus is shifted out because of learning. As we noted, because there are full spillovers, the second-period equilibrium looks just like the first and occurs at the tangency between indifference curves and the production possibilities schedule.

Basic Analytics: Inefficiency of Unfettered Markets

We can now see the essential trade-off. If the government can induce a small shift in consumption at time t from $\{C_A^*, C_M^*\}$ to $\{C_A^{**}, C_M^{**}\}$ where $C_M^{**} > C_M^*$, then there will be a small decrease in welfare the first period (which is of second order in magnitude), but the second-period production possibility schedule will shift out, by an amount reflecting the increase in growth (enhanced learning) resulting from the increased industrial production, generating a first-order improvement in welfare (see figure 7.2). Hence, welfare is unambiguously improved. *It always pays for government to encourage the learning sector.*

The analysis so far assumed that the labor supply was fixed, so that, say, a subsidy on industrial goods or a tax on agricultural goods did not lead to a change in labor supply. Assume that industrial goods and leisure are substitutes, so that when the individual consumes more industrial goods, she also increases her labor supply. Then as we increase C_M, we also shift out the production possibilities schedule, *further increasing* C_M, generating still more learning benefits. (The welfare effects of the increase in labor supply can be ignored as a result of the envelope theorem.) In contrast, if industrial goods and leisure are complements, then while it is still the case that it is unambiguously beneficial to increase C_M, the magnitude of the benefits are smaller.

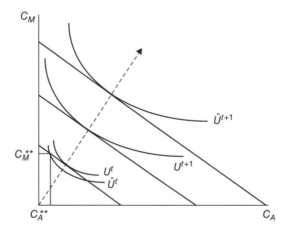

Figure 7. 2 An increase in C_M^t above C_M^{t*} lowers utility in period t slightly, but leads to a large increase in second-period utility. $\hat{U}$ represents that levels of utility each period as a result of the distortion from the competitive equilibrium.

Formal Proof

Two-period utility is given by

$$V^t + \delta V^{t+1}, \tag{4}$$

where δ is the pure rate of time discount, and V is the indirect utility function (the dual to the utility function), giving utility as a function of prices, p, and income, Υ:

$$V(p_A, p_M, \Upsilon),$$

where p_i is the price of the ith good. For simplicity, we assume here that the labor supply is fixed. Assume that the government can impose a tax or a subsidy on agricultural (craft) goods and/or on industrial goods, with a lump sum tax or subsidy representing the difference in revenues. For convenience, we let t_A be the tax on A goods, t_M be tax on M goods. We expect that optimality will require $t_M < 0$, that is, the optimal tax to be negative, a subsidy—and we will prove that to be the case. Then, without loss of generality, letting labor be the numeraire, normalizing the wage and labor supply at unity, and letting the cost of production of good i be unity,

$$p_A = 1 + t_A, \tag{5a}$$

$$p_M = 1 + t_M. \tag{5b}$$

Υ, income, is

$$\Upsilon = wL - S = 1 - S, \tag{6}$$

where S is the lump sum tax the first period.[6]

For simplicity, we assume that there is no way of making intertemporal lump sum transfers. It is easy to show in this model that in the second period, it is optimal for the government not to intervene, and the competitive prices will accordingly be

$$p_A^{t+1} = p_M^{t+1} = \psi(C_M^t). \tag{7}$$

To show that some government intervention is desirable, we simply differentiate (4) with respect to, say, t_M, evaluating the derivative at $t_M = t_A = S = 0$, taking into account the budget constraint

$$S + t_M C_M + t_A C_A = 0. \tag{8}$$

Setting $t_A = 0$ and differentiating social welfare with respect to t_M yields the result

$$-\delta \psi'(dC_M/dt_M)V_\Upsilon^{t+1}\Upsilon^{t+1} < 0, \tag{9}$$

where we have made use of the basic result that

$$V_{pi} = -C_i V_\Upsilon \tag{10}$$

and the fact that at $t_i = 0$ (using 8),

$$dS/dt_M = C_M. \tag{11}$$

dC_M/dt_M is the total derivative, taking into account both the direct effect of the increase in tax and the change in lump sum taxes. But because of (11), the latter effect is just equal to the compensation required to keep individuals just as well off after the tax increase as before. Hence, dC_M/dt_M is in fact the compensated price change, which is unambiguously negative. And that means that the welfare effect of an increase in the tax on industrial goods is unambiguously negative: *It is optimal to subsidize the industrial good*. While we have proved the result only for the case where the subsidy is paid for by a lump sum tax, it is easy to show that the result extends to the case where the subsidy is paid for by a tax on the A goods.

Optimal Interventions

The larger the government intervention, shifting C_M up increasingly (and C_A correspondingly down), the larger the first-period distortion and the higher the marginal cost of a further increase in C_M. As C_M increases, the greater the magnitude of learning, but with diminishing returns to learning, the smaller the marginal learning benefit becomes. Moreover, since the costs of learning occur in the first period, and the benefits later on, the value of the benefits have to be discounted.

It follows that there is an optimal intervention, where the marginal costs of increasing C_M just offset the discounted marginal benefits. It follows too that the higher the discount rate, the lower the benefit of learning, so the lower the optimal level of C_M.

We now derive a simple formula for the optimal tax intervention. We maximize social welfare with respect to $\{t_i, S\}$ subject to the budget constraint (8). The first-order conditions become (letting μ be the shadow price on the budget constraint):

$$
\begin{aligned}
-V_\Upsilon^t C_A + \mu[C_A + t_A(dC_A/dt_A) + t_M(dC_M/dt_A)] \\
- \delta\psi'(dC_M/dt_A)V_\Upsilon^{t+1}\Upsilon^{t+1} = 0,
\end{aligned}
\tag{12a}
$$

$$
\begin{aligned}
-V_\Upsilon^t C_I + \mu[C_I + t_A(dC_A/dt_M) + t_M(dC_M/dt_M)] \\
- \delta\psi'(dC_M/dt_M)V_\Upsilon^{t+1}\Upsilon^{t+1} = 0,
\end{aligned}
\tag{12b}
$$

and

$$
\begin{aligned}
-V_\Upsilon^t - \mu[1 + t_A(dC_A/d\Upsilon) + t_M(dC_M/\Upsilon)] \\
- \delta\psi'(dC_M/d\Upsilon)V_\Upsilon^{t+1}\Upsilon^{t+1},
\end{aligned}
\tag{12c}
$$

where

$$
\Upsilon^{t+1} = \Sigma \, C_i^{t+1}.
\tag{12d}
$$

Using the standard decomposition into price and income effects,

$$
dC_i/dt_j = (\partial C_i/\partial t_j)_U - C_j(\partial C_i/\partial \Upsilon),
\tag{13}
$$

and the symmetry of the Slutsky relations, and substituting the third condition into the first two, we obtain on the left-hand side the usual results from optimal tax theory:

$$
-\Sigma_i \, (t_i/p_i)[\partial(\ln C_j)/\partial(\ln p_i)]_U = \rho\psi'\Upsilon^{t+1}(C_M^t/C_j^t)[d(\ln C_M)/dt_j]_U,
\tag{14}
$$

where

$$
\rho = \delta V_\Upsilon^{t+1}/\mu.
\tag{15}
$$

ρ is the value of a dollar tomorrow relative to the value of a dollar today within the government's budget constraint.

We rewrite

$$\psi' \Upsilon^{t+1}(C_I^t/C_j^t) = -h\psi\Upsilon^{t+1}/C_j^t = -hL^{t+1}/s_jL^t,$$

where

$$h = -d(\ln \psi)/dC_I,\tag{16}$$

the elasticity of learning, and

s_j = fraction of labor allocated to commodity j in the first period.   (17)

Hence, letting

$$\acute{\eta}_{ij} = -[\partial(\ln C_j)/\partial(\ln p_i)]_U,\tag{18}$$

the (absolute value) of the elasticity of (compensated) demand, we can rewrite the optimal tax/subsidy formula (14) as

$$\Sigma \ (t_i/p_i)\acute{\eta}_{ij} = h\acute{\eta}_{Mj}\rho L^{t+1}/[s_jL^t(1 + t_j)]\tag{19}$$

The left-hand side of (19) represents the percentage (compensated) change of consumption of the jth good. If $\psi' = 0$ ($h = 0$), since (in this simple example) we are not raising any revenues, that would imply, not surprisingly, no taxation or subsidy: $t_A = t_M = 0$. The percentage reduction will be smaller the smaller the learning (h) and the smaller the (compensated) elasticity of demand of M goods with respect to the price of the jth good.

In this model, learning and learning externalities are the reasons for government intervention. Consider the simple case of separable demand equations, so

$$[\partial(\ln C_j)/\partial p_i]_U = 0 \text{ for } i \neq j.\tag{20}$$

We then obtain a simple formula for the optimal industrial subsidy:

$$t_M = -\ \rho h v/s_M,\tag{21a}$$

where

$$v = L^{t+1}/L^t, \tag{22}$$

the ratio of labor input in the two periods.

We have obtained a remarkably simple formula for the optimal industrial sector subsidy.[7] The industrial sector subsidy should be greater the higher the value of future income (ρ), the higher the learning elasticity (h), and the lower the share of industrial goods in production.

With separability,

$$[\partial(\ln C_M)/\partial p_A]_U = 0,$$

so

$$t_A = 0. \tag{21b}$$

There should be no subsidy or tax on the agricultural sector: The industrial subsidy is financed by a lump sum tax.

There is a natural intuition behind each of these results. When the future is relatively more important, we weight the benefits of learning (relative to the costs today, in terms of distorting consumption patterns today). When the learning elasticity is higher, the benefits from distorting consumption today are increased. When the share of the industrial sector is small, the social cost of the distortion, relative to the society-wide benefit, is small. When v is large, the benefits of learning are high, because of the higher scale of production *relative* to the costs, which are related to the scale of production the first period.

It is worth noting that the elasticity of demand does not appear in the equation. A low demand elasticity means that the distortion for a given size tax is small; but a given (percentage) tax induces little increase in consumption (production), and the benefit is related to the percentage increase in production. The two effects offset each other.

NO LUMP SUM TAXES Assume that lump sum taxes are not feasible, and the subsidy to the industrial sector has to be financed by a distortionary tax on the agricultural sector. We let τ_M denote the industrial subsidy. (In terms of our earlier notation, $tM = -t_M$.) Continuing within the optimal tax framework of the previous section, we seek to maximize with respect to $\{\tau_M, t_A\}$,

$$V^t([1 - \tau_M], [1 + t_A], 0) + \delta V^{t+1}(\psi(L_M^t), 0) \qquad (23)$$

where $\tau_M C_M = t_A C_A$. Here t_A is the tax that must be levied on agriculture (craft) to pay for the subsidy, so

$$dt_A/d\tau_M = (C_M/C_A) + \tau_M[d(C_M/C_A)/d\tau_M].$$

Again, because of our choice of units, $C_M^t = L_M^t$. This implies that

$$V_Y^t[C_M^t - C_A^t(dt_A/d\tau_M)] = -\delta V^{t+1}{}_Y \psi'(L_M^t)$$
$$(C_M^{t+1} + C_A^{t+1})dC_M^t/d\tau_M, \qquad (24)$$

or

$$V_Y^t C_M t_M\, d[\ln(C_M/C_A)]/d(\ln \tau_M) = \delta V_Y^{t+1} hL^{t+1}\, d(\ln C_M^t)/d\tau_M. \quad (24')$$

The left-hand side of (24) is the cost of the subsidy/tax—the distortion in consumption patterns—while the right-hand side is the learning benefit. Optimality requires that the (static) marginal cost of a subsidy equal the (dynamic) marginal benefit.

As expected, if $\psi' = 0$, the solution to (24) entails $\tau_A = t_M = 0$: There is no scope for distortionary taxation. But if the right-hand side of (24) is positive, it is optimal to tax A (agriculture) to expand M (industrial goods):

$$\tau_M = h\hat{\rho}(v/s_M^t)\beta_M/(\beta_M + \beta_A) \geq 0, \qquad (25)$$

provided

$$(\beta_M + \beta_A) > 0, \qquad (26)$$

where $\hat{\rho} = \delta V_Y^{t+1}/V_Y^t$, the discount rate for future income, reflecting both the pure discount factor δ and the normally lower marginal utility of income at $t + 1$ relative to t as a result of growth, and where[8]

$$\beta_M = d(\ln C_M)/d(\ln \tau_M) \geq 0, \text{ and} \qquad (27)$$

$$\beta_A = -d(\ln C_A)/d(\ln \tau_M) \geq 0. \tag{28}$$

These are total derivatives, taking into account the indirect effect of the increased price of agricultural goods. Thus, normally we expect the subsidy to increase consumption of industrial goods and reduce the consumption of agricultural goods. In particular, the ratio C_M/C_A under our assumptions of homotheticity depends only on the price ratio, which in turn depends only on τ_M.

$$d[\ln(C_M/C_A)]/d(\ln \tau_M) = \beta_M + \beta_A > 0, \tag{29}$$

provided the elasticity of substitution between the two commodities is greater than zero. The magnitude of the change in relative consumption as relative prices change depends on the elasticity of substitution.[9] When the elasticity of substitution is zero, there are neither benefits nor costs associated with the imposition of the subsidy/tax scheme.

Equation (25) gives results for the optimal subsidy similar to those in the lump sum case: a larger subsidy the more future consumption is valued, the higher the elasticity of learning, and the larger the scale of production next period, relative to this period. The one difference, though, is that now, the size of the subsidy also depends on the *relative* total elasticities of demand (taking into account both the direct and indirect effects) with respect to the subsidy of M goods and A goods. If A goods are relatively price insensitive, i.e., $\beta_A \approx 0$, then $\tau_M \approx h\hat{\rho} (v/s_\eta^t)$.

It is worth subsidizing the industrial goods even though, to finance the subsidy, one must impose a distortionary tax on the agricultural sector. But unlike the case where a lump sum subsidy is available, the magnitude of the subsidy is critically dependent on the magnitude of the elasticities of the demand curves (the elasticity of substitution).[10]

Market Structure and Innovation

We can use a variant of the above model to examine the effect of market structure on innovation. Return to figure 7.1, which shows the competitive equilibrium the first period. A monopoly in the industrial sector would normally be expected to produce less than the competitive level of output.[11] But a monopolist takes into account the future learning benefit that accrues to itself, and thus produces a larger output than it otherwise would. Figure 7.3 shows a situation where the learning benefit is so large that the firm produces more than would have been produced in competitive equilibrium. In that case, the production possibilities for the second period are "larger" in the second period than they would have been in competitive equilibrium: Schumpeter's conjecture that monopoly is good for innovation is correct, under these circumstances (to be delineated more precisely below).[12]

On the other hand, it is not necessarily the case that welfare is higher. First-period welfare is lower than in the competitive equilibrium, and second-period welfare may or may not be lower. If the second-period production possibilities curve is moved out only a little bit, then the loss of welfare the second period from the distortion exceeds the benefit from the enhanced innovation, and welfare is unambiguously lowered. (In figure 7.3, the production possibilities curve is moved out so much that second-period utility is much higher with monopoly than under competition, even taking into account the monopoly distortion.) Finally, we note that it is possible that the incentive of the monopolist to reduce output may be so great that, even though it takes into

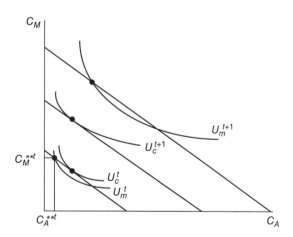

Figure 7.3 A monopoly may increase its production (relative to the competitive equilibrium) in the first period because it takes into account learning benefits. This means that the production possibilities curve in the second period is further out, so much so that utility in the second period is increased enough to offset the losses in utility during the first period from overproduction of industrial goods, relative to the static equilibrium. In this case, monopoly is better than competition. U_c represents the utility in the competitive equilibrium.

account learning benefits—which are ignored in competitive markets—output in the first period is smaller. There is then a loss of welfare in both the first and second periods; in the second period, both because of the monopoly distortion and because the production possibilities curve is lower because of the lower level of learning.

Analytics

The precise calculations are straightforward and provide some insights into the conditions under which monopoly enhances welfare. The profit-maximizing monopolist in the industrial sector maximizes

$$(p_M^t - 1)C_M^t + \delta[p_M^{t+1} - \psi(C_M^t)]C_M^{t+1}, \tag{30}$$

where, it will be recalled, we have normalized the first-period marginal cost of production to unity. This yields the first-order condition

$$(1 - 1/\eta_M)p_M^t + \delta v_M h = 1 \tag{31}$$

or

$$p_M^t = (1 - \delta v_M h)/(1 - 1/\eta_M), \tag{31'}$$

where we have assumed that the firm uses the same discount rate δ that society employs (i.e., there is no distortion in the capital markets), η_M is the elasticity of demand in the industrial sector, and

$$v_M = L_M^{t+1}/L_M^t,$$

the ratio of labor input into the *industrial* sector in the two periods. (If relative prices in the two periods were the same, under our assumption of homotheticity, $v = v_M$, but it should be clear that relative prices will not be the same.) In contrast, in the competitive allocation, $p_M^t = 1$. Using (31'), the monopoly price will be lower (the level of innovation will be higher) if and only if, at the competitive allocation, where $p_M^t = 1$,

$$1/\eta_M < \delta v h_M, \tag{32}$$

i.e., the learning benefit offsets the adverse effect of monopoly power. Monopoly will lead to more innovation if (a) the elasticity of demand is high (so that the monopoly distortion is low); (b) the discount factor is high—so that the present discounted value of the benefits of the learning is high relative to today's cost of distortion; (c) the learning elasticity is high, so that there are large benefits (private and social) to learning at the margin; and (d) v_M is high, so the scale of the industrial sector in the future is large relative to the scale today.[13]

These calculations confirm our earlier assessment. Even if there is more innovation under monopoly, however, it does not mean that welfare is higher. Society pays a cost, both today and in the future, from the monopoly distortions. If (32) is not satisfied, monopoly is unambiguously welfare decreasing, because there are both static and dynamic distortions. Only if the dynamic benefits are large enough to offset the static distortions is monopoly preferable to a competitive equilibrium.

Concluding Comments

Chapter 5 noted that, with constant returns to scale in production, the learning sector could only be competitive if there were full spillovers. Our analysis of that case has shown that there will be underproduction of the learning good and less innovation than would be socially desirable. A subsidy to the learning sector can correct this market failure.

Schumpeter argued for the advantages of monopoly. In the context of our learning model, the central advantage is that they internalize the learning externality. But as we noted, there is a large cost: a tendency to underproduction. In the case of investments in R & D, that implies less of an incentive for research. In the case of the learning models on which we focus in this book, it means less learning. We have delineated conditions in which the benefits of the internalization of the within-industry learning externality outweigh the costs of the monopolistic distortion of the market.

In any case, Schumpeter's enthusiasm for monopoly is not justified, for as we saw in the first part of the chapter, one can do better by government intervention—imposing a subsidy on the learning sector, paid for either by a tax on the other sector or, if feasible, by a lump sum tax.[14]

The next chapter shows how these results can be extended, in a straightforward way, to an economy with many sectors.

APPENDIX A

A Simple Model of Investment in R & D

In most of this book, we focus on how learning and learning spillovers affect the optimal production structure—leading to an industrial structure that might be markedly different from that which might emerge in an unfettered market economy. Here, we extend this work by looking at how knowledge spillovers affect the optimal pattern of R & D.

Assume there are two products, produced by a linear technology

$$Q_i = A_i(R_1, R_2)L_i,$$

where R_i is the amount of research on product i and L_i is the labor devoted to production.

$$E_i = L_i + L_i^r.$$

Total employment in sector i, E_i, is the sum of production and research workers. If $A_{ij} > 0$ $(i \neq j)$, this implies there are spillover benefits for product i from research on product j. For simplicity, we assume $R_i = L_i^r$, the amount of labor devoted to research in sector i.

Social welfare maximization entails

$$\max U(Q_1, Q_2) - L.$$

After some manipulation, the first-order conditions can be written

$$\alpha_1^1(L_1/L_1^r) + \alpha_2^2(L_2/L_1^r) = 1,$$

$$\alpha_2^1(L_1/L_2^r) + \alpha_1^2(L_2/L_2^r) = 1,$$

where $\partial(\ln A_i)/\partial(\ln L_j^r) = \alpha_j^i$.

The Role of Spillovers

With no spillovers $\alpha_i^j = \alpha_j^i = 0$, so

$$(L_i^r/L_i) = \alpha_i^i.$$

The ratio of employment in research in sector i to production labor is directly related to the elasticity of productivity. If the elasticity is high—research increases productivity a lot—then a large fraction of labor should be devoted to research.

It is easy to see that if there are externalities (i.e., $\alpha_i^j > 0$), research is increased. Consider the symmetric case, where $L_1 = L_2$ in equilibrium. Then

$$L_1^r/L_1 = \alpha_1^1 + \alpha_1^2.$$

With perfect spillovers,

$$\alpha_1^1 = \alpha_1^2,$$

so the effect is to double the ratio of research workers to production workers.

Comparison with a Market Economy

In a perfectly competitive economy with a large number of firms and perfect within-industry spillovers, there would be no research, as each would try to free ride on others: $L_i^r = 0$—clearly an underinvestment in research.

At the other extreme, assume that there were no spillovers. Then each firm would engage in some research. It would maximize output for any given input, i.e.,

$$\max A_i(L_i^r)(E_i - L_i^r),$$

generating

$$A_i'(E_i - L_i^r) = A_i,$$

or

$$\alpha_i^i = L_i^r/L_i,$$

an equation identical to that derived earlier for the optimal allocation in the case of no spillovers—highlighting the crucial role of spillovers in industrial policies. (The overall level of employment may, however, differ in the two situations.)

But there is another critical issue: Whether there are spillovers or not is, in part, a matter of industrial policy, e.g., concerning compulsory licensing, cooperative research efforts, and disclosure policies.

Thus, assume there are n firms in the industry, and that $A_i = A_{ii} + \beta \Sigma A_{ij}$. Government policy can increase β (the spillovers from research j to sector i) and thus the optimal amount of research. Moreover, if sector i has learning as well as research potential, and the other sector does not, then L_i will be much greater with $\beta >> 0$, and hence so will L_i^r.

More typically, sectors in which research is important are imperfectly competitive. Assume that again there is no knowledge spillover and that each sector faces an elasticity of demand of η. Then, as before, we can show that $L_i^r / L_i = \alpha_i^i$.

But now

$$U_i = p_i = A_i / (1 - 1/\eta),$$

where p_i is the price of the ith good (taking labor as the numeraire); while in the competitive case

$$U_i = p_i = A_i.$$

Production (output) is lower, i.e., for any given level of productivity (A_i), L_i is smaller; and hence L_i^r is correspondingly smaller. The exploitation of market power results in underproduction, and thus underinvestment in research, since the value of research is related to the cost savings—i.e., the level of production.

CHAPTER EIGHT

A Two-Period, N-Good Model with Endogenous Labor Supply

THE PREVIOUS chapter used a simple two-sector model to explain why markets by themselves are not in general efficient: If markets are competitive, there will be underproduction in the sector generating learning externalities, and thus less learning and innovation than is socially efficient. If the learning sector is monopolistic, monopoly power will result in worsening the problem of underproduction; but the fact that the monopolist internalizes the within-sector learning externality will lead to increased production. Which of these two effects predominates depends on an array of parameters, including the elasticity of demand in the learning sector, the discount factor, and the elasticity of learning. The chapter also analyzed government interventions—how the government can improve welfare by subsidizing the externality-generating sector and how it should balance out the growth benefits against the losses from the induced distortion.

A preliminary version of the analysis of this chapter was presented to a session of the World Bank's Annual Bank Conference in Development Economics in honor of Sir Partha Dasgupta in Stockholm, June 2, 2010 (Stiglitz 2010d).

This chapter generalizes the results of the previous chapter to a *competitive economy with N goods where labor supply is endogenous*. The next chapter focuses on a *monopolistically competitive economy*. The analysis confirms, qualifies, and generalizes the results derived for the two-sector case.

The analysis of the chapter, while straightforward, with results that are highly intuitive, is complex and depends on particular assumptions, for instance, about the nature of the spillovers. We consider, for example, both the case on which we focused in the last chapter, where there were perfect spillovers, and that where there are no cross-sector spillovers (or even within-sector spillovers). Accordingly, before presenting the calculations, we present the major findings. (The reader not interested in the detailed analytics can then proceed to the next chapter.)

Basic Intuitions and Results

The basic insight is that so long as there are any learning benefits, production in the first period in learning sectors goes beyond the level that would have occurred with static efficiency. Three of the factors that determine the benefit of that learning are those identified in chapter 7: how we discount the future (if we discount the future more, the benefit of this learning is less); how responsive future productivity is to today's production—the learning elasticity; and the scale of the next period's economy (relative to this period's), which determines the magnitude of the cost savings from greater productivity (in relation to the scale of the loss from the distortion in today's market). Production next period of a particular good will increase (relative to this period's) if the elasticity of marginal utility of consumption diminishes slowly, which translates into a more elastic demand curve; production next period of goods in general will increase (relative to this period's) if individuals respond to the lowering of prices as a result of increased productivity by working more (consuming less leisure, producing more goods), which depends on the elasticity of labor supply with respect to real wages.

Chapter 7 focused on a simple model with two goods, in one of which there is learning, but in which there is perfect spillover to the other sector. We noted there that if the sector generating the externality was, in a sense, small relative to the sector benefiting from the externality, other things being equal, it made sense to expand that sector more, i.e., to provide a higher subsidy to the sector generating the externality. The benefits of the distortion were high relative to the costs. Here, in a multigood context, there are more channels of interdependence, more ways by which a tax or subsidy on one sector can exert externalities on others. The previous chapter focused on technological externalities—how production of good M improved the productivity of labor in sector A. Now, many sectors can have their productivity improved, by different amounts, and the optimal subsidy to any sector has to take into account all of these spillovers.

Second, a subsidy to one sector, or a tax on another, affects the entire pattern of demand, as long as there are cross-elasticities. Some other sectors will expand, and there will be more learning and more learning spillovers; others will contract, and there will be less learning in these sectors, fewer spillovers. Hence, demand interdependence shifts the locus of learning, and government intervention has to take into account these interdependencies. One of the formulae described below highlights these demand interdependencies.

Finally, as we noted, learning could lead to an overall increase in labor supply, because goods become relatively cheaper. This increases the benefits of learning—the value of knowing how to produce something using, say, 1 percent less labor is proportional to the scale of production. By the same token, consumption subsidies this period (financed, say, by a lump sum tax) will increase labor supply, and this will result in more learning.

We derive below simple formulae that capture the learning benefits. The standard tax literature provides a number of alternative characterizations of optimal commodity taxation, depending on the simplifying assumptions used to describe the demand (and supply) equations. The most general is that there should be an equi-proportionate reduction in consumption along the compensated demand curves. A second, under the condition of separability, is that the tax should be inversely proportional to the demand elasticity (ignoring distributional considerations; see Atkinson and Stiglitz 1980). Since a tax on all goods in proportion is a tax on leisure, and effort will accordingly be discouraged, another formulation emphasized undoing this distortion by lowering taxes on complements to leisure and increasing those on substitutes (Corlett and Hague 1953).

These various formulations are discussed in the context of innovation below. We assume that there is no other need for government revenue. That means that optimal taxes, when there is no learning, should be zero. But when there is learning, we obtain simple formulae generalizing the results derived in chapter 7 for optimal subsidies.

While the general focus of our analysis is to argue that some sectors provide more learning spillovers to other sectors, and these sectors should be expanded relative to those with lower learning spillovers, we noted earlier that even in the case where all sectors are symmetric, markets are in general still not efficient, because there will be too little learning in earlier periods—in our model with learning by doing, too little production in earlier periods. We show that that is in fact the case, so long as there is some labor supply elasticity. That is, optimal government policy should be designed to encourage consumption (and labor supply) the first period (relative to what it would be in the static equilibrium), because in doing so, production capacities the second period are enhanced.

Beyond the introduction, this chapter is divided into five parts. First, we consider a "direct control" problem in which government can determine the amount of labor allocated to each sector. Second, we provide a price interpretation of this optimum. Third, we examine some special features of the symmetric sectors case. Fourth, we analyze optimal interventions using standard optimal tax theory, asking what taxes and subsidies the government should impose. We show how the optimum derived under the assumption that there was direct control can be implemented through taxes and subsidies, assuming that government can levy lump sum taxes. Finally, we analyze government intervention in more realistic contexts, in which government cannot impose such taxes.

1. The Basic Model: Optimal Production and Consumption

Assume as before (for simplicity) that utility is separable between goods in the two periods and between goods and labor:[1]

$$W = U(C^t) - v(L^t) + \delta[U(C^{t+1}) - v(L^{t+1})], \qquad (1)$$

where C^t is the vector of consumption $\{C_k^t\}$ at time t and L^t is aggregate labor supply at time t. The disutility of work is the same in all sectors, and L^t is aggregate labor input in period t:

$$L^t = \Sigma L_k^t \text{ and } L^{t+1} = \Sigma L_k^{t+1},$$

where L_k^i is the input of labor in sector k in period i.

Production is described by (in the appropriate choice of units)

$$C_k^t = L_k^t. \tag{2}$$

In this simple model, the more output of good j in period t, the lower the production costs in period $t + 1$. We assume

$$C_k^{t+1} = L_k^{t+1} H^k[L^t], \tag{3}$$

where L^t is the vector of labor inputs at time t $\{L_k^t\}$.[2]

The learning functions H^k and their properties are at the center of this analysis. This formulation assumes that there are full within-sector externalities, i.e., the amount of learning in sector k depends on the total production (input) in sector k. (Without loss of generality, if there are many firms in a sector and there are imperfect learning spillovers among the firms, we simply define the output of the different firms as different commodities, with these commodities being perfect substitutes for each other.)

In the following analysis, two properties of these learning functions will play a central role:

1. *Learning elasticity* — how much sectoral productivity is increased as a result of an increase in labor input. We define

$$h_k = d(\ln H^k)/d(\ln L_k^t) \geq 0, \tag{4}$$

where h_k is the (own) elasticity of the learning curve in sector k.

2. *Learning spillovers* — the extent to which learning in sector i spills over to sector j. $\partial H^k/\partial L_j^t > 0$, $j \neq k$, if there are learning externalities; or $\partial H^k/\partial L_j^t = 0$, $j \neq k$, if there are no learning externalities between sectors j and k.

As the discussion of chapter 3 emphasized, there may be larger spillovers from one sector to another, and more generally, the extent of cross-sector spillovers may depend as well on the production technologies being employed in the different sectors.

At various points in the discussion, we will find it convenient to focus on two special cases, one with no learning spillovers and one with full learning spillovers. In the special case *with no learning externalities*,

$$H_j^k = 0 \text{ for all } j \neq k,$$

and we write, for simplicity (with no learning spillovers)

$$C_k^{t+1} = L_k^{t+1} G_k(L_k^t). \tag{5}$$

In the other case, with *full learning spillovers*,

$$H \equiv H^k = H^j, \text{ all } j, k.$$

The previous chapter focused on the particular case where there is a set of sectors with learning (M) and another set with no learning (A), i.e., $H_A = 0, H_M > 0$.

Optimization of (1) with respect to $L_k^j, j = t, t + 1$ yields (in the obvious notation)

$$U_k^t = v'^t - B_k, \tag{6}$$

$$U_k^{t+1} H^k = v'^{t+1}, \tag{7}$$

where B_k is the learning benefit from increased output from (input into) sector k:

$$B_k = \delta \Sigma_j \, U_j^{t+1}(C^{t+1}) L_j^{t+1} H_k^j \tag{8}$$

Equation 6 simply says that in allocating labor in the first period, we take into account the learning benefits. The learning benefit is the increased output in *each* of the sectors as a result of increased learning, multiplied by the marginal utility of consumption of that good, all brought back to present values by the discount factor, δ. $B_k > 0$ implies that, so long as there are any learning benefits, production in the first period goes beyond the level that would have occurred with static efficiency (which entails $U_k^t = v'^t$). Obviously, *sectors with more learning benefits expand production more* (relative to the level of production in the equilibrium with no learning). So too, the smaller ξ is, the less we value the future learning benefits.

To see what that entails more precisely, we focus on the polar cases referred to earlier.

Case (a): No Spillovers

In the case of no spillovers, the only benefits from expanding production in sector k accrue to sector k:

$$B_k = \delta \xi_k h_k U_k^t(C^t), \qquad (9)$$

where

$$\xi_k = U_k^{t+1} C_k^{t+1} / U_k^t C_k^t.$$

The magnitude of the learning benefit depends on the discount rate (the larger ξ, the more we value future benefits) and the learning elasticity, h_k. Indeed, without spillovers, the learning benefit is proportional to the learning elasticity.[3]

One might have thought that because of the fixed-cost nature of learning, production in larger sectors would have increased more. But the magnitude of expansion of production entails a careful balancing of the marginal benefit of learning (the dynamic gain) and the marginal costs of the first-period distortion (the static cost). The formulas derived in this chapter analyze what that entails. In effect, they show that what matters is the learning elasticity and not the scale but *changes* in the scale between the two periods, captured by the variable ξ_k. The reason for this is that the cost of the distortion (relative to the size of the economy) is related to the size of the sector (relative to that of the economy); but the benefits of the distortion—the learning—accrue to that sector, and that sector only.

Normally, we would expect that, as a result of productivity increases, consumption of each good would increase. In the case of separability with respect to consumption,

$$U = \Sigma_k u_k(C_k),$$

and the effect on $U_k C_k = u'_k C_k$ of an increase in C_k depends on the elasticity of marginal utility for commodity k, η_k, where $1/\eta_k = -d(\ln u'_k)/d(\ln C_k)$:

$$d[\ln(U_k C_k)]/d(\ln C_k) = 1 - 1/\eta_k.$$

Because normally $C_k^{t+1} > C_k^{t}$,[4] ξ_k is greater than or less than unity, depending on whether η_k is greater or less than unity. If η_k is less then unity, marginal utility diminishes slowly, the elasticity of demand is greater than unity, and the value of learning is greater.

In the case of the logarithmic utility function, $\xi_k = 1$, so

$$B_k = \delta h_k U_k^t(C^t). \tag{10}$$

Case (b): Full Spillovers

The case of full spillovers can most simply be analyzed by rewriting our maximization problem as

$$\max W = U(C^t) - v(L^t) + \delta[U(H(C^t)L^{t+1}) - v(L^{t+1})]. \tag{11}$$

For simplicity, we assume homothetic preferences, which allows us to rewrite our utility function

$$U = U(\phi(C)),$$

where ϕ has constant returns to scale. This generates the first-order condition

$$U'^t \phi_k - v' = -\delta U'^{t+1} H_k [\Sigma_j \, \phi_j(C^{t+1})L_j^{t+1}] \tag{12}$$
$$= U'^t \phi_k[-\delta h_k \xi^*/\gamma_k],$$

where

$$\xi^* = U'^{t+1}\phi^{t+1}/U'^t\phi^t, \tag{13a}$$

$$\gamma_k = d(\ln \phi)/d(\ln C_k) = \phi_k C_k/\phi, \tag{13b}$$

and where we have made use of the result that with constant returns

$$\Sigma_j \, \phi_j(C^{t+1})L_j^{t+1}H = \Sigma_j \, \phi_j(C^{t+1})\, C_j^{t+1} = \phi. \tag{14}$$

(The later discussion will make clear that in the competitive equilibrium without learning, $U'^t \phi_k = p_k v'$, and γ_k has a natural interpretation: $\gamma_k = s_k$, the share of income spent on the kth commodity.)

We can now rewrite the first-order condition for first-period consumption:

$$U'^t \phi_k[1 + \delta h_k \xi^*/\gamma_k] = v'. \tag{15}$$

Again, the learning benefit is proportional to the discount factor and the learning elasticity, and inversely proportional to the "share" of sector k (γ_k). The smaller the share, the larger the relative spillover—the societal benefit relative to the distortion in the sector itself. Obviously, as before, if $U = \ln \phi$, then $\xi^* = 1$.

Case (c): Full Spillovers in Some Sectors and No Spillovers in Others

For simplicity, we focus on two sectors, labeled s for spillovers and 0 for no spillovers. (This is a generalization of the model of chapter 7, where we assumed that in the sector with no spillovers, $h = 0$.) Then our maximand becomes

$$\max W = U(C_s^t, C_0^t) - v(L^t) + \delta[U(H^s(C_s^t)L_s^{t+1},$$
$$H^s(C_s^t)H^0(L_0^t)L_0^{t+1}) - v(L^{t+1})], \tag{16}$$

(so production in sector s increases productivity in sector 0, but production in sector 0 only increases productivity in sector 0) yielding the first-order conditions

$$U_s^t - v'(L^t) = -\delta H^{s\prime}(C_s^t)[U_s^{t+1}L_s^{t+1} + U_0^{t+1}H^0(L_0^t)L_0^{t+1}]$$
$$= -\delta h^s(C_s^t)[U_s^{t+1}(C_s^{t+1}/C_s^t) + U_0^{t+1}C_0^{t+1}/C_s^t] \tag{17a}$$

and

$$U_0^t - v'(L^t) = -\delta H^s(C_s^t)U_0^{t+1}H^{0\prime}(L_0^t)L_0^{t+1}$$

$$= -\delta h^0(C_0^t)U_0^{t+1}C_0^{t+1}/C_0^t. \tag{17b}$$

Provided that the learning elasticities are similar, learning induces a far larger expansion in the sector with spillovers than the sector without. For instance, with logarithmic utility functions,

$$U = \alpha_s \log C_s + \alpha_0 \log C_0, \ \alpha_s + \alpha_0 = 1$$

$$U_s^t - v'(L^t) = -\delta h^s(C_s^t)/C_s^t = -\delta h^s U_s^t(1 + \alpha_0/\alpha_s),$$

while

$$U_0^t - v'(L^t) = -\delta\alpha_0 h^0(C_0^t)/C_0^t = -\delta h^0 U_0^t.$$

If, for instance, $h^0 = h^s$ (i.e., the learning elasticities are the same), the sector with spillovers is expanded much more than the sector without:

$$U_s^t = v'/[1 + \delta h(1 + \alpha_0/\alpha_s)],$$

$$U_0^t = v'/[1 + \delta h].$$

2. Price Interpretation

The equations describing the optimal allocation of resources have an obvious price interpretation. Let

$$U_k^t/v'^t = p_k^t = \text{marginal rate of substitution between good } k$$
$$\text{and leisure in period } t. \tag{18}$$

Let q_k^t = marginal rate of transformation between labor and good k in period t.

$$q_k^t = 1 \text{ for all } k, \tag{19}$$

and

$$q_k^{t+1} = 1/H^k, \text{ for all } k. \tag{20}$$

Then (7) implies that

$$p_k^{t+1} = q_k^{t+1}, \text{ for all } k. \tag{21}$$

In the first-best allocation, in the second period, the consumer price (equals the marginal rate of substitution) equals the producer price (equals the marginal rate of transformation).

The first-period allocation is somewhat more complicated. Equation (6) implies that

$$p_k^t = q_k^t - \Omega_k p_k^t = 1 - \Omega p_k^t = 1/(1 + \Omega_k), \tag{22}$$

where Ω_k is the marginal (normalized by the marginal utility) learning benefit from producing more of good k in the first period (this includes the learning benefits to *all* sectors):

$$\Omega_k \equiv B_k / U_k^t = \delta[\Sigma_j \, U_j^{t+1}(C^{t+1})L_j^{t+1}H_k^j]/U_k^t$$
$$= \delta\Sigma_j \, \xi_{jk} \, d(\ln H^j)/d(\ln C_k^t) > 0, \tag{23}$$

where

$$\xi_{jk} = (U_j^{t+1}C_j^{t+1})/(U_k^t C_k^t). \tag{24}$$

Optimal production entails producing in the first period beyond the point of the static efficiency condition, where the marginal rate of substitution equals the marginal rate of transformation. The extent to which we expand production depends on the direct learning effects *and* on the indirect benefits to other sectors. It is not just the direct learning benefits that count. If a sector has more spillovers to others, we might want to expand its production even if its own learning elasticity is lower.

We again consider our two polar cases. First, assume there are no learning spillovers, so $H_j^k = 0$ for $j \neq k$. Then

$$\Omega_k = \delta\xi_{kk}h_k. \tag{25}$$

In the case of a logarithmic utility function, $\xi_{kk} = 1$. The extent to which the marginal rate of substitution is less than the marginal rate of transformation (i.e., the extent to which production is expanded beyond the level of static efficiency) depends on the elasticity of learning. If marginal utility diminishes rapidly, sectors for which there is a lot of learning will have correspondingly smaller values of ξ_{kk}, diminishing the extent to which output is expanded. The higher δ (the less future utility is discounted), the more important the learning benefits are and thus the higher the level of production the first period.

Second, consider the case with full spillovers. Then

$$\Omega_k = \delta h_k \xi^* / \gamma_k, \tag{26}$$

where ξ^* and γ_k are as defined earlier (equations (13a) and (13b)).

Comparison with the Competitive Equilibrium

The price interpretation is useful because it provides an easy and direct contrast between optimal resource allocations and the competitive equilibrium without government intervention. (We will discuss the monopolistically competitive equilibrium later.) In the competitive equilibrium,

$$U_k^t / v'^t = q_k^t = 1 \text{ for all } k,$$

$$U_k^{t+1} / v'^{t+1} = q_k^{t+1} = 1/H^k, \text{ for all } k;$$

that is, production in the first period ignores *all* learning benefits but, conditional on the learning that has occurred, second-period production is efficient. Clearly, there will be underproduction in the first period, especially in those sectors in which learning is important.

3. Symmetric Case

The above analysis derived general formulas for analyzing optimal production/learning if government could directly control inputs/outputs in every sector. We also provided a price interpretation of the optimum. Much of our discussion focused on the desirability of increasing activities that generate learning externalities compared with those that did not.

But there is a broader macroeconomic issue: Even if all sectors were identical (symmetric), so that $1/n$th of the labor supply ought to (and, in market equilibrium, would) be devoted to each commodity, there may be too little output (labor supply) in the first period. If labor supply is inelastic and the number of goods is fixed at n, in the symmetric equilibrium, $1/n$th of the labor force is allocated to each good. It is obvious that the market equilibrium has the efficient amount of learning in each sector; there is no learning distortion, even though there are learning externalities. This is important, for it illustrates the large discrepancy between partial and general equilibrium analysis. (Partial equilibrium analysis would have led us to the conclusion that there was an underinvestment in learning.)

The symmetric equilibrium also provides an easy context in which to compare the market equilibrium with the optimum. For simplicity, we will assume no spillovers across sectors.

The social welfare maximization problem can be easily written as

$$\max U^t(L^t/n, L^t/n, L^t/n, \ldots) - v^t(L^t) + \delta[U^{t+1}(G(L^t/n)L^{t+1}/n,$$
$$G(L^t/n)L^{t+1}/n, G(L^t/n)L^{t+1}/n, \ldots) - v^{t+1}(L^{t+1})]$$

with respect to $\{L^t, L^{t+1}\}$, where n is the number of commodities, and where we have assumed separability between labor and goods but not necessarily between goods; where $G_k(L_k^t)$ is the learning function giving output per unit input[5]); and where, because of the assumption of symmetry, we can, without loss of generality, drop the subscript on the learning function.

The first-order condition can be written

$$\Sigma\, U_i^t/n - v^{t\prime} = U_i^t - v^{t\prime} = -\,\delta\Sigma\, U_i^{t+1}G'(L_i^t)L^{t+1}/n^2$$
$$= -\,\delta U_i^{t+1}G'(L_i^t)L^{t+1}/n.$$

In competitive equilibrium,

$$U_i^t - v^{t\prime} = 0,$$

so it is clear that (in general) there is too little production the first period. The only exceptions are the cases where L^t is fixed (i.e., cannot be increased) or $G' = 0$ (at the margin, there is no learning). Then, trivially, the market equilibrium is efficient.

The first-order condition for L^{t+1} is

$$U_i^{t+1}G(L^t) - v^{t+1\prime} = 0.$$

In competitive equilibrium, the price is $1/[G(L_i^t)]$, so that, conditional on the state of knowledge in the second period, output is efficient.

If the government were to subsidize first-period production by τ, so that the individual's first-order condition is

$$U_i^t - v^{t\prime}(1 - \tau) = 0$$

and sets

$$\tau^* = \delta U_i^{t+1}G'(L^t/n)L^{t+1}/(v^{t\prime}n), \qquad (27)$$

raising the revenue through a lump sum tax, then the government can induce the market to replicate the first-best optimum.[6]

It is useful to rewrite the above expression as[7]

$$\tau^* = \delta[v^{t+1\prime}L^{t+1}/v^{t\prime}L^t]h$$
$$= \delta\varsigma h, \qquad (27')$$

where ς is our new relative scale parameter, slightly different from that used earlier:

$$\varsigma = v^{t+1\prime}L^{t+1}/v^{t\prime}L^t. \qquad (28)$$

For instance, assume constant marginal disutility of work, $v' = 1$ (a constant) and logarithmic utility of goods, $U = \Sigma \ln C_i$. It is easy to show that in the case of symmetry, the results are the same if we had a single consumption good. For notational simplicity, we will assume that, and drop the subscript on C. Then

$$C^t = 1/(1 - \tau)L^t$$

and

$$C^{t+1} = \Psi,$$

so

$$L^{t+1} = C^{t+1}/\Psi = 1$$

and

$$\tau^* = \delta h(1 - \tau^*).$$

so that

$$T^{(*2)} = \delta h/(1 + \delta h).$$

For small δh, the solution can be approximated by

$$\tau^* \approx \delta h, \qquad (27'')$$

as before.

Other special cases can similarly be solved for explicitly. Assume, for instance, that we had a learning function that was linear (rather than constant elasticity), with

$$\Psi = 1 - \vartheta L, \qquad (29)$$

where ϑ is a small number (limited learning). Assume constant marginal utility of consumption ($U' = 1$) and quadratic disutility of leisure ($v = .5L^2$). Then it is straightforward that $L^{t+1} = \Psi = 1 - \vartheta L^t$, $\Psi' = -\vartheta$, and $L^t = 1/(1 - \tau^*)$. Hence, (27) can be rewritten as

$$\tau^* = \delta\vartheta[1 - T - \vartheta]$$

$$\tau^* = (\delta\vartheta[1 - \vartheta])/(1 + \delta\vartheta)$$

For small subsidies (small ϑ), τ^* can be approximated by

$$\tau^* \approx \delta\vartheta, \qquad (27'')$$

again, proportional to the discount factor and the learning parameter.

Even though we can impose lump sum taxes, subsidies distort static allocations. Optimal interventions balance these static losses with the dynamic gains. The above formulas show the outcomes of this balancing.[7,8]

4. Optimal Learning with Optimal Taxation: Lump Sum Taxation

So far, we have derived the optimal allocation (assuming that government directly controls production and consumption) and analyzed price interpretations of the resulting equilibrium. It may be useful to redo the analysis using more standard techniques in public finance. We begin by assuming that the government can only impose excise taxes, subsidies, and lump sum taxes. The government faces an indirect control problem. With lump sum taxation, assuming that first-period subsidies must be paid by a lump sum tax in the first period (i.e., there are no intertemporal budget constraints, so the government cannot borrow from the future to finance this period's deficits), we can write social welfare using the indirect utility function, giving the level of utility as a function of prices and "income":

$$V^t(p^t, -T) + \delta V^{t+1}(p_i^{t+1}, 0), \tag{30}$$

$$p_i^t = 1 - \tau_i, \tag{31}$$

$$p_i^{t+1} = 1/H^i, \tag{32}$$

where τ_j is the first-period subsidy to commodity j. Under our normalization, in a competitive market without subsidies, the (consumer) price of all goods would be unity; a subsidy on good j of τ_j brings down the competitive price to $1 - \tau_j$. In a competitive market, in the second period, the price is just the cost of production.

There are two spillovers from a subsidy on sector j:

1. An increase in the subsidy on commodity j affects demand (and supply) for commodity i. That in turn has two effects: an impact on learning in those sectors (the benefits of which can spill over to other sectors) and an impact on the government's budget constraint. For example, if demand shifts toward highly subsidized products, the government would face a budgetary shortfall, which would necessitate a decrease in the subsidy on some other commodities.

2. The expansion of sector j affects learning in sector i.

It is easy to establish that, provided the sectors are not too different, and there is learning in all of the sectors, it pays to subsidize consumption of every good in the first period.[9] But if sectors are very different, it may pay to impose a tax on a sector, even if there is some learning in that sector. If the learning elasticity of a sector is much larger than that of others, and that sector has large spillovers to others, and there is some sector that is a substitute for the high-learning sector, then it may pay to tax that sector, in order to encourage learning in the high-learning sector.

We can easily derive the optimal tax/subsidy rate,[10] the values of $\{\tau_i\}$ that maximize

$$V^t(p^t, -T) + \delta V^{t+1}(p_i^{t+1}, 0) \tag{33}$$

subject to (31) and (32) and to the government's budget constraint,

$$T = \Sigma \tau_i C_i. \tag{34}$$

The first-order conditions are given by

$$-V_{pj}^t - \mu[C_j^t + \Sigma \tau_j (dC_j^t/d\tau_i)]$$
$$- \delta\Sigma_k V_{pk}^{t+1} \Sigma_i [(1/H^k)^2]H_i^k \, dC_i/d\tau_j = 0, \tag{35a}$$

$$-V_I^t - \mu[-1 + \Sigma \tau_j (dC_j^t/dI)]$$
$$- \Sigma_k V_{pk}^{t+1} \Sigma_i [(1/H^k)^2]H_i^k \, dC_i/dI = 0, \tag{35b}$$

where μ is the Lagrange multiplier associated with the government budget constraint (34). Using the Slutsky equation and the same techniques used in the previous chapter, we obtain [subtracting (35b) from (35a)]

$$-\mu \Sigma \tau_j (dC_j^t/d\tau_i)_U + \Sigma_k V_{pk}^{t+1} \Sigma_i [(1/H^k)^2]H_i^k (dC_i/d p_j)_U = 0.$$

The term $[\Sigma \tau_j (dC_j^t/d\tau_i)U]$ reflects the spillovers to the budget constraint: The increase in output of sector i affects the aggregate subsidies and, therefore, the aggregate lump sum tax. We define, as before,

$$\delta V_I^{t+1}/\mu = \rho, \tag{36}$$

a kind of intertemporal marginal rate of substitution, reflecting the pure rate of time discount, the diminution of the marginal utility of income as a result of growth, and the shadow price associated with raising revenue. (In the absence of commodity taxes and subsidies, $\mu = V_I^t$, so V_I^{t+1}/V_I^t is just the individual's marginal rate of substitution. Normally, δ is less than unity, and with growth and diminishing marginal utility of income, V_I^{t+1}/V_I^t is less than unity, so ρ is less than one.) Then, using the standard "tricks" of optimal tax theory (combining the Slutsky equation with the symmetry of the compensated price elasticities), we can rewrite (18) as

$$-\Sigma_j \, (\tau_j/p_j)[\partial(\ln C_i)/\partial(\ln p_j)]_U = \rho\Phi_i, \qquad (37)$$

where $\Phi_i = -[(L^{t+1}/(1 + \tau_i)s_i^t L^t] \, \Sigma_k \, \{s_k^{t+1} \, \Sigma_j \, h_j^k[\partial(\ln C_j^t)/\partial(\ln p_i)]_U\}$ is the total net marginal learning benefit from encouraging the consumption (equals the production in a closed economy) of sector i, taking into account potential effects on other sectors, both through induced learning in other sectors (as a result of cross-elasticities of demand) and as a result of learning spillovers. The double sums reflect this. An increase in the subsidy on product i leads to an increase in consumption of i, which affects learning in i, but also in other sectors (hence the terms H_i^k); but through cross-elasticity effects, it also affects production in sector j, and this affects learning in that sector and every other sector.

$\Sigma_j \, h_j^k[\partial(\ln C_j^t)/\partial(\ln p_i)]_U$ reflects the total impact of a change in the price of good i on learning in sector k, taking these effects into account. Φ_i weights these learning effects by the relative share of these goods in the second-period consumption bundle. Φ_i also reflects the relative scale of the economy in the two periods—if L^{t+1}/L^t is large, Φ_i is large, reflecting the greater value of learning. Finally, as in chapter 7, we take into account the relative size of sector i. If it is small, the cost of the distortion will be small relative to the society-wide benefits.

Equation (37) can be interpreted similarly to the analogous expression in optimal tax theory: In the absence of learning (where $\Phi_i = 0$ for all i), the percentage deviation of consumption of good i (along the compensated demand curves) should be zero for all goods. Now we will make an adjustment: The percentage deviation should be larger for those sectors with larger marginal learning benefits, but those marginal learning benefits include not just the direct learning benefits but the spillovers to other sectors.

Qualitatively, we can see what is implied by considering the case of separable demand functions with no spillovers:[11]

$$\tau_i = \rho h_i^i \zeta_i, \tag{38}$$

where $h_i^i = \partial(\ln H^i)/\partial(\ln L_i)$, the (own) elasticity of the learning curve; and

$$\zeta_i = s_i^{t+1} L^{t+1}/(s_i^t L^t), \tag{39}$$

the ratio in sector i of labor input the second period into sector i to that in the first period.[12] ζi is itself a function of τ_i. As in chapter 7, the tax rate does not depend on the demand elasticities. With constant shares, in the case of no spillovers, the share effect drops out. With nonhomotheticity, the share of i will increase or decrease depending in part on whether the income elasticty is greater or less than unity. If the demand elasticity is greater than unity, the share will increase if the second-period learning effect (H_i for a learning sector is greater than for a nonlearning sector, so the price will be lower) outweighs the first-period subsidy effect (first-period production/consumption is encouraged as a result of the subsidy).[13]

Note that for a sector with no learning, $\tau_i = 0$. The subsidy for the learning sector is paid for by a lump sum tax. However, with non-separable demand functions, if a tax on the sector with no learning induces a shift to consumption of the learning sector (they are substitutes), it is optimal to tax that sector; if the goods are substitutes, it is optimal to subsidize the learning sector.

Full Spillovers

The other case that is easy to analyze is when there are full spillovers. Then $p^{t+1} = 1/[H(C^t)]$, and the above formula simplifies to

$$\Phi_i = -\{L^{t+1}/[(1 + \tau_i)s_i^t L^t]\} \Sigma_j h_j[\partial(\ln C_j^t)/\partial(\ln p_i)]_U, \tag{40}$$

where, in the obvious notation, $h_j = d(\ln H)/d(\ln C_j^t)$. Subsidizing a particular sector has a high benefit if it leads to an increase in production, directly or indirectly, of a good which has a large effect on learning (h_i is large.) Now, with separability of the demand curve:

$$\tau_i = \rho h_i [(L^{t+1}/s_i^t L^t)]. \tag{41}$$

Now, a small sector which exerts a large learning benefit for the entire economy should be subsidized more. Again, with separable demand functions, a sector for which there is no learning but which is a substitute for one that is should be taxed.

Symmetric Equilibrium and the Role of Labor-Supply Elasticity

We can simplify further in the special case of symmetry, discussed above. From symmetry, we know that all will face the same price, so we can write our optimization problem as (using the obvious notation)

$$\max V^t((1 - \tau_i), \ldots, -n\tau_i C_i) + \delta V^{t+1}(c_i(\tau_i, \tau_{j\neq i}), 0), \tag{42}$$

where c is the cost of production; i.e., $c_i = 1/H_i$, implying

$$-V_I^t(n\tau \, dC_i^t/d\tau) - \delta V_I^{t+1} \, \Sigma_i \, \{(n - 1)C_j^{t+1} \, \partial[c_i(\tau_i, \tau_{j\neq i})]/ \, \partial\tau_{j\neq i}$$
$$+ C_i^{t+1} \, \partial[c_i(\tau_i, \, _{tj\neq i})]/\partial \, \tau_i\} = 0, \tag{43}$$

or

$$\{-V_I^t(\tau/p) + \delta V_I^{t+1}(L_j^{t+1}/L_j^t)[(n-1)h_{ij}$$
$$+ h_{jj}]\}\{d(\ln C_i^t)/d(\ln p)\} = 0, \tag{44}$$

where

$$d\{\ln[c_i(\tau_i, \tau_{j\neq i})]\}/d(\ln \tau_i) = -\{(n - 1)[\partial(\ln c_i)/\partial(\ln C_j)]_{j\neq i}$$
$$[\partial(\ln C_j)/\partial(\ln \tau_j)]_{j\neq i} + [\partial(\ln c_i)/\partial(\ln C_i)][d(\ln C_i)/d(\ln \tau_i)]\}. \tag{45}$$

Under our assumptions of symmetry, when we increase τ_i, we increase all subsidies by the same amount, so the effect is n times greater. The total derivative of C_i and c_i with respect to reflects the sum of all of these effects.

There are direct benefits of learning (h_{jj}, the own elasticity of the learning curve) and indirect benefits (h_{ij}, the learning spillovers).

There are two solutions. If $d(\ln L^t)/d(\ln \tau) = 0$, then (as we argued earlier) there is no reason to interfere with the market. But in the more general case,[14]

$$\tau/(1 - \tau) = \rho\zeta[(n - 1)h_{ij} + h_{jj}], \tag{46}$$

where, as before, $\zeta = L_j^{t+1}/L_j^t$. And as before, the higher the learning and the more learning spillovers, the higher the subsidy. If labor supply is very elastic and there is substantial learning, then $L^{t+1}/L^t >>> 1$, so, again, the higher the subsidy. If there are significant spillovers and many sectors, it is the magnitude of the spillovers that really matters.[15]

We can rewrite (46) to bring out the role of the labor supply elasticity. ζ can be written as a function of τ, since L^t is a function of τ; and L^{t+1} can be written as a function of H, which itself is a function of τ. $\zeta(\tau) \approx \zeta(0) + \zeta'(0)\tau = \zeta(0)\{1 + [d(\ln \zeta)/d(\ln L^t)][d(\ln L^t)/d(\ln \tau)]\}$. But

$$d(\ln L^{t+1})/d(\ln L^t) = h\varepsilon_{Lw},$$

where ε_{Lw} is the wage elasticity of the labor supply. Thus,

$$d(\ln \zeta)/d(\ln L^t) = h\varepsilon_{Lw} - 1$$

and

$$d(\ln L^t)/d(\ln \tau) = \varepsilon_{Lw} \, d(\ln w)/d(\ln \tau) = \varepsilon_{Lw}\tau/(1 - \tau).$$

Thus, an increase in the subsidy increases the first-period real wage and increases learning, but whether it increases the scale parameter ζ depends on whether $h\varepsilon_{Lw} >$ or < 1. If the learning elasticity is high ($> 1/\varepsilon_{Lw}$), then ζ is increased.

$\zeta(0)$ itself is a function of H_o, how much learning there would be at a zero subsidy. At a zero subsidy, with some learning, the real wage the second period is higher (by H_o) as a result. Hence,

$$\zeta(0) \approx 1 + \varepsilon_{Lw}H_o.$$

Putting the results together, we obtain

$$\zeta(\tau) \approx [1 + \varepsilon_{Lw}H_o]\{1 + [h(\varepsilon_{Lw})^2 - \varepsilon_{Lw}]\tau/(1 - \tau)\}.$$

It should be clear that with a high value of h, $\zeta > 1$. With low values of h and H_o, however, it is possible that $\zeta < 1$.

Substituting into (46) and defining the total learning elasticity $h^* = [(n-1)h_{ij} + h_{jj}]$, we obtain

$$\tau/(1-\tau) \approx \rho h^*(1 + \varepsilon_{Lw}H_o)/[1 - \rho h^*\varepsilon_{Lw}(h^*\varepsilon_{Lw} - 1)(1 + \varepsilon_{Lw}H_o)]. \quad (47)$$

At a low value of h^*, this implies that

$$\tau/(1-\tau) \approx \rho h^*[1 + \varepsilon_{Lw}H_o]/[1 + \rho h^*\varepsilon_{Lw}(1 + \varepsilon_{Lw}H_o)]$$

$$\approx \rho h^*[1 + \varepsilon_{Lw}H_o].$$

It follows that the higher the labor-supply elasticity, the higher the subsidy rate.[16] (We already noted the limiting case of zero labor-supply elasticity. (47) suggests that even if the labor supply elasticity is small but positive, it will still be desirable to have a goods subsidy, in magnitude approximately equal to ρh^*.[17])

5. No Lump Sum Taxes

When government cannot impose lump sum taxes, there may still be room for industrial policies, as we have already noted in chapter 7. One sector may have more learning benefits, so that a tax on the other sector to finance a subsidy on the learning sector might be desirable, even though lump sum taxes are not feasible. Establishing this is a straight-forward generalization of the model in the previous chapter.

In this section, we explore one further complication. Assume the government may be able to borrow, even if private individuals cannot. It can impose taxes in the second period to repay the cost of first-period subsidies. For simplicity, we focus on the symmetric case; i.e., we focus on the benefit from government borrowing to finance current-period subsidies that lead to more learning (similar results hold for government investments in R & D). The government seeks to maximize[18]

$$\max V^t((1-\tau_i),\ldots,0) + \delta V^{t+1}(c_i(C_i(\tau_i,\tau_{j\neq i})) + t_i, 0)$$

$$\text{s.t. } \Sigma \tau_i C_i^t(1+r) = \Sigma t_i C_i^{t+1},$$

where r is the interest rate the government has to pay. In the symmetric case, we can, without loss of generality, simplify by assuming only one commodity; dropping the subscripts, we have $\tau C^t(1 + r) = tC^{t+1}$.

The first-order condition is

$$\tau[V_I^t C^t - \delta(1 + r)V_I^{t+1}C^t(1 + \beta^t + \beta^{t+1})] + \delta V_I^{t+1}C^{t+1}c'C^t\beta^t = 0,$$

where, as in chapter 7,[19]

$$\beta^t = d(\ln C^t)/d(\ln \tau) > 0$$

and

$$\beta^{t+1} = -d(\ln C^{t+1})/d(\ln \tau),$$

or simplifying,

$$\tau[1 - \rho(1 + r)(1 + \beta^t + \beta^{t+1})] + \rho(L^{t+1}/L^t)h\beta^t = 0.$$

$[1 - \rho(1 + r)(1 + \beta^t + \beta^{t+1})]$ is the benefit of borrowing money this period to be paid back next period. (In the absence of taxes, where $\tau = \beta^{t+1} = \beta^t = 0$, borrowing would be desirable so long as $[1 + r] < 1/\rho$). We focus on the case where, in the absence of learning benefits, it would not be beneficial to borrow, that is,

$$\rho(1 + r)(1 + \beta^t + \beta^{t+1}) > 1.$$

In that case, if there is learning, there is an optimal subsidy (financed by borrowing), given by

$$\tau^* = \rho(L^{t+1}/L^t)h\beta^t/[\rho(1 + r)(1 + \beta^t + \beta^{t+1})] - 1 > 0. \qquad (48)$$

The subsidy is higher the higher the learning elasticity h, the lower the interest rate, and the more sensitive first-period consumption (production) is to the subsidy (i.e., the higher β^t).[20]

Concluding Comments

In this chapter, we have shown how, with appropriate knowledge of the full learning functions and demand functions (and thus knowledge of the impact of a subsidy on all demands and learning), we can derive the optimal set of subsidies in a straightforward (if somewhat complicated) way.

The intuitions established in the previous chapter concerning the two-commodity case have been shown to be robust. We have seen the critical role played by learning elasticities, learning spillover, and the discount factor. We have derived a simple formula analogous to that familiar from optimal tax theory, this time showing that the percentage change in consumption of the ith commodity along the compensated demand schedules should be proportional to the society-wide learning benefit, taking full account of learning externalities. But perhaps the most surprising result is that applying this general formula to the case of separable utility functions, the optimal subsidy does *not* depend on demand elasticities (quite unlike the result in optimal tax theory). The reason is that both the costs (the distortion) and the benefit (consumer surplus associated with lowering the costs of production) are related to the (compensated) demand elasticities, in a fully offsetting way.

We had noted in the last chapter that when the elasticity of labor supply was positive, production subsidies were desirable even in the case of perfect symmetry (so there is no "learning" sector). Higher production today lowers production costs in the future. We obtained a general result confirming that with higher labor supply elasticities, higher goods subsidies the first period are desirable.

It should be obvious that implementing these optimal interventions requires considerable information concerning preferences and technology. The basic insights of the previous chapters are still relevant: Even without such detailed knowledge, if we can identify a set of sectors, like the industrial sector, with higher learning elasticities and higher learning externalities, it is desirable to encourage such sectors. Later chapters will show how it is possible to do so through broad-based measures, such as changes in the exchange rate.

First, however, we want to take a closer look at the design of interventions when markets are not fully competitive—an especially relevant situation because, as we have argued, when innovation and learning are important, markets are not likely to be fully competitive.

CHAPTER NINE

Learning with Monopolistic Competition

EARLIER CHAPTERS explained the dilemma facing learning economies: While in competitive markets, there are likely to be large learning spillovers, and thus underinvestment in R & D, in models with monopoly or monopolistic competition, the extent of learning spillovers may be reduced—the learning externalities are more internalized. Thus, a monopolist will produce beyond the point of maximizing marginal revenue—but monopoly itself can lead to lower welfare from reduced output, and the reduced output itself reduces the incentive to innovate (relative to what it would have been in the first best). Our earlier discussion showed how, in some very simplified contexts, these two effects play off. Chapter 5 showed, for instance, that matters were more nuanced than either Schumpeter or the conventional advocates of competition claimed. We delineated circumstances in which a monopoly might lead to more or less innovation than a duopoly, and in which monopoly might lead to higher or lower levels of welfare. While these simple models of, say, Cournot equilibrium do not capture the "spur" to innovation that competition is supposed to provide, we also showed that the

alleged spur to innovation may be much less than is widely thought—
and that the market can as well distort the pattern of innovation.

We can use an analysis similar to that of the previous chapter to
describe welfare-enhancing government intervention in the context of
an *n*-good economy. As before, industrial policy depends on the set of
instruments available to the government—for example, whether it can
undo the effects of monopoly and whether it can impose lump sum
taxes. Here, we assume that the government can do nothing about the
monopoly power of each firm but that in setting, say, a subsidy for any
product, it takes into account that markets are distorted as a result of
monopolistic competition.

Even then, precise prescriptions for the design of optimal intervention depend on what the government can do with, say, tax and subsidy
policies, and whether it can undo the adverse effects of monopoly. For
instance, if the government can impose a nondistortionary profits tax
and use it to subsidize production in the first and second periods, it can
presumably fully undo the effects of monopoly. If it can also undo the
effects of second-period monopoly, the formulae derived earlier can
be used. If it cannot undo monopoly, then providing a subsidy to a
monopoly to encourage it to produce more, because of the learning
spillovers to others, may be more attractive if it can nonetheless undo
the adverse distributional consequences of such subsidies.

The major difference between this case and those analyzed in the
previous chapter is that if there are no cross-sector learning externalities, the monopolistically competitive firm internalizes the learning
externality. However, the firm still does not internalize cross-sector
demand effects; that is, the actions of firm *j* (controlling product *j*)
affect the demand for product *i*, and therefore the equilibrium level of
innovation in that sector. But, as in the previous chapter, there are also
macro labor-supply effects which firms fail to take into account.

What makes the analysis still more complicated, though, is that even
in the absence of learning effects, the general equilibrium with monopolistic competition (either with a fixed or variable number of firms) will
not, in general, be Pareto efficient. Dixit and Stiglitz (1977) showed
that with free entry, with all firms facing the same fixed costs of entry,
symmetry, and constant elasticity of demand curves (and no learning),
the market equilibrium was efficient. However, when these idealized
conditions were dropped, it was not.

In the discussion here, we attempt to focus on certain simplified cases where the market distortions associated with learning can be identified.

This chapter is divided into three sections. After describing the behavior of the monopolist, we contrast the monopoly outcome with the competitive outcome, focusing in particular on the case of symmetry. Next, we describe the optimal government intervention, focusing then on the special case of a two-sector model, in one of which there is learning which spills over to the other.

The Behavior of the Monopolist

Using the notation of the previous chapter, the firm sets

$$(p_i^t + C_i^t \, dp_i^t/dC_i^t) = 1 - \delta C_i^{t+1} H_i^i/(H^i)^2 \tag{1}$$

or

$$p_i^t(1 - 1/\acute\eta_i) = 1 - \delta\zeta_i h_i$$

or

$$p_i^t = (1 - \delta\zeta_i h_i)/(1 - 1/\acute\eta_i), \tag{2}$$

where (as before)

$$\zeta_i = L_i^{t+1}/L_i^t,$$

the ratio of the input into sector j at time t to that at $t + 1$,

$$h_i = d(\ln H^i)/d(\ln L_i^t),$$

the (own) elasticity of productivity with respect to labor input (the learning coefficient), and

$$1/\acute\eta_i = -d(\ln p_i)/d(\ln C_i),$$

the elasticity of demand.

Second-period production is given by the solution to

$$p_i^{t+1} = [1 - H]/(1 - 1/\acute{\eta}_i). \tag{3}$$

The monopolist obviously doesn't take into account the consequences of its production or pricing decisions on the learning of other firms—either through spillover effects or through market effects. The latter can be important in the case of a nonseparable demand function. But the firm does take into account its own learning, and so sets a price (the first period) lower than it would if there were no learning. Firms with more elastic demand functions charge a lower price (and produce more the first period); but firms with a more inelastic demand show a greater sensitivity to learning (i.e., all firms lower their price as *h* increases, but those with a higher markup—lower price elasticity—lower their price more. They have to, in order to expand output.)

Assessing Monopoly Market Distortion

The nature of the overall market distortion is, however, complex. For instance, in the second period, because of the exercise of monopoly power, the benefits of learning will be smaller. However, given the lower level of output in the second period, ignoring spillovers, the firm appropriately values the benefits of learning, which it sees at the margin as saving labor.[1]

There can be distortions in both total labor supply in the first period and in its allocation.

The Case of Symmetry

To focus on the impact on labor supply, we consider a symmetric equilibrium in which all firms have the same demand and learning elasticities. The effect of monopolistic competition is to change real wages in the first period. If first-period labor supply elasticity is zero, this has no effect on learning. An awareness of the learning benefits drives up the real wage, but that is all that happens. First- and second-period output is unchanged.

But if there is a positive elasticity of labor supply, the analysis becomes more interesting. In the case of myopic monopolistic competition (where no weight is given to the value of future learning), first-period real wages are lowered as a result of monopoly power, labor supply is lowered, output is lowered, and learning is thereby lowered.

With myopic monopolies, in the symmetric case, monopoly is unambiguously worse than competition; even though neither takes into account the benefits of learning, growth is higher with competition than with monopoly.

With nonmyopic monopoly, whether learning (growth) is higher with monopoly depends on whether the benefits from recognizing the value of learning (which is taken into account by the monopolist and not in the competitive market) exceed the losses from the contraction in output as a result of monopoly power. That is, it depends on whether

$$[1 - \delta \zeta_i h_i]/(1 - 1/\acute{\eta}_i) < \text{or} > 1, \tag{4}$$

that is, on whether

$$\delta \zeta_i h_i > \text{or} < 1/\acute{\eta}_i. \tag{4'}$$

If the elasticity of labor supply is positive, if firms are not myopic, if the elasticity of demand is low, the elasticity of learning is small, the growth of labor input is low (or negative), or the rate of discount is high, then monopoly is worse than competition, even though the benefits of learning have been internalized.

Note that the elasticity of labor supply does not seem to enter equation (4). The elasticity of labor supply does, however, affect the magnitude of the welfare loss from monopoly, and it does affect the magnitude of ζ. In fact, matters are somewhat more complicated than equation (4) might suggest, because ζ_i is itself endogenous. Again assuming symmetry, then $\zeta_i = \zeta_j = L^{t+1}/L^t$. If the elasticity of labor supply is zero, this is unity. If the elasticity of labor supply is positive, then under competition, $\zeta_i > 1$, because of innovation. But under monopoly, there is a countervailing effect, as prices are lowered the first period (real wages are increased) as firms recognize the value of learning. There is thus some presumption that $\zeta_i^c > \zeta_i^m$. ζ_i^m can even be less than unity. The precise value of ζ_i^m depends on the elasticity of labor supply and the equilibrium value of H (the *level* of innovation, as opposed to h, the elasticity of learning). The higher the level of innovation (the higher H), the higher ζ_i, leading in turn to higher production the first period and, as a result, a still higher H. H and ζ are increased if the elasticity of labor supply is higher. At the same time, a higher marginal value of learning spills over into an offsetting effect—a higher demand for labor the first period, higher real wages the first period, a higher value of L^t, and therefore a lower value of ζ_i. So long as this second-round repercussion effect is smaller than the initial effect, and so long as there is a sufficiently high level of innovation, $\zeta_i > 1$; and the greater the elasticity of labor supply, the greater ζ_i. This means that *the greater the elasticity of labor supply, the more likely that the monopoly innovation level will be greater than the competitive level. On the other hand, with a sufficiently low elasticity of demand, low level of learning and learning elasticity, and high discount rate (low value of δ) the level of innovation with monopoly is lower than that with competition.*[2]

General Principles of Government Intervention

The general principles of government intervention should be clear. Government has to correct two market failures and must be careful that in correcting one, it does not exacerbate the other. Focusing only on learning, optimal policy entails encouraging production in the first period by a production subsidy financed (if possible) by a lump sum tax. If a lump sum tax is not possible but the country can borrow, it pays to finance the first-period subsidy with a second-period tax.

If it can only, say, impose a lump sum tax to finance a commodity subsidy in the first period, then it seeks to maximize with respect to t

$$V^t(p^t, -\Sigma\tau_i C_i) + \delta V^{t+1}(p_i^{t+1}, 0), \tag{5}$$

where

$$p_i^t = \kappa_i(1 - \tau_{ai}), \tag{6}$$

$$p_i^{t+1} = \kappa_i/H^i = \kappa_i c^i, \tag{7}$$

$$\kappa_i = 1/(1 - 1/\acute{\eta}_i), \tag{8}$$

the monopoly markup over marginal cost, and

$$c^i = 1/H^i.$$

When we introduce a subsidy, we partially undo the first-period monopoly distortion and correct the underinvestment in production/learning distortion.[3] If we could impose similar corrective taxation in the second period, we could achieve precisely the equilibrium described in the previous chapter for the case of competition.

Here, we assume we cannot; and if not, we have to take into account the fact that the benefits of learning are lower, because future production is lower. Hence, in general, optimal subsidies will be lower.

A Two-Sector Model

The more interesting case is that in which there are two sectors, one (manufacturing, M) with a full learning spillover and the other (agriculture, A) with no learning. In this case, it can be shown that not only is a subsidy on manufacturing desirable, there is even some presumption that it should be larger with monopoly than with competition.

We now have

$$\max_{\{M, A\}} V^t(\kappa_M(1 - \tau_M), \kappa_A(1 + t_A), 0)$$
$$+ \delta V^{t+1}(\kappa_M c(L_M), \kappa_A c(L_M), 0) \tag{9}$$

where, as before, the subsidy to manufacturing, τ_M, is financed by a tax on agriculture, t_A. The first-order condition is given by

$$V_I^t\{(\kappa_M - \kappa_A)C_M - \kappa_A C_A \tau_M \, [d(C_M/C_A)/d\tau_M]\}$$
$$= -\delta V_I^{t+1} c'(L_M)(\kappa_M C_M^{t+1} + \kappa_A C_A^{t+1}) \, dC_M^t/d\tau_M, \tag{10}$$

where, it will be recalled,

$$dt_A/d\tau_M = (C_M/C_A) + \tau_M \, d(C_M/C_A)/d\tau_M.$$

Instead of the condition for the optimal subsidy we obtained in chapter 7,

$$\tau_M = h\hat{\rho} \, (L^{t+1}/L_A^t)\beta_M/(\beta_M + \beta_A), \tag{11}$$

now we have

$$\tau_M = h\hat{\rho}\,(L^{t+1}/L_A^t)(\kappa^*/\kappa_A)\beta_M/[\beta_M + \beta_A + (1 - \kappa_M/\kappa_A)], \qquad (12)$$

where κ^* is the weighted average markup,

$$\kappa^* = s_M^{t+1}\kappa_M + (1 - s_M^{t+1})\kappa_A,$$

and $s_M = L_M/L$, the share of labor going into the manufacturing sector.

   If the markup in the two sectors is the same, (11) and (12) become identical. The industrial subsidy should be increased beyond this point to the extent that it corrects the distortion in the relative allocation of resources to the industrial sector caused by the industrial sector having a higher markup than the agricultural sector.

APPENDIX

Multiple Equilibria

In the monopolistic equilibrium, the higher total demand (and thus the firm's output) next period, the higher the value of learning, and thus the higher the level of production this period. But the higher the level of production this period, the higher learning, the higher real wages the second period, and, with a positive supply elasticity, the higher output the second period. Hence, we can write, in the case of symmetry,

$$C^t = Z(C^{e\ t+1}), Z' > 0, \qquad (A.1)$$

$$C^{t+1} = X(C^t), X' > 0, \qquad (A.2)$$

where C^t is consumption (aggregate, or of a typical good) in period t, and $C^{e\ t+1}$ is expected output in the second period. A rational expectations equilibrium requires $C^{e\ t+1} = C^{t+1}$ and $\{C^{t*}, C^{t+1*}\}$ to be solved simultaneously

$$C^{t*} = Z(C^{t+1*}) \qquad (A.3)$$

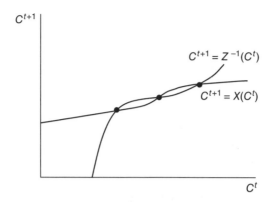

Figure 9.1 Consumption (production) during the first period is an increasing function of expected output in the second period, and consumption (production) during the second period is an increasing function of actual output in the first period. There can be multiple rational expectations equilibria.

and

$$C^{t+1*} = X(C^{t*}). \qquad (A.4)$$

But as figure 9.1 illustrates, because both loci are upward sloping, there can be multiple equilibria, a low-learning equilibrium, with low output in the first period and in the second, and a high-learning equilibrium. The locus Z can take on quite complicated shapes, because Z' depends on, for instance, how h (the elasticity of learning with respect to first-period production) changes with the level of production, how the elasticity of demand changes with the level of production, and on the elasticity of labor supply.[4] Clearly, if there is no elasticity of labor supply, C^t does not depend on C^{t+1} and there is a unique equilibrium.

There is some presumption that welfare is higher in the latter equilibrium than in the former.

CHAPTER TEN

Long-Term Growth
and Innovation

FINITE-PERIOD MODELS, such as that which we have employed in the previous two chapters, have gone out of fashion in economics in favor of infinite-period models. To make such models tractable, however, requires very special parameterizations, so that in practice neither model is really more general than the other. If there is to be a steady state with learning, since the output per unit of labor is increasing steadily, for the labor supply to any sector to be constant, either (a) the labor supply must be inelastic and relative prices must be constant or (b) utility of consumption must be logarithmic. Logarithmic utility functions have the unattractive property that the share of expenditure on each commodity is fixed. Normally, relative prices will be constant only with full spillovers (one of the cases we focus on, but clearly not general).

Alternatively, we can focus on asymptotic behavior, for instance, where the fraction of a person's (society's) time spent working in any particular sector approaches some bound. But again, these asymptotes are often of limited interest in the short run (and we are always in the short run), especially since, in the general case of these models, asymptotic allocations of labor to certain sectors go to zero.[1]

The problems posed by learning models are even more complicated in the case of, say, an exponentially growing population. Of course, with a finite earth, such models face a problem of asymptotically infinite density, which is, to say the least, uncomfortable. But more formally, if learning depends on labor input and labor input is always growing, then, with learning, steady-state growth depends on the delicate balancing of the effective increasing returns from learning with decreasing returns, either decreasing returns in the learning process itself or diminishing returns associated with a fixed factor such as land. There is no a priori reason to expect the two forces to just offset each other. One can find parameterizations in which this occurs, but we should not be fooled—they are very special.

Indeed, there is no theoretical reason to expect the episodic large innovations that have transformed our economy—electricity, computers, the automobile—to occur with regular periodicity and appropriate magnitude to sustain anything approximating a steady state.

In our own lifetime, we have seen dramatic transitions in the rate of population growth, to the point where it is even declining in many advanced industrial countries. There is a general consensus that the global population will level off (will *have* to level off) at around 9 billion.

In short, we shouldn't take steady-state models excessively seriously. They are meant to help us think through trade-offs. In some cases—for instance, when we are focusing on issues of the demographic transition—more insight might be obtained from looking at N-period models, where population is expanding in earlier periods and stationary in later periods. On the other hand, with a high enough discount rate, the distant future is of little moment, and a model focusing on the short run may provide a good approximation.

Of course, finite-period models have their own limitations. Clearly, behavior tomorrow depends on the future *beyond* tomorrow. In an n-period model, there is no incentive to invest in the nth period and little incentive to invest shortly before that.

Thus, both finite-period and steady-state models should be viewed only as tools to help us think through, in some simplified contexts, the complexities of multiperiod dynamics. The essential insights of the finite-period models in chapters 7, 8, and 9 are valid in much more general models—for instance, the notions that monopolies will take into account learning benefits in their production decisions; competitive firms will not; neither will take into account learning externalities; and that accordingly, there is a role for government intervention, to encourage sectors with greater learning spillovers (both direct and indirect.)

In this chapter, we briefly explore special cases in which a steady state exists. We structure the cases so that whatever is optimal at time t is optimal at time $t + 1$; in that case, policy is directed at choosing the optimum steady state.[2] In all of the cases, the central result is that it is optimal to permanently impose distorting taxes to encourage production in the learning sector.

In chapter 8, we explored models in which the government directly controls outputs (inputs), in which it has indirect control through taxes but can impose lump sum taxes, and in which it cannot impose lump sum taxes. We have also explored models in which learning is symmetric or asymmetric and in which there is and is not perfect competition. In this chapter, we investigate only two cases; the results can easily be generalized to the other contexts.

Logarithmic Utility Functions

We first assume a logarithmic utility function in goods,

$$u^t = \Sigma \; \alpha_i \ln C_i^t, \; \Sigma \; \alpha_i = 1, \tag{1}$$

and assume separability in utility between goods and leisure,

$$W^t = u^t - v(L^t). \tag{2}$$

At each moment of time, this implies (in static maximization)

$$\alpha_i / C_i^t = p_i v'(L^t),$$

which in turn implies that[3]

$$C_i^t p_i = \alpha_i / v'(L^t).$$

Expenditure shares are proportional to α_i and don't depend at all on costs. We focus on the direct-control problem where the government sets $\{v, L\}$, where v_i is the share of total labor allocated to the production of good i. In the short run, as before, we assume the cost of each good is unity. Then

$$W^t = \Sigma_i \, \alpha_i \ln v_i^t + \ln L^t - v(L^t),$$

so

$$W^0 \equiv \Sigma_i \, \alpha_i \ln v_i^0 + \ln L^0 - v(L^0),$$

from which it follows that static optimization entails $v_i^t = \alpha_i$, and $1 = v'(L^*)L^*$. Note that the short-run optimum L does not depend on productivity.

We assume that, as before, productivity at time $t + 1$ is related to productivity at time t by a learning function, which we now write as

$$P_i^{t+1} = P_i^t H_i^t(vL),$$

where P_i^t is output per unit labor at time t and vL is the vector of labor inputs. If L and v are the same at t and $t + 1$, then

$$u^{t+1} = u^t + \Sigma \, \alpha_i \ln H_i^t(vL) = u^t + g(vL),$$

where

$$g(vL) \equiv \Sigma \, \alpha_i \ln H_i^t(vL).$$

$g(vL)$ is the overall rate of productivity increase (measured here in terms of utility). It should be clear that, given the structure of the model, if $\{v, L\}$ is optimal for time t, it is optimal for time $t + 1$. We can write discounted utility[4] as

$$W = \Sigma \, W^t g^t = [W^0 + g/(1 - \delta)]/(1 - \delta),$$

from which it follows that W is maximized when

$$\partial W^0/\partial v_i + [1/(1 - \delta)](\partial g/\partial v_i) = 0$$

$$\partial W^0/\partial L + [1/(1 - \delta)](\partial g/\partial L) = 0,$$

from which it follows that we expand labor input beyond the level which would have maximized short-run welfare (i.e., that would have maximized W^0), and the extent by which production is increased beyond short-run utility maximization is greater in sectors that increase g the most. Moreover, in this model, industrial policy is a permanent feature of the economy.

It is easy to derive the implications for some special cases. Assume that there are two sectors, A and M, and there is learning only in the M sector. Then if there are no learning spillovers,

$$g = \alpha_M \ln H(\upsilon_M L),$$

and

$$W^0 = \alpha_M \ln \upsilon_M + (1 - \alpha_M) \ln(1 - \upsilon_M) + \ln L^0 - v(L^0).$$

The optimum values of υ_M and υ_A are[s]

$$\upsilon_M = \alpha_M[1 + h/(1 - \delta)]/[1 + \alpha_M h/(1 - \delta)]$$

$$= 1 - (1 - \alpha_M)]/[1 + \alpha_M h/(1 - \delta)],$$

and

$$\upsilon_A = 1 - \upsilon_M = (1 - \alpha_M)]/[1 + \alpha_M h/(1 - \delta)],$$

where, as before, h is the elasticity of the learning curve,

$$h = d(\ln H)/d(\ln (\upsilon_M L)).$$

The greater h, the larger the fraction of labor allocated to manufacturing. When $h = 0$, as expected, $\upsilon_M = \alpha_M$.

By the same token, work at each date is expanded beyond the static level, to the point where L^{**} now satisfies

$$L^{**} v'(L^{**}) = 1 + h\alpha_M/(1 - \delta),$$

or

$$1/L^{**} - v'(L^{**}) = -h\alpha_M/[(1 - \delta)L^{**}] < 0;$$

the static marginal disutility of work exceeds the value of the marginal output.

Both of these results confirm our earlier assertion that production (consumption) of manufacturing goods expand beyond the static level the greater the learning elasticity and the lower the discount rate. There is a greater input of labor, and a greater share of that input is allocated to manufacturing.

Alternatively, assume there are perfect spillovers. Then

$$g = \ln H(\upsilon_M L),$$

so

$$d(\ln g)/d(\ln \upsilon_M) = h,$$

an effect which is $1/\alpha_M$ greater than in the case with no spillovers. Hence, the optimum value of υ_M given by

$$\upsilon_M = [\alpha_M + h/(1 - \delta)]/[1 + h/(1 - \delta)] = 1 - (1 - \alpha_M)]/[1 + h/(1 - \delta)],$$

confirming our earlier assertion that production (consumption) of manufacturing expands beyond the static level more when there are spillovers than when there are not.

Fixed Labor Supply, No Lump Sum Taxation, Two Sectors

A second case where simple and intuitive results can be obtained is that where the labor supply is fixed and lump sum taxes are not allowed. We again focus on the case where there are two sectors, denoted A and M. Here, we have an additional problem in steady-state analysis: If there is differential growth in labor productivity in the two sectors, one sector gets a smaller, diminishing its share of overall expenditures, except in the special case of unitary elasticity of substitution (the logarithmic utility case just analyzed). Accordingly, we focus on the case with full spillovers, so that relative prices remain unchanged and, with homotheticity, so do relative shares. We assume a homothetic utility function of the form

$$U = U(C_M, C_A) = C_A^{-a+1} u(C_M/C_A),\ 0 < a < 1,$$

where, as before, $a = 1/\eta$ is the elasticity of marginal utility. As before, we impose a subsidy at the rate τ on manufacturing, paid for by a tax at rate t on agriculture. We can then write the indirect utility function as $V(1 - \tau, 1 + t, I)$. Static utility maximization entails maximizing V with respect to τ:

$$dV/d\tau = -C_A\tau\,[d(C_M/C_A)/d\tau]V_I$$

$$= -C_M\{d[\ln(C_M/C_A)]/d(\ln \tau)\}V_I$$

$$= -C_M(\beta_M + \beta_A)V_I = 0,$$

If the elasticity of substitution is greater than zero, the above equation holds if and only if $\tau = 0$ To see this, observe that

$$\beta_M + \beta_A = \tau d[\ln(C_M/C_A)]/d\tau.$$

where β_M and β_A are, as defined in earlier chapters, the [total] elasticity of demand of M and A, respectively, with respect to the manufacturing subsidy, taking into account the effect of the corresponding increase in the tax on A goods. An increase in τ changes the relative price, and the relative consumptions are unchanged if and only if the elasticity of substitution is zero.

But now assume that there is learning only in the manufacturing sector but perfect spillover to the agricultural sector. Productivity growth is thus $H(C_M)$. Again, we have structured the model so that the optimal subsidy at time t is the optimal subsidy at $t + 1$, and the present discounted value of utility is given by

$$U_0/1 - \delta H^{-\eta+1},$$

which is maximized at

$$\partial(\ln U_0)/\partial t + \delta\left[\frac{(1-\eta)H^{-\eta+1}}{1-\delta H^{-\eta+1}}\right]$$

$$[\partial(\ln H)/\partial(\ln C_M)][d(\ln C_M)/d\tau] = 0.$$

The above expression can be used, as before, to derive the optimal subsidy rate. The distortion from the static allocation is greater the greater the elasticity of learning $[h = \partial(\ln H)/\partial(\ln C_M)]$ and the higher δ (the more future utility is valued relative to today).

Cumulative Experience

We now take a somewhat different approach in which changes in productivity are based not directly on current production but on the change in cumulative experience. (Effectively, Arrow's original model was of this form, though he focused on investment, not production.) That is, we write, in the absence of spillovers,

$$Q^k(t) = H^k(t)L^k(t),$$

where now productivity depends on, say, discounted cumulative experience, E, according to the function

$$H^k,(t) = [E]^{b^k},$$

where b^k is the elasticity of productivity with respect to experience in the sector, and where experience, E, is defined by[6]

$$E = \left[\int_0^t L_k(x)e^{-z(t-x)}dx \right],$$

capturing the notion that experiences a long time ago have limited relevance for productivity today. In steady state, it is obvious that

$$d(\ln Q^k)/dt = (b^k + 1)n,$$

where n is the rate of growth of the population. Even though learning is endogenous, we obtain the standard Solow result that the long-term sectoral growth rate is determined by the rate of growth of population. The fact that learning is affected by experience is still important, because the aggregate growth rate is affected by the allocation of resources. Assume, for instance, as before, individual logarithmic utility functions

$$W^t = \Sigma \, \alpha_i \ln C^t_{\,i} - v(L^t), \; \Sigma \, \alpha_i = 1,$$

exponential labor force growth at the rate n, and a social welfare function of the form

$$W = \int \exp \{-r + n\} W^t,$$

where r is the discount rate, $r > n + g$, where g is the rate of growth of utility (which, given our assumptions about the utility function, in steady state is equal to the rate of growth of output), and where we have moved to a continuous time formulation. In steady state,

$$W = -\{[W^* + v(L^*)]/(n + g - r)\} + v(L^*)/(n - r)$$

With learning, in steady state, $W + v$ (that is, the utility derived from the consumption of goods) is increasing at the rate

$$g = \Sigma \, \alpha^k (b^k + 1) n.$$

Clearly, allocating more labor to sectors with higher learning elasticities will lead to higher rates of growth of utility (consumption). As before, let v_i and g be the fraction of the labor supply allocated to sector i. For simplicity, we can express W^* (in steady state) as a function of $\{L, v\}$. Then, if we want to choose the allocation that maximizes with respect to L and v

$$-\{[W^*\{L, v\} + v(L^*)]/(n + g(L, v) - r)\} + v(L^*)/(n - r)$$

we must distort the allocation of $\{L, v\}$, relative to static utility maximization, to increase long-run growth.[7] The optimum balances the two effects. Because increasing L increases cumulative experience, it increases productivity, and long-term social welfare maximization takes this into account. In the standard Solow growth model, an increase in L does not have any effect on long-term growth rates, just as an increase in the savings rate has no effect on the long-run growth rate.

Here, however, *both the overall level of labor supply and the allocation of labor do*. The rate of growth is endogenous and can be affected by industrial policy.

Asymmetric Equilibria and the Advantages of Specialization

Learning, as we have noted, introduces nonconvexities, which may make it desirable for countries to specialize. The learning curves introduced in the previous section suffer from diminishing returns and therefore don't capture this effect. If, for instance, in our model with logarithmic utility functions, there were two commodities, with $\alpha_i = \frac{1}{2}$, and symmetric learning curves with diminishing returns, then

$$v^* = \frac{1}{2}.$$

Assume that there are no learning spillovers (that is, productivity depends only on cumulative discounted experience within its own sector) and that H is (within a region) a convex function. Assume, for instance, that H "jumps" once E hits a critical threshold of E^*, as depicted in figure 10.1.

$$H^k = \left[\int_0^t L^k(x)e^{-z(t-x)}\, dx \right]^b, \text{ if } E \geq E^*,$$

$$H^k = \hat{H}, \text{ if } E < E^*,$$

such that $\hat{H} = 1 << E^{*b}$.[8] (See figure 10.1.)
   Assume further that

$$u^k = \ln C^k, \text{ if } C^k \geq 1,$$

$$u^k = 0, \text{ otherwise,}$$

where now C^k represents individual consumption. (We introduce this assumption because otherwise, as C^k goes to zero, the marginal utility of consumption goes to infinity, and we always produce both goods. In our formulation, however, this implies that utility is a nonconcave function of consumption, which strengthens the forces for specialization. See figure 10.2.)

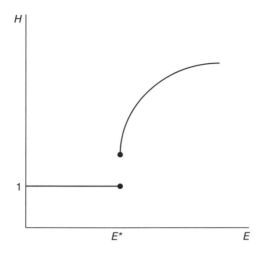

Figure 10.1 Productivity is a nonconcave function of experience. This implies that there are advantages to specialization.

It follows that if L is small enough, then optimality may require, say, $v_1 = 1$, $v_2 = 0$. The economy specializes in one of the two commodities. As we specialize in commodity 1, H^2/H^1 becomes small (there is no cumulative experience in producing good 2), so it becomes optimal both statically and dynamically not to produce good 2.

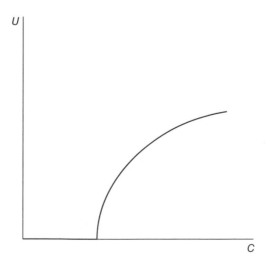

Figure 10.2 Utility is a nonconcave function of consumption.

Cumulative Learning from Output

A slight variant of the previous model focuses on output rather than input. The difference arises from that fact that with learning, output grows more rapidly than input.[9] Assume now that the relevant measure of "experience" is

$$E^k = \int_0^t Q^k(x)e^{-z(t-x)}\,dx.$$

For simplicity, we assume $H^k(t) = [E^k(t)]^b$, or

$$H^k(t) = \left[\int_0^t Q^k(x)e^{-z(t-x)}\,dx\right]^b.$$

Thus, in steady state (where the same fraction of labor is allocated to any sector every year), the rate of growth of the kth sector, g^k, satisfies the equation

$$g^k = bg^k + n = n/(1 - b),$$

where it will be remembered that $b < 1$. If $b > 1$, faster growth begets faster growth of experience, which begets even faster growth of output. The economy is unstable, with potentially super-exponential growth.

While the steady states of this model look very much like those of the earlier models, in which experience is based on labor input, more general versions of this model can give rise to multiple short-run equilibria. Assume that $H^k(E)$ does not have constant elasticity.[10] Then, assuming that at each date, L is fixed, but growing at the rate n,

$$g^k = h^k(E)\,d(\ln E)/dt + n + d(\ln v^k)/dt,$$

where, as before, $h^k(E) = d(\ln H^k)/d(\ln E)$. Since E and $d(\ln E)/dt$ depend on g^k, it would appear that there could be both high- and low-growth scenarios: A high level of expansion of a sector can lead to a higher elasticity of learning (e.g., if there is learning by learning) and a higher rate of growth of "experience," both of which support the higher expansion of the sector. The implications for optimal policy are similar to those discussed earlier: Even if two sectors initially appear symmetric, it may be optimal to focus on one of the two sectors to increase learning; but now it is possible that the increased growth induced by the faster learning is further reinforced by a higher learning elasticity.

CHAPTER ELEVEN

The Infant-Economy Argument for Protection: Trade Policy in a Learning Environment

CONVENTIONAL ECONOMIC wisdom is that free trade enhances economic efficiency and this promotes growth. Indeed, there are few propositions in economics about which there is greater consensus among conventional economists than those which assert the benefits of free trade.[1,2]

However, in the "learning" context upon which we focus here, spillovers (both technological and institutional) within countries but across industries may be fundamental to the process of growth. As we have already noted, there will be trade-offs between static (in)efficiencies and dynamic benefits. In the last set of chapters, we saw how production in earlier periods (especially in sectors with high learning elasticities and learning spillovers) was increased (beyond the level associated with static efficiency) in order to increase growth. In an open economy, the essential trade-off is between the static efficiencies associated with comparative advantage and the dynamic benefits associated with the faster learning that might come from alternative resource allocations, including those associated with beneficial local spillovers.[3]

We show that it is desirable for governments to intervene in the market, to encourage, possibly through trade protection, sectors in which there is more learning and more learning spillovers. We call this the infant-*economy* argument for protection: Learning benefits are likely to be especially high for countries for which there is a large knowledge gap between themselves and the more advanced countries.

Before presenting the argument in detail, we discuss a long-standing argument for protection that might seem similar, but in fact is not: the infant-*industry* argument for protection.

The Infant-Industry Argument for Protection

The infant-industry argument for protection held that developing countries should protect their "infants" so they could become more productive (learn-by-doing) and thus become competitive with the more advanced countries. Without such protection, the developing economies would be relegated to producing traditional goods marked by slow growth in productivity.[4]

As we argued in chapter 4, the industrial sector is subject to faster learning than agriculture,[5] so it was natural that countries would want to move into that sector. But industry was not their current comparative advantage; without some government intervention, they could not enter the industrial sector and therefore could not learn. Unfettered markets, it was feared, would keep a country from entering more dynamic sectors, especially if the learning is external to the firm (for then no firm would have an incentive to make the investments required to "catch up").

With protection, firms could enter these more dynamic sectors: As a result, for instance, of learning by doing, marginal costs would decline, and firms would eventually become competitive. Without protection, they could not survive to enjoy the benefits that come from that learning.

There is, in fact, considerable evidence for the validity of these infant-industry arguments—protection did play a critical role in the development of many European countries (see, in particular, Chang 2002). But critics point out that in many cases, the infants never seem to grow up, imposing high costs on society. We shall address these concerns later in this book—we believe that they are far less relevant for the infant-economy argument for protection than for the infant-industry argument. Indeed, we will explain why government subsidies may be desirable even if the subsidized sector *never* becomes fully competitive.

Moreover, these critics contend that if it were the case that these firms would eventually be competitive, they should be able to borrow today (see, e.g., Baldwin 1969). It is easy to show that in a long-run dynamic model (i.e., where firms maximize the present discounted value of their profits, taking into account future learning), the relevant marginal cost of production is *lowered* by the fact that producing today lowers the marginal cost that they will face in the future.[6] Thus, it would be optimal for them to operate at a loss today. Opponents of protection say that if these firms are really competitive, then they *should* be able to borrow to finance their learning—there is no need for government intervention.

Capital Market Imperfections, Imperfect Information, and the Infant-Industry Argument for Protection

However, especially in developing countries, firms cannot borrow, especially on the basis of future profits (not collateral). The theory of imperfect and asymmetric information has explained why that is so.[7]

The response to this (according to the critics of the infant-industry argument) is that government should then step in to correct *this* market imperfection, rather than creating a new political economy problem. If that can't be done in general, the government should (in this view) simply lend the money that the firm would have been able to borrow had capital markets worked better, at a commercial interest rate.

To some extent, this is in fact what the successful East Asian countries did (see Stiglitz 1996; Stiglitz and Uy 1996; World Bank 1993). They made capital more available to firms that they believed showed more learning potential. But they went beyond just correcting the failure in financial markets.

There are two reasons that simply correcting those failures will not suffice. The first, which is the subject of most of this book, is that markets and economies in which innovation (learning) is important are rife with market failures. Correcting one market failure—access to finance—leaves in place a rash of others, some of which are far more important. In the case of the East Asian countries, they were not just correcting financial market failures; they used access to scarce finance as an instrument of industrial policy, to encourage sectors with large technological spillovers.

The second response to the suggestion that firm subsidies or loans be used *instead of* (rather than in addition to) protectionism is that this approach does not fully take into account the information imperfections that give rise to capital market imperfections. The government may not be in any better position to judge which *firms* are likely to repay their loans than the capital market is. (As we explain below, assessing which industries or sectors have more learning potential and more learning spillovers requires quite different information.)[8]

In a sense, there is some, but not complete, similarity between the use of the patent system to finance research and the use of protection to finance new industries. Government funding of research can be much more efficient, avoiding some of the static and dynamic inefficiencies associated with the patent system (see chapter 15). But the government then has to decide *which* researchers should be funded, just as capital markets have to decide which entrepreneurs to finance.[9]

Both the patent system and protection, though, allow for self-selection. With the patent system, firms take their own chances; those that are lucky or smart will get a return. If firms misjudge, they bear the consequences. So too for protection, or, as we explain later, with other broad-based interventions, such as exchange rate adjustments.[10]

Why Not Entering the More Dynamic Sectors May Not Be a Disadvantage

This market failure we have just described, by itself, does not provide a fully coherent argument for trade and industrial policy. Underlying the infant-industry argument for protection is the belief that countries are disadvantaged if they cannot enter sectors with high productivity growth. This is, however, not necessarily the case.

The reason is that all countries will benefit from the learning in the more dynamic economies as a result of lower prices, so long as markets remain competitive. Moving into a more dynamic sector does not guarantee a country greater (innovation) rents. And those not in the sector benefit from the learning going on elsewhere, *so long as markets are competitive.*

This can be illustrated by a simple example. Consider a two-country, two-good model, in which we assume all persons have the same utility function: $\ln U = .5 \ln C_1 + .5 \ln C_2$.[11] Each good is produced by labor alone; the two countries are the same size; and country 1 specializes in good 1, while country 2 specializes in good 2. It is trivial to show that half of global income goes to country 1, half to country 2. If country 1 has rapid technical progress (endogenous or exogenous) but goods are produced competitively, prices will fall in proportion to productivity, so that while revenue per unit produced falls in proportion to productivity, revenue per hour remains the same. Country 2 benefits fully from country 1's learning. It should not envy the other country that has specialized in the seemingly more dynamic sector.

This analysis, however, assumes away two of the critical market failures in markets with learning and innovation that we highlighted in chapters 5 and 6: learning spillovers and imperfections of competition. Each of them alone provides a convincing rationale for trade and industrial policies, and the two of them interact to provide an even more compelling case for government intervention (and even more so in conjunction with the other market failures delineated earlier in the book). Most of our analysis focuses on learning externalities, but before turning to the implications of these spillovers, we comment briefly on imperfections of competition.

Imperfections of Competition

Chapter 5 emphasized that markets in which learning (innovation) is important are likely to be imperfectly competitive, and prices may be (significantly) above average and marginal costs.[12] Imperfect competition provides, in general, grounds for government intervention. But we normally think of the desired intervention as one form or another of competition policy. However, governments in exporting countries may not have incentives to enforce competition among their exporters. The government in, say, the developed country in which the incumbent monopoly is located has to assess the loss of profits to the monopolist and the loss in tax revenues which might accrue to the government from taxing those profits[13] against the gains to *its* consumers. It doesn't weigh the benefits to consumers in other countries; indeed, since it may garner for itself a share of the profits earned by the monopolist through taxes, it even benefits from the monopoly. Even if the government were not beset by "political economy" problems—undue influence from the incumbent monopolist—it might not be in its interests to intervene to encourage more competition.

Because the country of the incumbent already enjoys the learning spillovers from the presence of the industry, the benefits it receives from helping a competitor get established are also smaller than in the rival country. If there is to be a subsidy to establish a competitor, it would rather free ride on the efforts of others.

Like many of the policies considered in this book, there are important intertemporal trade-offs. Trying to create viable domestic competitors to foreign monopolists and oligopolists has a cost. With direct subsidies, the costs are borne by taxpayers. With protectionism, the costs are borne by consumers. But if successful, there will be a more competitive marketplace in the long run. In the case of protectionism, part of the trade-off may be less competition in the short run, but more in the long run.[14]

In short, the social benefits to the developing country from intervening in the market to put one or more firms in a position to be effective competitors may well be greater than the costs. Its consumers gain in the long run (though with protectionism, they may lose in the short run; in the case of subsidies, consumers may gain even in the short run), the country gains from the learning spillovers, and the country may be able to seize a fraction of the producer rents that accrue to foreign producers as a result of imperfections of competition.

Establishing a more competitive marketplace is, of course, a global public good, from which consumers everywhere benefit. But because it is a global public good, there are likely to be insufficient "investments" in creating a more competitive global marketplace.[15]

From the Infant-Industry Argument to the Infant-Economy Argument

This book stresses the importance of creating a *learning economy*. Our focus is thus not on particular sectors but on the broader economic system. In this chapter, we argue that protectionism can be an important instrument for helping infant economies grow by creating a learning society.

We provide the real answer to the critics of industrial and trade policy—a fully articulated rationale for protection based on market failures derived from information asymmetries and endogenous learning and innovation *with learning externalities.*

While earlier chapters (and earlier discussions within this chapter) highlighted that there were multiple market failures *inherently* associated with innovation (including imperfections in risk markets and in competition), this chapter will focus more narrowly on learning externalities.

In this perspective, industrial and trade policy is not focused on picking winners, though, to be sure, governments do not want to pick losers. Nor is it predicated on the belief that government can do a better job than the private sector of picking winners. *It is based on the notion that learning involves spillovers (externalities) that will be imperfectly internalized in a market economy.* Industrial and trade policies are concerned with identifying sectors or industries (firms, areas of innovation) which would generate large externalities or where the returns that could be appropriated by the innovating (learning) firm are a fraction of societal benefits. Governments in many countries have, in fact, done a credible job in making these selections, and our societies have benefited greatly as a result. Chapter 12 discusses these historical experiences.

The infant-economy argument for protection that we advance here does not even require identifying particular sectors with large spillovers or large capital-market imperfections. It simply argues that *on average* spillovers may be larger within some broadly defined sectors of the economy—sufficiently larger to warrant distortions in the conventional static allocation of resources.

In order to show more fully the role of trade policy, we continue the analysis of the simple two-sector model with an industrial (modern) and a traditional ("craft" or "agricultural") sector introduced in chapter 7, extending it to an open economy. Recall from that discussion that there are four key features to the model: (a) there are spillovers from the industrial sector to the crafts sector, for which firms in the industrial sector are not compensated; (b) such spillovers are geographically based, that is, only productivity increases in the industrial sector in the developing country affect productivity increases in the traditional sector;[16] (c) the industrial sector is the sector in which innovations are concentrated; and (d) among the important determinants of the pace

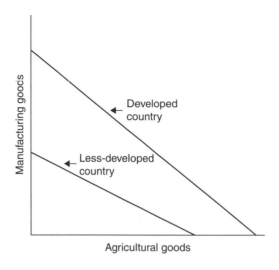

Figure 11.1 Comparative and absolute advantage.

The developing country has an absolute disadvantage in both goods, but a comparative advantage in agriculture.

of innovation in the industrial sector in the developing country (or of its impact on the traditional sector) is the size of that industrial sector.[17]

Earlier critiques of trade policies encouraging the development of the industrial sector in developing countries ignored the spillovers that are at the heart of the analysis here. They argued, first, that protection is costly: Korea could have more industrial goods and more agricultural goods by taking advantage of its comparative advantage, as illustrated in figures 11.1 and 11.2. Figure 11.1. shows that Korea (the less-developed country) has a comparative advantage in agricultural goods. By specializing in agriculture, its "consumption possibilities schedule" is unambiguously improved.

Second, critics of protectionism contended further: that Korea's comparative advantage wouldn't change as a result of protectionism. Korea would always have a comparative advantage in growing rice. Therefore, it was foolish for it to restrict imports of industrial goods, even if by doing so increased productivity in the industrial goods sector. It could never catch up, so the protection would have to be permanent. Year after year, the country would have been better off if it simply specialized in its own comparative advantage, growing rice.[18]

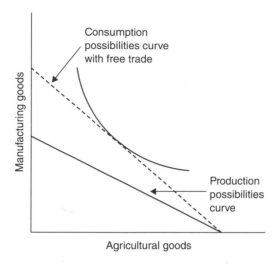

Figure 11.2 Free-trade equilibrium

By specializing in agriculture, the developing country could have a higher level of utility—more consumption of both goods. This is the free-trade equilibrium.

There are two errors in this line of reasoning. The first is that countries can and do catch up, at least in certain areas, and Korea provides a telling example. If catching up is possible, then *dynamic* comparative advantage differs from static comparative advantage.[19] Most importantly, *if dynamic comparative advantage is affected by today's resource allocation, then it is desirable to intervene in the market, to move away from static comparative advantage.*

But the second flaw is even more profound. The standard analysis ignores learning spillovers and the fact that there may be more learning, and more learning spillovers, associated with some sectors than others. *If there are advantages to industrialization (e.g., associated with learning and learning spillovers), as our earlier analysis suggests, then again it is desirable to intervene in the market, to move away from static comparative advantage.* Even if the infant never grows up—even if year after year there has to be a subsidy, even if there is no change in comparative advantage—the dynamic benefits of protection, the faster rate of growth which results, may (and under our assumptions will) exceed the static costs. The models we present below show that even if government subsidies (protection) do not change a country's comparative

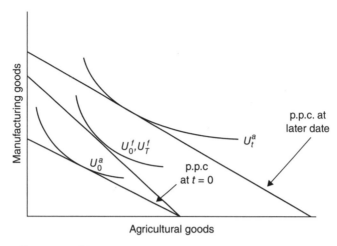

Figure 11.3 Quota autarky

With autarky, in the short run, welfare is lowered $U_0^a < U_0^f$. But in the long run, it is increased: $U_T^a > U_T^f = U_0^f$.

advantage, intervention may be desirable, because it enhances an economy's learning (and its ability to learn). That is, even if Korea's comparative advantage remained in agriculture, industrial protection might be desirable, because by doing so, one might also have a more dynamic agricultural (traditional) sector. Trade restrictions enhance the size of the industrial sector, the benefits spill over to the rural sector, and national income grows at a possibly far faster pace. Our concern is thus maximizing the learning not just of a particular firm or a particular industry but of the entire economy—creating a learning society.

Figure 11.3. shows that under autarky, in the short run, consumers are worse off. Moving from free trade to autarky lowers utility from U_0^f to U_0^a, where the subscript 0 refers to the period and the super-script refers to the trade regime: f for free trade and a for autarky. (Later, we will refer to U_T^f and U_T^a, utility at date T in the free trade and autarky regimes, respectively.) But because with autarky, Korea is producing manufactured goods—and learning—its production pos-sibilities schedule is moving out. At some later date, T, it has moved out so much that society is better off (even with the trade distortion) than it would have been had it remainedwith free trade. With free trade, there would have been no learning, so $U_T^f = U_0^f$. Thus, U_T^f is less than U_T^a. Whether the short-run costs are worth the long-run benefits depends on the pace of learning and the rate of discount. (Of course, countries don't have to choose between the extremes of autarky and free trade. The discussion below will identify the nature of the *optimal* trade intervention.)

In much of the modeling below, we shall assume two (or occasionally three) sectors, but the analysis can easily be extended to n sectors, along the lines of chapter 8.

A Simplified Model

We will consider a highly simplified world consisting of two economies—one developed (D) and the other less developed (L). (The limitation to just two economies is inessential; our model could equally well consist of multiple [identical] versions of each of the two types of economy.)

These economies produce two types of goods—one industrial (M) and the other agricultural/craft (A). (Again, we could easily extend the model to include a multiplicity of goods in each category.) Both are produced using only labor as an input, with technologies that at any point in time embody constant-returns-to-scale. We define, as in chapter 7,[20]

> $c_M^D(c_A^D)$ ≡ amount of labor per unit of industrial (agricultural) output in the developed economy.
> $c_M^L(c_A^L)$ ≡ amount of labor per unit of industrial (agricultural) output in the less-developed economy.

We assume that the developed economy enjoys absolute advantages in the production of both goods (i.e., $c_M^D < c_M^L$ and $c_A^D < c_A^L$), but that the less-developed economy enjoys a comparative advantage in agricultural/craft production. Thus,

$$c_A^D/c_M^D > c_A^L/c_M^L.$$

We further assume that the developed economy is very large relative to the less-developed economy; in particular, that it is capable of supporting the entire global demand for industrial output and at the same time producing significant amounts of agricultural/craft output.

Prices will be determined by the trade-off in the developed economy between the cost of producing the industrial good and the cost of producing the agricultural/craft good. If we designate the agricultural/craft good as numeraire with price unity, then the price of the industrial good in the developed economy will be

$$p_M^D = c_M^D/c_A^D,$$

and wages in the industrial economy will be

$$W^D = 1/c_A^D.$$

In the less-developed economy, again using the agricultural/craft output as numeraire with price unity, the wage level will be

$$W^L = 1/c_A^L,$$

which is, of course, lower than the wage level in the developed economy, since $c_A^L > c_A^D$.

Free-Trade Equilibrium

Since $c_M^D/c_A^D < c_M^L/c_A^L$, industrial production in the less-developed economy is not economically viable. It specializes in agriculture. The composition of consumption in the less-developed economy is then determined by the real price, p_M^D. The composition of output in the industrial economy is determined by the global demand (its own demand plus the imports of the less-developed economy) for industrial goods. Finally, note that, in this simple static equilibrium, all the gains from trade accrue to the less-developed economy.

This was seen earlier graphically in figure 11.1, where we show the production possibilities loci (scaled down to the size of the population) of the two countries. We note that the frontier of the developing country is inside that of the developed, but is flatter. As we noted earlier, and as figure 11.2 illustrates, in the free trade equilibrium for the developing country, it specializes in agricultural goods. Trade unambiguously makes it better off *in the short run*.

Dynamic Development

We now introduce technological progress into this static equilibrium. Formally, we will assume, first, that productivity improvement affects the industrial and agricultural/craft sectors equally (the case of perfect spillovers). Thus,

$$d(\ln c_M)/dt = d(\ln c_A)/dt, \tag{1}$$

so that

$$d[\ln(c_M/c_A)]/dt = 0.$$

Whatever increases productivity increases spillover fully from one sector within the economy to the other. This has one important simplifying implication: Productivity growth does not affect the price of industrial goods relative to agricultural/craft goods. (Our results require only that there be some spillovers from the industrial to the traditional sector within a country.) This means that there is no change over time in comparative advantage.

To repeat the arguments made earlier in the book, productivity growth results from (1) research and development efforts which, while originally devoted to one sector, have benefits that inevitably spillover to other sectors; (2) human capital improvements which, again, while they arise in one sector, inevitably migrate with labor to other sectors of the economy; (3) the accumulated knowledge and attention of managers and engineers which, although developed in one sector, also naturally migrate to other sectors; and (4) institutional developments, which, while they arise in response to the needs of one sector, have benefits to others.

Next, we assume, as earlier, that some sectors are more conducive to learning than others. As in chapter 7, we postulate that the rate of technological progress, g, is determined by the size of the industrial sector:

$$g = -d(\ln c_M)/dt = -d(\ln c_A)/dt = f[Q_M/(Q_M + Q_A)],$$

$$f(0) = 0, f' > 0, \tag{2}$$

where Q_M is the *output* of the industrial sector and Q_A is the *output* of the agricultural/crafts sector. This assumes that the forces driving productivity growth originate in the industrial sector of the economy and have an aggregate impact that is proportional to the (relative) size of the industrial sector.[21] (In a closed-economy model, output, Q_i, and consumption, C_i, are obviously identical. In an open economy, they are not.)

The process of productivity growth described by equations (1) and (2) has important long-run consequences for our two economies. The less-developed economy, with $Q_M^L = 0$, stagnates. Without an industrial sector, there is no productivity growth. In contrast, the developed economy experiences productivity growth at a rate

$$g^D = f[Q_M^D/(Q_M^D + Q_A^D)],$$

where the composition of output is determined increasingly by its own demands for output, because the less-developed economy becomes a progressively smaller part of the overall global economy. Asymptotically, g^D will converge to a rate of growth determined by the developed economy conditions alone. Over time, in the absence of protection, the less-developed economy falls further and further behind its developed counterpart.

The Role of Trade Policy

Consider now the consequences of a ban by the less-developed country on industrial imports (or equivalently, the imposition of prohibitively high tariffs). The result would be an immediate welfare loss as it substituted high-cost domestic industrial production for lower-cost imports from the developed economy. However, in the new autarkic equilibrium, industrial output in the less-developed economy would no longer be zero, and productivity growth would now occur. Just as in the case of the developed economy, a high-tariff, less-developed economy would produce a mix of outputs dependent on its own demands for industrial and agricultural/craft products at a fixed relative price

$$p_M^L = c_M^L/c_A^L.$$

If we designate the resulting industrial output by Q_M^{La} (and the corresponding agricultural output by Q_A^{La}), then the rate of productivity growth would increase from zero to

$$g^{La} = f[Q_M^{La}/(Q_M^{La} + Q_A^{La})].$$

Eventually the benefits of this dynamic improvement in productivity will outweigh the short-term inefficiencies associated with high-cost local industrial production. The country will be better off. Whether the present discounted value of welfare is higher depends on how high g^{La} is, and how low the discount rate. Thus, in this context, trade barriers may enhance rather than impair economic welfare.

If the discount rate is ρ, and if we assume a constant elasticity homothetic utility function (with an elasticity equal to $1 - 1/\eta > 0$),[22] then the present discounted value of utility under free trade is

$$\int U^f e^{-\rho t} \, dt = U^f/\rho,$$

while under autarky, it is

$$\int U_0^a e^{[(1-1/\eta)g^{La} - \rho]t} \, dt = U_0^a/\rho - (1 - 1/\eta)g^{La}.$$

Autarky is better than free trade, provided

$$g^{La} > \rho[1 - (U_0^a/U^f)]/(1 - 1/\eta),$$

i.e., so long as growth is high enough relative to the discount rate and so long as the loss of welfare from autarky is not too high. (Notice that because, with autarky, there is no change in the less-developed economy, U^f, the utility level is constant over time.[23] It also follows that if autarky is preferred to free trade at time 0, it is preferred to free trade at every date.[24])

In this model with full spillovers, the developing country *always* has a comparative disadvantage in the learning good; hence, if it is to continue learning, protection must continue. The infant never grows up, in the sense that agriculture remains the country's comparative advantage—and yet it is desirable to continue to provide subsidies to the learning sector.

Optimal Trade Interventions

Our analysis can be used to derive an optimal tariff balancing the long-term benefits of fostering industrial growth against the short-term costs of inefficient acquisition of industrial products. The methodologies introduced in chapters 7, 8, and 10 can be applied directly to this case. Figure 11.4 provides a heuristic interpretation: The static welfare costs increase with the size of the trade interventions. (Small interventions have second-order welfare effects, as in the usual Harbergerian analysis.) In figure 11.4, we model the trade intervention as an import quota on manufactured goods, which means that the residual between domestic demand (at the international price) and domestic production is met by domestic production. Thus, a quota translates into moving the "consumption possibilities" schedule from AM', downward to AM', and the equilibrium consumption moves down from E_0^f, the free-trade equilibrium, to E_0^q, the equilibrium with a quota. Utility in the short run is clearly lower, and the larger the trade restriction, the lower welfare is. The limiting case is that of autarky, discussed earlier.

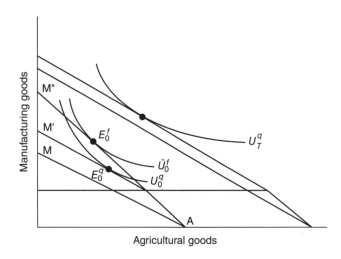

Figure 11.4 A quota

With a quota, the static distortion is lower than in autarky, and the growth benefits are smaller. But utility in the long run, U_T^q, is still higher than with free trade.

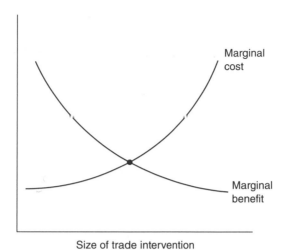

Figure 11.5 Optimal interventions

The larger the trade intervention (e.g., higher tariff or lower import quota), the higher the static (marginal) cost but, because of diminishing returns, the lower the marginal benefit. The optimal intervention occurs when the marginal benefits equal the marginal costs

Thus, it is clear that in the short run (say, at time 0) $U_0^f > U_0^q > U_0^a$, where, in the obvious notation, U_t^q refers to the level of utility at time τ in the quota regime.

But while the costs of intervention increase with the size of the intervention, so do the benefits. Growth increases with the size of the trade intervention, but there is diminishing returns. The optimal intervention entails the marginal cost equaling the marginal benefit. (See figure 11.5). Later discussions will derive more precise formulae, but it should be intuitively clear that the growth benefits at the margin will be higher the lower the discount rate (the more we value future income) and the higher the elasticity of growth rates to the increase in the size of the industrial sector (the higher the learning elasticity).

In the following sections, we explore in more detail the design of optimal interventions. (Readers not interested in the details of the calculations can skip to the concluding section.)

Optimal Intervention in a Two-Sector Economy

Assume, for instance, that the labor supply is (in the absence of intervention) fixed at unity. (This is just a normalization.)[25] For simplicity, we choose units so that the relative price of the two goods in the developed country is unity. If the developing country allocates a fraction, π, of its labor force to producing industrial goods, its income (using agricultural goods as our numeraire) is $Y = \pi k + (1 - \pi)$, where $k < 1$ represents the lower productivity associated with industrial production. We assume that a proportion, λ, of income is allocated to agricultural goods.

We assume a logarithmic utility function:

$$U = \alpha_M \ln C_M + (1 - \alpha_M) \ln C_A$$

$$= \alpha_M \ln(1 - \lambda) + (1 - \alpha_M) \ln \lambda + \ln Y = U^*. \qquad (3)$$

It is easy to show that U is maximized by maximizing Y, and Y is maximized at $\pi = 0$; that is, the country specializes in the production of agricultural goods. This is the conventional static result.

But now we assume that the country's rate of productivity increase is $g(\pi), g' > 0$; that is, the rate of productivity growth increases with the (relative) size of the industrial sector. In this section, however, we use, for simplicity, a discrete time formulation. There is full spillover from the industrial sector to the agricultural sector. Because of this assumption (and a similar assumption in the global market), the country's comparative advantage remains with agriculture. The problem facing the country in the next period is essentially the same problem facing the country this year. If consumption of both goods at $t + 1$ is $(1 + g)$ times consumption at t, $U^{t+1} = U^t + \ln(1 + g)$. $U^{t+n} = U^t + n[\ln(1 + g)]$. Hence, if ∂ is the factor associated with discounting utility, i.e.,

$$W = \Sigma \, \partial^t U^t,$$

and the present discount value of utility is[26]

$$W \equiv [U^* + \ln(1 + g)/(1 - \delta)]/(1 - \delta). \qquad (4)$$

And it is no longer the case that maximizing social welfare (W) entails $\pi = 0$. It immediately follows that optimality requires (for an interior solution)[27]

$$\partial U^*/\partial(\ln \pi) + g'\pi/[(1 - \delta)(1 + g)] = 0. \tag{5}$$

So long as $g' > 0$ (there is a marginal benefit to growth from expanding the industrial sector), optimality requires that $\partial U^*/\partial \ln \pi < 0$, i.e., $\pi > 0$. *The country should produce the industrial good, even though it is not its comparative advantage* (and, under our assumptions, *never will be*.) The dynamic benefits of learning exceed the static costs. Industrial policies pay off.

The greater the learning benefit and the higher δ (the lower the discount factor), the higher π, that is, the higher the optimal static distortion.

$$\partial U^*/\partial \pi = -(1 - k)/\Upsilon, \tag{6}$$

which is always negative, but the larger π is, the smaller Υ is and, therefore, the larger the marginal cost is. From (6), π^* is the solution to (assuming an interior solution)[28]

$$(1 - k) = [1 - \pi^*(1 - k)] g'/[(1 - \delta)(1 + g)]. \tag{7}$$

It should be clear that if k is near 1, then there is little distortion from increasing π, but a strictly positive benefit (so long as $g' > 0$), so that for small enough k, some trade intervention is always desirable. Similarly, the present discount value of the benefits goes to infinity as δ goes to 1 (no discounting), so that as long as the discount rate is small enough, trade intervention is always desirable.

It is also straightforward to show (a) the larger k is, the larger is the optimal value of π; and (b) the larger δ is, the larger is the optimal value of π.

In a manner analogous to our earlier analysis, we let the elasticity of the growth factor be

$$h = g'\pi/(1 + g).$$

Then we can rewrite (7) as

$$\pi = [1/(1-k)][h/(1 - \delta + h)], \qquad (7')$$

yielding the result that the higher the elasticity of growth (responsiveness of growth to an increase in π), the higher is the optimal π.

This framework requires industrial policies that allow for a limited industrial sector, even though the country has a comparative disadvantage in that sector in the short run and, in this model, even in the long run. That is, in our Ricardian model, with full spillovers, technological change does not change the country's comparative advantage.

In this model with a linear technology, the easiest way to implement the desired level of domestic production is through a quota, set at a level which ensures that at the equilibrium price, the desired amount of manufactured goods are produced at home. With increasing costs, there exists an optimal tariff, which would result in the desired level of domestic production.

Catching Up

So far, we have assumed that the rate of learning (cost reduction) is a function of the relative size of the industrial sector. But if we assume further that the rate of learning is a function of the gap in knowledge between the developed and less-developed country, then we can obtain partial or (depending on the functions) even full convergence.

Thus, we postulate that, instead of (2):

$$g = f(Q_M/Q_M + Q_A, \kappa), \qquad (2')$$

where, for purposes of this section, $\kappa = c_M^D/c_M^L$, the gap in productivity in the industrial sector.[29] We assume that $f_2 < 0$ for $\kappa < 1$, and $f_2 = 0$ for $\kappa \geq 1$; i.e., learning in the more-advanced country is unaffected by the state of the less-advanced country. We also assume that should the less-developed country surpass the more developed country in productivity in the industrial sector (even though its comparative advantage remains in the rural sector), the growth trajectory of the developed country is unaffected.[30]

If $f_1(0, \kappa)$ is large enough, for $\kappa < 1$, then $\pi > 0$ so long as $c_M^d/c_M^L > 1$. In other words, the benefits of the increased learning from increased industrial output outweigh the (small) distortion from moving away slightly from comparative advantage.

In steady state, the less-developed country may stay a certain distance behind; i.e., there may be a steady-state value of κ, denoted κ^*, such that

$$f(\pi^{D*}, 1) = f(\pi^L, \kappa^*). \tag{8}$$

It will be recalled that we have assumed, for simplicity, that the developing country is very small relative to the developed, so that the developed country's equilibrium value of π (essentially) depends on its own internal conditions.[31] This defines a positively sloped curve between κ and π^L: As κ increases, the pace of growth slows (there is less to learn). Thus, for the developing country to maintain the same distance from the frontier, π^L must be increased.

The steady-state solution is defined by the solution to (8) and the first-order condition for the less-developed country's welfare maximization.

$$W_\pi = 0, \tag{9}$$

which defines a negatively sloped curve, so long as the marginal return to growth from increasing π diminishes as κ increases.[32]

There is thus a unique solution (figure 11.6). It is possible that there is a steady state where $\kappa = \kappa^* < 1$ (implying the persistence of a knowledge gap of a given size) with a value of π^L that is less than π^{D*} (figure 11.6A).[33] But it is also possible that the only steady-state equilibrium is where $\kappa \geq 1$; i.e., eventually, the "L" country surpasses the "D" country in productivity in the industrial sector (figure 11.6B). (Japan has surpassed the United States in productivity in automobiles.) This might be the case where the "D" country has a high rate of time preference ($\delta^D < \delta^L$) and a high preference for agricultural goods ($\alpha_M^D << \alpha_M^L$).

In both of these cases, to maintain growth, $\pi > 0$. In other words, in the first case, even though the country is benefiting from spillovers, if it didn't have an industrial sector, it would get fewer spillovers and the gap between it and the advanced country would increase. *The infant never fully grows up*, but to keep up with big brother, he has to continue to

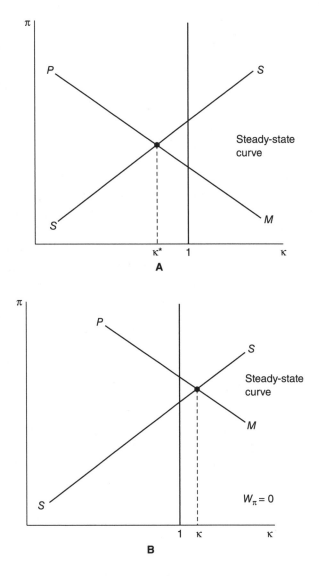

Figure 11.6 Catching up: Steady-state equilibrium

Normally, there is a unique equilibrium. A. The steady-state equilibrium entails the catching-up firm remaining always behind. B. It is possible, however, that the only steady-state equilibrium is where the small developing country actually surpasses the developed country. C. Steady-state equilibrium entails no trade intervention.

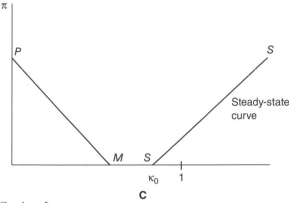

π

P

S

Steady-state
curve

M   S

κ_0 1

C

Figure 11.6 (Continued)

have industrial protection. In the second case, there are no spillovers—in the long run, the developing country becomes technologically superior in manufacturing. But even though it is technologically superior, its comparative advantage remains in agriculture. (This situation, while a conceptual possibility, is not very plausible. We comment on it further in the concluding section of this chapter.)

There is a third possibility, depicted in figure 11.6C, in which the spillovers from the advanced country flow sufficiently freely that the steady-state curve intersects the horizontal axis at a high level of κ. Thus, even without industrial and trade policies, the backward country can keep up with the developed country, with only a modest gap. We denote that critical value of κ by κ_0. If at κ_0 the marginal return to learning (from creating an industrial sector) is small enough (i.e., f_π is small enough), then the $W_\pi = 0$ curve will hit the horizontal axis to the right of κ_0, implying that the steady-state equilibrium entails $\pi = 0$. In other words, in steady state there is no industrial policy (though there will be in early stages of development, when κ is very small). The less-developed country passively gains from the gradual spillovers as they transmit themselves across national boundaries.

While we might normally expect that as the gap between the developed and less-developed country narrows, the less-developed country distorts its production less (i.e., its optimal value of π is smaller), it is possible that the opposite is true. As we noted in earlier chapters, if there is a very large gap, the knowledge base may be so low that the

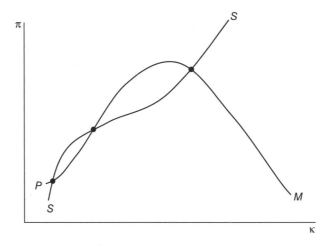

Figure 11.7 Catching up: Multiple steady-state equilibria

If the gap between the advanced and developing country is large, there can be little learning by the developing country, and it can get caught in a low-level equilibrium trap.

(marginal) benefits of learning are low. In this case, there can exist multiple equilibria—a low-level, large-gap equilibrium, and another high-level, low-gap equilibrium. (See figure 11.7.)[34]

Nontraded Sector and the Desirability of Exchange Rate Intervention

International trade agreements restrict taxing imports and subsidizing exports (or at least doing so too openly), so the relative producer prices of agricultural and manufactured goods must be the international trade price. Even in these circumstances, though, there is a role for industrial policy, through the exchange rate. In this section, we will show how a low exchange rate can be used to encourage the expansion of manufacturing. But to accomplish this, the country may need to have a trade surplus. Learning may be so valuable that a poor country decides not to spend all the foreign exchange it has available, highlighting the fact that the knowledge gap is more important than the resource gap. The learning benefits that arise from the "distorted" production and the delayed consumption and investment exceed the direct benefits of either consuming or investing today.

To see this, we extend the model by incorporating two additional goods, nontraded consumption goods, NT, and public goods, G. Let us assume a more general homothetic utility function, with the obvious notation

$$U^* = U(C_M, C_A, C_{NT}, G). \tag{10}$$

We generalize the production technology to

$$F(Q_M, Q_A, Q_{NT}) = 0, \tag{11}$$

where we have assumed, for simplicity, that there are three produced goods. To put the problem in a more familiar setting, we assume that the country has (like China) already established a comparative advantage in manufacturing but is still poor. Its focus is on growing faster. Thus, it wants to export more. The output of manufactured goods is used for government goods, consumed at home, or exported:

$$Q_M = C_M + G + X, \tag{12}$$

while

$$Q_A = C_A - M. \tag{13}$$

The output of agricultural goods is equal to consumption minus imports (of agricultural goods), or equivalently, consumption of agricultural goods is equal to output plus imports. By definition, the output and consumption of non-traded goods is identical.

Trade balance requires

$$S = X - M = 0. \tag{14}$$

In the standard international trade problem, there are five relative prices: taking the nontradable consumer price as unity, there are p_M and p_A, the consumer prices of manufactured and agricultural goods; and the three producer prices (all relative to the nontraded consumption good). Countries thus want to encourage the production of the industrial goods by raising the producer price, relative to other producer prices, either through subsidizing manufactured goods or taxing other goods. Since it is only relative prices which matter for determining where on a country's production possibilities schedule it will operate, it doesn't really matter whether we encourage manufacturers or discourage other sectors. We will assume that the restrictions imposed by international agreements see through this and insist that the relative price of imports and exports is fixed at the international level (which we normalize at unity). This means that there is only one relative producer price, the price of nontradables relative to tradables, which we refer to as the real (producer) exchange rate. Initially, we will assume that there are no consumption taxes, so consumer and producer prices are identical.

We can express income in terms of the nontradable price. If the government imposes a lump sum tax of T,

$$Y = Q_{NT} + e(Q_M + Q_A) - T = Y(e, T). \qquad (15)$$

At any value of e, firm profit maximization implies a particular value of $\{Q_i\}$, so that Y is just a function of e and T. Government expenditures equal lump sum tax revenues,

$$eG = T. \qquad (16)$$

(Recall that, for simplicity, we assume that government goods are manufactured and, hence, cost e.)

From individual utility maximization, we derive demand functions, which generate, in a straightforward way, the equilibrium exchange rate (and the equilibrium levels of consumption and production of each good). It is the solution to

$$C_{NT}(e, Y(e, T)) = Q_{NT}(e). \qquad (17)$$

The solution to (17) gives the equilibrium value of e for any T. The government then chooses the T that maximizes U^*. At e^*, the corresponding exchange rate, there is trade balance:

$$Q_M(e) - C_M(e, T) - G = C_A(e, T) - Q_A(T). \qquad (18)$$

This is the standard static problem. But now, the government takes into account the value of learning that comes from producing more industrial goods. To simplify, we assume that it now maximizes

$$U^* + \mathscr{L}(Q_M),\tag{19}$$

where the second term refers to the learning benefit from production of manufactured goods, subject to having a nonnegative trade surplus,

$$S = Q_M(e) - C_M(e, T) - G - [C_A(e, T) - Q_A(e)] \geq 0,\tag{20}$$

and a nonnegative budget surplus,

$$T \geq eG.\tag{21}$$

As it lowers the exchange rate (increases e), the country produces more manufactured goods but fewer nontraded goods. Normally, this would create a disparity between the supply and demand for nontraded goods, giving rise to inflation (one of the reasons that trade intervention is often associated with inflation). But if the government is aware of the problem, it can take other measures. As (17) illustrates, it can increase the lump sum tax, which will decrease income and thus decrease the demand for nontradable goods. Solving (17) for dT/de, it is easy to see that as the exchange rate decreases (e increases), production of the tradable goods increases and consumption decreases. Thus, the trade surplus increases:

$$dS/de = d[Q_M(e) + Q_A(e)]/de - d[C_M(e, T) + C_A(e, T)]/$$

$$de - dG/de > 0,\tag{22}$$

so long as the government does not respond to the increased tax revenue by spending too much (on tradable goods). (If the government spends all of its revenues, then

$$dG/de = -T/e^2 + (dT/de)(1/e).$$

$$dG/de < 0,$$

provided, from (17),

$$d(\ln T)/d(\ln e) < 1. \tag{23}$$

But even if (23) is not satisfied, (22) may still be satisfied even if government spends all of its revenues.] While a decrease in the exchange rate leads to a trade surplus, it also leads to a welfare increase. Differentiating (19) with respect to e, evaluating at e^*, using the envelope theorem, we have:[35]

$$d[U^* + \mathscr{L}(Q_M)]/de = (dU^*/dT)(\mathrm{d}T/\mathrm{de}) + \mathscr{L}(Q_M)(dQ_M/de)$$

$$= \mathscr{L}(Q_M)(dQ_M/de) > 0.$$

The loss of welfare from the distortions associated with trade intervention (the induced taxes to reduce the demand for nontraded goods, the resulting distortion in the allocation between private and public goods) has, at the market equilibrium (which is optimal) second-order effects, while the learning benefits from increased production of manufactured goods have first-order effects.

There are other ways, of course, that the country can maintain equilibrium as it seeks to increase industrial production. One is to impose consumption taxes. Assume A goods are complements for nontraded goods, and M goods are substitutes. Then a tax on A goods used to finance a subsidy on M goods will result in reduced demand for nontraded goods, restoring demand and supply for the nontraded goods. The welfare effects of these consumption distortions are second-order, while the welfare benefits of the increased production of manufactured goods are first-order.

Note that, as in our earlier analysis, with homotheticity and constant elasticity, the world at time t looks the same as it does at $t + 1$. It thus may be optimal for the country to maintain a low exchange rate—with a trade surplus—forever. It never uses the surplus, for were it to do so, it would affect the exchange rate, its ability to export manufactured goods, and thus the extent of its learning.

Non-Steady-State Analysis

We should emphasize the sensitivity of this analysis to the assumptions that we have imposed to allow for a steady-state analysis. A fuller analysis would take into account the fact that as the country closes the knowledge gap between itself and the advanced industrial countries, learning benefits may decrease, perhaps to the point at which the cost of running a surplus—the lost utility from the forgone consumption—exceeds the learning benefit.[36] The marginal benefit of learning may decrease; the marginal cost associated with the static distortion (and the opportunity cost of not using the ever-increasing surplus) may increase. The country might then want at first to bring S down to zero—to stop growing reserves—and then to consume its accumulated surplus.

Other factors would also, of course, affect the country's desired level of surplus. A country with an aging population might want to put aside savings and then, as the aging population enters into retirement, reduce that surplus. Such demographic transitions are not analyzed well in steady-state models.

Out-of-steady-state analysis requires taking into account *changes* in the exchange rate over time—how current policies affect exchange rates and how changing exchange rates affect intertemporal trade-offs. Because the exchange rate in later periods, when the country is more advanced and when it is running a trade deficit, is likely to be higher than in earlier periods, it experiences a capital loss on the cumulated reserves. This lowers the dynamic benefit of the surplus, implying that it is desirable to have a lower level of learning (and surplus) than would otherwise be the case.

So too, the analysis needs to be modified if learning is related to the level of investment. Then the government will want to increase the capital intensity of production. If in early stages of development, capital goods are imported, it may wish to have a high exchange rate in early years, followed by a lower exchange rate in later years, as the investments bear fruit and the country starts to exports. This will result in high returns to investing in early years, and consequently high levels of learning and growth.[37]

On the other hand, if, as we have argued, in the earlier stages of development, learning benefits are sufficiently large that the country accumulates a surplus, at the margin, an increase in the price of tradables (a further reduction in the price of nontradables) as a result of a decrease in the exchange rate has a positive effect—it receives more for what it sells; while in later periods, when the country has a trade deficit (as it uses up its surplus), a decrease in the exchange rate (the price the country has to pay for the goods it buys) has a negative effect.[38] This provides further impetus for lowering exchange rates (further below equilibrium levels that would prevail in the absence of intertemporal effects) in earlier stages and increasing them later—exacerbating patterns of "global imbalances."

Concluding Comments

This chapter has overthrown several long-standing presumptions concerning trade, growth, and government policy. We have shown that, in a learning economy, free trade is not, in general, desirable. Growth—and societal welfare—is maximized with some trade intervention to encourage the industrial (learning) sector. While we have criticized the infant-industry argument for protection, we have provided an alternative, more general argument—the infant-economy argument for protection. We have constructed simple models in which it is true that intervention can be desirable, *even if the infant never grows up.* We have provided a simple characterization of the optimal intervention.

Constraints on the set of interventions, such as those arising out of international trade agreements, may be welfare reducing. In response, it may be optimal for governments to intervene in the exchange rate—to such an extent that it may be desirable for them to run surpluses. In some simple models, it may even be desirable for them to run surpluses in perpetuity.

With these interventions, developing countries may be able to close the knowledge gap that separates them from more-developed countries. Depending on the nature of the spillovers from the developed to developing countries, eventually, the knowledge gap may be closed, or there may be a long-run equilibrium in which there is no convergence—there is a persistence in the relative gap. There is some evidence that, in many cases, gaps in per capita income have persisted—far more than one would have expected, say, from the Solow growth model, which had predicted convergence.[39] Such growth patterns are consistent with the analysis presented in this chapter.

We have also seen that there is a possibility of multiple equilibria—a developing country can get trapped in an equilibrium with a low level of per capita income (large knowledge gap) relative to the more developed country—a gap so large that investments in learning have a low return. When there are such multiple equilbria, history matters. The policy of structural adjustment foisted on African countries in the latter part of the twentieth century, which led to the deindustrialization of sub-Saharan Africa, may have contributed to some countries in that region being trapped today in such a low equilibrium (see Noman and Stiglitz 2012a, 2012b, 2012c, and the references cited there).

We should note that one of the reasons that our analysis differs from the conventional wisdom that emphasizes the virtues of trade is that it is often assumed that the best way that countries learn is through trade. Since trade barriers restrict trade, they restrict learning. We have, by contrast, highlighted the role of production (and investment) within a country. Properly formulated, the two hypotheses need not be in contradiction. We are not arguing for autarky. Learning can be a function both of domestic production in general and of exports in particular. Having demanding buyers and competing in a global marketplace can facilitate learning. In this perspective, though, it is not trade in general, and not imports, that generate learning. Thus, trade liberalization which destroys a country's domestic production will destroy its learning in these sectors, with adverse effects on societal learning, if there are significant learning spillovers from these sectors to the rest of the economy. As we argued in this chapter, if trade liberalization leads the economy to specialize in sectors where there is little learning, the economy will not grow as well as it would with protection. What matters is not trade, but what is traded, and in particular, what is produced and exported.

In the following paragraphs, we describe two other broader implications of the analysis of this chapter.

Global Imbalances

Some countries have been criticized for contributing to global imbalances by accumulating excessive reserves. In static models, it has seemed irrational for developing countries—suffering from capital shortages and with constrained consumption—to do so; just as it has seemed peculiar that the United States, with an aging population, is running long-term deficits. This chapter shows, however, that once dynamic learning benefits are taken into account, with sufficient constraints on industrial policies, such as those imposed by the World Trade Organization, the accumulation of reserves by a developing country beyond a level required for precautionary reasons to manage global volatility, may be reasonable if the learning benefits are large enough.

With these restrictions, governments are forced to undertake second-best measures, such as the exchange-rate interventions described earlier. The effect of these interventions almost surely is to lower growth from what it otherwise would be—reducing the pace at which the gap between developing and developed countries is closed. They also increase the welfare costs of intervention, since they reduce the set of interventions that are permissible.

But these restrictions have another, unintended consequence. It now may be desirable for developing countries to even perpetually run surpluses. Even taking into account the high opportunity cost of not consuming/using these surpluses *now*, reserve accumulation is desirable because of the learning benefits. Were they to raise their exchange rate, output in the industrial sector and learning would diminish. (We do not pursue here the global macroeconomic effects of these surpluses, nor the role of the dollar reserve system in giving rise to global imbalances.[40])

Interestingly, while this policy leads to a lower level of imports initially, because of the induced growth, over the longer run, the country's level of imports is actually increased.[41] It is perhaps not an accident that China's reserves and surpluses soared after it joined the WTO, as it faced new restrictions on its industrial policies simultaneously with new opportunities to export.

Changing Comparative Advantage

The central model that we explored in this chapter is one in which there are full spillovers, so that if the less-developed country initially has a comparative advantage in agriculture/crafts, it always does. That means that if the country wants to have an industrial sector, it must *permanently* provide some protection. It is incorrect to say that the infant never grows up: Productivity in manufacturing may increase enormously, and the gap between productivity in that sector in the developed and developing country may narrow markedly. But because of the assumption of full spillovers, *comparative* advantage never changes. As we have repeatedly emphasized, even if it were true that infant industries sometimes never *fully* grow up, the support provided by the government to the industrial sector pays off: The economy is on a longer-term, faster growth trajectory than it otherwise would have had.

But Korea represents the more typical story, where, as it learns, productivity in the industrial sector increases faster than in agriculture, so much so that *eventually* the country's comparative advantage changes. That means that *eventually* government intervention to maintain a (relatively) large, larger than would be the case under unfettered market forces, industrial sector is no longer required. But as the discussion of the previous section points out, even after the country achieves some success in improving manufacturing capacities, it may still want to intervene, to produce *more* manufacturing goods than it otherwise would have produced. (Of course, this will not be the case in the Ricardian model, where, with a linear technology, a small country either specializes in the production of agricultural goods or manufacturing goods.)

Looking Forward

The analytic discussions of part II of this book provide the foundations of the policy discussions of part III. We have established the desirability of government intervention to encourage the industrial sector and to help create a learning economy and society. There are many ways by which this can be done and many policies which affect the economy's learning. The following chapters focus on some of the most important of these. Not surprisingly, as we will explain, the most successful countries have, at critical junctures in their growth, undertaken these policies.

APPENDIX A

Trade Interventions and Optimal Tax Theory

It may be useful to set our analysis from the first section of this chapter into the context of optimal tax theory. The classic works of Diamond and Mirrlees (1971a, 1971b), showed that production efficiency was optimal. That implied that it was not desirable to interfere with trade efficiency. There should be no trade taxes.

Our general analysis differs from that classic theory by assuming that there is a social value to the production of manufactured goods. In Diamond and Mirrlees, all that society values is *consumption*. Once we recognize that there is a value to the domestic production of manufacturers, it follows that we want to distort production patterns to increase the output of manufacturing, reversing the Diamond-Mirrlees presumptions.

Once we introduce restrictions on the set of admissible taxes, we are in the third-best world explored by Dasgupta and Stiglitz (1971, 1972), which showed again that there was a presumption in favor of distorting production efficiency, including imposing trade interventions (Dasgupta and Stiglitz 1974; Blitzer, Dasgupta, and Stiglitz 1981). The basic insight of that literature is that one uses the set of admissible taxes to partially substitute for the restricted taxes. If we cannot directly encourage the production of industrial goods in a targeted way, we encourage the broader class of goods that we are allowed to promote, "tradables." To ensure that the demand and supply of nontradables is equilibrated, we have to introduce still further distortions in the economy, but (at least for small trade interventions) these have small welfare costs, e.g., consuming less today than we otherwise would, consuming more tradables than we otherwise would. These changes in consumption can be induced either directly (as a result of consumption subsidies) or indirectly (through government expenditure programs directed at manufacturing goods).

APPENDIX B

Optimal Policies for Leaders and Followers

Acemoglu, Robinson, and Verdier (2012) have put forward an interesting hypothesis that technological leaders and followers should follow different economic strategies. Optimal economic policies for advancing the technological frontier are different from those that optimize "catching up," borrowing technologies from others. They suggest that the Nordic welfare model may be all well and good for the follower, but the American style of cutthroat capitalism is better suited for the countries at the frontier. We put aside the contention that the

Scandinavian countries are followers: It is hard to reconcile such a view (at least within the context of the models discussed in this book) with results that suggest that their standard of living is at least comparable to, and may well exceed, that of the United States (postulated to be the technological leader).

Central to their conclusion is their assumption that cutthroat competition is optimal for innovation. In other words, their results are a direct consequence of their assumptions. Elsewhere in this book, we have noted the importance of the (inherent) absence of a full set of risk markets. It could be argued as well that the Nordic model, with heavier public investments in education, technology, and infrastructure and heavier investments in social protection, increases the capacity for innovative risk taking. While it is true that the optimal policy of the leader and the follower will be different, it is not necessarily the case that the leader has less of a "social model" than the follower.

This can be seen most simply by a direct generalization of our catching-up model. We generalize equation (2′), which describes the rate of growth of the economy, to

$$g = f(\dot{Q}_M/Q_M + Q_A, \kappa, \varsigma), \qquad (2'')$$

where ς is a measure of the extent of society's social protection/social investment. (Obviously, this is an oversimplification, since there are many dimensions to social protection and social investment.) We assume (contary to Acemoglu, Robinson, and Verdier)

$$\partial g/\partial \varsigma > 0.$$

We also assume that there is a short-run social cost of these measures (at least beyond a certain level, ς^*, that maximizes short-run utility). Thus, we write the short-run (momentary) utility as $U^*(\pi, \varsigma)$, with $\partial U^*/\partial \varsigma < 0$ for $\varsigma > \varsigma^*$.

The leader (the large, developed country) maximizes long-term social welfare with respect to ς, taking into account the short-run costs and the long-run benefits. It immediately follows that the leader sets $\varsigma > \varsigma^*$.

The follower goes through a similar exercise, but for the follower, $\kappa < 1$ (in contrast to the leader, where $\kappa = 1$, by definition), and $\pi^L < \pi^D$ (where, it will be recalled, the superscript L refers to the less developed country, D to the developed, and π is the share of the labor force in manufacturing). The marginal growth benefits of increasing ς will be affected by the growth cross-elasticities between ς, κ, and π. Assume, for instance, that there is less risk associated with the kinds of "research" required for catching up and that the levels of social investment required for catching up are less than those associated with moving the frontier forward. Then the optimal level of ς for the follower will be lower than for the leader. The Nordic model includes exactly the kind of policies that one would expect to see in a leader. It is not optimal for all countries to follow the same model, but those countries that aspire to be on the frontier should.

PART THREE

Policies for a Learning Society

CHAPTER TWELVE

The Role of Industrial and Trade Policy in Creating a Learning Society

INDUSTRIAL POLICIES—meaning policies by which governments attempt to shape the structure of the economy, including the choice of technique and the sectoral allocation of the economy—are back in fashion, and rightly so. The major insight of welfare economics of the past fifty years is that markets by themselves in general do not result in (constrained) Pareto efficient outcomes (Greenwald and Stiglitz 1986).

By now, there is a rich catalog of market failures, circumstances in which the markets may produce too little of some commodity or another, too much of another, or may result in too little employment, and in which industrial policies, appropriately designed, may improve matters.

This chapter focuses on one of the central reasons for industrial policies, one that has been at the center of this book: Markets on their own do not create a learning society; the structure of the economy that

This chapter is based partially on Greenwald and Stiglitz (2014a, 2014b) and Charlton and Stiglitz (2005, 2012), and borrows liberally from those papers.

results from market forces results in less learning—and less growth—than there could or should be.

We believe that one of the objectives of economic policy should be to create an environment that enhances both learning and learning spillovers. As we argued in chapter 1, creating a learning society is more likely to increase standards of living than small, one-time improvements in economic efficiency or improvements that derive from the sacrifices of consumption today to deepen capital.

Earlier chapters have described the key determinants of learning and have explained why markets by themselves do not create as effective a learning economy and society as can be created. The critical reasons are that:

Learning involves spillovers (externalities) that will be imperfectly internalized in a market economy, and

In circumstances in which learning might largely be internalized—where there is a monopoly—the distortions created by the monopoly itself require government intervention.

Furthermore, we have described, using simple analytic models, how intervention might lead to higher growth and societal welfare.

This chapter moves from the broad analytic discussion of the previous five chapters to the central policy debates. Industrial policies have been highly controversial, and trade policies, including those designed to help restructure the economy, even more so. In this chapter, we explain why many of the arguments used against these interventions are misplaced and suggest how trade and industrial policies might more effectively contribute to creating a learning economy.

The chapter is divided into nine sections. In the first, we explain why much of the debate about industrial policies is misplaced—whether governments want to or not, they are, in practice, always engaged in industrial policies. In the second, we focus more narrowly on developing countries, arguing that these policies are especially relevant to such countries. In doing so, we refute the long-standing Washington Consensus presumption *against* industrial policies. In the third, we turn to the objectives of industrial policy. This is followed by a more extensive discussion of trade policy as an instrument of industrial policy, a continuation of the analysis of the previous chapter. The fifth section focuses on one of the most important issues of industrial policy facing many developing countries—how to make the most of their natural resources. The final four sections of the chapter contain more general reflections on industrial policy—its historical role, the role of political economy, and strategic considerations.

1. The Inevitability of Industrial Policies

Governments are inevitably involved in industrial policy, in shaping the economy, both by what they do and what they do not. If they don't manage the macro-economy well, then more cyclically sensitive industries will be discouraged. If they use interest rate adjustments to stabilize the economy, interest-sensitive sectors will suffer. If they don't stabilize the exchange rate, then nontraded sectors are encouraged.

Moreover, in almost all countries, governments play a central role in education, health, infrastructure, and technology; and policies and expenditures in each of these areas—and the balance of spending among these areas—also shapes the economy.

Markets don't exist in a vacuum, and each of the laws and regulations that structure our economy—such as laws governing bankruptcy and corporate governance—shape the economy. Development economics routinely emphasizes as central to growth the study of institutions.[1] All the rules and regulations, the legal frameworks and how they are enforced, affect the structure of the economy. Therefore, unwittingly, government is always engaged in industrial policy. American laws giving priority to derivatives in the event of bankruptcy was an industrial policy that encouraged derivatives. American laws providing that student loans cannot be discharged, even in bankruptcy, discouraged the education sector. At the same time, the absence of effective regulation of its predatory for-profit education institutions encouraged such institutions.[2] Tax systems that tax financial speculation more lightly than other forms of economic activity encourage resources to move into financial speculation.

In short, all governments have an industrial policy, explicit or otherwise. The only difference is between those who construct their industrial policy consciously, and those who let it be shaped by others, typically special interests, who vie with each other for hidden and open subsidies, for rules and regulations that favor them over others.

Even the agenda of financial market liberalization was an industrial policy—one pushed by the banks and the financial sector, the effect of which was to lead in many countries to a bloated financial sector, rife with explicit and implicit subsidies (reaching record levels in the crisis of 2008–2009), diverting resources from other uses that arguably would have led to higher sustained growth. It was an industrial policy that led to more macroeconomic instability, which, as we explained in chapter 4 above, itself adversely affected learning.

The Instruments of Industrial Policy and a Guide to Part 3

We have explained how government, in all of its policies, laws, and regulations, needs to be mindful of their effects on the structure of the economy and on the creation of a learning society. Earlier chapters explained why government intervention to promote learning was desirable. But there are many forms this intervention can take, many actions by which the government can help shape the economy. Since we have argued that virtually all actions undertaken by the government have some effects in shaping the economy, our analysis has to be confined to those where the impacts are largest, or which are explicitly directed at shaping the economy. This and the following four chapters look at several of the key policies: This chapter at industrial and trade policies, the next at financial policies, chapter 14 at macroeconomic policies (including exchange rate policies) and investment policies, and chapter 15 at intellectual property.

2. The Special Importance of Industrial Policies for Developing Countries

Closing the Knowledge Gap

Earlier, we emphasized that what separates developed from developing countries is not just a gap in resources, but a gap in knowledge (Stiglitz 1999b, World Bank 1999). Much of the difference in per capita income between these countries and the more advanced is attributable to differences in knowledge. If this is so, then development strategies should be centered on promoting learning, closing the knowledge gap between more- and less-developed countries. Policies that transformed their economies and societies into "learning societies" would enable them to close the gap more rapidly, with marked increases in incomes.[3] Development entails learning how to learn (Stiglitz 1987c). As we argued earlier too, the fact that some countries and firms have "learned how to learn" helps explain why the last two centuries have seen such remarkable increases in standards of living, in comparison to the millennia that preceded them, which were marked by stagnation.

How Structural Adjustment Policies Stifled Growth

But rather than promoting the learning sectors, the policies foisted on developing countries by, say, the international economic institutions, have actually discouraged the learning sector (industry) in many developing countries, especially in Africa (see, e.g., Noman and Stiglitz 2012a, 2012b, 2012c; and the references cited there). The result is that over the past thirty years, Africa has suffered from deindustrialization. The quarter century from the early 1980s was a period of declining per capita income and increasing poverty.

Structural adjustment policies advocated by the IMF and the World Bank were predicated on the belief that by eliminating "distortions" in the economy, Africa would grow faster—by constructing an economy based on principles of free and unfettered markets. The reigning dogma was that with the government restrained to ensuring macro-stability, which typically just meant price stability, economic performance would increase and all would benefit. In focusing on static efficiency, these international institutions totally ignored learning and the associated dynamics.

But this was not the only way that the structural adjustment programs impeded the development of a learning economy. Much learning occurs on the job—but if there is to be on-the-job-learning, there has to be jobs. It was recognized, of course, that eliminating trade protection would result in the loss of jobs, some in agriculture, many others in industry. The strongly held belief, however, was that these workers would quickly find jobs in new industries, consistent with the country's comparative advantage. Moving resources from inefficient protected sectors to more efficient competitive sectors would raise incomes.

Things didn't turn out as the advocates of these policies had hoped. Rather than growth, there was decline. Job creation often (or even typically) didn't keep pace with job destruction, and so workers moved from low-productivity protected sectors to even-lower-productivity unemployment, open or disguised.[4]

The Washington Consensus and Learning

The structural adjustment policies in Africa were associated with a set of economic doctrines that shaped the policies demanded of developing countries if they were to receive assistance from the West. For more than a quarter century, policies, especially in developing countries, were dominated by a set of ideas that is commonly called the Washington Consensus. It was these ideas that led to the structural adjustment policies that in turn led to Africa's deindustrialization,[5] with such adverse consequences for its growth and the well-being of its citizens.

The Washington Consensus policies were predicated on the assumption that markets, by themselves, are efficient; and that therefore the major source of inefficiency or mal-performance of the economy arises from government intervention. Hence, the first item in the reform agenda is to eliminate these interventions with the market. The only (or at least the main) economic role of the government was to ensure price stability and property rights (including the enforcement of contracts).[6]

Thus, the Washington Consensus, and the ideology on which it was based, gave short shrift to market failures. When they grudgingly admitted to market failures, they suggested that government was not capable of correcting these market failures, because of "political economy" reasons.

This chapter explains why both parts of these doctrines were wrong: Market failures are pervasive, and governments—even in developing countries—can improve matters, and have done so, even if they have not "perfectly" corrected them.

In their aversion to industrial policies, the Washington Consensus policies focused on static efficiency. They didn't even consider what the consequences for innovation and learning were. If there was learning and technological progress, it was assumed to be exogenous, outside the purview of policy, and certainly outside the purview of the economic policies on which they focused. That this was so was striking, given the observation, made earlier, that development is so much about learning and economic transformation.

LEARNING AND ONE-SIZE-FITS-ALL POLICIES One critique of the Washington Consensus is that it has attempted to impose one-size-fits-all policies. Such policies may be particularly inappropriate when it comes to creating a learning society.

A critical aspect of "learning" is that it takes place locally and must adapt to local differences in culture and economic practice. Thus, "learning" prescriptions that work in some environments will not work in others. For example, in some economies, especially in East Asia, close relationships between government and business seem to have helped development; potential conflicts of interest have been contained, and there have been marked benefits from effective coordination (see World Bank 1993). But such relationships can easily evolve toward "crony capitalism," and the associated corruption may impede development.[7] Learning how to relate to government has value in most economies, but in some, the skills required may concern those related to bidding processes, in others to interpersonal connections. American firms have had to learn to adapt to the Foreign Corrupt Practices Act.[8] Labor norms differ too among countries, and personnel policies have to accommodate such differences. Differences in consumer preferences and norms as well as in distribution channels necessitate different "learning" about marketing. Most importantly, and perhaps obviously, relative factor prices may differ, so that the returns to learning how to save on the utilization of one factor versus another may differ.[9]

These cross-country differences have numerous implications. It helps explain why learning in a firm may spill over more easily to other firms in the same country than to firms in other countries. The learning in one country may simply be less relevant to production in the other country.

They help explain too why it is that in some economies public enterprises function well, while in others they do not.[10] (Functioning well means, of course, being able to learn and adapt—and in countries that have more broadly created a learning society, or at least one where learning permeates an important segment of society, even public enterprises can learn and adapt.)

They also help explain the limitations of globalization: Local firms have a competitive advantage in having more knowledge about local circumstances (see Greenwald and Kahn 2009). Much financial information is chiefly available locally, and even when information is available, outsiders may have less of an understanding of the nuances of the country's distinctive institutional structure—as foreign investors have learned to their cost about U.S. mortgages. Thus, effective capital deployment will often require local financial institutions.

Unfortunately, Washington Consensus policies which pushed capital and financial market liberalization did not take into account the importance of this local knowledge. Foreign banks succeeded in attracting depositors away from local banks, because they were perceived as safer (and in some cases, may have been, because they had the implicit guarantee of governments with deeper pockets). But foreign banks were at an information disadvantage relative to local banks about small- and medium-sized local firms, and it was thus natural that lending be diverted away toward loans to government, consumers, and large domestic firms (including local monopolies and oligopolies). But in doing so, local learning and entrepreneurship may have been undermined and growth weakened.[11]

Industrial Policy and the Distinctive Circumstances of Developing Countries

There are several other reasons that in developing countries industrial policy should play an even more important role than it does in developed countries. The first two concern the fact that these countries are laying down the foundations that will provide their economic structures for decades to come.

We have emphasized how legal frameworks—the laws and regulations that govern a society and an economy—simultaneously *shape* the economy. They constitute a kind of industrial policy. But a key issue in development is the formulation of these laws, when they don't exist, and reforming the laws, often inherited as part of their colonial legacy, when they do. Developing countries have to be aware that the legal frameworks they choose are shaping their economy today—with important consequences for their future.

So too, the physical infrastructure that they invest in will increase the returns to some kinds of private investment and reduce that of others.

Investments developing some ports or roads will lead to the development of the surrounding areas, at the expense of areas which might otherwise have been developed.

In both of these instances, the groups lobbying (for the institutional and physical infrastructure that serves their interests) are the firms that exist today—those that might exist with a different institutional and physical infrastructure have little or no voice.

Earlier, we noted that all countries have an industrial policy—but the industrial policy which is chosen by developed countries is chosen to advance their own economies, or special interests in their own economy. Even if it were easy to borrow these ideas from the developed countries, and even if it is possible to design industrial policies that enhance the flow of knowledge from developed to developing countries, strengthening cross-border flows of knowledge should not be the only focus of developing country industrial policy. For instance, environmental impacts are important for all countries, but especially for developing countries. The fact that natural resources and the environment are "underpriced" means that there are insufficient incentives to allocate resources (including those devoted to learning) toward the environment and natural resources—so more resources gets expended on saving labor.

This highlights a difference between developed and developing countries, and a reason why it is important that developing countries have their own innovation policies and an industrial policy which promotes indigenous learning. Much of innovation in advanced industrial economies has been directed toward saving labor. But in many developing countries, labor is in surplus and unemployment is the problem. Labor-saving innovations exacerbate this key social challenge. (See chapter 6.)

Even when labor-saving innovation does not result in unemployment, it will have adverse distributional consequences, lowering wages. With inequality already so high in many developing countries, this should be of concern.

Behind this analysis are two general theoretical observations: First, when innovation is important, history matters, as the discussion of chapter 3 emphasized. Technology that is developed today affects the kinds of technological developments that it pays to make later.

Moreover, factor prices in developing countries differ from those in developed countries, and in both, factor prices differ from shadow prices, because of a variety of market failures.

These observations have, in turn, three important policy implications: In both developed and developing countries, industrial policies have to be strategic—to take into account not just the country's circumstances today, but its likely long-run situation. What matters is not static comparative advantage but dynamic comparative advantage. (What this entails will be discussed at greater length below.) Second, both the direction of innovation which firms would undertake and that which governments should undertake can differ markedly between developed and developing countries. And third, in both developed and developing countries, governments need to shape the direction of innovation and learning. As we emphasized in chapter 6, economies have a choice of the direction of innovation—whether it is, say, resource saving or labor saving. Those choices should reflect scarcity values—what the relative shares of different factors would be if factor prices reflected true scarcity, i.e., if market prices and "shadow" prices were equal.

3. The Objectives of Industrial Policy

While this book focuses on the role of industrial policies (broadly understood, in the manner described earlier in this chapter) in promoting growth through learning, governments have to simultaneously be cognizant of other social and economic consequences. Industrial policy is usually conceived of as promoting growth, but it should be seen more broadly, as any policy redirecting an economy's sectoral allocation (or other production decisions, such as the choice of technique or the nature of innovation) where market incentives, as shaped by rules and regulations, are misaligned with public objectives. Governments are concerned about employment, distribution, and the environment in ways in which the market is often not. Thus, in those countries with persistent high levels of unemployment, it is clear that something is wrong with market processes: labor markets are not clearing. Whether the explanation has to do with inherent limitations in markets (e.g., imperfect information giving rise to efficiency wages[12]), unions, or government (e.g., minimum wages), the persistence of unemployment implies that "correcting" the underlying failures may not be easy. The social costs of unemployment can be very high, and it is appropriate for government to attempt to induce the economy to move toward more labor-intensive sectors or to use more labor-intensive processes.

In the following four sub-sections, we illustrate four key objectives of industrial policy beyond creating a learning society. In each of these instances, shadow prices differ from market prices. And in each of these cases, there are externalities generated by market participants (analogous to the learning externality which is at the heart of the analysis here) that market participants (without appropriate government intervention) do not take into account.

Structural Transformation

It has increasingly been recognized that development requires the structural transformation of the economy (see Lin 2010, 2012; Lin and Monga, forthcoming; and Stiglitz 1998b). Markets themselves are not very good at such structural transformations, partly because the sectors that are being displaced—resources that have to move from one sector to another—typically suffer large capital and income losses and are thus not well placed to make the investments required for redeployment; and well-understood capital market imperfections (based on information asymmetries) limit access to outside resources (see Delli Gatti et al. 2012, 2013). One of the main impediments to the easy flow of resources from one sector to another is, of course, the lack of appropriate skills; a greater focus on "learning" would have led to policies that would have enhanced the relevant capabilities of the workforce.

Unemployment

In standard economic models, there is no unemployment—and no job vacancies. The demand for labor always exactly equals the supply, and this is true for each type of labor. But neither assumption is true. But markets, in their structuring of innovation, focus on the costs they face, not societal costs. With many countries facing high unemployment, there is an imperative to create more jobs. High unemployment means that the market price of labor almost surely is markedly higher than the "shadow price," the opportunity cost of labor. Government should encourage labor-intensive sectors and technologies. To the extent possible, government should be sensitive to the kinds of labor that are being demanded, using both industrial and educational policies to bring the demand and supply of, say, school leavers and university graduates into better alignment.[13]

Environment

If the shadow price of labor is often far less than the market wage, just the opposite is true of the environment, where firms typically do not pay for the full consequences of their actions. The consequences for investment—including investments in R & D—are obvious. Firms in many countries are searching for labor-saving innovations, even in countries with high unemployment, when from a social perspective, there are high returns to innovations that protect the environment.

Inequality

Many developing countries have been marked by high levels of inequality.[14] Industrial policies can affect the extent of inequality by increasing the demand for lower-skilled workers, driving up their wages, and lowering their level of unemployment. While policies focusing on distribution have traditionally been centered on tax and transfers, it has long been recognized that it may be better (more efficient) to have policies that change the before-tax-and-transfer distribution of income. Such policies reduce the burden imposed by distortionary redistributive policies (Stiglitz 1998b).

But there are further reasons that we should be concerned about growing inequality than just a sense of social justice. It can lead to increased political and social instability. There is, moreover, a growing understanding, even within the IMF, that inequality may lead to lower economic growth, more economic instability, and a weaker economy (see Stiglitz 2012c, 2011; Berg and Ostry 2011; and the references cited there). While there are many channels through which these adverse effects operate (e.g., inequality diminishes the aggregate demand for domestic nontraded goods, and central banks often take offsetting actions—lowering interest rates and relaxing regulations and their enforcement—which give rise to unsustainable bubbles), one may be of particular importance in developing countries, where there is a need for heavy public investments in infrastructure, education, and technology.

In a society with very little inequality, the only role of the state is to provide collective goods and correct market failures. When there are large inequalities, interests differ. Distributive battles inevitably rage, and to prevent redistribution, wealthy elites often try to circumscribe the powers of government. But in circumscribing government, they also restrict government's ability to perform positive roles. As we have argued here and elsewhere, government needs to play an important role in any economy, correcting pervasive market failures, but especially in the "creative economy."

Thus, our critique of noninclusive growth goes beyond that it is a waste of a country's most valuable resource—its human talent—to fail to ensure that everyone lives up to his or her abilities. Noninclusive growth can lead to democracies that do not support high-growth strategies. There can be a vicious circle, with more inequality leading to a more circumscribed government, leading in turn to more inequality and slower growth.

The analysis of this section has several obvious but important implications: Earlier, we argued that developing countries cannot just "borrow" or even simply adapt technology from more-developed countries. There is a need for a new model of innovation. Here, we have identified some objectives that are of particular relevance to developing countries—innovation needs to be directed (through industrial policies) at saving resources, protecting the environment, improving the distribution of income, and helping restructure the economy. These objectives may be intertwined—industrial policies that promote more inclusiveness may promote more learning; better environmental policies may lead to a better distribution of income (Dasgupta 1993).

4. Trade Policy

Many of the industrial policies discussed in earlier parts of this book entailed government expenditures—subsidies to sectors which should be expanded or investments in R & D and education to enhance the competitiveness of the learning sectors. But governments in developing countries (and even in developed countries) have a hard time raising revenues (see, e.g., Aizenman and Jinjarak 2009). In the absence of lump sum taxes, all taxes are distortionary, and thus there is a real cost to providing such subsidies. (Our analysis in the preceding chapters took those costs into account in designing the optimal interventions.)

It is thus natural that governments try to shape their economy using tools that raise revenues rather than use them. Tariffs and auctioned quotas can do that (see Dasgupta and Stiglitz 1971, 1972, 1974; Emran and Stiglitz 2005). This helps explain the widespread use of trade policy as part of industrial policy.

But turning to trade policy encounters several problems. First, there is the widespread theoretical presumption in favor of free trade—dating back to Adam Smith and his attack against mercantalism; David Ricardo, who developed the theory of comparative advantage; and nineteenth-century liberal economists such as John Stuart Mill. Samuelson (1938) formalized the welfare benefits of free trade. And neoliberal doctrines of the latter part of the twentieth century, discussed earlier in this chapter, reinforced this presumption.

But the stringent assumptions required to prove the result that free trade was desirable only highlighted the limited scope of the result. The analysis assumed perfect markets—perfect competition, perfect risk markets, full employment, and, most important from our perspectives, no externalities and, especially from the perspective of this book, no learning externalities. When any of these assumptions is dropped, free trade is *not* desirable.[15] Chapter 11 showed that in a learning economy, growth and long-term welfare could be enhanced with trade interventions. The result that there should be no tariffs vanished even in the absence of limitations on government's ability to raise revenues. Thus, advances in modern economics have reversed the earlier presumption: Now there is a presumption *against* free trade. And this presumption is even increased when account is taken of possible adverse distributive consequences. Trade liberalization has been associated with increasing inequality.[16]

Second, whatever the theoretical presumptions, there is a widespread belief that, empirically, trade is good for growth. While some earlier cross-country regressions seem to confirm this politically popular view, upon closer examination, the evidence does not support the conclusion.[17] It appears that once the "misattribution of macroeconomic phenomena (overvalued currencies or macroeconomic instability) or geographical location (in the tropical zone) to trade policies . . . are corrected, any meaningful cross-country relationship between trade barriers and economic growth evaporates" (Helleiner 1994).

That trade liberalization *by itself* would not ensure growth should have been obvious from the large disparities that exist within developed countries: There are no trade barriers between north and south Italy (no barriers even to the movement of capital), and yet there have been persistent large differences in income. So too for the United States, until the federal government undertook actions (including assistance) that narrowed (but far from eliminated) the gap in income between the North and the South.

There is another way of seeing that trade (and trade liberalization) *cannot* be at the center of the explanation of successful growth: Trading opportunities available through globalization are universal; yet growth has been highly particular, both across countries (even among those that have liberalized) and within individual countries over time. It is particular local conditions that determine whether the universal trade opportunities lead to growth.

Much of the presumption that openness leads to growth is based on the observed correlation between growth and trade.[18] But that correlation does not prove causality: Is it trade that has caused growth, or vice versa? One way to get insight into this issue is to look not at trade, but at trade liberalization. Free trade is about trade liberalization. Developing countries that have grown more may have done so because they've exported more, not because they liberalized; they may have succeeded in exporting more because of enhanced learning, which could have been impeded by liberalization. The evidence supports this hypothesis—that for the most part causality goes from growth to trade. The United Nations Development Programme (UNDP 2003), among others, presents evidence that trade liberalization was *not* associated with higher economic growth. Similarly, the marked reductions in trade barriers facing the least-developed countries (under Europe's "Everything But Arms" initiative or the United States' AGOA) have not had the hoped for benefits in terms of an expansion in trade.[19]

This book (focusing on learning) helps explain why we should not be surprised at the result that trade liberalization may be adverse to growth, and in section 6 of this chapter, we present evidence that is consistent with these perspectives.

The third objection to trade interventions (as to other forms of industrial policy) concerns *political economy*: Even if theoretically, there is a presumption against free trade, even if the evidence that trade is good for growth is, at best, weak, and even if the most successful countries employed trade policy as an instrument for economic growth, today's less-developed countries, it is alleged, are incapable of using trade policy as an effective instrument. Opponents claim that, more likely than not, it will be abused. We will confront this objection in section 7 of this chapter.

The final set of difficulties in the use of trade policies as an instrument of industrial policy arise from international trade agreements. In recent years, the WTO has attempted to restrict the use of such policies. These WTO restrictions on industrial policies and domestic sourcing (and possibly other restrictions on financial markets) may impede the ability of developing countries to foster learning, to garner for themselves the full learning benefits of foreign direct investment, or force them to employ second-best methods for promoting learning within their economies. Though the advocates of these restrictions surround them with neoliberal ideology, arguing that these restrictions are best for the countries themselves, the hypocrisy of countries like the United States and many in Europe attempting to restrict others from undertaking policies that were at the center of their own development has not gone unnoticed.[20]

The central result of earlier chapters was that while targeted subsidies may be the most effective way of promoting development and learning, trade policy (implemented through tariffs, quotas, or exchange rate policies) may be an effective instrument as well, as the last chapter demonstrated.[21] Though there are static costs associated with such interventions, the dynamic benefits can well exceed the costs. Chapter 11 showed that even though WTO constraints may impose a high cost on developing countries, trade intervention through managing exchange rates is still desirable, and later chapters will illustrate that there are other policies that can help shape the economy that can escape WTO strictures.

While trade policy can be, and has been, an important instrument for creating a learning economy, the learning perspective also can strengthen the rationale for regional integration: It may well be that individual national markets may be too small to support robust local industries. In that case the natural extension of the basic policy is to combine local economies at similar stages of industrial development into free-trade areas which are then protected by common uniform external industrial tariffs. Such extension has the added benefit of enhancing local competition.

Given space limitations, we cannot comment in depth on the form and design of trade policy. We make only two comments, elaborating in part on observations made earlier. First, our learning perspective emphasizes that what is important is not static comparative advantage but dynamic comparative advantage. As we explained in chapter 1, however, what that entails is more complicated than is often suggested. Indeed, we have argued that even the concept of static comparative advantage is more subtle than is widely recognized, once the (partial) mobility of capital, labor, and knowledge is taken into account. Three specific conclusions emerge from the discussions (including of chapter 1): (a) Countries cannot simply look to what other countries have done at similar stages of development. History matters. Changes in technology and the global marketplace mean that what worked for, say, Korea fifty years ago may not work for a country in a similar position today. (b) Given the difficulties of determining a country's (static or dynamic) comparative advantage, Lin's argument (2012, 2014) that countries should be careful about pursuing industrial policies that "defy" comparative advantage may not be of much help. (c) Countries have to be strategic—because history matters, they have to take into account how enhancing capabilities today (through trade policies) will affect their potential for capability enhancement in the future.

Second, more finely honed interventions require more information and may raise more political economy problems. Thus, while in the absence of these limitations, more finely honed interventions would be able to improve the dynamic-static trade-offs—getting more growth with a smaller sacrifice in current consumption/utility, taking them into account may imply the desirability of broader interventions. We explore this notion further in section 7.

5. Making the Most of One's Natural Resources

Many of the less-developed countries, especially in Africa, are highly dependent on resource exports. Linkages between natural resource production and learning there and in other sectors are typically weaker than, say, between manufacturing and the rest of the economy, helping to explain why there is typically such a large gap between the state of technology in the mining and natural resource sector and other sectors of African economies, and explaining in part why the abundance of natural resources has often not been accompanied by the hoped for increases in standards of living.

The latter failure, which has become known as the "resource curse" or the "paradox of plenty" (Humphreys, Sachs, and Stiglitz 2007; Stiglitz 2006a;) is partly explained by macroeconomic problems of high volatility and noncompetitive exchange rates that mark resource-rich countries. High volatility and high exchange rates are especially bad for creating a learning economy[22] and thus for long-run increases in standards of living. But there are well-known effective policy responses, including stabilization and sovereign wealth funds and care in borrowing from abroad, especially in periods of commodity price booms.

But industrial policies have not played as important a role in addressing the problems of the resource curse as they should. This is partly because the issues on which we have focused in this book have not received the attention that they should.

Historically, those countries with an abundance of natural resources (especially those in Africa) were thought of simply as a source of raw materials. In the development of the mines, little or no attention was given to how that development might affect the broader development of the economy (other than through the availability of resource rents). Transportation systems were designed to move the resources out of the country, not to promote the broader development of the country.

Trade policies in developed countries in the postcolonial era reinforced these colonial-era policies. Escalating tariffs,[23] for instance, discouraged the development of value-added activities within such countries. Neoclassical economics reinforced these patterns of development: because most African countries do not today have a static comparative advantage in these value-added activities, they have been discouraged from developing them. The only circumstances in which such activities might make sense (from that perspective) are when transportation costs offset these disadvantages; i.e., it may make sense to do some processing if in doing so the costs of transportation are thereby reduced.

But from a learning-development perspective, matters look markedly different. One of the reasons that African countries may not have done as well as others is that the "natural" (market-driven) learning spillovers from mining and natural resource industries to the rest of the economy are less than those from, say, manufacturing—or are at least less so, in the absence of government intervention.[24] In this view, then, the high exchange rate and high volatility marking most natural-resource-dependent countries has led to an economic structure that has discouraged activities with large learning spillovers. Better macro-policies (leading to less volatility and lower exchange rates) can go some way in correcting this distortion. But so can industrial policies, by leveraging off the countries' resource base (in which at least some countries have a degree of monopoly power).

This entails exploiting upstream, downstream, and horizontal linkages (Hirschman 1958), and linkages that might be associated with processing and resource extraction itself. Some developing countries (like Malaysia) have actually succeeded in developing capabilities in resource extraction by imposing employment and training conditions on foreign operators.

Even if much resource extraction technology itself is not closely linked with other technologies which might provide the basis of broader growth and learning, many of the sub-activities entailed in the long and complex process of removing natural resources do. Buildings have to be built and people have to be hired. Workers have to be fed. There is a demand for people and vehicles for transportation and logistics. In short, for many natural-resource-rich countries, the exploration and development of these linkages can be the basis of an effective industrial policy, one which enhances the capabilities of the people and firms within them. (For a more extensive discussion, see Jourdan, forthcoming.)

6. History

There is ample evidence that many countries have successfully used trade and industrial policies. Indeed, are few successful economies in which the government has not successfully employed industrial *and* trade policies, broadly understood, and including trade restrictions. This is true not just for developing countries, like Korea, but also for developed countries like the United States.[25] Moreover, such policies can be used not only by countries with highly trained bureaucracies, but by countries at early stages of development. At the time that many of the East Asian countries began their industrial policies, not only was their economic development lower than some of the less-developed countries today, but so too was their political development.

To understand the role of government in this arena, we need only think of the history of the United States, where the development of agriculture, the main "industry" in the nineteenth century, was promoted by government. The history of telecommunications—from the first telegraph line to the development of the Internet—entails one form of government support after another. Even the first browser was supported by the government. So too, in Brazil, we can think of the development of sugar-based ethanol and the Embraer airplane—and a host of other export-enhancing government interventions. In each of these cases, the social returns from these government-supported innovations are so high that they would support many less successful ventures.

The success of the most successful countries in development after World War II—those in East Asia—is largely attributable to their recognition of the importance of learning and the role of government in promoting it. Korea, for instance, paid little attention to its static comparative advantage. Its static comparative advantage would have led that country to focus on rice farming. But it knew that even if it became the most productive rice farming country in the world, its prospects would be limited. Only by focusing on sectors from which it could learn, and on the basis of which it could close the knowledge gap with more advanced countries could they achieve the growth they desired. Thus, Korea developed complementary industrial, education, and technology policies, and it succeeded, increasing its per capita income more than eightfold in a span of less than four decades.

Had it followed the dictates of the Washington Consensus policies, it would have eschewed industrial policies and focused investments in education at the primary level—and it would have, at best, been a middle-income rice-growing country. History has shown that not only have countries like Korea that adopted industrial policies done well, but also that those that have not have suffered, illustrated by the impact of the structural adjustment policies in Africa, which eschewed industrial policies, leading to deindustrialization and low or negative growth.

Interestingly, Korea followed a strategy that was a mixture of the broad-based export promotion policies we have advocated as part of an infant-economy strategy and a more targeted approach (e.g., promoting chips and heavy industries and chemicals). Whether they would have done still better had they limited themselves only to broad-based strategies is an exercise in counterfactual history, for which the answers are at best debatable.

Historical Experiences with Trade Interventions

Historical evidence provides considerable support for the efficacy of learning-related trade restrictions.[26] While the most successful countries, both today (in East Asia) and historically (including the United States) have used a variety of instruments as part of their industrial policies, among the most important have been trade interventions. They have not only engaged in trade restrictions, but those restrictions were an explicit part of their growth strategies. Indeed, Rodrik (2001) argued that the three primary models of successful development in the twentieth century *all* relied on managed trade regimes: import substitution as practiced by a number of countries in the 1960s, outward oriented industrialization as practiced in East Asia in the 1980s, and the state-directed capitalism of China in the 1990s. Chang (2002) showed that almost all of today's rich countries used tariff protection and subsidies to develop their industries, and "Britain and the USA, the two countries that are supposed to have reached the summit of the world economy through their free-market, free-trade policy, are actually the ones that had most aggressively used protection and subsidies."

Of course, all of these countries, including the East Asian tigers, did engage in trade—but it was promoting exports, expanding the learning sector, not trade liberalization as is usually understood, opening up domestic markets broadly to foreign imports. Trade interventions have sometimes not worked out well. They have at times been used as protectionist tools by special interests, rather than to redirect society's resources toward creating a learning society. But the history of successful interventions suggests that failure is not inevitable. Hopefully, countries will learn from the failures (and successes) of the past, so that the returns from future interventions will presumably be greater than those from past interventions, a point to which we return later in the chapter.

Not surprisingly, countries like Myanmar, that pursued xenophobic policies that cut themselves off from others—both from trade and from learning—did not fare well.

In short, our analysis suggests that well-designed trade policies such as those in East Asia, centered on learning and the acquisition of technology, have done a far better job of promoting growth and learning than either of the extreme policies of full liberalization or full autarky.

War Time

Perhaps even more telling concerning the relationship between trade, growth, and learning is the fact that war times, in which trade is interrupted, have often seemed to be periods of enormous dynamic gains.[27]

Our learning perspective provides an interpretation of these seemingly anomalous experiences. Forced to rely on their own production capacities, economies increased their industrial production and, with it, their learning. Moreover, the exigencies of the moment "forced" the economies to learn more quickly than they might otherwise have done.

Does Latin America Demonstrate the Failure of Industrial Policies?

Some have argued that even if industrial policies were successful in East Asia, and even if they worked in times of war, they were a dismal failure in Latin America, and blame that continent's lost decade on its pursuit of industrial policies. Even if that conclusion were true, it would only imply that the form of industrial policy pursued in Latin America (import substitution versus the export-led growth of East Asia) was flawed, not that industrial policies per se were doomed to failure.[28]

But the conclusion that industrial policies were a failure in Latin America is, at best, contentious, at worst, simply wrong. Brazil, the most ardent adopter of such policies, had an impressive growth rate of almost 6 percent in the three-quarters century before 1980. Industrial policies played an important role in that country's success in this period. The lost decade was a result of Latin American countries' excessive indebtedness in the 1970s, the period of the oil shock—understandable, perhaps, given the low, or even negative, real interest rates at which the petro-dollars were being recycled—followed by an unprecedented increase in interest rates, a result of the United States suddenly switching its monetary policy regime to monetarism.

The lost decade of the 1980s was, in short, a result of a macroeconomic shock, not a failure of microeconomic policies. The subsequent adoption of the Washington Consensus policies, which eschewed industrial policies, prolonged the subsequent period of slow growth. The more recent revival of growth, for example, in Brazil, has much to do with the government once again undertaking activist policies (Bértola and Ocampo 2012).

China and India

What about countries like India and China, which have liberalized and grown? A closer look at the timing shows that their take-off occurred prior to trade liberalization. Serious trade liberalization occurred *after* the trend rate of growth had increased. In both cases it was associated with "internal liberalization."[29] Reducing domestic distortions while maintaining external barriers provided precisely the conditions for the dynamic gains identified in this book.

History Shows That Industrial and Trade Policies Can Work

In short, the historical experience shows that industrial policies can work. They have worked in a variety of countries in a variety of circumstances, with a variety of strategies and instruments. Even instances of seeming failure need to be interpreted with caution. Good policies involve some risk—if every public or private investment succeeded, it would indicate insufficient risk taking.[30]

There are undoubtedly instances where industrial policy has failed because of abuses. But the relevant question is: Are the problems inherent in political processes? The next section shows that they are not, but that limitations in the political processes may affect the form that industrial policy should take.

7. Political Economy

A persistent criticism of industrial policies is that, even if market allocations are inefficient, even if market prices differ from shadow prices, government attempts to correct these failures will simply make matters worse. There is, it is alleged, just too much potential for misuse.

Some go so far as to suggest that abuse is almost inevitable, because of a proclivity for rent seeking. Even if government doesn't *abuse* these policies, at least in developing countries it doesn't have the competency to implement them effectively.

Of course, most of these critics also believe that industrial policies are not needed: one should rely on the private sector. Government shouldn't be in the business of picking winners, of trying to outsmart the market. One should leave decisions about resource allocations to the market. As a former chairman of the U.S. Council of Economic Advisors famously is said to have claimed: It doesn't make any difference whether we produce potato chips or computer chips.

We have already provided answers to several of these perspectives. Market failures *are* rife. The objective of industrial policies is to correct these market failures.

That abuses are not inevitable is also clear: There is neither theory nor evidence in support of such a conclusion. The historical experiences cited in the previous paragraphs provide convincing evidence to the contrary. To be sure, there are instances of government failure, but none with the consequences or on the scale of the losses resulting, for example, from the failures of America's financial market before and during the Great Recession. As we noted, virtually every successful economy has employed industrial policies successfully, at one time or another (see Chang 2002, 2003; and the references cited there). And this is most notable in the case of East Asia.[31]

But then the question is raised, can there be effective industrial policies in countries with significant deficiencies in governance. The implication is that, while with "ideal government" intervention might improve matters, in the "real world—outside of a few isolated successes— interventions do not necessarily do so. The argument has been put that even if such policies contributed greatly to the success of East Asia, elsewhere they were less successful, because they were abused. These critics go on to say that, given the widely acknowledged deficiencies in governance in many African countries, they should shy away from such policies.

The critics point to Latin America and its lost decade as a prime example of the failure of industrial policies, but we have argued that Latin America's failure was a result not of its industrial policies, but of its debt and macroeconomic policies. We have also pointed out that at the time Korea and some of the other East Asian countries undertook industrial policies, they were as economically and politically under-developed as many of the poor countries of the world today that are debating adopting such policies.

Framing the Question the Right Way

The strongest objection to these objections to industrial policy is that they frame the question the wrong way. The question is not whether in some cases such interventions have failed, but whether in some instances they have succeeded. The answer to that is unambiguously, yes. Indeed, the discussion in the previous section suggests that there are few, if any successful countries that have not engaged in industrial policies.

Even with some failures, average returns have been positive. Indeed, again as we have already noted, good industrial policy entails risk taking, and with risk taking, we should expect some failures.

But even if average returns were sometimes, or often, low, the question today facing a country contemplating adopting industrial policies is whether it can learn from the successes and failures of the past, whether it can construct an industrial policy that has prospects of working.

Industrial Policies Are Not About Picking Winners

There is a second way in which the standard objections to industrial policy have framed the issue incorrectly. Industrial policies are not about picking winners. They are about correcting market failures in general, and creating a learning society in particular. It is now widely accepted that there can be important market failures arising from large negative externalities (e.g., from pollution or from excessive risk taking in the financial sector) and that there is an important role for government in correcting these market failures. Except among the extreme right, there is a general consensus that, even if government interventions may not have been perfect, we are a lot better off as a result of these interventions, which have curbed air and water pollution. We are concerned here with an equally important set of *positive* externalities, and we believe that government can be equally effective in (partially) correcting these externalities. Indeed, as the previous discussion has made clear, many governments (both in developed and developing countries) have a credible record of industrial policy interventions.[32]

Policies to Address Political Economy Problems

Moreover, these successes were not just accidents. The thrust of the book *The East Asian Miracle* (World Bank 1993; see also Stiglitz 1996; Khan 2012; Stiglitz and Uy 1996) is that the East Asian countries used systemic procedures that limited the scope for abuse and increased the likelihood of identifying firms and sectors whose expansion would have society-wide benefits. First, the subsidies were limited—indeed, one of the main benefits government granted was access to credit. (With credit rationing, there is a difference between the shadow price of credit and the market price of credit; but the terms at which they got credit were still largely commercial.) Second, the government, to a large extent, employed contests for the allocation of the credit and other subsidies: those companies that demonstrated success in export markets gained preferential access to credit. It was not just profits that determined the allocation of credit; for higher profits might signal a better ability to exploit monopoly profits. But success in international markets demonstrated broader marketing and technical competencies. In effect, the government channeled rent seeking—the benefits of access to government subsidies and access to credit—making it socially constructive. Competition for rents led to firms that learned more and became more competitive in the global marketplace.

(In other countries, though, rent seeking has diverted resources away from growth-inducing activities, and even when resources are allocated to innovation, the innovation may not be growth inducing. Firms have devoted their resources to learning how to circumvent regulations designed to make the economy more stable and to learning how to exploit consumers and the firm's monopoly power better. Markets don't work well when private returns are not well aligned with social returns; and in those circumstances, incentives to innovate and learn are also distorted, as we have repeatedly noted.)

Governance and Institutional Reform

The fact that there have been some failures in industrial policy and some successes means that countries contemplating such policies need to think carefully about their design. There are institutional reforms that reduce the likelihood of abuses and increase the likelihood of successful interventions. East Asia provides examples of effective institutional designs that harnessed the drive for rent seeking in a socially constructive way. Other institutional innovations, including peer review, improvements in competitive bidding and allocational processes and transparency, time-limited programs, and the design of partnership arrangements (where those receiving assistance have to contribute significant amounts of equity) have contributed to reducing the scope for abuses and improving the efficacy of industrial policies. Some of these institutional improvements—including those related to the performance of development banks, such as Brazil's BNDES—show that there has been learning from the failures (and successes) of the past.

IMPLICATIONS OF GOVERNANCE DEFICIENCIES FOR THE DESIGN OF INDUSTRIAL POLICIES Reforming political processes is slow, and it may not be possible to make reforms fast enough to reduce the likelihood of abuses of certain forms of industrial policies to a tolerable level or to enhance the likelihood that they will be successful to the point where undertaking such policies seems advisable. The implication of deficiencies in governance is that *one needs to tailor the design of the instruments of industrial policy around the capabilities and governance of the public sector.*

This poses an important trade-off. Chapter 11 focused on the infant-economy argument for protection, centering on encouraging the industrial sector more broadly. An implication of the infant-economy argument is that trade restrictions should be broadly and uniformly applied to industrial products. Since the benefits sought are broadly rather than narrowly determined, there should be no attempt to support particular industries or, more precisely, to identify sectors in which there are larger spillovers. Broad-based measures such as exchange rate interventions require only that the government ascertain that the sectors that would be encouraged by such interventions, such as in the determination of the exchange rate, have more societal learning benefits than the sectors that would be discouraged—and there is ample evidence that that is the case (evidenced, in particular, by the success of export-led growth strategies). Firms and sectors within the economy self-select, and the expansion of firms and sectors with greater learning enhances the dynamism of the economy.

On the other hand, more targeted interventions can, if well designed and executed, lead to even more learning and faster rates of growth. Some countries have shown that they can manage the political economy problems of more targeted interventions. As we noted, the East Asian countries did so by using rule-based systems in which interventions were linked to past export success.

Ultimately, the test of the effectiveness of uniform infant-economy tariff policies is how well they have worked in practice and here, at least superficially, the historical record is encouraging. The trade policy of the newly formed European Economic Community was, in the 1950s, one of high but relatively uniform external tariff barriers. The growth of the Community behind these barriers was rapid. Similarly, Asian economies like Japan, Korea, China, Taiwan, and Singapore while they did have some targeted interventions which, by and large, they managed well, have tended to favor broad rather than narrowly tailored barriers to trade, and they have all experienced strong growth. Finally, in its early history the United States, too, tended to favor high and broadly applied industrial tariffs and succeeded in fostering high levels of growth.

Of course, there is no form of intervention that completely "solves" the political economy problem: Sectors that benefit from exchange rate intervention may lobby for the maintenance of that intervention even in the absence of learning benefits. Still, arguably, the political economy problems can be better managed with such broad-based interventions than with more narrowly directed interventions, which lead to the creation of narrowly focused special interests concerned with sustaining particular tariffs beyond their natural economic lifetimes. Properly designed, both the costs and the benefits of a uniform industrial tariff system should be widely dispersed. Moreover, a broadly based industrial tariff system should be, to some extent, naturally self-limited. Successful local industries should begin to export and, therefore, be naturally predisposed in favor of free trade.

A Methodological Response to the Political Economy Critique

There is also a methodological response to the political economy critique of industrial policies: Whether such political economy objections are true or not, the conclusion is based on political analysis, not economic analysis. And the political analysis is often more simplistic than economic analysis.

Moreover, similar questions can be raised about every other aspect of policy. Many governments have not used monetary and financial regulatory policy well; in some cases, the misuse can be traced to problems of governance. Many have argued that regulators and central banks in some advanced industrial countries were captured by special interests in the financial markets, and this played an important role in the 2008 global economic crisis (see, e.g., Stiglitz 2010b; Johnson and Kwak 2010). But few would argue that as a result, governments should eschew the use of monetary and financial regulatory policy.[33]

LIBERALIZATION AND POLITICAL ECONOMY Finally, we note that liberalization is itself a political agenda. As we previously commented, markets do not exist in a vacuum. There are always going to be rules and regulations, even in a liberalized world. And the design of those rules and regulations will shape markets. The rules and regulations that were adopted in the process of "liberalizing" and deregulating financial markets in the United States and U.K. led to bloated financial institutions backed by implicit guarantees from the monetary authority and ultimately the taxpayer—an industrial policy of deregulation and favorable regulation that distorted the economy.

8. Some General Reflections on Industrial Policy

Theory of the Second Best

Industrial policies distort consumption from what it otherwise would have been. Conventional economics (such as the Washington Consensus policies) emphasized the costs of these interventions. We have emphasized that when there are market failures (as is always the case when there are learning externalities), there will be benefits. Optimal policy weighs the benefits and costs as the margin.

The economics of the second best is particularly relevant here: R & D and learning give rise to market imperfections, sometimes referred to as distortions, where resources are not allocated in a "first best" way. Well-designed distortions in one market can partially offset distortions in others.

We use the word *distortions* with care: Common usage suggests that governments should simply do away with them. But as the term has come to be used, it simply refers to deviations from the way a classical model with, say, perfect information might function. Information is inherently imperfect, and these imperfections cannot be legislated away. Nor can the market power that arises from the returns to scale inherent in research be legislated away. That is why simultaneously endogenizing market structure and innovation is so important, as we noted in chapter 5. Similarly, the costs associated with R & D (or the "losses" associated with expanding production to "invest" in learning) cannot be ignored; they have to be paid for. Monopoly rents are one way of doing so, but—as we argue here—a far from ideal way.

As always in the modern economics of the public sector, the nature of the optimal interventions depends on the instruments and powers of government. Whether the government can abolish monopolies or undo their distortionary behavior has implications for the desirable levels of research and learning. It makes a difference, too, if the government can raise revenues to subsidize or support research or learning only through distortionary taxation rather than through lump sum taxes. But even when the government can only raise revenues through distortionary taxation, there are ways of doing so and spending the proceeds that increase societal well-being and the speed of innovation. (But the optimal investment in innovation is likely to be less with distortionary taxation than with lump sum taxation.)

Industrial Strategies

A key issue of industrial strategy is not only the direction (e.g., should Korea have attempted to reinforce its comparative advantage in rice, or to create a comparative advantage in some other area?), but also the size of the step. Should governments try to promote a nearby technology (product), nudging along a gradual, evolutionary process that might eventually have occurred anyway? Or should it take a big leap? The latter is riskier, bringing perhaps greater returns if successful, but also a higher probability of failure.

We have not formally modeled this critical decision, so the following remarks are only meant to be suggestive: The difficulties in learning increase significantly the bigger the leap; but so may the benefits. There are natural nonconvexities in the value of information/knowledge (Radner and Stiglitz 1984), implying that it pays to take at least a *moderate* step: small incrementalism is not likely to be optimal.

By the same token, using another analogy to corporate strategic policy, it pays to move to a part of the product space where there are rents which can be sustained (e.g., as a result of entry barriers, arising, for instance, out of returns to scale or specific knowledge). This almost surely entails not doing what others are or have been doing.

Among the most important insights of the theory of learning that we have developed is that, because history matters, decisions taken today concerning the direction of learning and innovation can have long-run consequences. Had Korea made different decisions in earlier decades, its economy today would look markedly different. The commodities which constitute its current static comparative advantage would be different, and its learning capabilities would be different. Because there are these long-term consequences, countries can't avoid making guesses about the evolution of the global economy. As we have argued, they can't or shouldn't simply follow patterns of development undertaken by countries at similar stages of development a quarter or half century ago.

Industrial policies are inherently risky; but it is even riskier not to have an industrial policy.

9. Concluding Remarks

Earlier, we argued that countries have no choice but to have industrial policies; budgetary policies and legal frameworks inevitably shape the economy. We have argued that countries need to be more conscious of the effects of policies in shaping the economy—and more active in doing so, with a particular focus on creating a learning and innovative economy. Markets don't do this on their own.

For developing countries in Africa and elsewhere, as they attempt to reindustrialize, to restructure their economies to become more integrated into the global economy and move away from excessive dependence on commodity exports, to raise standards of income, increase employment, reduce poverty and inequality, and protect a fragile environment, industrial policies are of especial importance. We have explained why the widely cited objections—that though industrial policies may have worked in East Asia, they are inappropriate for Africa or other developing countries because of deficiencies in governance—are at best unpersuasive, at worst wrong. We have argued further that what is required is more than just creating a business-friendly environment, allowing the market to shape the economy on its own. Such policies are necessary, but they are not sufficient.

The debate today should not be about whether governments should pursue policies that shape the industrial structure of the economy. Inevitably, they will and do. The debate today should center around the directions in which it should attempt to shape the economy and the best way of doing so, given a country's current institutions and how they will evolve—recognizing that the evolution of the institutions themselves will be affected by the industrial policies chosen. In the past, trade interventions have been an effective instrument of industrial policy; and although WTO strictures may limit the scope and form of trade interventions, they have not undermined the desirability of such interventions. Governance issues are, of course, relevant in all countries and are important in shaping the form that industrial policy takes and the instruments that are appropriately used. They strengthen the argument for broad-based interventions, such as those associated with exchange rate policy.

The belated recognition of the potential of these policies comes at a fortunate time, for changes in the global economy may afford the countries of Africa and some other regions that have lagged a distinct opportunity to transform their economies in a way that will, at long last, narrow the gap that separates their standards of living from that of much of the rest of the world.

CHAPTER THIRTEEN

Financial Policy and Creating a Learning Society

IF THERE are powerful arguments for broad barriers to imported industrial goods, those apply equally to restrictions on capital movements. Capital and financial services *within* a country can support learning; in contrast, financial services provided by foreigners can lead to a redirection of investment and learning *out of the country*, impeding the creation of a learning society. By the same token, the availability within a country of low-cost capital can encourage learning investments in the country. We saw in earlier chapters that complements to learning activities ought to be encouraged, and lowering the domestic cost of capital (by restricting capital outflows) may do so. This is especially so if learning is directly related to the level of investment, as Arrow originally hypothesized. Moreover, in a world of credit rationing, access to capital can be a key instrument of industrial policy.

There are further links between financial policy and learning. A poorly designed financial sector and poorly designed financial policies can lead to macro-instability, and as we noted in chapter 4, macro-instability impedes learning. (We will postpone the analysis of the links between financial policy and macro-stability to chapter 14.)

In short, a key objective of government policy should be to create a financial sector that fosters learning and helps create a learning economy. Standard policies (such as those advocated within the Washington Consensus) have simply ignored the effects of the financial sector on learning and have, as a result, fostered a financial sector which we believe is often not only not conducive to learning, but inimical to it. This chapter will explore briefly the various links between financial sector policies and learning. What emerges from our analysis is a set of policy recommendations that is markedly different from those of the conventional wisdom. Underlying the analysis is the pervasiveness of externalities. While recent literature has emphasized the overall importance of externalities within the financial sector and between the financial sector and the real sector,[1] we emphasize here that private returns are often markedly different from social returns because of learning externalities.

The chapter is divided into four sections. The first focuses on financial market liberalization, opening up of countries to foreign financial institutions. The second centers on capital market liberalization, policies aimed at allowing the free flow of capital into and out of a country. The third takes up the issue of financial policy as an instrument of industrial policy—including how we can shape the financial sector in ways which encourage the development of learning sectors.

There is a certain symmetry between labor and capital. If creating a learning economy entails restrictions on the free flow of capital, it should be apparent that there are even more compelling arguments for shaping labor movements. In the concluding section of the chapter, we touch upon some key aspects of this complex issue.

1. Financial Market Liberalization

Information externalities are at the center of the debate over financial market liberalization. Western governments (directly, and through the international financial institutions) have strongly pushed developing countries to deregulate and liberalize their financial markets.

Deregulation ignored, of course, the market failures which had led in the first place to the demand for regulation of the financial sector. While a full discussion of these would take us beyond the confines of this book, suffice it to say that the actions of the financial sector can and do impose large externalities on the rest of the economy;[2] that there is a proclivity for the financial sector to engage in excessive risk taking; and that, as a result, economies with unregulated and underegulated markets are likely to have excessive volatility. This volatility imposes huge costs on society—most obviously on workers, but also on the public fisc, both directly, as it bails out banks in an attempt to prevent matters from getting worse, and indirectly, as the economic downturns have huge budgetary consequences, with declining revenues and increasing social expenditures.

Financial sector liberalization focuses on opening up a country's financial markets to banks and other financial institutions from abroad. It was one of the central initiatives of the Uruguay round trade negotiations. Ironically, even as the United States was pushing others to open up their financial markets, the United States had not yet even allowed interstate branch banking within its borders. Such restrictions (finally eliminated in 1994[3]) were introduced in the nineteenth century, because those outside the eastern United States worried that if the large New York banks were allowed into their markets, they would siphon off deposits, impeding the development of these other parts of the country—concerns closely related to justifiable worries of many in the developing world that have resisted full financial market liberalization.

One of the earlier justifications for such liberalization was that the domestic banks in developing countries would *learn* good practices from Western banks. In the aftermath of the global financial crisis, that argument seems less persuasive: They might have learned how to engage in more effective exploitation of the poor, through predatory lending and abusive credit card practices, and they might have learned about how to engage in deceptive off-balance-sheet accounting, but it is clear that there may be negative externalities associated with such socially unproductive learning.[4]

The evidence presented in papers such as Rashid (2011); Yeyati and Micco (2007); Detragiache, Tressel, and Gupta (2008); Mian (2006); and Bayraktar and Wang (2004) is that financial market liberalization is not associated with faster growth in developing countries. A closer look at the evidence suggests some of the reasons (alluded to earlier) why this may be so.[5] Foreign banks lend less to small and medium-sized enterprises. And for good reason.

If an English bank opens a branch in Latin America, the managers know a lot more about investment opportunities in England than they do about investment opportunities in Latin America. Given the asymmetries of information, therefore, the natural tendency is going to be to take the financial resources and move them out of Latin America to England. And to the extent that it lends domestically, it will be in areas requiring less information—lending to domestic large enterprises, including monopolies, and to government.[6]

Just as the infant-economy argument argues for protection of the industrial sector, this analysis provides an analogous infant-economy argument for protection of finance. That is, it is desirable to develop domestic competency in the allocation of resources and management of risk, focusing on the particular facts and circumstances of the domestic economy. In the case of banks, even if domestic institutions were more competent (in allocating capital, managing risks, lowering transactions costs) foreign banks may have an advantage, if domestic depositors or others that transact with the foreign institution *believe* that they are safer than domestic institutions.[7] They may be safer either because they are truly more sound, or simply because depositors (and others who transact with the bank) believe their richer governments stand behind them.[8] Those governments have the capacity and willingness to bail out their national banks, a belief that turned out to be largely true in the 2008 crisis but not in the Argentinean crisis.[9] Whether these beliefs are justified or not, if individuals hold these beliefs, then they will demand higher interest rates for deposits in domestic banks. In short, these beliefs put domestic financial institutions at a disadvantage.

Now, obviously, one would like to be able to test this idea empirically, and there is a set of data on which one can do so. The less-developed part of the United States economy includes the states of the old confederacy (Alabama, Arkansas, Florida, Georgia, Louisiana, Mississippi, North Carolina, South Carolina, North Carolina, Tennessee, Texas, and Virginia). One can look at the relative development of those states in the period where the United States had only state banking and there was no interstate banking. That basically was the regime over the twenty years from 1850 to 1870. (There are other big changes over this period, most notably that have to do with the war, and that's why one wants to look at growth over a longer period.)

Between 1850 and 1870 the relative income, that is, the income in those southern states relative to total U.S. income, grew by 15 percentage points.[10] Growth was slightly higher in the poorer states of Alabama, Mississippi, and South Carolina than it was in the richer states of Georgia, Virginia, and North Carolina. If one looks at the subsequent period of national banking, from 1870 to 1890, the catch-up is much, much slower: on average only 6 percent, and it is skewed toward the richer states: Virginia, Georgia, and North Carolina in particular. In fact, growth almost stops dead in its tracks in Alabama and Mississippi. Our hypothesis of what happened is simple: With local banking, local savings went to local entrepreneurs, and local financial institutions had incentives to develop the competency of judging among these. With national banking,[11] funds flowed out of the poorest states, which were afflicted with a low level of human capital and poor infrastructure.

Similar patterns seem at work today in developing countries. With financial market liberalization, foreign banks can attract funds away from domestic banks—or domestic banks will have to pay a higher interest rate to retain their depositor base. But, as we noted earlier, foreign banks have less information and less competency in judging among domestic small and medium-sized enterprises. Funds get diverted either back to the home country (about which they have superior information) or countries similar to or with close trade and financial ties to the home country. Any funds remaining within the developing country get allocated to seemingly more "secure" investments—loans to domestic monopolies and oligopolies and to the government.[12] To the extent that local banks are able to retain their depositor base by paying higher interest rates, the additional costs get passed on to local borrowers, putting local small and medium-sized enterprises at a disadvantage.

2. Capital Market Liberalization

Capital market liberalization (allowing the free mobility of capital in and out of a country[13]) has long been one of the most contentious areas of developmental policy. The IMF tried to change its charter, to allow it to force countries to liberalize their capital markets, in 1997—just as the East Asian crisis struck. The crisis was, in no small part, a result of the liberalization of capital markets in East Asia—which led to capital at first rushing in and then, when sentiment changed, rushing out (see Stiglitz 2002a; Furman and Stiglitz 1998). Interestingly, fifteen years later, in the aftermath of the global financial crisis of 2008, the IMF changed its position, recognizing that capital controls can play an important role in macroeconomic stability (IMF 2012b).

Ironically, capital market liberalization was supposed to bring both greater stability and growth. Capital would (in the standard theory that was part of the conventional wisdom and that underlay the Washington Consensus policies) flow into the country when it was needed—in a countercyclical way. And capital would flow from rich countries with a high capital to labor ratio to poorer countries with a low capital to labor ratio, enhancing growth in GDP in the latter and increasing global efficiency.[14] On both accounts, the standard theory failed: capital flows were largely pro-cyclical; overall, capital flowed out of developing countries; and, not surprisingly as a result, countries that liberalized their capital account had both more instability and lower growth.[15] (It was remarkable that these theories gained the ascendency that they did, given the overwhelming empirical evidence suggesting that capital flows were pro-cyclical.)

In the next chapter, we'll discuss briefly the impact of capital market liberalization on macro-stability. Here, we focus on the impact on the structure of investment—and thereby on learning.

What was so striking about East Asia was that with its very high savings rate, there was little need for capital inflows (unlike other parts of the developing world). What happened was that capital flowed in—and simultaneously flowed out. The countries typically borrowed at a much higher interest rate than they lent. They "invested" in U.S. government bonds, but borrowed from private (foreign) financial markets. In effect, capital market liberalization meant that they were outsourcing the allocation of capital to Western financial institutions. But, as our earlier analysis of banking suggested, these foreign financial institutions were less well informed about local conditions. In the case of several of the countries, money flowed particularly to real estate—helping create a real estate bubble. Thus, money flowed into sectors in which there was less learning.[16]

There were even more adverse effects on the structure of the economy (with respect to creating a learning economy) in the aftermath of the crises which regularly followed capital market liberalization (the East Asia crisis itself being but one example). Money flowed into these newly liberalized economies in a wave of irrational exuberance, but when attitudes changed, money flowed out. The sudden fall in the exchange rate created a currency crisis, which in many cases was translated into a financial and economic crisis. What happened next in Thailand illustrates the adverse effects. The IMF "rescue" package (designed to rescue the foreign lenders, not to protect the Thai economy) demanded high interest rates and large government cutbacks in spending. The result was a major economic downturn, with small and medium-sized domestic firms particularly hard hit and with major cutbacks in human investments (education and health). In effect, the attempt to arrest the fall in the currency—to enable firms that had borrowed in foreign exchange to be in a better position to pay back their debts—came at the expense of local entrepreneurs. In this case, the policy interventions were particularly unfortunate. The bail-out package had a barely noticeable effect on the exchange rate. Even if it had, much of the foreign-denominated lending was for real estate, and the real estate sector was already dead, with the breaking of the real estate bubble, and would not have been brought back to life even if the currency had been stabilized. But the high interest rates put a large fraction of smaller enterprises into bankruptcy—businesses that had never gambled by taking on foreign-denominated loans to finance activities the returns to which would accrue in baht. And yet the damage to the growth prospects of the economy could be long lasting.[17]

Capital market liberalization had a more direct effect on "learning," even in countries that did not experience a crisis. Because the allocation of capital was outsourced to Western financial institutions, there was less learning within the less-developed countries about the processes of capital allocation, risk management, etc.

Capital Outflows

Much of the discussion of recent capital market liberalization has focused on allowing capital inflows. But historically, restrictions on capital outflows have been even more important.

China restricted the outflow of capital, though it allowed an inflow of foreign direct investment. The effect of these capital market restrictions almost surely was to lower the cost of capital below what it otherwise would have been, facilitating domestic investment. If, as Arrow suggested, learning is related more to investment than to production, the result is more learning.

The general point (from the perspective of this book) is that if there are externalities associated with investment, when the money is invested abroad, those within the country don't benefit (at least as much) from these externalities.[18]

3. Finance and Industrial Policy

One of the reasons that markets fail to allocate resources efficiently to "learning" is capital market constraints and imperfections. R & D is hard to collateralize,[19] and optimal learning entails expanding production beyond the point where price equals short-run marginal costs. Imperfections of information often lead, especially in developing countries, to credit and equity rationing.

The United States provides an illustration of a country with a large financial sector (before the 2008 crisis, profits in that sector amounted to 40 percent of all corporate profits) but in which the financial sector did not, for the most part, focus on "learning sectors." Before the crisis, funds flowed freely into real estate and consumer loans, with only a small fraction of the funds going into new enterprises in learning sectors. In spite of its widely vaunted venture capital firms, which did play an important role in financing high-tech industries, these venture capital firms were a small fraction of the overall financial sector. The misallocation of resources—with implications for long-term growth—is all the more striking given the extraordinarily low (real) interest rates.

The previous chapter discussed the role of government in shaping the economy through industrial policy. We emphasized that, whether government likes to or not, whether the government does so deliberately or not, it inevitably shapes the economy. It is important, we argued, that it be conscious of how laws, regulations, and policies affect the economy, and attempt to do what it can to create a learning economy. The United States again illustrates what we had in mind: Loose financial regulations and deficiencies in corporate governance helped create an overbloated, dysfunctional financial sector.[20]

On the other hand, government regulation of the financial sector—and in some cases, direct government control over financial resources—can be effective instruments for directing resources to the creation of a learning economy. Even in the United States, usually viewed as a country in which the private sector dominates finance, at times government has played an active role in directing financial resources, e.g., through the Export-Import Bank and the Small Business Administration. Interestingly, a key instrument of industrial policy in East Asia was *access* to finance, often not even at subsidized rates (Stiglitz and Uy 1996). By steering finance to "learning" sectors, overall growth can be enhanced.

There are several other aspects of "learning" in the design of financial policy. In the following paragraphs, we discuss a few of the more important of these.

Financial Restraint[21]

Creating a vibrant financial sector focused, for instance, on lending to the industrial sector is not easy. Traditionally, banks focused on very short-term lending, trade credit, collateralized by the goods being bought and sold. At the core of successful lending is information—identifying who are good borrowers and then monitoring them to ensure that the funds go to where promised and that the borrower behaves in ways which enhance the likelihood of repayment. For reasons that are now well understood (see Greenwald and Stiglitz 2003), such information is best produced within institutions (banks or venture capital firms). As the U.S. precrisis attempt at developing a market-based system based on securitization shows so forcefully, capital markets are not a good substitute for such institutionally based financial flows.[22]

But within such institutions, there are strong agency problems (managers take actions to increase their own well-being, at the expense of other stakeholders, including shareholders), and the actions of financial institutions, especially large ones, give rise to significant externalities (when a bank fails, it has significant consequences for others). That is why governments all over the world subject banks to strong regulations. The question is: What kinds of regulations will be most effective in promoting long-term economic growth?

Much of the post-2008 crisis literature has focused on how to avoid excessive risk taking, to ensure macroeconomic stability. We focus here on a more basic question: how to ensure that finance flows to the "right" sectors and at terms that are pro-growth.

The East Asian countries, as we have already suggested, were remarkably successful in doing so. One instrument that they used was financial restraint: restricting both entry into banking and deposit rates *mildly*.[23] Financial restraint increased the franchise value of banks, and this encouraged them to undertake more prudential lending. The greater safety of the banking system more than offset the effect of the slightly lower interest rate, to ensure a strong flow of funds into the financial sector. (Governments in the region took other actions to encourage savings, so that even though real interest rates paid to savers were very low, savings rates were very high.)

There was enough competition within the banking system (accompanied perhaps by government pressure) that the lower deposit rates got translated into lower lending rates,[24] while incentives (and again, government pressure) ensured that much of the spread got reinvested in the banks, enabling them to expand lending in subsequent periods. The greater franchise value of the banks also induced them to act more prudently.

In short, government policy led to a more stable banking system, one which had the capacity to focus on more long-term lending. But government policy went further in encouraging lending to the learning sectors.

Access to Credit for Learning Sectors

As we have noted, because of the pervasiveness of externalities and other market failures, funds do not necessarily flow to sectors which might be most conducive to long-term growth, e.g., as a result of learning externalities. Regulatory policies can be used to shape the flow of funds, for instance, by putting restrictions on the maximum fraction of funds that can go into real estate or into consumer loans, or on the minimum fraction of funds that can go into, say, the industrial sectors. Tax and regulatory policies (such as those affecting derivatives and credit cards) can also encourage banks to devote both human and financial resources to wealth-creating lending activities, rather than to speculative activities or to predatory lending.

We noted earlier the dependence of the flow of funds on information, and government policies can help shape the flow of information, e.g., by insisting that banks open up branches outside the capital city.

Broad-based restrictions (as opposed to more narrowly focused policies that direct lending toward a particular firm) have a political economy advantage: The bank is not directed to put funds into a particular firm. It has to find, within the given category, the best set of borrowers, i.e. those most likely to repay. As we noted earlier, there is a trade-off. Such broad-based regulations may not succeed in targeting firms with the highest learning externalities, but the political economy advantages may more than offset the reduced effectiveness of targeting.

In some cases, however, relying on the private sector to allocate funds in ways that are most socially productive (especially when learning is important), using regulation to curb abuses and to partially correct the market failures arising from pervasive differences between private and social returns, may be less effective than government directly allocating funds itself. (The presumption that the private sector was a better allocator of scarce capital was clearly undermined by the events leading up to the 2008 financial crisis.) Thus, many developing countries have found development banks to be an important and effective instrument for managing the flow of funds to projects and enterprises which are viewed to have large externalities to others. While earlier development banks had been criticized for making politically connected loans with low social payoffs, in more recent years, countries around the world have found ways of managing these agency and political economy problems.[25]

There are some "half-way" houses, where the government provides some of the capital or absorbs some of the risk associated with lending to certain sectors (small businesses, R & D ventures). Government might, in particular, absorb some of the macroeconomic risks, forcing the bank to focus on commercial risks—the viability of the project, on the assumption that the government maintains the economy at or near full employment.[26] These mixed systems are designed to curb the political economy problems that sometimes arise with government programs: Funds are only provided if there is some private lender that is willing to bear *some* of the risk in return for some of the return.

Access to Credit for New Entrepreneurs and Small and Medium-Sized Enterprises

Emran and Stiglitz (2009) have stressed learning about who is a good entrepreneur. The problem, as we noted earlier (chapter 3), is that because of "poaching," the benefits of identifying who is a good entrepreneur may not be appropriated by the lender; those who establish themselves as good entrepreneurs will be recruited away by other banks (or firms). Even if the initial lender retains them, it will be forced to lend at a competitive interest rate—too low to recoup the losses incurred in lending to untried entrepreneurs, some of whom turn out to be incompetent.[27] There will be too little lending to new entrepreneurs. Government regulations can, however, mitigate the problem, e.g., by imposing restrictions on new entry into banking. But there is an economic cost of such regulations, and it may be preferable for governments to intervene more directly. That is one of the reasons that governments in many countries (including the United States) have government-funded programs to encourage lending to small and medium-sized enterprises. In some cases, these entail lending directly; in others, the absorption of part of the risk.

The learning externalities associated with small and medium-sized enterprises may be particularly significant, because of the high turnover of such firms. There is a higher likelihood that the personnel from such firms wind up in a relatively short time in some other firm, carrying with them the knowledge that they have acquired.[28]

4. Concluding Comments: Restrictions on the Movement of Labor

This chapter has questioned the contention that the free and unfettered movement of capital—within and between countries—is desirable. We have shown that there is a role for government financial regulations, not only in promoting greater macro-stability, but also in affecting the structure of the economy. Financial and capital market liberalization has often resulted in fewer resources going into sectors generating learning externalities and has therefore produced lower economic growth. There are likely to be stronger spillovers from lending by domestic financial institutions than from lending by foreign financial institutions. Restrictions on capital flows and on the provision of financial services by foreign firms are often effectively restrictions on the importation of foreign financial services, and just as we have argued that restrictions on the import of industrial goods may be desirable, there is an even more compelling case for restrictions on the import of foreign financial services.

Financial policy can also be an important tool for industrial policy. But even when the government is not directly using the financial sector to encourage some sector, or discourage another, broader financial sector policies can be used to help create a financial sector that is more focused on lending, and especially lending to activities that generate learning externalities. We have also suggested that while regulation of private financial institutions may be an effective tool for accomplishing these goals, government actions may need to go beyond this, creating government-run institutions (development banks) or programs that provide partial guarantees to private institutions.

Similar arguments, perhaps with even more force, though probably more controversially, apply to the free movement of labor across borders. Consider, for instance, the problem posed by the brain drain.[29] It is probably not a coincidence that the successful history of growth in Latin America seems to evaporate about the time when U.S. immigration laws changed, in 1965. In effect, those new policies enabled them to "import jobs from" (that is, get jobs in) the United States for their best and most talented people, who then don't disseminate the learning on a local basis, as they would have done if they had stayed in Latin America.

We should emphasize that we are not necessarily arguing for restrictions on out-migration, only noting that there are growth consequences—externalities—that should not be ignored. There are policies that could mitigate some of the costs, e.g., international agreements that would require those emigrating from a country to repay investments in human capital. But while these policies partially address the fiscal consequences of migration, they do not adequately address the more fundamental problem of learning externalities.

At the same time, there are some instances when returning migrants bring back with them not only money (which has often been emphasized in the recent literature on migration and development) but also knowledge—sometimes called "cultural remittances." Migration *can*, if properly structured, facilitate cross-border movements of knowledge and learning. It can thereby help create a learning economy.

CHAPTER FOURTEEN

Macroeconomic and Investment Policies for a Learning Society

CHAPTER 4 explained the key reasons that macroeconomic volatility is bad for a learning economy, and accordingly, why policies which exposed countries to more volatility can have adverse effects on learning—quite apart from whatever other positive or negative effects are associated with such policies.

This chapter looks at four broad issues regarding how government macroeconomic and investment policies can help create a learning economy. The first looks at financial and capital market liberalization. The last chapter explained why such policies may not be desirable, as a result of their impact on the *structure* of the economy—they change the structure in ways that slow learning. Here, we use an information-theoretic analysis to help explain why such liberalization may systemically be associated with more macro-instability. The second looks at exchange rate policy. With the advent of increasing international restrictions on the use of trade and industrial policy, adjustments in exchange rate have become increasingly important as a tool. Moreover whether and how the government manages the exchange rate—both the level of the rate and its volatility—affects the structure of the economy and the extent to which there is learning, and thus growth. The third looks at foreign direct investment (FDI), asking how and when it can be used to promote a learning economy. (The previous chapter and section 1 of this chapter focused on *financial* flows, not FDI.) The fourth examines the role of government investment.

1. Financial Policy and Macro-Stability

It has been widely noted that capital market liberalization is often associated with greater macroeconomic instability. To advocates of capital market liberalization, especially those wedded to the standard neoclassical model assuming perfect markets (including the absence of any information asymmetries), this seemed a puzzle. Of course, for anyone observing actual patterns of capital flows, it would have been more of a mystery had it turned out that capital market liberalization was stabilizing, for such flows tend to be pro-cyclical.

In the discussion below, we suggest one of the reasons that capital market liberalization is often associated with instability.

Imagine that a foreigner invests his money in a country, alongside local investors. The local investors, let's say in the banking system, know a lot more about what's going on than foreigners do. They have a better sense of what difficulties (either economic or political) can be easily resolved, which cannot be. When a firm fails, they can better ascertain whether the failure was due to idiosyncratic events confronting the firm, or whether they are systemic effects likely to affect others. So when there is trouble within a country, they are going to know to take their money out of the country before foreigners do. But foreigners know that they are in this disadvantageous position; they know that there are these information asymmetries and that they observe things only with error. Accordingly, they set a lower threshold at which they take their money out—even slightly adverse signals may lead to large capital outflows by foreigners.

In practice, that has three implications. The first is that countries that restrict capital movements will have more stability (see, e.g., Stiglitz and Ocampo [2008] and the articles cited there).

Second, crises will be *disproportionately* generated by overseas investors because they are the uninformed investors who react often even to small signals.[1,2]

But the third and most surprising implication of this is that the countries that are successful at "exporting" financial services (that is, to selling their financial services to outsiders) ought to be small countries, because in small countries there are fewer locals who are at an informational advantage over foreigners. These issues of instability and redistribution between the locals and the outsiders will be less severe. This perhaps explains why it is the small countries like Switzerland, Luxembourg, and Iceland which turn out to be (disproportionately) the financial centers.[2] (However, as several of these countries have learned at great expense to themselves, there are real costs, including to macro-stability, from having an outsized financial sector.)

Financial Market Liberalization

Financial market liberalization, like capital market liberalization, was supposed to enhance macroeconomic stability. The argument was that strong international banks would be able and willing to continue the flow of funds to, say, a developing country whose own financial institutions were going through a period of weakness.[3] But there is evidence that it has not done so (Rashid 2012). One of the reasons is that just noted: foreign banks are at an informational disadvantage and so are more prone to pull money out of a country in response to adverse signals.

But another is that foreign banks can be a source of economic volatility, especially if they come to take a large share of the domestic financial sector. Because foreign banks are less informed about foreign borrowers, they view such lending as riskier. When banks face an adverse balance sheet shock (e.g., in the event of an economic crisis at home), they become more risk averse. They respond by pulling back most on the riskiest lending—including lending abroad (Greenwald and Stiglitz 1993, 2003).[4] These responses become even stronger under home government pressure, when the government has put in funds to rescue the bank (or potentially might do so). The justification for such bailouts is that they are necessary to maintain the flow of credit *within the country*, but citizens will then expect that the flow of credit in fact go to their own country, not abroad. Hence, there will be demands that banks allocate scarce lending resources to home country borrowers. There is some evidence that this occurred during the 2008 global financial crisis.

The consequence, of course, is that financial market liberalization may lead to the transmission of problems in one country to another. It can be an important way for macroeconomic instability to move across borders. In fact, there is considerable evidence that much of the instability in developing countries during the era of global financial market liberalization came from outside the boundaries of the countries: Volatility in capital flows and global risk premiums have become an important source of macroeconomic instability.

2. Exchange Rate Policy

Exchange rate volatility is closely associated with macroeconomic instability. It is both cause and consequence. In a world of flexible exchange rates, changes in beliefs about the future value of the exchange rate can induce large financial flows and lead to large changes in the exchange rate today, with large macroeconomic consequences, e.g., for trade.

The exchange rate affects the competitiveness of the economy—the ability of exporters to export and of import-competing firms to compete with imports. The consequences of an appreciation of the currency (say, as a result of the inflow of capital or foreign aid) can be severe: If the exchange rate increases by, say, 25 percent, there is no way that (in the short run) productivity can compensate or for there to be offsetting adjustments of wages and the prices of other inputs. Moreover, there are important hysteresis effects (just as there are with large movements in the interest rate): A firm that dies because it can't compete as a result of a high exchange rate is not brought back to life when the exchange rate subsequently falls. (Capital market imperfections imply that especially small and medium-sized firms will be unable to obtain the capital required to tide them over.)

By the same token, it is expensive for firms (especially small and medium-sized domestic firms) to manage exchange rate volatility, especially in emerging markets and in the least-developed countries. In many of these countries, there may be no markets in which firms can hedge their exchange rate risks. But even if there are markets for hedging, there is a cost to doing so.

Thus, like it or not, exchange rate policy affects the industrial structure. Some sectors, some technologies, and some kinds of firms are discouraged relative to others. A decision not to actively manage the exchange rate will result in a more volatile exchange rate, more macroeconomic instability, and a smaller traded goods sector more dominated by large firms than would otherwise be the case. In the context of Africa, the decision of many resource-rich countries to allow their exchange rate to appreciate has contributed to deindustrialization and even the weakening of the agriculture sector.

There are several implications of this analysis. First, governments need to adopt policies that make exchange rates less volatile, e.g., capital controls (or more generally, they have to adopt a portfolio of tools for capital account management).[5]

Second, governments need to keep exchange rates "low" so as to make domestic firms more competitive—to expand exports and import-competing sectors. This is especially true because low exchange rates help export sectors like manufacturing, which have higher learning elasticities and generate more learning externalities. (There may be further macroeconomic—and learning—benefits if the lower exchange rate allows the country to operate closer to full employment.[6])

But a concern about industrial policy means governments need to be attentive to *how* they intervene to stabilize and lower the exchange rate. If to prevent a large decline in the exchange rate they increase interest rates (as was the wont of the IMF), while they may thereby save large numbers of enterprises that have taken on foreign denominated debts, at the same time they may kill other enterprises that were more prudent and took on only domestic debt. The effects may be particularly adverse to small and medium-sized enterprises (which typically do not take on foreign debt, because they do not have access to international markets)—as was evident in the East Asia crisis (Furman and Stiglitz 1998). Again, if these small and medium-sized enterprises play an important role in creating and disseminating knowledge and learning, such policies can be particularly counterproductive. In any case, governments should be aware that whether and how governments intervene in managing the exchange rate has implications for economic structure—and for learning.

There are alternative ways of stabilizing the exchange rates and, even more so, keeping exchange rates low, which may be less costly. Low interest rates benefit domestic firms on two accounts, both directly and indirectly, through effects on exchange rate. Direct intervention, with the consequent buildup of reserves, may be a particularly effective way of smoothing the exchange rate, avoiding at the same time volatility in interest rates.[7]

Some have suggested that it is impossible to push the *real* exchange rate down for more than a short period of time. But such arguments are based on a confusion. It is impossible to keep exchange rates above the "market" level through direct intervention, because to do so requires selling dollars (or other hard currency), and countries only have limited amounts of these in their reserves. But to push the exchange rate down requires selling one's own currency, and buying dollars (or other hard currencies), and this countries can easily do.

There are other instruments available for affecting especially the *level* of the exchange rate. Any regulation that affects the flow of money out of or into the country affects the exchange rate. Thus, making it easier for foreign companies to invest in the country leads to the appreciation of the currency; making it more difficult leads to the depreciation of the currency. In assessing foreign direct investment policy, one has to weigh the benefits of access to markets or technology or training with the costs to the rest of the economy from the exchange rate appreciation (including the adverse effects on learning). Capital market liberalization similarly can lead to an influx of capital and an appreciation of the currency. By the same token, loosening restrictions on citizens of the country investing their money abroad lowers the exchange rate.[8] Since most countries have a broad array of regulations affecting inward and outward investment, there is, in a sense, no "free market" exchange rate. Through these regulations and through interest rates, as well as through direct interventions, governments set the exchange rate, either intentionally or not.

A lower exchange rate represents a broad-based mechanism for industrial policy—firms themselves decide whether they can compete at that lower exchange rate. The government has identified broadly that the export sector has more learning externalities and therefore that sector should be encouraged relative to others, but it doesn't have to identify precisely which subsectors or firms should be encouraged. The market does that.

This has an advantage and a disadvantage, which we have briefly noted in earlier chapters. More finely tuned targeting may increase the overall (dynamic) efficiency of the economy; after all, each firm or sector takes no account of the extent of the benefits that accrue to others. A more targeted approach can offset the externality associated with research or learning in each sector. On the other hand, government attempts at fine tuning may encounter more severe "political economy" problems.

There are two questions about the use of each of the instruments. First, what really matters is the real exchange rate. The question is: Can government affect, at least more than just briefly, the real exchange rate? Here, the critical question is the extent and speed of "pass through." For very open economies, importing and exporting a large fraction of their goods, lowering the nominal exchange rate leads to increases in nominal prices, which can undo the benefits, unless, say, monetary authorities take actions to dampen the potential inflation, but such actions themselves have costs (e.g., higher unemployment). It is clear, however, that many countries have managed to lower their *real* exchange rate for an extended period of time and have done so at the same time that they have promoted growth.

Second, what are the costs of each of the interventions, and do the benefits exceed the costs? Some worry that the cost of preventing inflation from direct intervention is too high. The East Asian countries have managed to intervene in the exchange rate over long periods of time without facing either high inflation or high costs of avoiding inflation. But, at least in China, there is another growing concern: to keep the value of their currency low, they have bought dollars, which yield a low return. Worse, dollars are depreciating relative to the RMB, implying that they are experiencing a (paper) capital loss.

Industrial policies can intervene in relative prices in ways which avoid these costs (and which can in fact be more targeted than lowering the [real] exchange rate), e.g., by sectoral subsidies (including subsidized interest rates) or infant-industry protection. But, as we noted earlier, international trade agreements restrict the use of industrial policies. The only instrument left may be the exchange rate. Our earlier discussion (chapter 11) showed that the benefits of expanding exports are sufficiently great that it may be possible that optimal policy requires the country to build up reserves forever, never to use them (essentially like throwing money away). The benefits of learning exceed the costs of the "forced saving" required to ensure that the exchange rate remains competitive.

3. Investment Policies

In some (but not all) of the successful countries, foreign direct investment (FDI) has played an important role. For some countries with limited access to finance, FDI can be an important source of funds.

But even in those countries with high savings rates, champions of FDI extol its virtue in terms of the transfer of knowledge. But this doesn't happen automatically; the learning spillovers are more important for some forms of FDI than others; and there are ways of transferring knowledge other than by FDI. While FDI may be one way of acquiring knowledge, there may be other ways of doing so, which simultaneously induce more learning. Whether that is the case may depend on the admissible rules governing FDI (which we will discuss shortly).

It is worth noting that as we look around the world at countries that have been most successful in development, some have succeeded with little FDI (Korea and Japan), while in others, FDI has played an important role. For the most part, though, the countries that have relied on FDI have not succeeded in creating global enterprises of the likes of Samsung, Toyota, and Sony.

Foreign firms have both advantages and disadvantages in promoting learning. On the one hand, knowledge often moves more freely within the boundaries of the firm than across firm boundaries. Within-firm knowledge may thus be the most effective way of moving knowledge across national boundaries.

On the other hand, firms actively work to limit the knowledge so transferred from seeping out beyond the confines of the firm. In spite of such efforts, though, knowledge is transferred—and this is in fact one of the main justifications for encouraging FDI.

But firms may feel that keeping knowledge within the confines of the firm may be more difficult outside the home country, and thus they may restrict the flow of knowledge across borders, consigning, say, developing countries to using less advanced technologies. In this case, FDI may not be the best way for developing countries to close the knowledge gap. (Western companies and governments sometimes claim that they would more readily use more advanced technologies in developing countries if these countries more effectively enforced intellectual property rights. But there is little convincing evidence to support this hypothesis. The next chapter discusses intellectual property rights more broadly.)

In many, perhaps most, cases, entrepreneurial spillovers may be larger in the case of domestic enterprises than foreign, since domestic firms are likely to be more firmly embedded within the local community. Government policy should, accordingly, provide some preference for domestic firms relative to foreign firms, except when there are strong learning benefits that are specifically related to foreign firms, e.g., because the foreign firm brings knowledge that is not locally available and can't be otherwise acquired.

One question governments attempting to create a learning economy through FDI needs to ask is: What kind of FDI is likely to be most beneficial? The theory of localized technological change (Atkinson and Stiglitz 1969), discussed in chapter 3, explains that the spillovers from learning associated with one technology are more likely to be greater for "nearby" technologies. What matters is both the *relevance* of the knowledge associated with one technology for the improvement of another and the *capacity* of those employing one technology to learn from another. Accordingly, spillovers may well be stronger across sectors for similar technologies than within the sector for markedly different technologies. Thus, just-in-time inventory practices have benefits for many sectors in which inventories play an important role.

Much of the knowledge which is embedded in, say, mining technologies is of limited relevance to most other sectors of the economy. Thus, the learning benefits of FDI associated with resource extraction are likely to be much more limited than those associated with, say, manufacturing, and this may help explain why so many resource-dependent economies remain "dual" economies, with few spillovers from the natural resource sector to the rest of the economy. If this is so, it means that FDI in this area—one which has dominated in Africa—is of much less benefit than FDI in other areas. (But as chapter 12 emphasized, there are still ways in which industrial policies can play an important role in natural resource economies. The limited spillovers are, in part, the result of the absence of adequate industrial policies.)

By the same token, the benefits of export-processing sectors are often disappointing (beyond the direct job creation and limited tax revenues that they generate). Weak links to the rest of the economy mean that spillovers are limited, and the low-technology, labor-intensive processes in which they specialize would, in any case, give rise to few spillovers. At the same time, government-sponsored industrial and research parks, promoting clusters of related activities, can promote growth by generating and capturing learning spillovers.

While it may be easiest to learn about adjacent technologies, the benefits of such learning may be more limited than that associated with making larger steps (sometimes referred to as leapfrogging.) There is, then, a complicated optimization problem: Both the costs and benefits increase the larger the step. Moreover, one wants to move toward technologies from which one can learn the best going forward, and that may not always be easy to assess from one's current vantage point. Korea and Japan's industrial development was characterized by strategies that involved moving some distance from the technologies that they were then employing.

Government Subsidies for and Regulation of FDI to Promote Learning

Government subsidies for FDI have typically been justified in terms of the government revenue and employment generated. But our analysis suggests another rationale: learning. But if this is so, then subsidies should be larger for those sectors and technologies which are likely to have large spillovers and for firms that are willing to engage in practices that enhance the likelihood of such learning.

Government policies can also affect the extent of spillovers. Compulsory employment and training programs and domestic procurement requirements (programs that compel firms to source locally) are more likely to lead to learning spillovers. The success of Malaysia's FDI was partially attributable to these requirements. The benefits of learning can more than offset the social costs of the distortion.[9]

It is worth noting that trade and investment agreements have typically circumscribed the use of these kinds of interventions and have tended to insist on foreign firms being given equal—or in some cases preferable—treatment with domestic firms.[10] Like other aspects of Washington Consensus and neoliberal policies, these provisions need to be reexamined through the prism of learning.

Outward-Bound Investment

China and other emerging markets are increasingly engaged in buying foreign firms. This can be seen as an alternative, and sometimes more effective, way of acquiring knowledge. Ownership of a firm gives them the right to transfer the technology. The new owners may seek to acquire the technology and transfer production to their country, where the subsequent learning will occur. The result is that the country that had been the technological leader in a particular arena will lose its dominant position. More broadly, from the perspective of societal learning, the locus of such learning will change too: More will occur in the country of the acquiring firm.

There is much to be said for China's learning strategy: First it developed the ability to learn, through investments in education and foreign direct investment in China. As foreign governments and firms saw China and Chinese firms as more of a competitive threat, FDI became a less effective way of learning (at the margin) compared to buying foreign firms—which became increasingly feasible with China's mounting resources. At this point, for the most part, the "rules of the game" worked in favor of China—there were relatively few restrictions on the acquisition of firms, even when the intent and consequence was clear, the acquisition of technology and the shift in the locus of production. (An important exception was U.S. restrictions on the acquisition of high-technology industries. But here, U.S. restrictions on high-technology exports provided China with an even greater impetus to develop its own capacity, acquiring technology from other countries not imposing such restrictions.)

4. Government Investment

We have argued that governments cannot avoid questions of industrial policy, for they have to make decisions about the direction of public investment, say, in education and infrastructure. These decisions have to be based on beliefs about the future directions of the economy, which are in turn affected by these public decisions. But the policies with which we are concerned go well beyond this. For government can use public expenditure policies to partially compensate for deficiencies in market allocations.

To see what this implies, let's extend our earlier learning model (presented in chapter 8) by introducing Public Goods, denoted by G, into the first-period utility function.[11] (G is a vector of public goods.) For simplicity, we assume that we can impose a lump sum tax to finance them and that there are full spillovers. We focus on the direct-control problem, where we choose the level of spending on each private and public good. Focusing on the first period, we find[12]

$$\max_{\{L^t,\, L^{t+1},\, G\}} U^t(L^t, G) - v(\Sigma_i L_i^t + \Sigma_i G_i^t) + \delta\{U^{t+1}[L^{t+1}H(L^t, G)]\}, \quad (1)$$

where the output of public good G_i in period t is just equal to the labor input in its production, the output (consumption) of good i in period t, C_i^t, is just equal to the labor input, L_i^t, the output of good i in period $t+1$ is just $L_I^{t+1}H$, and where, in the obvious notation, L^t, L^{t+1}, and G stand for the vector of labor inputs at t and $t + 1$ and production of public goods, respectively In turn, H is the level of productivity in the second period, which depends not only on learning-by-doing in the private sector the first period (on the vector L^t), but directly on investments in public goods the first period, G. The first-order condition with respect to G_k is:

$$U_{Gk}^t - v' + \delta\Sigma\, U_i^{t+1}\, L_i^{t+1}H_{Gk} = 0. \tag{2}$$

In deciding on the optimal level of investment, we look not just at the direct benefits, but also at the learning benefits.

But in the absence of subsidies on private goods that take into account the learning benefits and spillovers, the provision of the public good can have another benefit. By expanding the production of public goods which are complements to goods with high learning elasticities and large externalities, the government can help create a more dynamic economy. To see this, we reformulate our optimization as an indirect-control problem (still assuming the public good is financed by a lump sum tax):

$$\max_{\{p^t,\, p^{t+1},\, G\}} V^t(p^t, I^t - T, G) + \delta V^{t+1}(p^{t+1}, I^{t+1}) \tag{3}$$

where V is the indirect utility function, giving the level of utility as a function of prices, income, I, net of lump sum taxes, T, and public goods, G. Assume, for simplicity, that the government is not allowed to provide subsidies to private goods but can finance public goods. In the absence of product subsidies, equilibrium is characterized by price equaling marginal cost, or

$$p^t = 1;\, p^{t+1} = 1/H(L^t, G). \tag{4}$$

Moreover, we assume that the public goods are financed by the first-period lump sum tax, i.e.,

$$T = \Sigma\, G_i. \tag{5}$$

An increase in G_i, financed by a lump sum tax, has complex income and substitution effects on the demand for each commodity. For instance, if some public good is a close substitute for some private good, the lower spendable income as a result of the additional provision of the public good, combined with the availability of a public substitute, will lead to a reduction in the private demand for that good. However, if the public good were a strong enough complement (e.g., a free road to a ski resort), it might increase the demand for the good (trips to the ski resort.) We denote by $dL_j^t/dG_i = dC_j^t/dG_i$ the change (the total derivative) in the demand for (consumption and supply of) good j as a result of an increase in public good i.

Hence, optimizing with respect to G_i yields[13]

$$V_{Gi} - V_I^t = \partial V_I^{t+1}\{\Sigma\, L_k^{t+1}\, [H_{Gi}/H^2 + \Sigma j\, (dL_j^t/dG_i)(H_j/H^2)]\}. \quad (6)$$

The first term (H_{Gi}/H^2) on the right -hand side is the direct learning benefits, the second term $[\Sigma j\,(dL_j^t/dG_i)(H_j/H^2)]$ is the indirect effects on learning as the composition of demand changes. (If G_i is a public investment good, then an increase in G can increase the productivity of second-period inputs of labor not just through learning effects, but as a result of complementarities between these public investments and labor.)

We expand the production of public goods not only to take into account the learning benefits, but also the indirect effects in inducing more consumption of some goods and less of others, taking into account the total net effect on learning. In a more dynamic (longer-term) model, we would take into account the effect of the first-period learning on the structure of demand the second period, and hence on second-period learning; and the direct benefits of learning on the production of public goods themselves. These multiperiod learning effects highlight the importance of longer-term strategic policies discussed earlier.

5. Concluding Comments

This chapter has explained the important role of government in establishing an environment that is conducive to creating a learning economy, through public investments that support private-sector investments in learning sectors or by creating a stable macroeconomy.

Virtually every policy of the government can be reexamined through the prism of learning, but doing so would take us beyond the confines of this short book. We should, however, mention four in particular.

Education

The first is education. Nothing is more important than educating young people for creativity, and an education system that is focused on learning how to learn and on lifetime learning. Much attention is focused on learning in our educational institutions, but far more important is the education that occurs elsewhere, including on the job. Recognizing the complementarity between these different forms of education and designing formal education systems and on-the-job training programs that are complementary to each other and which, together, maximize overall learning is essential to creating a learning economy. We will have a little more to say about education in chapter 16.

Social Protection

The second policy area is social protection. We don't typically think of systems of social protection as part of our "learning society" policy framework, but they are—for learning is risky. We argued here and in chapter 4 that risk has an adverse effect on creating a learning society. What matters, though, is not just the level of risk but how risk is managed. The adverse effects of "trying and failing" are lower in a society with a good system of social protection. In short, there can be more risk taking in societies with better systems of social protection.[14]

Legal Frameworks

There are other aspects of a country's legal and economic framework that can affect risk taking as well. Bankruptcy laws give an individual a fresh start, and thus good (and especially debtor friendly) bankruptcy laws can encourage risk taking. Such bankruptcy laws also may encourage better lending practices. Many believe that it is not an accident that the worst lending in America's mortgage market occurred as the United States "reformed" its bankruptcy laws to make the discharge of debt more difficult (Stiglitz 2010b). And as we have previously noted, a badly designed bankruptcy law, combined with deficient regulation of for-profit predatory educational institutions and the high cost of public education, discourages investment in tertiary education.

Innovation System

An important aspect of a country's economic and legal framework that is crucial in determining whether the country becomes a learning society is a country's "innovation system," including the set of laws and institutions that support explicit investments not only in education but also in research. Most important are investments in basic research by the government, which do much to define the opportunities available for others to make advances. How those advances are incentivized and financed, and how knowledge is shared, has much to do with creating a learning economy. A central feature of any country's innovation system is the country's intellectual property regime, the subject of the next chapter.

CHAPTER FIFTEEN

Intellectual Property

INTELLECTUAL PROPERTY provides a final application of the general ideas we have attempted to develop in this book. Intellectual property rights (IPR) are supposed to provide incentives to encourage innovation. As such, a discussion of IPR fits squarely into any analysis of policies centered on creating a learning society. Our concern here is that the provisions of the intellectual property regime that has become dominant around the world (reflected in the TRIPS provisions of the Uruguay Round global trade agreement) do not maximize learning. This was evident even at the moment of their creation. They were explicitly not driven by a broad focus on enhancing societal innovation

This chapter draws heavily upon Stiglitz (2004, 2006a, 2008b, 2013a); Henry and Stiglitz (2010); and Dosi and Stiglitz (forthcoming). There is a large literature on the subject, which we cannot do justice to in this brief discussion. See the references in the above cited papers, as well as the recent books on intellectual property by Perleman (2002); Jaffe and Lerner (2004); Lundvall (2010); Fink and Maskus (2005); Jaffe, Lerner, and Stern (annual); and Cimoli et al. (2013). See also Grandstrand (2005).

or even well-being (though the rhetoric advanced in their support sometimes suggested otherwise). They did not maximize learning and the pace of progress for the United States and other advanced industrial countries; they were even worse for developing countries. Rather, they were designed to maximize rents of the entertainment and pharmaceutical industries. That was why the Council of Economic Advisers and the Office of Science and Technology Policy opposed them.[1]

In this chapter, we attempt to explain some of the reasons that these standard IPR provisions do not maximize learning and what might be done about it. And while we shall have much to say about the consequences for developing countries, there is dissatisfaction even within the United States. Many in the software industry, for instance, have been agitating for changes. As we note at the end of the chapter, there have in fact been some dramatic changes to the U.S. intellectual property regime in recent years, though mostly through court rulings, rather than through legislation.

1. IPR and the Relationship Between Social and Private Returns

Given our emphasis in this book on learning externalities, it might be thought that we would support the conventional wisdom, that the stronger the intellectual property rights, the better. For at least with strong intellectual property rights, it would seem that more of the returns to the innovation would be captured by the innovator. This would reduce the gap between social and private returns.

The problem is that the disparity between private and social returns is multifaceted, and, as the discussion of part 1 hinted, stronger IPR may not lead to more innovation and, more broadly, may lower social welfare. Later sections of this chapter will explain that there are other ways of financing and incentivizing innovation that may lead to a faster pace of innovation or higher levels of social welfare. The problems are exacerbated with poorly designed IPR regimes; some of the problems with current IPR regimes could be ameliorated through reforms in the IPR regime discussed in the next section.

We can organize the distortions introduced into the economy system by IPR into two categories: IPR gives rise to a static inefficiency, and (especially inappropriately designed) IPR regimes may even impede the pace of innovation.

Static Inefficiencies

As we noted in chapter 5, knowledge is a public good, so any restriction on the use or dissemination of knowledge introduces an inefficiency. Moreover, IPR gives the owner of the knowledge (patent) exclusive rights over the use of that knowledge. It thus confers monopoly power over knowledge, which can give rise to monopoly power in production, which, in turn, introduces a distortion in production.

There are some circumstances in which these static costs can be especially high. For instance, monopoly drug prices make lifesaving medicines unaffordable to the poor in countries without public health insurance, resulting in large numbers of unnecessary deaths. And in developing countries with limited budgets, when governments pay monopoly prices to the drug companies, there is less left over for other health needs or to pursue broader developmental objectives.

Typically, advocates of IPR argue that a well-designed IPR regime balances these well-recognized static costs against the dynamic benefits of faster innovation. But, as we now explain, IPR may not even result in faster innovation.

Dynamic Inefficiencies

In chapters 5 and 6, we explained why a monopolist may have less incentive to engage in innovation than is socially optimal, simply because production is lower.[2] Here, we explain further why a strong intellectual property regime may not lead to rising living standards. First, it may not lead to more innovation. Second, the innovation that does occur may not be well directed.

DOES STRONGER IPR LEAD TO MORE INNOVATION?[3] Earlier, we explained why Schumpeter's argument that Schumpeterian competition would provide a spur for innovation was wrong: The incumbent can get sufficiently far ahead of potential competitors that they would be discouraged from entering the fray; the monopolist could then simply rest on its laurels. Because stronger IPR can give rise to stronger monopoly power, these problems can be exacerbated by strong IPR regimes, which result in a less competitive marketplace.[4]

We have seen too how a monopolist may create entry barriers, engaging in a variety of entry-deterring practices that stifle innovation—as Microsoft so ably demonstrated. Its control of the PC operating system meant that it could (and in fact did) foreclose, or at least reduce, competition in the provision of applications. It took especially strong actions against innovations that were a threat to its dominance.

We also noted that, because monopoly restricts production, the level of innovation will be less than the socially optimal level (though possibly more than with competition, where the level of production of each producer is even smaller).

A major theme of this book is that there are always knowledge spillovers, but market participants won't take these societal benefits into account in deciding on the level of investment in innovation. This is even true under Schumpeterian competition, where there is a succession of monopolists, even when the innovation in one sector is of no benefit to those in other sectors. In this situation, the innovation that occurs at time t sets the base from which successor innovations take off, but each innovator fails to take into account the benefits it confers to the monopolists that follow.[5]

There are still other reasons that stronger IPR regimes may not lead to a faster rate of innovation, a number of which we mention briefly below.

Follow-On Innovation The most important is that knowledge is the most important input into the production of knowledge, into learning. Every innovation is based on prior innovations. Thus, to *maximize learning*, one must strike a balance, between the benefits to the producer and the potential benefits to subsequent (follow-on) users.[6] Those in the drug industry, for instance, while they want to preclude others from using their innovations in follow-on research, seek to be sure to have the ability to use the innovations of others in theirs. These concerns were part of the original "deal" in creating our intellectual property regime: Those who seek protection of patents are required to disclose enough information to have the innovation replicated by others. Others could use that knowledge in their own learning, even if they could not use the product itself in their own developments. In practice, however, disclosure is typically inadequate, and some who have sought intellectual property protections have simultaneously fought hard against disclosure. (Microsoft is the most notable case. They have resisted disclosure of source code and, when required to do so, complied only after heavy fines have been imposed.)

Enclosing the Knowledge Commons Every idea builds on others. Patents are supposed to protect only new knowledge. But the boundaries of knowledge are not precise (in contrast to land, where we can demarcate boundaries precisely), and, inevitably, to some extent patents may extend to preexisting knowledge. To the extent that that is the case, they provide a return to the patent holder; but there is a *negative* societal return, since the patent will discourage innovations that might have made use of this otherwise freely available knowledge. Boyle has referred to such patents as "enclosing the commons" (Boyle 2003).

Patents of traditional knowledge, to be discussed further below, are the most dramatic example of a patent extended to preexisting knowledge.

Of course, patents shouldn't be granted for preexisting knowledge, but it is often difficult to ascertain the boundaries of existing knowledge. The patented knowledge may, of course, not be known to the patent examiner, and, especially in the case of traditional knowledge, it may not have been published. It may not be easy to publish knowledge that is so widely known as to be considered "common knowledge."

Encouraging Secrecy The basic model of science—a model that has proved enormously productive—entails openness and the sharing of knowledge. But intellectual property not only interferes with the dissemination and transmission of knowledge, but it encourages secrecy, which impedes learning. Indeed, the extension of IPR to universities, under the Bayh-Dole Act, has encouraged a culture which is antithetical to the openness that has traditionally characterized such institutions.[7]

Litigation Risk and Ambiguous Boundaries These problems are exacerbated by the absence of well-defined boundaries for knowledge, which we have already noted. Did or should George Baldwin Selden's original patent for a four-wheeled, self-propelled vehicle include all such vehicles or only the one he sketched out?[8] And because all knowledge is based on prior knowledge, one faces a difficult decision: When is a new idea really new, rather than a minor wrinkle on an old idea, or a different expression or representation of an old idea? Patent laws have addressed this question through standards of "novelty" and "obviousness." But there is inevitably ambiguity, and where the standard is drawn raises all the questions we have been discussing, balancing out the impediments to further innovation with the (alleged) benefits of induced innovation. There is thus always a critical issue in defining the scope of the patent.[9]

What is clear is that the patent offices have found it difficult to draw the line in ways which many, if not most, in the scientific community view as balancing the concerns appropriately. Too much weight is given to the current producer, too little weight to future users.

The difficulties posed by defining boundaries give rise to litigation. Lawyers have recognized the problems posed by these ambiguities and have had a field day. The litigation and the uncertainty surrounding litigation themselves becomes impediments to innovation.

The problem is compounded by the underfunding of the patent office, which limits the amount of time that patent examiners have to examine any patent, leading to the issuance of too many patents. Particularly before the eBay decision described below, those who received these "weak" patents (patents that were unlikely to survive a challenge) were nonetheless able to extract considerable rents out of other innovators, with adverse effects on innovation (see Farrell and Shapiro 2008).

Patent Thickets[10] Today, most products are sufficiently complex that their production may require using many separate items of knowledge. If each piece of knowledge is protected by a patent, this engenders a complex bargaining problem. Unless the owners of these separate pieces of IPR can agree, the product cannot be produced.

The problems are even worse. Anybody engaged in writing a software program, for instance, even doing so with complete originality, faces the risk that in doing so she may have trespassed on one of the hundreds of thousands of related software patents or that she may have come close enough to trespassing to make herself libel to litigation. No one can keep up with the myriad of patents being issued—if one did, it would be difficult to have time to engage in research. In this sense, the patent system itself has become a roadblock to innovation.

There is a long history of patent thickets serving as obstacles to innovation. Early in the twentieth century, the development of the airplane was impeded by conflicting patent claims by the Wright Brothers and Glenn H. Curtis. It was only with World War I, when the government forced the creation of a patent pool, that progress occurred in the United States.[11,12]

Holdups and Patent Trolls More recently a whole industry has developed—firms (called patent trolls) buy up patents, waiting until someone successfully produces a product that *might* have infringed on their patent. When they find such a product, they sue, in effect holding up the producer for ransom. To the extent that they can get more for themselves, there is less left over for the real innovators.

The holdup problem has been exacerbated by provisions in our patent system that allow the owner of a patent—even a patent whose legitimacy is under question—to exclude anyone else from using that knowledge.[13] The BlackBerry suit shows what can happen. They were held up for ransom by the owner of patent(s) that were under dispute. Blackberry proposed a settlement, widely viewed to be fair (or even overgenerous), suggesting that if it turned out that the patents were not valid, a fraction of the payments be returned to them. The offer was refused. BlackBerry had no choice: It had to either accept the terms or shut down.

In the United States, a pathbreaking decision of the Supreme Court in a case called *eBay Inc. v. MercExchange, L.L.C.* may have profound implications for such suits.[14] In the past, patents have typically been enforced through injunctions—others cannot trespass on a patent without the permission of the patent holder, who can extract as much "rent" as he wishes. This is in contrast with many other areas of the law, where there is compensation for violating someone's rights or property. The Supreme Court itself has raised questions about the consequences of what might be termed excessive enforcement, when patent holders take actions that in effect exclude from the market those who *might* infringe upon the patent. In *eBay*, the Court ruled that a permanent injunction (against infringement) would only be granted if a four-part test was satisfied:[15]

A [patent] plaintiff must demonstrate: (1) that it has suffered an irreparable injury; (2) that remedies at law, such as monetary damages, are inadequate to compensate for that injury; (3) that, considering the balance of hardships between the plaintiff and defendant, a remedy in equity is warranted; and (4) that the public interest would not be disserved by a permanent injunction.

An extreme version of exclusion to protect intellectual property is still part of America's trade laws, where a firm that the International Trade Commission finds has violated an American's intellectual property rights can have the infringing products excluded from importation into the United States.[16]

There are other reasons that stronger IPR may not lead to a faster rate of increase in standards of living. Even if stronger IPR increased investment in innovation, the innovations that were encouraged may not contribute to long-term well-being as much as alternative allocations of research investment. Distortions in the pattern of innovation arise from marked discrepancies between social and private returns to innovation.

DISCREPANCIES BETWEEN SOCIAL AND PRIVATE RETURNS AND DISTORTED INCENTIVES We noted in earlier chapters that the social return to an innovation is simply the fact that the product arrives on the market *earlier* than otherwise would have been the case. The private returns are the (incremental) rents accruing to the innovator. Much innovation is directed at seeking and preserving rents rather than enhancing societal well-being. Not only may social and private returns have little relationship with each other, stronger IPR regimes may exacerbate the discrepancies and, therefore, the misallocation of scarce research resources. The following illustrate the nature of the disparities.

Enhancing Market Power Many patents (and the research behind them) are focused not so much on producing a product that is better, valued more by consumers, or cheaper, but rather on enhancing market power, e.g., by extending market dominance. One form this takes is called "evergreening," where a patent holder makes what are fairly obvious slight improvements in the product (drug) to extend the patent and, thus, the firm's market dominance. For instance, a pharmaceutical company, toward the end of the lifetime of a patent, introduces and patents a timed-dosage variant of the pill. Because of the patent, no other producer could have done so. And because the timed-release version is preferred, the effective life of the patent is greatly extended.

(The patent authorities should not, of course, grant these evergreening extensions. Some developing countries have expressed strong reservations, but the practice remains common within developed countries.)

The pharmaceutical companies have become experts in extending the effective life of their patents, warding off generics. In doing so, they have made extensive use of trade agreements, which impose a variety of further restrictions. One of the most effective and objectionable is called data exclusivity. A generic producer typically must get approval of its drug, showing the drug's safety and efficacy. This should be easy: All it should have to do is to show that it is equivalent to the patented drug, which has been shown to be safe and effective. But the drug companies say that that is, in effect, using their data (even when the data was partially produced or financed by government), and thus is an intrusion on what should be their intellectual property. But not allowing the generic producer to use the data is an effective way of foreclosing their entry, because it would be unethical to test the generic against a placebo when there is a known product which is effective and safe. Many trade agreements between the United States and developing countries include a provision on data exclusivity (see Charlton and Stiglitz 2005).

Patents can, and often are, used as a barrier to entry. Particularly if the patent is broad, or if monopoly power in one area can be leveraged into monopoly power in another (e.g., Microsoft's dominance in the PC operating system allowed it to extend its dominance into applications, such as word processing), the private return may substantially exceed the social return; the social return to such innovations can even be negative.

Circumventing Patents At the same time, patents sometimes give rise to research of limited social value, as others try to innovate around a patent. The social return on a "me-too" invention (designed simply to circumvent an existing patent and to share in the monopoly rents) is zero.[17]

In short, the patent system not only does not reward inventors on the basis of their marginal contributions, but sets up a distorted set of incentives for innovations, where inventive activity is often directed first at creating market power, and then, by others, at overcoming the artificially created market power.

Patents of Traditional Knowledge There are many other distortions arising from the patent system. There may be relatively low—or even negative—social benefits to allowing patents of traditional knowledge, such as medicinal uses of turmeric. Such patents obviously don't generate new knowledge—the knowledge was already there, and even widely known (except to the patent examiner), but there may be high costs to such patents, since they may impede the use of knowledge. (There are, of course, benefits to transmitting knowledge, e.g., from the sources of traditional knowledge to elsewhere, but these benefits are usually not rewarded with IPR.)

Socially Unproductive Patent Races The patent is granted to the first to make a discovery (or to apply for a patent), and this can give rise to a race to be the first. In the case of decoding the human genome, there was a well-funded international effort, engaged in a systematic scientific process. But others attempted to short circuit this process, identifying some genes with large market value and racing to beat the more methodical approach. In the case of Myriad and the genes related to breast cancer, they succeeded. But the very limited social benefits of having this knowledge slightly earlier has been dwarfed by the social costs of the impediments (charges) that have been placed on the use of this knowledge.

Mispricing and Perverse Incentives In the market economy, prices are supposed to guide resource allocations—including the allocation of resources to innovation. But if prices are misaligned, then private returns will not accord with social returns.

The financial sector provides the most obvious example (to which we have alluded on several occasions), where much of the returns from innovation were associated with circumventing regulations (intended to reduce externalities, enhance financial stability, and prevent fraud, predatory lending, and market manipulation.) While these financial innovations were highly lucrative (even though they were not protected by patents), they had adverse effects on the economy.

Stronger intellectual property rights could have simply exacerbated this and similar distortions.

Similarly, there is underinvestment in innovations that protect the environment (e.g., reducing greenhouse gas emissions), simply because there is no market price associated with such emissions. But with high unemployment, especially of unskilled labor, there is overinvestment in innovations to further reduce the demand for unskilled labor—which simply create more unemployment and thereby impose high social costs on society.[18] Again, stronger intellectual property rights might exacerbate this problem.

Knowledge Pool One of the most important determinants of the pace of innovation (the increase in living standards) is the set of opportunities—the pool of knowledge that can be drawn upon. Every innovation adds to the pool of knowledge, but with IPR—including the "enclosure of the commons," the patent thicket, and the potential for holdups—every innovation also takes out from the effective *publicly available* pool of knowledge. The net effect is ambiguous. Indeed, earlier in this book, we showed that in plausible circumstances, it could be negative. In that model, the adverse effect on the pool of publicly available knowledge of tougher IPR regimes was so strong that the pace of innovation was reduced.

In this section of the chapter, we have identified the static costs and potential dynamic benefits. Advocates of a strong IPR regime typically underestimate static losses, overestimate dynamic benefits, and disregard "balance." Even as they note that IPR may create monopoly power, they emphasize its temporary nature, ignoring the research (noted above) showing that such power can persist and that attempts to maintain monopoly distort resource allocations. Poorly designed IPR regimes may even impede innovation.

Later in this chapter, we will explain that there are alternative ways of financing and incentivizing innovation. First, however, we discuss how reforms in the IPR system may reduce the adverse effects of the IPR system while increasing innovation.

2. Reforming the IPR System[19]

There is not just one IPR system. Details matter, and different countries have chosen different rules. This book is concerned with creating a learning society; some rules are more conducive to creating a learning society than others. The effects can be indirect or direct: Rules that allow for monopolization (e.g., longer and broader monopolies) may reduce innovation because of the adverse effects on competition; the Bayh-Dole bill may have reduced the flow of knowledge within universities and the flow of knowledge into the knowledge commons.

Many details of an IPR regime are critical: what can be patented, the standards used for granting patents, the length and breadth of the patent, restrictions on the patent, how the patent is enforced, and rules governing the granting of the patent. In each dimension, there are complex trade-offs, e.g., between providing incentives for innovation on the one hand and introducing inefficiencies in the dissemination of knowledge and impeding follow-on innovations on the other. One of the reasons that there is a broad consensus against patenting mathematical theorems or other insights from basic research is that the disadvantages of patenting far exceed the advantages. Other patents, such as those for business processes, impose other costs, e.g., in terms of litigation risks.

Some of the recent changes in IPR regimes have not always carefully balanced costs and benefits. The extension of the life of copyrights (seventy years after the death of the author) probably imposed more costs than any benefits from improved incentives.

On the other hand, some recent court decisions have shown an awareness of some of the inefficiencies associated with the prior patent regime. We have already mentioned the eBay decision.

With weak standards of "novelty" and "nonobviousness," patent owners can "evergreen" their patents, thereby extending the patent life. There is a legitimate debate about the optimal length of the life of a patent[20]—but such indirect ways of extending it almost surely have greater costs than any associated innovative benefits. The costs can be particularly high in the case of drugs in developing countries.

There have been some excessively broad patents (for instance, the original U.S. automobile patent); the greater the breadth, obviously, the greater the value of the patent, but the greater the impediments for follow-on inventors.

Other details of the IPR regime can reduce the costs relative to the benefits. As we noted, historically, to get a patent, knowledge had to be disclosed, which meant, in principle, that others could make use of that knowledge for their research. Patent rights can be viewed as an exchange, where the "public" grants a temporary monopoly right, circumscribed, in return for the revelation of information. More recently, some in the software industry have been arguing for stronger intellectual property rights *without* disclosure. (In the end, some may choose not to seek intellectual property protection, preferring to rely on trade secrecy.)

The following sections focus on a set of key issues in the design of an IPR system.

WHAT CAN BE PATENTED   Only certain things can be patented. The applicant is supposed to demonstrate, for instance, a certain standard of novelty. Even then, theorems cannot be patented. Some countries have restricted the granting of patents to *processes* for producing chemicals, not to the molecules themselves. The Supreme Court of the United States has recently rejected the right to patent naturally occurring genes.[21] This is a position taken by many other countries. America's business process patents have been widely criticized as extending the reach of patents too far.

BREADTH OF PROPERTY RIGHTS A common misperception is that, once a patent is granted, the grantee has the right to do anything with it during its life time, an uncircumscribed ability to exercise monopoly rights. Property rights do not, in general, and should not, give the owners of property uncircumscribed rights, and this is especially true for intellectual property rights. Intellectual property rights are not an end in themselves; they are a social construction, a means to an end—to promote societal well-being—which is accomplished through careful definition and design.

Examples in which public interest concerns circumscribe ordinary property rights abound; the general principle is that an owner of property cannot do things with her property that might adversely affect others.

U.S. patent law illustrates these issues by excepting patent protection for government use. Under 28 U.S.C. 1498, the government is authorized to use any patent or copyright, a right which can be extended to any contractor, subcontractor, or employee working for the government. While there is extensive debate about the justification for this, the view taken by the United States Court of Federal Claims in the 1990s is telling. It recognized that the granting of a patent was a limited grant—just as it was limited in time, so too it was limited in use. Government use represents a power reserved to the government when it initially grants the patent: "The government cannot 'take' what it already possesses, the government [has] the absolute power to take a compulsory, non-exclusive license to a patented invention at will."[22] While other courts have challenged this interpretation, the Court of Federal Claims decisions make clear that reasonable people, even in advanced industrial countries, balancing interests and looking at the costs and benefits of stronger intellectual property rights, have come to the conclusion that these rights should be heavily circumscribed.

The question, accordingly, is not whether intellectual property rights need to be circumscribed to advance broader social objectives, but how much and in what manner.

CURTAILING ABUSES OF MARKET POWER THROUGH LIMI-
TATIONS ON INTELLECTUAL PROPERTY RIGHTS Intellectual
property rights, by definition, create a monopoly power over the use
of knowledge, but this is not a license for monopoly abuse. But what is
meant by an *abuse* of monopoly power? And what should be the appropriate remedy? There is a broad consensus that Microsoft overstepped
the boundaries by leveraging its market power over operating systems
into other arenas. Of particular concern is that in doing so, it may have
actually stifled innovation. But while both American and European
antitrust authorities have concurred on this, they have proposed different remedies, perhaps partly based on differences in judgments about
the "balancing" of static and dynamic effects.[23]

One of the responses to abusive, anticompetitive practices has been
to restrict the use of patents, effectively insisting on compulsory licensing, sometimes through forming patent pools. In the consent decree in
the case of the antitrust action against AT&T in the 1950s, AT&T had
to make its patents available to anybody wanting to use them.[24,25]

Another proposed reform that has gained favor among some academics is limiting the life of intellectual property protection as a way
of limiting abuses, increasing market competitiveness, and spurring
innovation. If Microsoft's operating system had only a three-year protection, then it would be spurred to make significant improvements in
each subsequent release.[26]

Again, what is clear is that there is no unanimity even among the
advanced industrial countries on what appropriate balancing entails.
(Emerging markets and developing countries should be particularly
wary of monopolization; in certain sectors, because markets are less
perfect, the threat of monopolization is greater. As we explained earlier,
monopolies, once created, tend to persist.)

COMPULSORY LICENSES Besides the restrictions arising from the
threat of excessive monopolization, the two most important instances
in which patent rights have been circumscribed have been when there
is a threat to public health or in response to global warming. The 1992
Rio Agreement created a framework for addressing problems of climate change by providing for compulsory licenses for obtaining access
to technology related to mitigation of emissions. The 1994 TRIPS
agreement provided for compulsory licenses for lifesaving medicines.
(Effective enforcement of this provision has, however, been difficult,

since the United States has repeatedly put enormous pressure on governments that have threatened to issue compulsory licenses not to do so. This has remained true even after a global civil society movement succeeded in getting an international agreement clarifying the rights to issue compulsory licenses in the case of lifesaving medicines. [See Charlton and Stiglitz 2005; Stiglitz 2006a.])

THE PROCESS OF GRANTING AND ENFORCING PATENTS Institutional details matter. Nowhere is that more evident than in the way that patents are granted and enforced. Different countries have approached these issues in different ways. In Europe, there is a process of *opposition*: Those who believe the patent should not be granted have an opportunity to express their views to the patent office *before* a patent is granted. There is no such provision in the United States, exacerbating the bias toward excessive patenting that arises from the very structure of the patent system. Patents, as we have noted, privatize knowledge, but challenging a patent converts what would otherwise be a private good into a public good. Thus, challenging is itself a public good and, as in other arenas, the private sector will underinvest in the provision of this public good.

DESIGNING AN IPR REGIME TO PROMOTE LEARNING The previous paragraphs have identified a large number of central issues in the design of an IPR regime. Choices affect the level of competition in the economy, and access to and the affordability of medicine—and thereby both the health of citizens and (since in most countries, governments pay a large proportion of medical costs) that of the government's budget. Our focus in this book, however, is on innovation and learning.

The direct effect of IPR is to impede the flow of knowledge and therefore impede the learning process. We have seen that there is an indirect effect—encouraging secrecy—which can be particularly adverse when IPR is extended to traditionally open institutions like universities. Offsetting these costs allegedly are the stronger incentives for innovation and for the acquisition of information. In the case of poorly designed IPR regimes (and the United States and most other countries do not have well-designed IPR regimes), even that effect may be limited—or worse, innovation may be stifled. And even when there are increased incentives for R & D, research may not be directed in ways which increase standards of living, let alone the pace of innovation.

This section of the chapter has outlined some critical details in the design of the IPR regime; a poorly designed IPR regime *on balance*—taking into account the benefits of improved incentives and all the other adverse effects we have noted—leads to a lower pace of innovation; with appropriate design, the balance between the benefits and costs of IPR can be changed.

But as we noted earlier in the chapter, IPR is only one way of incentivizing and financing R & D and learning. IPR needs to be seen as part of a country's innovation system, and there needs to be a balance between IPR and other approaches. This is the subject of the next section.

3. IPR and the National Innovation System[27]

So far, our discussion has focused on the potential disadvantages of the IPR system—that it inevitably gives rise to static inefficiencies that and excessively strong, poorly designed property rights may actually impede innovation and growth. This brings us naturally to the critical question: Are there better alternatives to IPR for producing and financing knowledge?

Alternatives to IPR

Advocates of stronger intellectual property rights give the impression that they are essential for innovation. A moment's reflection should make it obvious that there are many alternative ways to finance and reward innovation. There are, for instance, other ways of appropriating returns from innovation (trade secrets, first-mover advantage) besides patents and copyrights, and in many areas these are highly effective. In fact, as we have already noted, many of the most important advances in knowledge are not protected by intellectual property rights and were not motivated by monetary gains. The basic mathematical advances that provided the underpinnings of the computer and the discovery of DNA which underlies so many advances in modern medicine are but two of a large number of examples.

GOVERNMENT-FUNDED RESEARCH   One of the more important alternative ways of financing research is through government support. The United States and other governments finance much of the basic research upon which pharmaceutical companies base their innovations. The Internet, which has spawned myriad innovations since the 1990s, was based on research that was supported, and largely conducted, by U.S. and European governments. The fact that so much of the successful innovation in the United States has occurred in research parks adjacent to universities suggests that these firms are benefiting from knowledge produced in the universities; and university research is, by and large, funded by foundations, government, and university endowments— but not motivated by the search for profit.

More generally, Mazzucato (2013) in her book, *The Entrepreneurial State*, has shown persuasively the critical role that the state has played in promoting the large transformative innovations and the smaller innovations, the cumulative effect of both of which has been to create the modern economy.

OPEN SOURCE   More recently, the open-source movement has been an important source of innovation. While its original successes were in software, it is now demonstrating its effectiveness in other arenas, such as biotechnology (see Henry and Stiglitz 2010; Hertel, Krishnan, and Slaughter 2003; Lerner and Tirole 2002; Weber 2005). It highlights and strengthens the collaborative nature of research that is the hallmark of academia, and the open architecture facilitates follow-on research—in contrast to the patent system, which closes it down or at least makes it more difficult. As in academia, in some instances nonpecuniary returns play a crucial role in motivating research; in other cases, firms have found a variety of ways of appropriating returns, e.g., through the sale of services or tailoring software based on open source to the needs of particular clients.

PRIZES   The prize system represents another alternative to the patent system. This entails giving a prize to whoever comes up with an innovation, or at least those innovations that meet announced objectives.[28] For instance, the person who finds a cure or a vaccine for AIDS or malaria would get a big prize. Someone who comes up with a drug with slightly different side effects than existing drugs (but which is otherwise no more effective) might get a small prize. The size of the prize is calibrated by the magnitude of the contribution.

The idea is an old one.[29] The U.K.'s Royal Society for the Encouragement of Arts, Manufactures and Commerce has been advocating and using prizes to incentivize the development of needed technologies for more than a century. For instance, an alternative was needed for chimney sweeps, those small, underfed boys who used to be sent down chimneys. It was not good for their health, but not cleaning chimneys meant increasing the risk of fire, with serious consequences. So the Royal Society offered a prize to anybody who invented a mechanical way of cleaning chimneys. The prize provided an incentive—and it worked.[30] A patent system might also have motivated the development of a mechanical device (though it did not), but if it had, there would have been a problem: The owner of the patent would have wanted to maximize the return on the innovation by charging a high fee for its use. That would mean that only rich families could have afforded to use the mechanical device, and young boys' lives would have continued to be put at risk. With the prize system, everyone could benefit from this socially important innovation.

The current patent system can, of course, be viewed as a prize system. It is an inefficient one, however, because the "prize" is a grant of monopoly power, and with monopoly power there are incentives to restrict the use of the knowledge. One of the characteristics of a desirable innovation system is that the ideas and innovations, once developed, be widely used and disseminated; the patent system is designed to restrict the use of knowledge. With the prize system, the competitive market ensures efficient dissemination; giving licenses to a large number of people uses the force of competition to drive down the price and to increase the use of the knowledge. With both patents and prizes, market forces are used: one is the incentive of a monopoly to restrict knowledge and raise prices, the other is the force of competitive markets to drive down prices and extend the benefit of knowledge widely.[31]

Moreover, the prize system has the advantage of creating fewer incentives to waste money on advertising and to engage in anticompetitive behaviors designed to enhance monopoly profits. Drug companies spend more on advertising and marketing than they do on research. These marketing expenditures are designed to reduce the elasticity of demand, which allows the owner of the patent to raise prices and increase monopoly profits. From a social point of view, these expenditures are dissipative.

The patent system also distorts the pattern of research. Drug companies have insufficient incentives to develop medicines for the diseases that tend to afflict poor people, simply because there is no money in those drugs. One of the widely discussed ideas for addressing this problem is a guaranteed purchase fund, in which the World Bank or the Gates Foundation would guarantee one or two billion dollars for the purchase of the drug to those who develop a vaccine or cure for AIDS, malaria, or some other disease afflicting the developing world. In effect, there would be a certain market. The guarantee of one or two billion dollars for the purchase of the drug would act as a prize, and a sufficiently large guarantee would provide a clear motivation for research. These guaranteed purchase funds, however, would still maintain the inefficiency of the monopoly patent system, unless there was an accompanying commitment that would make the patent accessible to all at reasonable royalties for purchases beyond the guarantee. The discoverer receives the "prize"—the monopoly profits—by charging monopoly prices. The poor, who get the drugs through the guaranteed purchase fund, do not, of course, pay the monopoly price. But the funds are limited, and when they are used up, without such a commitment, a government that wants to provide to its citizens, say, the malaria medicine that has been bought through the guaranteed purchase fund, will have to pay the full monopoly price.

Money spent purchasing this drug at the monopoly price is money that cannot be spent on the country's other health needs or in supporting basic research or education (each of which could have greater benefits in enhancing societal learning). It may be far better to use the money for the guaranteed purchase fund in a way which spurs competition in providing the drug, to offer a prize, or to buy the patent, and to allow anyone willing to pay a limited licensing fee to produce it.

OTHER MARKET-BASED MECHANISMS Of course, even in the absence of these explicit mechanisms for incentivizing research (patents and prizes), firms undertake research and learning. Firms appropriate returns through natural markets using non-IPR mechanisms such as the advantages that arise from being first or trade secrets. Some industries rely upon such mechanisms even when access to the patent system is possible (partially because they are concerned with the disclosure requirements of the patent law).

Finally, we should note that traditional discussions of intellectual property rights have perhaps overemphasized the importance of monetary incentives. As we emphasized in chapter 3, many, if not most, of the most important advances have been otherwise motivated—by a simple quest for knowledge and peer recognition (see, e.g., Dasgupta and David 1994).

A Portfolio Approach to Innovation

We have described briefly alternative ways in which innovation and learning are financed and motivated. Intellectual property rights should be part of an innovation system that also includes open source, prizes, and government-supported research and grants (which are probably the most important component of the innovation system in supporting basic research). Each of these has its strengths and weaknesses.

Any innovation system has to solve the problems of finance, selection (who gets research money), and incentives. There are, in addition, problems of coordination of research efforts. And different systems have associated with them different implications for the dissemination of knowledge and different transaction costs.

Every country should have a portfolio of instruments. The nature of the portfolio will affect the extent to which the country is successful in creating a learning society; it will affect the innovativeness and efficiency of the system—including the uncertainty and transaction costs facing market participants. In our view, too much weight has been assigned to patents in the current portfolio in the United States. Table 15.1 provides a chart of some of the attributes of the alternatives.

SELECTION The first attribute listed is *selection*. One problem facing any innovation system is how to select those to engage in a research project. The advantage of the patent and the prize system, as well as "open source" is that they are decentralized and based on self-selection. Those who think that they are the best researchers make the decision to undertake the research. They make the investment, risking their own money, in the belief that they have a good chance of winning the prize (the formal prize or the prize of the patent) or of contributing to the advancement of learning. The prize and patent systems have this advantage over government-funded research, in which there is a group of peers (or bureaucrats) deciding on the best researcher. There is obviously also a concern about "capture" of the research-awarding process, e.g., by political or economic interests whose agendas may be separate from or even counter to the advancement of science and technology.

TABLE 15.1
Comparing Alternative Systems

Attribute	Innovation System				
	Patent	Prize	Government-Funded Research	Open Source	Non-IPR Market Appropriation
Selection	Decentralized, self-selection. Lacks coordination.	Decentralized, self-selection. Lacks coordination.	Bureaucratic. More coordination possible.	Decentralized, self-selection. Sometimes "self" coordination.	Decentralized, self-selection. Lacks coordination.
Finance (tax)	Highly distortionary and inequitable.	Can be less distortionary and more equitable.	Most efficient.	May be underfinanced. Foundations, government, by-product of other activities.	Likely to be less distortionary than patent.
Risk	Litigation risk.	Less risk.	Least risk.	Limited.	Limited.
Innovation incentives	Strong but distorted.	Strong, less distorted. Requires well-defined objectives.	Strong nonmonetary incentives.	Strong, often nonpecuniary.	Strong, less distorted.
Dissemination incentive	Limited—monopoly.	Strong—competitive markets.	Strong.	Strong.	Limited—returns depend on secrecy.
Transaction costs	High.	Lower.	Lower.	Low.	Low.

FINANCE With respect to *finance*, the patent system is the worst of the systems. We can think of IPR as a method of funding research—a highly distortionary method. Price exceeds marginal cost by a considerable amount, for a limited period of time, and the resulting monopoly profit not only provides the incentives, but also the resources for innovation. This gap between price and marginal cost can be thought of as a tax, part of the proceeds of which are used to finance research. In the last seventy-five years, there has been considerable research into the optimal way of raising (tax) revenues. The implicit taxation of IPR (even if *all* the proceeds were devoted to R & D) is *not* an optimal way of raising revenues. Its principal virtue is that it is a benefit tax; that is, only those who benefit from the innovation pay for it. But in most arenas, we do not employ benefit taxes, largely because the additional distortions associated with such taxes are generally not viewed as worth the slight gain in "equity." In the area of lifesaving drugs, such an argument is even more compelling, because typically those who need the drugs are already suffering from having a life-threatening disease. In these circumstances, levying a "benefit tax" by forcing them to pay for the drugs to keep them alive may be viewed as not only inefficient but inequitable. In the case of drugs, the "monopoly tax" is an inefficient way of funding research for yet another reason: A large fraction of the revenue does not reach its target—it is spent on marketing and advertising, rather than on research.

Within the United States, the distortions in consumption associated with monopoly pricing as a basis of research funding for medicines may be limited for those who have health insurance or are covered by Medicare, because so much of the funding for health care, including drugs, is from third parties, and there may be accordingly little price elasticity. Internationally, however, this is not true. In all countries with governments picking up a significant fraction of the cost of medicines, monopoly pricing represents a transfer from ordinary taxpayers to the pharmaceutical companies. And even in the United States, there are large distortions (including in patterns of research) arising out of rent-seeking—in the quest to garner monopolistic returns. But especially in developing countries (and even in the United States and the few other developed countries where governments do not guarantee access to lifesaving medicines), high prices effectively deny access to lifesaving drugs for large numbers of people. Everywhere, for the poor without insurance, monopoly pricing may result in their not getting medicines that they need—they especially bear the burden of monopoly. More generally, the in-effect benefit tax is regressive. A more equitable system of financing would be progressive and those more able to pay would pay more—and indeed a larger share of their income. Indeed, one can argue that in countries where individuals have to pay a larger share of their drug costs, not charging prices above marginal cost for lifesaving drugs may be a desirable way to provide assistance to poorer people who have the misfortune of suffering from disease. A system of direct payment for the underlying research combined with marginal-cost pricing would make what is going on more transparent, would be a more equitable system of finance, and would lead to better resource allocations.[32]

In short, the patent system is highly distortionary and inequitable in the way in which funds to support research are raised—by charging monopoly prices, e.g., on the sick.

INCENTIVES The main purported advantage of the patent system is that it provides good incentives. Innovation incentives are strong in the patent system, but they are distorted, whereas the prize system can provide equivalent incentives that are less distorted. As we have noted, incentives are distorted under the patent system because there are also incentives to engage in research to innovate around a patent, to spend money in ways that extend the effective life of the patent, to develop a holdup patent, to enclose the knowledge commons, and to extend and to enhance market power. These innovation distortions are in addition to the other market distortions, such as those associated with marketing expenditures and practices attempting to make demand curves less elastic or otherwise to extend and enhance market power.

Moreover, earlier chapters have explained the impact on why innovation of the patent system may actually be very limited—in fact the patent system may be adverse to innovation: The patent system helps create monopolies, and monopoly incentives may be attenuated. Moreover, the patent thicket and holdups have adverse effects on innovation, as are the attempts by an existing monopolist to foreclose innovative entry of others. And patents create significant impediments for follow-on research.

RISK AND COORDINATION Research is inherently risky: it is an exploration into the unknown. There is, however, a big difference in the nature of the *risk* faced by researchers operating in the difficult systems. Moreover, one of the disadvantages of both the patent and the prize systems is the lack of *coordination*. From a societal point of view, there is a risk of excessive duplication.[33] The lack of coordination increases the cost of doing research.

One of the risks that each researcher faces is not knowing how many other people are engaged in that research. This increases the risk that someone else will make the discovery first, and thus get the patent or prize. Government-funded research can be more coordinated.

Coordination is important not just with respect to the number of researchers or research projects, but the portfolio of research projects. The optimal portfolio takes into account the marginal contribution of each project, given the other projects undertaken—the increased likelihood of a discovery, or that the discovery will occur sooner than it otherwise would have occurred. (See the discussion in chapter 6.)

We have already noted another important source of risk associated with the patent system: that of costly litigation, with uncertain outcomes.

Thus, with respect to risk and coordination, the patent system is the worst and the government-funded system is the best, because it has the advantages of paying for the input rather than the output. That is to say, a researchers gets money for their time and other resources spent doing the research, whereas in the prize and the patent systems researchers are rewarded only if their research is successful—and successful before their rivals.

The patent system imposes more risk than the prize system, because under the patent system, there is an additional source of uncertainty: the value of the "prize," which depends on the magnitude of the monopoly rents which the winner of the patent can extract.

One of the reasons that risk is important is that in equilibrium consumers have to pay for the risk borne by researchers. People and firms are risk averse,[34] and if they must bear risk, they have to be compensated for doing so. The patent system makes society bear the cost of that risk in an inefficient way. Under the government-financed research system, not only is risk lower, but it is shared by society in a more efficient way.

TRANSACTION COSTS The transaction costs associated with running IPR regimes are very high. Some have claimed that in the United States there is more spending on IPR lawyers (to obtain patents, to pursue patent claims, and to defend against patent claims made by others) than there is on research. While getting precise numbers is difficult if not impossible, it is clear that the transaction costs are considerable, and greater than in the other ways by which innovation can be funded and incentivized.

DISSEMINATION Widespread access to and dissemination of knowledge is one of the most important attributes in assessing the impact of alternative mechanisms within the innovation portfolio (recall that knowledge is a public good, in the sense that there is no marginal cost in an additional individual or firm making use of that knowledge), and here the patent system is particularly deficient. It is designed to impede access to knowledge. Lack of access to knowledge not only leads to a static inefficiency but impedes further innovation. It can be a major impediment to creating a learning society. The hallmark of the alternative mechanisms (open source, government-funded research, the prize system) is that knowledge is made available for free or for a limited licensing fee.

This discussion has made clear that, on most accounts, the prize system dominates the patent system. The prize system provides high returns to innovators who develop innovations of high social value. (Indeed, the prize can be better aligned with social benefits than can the random prize associated with the award of monopoly rights through the patent system.) And then the benefits of this knowledge can be more widely disseminated through the use of competitive production. Moreover, the prize system avoids not just the static but also the dynamic distortions associated with monopoly—including the incentive to impede follow-on innovations (that would reduce the monopoly rents of the patent holder).

But the prize system has one limitation: It does not work when the objective is not well-defined. (There are, however, many areas, such as health, energy conservation, and carbon emissions reductions, in which there are well-defined objectives.) That is why the prize system will never replace the patent system.

At the same time, in basic research—the foundation on which everything else is built—government-funded research will continue to remain at the core of the innovation system. No one has proposed otherwise: The costs of restricting the usage of knowledge associated with the patent system far outweigh any purported benefits. The debate today revolves only around applied research, which entails translating the knowledge acquired in basic research into applications.

4. Intellectual Property and Economic Development[35]

Throughout this book, we have emphasized that what separates developed from less-developed countries is a gap in knowledge—not just a gap in resources. The most successful countries have been the most effective in reducing that gap quickly. Intellectual property rights (and especially a poorly designed IPR system) may impede both access to knowledge and the creation of a learning society in these countries.

We have explained that any IPR regime involves trade-offs between static inefficiency and dynamic gains—any restriction on the use of knowledge induces a static inefficiency,[36] even more so if it gives rise to monopoly power—but that the dynamic gains from the current IPR system may be limited, both because of abuse of monopoly power and the problems posed by the difficulties of defining boundaries precisely, giving rise to patent thickets. Holdups use the patent system to divert to themselves profits that would otherwise accrue to the real innovators. Risk is increased both as a result of litigation and a lack of coordination. And most importantly, impediments in access to knowledge slow down follow-on research. But even if there were significant dynamic benefits, the optimal trade-off for a developing country is different from that for a developed country. Developing countries have much to benefit from learning from those in the developed countries. There can be direct learning benefits, but also, as we have emphasized, indirect benefits, as learning in one industry or one firm spills over to others.

That is why there is a need for a development-oriented intellectual property regime. The intellectual property regime which is appropriate for the advanced industrial countries will not be appropriate for developing countries or emerging markets.

On October 4, 2004, the General Assembly of the World Intellectual Property Organization (WIPO) called for such a regime.[37] Such a regime would begin by asking, How can one more effectively increase sustainable learning by developing countries? (See Stiglitz 2004.)

There were two critical ideas in the WIPO resolution. It recognized that intellectual property "is not an end in itself."[38] And it reiterated WIPO's mission to "promote creative intellectual activity" and "the transfer of technology to developing countries." The new development agenda calls for ascertaining how different intellectual property regimes affect developing countries.

Both the design of the IPR regime and the broader national innovation system has to reflect the differences in circumstances. That is why the attempt at excessive harmonization under TRIPS (the Agreement on Trade Related Aspects of Intellectual Property Rights that was adopted as part of the Uruguay Round trade negotiations) was so misguided.[39]

For an emerging market, access to knowledge is essential for its future growth. Intellectual property should not be used as an impediment to its development. The liability system (in effect, granting a compulsory license at fair compensation for the use of knowledge) is one way of ensuring access to knowledge. Even more modest reforms, such as allowing the use of intellectual property so long as there is a challenge (with appropriate compensation paid if the patent is upheld) would be preferable to the existing system (see, e.g., Lewis and Reichman 2005; Shapiro 2007).

While it may eventually be possible to devise simple rules for judging when, for instance, a compulsory license should be granted, intellectual property rights, especially in developing countries, are at an early stage of development. Simplicity—and the limited capacity of developing countries to engage in expensive litigation—argues that there should be strong presumptions in favor of limiting intellectual property rights when there is an apparent health, competition, or developmental objective. That is, the burden of proof should be placed on the original holder of the patent that there is not a legitimate health, competition, or developmental objective.[40]

Learning in developing countries occurs through several channels, some of which we have discussed in earlier chapters: mobility of people, open-source forms of knowledge dissemination, investment goods, imitation and reverse engineering, formal licensing, intrafirm technology transfer (e.g., through multinational corporations), foreign direct investment, and the acquisition of firms with technology.[41] A few developing countries (notably China) have begun to undertake significant investments in R & D and made extensive use of the patent system. Advocates of stronger IPR have argued that strengthening the patent system would enhance innovation and learning and would increase the willingness of firms from the advanced countries to undertake research, or even move advanced production which could be the basis of learning, to developing countries. But they ignore the fact that the patent system would impede learning through many of the channels through which learning has typically occurred and that these channels have historically played a critical role. The implication is that stronger (and especially poorly designed) intellectual property rights may have an especially adverse effect on learning and innovation in developing countries.

5. Concluding Comments

Intellectual property regimes are supposed to encourage innovation by providing incentives to do research, enhancing the ability of innovators to appropriate the returns. But intellectual property interferes with the dissemination and transmission of knowledge and encourages secrecy, which impedes learning. Increasingly, there is an awareness of these and other adverse effects, especially for developing countries, of intellectual property regimes, as developed in the advanced industrial countries. Knowledge is the most important input into the production of knowledge, and by restricting the availability of knowledge IPR inhibits the production of further knowledge (learning). The patent system gives rise to monopoly power; monopolies restrict production, thereby reducing incentives to innovate. The patent system can give rise to a patent thicket, a complex web of patents, exposing any innovator to the risk of litigation and holdup.

There are two implications of this analysis. The first is that, given the critical role of closing the knowledge gap for successful development, the appropriate intellectual property regime for developing countries and emerging markets is likely to be markedly different from that appropriate for the advanced industrial countries. In this area, even more than in others, one-size-fits-all policies are inappropriate.

Second, there are alternative ways of designing an innovation system, with greater emphasis on prizes and on open source. Patents will play a role, but the details of the patent system matter: a good patent system, for instance, has to pay more attention to disclosure, to problems of holdup, and to designing better systems of challenging patents.

This book has argued that creating a learning society provides a prism through which all the policies and institutions of a society need to be examined. This is especially so in the case of policies and institutions that are *supposed* to promote innovation and learning.

CHAPTER SIXTEEN

Social Transformation and the Creation of a Learning Society

WHILE WE have been discussing the *economics* of learning and creating a learning economy, that subject cannot be separated from broader aspects of societal transformation. Much of this book, for instance, has focused on policies that change sectoral composition in ways that would promote learning. But at the root of success is changing mindsets (see Stiglitz 1998c). Change has to be viewed as both possible and desirable, and there has to be an understanding that underneath change is *learning*.

In many ways, understanding how to change mindsets is more difficult than coming to an understanding of what economic policies would facilitate learning. But in creating a learning society, the two are inexorably linked. We want not just to identify what policies might lead to creating a learning society, but also to get them adopted. That requires political systems and mindsets that recognize the virtues of creating a learning society.

This chapter draws heavily from Stiglitz (2010b); and Hoff and Stiglitz (2010, 2012).

The neoclassical model ignores learning, not only paying no attention to the importance of the allocation of resources to learning and research and development, but also assuming that all firms employ best practices—so they have nothing to learn. Not surprisingly, the neoclassical model was not helpful in understanding what is entailed in the creation of a learning economy. Worse still, we have emphasized that the policies that are based on that model are often counterproductive—they impede learning. So too, the neoclassical model which assumes beliefs and preferences are fixed is not helpful in understanding changing mindsets.

As we noted in chapter 3, it is not an accident that the change in mindsets that we associate with the Enlightenment was closely associated with the changes in technology that had brought about the dramatic changes in living standards that mark the past two hundred years. And yet, as important as the Enlightenment was to creating the modern economy and society, even in the advanced industrial countries, there are strong forces countering the Enlightenment—questioning basic tenets of science, including and especially those involving evolution.[1]

In developing countries, these issues are all the more important, as Hirschman emphasized in his writings (see, e.g., Hirschman 1958). For instance, race and caste are social constructs that effectively inhibit the human development of large parts of the population in many parts of the world and impede change. The study of how these constructs get formed, and how they change is thus a central part of developmental studies. Similarly, Myrdal (1968), in his studies of South Asia, argued, in effect, that certain social constructs affect behavior and were part of what might be called a dysfunctional *economic* and *social* equilibrium that could persist. But he did not address the question of the mechanisms by which such social constructs are created. And what happened in Asia subsequent to his writing showed that societies could evolve. Myrdal also didn't address the question of the mechanisms by which such social constructs evolve, or collapse.

Nor did either Hirschman or Myrdal ask how we might reconcile such constructions of the developmental process with the usual approaches taken by economists,which, for instance, highlight some notion of rationality.

The objective of this chapter is to provide a very preliminary discussion of these aspects of creating a learning society, amplifying on the earlier discussion in chapter 3, and doing so in ways that touch upon the relationship between the approach taken here and that of the standard economic model. This chapter is divided into two sections, beyond the introduction and conclusion. In the first, we present a general approach to societal evolution of beliefs (including beliefs about change) that provides the foundations of an understanding of both societal rigidities and societal change; it provides insights both into the impediments to creating a "learning society" mentality and into how learning mindsets can be created. The second describes the links between democratic ideology and learning societies.

1. Toward a General Theory of the Social Construction of Beliefs and Societal Transformation

Recent work by Hoff and Stiglitz (2010, 2011) has attempted to construct a general approach to societal evolution that clarifies the critical — and unrealistic — assumptions about individual behavior and cognition that underlie what has become the dominant developmental model within the economics literature. This work, at the same time, provides some insights into why Myrdal's (1968) bleak predictions concerning Asia's prospects could have been so far off the mark. The theory proposed by Hoff and Stiglitz, and discussed more briefly here, centers on *what collective beliefs* (sometimes referred to as ideologies) *are an equilibrium*, and how they change. The analysis below is divided into two steps. The first focuses on how, at any moment of time, beliefs are formed and what might be meant by *equilibrium beliefs*; the second addresses how beliefs change.

Equilibrium Beliefs

Our theory of equilibrium beliefs is based on three critical hypotheses:

1. *Individuals' perceptions — how they receive and process information — are affected by individuals' prior beliefs.* Well-documented results in psychology show that individuals recognize and process information that is consistent with their prior beliefs in a way that is different from the way they treat other information.[2] This view, based on strong evidence and referred to as *confirmatory bias*,[3] is markedly different from the dominant view of economists, predicated on "rational

expectations," where it is assumed that individuals process all information fully and rationally. Such theories are hard to reconcile with both the psychological evidence and the persistence of differences in human views and beliefs.[4]

There are two important corollaries of this. This hypothesis alone can help explain *equilibrium fictions*. That is, equilibrium can be based on beliefs that (to the individual) seem self-confirming even when, in a fundamental sense, they are wrong (see Hoff and Stiglitz 2010). Moreover, it explains why different individuals can have persistently different beliefs—for each, the data that one person sees and how that person processes it confirm that person's prior beliefs. There is no process of consensus building even about the nature of the world, let alone what might be done to improve it.

In this book, however, we are concerned with explaining not just the persistence of disparate beliefs among individuals, but how some societies come to share certain beliefs that are conducive to learning, creating a learning society. Here, we introduce two further hypotheses.

2. *The information most individuals receive comes from other individuals, and how they assess that information (the weight they assign to it) depends on their prior beliefs and their social connections.* The role of society in determining our perceptions goes even further. The cognitive frames which shape perceptions are largely socially determined.[5] They are what is sometimes called social constructs. But in describing them as social constructs, it is important to recognize, as Hoff and Stiglitz emphasize, that they are not necessarily consciously constructed. By "social construct" we simply refer to anything that is collectively made by people. Collective beliefs can emerge endogenously and spontaneously from individual behaviors.[6]

This is a major difference from the neoclassical perspective.[7] Even the categories into which information is placed are often social constructions. Individuals do not choose their "software" in isolation, but within a social context. From among the infinite set of potentially observable data and the infinite ways in which that data could be processed, individuals choose a finite set of data and process them in particular ways; they are limited by the finite set of *socially* constructed categories that are themselves a part of what are called *ideologies* (or *belief systems*).[8]

These hypotheses helps explain why different groups can come to believe different things, and why those differences in beliefs can persist, even when the "reality" that each confronts—the true empirical evidence—is the same.

In the end, we are interested in explaining *behavior* (e.g., individuals' performance or the choices they make, including how they allocate time and the sources of information they seek out). That brings us to our third hypothesis.

3. *Perceptions (beliefs) affect actions (choices).*[9] Perceptions about being powerless, less productive, or being unfairly treated affect behavior. Those who think that they will not do well won't in fact do well. If one believes that change is not possible, or that most changes are for the worse, then one won't undertake actions that facilitate and promote change.

The real power of the theory arises from the interactions of the three hypotheses. Individual behavior is based on beliefs that are more complex (or at least different) in their formation than is reflected in standard Bayesian theories about the determination of individual's subjective probabilities of the occurrence of different states of nature.

As in Rational Expectations models, beliefs affect behavior, which affect outcomes, which affect beliefs. But unlike in a rational expectations model, *beliefs also affect what is perceived* and how information is absorbed and filtered. Biases—at every stage of the formation of beliefs—shape perceptions and widen the set of possible equilibria. If individuals come to believe that a certain group of individuals (members of some caste) are less efficient or productive, information that is consistent with that belief will be absorbed more easily than information that is inconsistent with that. Those from other castes will come to believe that their discriminatory attitudes are not discriminatory, but reflect "reality"—for that is how they perceive it. These beliefs are reinforced because they are held by others in the peer group. Even worse, because those who are discriminated against may come to share such perceptions, it may affect their efforts. To some extent at least, the beliefs become self-fulfilling.

The dependence of performance on perceptions, combined with the earlier hypotheses on confirmatory bias and the social construction of beliefs, means that the set of "fiction" equilibria is widened. There can be multiple equilibria.[10]

Just as beliefs affect *individual* actions and performance, widely held beliefs affect *collective* actions. If there is a widespread belief concerning the importance of education and the effectiveness of public education, it is more likely that there will be collective actions in support of public education. And again, there can be multiple societal equilibria.

There can be a high-learning equilibrium, in which members of society believe that change is possible and that education is an important instrument for bringing about change. Such a society will make public and private investments and adopt policies that sustain a learning society, and the outcomes will confirm their prior beliefs—especially when the salience of possible failures is discounted. But other societies can be trapped into a low-learning equilibrium. If individuals believe that change is not possible, they will not make the investments that make change possible.[11]

The Persistence of Socially Dysfunctional Beliefs and Policies

An understanding of the persistence of dysfunctional beliefs systems and the creation of belief systems that might be more conducive to learning is of no less importance for developed countries than for developing countries. The 2008 crisis provides evidence of the relevance of the ideas that we have presented: Those wedded to the notion that markets were always efficient and stable perceived the crisis markedly differently from those who are more skeptical of these perspectives.

To most observers, the crisis (the bubble and the reckless lending that preceded it) demonstrated that markets were not necessarily efficient and stable and that these market failures could be *very* costly. Those who believe nonetheless that markets are fundamentally efficient found alternative interpretations. In "processing" the vast array of "information" about the economy, their prior beliefs led them to discount information suggestive of market inefficiency and instability. While in 2008, it was virtually impossible to ignore that things had gone badly wrong, they sought to blame government—it was the government's attempt to push poor people into housing that was to blame. They held that view in the face of overwhelming evidence to the contrary.[12] When such arguments couldn't work, free market advocates simply said that it was a once-in-a-hundred-year tsunami, that no theory can be expected to explain such unusual events They failed to recognize that the tsunami was actually *created* by the market.[13]

Such considerations are equally important when it comes to theory. Even general theorems (such as that of Greenwald and Stiglitz [1986,

1988]) showing that markets are essentially never efficient if there are information imperfections and imperfect risk markets (as there always are) are "discounted." Theorems, of course, are propositions that follow logically from the assumptions. For a long time, those who believed that markets are efficient tried to find a logical flaw or to question the assumptions of our analyses. But the framework was general essentially that used in standard economics—except that there were imperfections in risk markets and in information. No one could deny the small modification that we had made: that information was imperfect and risk markets incomplete. The only recourse was to dismiss these imperfections as *quantitatively insignificant*. Of course, for those who believed in the efficiency of markets there was no data on the basis of which they could establish such a result. And, anticipating this kind of response, we had gone further, showing that even small imperfections of information had large effects, fundamentally changing the nature of the equilibrium (see Rothschild and Stiglitz 1976; Stiglitz 2002b). Again, devotees of free markets had a way of "framing" the analysis. Either they dismissed the result as a theoretical curiosity or countered that even if markets were not perfect, government attempts to correct the market failure would make things even worse.

Societal belief systems are so important because of the role they play in shaping policy. Chapter 15 analyzed, for instance, intellectual property rights. Certain belief systems that led to and supported the notion that the stronger the IPR regime the better, led to systems of intellectual property rights that, we suggest, impede the creation of a learning society. Neoclassical ideologies which focused on the static efficiency of the economy led to and supported the notion that governments should not undertake trade and industrial policies that might help create a learning society. Beliefs about the virtues of financial innovations led to and supported economic policies that increased macroeconomic instability and undermined resource allocations that would have better supported a learning society.

We've referred to "societal belief systems," but of course this discussion should have made clear that there can exist at the same time groups (within the same or different countries)—subcultures—who have markedly different beliefs—including beliefs about the desirability of change and the effectiveness of alternative policies or actions in creating a learning society.

Changes in Perceptions and Beliefs

Beliefs do change, and with changes in belief, policies and behavior change also. The Enlightenment represented a change in mindsets, one which was conducive to creating a learning society and which provided the basis for scientific enquiry, the fruits of which have been, as we have noted, fundamental to increases in standards of living. But the changes brought about by the Enlightenment were no less profound in the area of social organization. Beliefs about the sources of authority were changed in a fundamental way.

An understanding of how belief systems change—and the extent to which and how those (like governments) who seek to deliberately change belief systems can do so—is, or should be, a core part of the analysis of economic development and history.

Sometimes change occurs very slowly; at other times, seemingly rapidly. Consider, for instance, that for thousands of years, certain types of differential treatment of women was considered not only acceptable, but natural, essentially inevitable; and then in a span of around a hundred years, such behavior came to be viewed as unacceptable in most parts of the world.

Such changes in societal beliefs are sometimes motivated by changes in economic circumstances. But belief systems often have a life of their own, leading to their own evolution. The two processes are typically intimately intertwined. Historical analyses have often focused on how, for instance, changes in the scarcity value of labor (as a result of a change in technology or a plague) might lead to an attempt by those in power to maintain their economic power by imposing restrictions on workers. Belief systems would then evolve to explain and justify these restrictions.

A set of collective beliefs (ideologies) that serves a society—or some group in society—well under one set of economic circumstances may serve it less well under another. And thus, when circumstances change, there will be "forces" to change the underlying beliefs.

It should be clear that particular belief systems may serve the interests of some groups in society over others. Notions of slavery or caste (notions that members of a particular race or caste are in some way inferior) are advantageous to some groups but obviously are disadvantageous to others.

Because belief systems affect the equilibrium, e.g., by shaping perceptions, elites have a strong incentive to influence people's beliefs. (In contrast, in standard economic equilibrium of the rational expectations variety, this is not relevant—cognitive frames play no role.) But the elites cannot simply "choose" the cognitive frames that work best for themselves (nor can nonelites). The task of choosing cognitive frames and imposing them on others is more complicated and is itself constrained by higher-order beliefs, the "ideologies" to which we referred earlier. Even those in power typically do not control all the determinants of the evolution of beliefs. Cultures are always contested.

We have noted, however, that while economic interests and circumstances help explain the evolution of beliefs—and their failure to change in some circumstances—belief systems can have a life of their own. Whether the writers of the Declaration of Independence intended that the notion that all men are created equal extend to women and slaves may not be clear. Once a notion like that is accepted, however, it is inevitable that the meanings get reexamined and reinterpreted.

The broad ideologies—which both define the categories, the prisms, through which we see the world and what particular beliefs are viewed as acceptable—change, but typically slowly, so slowly that at any moment of time they can be viewed as state variables. An institution (like Jim Crow) may be accepted at one time and not at another.[14] It may be part of an equilibrium at one time, and not at another.[15]

Institutions function because they have legitimacy, because they are accepted. The acceptance and performance of institutions depend not only on economic variables, but also on the set of general beliefs about the world.

Incorporating "cognitive frames" (ideologies) as state variables provides part of a general theory of societal change that is markedly different from traditional theories, in which only capital and the distribution of power and wealth are state variables. If beliefs have the profound effects that we have suggested they do, and if at times they change, and at others they do not, then a central part of understanding societal evolution is understanding the dynamics of these changes in beliefs—and the circumstances under which rigidities might arise.

In some ways, the latter task is easier than the former. We've explained the concept of equilibrium fictions; if individuals' beliefs are partially or largely dependent on the beliefs of others with whom they interact, there can be a Nash equilibrium in beliefs that can persist, which discounts new information that might contradict those beliefs. Indeed, a set of beliefs that may have been functional at one time, but is no longer so, can persist after the economics or technology that had led to the adoption of the beliefs has changed.

At the same time, if ideologies change, the equilibrium can change, with little or no change in underlying "fundamentals." Changes in views about gender have had profound economic consequences but are themselves only to a limited extent explained by underlying changes in technology or the economy. (Changes in economics may help explain the increased availability of public education, but the extension of public education to women, and the implications of that for societal change, almost surely were driven as much by beliefs about equality as by economics.)

We turn now to one particular set of beliefs that has had enormous importance in shaping societies in recent decades.

2. Democracy and the Creation of a Learning Society

Ideas concerning human rights and democracy have been among the most important in shaping our economy and society. In the United States and Europe, these ideas eventually led to the abolition of slavery, though there were large groups for whom the continuation of this institutional arrangement was advantageous, and those who opposed it reaped little economic gain from the abolition.

Democratic ideals question authority. When America's Declaration of Independence said, *All men are created equal*, it didn't mean that they were of equal physical or mental capacities, but of equal rights, including the right to put forth their ideas into a competitive marketplace of ideas.

But it is exactly that same frame of mind which is so essential for creating a dynamic, learning economy and society. Democracy and an open society are intrinsically interlinked with a learning economy and society. A more open society generates more ideas, a flow of "mutations," which provides not only excitement but the possibility of dynamic evolution, rather than stasis.

Unfortunately, even if in the long run, a more dynamic society benefits most members of society, in the short run, there can be (and normally will be) losers. And not surprisingly, those who might lose seek to prevent such changes through any means they can. The political process is one way that is often taken. Those who seek to maintain inequalities in wealth and power do so not only through policies (economic, legal, etc.) which perpetuate existing bases of power and wealth, e.g., by creating entry barriers; but also through policies which attempt to maintain the legitimacy of these inequities of wealth and power. Media policies (control of the airwaves, right-to-know laws, and so forth) thus become important instruments for shaping public perceptions, and thus public policies. The political processes themselves evolve over time, shaped not just by history but by economics, especially in countries, like the United States, where money has such influence in the political process. Firms have learned that they can partially shape individuals' preferences. Those with wealth have more recently learned how to use such tools to shape perceptions in ways that lead to outcomes in the political process that are more favorable to themselves. Sometimes, this entails creating a less open and transparent society—a more open society might lead people to question the persistent inequities, a more transparent society might expose the nefarious ways by which inequities are maintained. When that happens, the long-term success of the economy may be put into question.[16,17]

Inclusive Growth

So far, we have emphasized the importance of creating a learning economy and society, suggested that success requires not just an economic transformation but a social transformation, and argued that, over the long run, democratic and open societies will be more dynamic. But, as we have noted, democratic processes can be shaped, and there are incentives on the part of some to maintain existing inequities. Democratic processes can then lead to the antithesis of an open and transparent society.

There is thus at least one more requirement for long-term success: inclusive growth. It is now generally accepted that trickle-down economics doesn't work. Higher GDP does not necessarily mean that all, or even most, benefit. The critique of many of the Washington Consensus policies, though, was not just that they were not pro-poor, that is, that the poor did not share in the benefits. Rather, it was that they were anti-poor. Policies that lead to greater volatility (which arguably capital and financial market liberalization do) are anti-poor. It is the poor that bear the brunt of crises—nowhere evidenced more than in the 2008 crisis (see also Furman and Stiglitz 1999). Policies that lead to higher levels of unemployment are anti-poor. Trade liberalization destroys jobs, so that unless such liberalization is accompanied by measures that lead to job and enterprise creation, it can be anti-poor. That is why it is so important that trade liberalization be accompanied by appropriate financial sector and aid-to-trade measures to ensure that job creation occurs in tandem with job destruction. Markets, on their own, do not ensure this, even in seemingly well-functioning advanced industrial countries.

One of the big advances in development in recent years is that we understand not only that some policies lead to anti-poor or non-pro-poor growth, but that we have instruments and policies (from broad policies, like micro-credit, to specific instruments, like more efficient cookstoves) to enhance the likelihood that the poor share in the growth that occurs.

The Political Economy of Inclusiveness and Openness

Our argument for why inclusive growth is so important goes beyond the standard one that it is a waste of a country's most valuable resource, its human talent, to fail to ensure that everyone lives up to his or her abilities. Rather, it is based on political economy, on an analysis of how inequality affects political processes in ways which are adverse to long-term learning and growth and inclusive democracy.[18]

Earlier we argued that government needs to play an important role in any economy, correcting pervasive market failures, but especially in the "creative economy," e.g., financing basic research and providing high-quality education. Moreover, innovation is always risky, and in societies with better systems of social protection, individuals are willing to take more risk. Also, societies (like some in Scandinavia) in which there are stronger social protections are more willing to expose themselves and their citizens to growth-enhancing risks, such as those associated with openness.

Consider, for a moment, a society in which there is little inequality. The only role of the state, then, is to provide collective goods and correct market failures. A consensus can be developed on what that entails—since interests are aligned.

But this is not so in societies in which there are large inequalities. Then interests differ. Liberals may want to use the state to redistribute income. While ostensibly conservative high-income individuals may claim that they are only trying to prevent such redistributions, a more careful look at the policies they advocate often reveals that they entail redistributions toward themselves; at the very least, they entail ensuring that the government does not ask them to contribute too much for the support of the public good and that it does not curtail their activities exploiting the poor and extracting for themselves a disproportionate share of public assets. Distributive battles inevitably rage.

Often, the battle takes the form of an attempt to circumscribe government (e.g., an "independent" central bank that is, in reality, accountable mainly to the financial sector, or budget constraints that severely limit the scope of government activity, even when there are very high return investment opportunities in the public sector).

Many in the United States are concerned that the country has embarked on an adverse dynamic, moving it toward an equilibrium in which there will be greater inequality and, as a consequence, toward a less dynamic economy and society. As social protections erode and public investments weaken, including in education, inequality increases. The rich turn to private education, private parks, private health insurance, etc., even though public provision might be far more efficient. Rather than working to improve the efficiency of the public sector, those who seek to limit the scope of government work to tear down the public sector, to undermine its credibility, knowing that if they succeed, then there will be a broader consensus for limiting the role of government and thus limiting the extent to which the government can engage in redistributive activities, *even if in doing so, the government is limited in its ability to engage in collective wealth enhancement.* As this happens, inequalities increase, confidence in public provision erodes, and the state takes on a less important role. It is problematic to gauge whether, in the end, even those at the top benefit; but what is not questionable is that the vast majority in the society lose out.

A casual look around the world suggests that different societies have taken different courses. The Scandinavian countries, by and large, have limited inequalities, have efficient and large public sectors and high standards of living for the vast majority of their citizens, and have succeeded in creating inclusive dynamic economies and societies. There are important differences among the political parties in these countries, but still, there is a broad consensus about most of the elements of the "social contract." America in more recent years has taken a different course. The image of a society with a high degree of social mobility is belied by the statistics, which suggest that such mobility is less than in many "old" European countries. The consequences for the United States are decreasing standards of living for the majority of citizens combined with increasing social pathologies.

There is not a consensus about whether government in a large country such as the United States can achieve the efficiency and effectiveness in the public sector approaching that achieved by the Scandinavian countries. But a major import of the analysis of this book is that even if it can't, it does not mean that markets should be left to themselves. Rather, it means that the instruments have to be adapted to the capabilities of government—and that efforts should be made to improve those capabilities.

3. Concluding Comments

In this chapter we have touched on a broad terrain. Economics, politics, and society are interconnected. Too often, economists have lost touch with these broader dimensions—though we have also argued that much of the conventional wisdom of economists even missed out on the most important *economic* elements in creating a dynamic and creative society.

In discussing the importance of creating an open, democratic, and inclusive society as necessary conditions for creating a dynamic economy and a learning society, we don't want to underestimate the importance of these as ends in themselves. Creativity, voice, and security are all important ingredients to individual well-being and a sense of dignity. The central message of the International Commission on the Measurement of Economic Performance and Social Progress was that GDP was not a good measure of well-being, and policies which narrowly focused on increasing GDP were misguided (Stiglitz, Sen, and Fitoussi 2010).

We have not devoted much attention to specific policies by which we can create a more open and inclusive democracy, or by which we might transform society, enhancing the culture of learning. Nor have we explained how the interplay between changes in economics, politics, and technology, on the one hand, and the self-evolution of belief systems on the other led to the evolution of the Enlightenment; that is a subject which goes beyond the scope of this book. Nor have we had much to say about why the principles of the Enlightenment and the associated learning mindset have still not become universally accepted, or why, even in countries where they are generally accepted, there are segments of society within which these views are not widely accepted. What we have emphasized, however, is that beliefs (the learning mindset) affect not only individual behavior but also collective actions—including policies which affect the extent to which society learns and the pace of economic progress.

We end with three notes. First, we have stressed the importance of equilibrium fictions, beliefs that persist in spite of evidence to the contrary. Two such fictions that have been persistent are (a) the belief in the efficiency of unfettered markets and (b) the importance of "strong" intellectual property rights. (Even the idea that there is such a thing as an unfettered market—that markets *could* be left to themselves—is a fiction, for markets need rules and regulations, and these rules and regulations have to be agreed to collectively.) The irony is that these beliefs—often held to be at the center of creating a dynamic learning economy—may actually have precisely the opposite effect, especially in developing countries.

Second, at the center of the task of creating a learning society is the education system and how it inculcates attitudes toward change and skills of learning.

And third, while policies reflect societal attitudes, which in turn reflect mindsets of the members of society, they also help shape mindsets. Policies which enhance risk taking may lead to mindsets which are more accepting of risk. Intellectual property regimes which encourage secrecy lead to mindsets which value transparency and openness less.

It is, of course, not just public policies that affect learning and mindsets—so do the decisions made by firms. Firms can decide to cultivate an atmosphere of secrecy, which impedes the flow of knowledge within and between firms, or they can encourage more openness. What matters is not just democracy at the level of the nation, but also democracy within the workplace (see, e.g., Stiglitz 2001a, 2001b). Attitudes that question authority can help create a culture of learning at the level of the firm—and that culture can have society-wide benefits. There are, thus, not just "learning" and "technological" externalities, but "mindset" externalities. While the level of innovation is affected by success in creating a learning environment, some kinds of innovation may be conducive to enhancing a learning environment; others can be adverse.

Innovations that strengthen the ability to monitor, for instance, may strengthen hierarchical relationships (see Braverman and Stiglitz 1986).

We have stressed in this book that the decisions taken by firms—including the direction of innovation—are themselves shaped by public policy. As we evaluate the consequences of the various policies discussed in the first sixteen chapters of this book, we must be mindful of their long-term effects in shaping our society.

CHAPTER SEVENTEEN

Concluding Remarks

IT HAS been more than sixty years since our teacher Robert Solow showed persuasively that most of the increases in standards of living were due to technological progress and learning, and since Kenneth Arrow began the analysis of endogenous learning. If we were to evaluate the impact of their work by the number of citations—and even more, on the scholarly work that their papers inspired—the influence of their path-breaking insights has been staggering.

But at another level, the impact on the evolution of economics has been disappointing. True, everyone speaks today of the innovation economy or the knowledge economy, and there have been important advances (some referred to in this book) in the analysis of, say, patents and patent races, and network externalities, to take but two examples.

But the full implications of their work for the neoclassical model, which was central, for instance, to Solow's analysis, have still not been taken on board. And the implications for policy have been even less absorbed into mainstream thinking. This book can be seen as an attempt to fill that void.

Some forty years ago, the revolution brought about by information economics questioned all the standard results and conclusions. Equilibrium might not exist. When it did exist, it could look markedly different from that depicted by the standard model. (Supply might not equal demand. There could be credit rationing and unemployment. Equilibrium might not be characterized by a single price. There might be price dispersions. Price might systemically exceed marginal cost. Market equilibrium was not in general Pareto efficient.) The impact on both theory and policy was profound.

But information can be thought of as a particular kind of knowledge (see Stiglitz 1975a), and we might have expected that the knowledge revolution would have equally profound effects. The objective of this book has been to show the potential that the economics of learning and innovation has for revolutionizing both economic theory and policy. We have questioned, for instance, some of the basic tools used by economists: If most firms are operating below "best practices," does a production possibilities curve based on the assumption that firms are all efficient—or that their knowledge is fixed—make sense? Is it a useful tool *at all*?

We have shown that comparative advantage needs to be reexamined, especially in light of the increasing mobility of skilled labor and capital: A country's long-term comparative advantage is based in part on its comparative learning capabilities.

We have explained why, in a learning economy, there is no presumption that the market economy, on its own, is efficient—in either a static or dynamic sense. Indeed, the presumption is to the contrary. That means that there are policies that can lead to higher sustained growth. But many of the policies that enhance economy-wide learning are the opposite of those derived from the standard neoclassical model. A focus on short-run allocative efficiency may lead to slower growth. Industrial policies—including interventions in trade—will typically be desirable, and they may even be a permanent part of an economy's policy framework, not just in the early catch-up stage.

We have attempted to provide an analysis of factors that increase a society's learning capabilities and enhance its learning. This analysis provided us with a new theory of boundaries of the firm—different from that of Coase (1937)—focusing not on minimizing societal transaction costs, but rather on maximizing learning, recognizing that knowledge can flow more freely within a firm.

We have stressed the importance of viewing learning from a societal perspective. Learning externalities are pervasive, and it is a mistake not to take them into account. Firms, of course, do not, and that means there is no presumption that the market equilibrium—where the market draws the boundary of the firm—is efficient or maximizes societal learning. There is even less of a presumption that the attempts of firms to impose barriers on what other firms can learn from them lead to an optimum.

Most importantly, our focus on learning has provided a new prism through which virtually every aspect of policy—indeed, every aspect of a country's legal framework—needs to be reexamined. And while this is true for all countries, it is especially true for developing countries.

The construction of simple equilibrium models incorporating learning turns out to be a difficult task, because one has to solve simultaneously for market structure and (investments in) learning and innovation. The traditional way that question has been posed, e.g., whether monopoly or competitive structures are more conducive to innovation, is on that account at least partially misleading. (Of course, government can take actions which foster competition, or it can overlook anticompetitive practices.) Beliefs about future growth and industrial structure, moreover, affect current production, learning and even industrial concentration. We have shown that there may, in fact, be multiple equilibria—a high-growth equilibrium in which it pays to invest a lot in learning today, and as a result there is more growth, and a low-growth equilibrium.

We have examined policies directly aimed at the structure of the economy (like industrial and trade policies) as well as macro-policy. We have also argued that macro-stability is desirable not just because risk-averse individuals dislike volatility, and not just because with higher volatility there may be a larger output gap (a larger gap, on average, between the economy's potential and actual output) and more inequality,[1] but because macroeconomic volatility creates an environment which is adverse to learning. Whatever benefits might arise from the economic restructuring that economic downturns force upon economies are overshadowed by the costs of the losses in learning and innovation. We have shown how policies like financial and capital market liberalization may not only directly lead to an economic structure which is less conducive to learning, but may also create more macroeconomic volatility, with further adverse effects on learning. We have shown too how standard intellectual property rights may impede learning. And we have discussed possible reforms in the IPR regime which may be more conducive to learning. Even more importantly, we have argued that IPR needs to be seen within a broader context—that of a national innovation system, in which open source, prizes, and public investments in research and learning need to be given more emphasis, and IPR less.

We have shown too how government tax and investment policies can be used to foster a learning economy and society. But the list does not stop here. Alternative monetary policies and institutions, investment treaties, education and technology policies, legal frameworks for corporate governance and bankruptcy, indeed, the entire economic regime needs to be reexamined and reevaluated through the prism of learning. We have observed that even systems of social protection can affect learning: Investments in learning are risky, and in economies with good social protections, because there is better risk mitigation, individuals can undertake more risk. There can be more learning. Anxiety impedes learning, and good systems of social protection reduce anxiety. A corollary of the analysis of chapter 16 is that more democratic workplaces may be more conducive to learning, and labor laws that promote such working conditions may therefore be more conducive to learning.

Although in this short book we have been able to address only a few of the many ways that policies need to be reexamined from a learning perspective, our analysis has overthrown many long-standing presumptions:

- We have shown that there is an *infant-economy argument for protection*. Protecting a learning sector with large externalities (which we have argued is typically the industrial sector) leads to faster growth and improved welfare and standards of living, and can support convergence between developing countries and the more advanced countries. Not providing such protection can lead to stagnation. It may be desirable to provide this protection even if the economy never fully grows up.
- There are strong arguments for using the exchange rate as an instrument to encourage the learning sector, especially in the presence of restrictions on the use of industrial policy; it may pay even for a developing country to have a trade surplus—the benefits from learning outweigh the costs of forgoing consumption or investment. And it may even be desirable to engage in this intervention *forever*.

• Broader industrial policies are desirable. Industrial policies are not about picking winners, but correcting pervasive market failures, and especially the market failures associated with learning. Such policies should go beyond just creating a business-friendly environment. In some idealized models, we have derived general formulae for the optimal intervention.

• Financial and capital market liberalization may have an adverse effect on learning, both because of the resulting weaker flow of funds to firms and sectors where learning and learning externalities are more important, and because such policies undermine learning in the financial sector.

• Foreign direct investment can enhance learning, but the extent to which it does will depend on policies, like requirements concerning domestic procurement and employment, which are often criticized within the standard paradigm and often restricted by trade and investment agreements.

• Stronger intellectual property rights—and especially poorly designed IPR systems (and the IPR system in the United States, for instance, is *not* well designed)—can actually impede learning and the creation of a learning society, because they impede access to knowledge, because they encourage a culture of secrecy, which can be antithetical to the openness that facilitates the creation of a learning society, and because the resulting adverse effects on the knowledge pool, which defines the opportunity set facing innovators, discourages investment in innovation.

Three ideas have been key to our analysis. The first we have already referred to: There is no presumption that markets by themselves are efficient. Indeed, while we have highlighted the importance of learning externalities, we have detailed a host of market failures associated with learning. And we have noted that the spillovers from the expansion of industrial firms are not just technological: There are institutional spillovers (e.g., associated with the creation of a financial and educational system), and the revenues raised from the taxation of industry help finance a host of public investment goods that enhance learning and productivity. (Chapter 14 discussed how public investment should be allocated to maximize societal learning benefits.)

We have noted that markets where learning (innovation) is important are likely to be far from perfectly competitive. The only case where, putting aside various sources of diseconomies of scale, competition is viable in the long run is that where there are perfect learning spillovers. But then each firm will try to free ride on the investments in learning and innovation of others, and there will be an underinvestment in learning.

Indeed, in simple models, the economy converges to a monopoly. (With strong Bertrand competition, in the absence of any offsetting diseconomies of scale or scope, a monopoly may emerge immediately.[2]) We have shown that attempts by Schumpeter and others nonetheless to trumpet the virtues of the market economy have not been totally persuasive. Schumpeter was overly optimistic in emphasizing the temporary nature of monopolies—we have shown that they have the ability and incentives to engage in behaviors which allow their monopoly to persist—with adverse effects both on short-run efficiency and long-run innovation. We have shown that those who, following Schumpeter, suggested that potential competition (competition for the market) was an effective substitute for competition in the market were also wrong. Incumbents can deter entry and maintain high profits. Schumpeterian competition does not lead to an efficient allocation of resources to learning and innovation.

We show that one of Schumpeter's propositions is, in general, correct: An increase in competition may lower innovation. But the level of innovation under limited competition (including monopoly) may well be (indeed, in general will be) less than is socially optimal. There are government interventions that can improve welfare and innovation. Though the relationship between the level of competition and the level of innovation is a complex one (and varies greatly depending on particular assumptions), we have suggested that perhaps the real reason that competition may be important goes beyond the standard model of profit maximizing firms, focusing on issues of agency, managerial capitalism, and corporate governance.

We have argued, furthermore, that the failures of the market relate not just to the level of learning and innovation, but also to the direction. Too much effort is expended to get, and maintain, market power. Too much effort is also expended on circumventing existing patents. There are large divergences, even with well-designed patent laws, between social and private returns.

One of the manifestations of these distortions is that there may be excessive efforts at saving labor and insufficient efforts at protecting the environment. The result is that the market equilibrium will be characterized by high levels of unemployment—higher than it would be with appropriate government intervention in the innovation process. This distortion is particularly evident in the midst of recession, with high levels of unemployment of unskilled workers, and yet where significant efforts continue to reduce the need for workers.

The second key idea is that we must view markets and government as complements, as working together. It is not a choice of markets *or* government, but of designing an economic system in which they interact constructively. Indeed, as we have repeatedly emphasized, markets don't exist in a vacuum; governments set the rules of the game, and how those rules are written is one of the key determinants of whether a learning economy and a learning society gets created. Government can, for instance, help correct the "market failures" that we have argued are endemic in a learning economy. It can provide education opportunities that enhance individuals' capacity and desire to learn. It can provide a system of social protection that provides individuals with the security needed to undertake the risks associated with new ventures. It can support basic research, which underpins the major advances in technology. And it can help prevent the excesses in financial markets that are systematically associated with macroeconomic volatility.

The third key idea is that the design of a learning society is likely to involve complicated trade-offs. We have focused in particular on the trade-off between static efficiency and learning. Many of the policies discussed earlier (including the infant-economy argument for protection) entail a loss in the short run but a gain in the long run. Stronger intellectual property rights, more secrecy, and restraints on the mobility of workers might (all other things being held constant, including the opportunity set facing firms, the pool of knowledge from which they can draw) provide stronger incentives for investments in learning and innovation. But at the same time, they reduce the flow of knowledge; and because knowledge is the most important input into the production of knowledge, they may actually result *overall* in less learning and innovation, and even less investment in learning.

There are other complex trade-offs. Government can design more finely tuned policies which in principle could, if the government had the requisite information and could avoid the political economy problems associated with vested interests, lead to higher economic growth. But in many societies, the distortions associated with such policies arising from vested interests have had adverse effects. In such societies, broad-based policies, such as those associated with managing the exchange rate, are preferable to more finely tuned policies.

But the more general lessons that emerge from combining our theoretical analysis with historical experience are these: Political economy considerations should not affect whether economies engage in industrial and trade policies to help create a learning economy; they should influence only the choice of instruments. Many countries have learned how to manage these political economy problems, and these successes provide experiences from which other countries can learn.

Indeed, looking over the wide sweep of history, almost every successful economy has, at one time or another, engaged in the kind of industrial and trade policies which our analysis suggests.

Social innovations are no less important than the technological innovations upon which economists traditionally focus: The progress of human society has as much to do with such innovations—including innovations concerning how to manage large organizations and organizational learning and how to promote societal learning more broadly, including through industrial and trade policies—as it has to do with improvements in technology.

So too, there are complex trade-offs within firms. A centralized and more hierarchical structure may facilitate coordination (leading to a better designed portfolio of research projects, avoiding costly duplication). It may also lower the risk of undertaking bad projects—projects with a low probability of return. But such organizational designs may, at the same time, stifle innovation and make it more likely that good projects get rejected (see Sah and Stiglitz 1985, 1986).

Achieving balance between centralization and decentralization is a challenge which has to be confronted at every level—within the firm and within society as a whole. As we have noted, with pervasive externalities associated with learning and imperfections of information, there is a presumption that decentralized markets will be Pareto inefficient.[3]

We observed, however, that there again may be multiple equilibria—none of which are efficient; the economy may get trapped in a bureaucratic equilibrium in which innovation is stifled, or in an excessively free market equilibrium, in which imperfectly competitive firms focus innovation on rent seeking.

While we have emphasized the importance of trade-offs, we have also emphasized that there are a variety of policies which can increase both output in the short run and growth and learning. A poorly designed intellectual property regime combined with ineffective enforcement of antitrust laws could lead to lower output today and lower growth.

Most of this book has employed conventional economic models, for instance, with individuals having well-defined preferences; we have explored the consequences of changing only one assumption—we have assumed that learning (as well as market structure) is endogenous. This book has been an exploration of the profound implications of changing that single assumption. Most of this book has modeled learning in a fairly mechanistic way, keeping within the standard paradigm. Yet, as chapter 16 emphasized, both at the level of the individual and society, what is most important is having a learning mindset. Attitudes toward learning are largely socially determined and are affected obviously by societies' experiences. But what experiences a country is exposed to and how those experiences are perceived are themselves affected by beliefs. There can be equilibrium fictions—belief systems that persist because they seem to be confirmed by the world *as perceived by individuals*. While we have only hinted at how beliefs are formed—why dysfunctional belief systems may persist or why, at some time, they may change rapidly—they are at least in part, and perhaps largely, social constructions. Public policies and individual and firm actions are shaped by these belief systems; but at the same time, public policies also shape beliefs. We have noted the irony that certain prevalent beliefs about what is required to create and maintain a learning society may actually impede creating a learning society—that, for instance, beliefs about the importance of strong intellectual property may actually be leading to less openness, creating a culture that is adverse to learning and innovation.

The issues we raise are relevant for all countries, but perhaps especially so for developing countries, as they struggle to close the knowledge gap that separates them from the more developed countries. The Washington Consensus policies, derived from an excessive reliance on the neoclassical model, paid no attention to learning. In focusing exclusively on static efficiency, these policies may have actually resulted in growth and standards of living that were lower than they otherwise would have been. Fortunately, the most successful countries, especially those in East Asia, paid little attention to these policies. Learning was at the center of their development strategies. But unfortunately, not all countries had a choice: Those dependent on the West for foreign assistance, and especially those in sub-Saharan Africa, had to follow these policies. They experienced as a result low (and often negative) growth and deindustrialization.

Countries might like to pretend that they can avoid the issues that we have raised. Standard policies are complicated enough—why complicate them further by worrying about learning? They might hope that they can avoid, for instance, matters of industrial policy—following the neoliberal doctrines that these are matters to be left to the market. But they cannot. The choice they make in each of the arenas that we have discussed will affect the future growth of the economy.

We end where we began: Increases in standards of living have more to do with learning, the focus of this book, than with allocative efficiency, the subject which has been the preoccupation of economists. That this is so holds out enormous prospects for the well-being of those in the developing world: Accumulating resources is a slow process compared to the speed with which gaps in knowledge can be reduced.

But there is more at stake than just an increase in material standards of living: There are profound differences between a stagnant society and a dynamic one, a society in which individuals are struggling to meet the basic necessities for survival, and a society enjoys the prosperity that modern technology can provide, enabling individuals to live up to their full potential.

The policies that we have described that can help create a learning economy and society inevitably will shape not just the economy, but society more broadly, for the betterment of both, raising still further living standards now and in the future.

PART FOUR

Commentary and Afterword

CHAPTER EIGHTEEN

Introductory Remarks for the First Annual Arrow Lecture

MICHAEL WOODFORD

John Bates Clark Professor of Political Economy, Columbia University

THE INTENTION of this lecture series is to showcase new ideas in economics. It is named in honor of Kenneth Arrow, one of the most distinguished alumni of our PhD program in economics. Ken Arrow is, of course, one of the founders of modern economic theory, with fundamental contributions in many areas. When the Noble Prize in Economic Sciences was established several decades ago, Ken was one of the first people to be honored with the new prize, and I think this was hardly a surprise. One of his groundbreaking accomplishments, of which we are especially proud at Columbia, was his Columbia dissertation, subsequently published as a book called *Social Choice and Individual Values*. This book opened up a new area of inquiry in political and economic theory that has come to be known as social choice theory, and it is still very important.

The commentaries that follow these introductory remarks are based on the discussion that took place immediately after the lecture.

Among Ken's other fundamental contributions to economic theory, of which there are many, I would like to mention only two: first, his work on the theory of general competitive equilibrium, especially the extension of that theory to deal with economies with trading in financial assets. This work, apart from its interest for abstract economic theory, has been the foundation for extensive further developments in financial economics. In recent decades, this has been an area of economics that is not only intellectually fascinating, but that has also changed the world. Second, his work laying the foundations for what has come to be known as the economics of information, which stresses the pervasiveness in economic life not merely of incomplete information about the state of the world, but of asymmetries of information, and which shows how economic arrangements are profoundly shaped by the incentives that result from those asymmetries of information.

When I say that Ken's work has been of fundamental importance, I mean that, above all, because of the extent to which others have been able to take those ideas and run with them. In the case of Ken's idea on the consequences of information asymmetries, there are few economists who have run further with the basic idea than Bruce Greenwald and Joseph Stiglitz. Bruce and Joe are both from Columbia University faculty. Bruce Greenwald is the Robert Heilbrunn Professor of Asset Management here at the Graduate School of Business. He is also director of the Heilbrunn Center there, and well-known off campus as an expert on value investing, among many other topics.

Joseph Stiglitz needs even less introduction. He is a University Professor, with appointments in the Business School, the Department of Economics, and the School of International and Public Affairs, and is also the chair of the Committee on Global Thought and president of the Initiative for Policy Dialogue. His numerous honors include the John Bates Clark Medal of the American Economics Association, which many people argue is even harder to get than the Nobel Prize. He has received a Nobel Prize in Economics as well. He is also very well-known to the public as the former chair of President Clinton's Council of Economic Advisers and the former chief economist of the World Bank.

Bruce and Joe have maintained an extremely fruitful research collaboration for at least twenty-five years. The persistent theme of their work has been the consequences of information asymmetries, which they have applied to problems that include credit market problems,

problems in labor markets, understanding business cycles, and monetary economics, among other areas.

We are also pleased to have two very distinguished discussants for the Arrow Lecture, in addition to Ken Arrow himself. Philippe Aghion, the Robert C. Waggoner Professor of Economics at Harvard University is an authority on economic growth and, among other things, author of a leading textbook in that area, *Endogenous Growth Theory* with Peter Howitt, and coeditor of the *Handbook of Economic Growth* with Steve Durlauf.

Our second discussant is Robert Solow, Institute Professor Emeritus from MIT. Bob Solow is another one of the founders of modern economics as a field, and he is considered by many of us to be the father of the modern theory of economic growth. This was certainly one of the parts of his work that was especially stressed by the Nobel committee when he got his prize. But those who were fortunate enough to study at MIT in any of the several decades when Bob was on the faculty there—and I think also anyone who reads *The New York Review of Books*—know that Bob is worth listening to on almost any topic.

CHAPTER NINETEEN

Further Considerations

JOSEPH E. STIGLITZ AND BRUCE C. GREENWALD

Joseph Stiglitz: The main point of this lecture is to pose the question that Ken emphasizes (in chapter 22), which is, How do we create societies that are better at learning? How do we solve these problems of moving people, firms, and societies to the "frontier"? Maximizing the value of output in the short run, as is conventional in static analysis, does not necessarily optimize learning, does not necessarily move firms or countries rapidly to the frontier, and therefore does not necessarily maximize growth or societal welfare. We use tariffs as a way of trying to dramatize this point, but in fact there are many other instruments that affect learning.

One instrument used by China and many of the East Asian countries is exchange rate policy, specifically an undervalued exchange rate. Such an intervention is in the spirit of this discussion, especially so because it is broad-based. It is, in a way, a more self-correcting instrument, because pushing down the exchange rate through direct intervention leads to a trade surplus and the growth of reserves, and as reserves increase, the political pressures to do something with them increases. Exchange rate intervention may give a slight competitive advantage to manufacturing exports, and especially when there are the large externalities that we have described here, this promotes overall economic growth. It can create a backlash from one's trading partners, but in general there are ways of talking about it that mitigate such risks. You don't call it exchange rate management (or manipulation); you call it building up reserves, necessary for economic stability, given the large magnitude of global fluctuations.

The story of Korea may illustrate what we had in mind and what motivated our work. Korea's static comparative advantage forty-five years ago was in growing rice. If they had had free trade, they would have continued growing rice, which is what the World Bank and IMF suggested that they do. Korea's response was this: Even if we are the best rice-growers in the world, we will be poor, and pursuing our static comparative advantage in growing rice is not a way to develop. So they intervened in a variety of ways. If Korea had had free trade, Korea would have continued growing rice, and if Korea had continued growing rice, the country would not have "learned"; there would not have been the structural transformation that enabled Korea to grow so rapidly over the past four decades. They shifted production in a way that led to more learning, with benefits not only to the protected industries, but to all of society.

There is a very important issue related to the best way to achieve more learning. One of the criticisms of the infant-industry argument is that it entails government picking winners, something that critics of such policies say it is unqualified to do. We think that is not the right way to frame the discussion—though, of course, you do not want to pick losers. But the real issue is in identifying spillovers, externalities, and areas where society could learn more. Further, countries must identify the best way of doing that broadly, while noting that even if government were not very good at picking particular firms or even particular industries, it can make a judgment that a whole category of industries, maybe a whole industrial sector or a service sector, is better than agriculture in promoting learning. We have considerable scope in how broadly we define our interventions. There are thus interventions that can help shift the structure of the economy to make it more of a learning society and increase the pace of productivity.

Bruce Greenwald: The whole thrust of our work is that, in practice, information dissemination and absorption looks much more important than information creation. What you need to achieve more efficient information dissemination and absorption is some sort of institutional structure. I think that we could have substituted "urban" and "rural" for "industrial" and "craft," in our discussion, and that might have brought home what we have in mind much more compellingly. We want to have institutions in place that create better dissemination and utilization of information.

I want to talk about one specific example because it illustrates fairly usefully the main idea. Behind some of what we have said are very detailed studies of individual industries by Bob that were supported through the Sloan Foundation. So we know at the firm level, in certain cases, what the "technologies" were that led to 30 percent improvements in productivity in a year and almost 50 percent in two years. One particular case consisted of a woman going from one firm, where she had successfully promoted cutting costs without cutting output by 30 percent in two years and, moving to another firm, succeeded in cutting costs there by 35 percent in two years. This dramatic example provides a sense of how that might be possible and achievable.

That kind of learning is not going to happen across borders, at least not as easily. The crucial things about borders are language issues and historical patterns of dealing with each other. So in a sense, the paper is really about locating the impediments to dissemination of knowledge and information, considering the measures that might reduce those impediments, and in doing so, creating modern, developed standards of living in places where they do not yet exist. Conventional analyses have often begun by emphasizing competition, and that is clearly of first-order importance, especially if you look at what happens in the absence of competition (evidenced by the socialist experience). That was completely noncontroversial. We thought, in writing this essay in honor of Ken, we owed Ken more than that.

The second point I want to emphasize—and again it is absolutely striking—is that the biggest cost to a recession is not the immediate unemployment. In fact, what happens in a recession is that productivity growth drops *and it never recovers*. This productivity growth seems lost forever, and the total (present discounted value) loss in output and consumption is much more substantial than just the temporary loss of output. That is why the second thing we focused on was stability, and we thought that was noncontroversial—though typically not adequately recognized. So then we got to spillovers and trade, and we thought we could make trouble there, that what we said would provide stimulus for discussion.

Joseph Stiglitz: I want to add one point about why stability is important. There is a large amount of tacit information embedded within organizations and within firms, and when firms get destroyed, the networks and flows of information get destroyed along with them. We are about to have a very significant wave of firm destruction because of the crisis. There has always been a Schumpeterian debate about the role of downturns as cleansing out the inefficient firms and the dynamic benefits of killing off the bottom, versus the other side, wherein you also kill a lot of firms who were not at the bottom.

In the East Asia crisis, at the World Bank, we did some studies where we looked at the characteristics of the firms that were being killed, and it turned out their main failure was to have a bad chief financial officer—one who had led the firm to take on too much debt. In terms of productive characteristics, they did not differ significantly from the other firms. We are probably going to see some of the same thing going on here in this crisis. There are some firms that wound up taking derivative positions, that otherwise might have been perfectly efficient, but they are at risk of dying, too. And when they die, knowledge will die with them. And that is one of the reasons why probably, at the end of this, we will have a lower productivity economy than we otherwise would have had.

I really want to especially thank Bob and Philippe and particularly Ken for allowing us to honor him for his tremendous contribution to the economics profession and to our society.

CHAPTER TWENTY

Commentary: The Case for Industrial Policy

PHILIPPE AGHION

Robert C. Waggoner Professor of Economics, Harvard University

USUALLY IN such times, I would say it is a great honor to be here, but in this case the word *intimidating* may be equally appropriate: to be asked to discuss a paper by Joe Stiglitz and Bruce Greenwald, in the first Arrow Lecture at Columbia University, with Ken Arrow next to me, and with the other discussant being Bob Solow!

The task was all the more challenging that there was no paper to read in advance, no slides. I am just told that I will receive a 3:00 a.m. phone call at some point, and Joe will be on the line, and he will tell me a bit what is planned. So this has been an experience of guessing about what I am about to learn, an experience of learning by guessing.

The Setting

In the aftermath of World War II, many developing countries have opted for policies aimed at promoting new infant industries or at protecting local traditional activities from competition by products from more advanced countries. Thus, several Latin American countries advocated import substitution policies, whereby local industries would more fully benefit from domestic demand. East Asian countries like Korea or Japan, rather than advocating import substitution policies, would favor export promotion, which in turn would be achieved partly through tariffs and nontariff barriers and partly through maintaining undervalued exchange rates. For at least two or three decades after World War II, these policies, which belong to what is commonly referred to as "industrial policy," remained fairly noncontroversial as both groups of countries were growing at fast rates.

However, the slowdown in Latin America as of the 1970s and in Japan as of the late 1990s contributed to the growing skepticism about the role of industrial policy in the process of development. Increasingly since the early 1980s, industrial policy has been raising serious doubts among academics and policy advisers in international financial institutions. In particular, it was criticized for allowing governments to pick winners and losers in a discretionary fashion and consequently for increasing the scope for capture of governments by local vested interests. Instead, policy makers and growth/development economists would advocate general policies aimed at improving the "investment climate": the liberalization of product and labor markets, a legal and enforcement framework that protects (private) property rights, and macroeconomic stabilization. This new set of growth recommendations came to be known as the "Washington Consensus," as it was primarily advocated by the IMF, the World Bank, and the U.S. Treasury, all based in Washington, D.C.

The Washington consensus advocates did have a case: For example, recent empirical work by Frankel and Romer (1999) and Wacziarg (2001) would point to a positive effect of trade liberalization on growth. Thus, Wacziarg (2001) showed that increasing trade restrictions by one standard deviation would reduce productivity growth by 0.264 percent annually. Similarly, Keller (2002, 2004) showed that 70 percent of international R & D spillovers are due to cross-country trade flows, and more recently, Aghion et al. (2008) pointed to large growth-enhancing effects of the trade liberalization and delicensing reforms introduced in India in the early 1990s, particularly in more advanced sectors or in Indian states with more flexible labor market regulations.

The main goal of this discussion is to discover whether a case can still be made for policies aimed at supporting or protecting some local sectors, or whether the proponents of a full and unconditional liberalization have definitely won the debate. The discussion is organized as follows. I first summarize the infant-industry argument as it is traditionally stated and then discuss recent empirical work that refutes this argument. I then develop counterarguments in light of recent economic history. I then propose a new approach to industrial policy based on the notion of governance.

The Infant-Industry Argument

The story of the infant-industry argument in a nutshell is as follows: You have some new activities in the economy. Those new activities may have high-growth potential, because there will be a lot of learning by doing down the road, but they start out having very high costs. If you just open trade right away, there is no room for learning in these activities, because these activities will not be profitable. Also consider that there are knowledge externalities between these new activities and the rest of the economy. Because there are knowledge externalities, of course, you could always say, well, the activity has a high initial cost, but if you are an entrepreneur, you know that costs will be high in the beginning but then you will have high yields later on, so you decide to undertake the activity.

The problem is that the benefits are not just for the activities, they are for the whole economy. The entrepreneur in that particular sector does not internalize all the learning or growth gains that will be generated. As a consequence, the entrepreneur may not undertake that activity unless some protection is introduced. Someone needs to step in to subsidize your enterprise or protect you in some way. By doing that, in fact, you induce positive dynamic externalities from temporarily protected activities that will speed the knowledge over to the rest of the economy.

But now come the critics, starting with Krueger and Tuncer (1982), who looked at Turkish data from the 1960s and whether the infant substitution policies implemented by Turkey in the early 1960s had any growth effects. They used firm samples and industry samples. What they found is that, first, there is no systematic tendency for more protected firms or industries in Turkey to have higher productivity growth as a consequence of the infant substitution policy than less protected industry. And second, they argue that on the basis of their empirical analysis, they don't see any apparent tendency for new activities to show higher rates of growth than the industry to which they belong.

More generally, since the early 1980s, industrial policy has come under disrepute among academics and policy advisers, in particular for preventing competition and for allowing governments to pick winners and losers in a discretionary fashion and consequently for increasing the scope for capture of governments by local vested interests.

Why Rethink the Issue?

Three phenomena that have occurred in the recent period invite us to rethink the issue. First, climate change and the increasing awareness of the fact that without government intervention aimed at encouraging clean production and clean innovation, global warming will intensify and generate all kind of negative externalities (droughts, deforestations, migrations, conflicts) worldwide. Second, the recent financial crisis, which revealed the extent to which laissez-faire policies have led several countries, in particular in southern Europe, to allow the uncontrolled development of nontradable sectors (in particular real estate) at the expense of tradable sectors that are more conducive to long-term convergence and innovation.[2] Third, China, which has become so prominent on the world economic stage in large part thanks to its constant pursuit of industrial policy. Also, we now see an increasing number of scholars (in particular in the United States) denouncing the danger of laissez-faire policies that lead developed countries to specialize in upstream R & D and in services while outsourcing all manufacturing tasks to developing countries where unskilled labor costs are lower. They point to the fact that countries like Germany or Japan have better managed to maintain intermediate manufacturing segments of their value chain through pursuing more active industrial policies and that this in turn has allowed them to benefit more from outsourcing the other segments.

As mentioned above, the most recurrent counterargument to industrial interventionism is the "picking winners" argument. True, industrial policy is somewhat always about "picking winners," but as Vincent Cable, the current U.K. Business Secretary points out, "the 'winners' in this sense are the skills we judge we will need for the future, and the sectors they support." However, we will argue below that the picking winners argument loses bite, first when the government chooses to pick sectors, not particular firms, and, second, when it "governs" its sectoral interventions in a way that preserves or even enhances competition and Schumpeterian selection within the corresponding sectors. A second criticism of traditional industrial policy is the risk of capture and rent-seeking behavior that it involves. Here again, setting clear principles for the selection of sectors and for the governance of support to these sectors (competitiveness, exit mechanisms, etc.) should help address this criticism.

More fundamentally, a main theoretical argument supporting growth-enhancing sectoral policies is the existence of knowledge spillovers. For example, firms that choose to innovate in dirty technologies do not internalize the fact that current advances in such technologies tend to make future innovations in dirty technologies also more profitable. More generally, when choosing where to produce and innovate, firms do not internalize the positive or negative externalities this might have on other firms and sectors. A reinforcing factor is the existence of credit constraints, which may further limit or slow down the reallocation of firms toward new (more growth-enhancing) sectors. Now, one can argue that the existence of market failures on its own is not sufficient to justify *sectoral* intervention. On the other hand, there are activities—typically high-tech *sectors*—which generate knowledge spillovers on the rest of the economy and where assets are highly intangible, which in turn makes it more difficult for firms to borrow from private capital markets to finance their growth. Then there might indeed be a case for subsidizing entry and innovation in the corresponding sectors and to do so in a way that guarantees fair competition within the sector. Note that the sectors that come to mind are always the same four, namely, energy, biotech, information and communication technology, and transportation.

Rethinking the Design and Governance of Industrial Policy

To my knowledge, the first convincing empirical study in support for properly designed industrial policy, is by Nunn and Trefler (2010). These authors use micro data on a set of countries to analyze whether, as suggested by the argument of "infant industry," the growth of productivity in a country is positively affected by the measure to which tariff protection is biased in favor of activities and sectors that are "skill-intensive," that is to say, use more intensely skilled workers. They find a significant positive correlation between productivity growth and the "skill bias" due to tariff protection. Of course, such a correlation does not necessarily mean there is causality between skill-bias due to protection and productivity growth: The two variables may themselves be the result of a third factor, such as the quality of institutions in the countries considered. However, Nunn and Trefler show that at least 25 percent of the correlation corresponds to a causal effect. Overall, their analysis suggests that adequately designed (here, skill-intensive) targeting may actually enhance growth, not only in the sector which is being subsidized, but also the country as a whole.

More recently, Aghion et al. (2012) argue that sectoral policy should not be systematically opposed to competition policy. First, they develop a simple model showing that targeted subsidies can be used to induce several firms to operate in the same sector and that the more competitive the sector, the more this will induce firms to innovate in order to "escape competition" (see Aghion et al. 2005). Of course, a lot depends upon the design of industrial policy. Such policy should target sectors, not particular firms (or "national champions"). This in turn suggests new empirical analyses in which productivity growth, patenting, or other measures of innovativeness and entrepreneurship, would be regressed over some measures of sectoral intervention interacted with the degree of competition in the sector, and also with the extent to which intervention in each sector is not concentrated on one single firm, but rather distributed over a larger number of firms.

Data showing how much state aid each sector receives are not available for EU countries, unfortunately. Thus, to look at the interaction between state subsidies to a sector and the level of product market competition in that sector, Aghion et al. (2012) use Chinese firm-level panel data. More precisely, they look at all industrial firms from the Chinese National Business Survey. This is an annual survey of all firms with more than 5 million RMB sales. The sample period is 1988–2007, and the survey contains information on inputs and outputs, firm-level state subsidies, foreign investment and others. Product market competition is measured by 1 minus the Lerner index, which in turn is calculated as the ratio of operating profits minus capital costs over sales. Aghion et al. show that TFP, TFP growth, and product innovation (defined as the ratio between output value generated by new products to total output value) are all positively correlated with the interaction between state aid to the sector and market competition in the sector. Thus, the more competitive the recipient sector, the more positive the effects of targeted state subsidies to that sector on TFP, TFP growth, and product innovation in that sector. In fact, Aghion et al. show that for sectors with a low degree of competition, the effects are negative, whereas the effects become positive in sectors with a sufficiently high degree of competition. Finally, Aghion et al. show that the interaction between state aid and product market competition in the sector is more positive when state aid is less concentrated. In fact, if one restricts attention to the second quartile in terms of degree of concentration of state aid (this refers to sectors where state aid is not very concentrated), then state aid has a positive effect on TFP and product innovation in all sectors with more than the median level of product market competition.

Conclusion

In this discussion we tried to argue that, in spite of well-taken arguments against infant industry and in favor of competition-enhancing policy, adequately targeted sectoral intervention, e.g., to more skill-intensive or to more competitive sectors, can enhance growth. Also, we have argued in favor of not concentrating subsidies across firms in a sector. However, this is just the starting point in what we see as a much broader research program on how to *govern industrial policy* so as to make it more competition friendly and more innovation enhancing. In particular, how can industrial policy be designed so as to make sure that projects that turn out to be nonperforming will not be refinanced? How should governments update their doctrine and practice of competition policy so as to factor in renewed thinking on how to design and implement industrial policy? The conjunction of the debate on climate change, of the recent financial crisis, and the new dominance of China on the world market, reinforce our conviction that while market competition is certainly a main engine of growth, specialization cannot be left entirely to the dynamics of laissez-faire. Also, one increasingly realizes that the specialization model whereby the most advanced countries would focus on upstream R & D and services and outsource everything else to emerging market economies may not be sustainable in the long run.

CHAPTER TWENTY-ONE

Commentary

ROBERT SOLOW
Institute Professor Emeritus, Massachusetts Institute of Technology

THERE WILL be an inevitable change of pace because, unlike Philippe Aghion, I am not the Energizer Bunny. Even when I was Philippe's age, I was not the Energizer Bunny. I do share one handicap with Philippe, perhaps a little bit worse. I too had a three- or four-minute conversation with Joe about the content of the lecture I would be discussing, as a result of which I was totally misled. I thought that the focus would be on industrial policy aimed specifically at sectors that are fast learners or big "spillers over" if that is a noun. That may have been Philippe's inference too, because his comments were aimed there. But in fact, I have heard Bruce talking about much broader kinds of subsidies and protections, about the infant-economy argument, as he put it. So I have tried to think on the fly, and I will make some brief comments on the lecture that we have heard.

But first I want to say that my wife Bobby's and my association with Ken and Selma Arrow goes back, probably, to the summer of 1951. We spent that summer at the RAND Corporation working together on a joint project that, in the end, Ken finished. On the side, we wrote a short paper together. We discovered that Kenneth and I share a birthday along with many other things, both inside and outside of economics. Ken Arrow and I have been friends, and our families have been friends, for almost 60 years, which is longer than many people in this room have been alive.

I think it was a splendid idea for Columbia University to establish this lecture series in Kenneth Arrow's honor, and I am delighted to participate in the first of them. It is not going to be as easy as Michael Woodford suggested. It will be difficult to maintain the high moral and intellectual standards that you will naturally seek in a series dedicated to Ken. The world will know, from the publications, how well you succeed. I wish you bon voyage and good luck.

Commentary

There is a particular aspect of the prescription for broad tariff protection in developing countries that worries me. I was a member of the Commission on Growth and Development sponsored by the World Bank and led by Michael Spence. One of our clear findings was the great importance of integration into the world market for any poor country that wants to create a durable episode of rapid economic growth. The fundamental reason why this matters so much is that the world economy provides a large and price-elastic market for growing industries that produce tradables. We members of the Commission thought that it is very important for a developing country to be able to create and establish a comparative advantage in one or more manufacturing industries and that this requires the fairly rapid achievement of scale and technological improvement.

The first question that arose in my mind as I was listening to the lecture is that it would take a lot of abstemiousness on the part of the rest of the world to accept such broad tariff protection in developing countries while at the same time remaining open to exports from those same countries. Those exports are the only way that scale can be achieved early in the process. It seems doubtful that even a large developing country, like Brazil a few years ago, will be capable of developing manufacturing industries on the basis of internal demand only. So this asymmetry between the infant economy's need for outward openness and inward protection is a source of potential difficulty. One can imagine tolerance for the protection of an infant industry here and another there; the infant economy would be a harder sell.

A second problem that arose for me in the Greenwald-Stiglitz program is this: How do you prevent broad tariff protection from leading to rent-seeking and laziness? Where do the incentives come from to use the broad protection to be given the infant economy in order to achieve higher productivity, learning, improvement in technology, and rapid growth instead of dissipating it in the collection and consolidation of rents? Leaving this to chance or patriotism does not seem like a sound way to proceed. Of course, this point has been directed at the whole infant-industry argument in the past; the infant economy may be more vulnerable because one bad apple infects the rest.

I can be more concrete about this. I once took part in a series of studies done through the McKinsey Global Institute, which is the non-client research arm of the McKinsey firm. We focused on studying a few manufacturing industries plus some others, like construction and banking. We looked closely at the performance of the same industry in a half-dozen developed economies, including the United States. In each case, we picked out the best-practice firms, wherever they were, the ones with the highest level of productivity and best general performance. Once we had established the performance gaps, the amount by which firms in this industry in various countries lagged behind observed best practice, the next question was to ask why, to try to figure out the main factors in creating the performance gap. We took account of both the usual sorts of data and the reports of McKinsey consultants familiar with the industry.

What we discovered, very convincingly, at least to ourselves, was that you could not account for the cross-country differences in industrial efficiency and productivity in any of the routine ways. You could not account for the performance gaps by the unavailability of skilled labor. Nor could you appeal to differences in the availability of capital or achieved capital intensity; indeed, often the countries that lagged in the auto or steel industry, or in retail banking or in residential construction were more capital intensive than the best-practice leader. The McKinsey people were absolutely convinced that you could not account for productivity gaps by differences in access to technological know-how.

In the end, the group tended to conclude that observed productivity gaps were mainly a matter of deficiencies in management and that the main source of deficiencies in management was the absence or weakness of competitive pressure. And the most important obstacle to competitive pressure was formal or informal protection. Firms and industries exposed to competition from best practice were driven toward best practice.

Most of these comparisons were among industries in developed industrial economies. But the group found much the same chain of causation when it looked at "emerging" economies like Brazil and post-communist Russia. (There was a similar study of India, but I was not part of it.) So I think the results just described are applicable to today's discussion. I am not entirely clear about the breadth of the protection Bruce and Joe would extend to developing and emerging economies: Are we talking about a universal tariff, or tariffs protecting a selected group of industries, selected perhaps in the hope that they are fast learners or big spillers-over (which, of course, they would all claim to be). But we are talking about something broader than the isolated infant industry. It is an important issue: Where does the pressure to conform to best practice, or at least to approach it, come from in this kind of system?

On a more general level, I wonder where in this approach to industrial policy—with which on the whole I am sympathetic if not sold— attention is paid to the notion of comparative advantage. We are talking about broad protection. Developing countries can hope to develop and maintain comparative advantage in some sectors instead of others. We have to keep in mind that, in the modern world, comparative advantage, especially in manufacturing, doesn't usually rest on the things that our old textbooks thought about, like natural-resource availability, proximity to markets, good harbors, that sort of thing.

I started this morning in Springfield, Illinois, communing with Abraham Lincoln—a profitable exercise, I found. To get here I had to fly from Springfield to Chicago and then to New York. I flew from Springfield to Chicago in a regional jet manufactured in Brazil. Many of you have been on similar flights. I can imagine asking myself sixty years ago: Why should Brazil have a comparative advantage in the manufacture and export of small commercial jet aircraft? I don't suppose it can have much to do with the abundant timber resources of the Amazon. I don't know the history (though I would love to read about it), but I presume that somehow, not at all inevitably, an infant aircraft industry was established in Brazil.

Presumably it managed to get a head start, create a skilled labor force, and imitate known technology. Somehow it managed to wedge itself into a growing world market and get up to scale. It cannot have been easy, though a large country like Brazil must need small jets. But now it would be much harder for some other developing country to establish a profitable industry based on small commercial jet aircraft. The same chancy story will have to be repeated elsewhere. Malaysia has a flourishing electronics industry. Heckscher and Ohlin would have a hard time imagining where the comparative advantage of Malaysia in small electronics came from, why there rather than elsewhere. I wonder how the system Bruce and Joe are proposing will deal with such issues as footloose stopped to watch advantage and first-comer advantage.

So, pending my reading of this—infant?—paper, I am willing to play along. I rather liked what Joe told me by telephone that the trick was to detect and assist dynamic externalities. I would even grab the occasional dynamic internality while trying to work out how to detect dynamic externalities, encourage them, and avoid the pitfalls I mentioned earlier. I told you that I started this morning in Lincoln country. There is a Lincoln story that I did not notice in the Lincoln Presidential Library and Museum, but that I remember from my schoolboy days and that has stuck with me. During his early days in Kentucky, Abe was walking in the woods when he came upon a preacher engaged in a hand-to-hand physical struggle with a bear. Abe is reputed to have stopped to watch, cheering alternately: "Go it, preacher; go it, bear."

So I say, Go it, Bruce; go it, Joe. Let's hope it comes out right.

CHAPTER TWENTY-TWO

Commentary

KENNETH J. ARROW
Professor Emeritus, Stanford University

THIS IS a very moving occasion. I have been identified as a product of Columbia University. I started my university studies many years ago in the fall of 1940, and I don't know how many generations of professors have come and gone since then. There are obviously probably not many people in this room who were born at that point, except Bob. [Robert Solow interjects, "I was a freshman in September 1940."]

But this is not the time for reminiscing, because what was taught under the heading of economics was so very, very different from what is taught today in so many ways I cannot even begin to describe.

Back then, institutionalism was the dominant approach. People like Wesley Clair Mitchell, Arthur Burns and Simon Kuznets (who was at the National Bureau of Economic Research at Columbus Circle at the time) were very influential in developing many wide-ranging ideas to do with the central issues of the day surrounding business cycles. In some sense it may be that Bruce Greenwald and Joe Stiglitz in their paper are revisiting and reviving the plurality of ideas and viewpoints prevailing then. I am also moved, of course, by the tribute to me in having the set of lectures in my old institution named for me and it is, I hope, a legacy that will be carefully tended. And it's certainly starting out with a bang. I'm also grateful for having so many people here who are just good friends of mine, with varying degrees of length.

Now, as for the Stiglitz-Greenwald paper as in the written version, which I got only two days ago. I was more aggressive, I think, than Bob and Philippe, and I said I want to see a paper and one was produced! I read it on the plane coming here. That was my first chance to look at it.

Commentary

In my comments, I will concentrate on the issue of learning and knowledge that the paper emphasizes, since this is a topic of great interest to me. What strikes me most strongly about the paper and the underlying model and logic is that the issue of knowledge spillovers and their effects on growth is not necessarily limited to a discussion of foreign trade at all. In fact, suppose you have a world government or a single closed economy, these issues would arise nonetheless. Of course, the instruments that would be used in such cases would differ from those being considered here –broad and narrow tariffs—but the same insights would apply.

Before that exercise however, I would like to begin by briefly mentioning a central related theme that the paper invokes, but does not follow up in great detail. Greenwald and Stiglitz begin with the observation that most firms are operating below their efficient frontiers, whether in the United States or abroad. There are several possible reasons for this phenomenon including management styles, social cohesion within plants and others, but what has been established in the best empirical work is that there is substantial variation in efficiency. Richard Nelson and Sidney Winter's famous book on evolutionary economics (*An Evolutionary Theory of Economic Change*, 1982) provided examples of such large variation in both the United States and the Philippines. Another striking example of existing inefficiencies (provided in the current paper) is the study of firms facing strikes that were able to produce the end product with one-third the pre-strike number of workers.

Apart from being a sub-optimal outcome from a social welfare point of view, such gross productive inefficiencies constitute somewhat of an embarrassment from the viewpoint of standard economic theory.

Why don't competitive pressures, even mild ones, wipe out these inefficient firms? How do they survive? While there have been some answers provided—my colleague, Nicholas Bloom for example suggests that managerial differences explain differences in productivity across countries—I am still not completely clear on why these inefficiencies persist. This is an important issue which bears further thinking about.

While the Greenwald-Stiglitz paper alludes to the issue of competitive pressures and the effect on efficiency from tariffs and protection, it really does not pursue this question very much. Nor does it explore deeply another issue that it poses—that of macroeconomic stability. Instead, the dominant theme of the paper is the question of spillovers and learning and how the presence of such effects may justify the adoption of industrial policies (the 'infant economy' argument).

The persistence of inefficient firms and large differences in productivity mentioned in the paper suggest that spillover effects are not operating very well. This is especially so for firms producing the same product in competitive markets. Under these conditions, one should expect that there are large spillover effects since there is the most to learn from rival firms. If such inefficiencies persist in narrowly circumscribed situations such as this, there is certainly a puzzle.

What we know about spillovers is that they tend to be local and that therefore geography matters. Certainly the latter point has been emphasized by the literature on agglomeration. Silicon Valley and Route 28 in the Boston area are dominant in the high technology sector, even though they do not possess any obvious physical comparative advantage in producing computer chips and software. In fact, they may possess some disadvantages: in the case of the Silicon Valley, the physical confines of being between a bay and a mountain ridge and the consequent lack of available inexpensive land acts as a deterrent to manufacturing activity, yet the headquarters and research laboratories of leading firms remain there.

The usual explanation for this is that information and learning happen most effectively when people meet face-to-face and exchange ideas. Despite their devotion to the abolition of distance and space as an obstacle to communication these firms rely on face-to-face meetings for their innovation and growth. The interesting thing about knowledge is that it has an ability to spread rapidly and effectively. To extend the Jeffersonian formulation, these individuals and firms are lighting candles all over the place.

Now, this is an example of spillovers of knowledge and know-how in firms or industries which are similar, and in which learning from each other is therefore rewarded most directly. Greenwald and Stiglitz's paper however address different, more diffuse spillovers between segments of the economy they call 'Industry' and one they call 'Agriculture'. By this they do not mean necessarily the sectors of the economy defined by the national accounts, but between a progressive dynamic sector with more knowledge and one with lesser knowledge.

What are the kinds of spillovers that are involved between such sectors, and does productivity growth occur through such spillovers? This is not clear. If one looks at U.S. history, it is hard to make the case that agriculture is a "backward industry." The rate of growth of productivity in agriculture in the United States has been quite comparable to that of non-agricultural sectors. Further, it is difficult to trace the sources of that productivity to learning through industry. Hybrid corn, as I learned from Zvi Griliches many years ago, was one of the big factors in increasing agricultural productivity and was certainly something not done by industry. The idea that industry is the progressive sector of the economy has of course taken many earlier forms, including ideas suggesting greater opportunities for obtaining economies of scale or for technological progress. As such the broad idea that there may be efficiency gains from knowledge spillovers between these sectors still holds.

Knowledge is a free good. The biggest cost in its transmission is not in the production or distribution of knowledge, but in its assimilation. This is something that all teachers know. One of the advantages of trade is that it facilitates the spreading of information of technological knowledge. The fact that there is contact—that ideas are flowing—leads to spillover effects, learning, and greater competition. When foreign direct investment pours into China, for example, investing other firms.

While Greenwald and Stiglitz focus on spillovers and trade, most of these problems they consider arise in a closed economy. For example, if it is true that the larger the more progressive sector, then the greater the growth rate, then there is a case for intervention even in a closed economy. Obviously tariffs are not a policy instrument but one could tax diminishing returns industries and subsidize increasing returns industries. This is in fact an older point made by Alfred Marshall. Following from this, even in a world of international trade, would not the subsidy at a domestic level be superior to a tax? This is a lesser important point than the ones I have made before, but the focus on distorting trade flows does not seem so obvious.

There is of course, the historical case to be made for trade protection, since countries which have succeeded have had greater protection. The prime example is the United States, and in fact Alexander Hamilton's early ideas about these matters during the late 18th century were taken up by continental economists like Friedrich List and spread across Europe. Yet protectionism also culminated in the Smoot-Hawley Tariff of 1930, which is widely thought to have been a very destructive policy and one which prolonged and exacerbated the Great Depression.

Having noted this, I think the fundamental concern evinced in the paper, the emphasis on moving the efficient frontier in the long run, is very important. That is the real technological limit to growth and welfare. At the same time the idea that at any moment we are well below the frontier is a truth which is very hard to explain. These kinds of ideas require more discussion.

I want to close by saying that I am grateful for the occasion to comment on this paper.

Afterword: Rethinking Industrial Policy

Robert C. Waggoner Professor of Economics, Harvard University

INDUSTRIAL POLICIES were implemented after World War II in a number of countries, with the purpose of promoting new infant industries and of protecting local traditional activities against competition by products from more advanced foreign countries. Thus, several Latin American countries advocated import substitution policies whereby local industries would more fully benefit from domestic demand. East Asian countries like Korea and Japan, rather than advocate import substitution policies, favored export promotion, which was achieved partly through tariffs and nontariff barriers and partly through maintaining undervalued exchange rates. And in Europe, France engaged in a so-called Colbertist policy of targeted subsidies to industries or to "national champions." For at least two or three decades after World War II, these policies remained fairly noncontroversial, as countries implementing them were growing at relatively fast rates.

However, the slowdown in Latin America as of the 1970s and then in Japan as of the late 1990s contributed to the growing skepticism about the role of industrial policy in the process of development. Increasingly since the early 1980s, industrial policy has raised serious doubts among academics and policy advisers in international financial institutions. In particular, it was criticized for allowing governments to pick winners and losers in a discretionary fashion and, consequently, for increasing the scope for capture of governments by local vested interests. Instead, policy makers and growth and development economists now advocate nontargeted policies aimed at improving the investment climate: the liberalization of product and labor markets, a legal and enforcement framework that protects (private) property rights, and macroeconomic stabilization. This new set of growth recommendations came to be known as the "Washington Consensus," as it was primarily advocated by the IMF, the World Bank, and the U.S. Treasury, all based in Washington, D.C.

The view that more competition, more entry, and more trade liberalization are key to generating more innovation and more growth was not just ideological. It has been supported by a whole set of recent empirical studies.[1] Yet over the past three years, we have seen governments in advanced countries such as Germany, France, and the United States advocate sectoral intervention to fight the recession and foster long-run growth. Are these governments misguided or instead had we gone too far in opposing any form of government intervention targeted at particular firms or sectors, i.e., in opposing any form of industrial policy? In this discussion, I will push the latter view. More specifically, I will point at new arguments in favor of sectoral intervention even in the context of advanced economies where competition and innovation play a central role.

The discussion is organized as follows. Section 2 summarizes the infant-industry argument as it has been clearly stated in particular by Stiglitz, and then it discusses recent empirical work that partly refutes, partly supports this argument. Section 3 develops a first argument in favor of a "new industrial policy" in developed economies, which is based on the idea that innovation activities in a pure laissez-faire economy may go in the wrong direction. Section 4 develops a second argument, which, like the initial infant-industry argument, emphasizes the existence of cross-sectoral learning spillovers, but it proposes a different strategy to test for such spillovers. Section 5 concludes by mentioning two more arguments in favor of a new industrial policy. First, sectoral policy may help foster competition and thereby also innovation. Second, growth and innovation in credit-constrained sectors benefit from countercyclical government support.

Industrial Policy in Catching-Up Countries: The Traditional Infant-Industry Argument

The Argument in a Nutshell

The infant-industry argument, nicely formalized by Greenwald and Stiglitz (2006),[2] can be summarized as follows: consider a local economy which comprises a traditional (agricultural) sector and a nascent (industrial) sector. The industrial sector's new activities involve high costs initially. However, production and the resulting learning by doing reduce these costs over time. Moreover, suppose the existence of knowledge externalities between these new industrial activities and the traditional sector. Then two conclusions immediately obtain in this setting. First, full trade liberalization will make it very costly for domestic industrial sectors to invest in learning by doing: doing so involves producing but not selling in the short run since domestic costs are initially higher than foreign costs. Second, the social benefits from learning by doing are not fully internalized by industrial sectors, since they do not internalize the knowledge externalities they have on the agricultural sector. It is the combination of these two considerations which justifies domestic policies aimed at (temporarily) protecting nascent industries. Such policies may either take the form of targeted subsidies or import restrictions, or they may involve nontargeted policies, for example, maintaining undervalued exchange rates which will benefit the local industry as a whole as long as it does not import too many inputs from abroad.

Criticisms

The main objections to the infant-industry argument have been empirical. Thus, Krueger and Tuncer (1982) saw no systematic tendency for nonprotected firms or industries in Turkey over the 1960s to display higher productivity growth than less-protected industries; moreover, they saw no apparent tendency for a new industrial activity to display higher rates of growth than the overall industry to which it belongs.[3]

However, the most compelling case against the traditional infant-industry argument was recently made by Nunn and Trefler (2007). Nunn and Trefler's argument goes as follows: If we were to believe the above infant-industry argument, then we should see a positive correlation between growth and the extent to which the domestic tariff structure is skill-biased, the idea being that learning by doing on new activities with knowledge spillovers on the rest of the economy should require more skills than other activities. Thus, Nunn and Trefler regress average per capita GDP growth, measured by the log of $(\frac{y_{c_1}}{y_{c_0}})$, where yc_1 (respective to coefficient yc_0) denotes per capita GDP at the end (respective to the beginning of the period), on the extent to which the tariff structure is skill-biased (which in turn is measured by the correlation coefficient between skill intensity and the level of tariffs across sectors). A straight cross-country regression, with region and cohort fixed effects, shows a positive and significant correlation between growth and the skill-bias of the tariff structure.

Thus, at first sight, Nunn and Trefler's regression results seem to confirm the infant-industry argument. However, Nunn and Trefler push the analysis further by regressing, for each sector in each country, per capita growth on both the country-level measure of skill bias of tariffs and a new (industry-level) tariff-skill interaction term. This latter term interacts the tariff for that particular industry with the ratio of skilled over unskilled labor in that same industry. The intriguing result is that the coefficient for this industry-level tariff-skill interaction drops significantly. In other words, the positive coefficient on the aggregate measure of skill-biased tariff found in the previous regression reflects something more than simply the growth effect of protecting more skill-biased industries. Actually, Nunn and Trefler argue that the explanation for the positive coefficient also involves a third variable, namely, the quality of local institutions, which is positively correlated with growth and also with the government's propensity to emphasize skill-intensive sectors.

Industrial Policy in Catching-Up Countries: Industrial Niches

The notion that the existing pattern of specialization may limit the evolution of comparative advantage over time has not received much attention in the growth literature so far. For example, in Romer's (1990) product-variety model, the current set of inputs display the same degree of imperfect substitutability with respect to any new input that might be introduced, and therefore do not make one new input more likely than any other. This property stems directly from the fully symmetric nature of the Dixit-Stiglitz model of product differentiation upon which the Romer model is built. However, an important insight that emerges from the work of Alwyn Young (1991), Lucas (1993), and more recently Hausmann and Klinger (2007) is that successful growth stories involve gradual processes whereby neighboring sectors experiment with new technologies one after the other because experimentation involves learning by doing externalities across sectors.

To illustrate the case for targeted intervention based on the existence of cross-sectoral externalities in the simplest possible way, consider the following toy model. Individuals each live for one period. There are four *potential* sectors in the economy, which we number from 1 to 4, but only one sector, namely, sector 1, is active at date zero. Thus, the economy at date 0 can be represented by the 4-tuple

$$\Omega_0 = (1,0,0,0),$$

where the number 1 (resp. 0) in column i refers to the corresponding sector i being currently active (resp. inactive). At date t, a sector that is active produces at the frontier productivity level $\bar{A}_t = (1+g)^t$. Once activated, a sector automatically remains active forever. Aggregate output at date t is

$$\Upsilon_t = A_t = N_t \bar{A}_t,$$

where N_t is the number of active sectors at date t.

R & D investments activate new sectors, but there is a cost of learning about faraway sectors. Specifically, there is a fixed R & D cost $\gamma(1+g)^t$ of activating a sector in period t, but this is only possible if (a) the sector is adjacent to an already active sector or (b) the R & D cost $\gamma(1+g)^{t-1}$ was also incurred in that sector in the previous period.

Consider first the economy under laissez-faire. Being populated by individuals who live only one period, the economy will never invest in a sector that is not adjacent to a sector already active. At best, a local entrepreneur will find it optimal to activate a sector adjacent to an already active sector. This will be the case whenever $\gamma < \theta$, where θ is the fraction of output that can be appropriated by a private innovator. Note, however, that if $\theta < \gamma$, then private firms will not explore new sectors, even neighboring ones, even though it might be socially optimal to do so.

Coming back to the case where $\gamma < \theta$, in this case the laissez-faire sequence of active sectors will be:

$$\Omega_1 = (1,1,0,0),$$

$$\Omega_2 = (1,1,1,0),$$

$$\Omega_t = (1,1,1,1), t \geq 3.$$

Now consider a social planner. The social planner will invest in sector 2 in period 1, whenever the cost $\gamma(1+g)$ of doing so is less than the net present revenue of activating sector 2, namely,

$$\sum_{t=1}^{\infty} \frac{\bar{A}_t}{(1+r)^t} = \frac{(1+g)}{(r-g)},$$

that is, whenever

$$\gamma < \frac{1}{r-g}.$$

For g sufficiently close to γ or for γ sufficiently small, this inequality is automatically satisfied. In this case, it will also be optimal to invest in sector 3 in period 2, because at that date sector 3 will be adjacent to an already active sector (namely, sector 2).

In addition, whenever γ is sufficiently small, it will be optimal to invest in sector 4 in period 1, because that will allow sector 4 to be activated in period 2, whereas otherwise it can only be activated in period 3. Investing in period 1 instead of period 2 in sector 4 will yield an additional

$$\bar{A}_2 / (1+r)$$

and will cost an additional $\gamma(1+g)$. Thus, if γ is small enough, namely, if

$$\gamma < \frac{(1+g)}{(1+r)},$$

the optimal sequence of active sectors will be:

$$\Omega_1 = (1,1,0,0),$$

$$\Omega_2 = (1,1,1,0),$$

$$\Omega_t = (1,1,1,1), t \geq 3.$$

The laissez-faire equilibrium is suboptimal because people do not invest far enough away from already active sectors. In this example, output will be lower than optimal in period 2 ($3\bar{A}_2$ versus $4\bar{A}_2$) because individuals were not far sighted enough to invest in sector 4 in period 1, because it was too far away from already active sectors.

Thus, this model suggests a role for targeted industrial policy: namely, to overcome the potential underinvestment in new sectors. In particular, if targeted subsidies were to be implemented by a government, we conjecture that such subsidies should be more growth enhancing: (i) if they target sectors that are currently inactive but close "input-wise" to already active sectors, and (ii) if the country experiences low levels of financial development or low labor mobility or low average levels of education. Part (i) implies that the targeted sectors are more likely to benefit from learning-by-doing externalities from already active sectors. Part (ii) makes it less likely that market forces will spontaneously take advantage of these externalities.

The idea that the product space is heterogeneous, with an uneven density of active product lines, and that the current density distribution of active sectors affects the evolution of comparative advantage is taken to the data by Hausmann and Klinger (2006). Hausmann and Klinger measure the relatedness between two product lines by the probability $\varphi_{i,j}$ that, on average, countries export enough of the two goods simultaneously.[4] Next, Hausmann and Klinger define the density around good i in country c as the average relatedness of that product with other products exported by the same country, namely,

$$density_{i,c,t} = \frac{\Sigma_k \phi_{i,k,t} x_{c,k,t}}{\Sigma_k \phi_{i,k,t}},$$

where $x_{c,k,t}$ is the volume of export of product k by country c at time t.

A main finding by Hausmann and Klinger is that the probability of a country exporting product i in year $t+1$ is positively and significantly correlated with the country's density around product i in year t. This in turn provides empirical support to the idea that countries move toward new product lines that are adjacent to existing lines, even though this may be suboptimal, as discussed above.

Two arguments at least can be opposed to targeted interventions of the kind suggested in this section: (a) such policies may serve as a pretext for government favors, particularly if input-output information can be manipulated by politicians or bureaucrats; (b) what guarantees that temporary support to industries will be terminated, especially if the investment turns out to be inefficient? One possible answer to these two objections would be to involve third parties (for example, private partners) which would access input-output information and would also act as cofinanciers.

Industrial Policy in Developed Countries: Redirecting Technical Change

Previous work based on Acemoglu, Aghion, and Zilibotti (2006) argued that the closer a country or sector is to the corresponding world technology frontier, the more growth relies on frontier innovation rather than on imitation. In the above two sections, I discussed instances where industrial policy might help in the catching-up process. In this and the next section, I argue that even in a developed economy already endowed with a full range of sectors and activities, and where frontier innovations are a main driving force of the growth process, there is a case to be made for industrial policy. The main idea in this section is that a laissez-faire economy may sometimes innovate in the wrong direction, i.e., in a direction which may be detrimental to long-run growth. In this case, subsidizing research and production in particular sectors, at least temporarily, can help "redirect" research efforts so as to enhance long-run growth.

More specifically, Acemoglu et al. (2009) develop an endogenous growth model in which a consumption good (or final good) can be produced using a clean or a dirty input. Only the production of dirty inputs harms the environment. The environment in turn affects consumers' utility. Inputs are produced with labor and machines, and innovation can improve the efficiency of production of either type of machines. Innovation results from the work of scientists who can try to improve either the quality of dirty machines or the quality of clean machines. An important assumption is what Acemoglu et al. refer to as the "building on the shoulders of giants" effect, namely, that technological advances in one sector make future advances in that sector more effective.

Innovators direct their efforts to the sector where the expected profits from innovation are the highest. Thus, under laissez-faire, when the dirty technology enjoys an initial installed-base advantage, and given the "building on the shoulders of giants" effect, the innovation machine will work in favor of the dirty technology. The clean technology may never take off unless the government intervenes. What Acemoglu et al. show is that the laissez-faire equilibrium will typically lead to environmental disaster: environmental quality falls below the level at which it can be regenerated, and therefore utility collapses. Where the dirty technology is based on exhaustible resources, this may help to prevent such a disaster, as the dirty technology is eventually priced out of the market. But even in this case, the innovation machine left on its own works suboptimally, favoring the dirty technology for too long.

A critical parameter for the effectiveness of policy intervention is the extent to which the dirty and the clean technology are substitutable. In particular, when the clean and dirty technologies are sufficiently close substitutes, a temporary policy involving both, a tax on dirty input production (e.g., a "carbon tax") and a subsidy to clean research activities will be sufficient to avoid an environmental disaster and thus to guarantee long-run growth sustainability. Indeed, by redirecting technical change toward clean innovation, such a policy will make clean technologies catch up and eventually leapfrog dirty technologies, at which point, by virtue of the "building on the shoulders of giants" effect (but which now plays in the right direction), private firms will spontaneously choose to innovate in clean machines.

Thus, the optimal policy is targeted, i.e., it is directed toward clean production and innovation, but it also relies on a complementarity of roles between the government and the private sector. Delaying such directed intervention not only leads to further deterioration of the environment. In addition, the dirty innovation machine continues to strengthen its lead, making the dirty technologies more productive and widening the productivity gap between dirty and clean technologies

TABLE I
Delaying Action Is Costly

Discount rate (%)	I	1.5
Lost consumption, delay of 10 years (%)	5.99	2.31
Lost consumption, delay of 20 years (%)	8.31	2.36

Source: Calibrations from the AABH (2009) model.

even further. This widened gap in turn requires a longer period for clean technologies to catch up and replace the dirty ones. As this catching-up period is characterized by slower growth, the cost of delaying intervention, in terms of forgone growth, will be higher. In other words, delaying action is costly. This is illustrated in table I.

Not surprisingly, the shorter the delay and the higher the discount rate (i.e., the lower the value put on the future), the lower the cost will be. This is because the gains from delaying intervention are realized at the start in the form of higher consumption, while the loss occurs in the future through more environmental degradation and lower future consumption. Moreover, because there are basically two problems to deal with, namely, the environmental one and the innovation one, using two instruments proves to be better than using one. The optimal policy involves using (i) a carbon tax to deal with the environmental externality and, at the same time, (ii) direct subsidies to clean R & D (or a profit tax on dirty technologies) to deal with the knowledge externality.

Of course, one could always argue that a carbon tax on its own could deal with both the environmental and the knowledge externalities at the same time (discouraging the use of dirty technologies also discourages innovation in dirty technologies). However, relying on the carbon tax alone leads to excessive reduction in consumption in the short run. And because the two-instrument policy reduces the short-run cost in terms of forgone short-run consumption, it reinforces the case for immediate implementation, even for values of the discount rate under which standard models would suggest delaying implementation.

In fact the Acemoglu et al. model allows one to calibrate the cost of using only the carbon tax instead of a combination of a carbon tax and a subsidy to clean R & D. This cost can be expressed as the amount of "lost" consumption in each period expressed as a percentage of the level of consumption which would result from optimal policy, which involves using both types of instrument. Using a discount rate of 1 percent, this cost in terms of lost consumption amounts to 1.33 percent.

An alternative way of showing the higher cost when using only one instrument (i.e., the carbon tax) rather than a combination of carbon pricing and more industrial-policy looking subsidies is to express how high the optimal carbon tax would have to be when used as a singleton relative to its optimal level when used in combination. Simulating this scenario in the Acemoglu et al. model reveals that the carbon tax would have to be about 15 times higher during the first five years and 12 times higher over the following five years. The intuition behind the initial high differential is that the early period in particular is key to inducing the catch-up by clean technologies. By the same token, using only the subsidy instrument, while keeping the carbon-price instrument inactive, would imply that subsidies would have to be on average 115 percent higher in the first ten years compared to their level when used in combination with a carbon tax.

The good news is that government intervention to trigger green innovation and growth (through pricing carbon and subsidizing clean technologies) can be reduced over time. As soon as clean technologies have gained sufficient productivity advantage over dirty technologies, the private innovation machine for these clean technologies can be left on its own to generate even better and more efficient clean technologies. And with cleaner technologies in place, the environmental damage problem, which the carbon tax needs to address, gradually disappears. However, the longer intervention is delayed, the longer intervention will have to be maintained.

In fact, simulations with the Acemoglu et al. model indicate how the carbon tax and the clean innovation subsidy should be set optimally over time. The graphs in Acemoglu et al. show (i) that subsidies for new clean technologies should be granted immediately, but can be quickly reduced as soon as innovation has taken off for these technologies and (ii) that the carbon tax can decrease over time. With the emergence of perfectly clean backstop technologies that have zero emissions, and with the innovation gap between clean and dirty technologies eliminated and the stock of past emissions diminishing, the environmental externality gradually disappears, thus reducing the need for a carbon tax over time.

Industrial Policy, Competition, and the Business Cycle

Industrial policy should not be systematically opposed to competition policy. In particular, in current work with Mathias Dewatripont and Patrick Legros, we argue that targeted subsidies could be used to induce several firms to operate in the same sector, instead of escaping competition through excessive horizontal differentiation. This in turn may enhance innovation for two main reasons. First, it helps maintain a higher equilibrium degree of competition (i.e., by reducing horizontal differentiation), which then induces firms to innovate vertically in order to escape competition. Second, inducing several firms to operate in the same sector favors technological progress because firms operating in the same sector are more likely to benefit from knowledge spillovers or communication among them. Of course, a lot depends upon the design of industrial policy. Such policy should target sectors, not particular firms (or "national champions"). And appropriate exit mechanisms should be put in place, for example, through cofinancing arrangements between the public and the private sector, so that public funding would be eventually withdrawn from sectors where targeted intervention proves to be unprofitable ex post and therefore no longer attractive to private investors.

This in turn suggests new empirical studies in which productivity growth, patenting, or other measures of innovativeness and entrepreneurship would be regressed over some measures of sectoral intervention interacted with the degree of competition in the sector, and also with the extent to which intervention involves a partnership between the public and private sector or more generally allows for exit mechanisms.

Finally, the recent crisis suggests an additional argument in favor of government support to firms and sectors, which is related to the business cycle. In particularly, recent work by Aghion, Hemous, and Kharroubi (2009) uses a sample of forty-five industries across seventeen OECD countries over the period 1980–2005 to show that growth in industrial sectors that are more dependent upon external finance (using Rajan and Zingales's [1998] methodology) benefits more from more countercyclical fiscal policies, i.e., from policies that involve larger deficits in recessions (compensated by bigger surpluses during booms). Moreover, it is more the expenditure side than the revenue side of governments' budgets whose countercyclicality matters more for growth in such sectors. A natural issue, then, is whether government support should be targeted to particular sectors, those that suffer most from credit constraints, or whether it should remain untargeted. There also, the issue of exit is paramount: Countercyclicality requires that government subsidies be reduced or phased out when the economy comes out of the recession.

Whether these latter arguments are in some cases stronger than the powerful political economy counterargument(s) needs to be assessed depending upon characteristics of the country or the sector and also with regard to the economy's location in the business cycle. In any case, the general recommendation made by the Commission on Growth and Development (2008) with regard to industrial policy strikes us as stemming from common sense: namely, experiment, and then make sure you can stop the intervention if it turns out not to be efficient.

Notes

Introduction

1. Or, more accurately, if there was innovation, it was exogenous, not affected by what market participants did.

2. There are, of course, other exceptions. For instance, if risk markets are incomplete, free trade can lead to a Pareto inferior equilibrium; free trade increases risk, inducing investment away from high-risk/high-return sectors (see Newbery and Stiglitz 1982).

3. Note that this critique of the infant-industry argument is distinct from the usual criticisms based on political economy—that there is "capture" by vested interests. We deal with these issues below.

1. The Learning Revolution

1. How they make those choices will, of course, have profound effects on *measured* growth, since increasing leisure does not show up in conventionally measured GDP (see Stiglitz, Sen, and Fitoussi 2010).

2. This point was emphasized by Keynes (1930). See Stiglitz (2008d) as well as other chapters in Pecchi and Piga (2008).

3. The difference was referred to as the Solow residual. While technical change accounted for *most* of the residual, there were other factors, including the reallocation of labor from low productivity sectors to high productivity sectors (see Denison 1962).

4. Griliches and Jorgenson's work (1966, 1967), which entailed using alternative calculations of the value of capital, suggested a much smaller role for technical progress. Further problems were identified in the quantification of labor input, as economists attempted to assess the role of human capital

in economic growth (Klenow and Rodríguez-Clare 1997; de la Fuente and Doménech 2006).

5. There was a large literature describing how new technologies were "embodied" in capital goods. See, e.g., Solow (1962b) and the discussion and references cited in Stiglitz and Uzawa (1969).

6. For any doubters: Engage in a thought experiment in which primitive farmers accumulated more hoes, or even built more irrigation canals. If that primitive accumulation was *all* that had occurred during the past 200 years, standards of living would be incommensurately lower than they are today.

7. As Solow (1956) pointed out, an increase in the savings rate simply leads to an increase in per capita income, not to a (permanently) higher rate of growth. See the further discussion in the next chapter.

8. See Stiglitz (1998c), which describes development as a "transformation" into a society which recognizes that change is possible, and that learns how to effect such changes.

9. This work includes that of Kaldor (1957, 1961); Kaldor and Mirrlees (1962); Uzawa (1965); Nordhaus (1969a, 1969b); Atkinson and Stiglitz (1969); Inada (1963); and Shell (1967) and the papers contained in that volume. Not only did this early research address the question of the rate of technological progress, but also the direction (see Kennedy 1964; Samuelson 1965; Fellner 1961; Drandakis and Phelps 1966; Ahmad 1966; and others).

Of course, economic historians have long sought to explain the rate and direction of innovation (see, e.g., David 1975; and Salter 1966). Hicks (1932) made even earlier contributions to this field. More recent work building on these traditions includes Stiglitz (2006b).

A major stumbling block in the development of endogenous growth theory was that technological progress introduced a natural nonconvexity into the production function: if the economy was characterized by constant returns to scale in conventional factors, then, if technological progress were made endogenous, it would exhibit increasing returns in all factors. That is, if $Q = F(K, AL)$ is homogenous of degree one in K and L, where Q is output, A is the state of technology (technological progress is pure labor augmenting), K is capital, and L is labor, and if $A = A(L_R, K_R)$ describes the level of technology as a function of resources (capital and labor) devoted to research, then Q exhibits increasing returns overall. This posed problems both for normative (optimization) and descriptive models. Only under special values of the parameters of special formulations of the production function would a steady state exist. One could easily construct models that "worked," e.g., by assuming that $d(\ln A)/dt = \phi(L_R e^{-nt})$ where n is the rate of growth of population. Then, in a steady state with a fixed fraction of income saved, s, and with a fixed fraction of the labor force γ allocated to research, $d(\ln A)/dt = \phi(\gamma)$, and $d(\ln Q)/dt =$

$n + \phi(\gamma)$. But in the more general case, with say a fixed proportion of the labor force allocated to research, it is easy to see that in the limit $d(\ln A)/dt$ may either rise to some upper bound or fall to some lower bound. One could, alternatively, assume that there was a fixed factor, say land. In the absence of technological change, if the elasticity of substitution was less than unity, with increasing population, growth in income per capita would eventually halt. Technological change could offset the effects, say if it were "land" augmenting. But again it seemed a borderline case, where if a fixed proportion of the labor supply (or capital, or output) were allocated to land augmenting technological progress and similarly for labor augmenting progress, somehow the pace of innovation just offset the effects of the diminishing land per capita.

There was a second problem, discussed below: The nonconvexities naturally led to imperfections of competition.

10. This work includes the early work of Dasgupta and Stiglitz (1980a, 1980b) trying to endogenize both market structure and the rate of technological progress, subjecting some of Schumpeter's conjectures to more rigorous analysis. Other work includes that of Gilbert and Newbery (1982). Romer's (1986, 1990) work provided inspiration for much of the later work in this area. See Aghion and Howitt (1998) and Romer (1994) for surveys.

11. Arrow's 1962 papers (1962a, 1962b) are the classic references. Key properties of knowledge and its production (knowledge as a public good, nonconvexities associated with the production of knowledge, inherent capital market and risk market imperfections) are discussed at length below, with further references. See, in particular, Stiglitz (1987b; based on a 1978 lecture).

12. We do not, unfortunately, use the framework that we develop in this book to provide answers to two key historical questions: What happened to suddenly change the world, to initiate the process of becoming a "learning society"? And why did this process begin where it did and when it did? A few reflections on these questions are contained in later chapters.

13. The concept of "learning to learn" is developed by Stiglitz (1987a).

14. Gordon "suggests that it is useful to think of the innovative process as a series of discrete inventions followed by incremental improvements which ultimately tap the full potential of the initial invention" (2012, 2).

15. This idea gave rise to a vast literature on "embodied technological progress," closely related to work on "vintage capital," referred to earlier in note 5. The dynamics of economies with "putty clay" (where technology is fixed, once the machine is made) are markedly different from those of the "putty-putty" models that dominate in modern macroeconomics (see Solow 1959; Solow et al. 1966; Cass and Stiglitz 1969).

16. That is, taking into account the costs of creating markets or obtaining information (Greenwald and Stiglitz 1986, 1988).

17. Although Arrow did not frame the market failure in this way, it was clear from his analysis that knowledge was a public good, in the sense that Samuelson had defined public goods a few years earlier (Samuelson 1954). See the discussion below.

18. Of course, the principles are often contested, and the political influence of banks has, so far, been successful in resisting the adoption of many of the regulations around which there is broad consensus, at least among economists not associated with the financial sector.

19. Because industrial policies were often looked upon disparagingly in the years in which neoliberal economic doctrines predominated, some political leaders have looked for other terms to describe such policies, such as "proactive business policies." Alternatively, they have focused on particular categories of such policies (which typically meet with greater approval), such as export promoting policies. We will stick with the more conventional nomenclature.

20. This perspective was reflected in *Knowledge for Development*, the first World Bank Development Report done during Stiglitz's tenure as chief economist of the World Bank (World Bank 1999; see also Stiglitz 1998c, 1999b).

21. Most clearly articulated by Samuelson (1948).

22. For a more general discussion of leapfrogging (in the context of patent races), see Fudenberg et al. (1983).

2. On the Importance of Learning

1. Later discussion will explain why we also do not believe that these differences can be explained by the usual kinds of static inefficiencies, e.g., associated with distorted incentives.

2. To be sure, there may be problems of identification—when changes in capital are required to put into place changes in technology.

3. We recognize that the magnitude and sources of China's increase in productivity have been the subject of some controversy. For a contrary view, see Young (2003), who estimates productivity growth of only 1.4 percent for the nonagriculture sector from 1978 to 1998. There are many pieces of evidence collaborating the rapid increase in standards of living and output, e.g., trade statistics, and we suggest below why studies suggesting that total factor productivity growth was low are unconvincing.

4. Studies that suggest that total factor productivity growth has been low typically ignore the lag structure involved in human capita (see, e.g., Fleisher,

Li, and Zhao 2010). Moreover, many of these studies simply assume that the factor shares represent competitive returns; in the East Asian countries (and especially China), there is a presumption that that is not the case.

It is hard to reconcile a real return to investment in excess of 10 percent (or even 5 percent) with the patterns of investment, e.g., heavy investment in low-return infrastructure, or investments in U.S. government bonds, yielding real returns that are low or even negative (though the social returns to reserves may be somewhat higher, especially in the early years, when reserves were smaller; chapter 11 presents an alternative explanation for the accumulation of reserves). Studies that suggest low rates of factor productivity growth implicitly are assuming high rates of return to investment (or that is an implicit implication of their econometric analysis).

5. As we emphasize in Chapter 3, incentives are relevant not just for investment and labor supply, but also for learning.

6. For a recent discussion, see Zhu (2012), who argues that productivity growth has been central to economic growth since 1978. As Zhu notes, China's capital-output ratio has grown little since 1978. While in the initial period of "reform"—1978 to 1988—productivity growth came from agriculture, but between 1978 and 2007, non-state-sector "productivity growth contributed 2.27 percentage points per year to aggregate productivity growth" (p. 119). As we emphasize later in this chapter, improvements in allocative efficiency result in a one-time gain in productivity, not the persistent improvements that were observed, say, in China. (By contrast, Zhu argues, "Overall, gradual and persistent institutional change and policy reforms that have reduced distortions and improved economic incentives are the main reasons for the productivity growth" [p. 104].)

7. Though some studies do show high levels of TFP (total factor productivity growth) for the manufacturing sector in Eastern European countries, the small size of these sectors meant that there was relatively little impact on aggregate productivity. Brandt et al. (2012) find for 1998 to 2007, (p. 340) "firm-level TFP growth of manufacturing firms averaging 2.85 percent for a gross output production function and 7.96 percent for a value added production function."

8. In some countries, like the Czech Republic, multinationals did successfully bring in best practices. The highly educated labor force facilitated the requisite learning. In several of the seemingly successful countries of Eastern and Central Europe, the 2008 crisis made it evident that at least a significant part of this was related to a real estate boom/bubble.

9. Persistent differences across regions in many countries (such as Italy) are evidence of the deficiencies in the standard explanations focusing on artificial barriers to the movement of goods, services, or factors.

10. See, e.g., Foster, Haltiwanger, and Krizan 2001 for a survey. Hsieh and Klenow (2009) find very large gaps in the marginal products of capital and labor across plants within India and China.

11. This analysis does not explain the sources of the differences in learning ability. For example, is it due to differences in management/culture or differences in investments in learning?

12. The unemployment rate in the United Kingdom soared from 4.7 percent in 1979 to 11.2 percent in 1986 (OECD 2011), even as industry production, for instance, increased by nearly 5 percent over the same period (after recovering from an initial drop in the beginning of the decade). (World Bank data accessed through Google Public Data Explorer, GDO production, constant 2000 U.S.$, disaggregated by sector, http://www.google.com/publicdata/directory, accessed February 26, 2013).

13. One alternatively might have argued that the strike provided greater incentives for efficiency. But if that were the major explanation, why hadn't management adopted incentive structures to encourage these greater efficiencies, which would have saved enormous amounts of labor? The savings would have provided more than adequate compensation for the additional effort. Moreover, this and similar episodes exhibit hysteresis effects: once the organization has learned how to be more productive, productivity remains at relatively high levels even after the exigency which gave rise to the productivity rise is resolved.

14. A single episode of a productivity increase might be attributable to the removal of a static inefficiency; repeated increases should be seen much more as evidence of episodic learning—including possibly learning about how to remove certain static inefficiencies.

There are often periods of negative productivity change. Such periods reinforce the conclusion that much of the action in productivity occurs well *inside* the production possibilities curve.

15. Interestingly, some of the learning involved learning from foreign firms, e.g., about quality circles and just-in-time production (see, e.g., Nakamura, Sakakibara, and Schroeder 1998).

16. Total investment in the United States held steady at between 18.6 percent and 20.9 percent between 1995 and 2001, beginning at 18.6 percent and ending the period at 19.3 percent From 1981 to 1994 it ranged from 17.1 percent in 1991 to 22.3 percent in 1984, tending to decrease over the period (see the World Economic Outlook database of the International Monetary Fund, available at http://www.imf.org/external/pubs/ft/weo/2012/02/weodata/index.aspx, accessed February 26, 2012). Gross expenditures on R & D during the same period increased slightly from 2.5 percent to 2.7 percent; from 1981 to 1994 it ranged from 2.3 percent to 2.8 percent (see the indicators of the National

Science Board, available as table 4-19 at http://www.nsf.gov/statistics/seind12/c4/c4s8.htm#top, accessed February 26, 2013).

17. Some of the learning was related to computerization; some of the learning was learning how to exploit differences in costs between, say, the United States and China by constructing a global supply chain.

18. With monopolies in the consumer goods industries, the economy still operates along the production possibilities curve, but not at the point along that curve which maximizes societal welfare. With monopolies or imperfections in competition in inputs, however, the economy will not operate along the production possibilities curve.

19. The distinction is really artificial, once we take a broader account of production and value production correctly. That is, we need to take into account not only the good things that firms produce (steel) but the bad things (pollution) that are a byproduct of the good things that they produce. Once we do that, claims that controlling pollution may be good for consumers but bad for GDP make little sense. See the International Commission on the Measurement of Economic Performance and Social Progress (Stiglitz, Sen, and Fitoussi 2010).

20. We do not explore here those distortions or their interactions with learning and productivity growth. Our 2003 book lays out our interpretation of these macroeconomic disturbances. In Greenwald, Salinger, and Stiglitz (1990), we lay out the links between productivity growth and the business cycle (see also Stiglitz 1994c, 2006b; Greenwald, Levinson, and Stiglitz 1993).

21. With learning externalities (a major focus of this book), if learning is a function of investment, then individual decisions concerning learning will systematically result in too little investment.

22. Again, this was a major point made by the International Commission on the Measurement of Economic Performance and Social Progress (see Stiglitz, Sen, and Fitoussi 2010). There is now a large movement attempting to find and employ better metrics of economic performance and social progress.

23. For a developing country, facing a constantly moving frontier, there is a huge "one-time" gain in reducing the gap with the frontier, a gain which is an order of magnitude greater than the one-time gain from eliminating allocative inefficiencies. Once the gap is narrowed (or even better, eliminated), then productivity can only increase at the rate at which the frontier moves out.

24. We have noted that some of the disparities between what the economy or firm could produce and what it does can be related to distortions—allocative inefficiencies—within firms, but eliminating these inefficiencies can provide a one-time gain in productivity but not the kind of sustained increases in productivity with which we are concerned.

25. This formulation assumes that there are no learning spillovers across the firms that are at the frontier (or that there is a single firm on the frontier).

26. More generally, the nonconvexities associated with the production and acquisition of knowledge imply that the profit functions may not be single-peaked. Even if firms started with the same knowledge base, there might be no equilibrium in which all acquired knowledge grows at the same pace. The only equilibrium may entail some firms saving on investment in R & D and "poaching" off the knowledge acquired by others. The present discounted value profits for the two strategies might be the same. Later chapters will show that even if there exists a symmetric equilibrium, it is unstable. Chapter 11 develops an analogous model where some countries lag behind others in equilibrium.

3. A Learning Economy

1. In particular, beginning with the work of Stiglitz (1975a, 1975b), Rothschild and Stiglitz (1976), Akerlof (1970), and Spence (1973).

2. Hayek (1945) called attention to the problem of dispersed information — explaining it was precisely because information was so dispersed that central planning could never work. But somewhat inconsistently, he believed that the price system provided an efficient way of aggregating and transmitting information. As Stiglitz (1994c) has argued, if that were the case, then market socialism would have worked. Hayek never formalized his ideas. Later Chicago economists put forward the efficient markets hypothesis, but they too never created formal models to see whether markets efficiently aggregated and transmitted information. Grossman and Stiglitz (1976, 1980) showed that, in fact, they did not. The crisis of 2008 seems to have settled in most people's minds any lingering doubts about the efficient markets hypothesis.

3. Though, of course, there were other reasons for the failure of our regulatory system, e.g., related to special-interest politics.

4. The concept of learning to learn was developed in Stiglitz (1987a).

5. In 1977 Paul MacCready won the £50,000 Kremer prize offered by the Royal Aeronautical Society for a human-powered airplane with his Gossamer Condor (see http://aerosociety.com/About-Us/specgroups/Human-Powered/Kremer).

6. See Kanbur (1979) and Kihlstrom and Laffont (1979) for the canonical presentation of entrepreneurship in the setting of occupational choice. Emran and Stiglitz (2009) explain why competitive markets may do a bad job learning about who are good entrepreneurs.

7. To be sure, many developed countries showed in the 2008 crisis that they too had much to learn about risk management.

8. Supporting evidence includes Asher (1956) and Alchian (1963) on airframe production, Zimmerman (1982) on nuclear power technologies, Lieberman (1984) on production and investment in chemical process industries, and

Hollander (1965) on R & D. More recent studies include those focusing on learning by management, in rayon, in semiconductors, and in fuel-cell technology. See, e.g., Walters and Holling (1990); Jarmin (1994); Dick (1991), Gruber (1998); Argote, Beckman, and Epple (1990); Argote and Epple (1990); Barrios and Strobl (2004); and Schwoon (2008). Thompson (2010) provides a recent survey.

9. Arrow's work also gave rise to an extensive theoretical literature. See, in particular, Spence (1981); Fudenberg and Tirole (1982); Jovanovic and Lach (1989); Malerba (1992); Lieberman (1987); Leahy and Neary (1999); Ghemawat and Spence(1985); Young (1991, 1993); and Dasgupta and Stiglitz (1988a). As we note in chapter 5, some of these papers assume market structures that could not plausibly survive in the long run.

10. Warren Buffett, in his 2001 chairman's letter to Berkshire Hathaway investors, available at http://www.berkshirehathaway.com/2001ar/2001letter.html.

11. By the same token, societies (individuals) can develop capacities for learning how to use their leisure well, or they can enhance their capacities to enjoy consumption goods. (This can be thought of as improving individuals' capacities to translate inputs of time and goods into "enjoyment.") Thus, learning also can have large effects on consumption behavior (see Stiglitz 2008d).

12. Later in this chapter and in chapter 16, we will discuss societal characteristics that may facilitate learning and learning to learn.

13. See, in particular, the appendix to chapter 4.

14. An interesting aspect of a failure to adapt is that the school year in many countries is still related to the agricultural calendar—decades after that sector's decline to but a few percent of the labor force.

15. While we emphasize in this book technological knowledge, which enhances the ability to transform inputs into outputs, at every level there are other forms of "learning," e.g., changes in institutions or changes in beliefs, say about the way the economy or society functions. As we explain later, such changes in beliefs may not be based on an accurate analysis of the world and may in fact be counterproductive in terms of creating a learning society (see, e.g., Hoff and Stiglitz 2010, 2011; and the papers cited there).

16. Famously, Google has had a policy of allowing employees to dedicate 20 percent of their workweek to pursuing independent projects.

17. There is a small, but important, literature on an economy's innovation system (Nelson 2004, 1993; Freeman, 1987; Lundvall, 2010). There is also some writing on the "creative economy" (e.g., Florida 2002). Closer to what we have in mind is the work on, for example, agglomeration externalities. Moretti (2011), in his survey, groups the sources of agglomeration externalities in local markets into three broad bins: thick labor markets, thick markets for intermediate inputs, and knowledge spillovers. We might think of the latter as

(in our vocabulary) "learning spillovers." Moretti provides references for the current state of knowledge about learning.

18. Earlier, we noted another aspect of learning—learning the comparative advantages (skills) of different individuals. This is a central function of educational systems and is referred to as "education as a screening device." Because of marked differences between social and private return to such screening, market allocation of resources to such screening are not efficient (see Stiglitz 1975b, 2009).

19. There are other differences between young and old that may affect learning behavior. The major asset of the young is their human capital, and there is considerable uncertainty about the value of their human capital. One rational response (but not the only possible response) to this uncertainty is to increase investment in learning.

20. The new learning may, in fact, make the knowledge of those who are older obsolete. While, in the context of the standard competitive paradigm, individuals take the value of assets (including human capital) as given, in the small-scale microeconomics of the workplace, an increase in knowledge (learning) by one party can affect the value of human capital of others.

21. It is worth noting that similar considerations may have played an important role in explaining some of the differences in the transition from Communism to the market between, say, Russia on the one hand and Poland on the other. Russia had large, centralized firms, and these were, for the most part, retained as part of the transition. These firms were dominated by older managers. In contrast, Poland had more medium-sized firms and divided more of its large firms up in the process of the transition, providing a greater role for younger managers (see, e.g., Stiglitz 2002a, 2000c; Ellerman and Stiglitz 2000, 2001).

22. Letter from Isaac Newton to Robert Hooke, February 5, 1676.

23. See, e.g., the discussion in Henry and Stiglitz (2010). The far-reaching America Invents Act of 2011, which came into force in March 2013, has significantly deemphasized the need for disclosure in order to enforce patents. The law and related documents may be viewed at http://judiciary.house.gov/issues/issues_patentreformact2011.html (accessed on January 8, 2013).

24. Moreover, as we noted before, the patent system has encouraged a culture of secrecy, and some worry that the intrusion of IPR into the academic setting, through the Bayh-Dole Act, has had similar effects in universities, undermining the traditional academic norm of openness.

25. The General Assembly of WIPO adopted the Brazilian and Argentinean proposal for a developmentally oriented intellectual property regime on October 4, 2004.

26. And again, there is a worry that intellectual property creates incentives that undermine this traditional model.

27. Moreover, transportation systems are often centered around national hubs. It is easier to move within a country. Institutions and institutional knowledge are also likely to be local.

28. We again note that not all ideas are actually conducive to learning. As we argue extensively in this book, Washington Consensus policies which spread through globalization may have impeded learning.

29. This has provided one of the rationales for why advocates of trade liberalization, such as Grossman and Helpman (1991), suggest that enhanced trade will lead to more learning. As we explain later, there may be other, more than offsetting, effects.

30. But again, the effects can be ambiguous, as individuals are able to create on the Internet communities of like-minded people, reducing the exposure to new ideas (see Sunstein 2001).

31. The ideas in this paragraph are developed more extensively in Stiglitz (1998c). Chapter 16 (based on Hoff and Stiglitz 2010, 2011) elaborates on the role of cognitive frames and how they are shaped.

32. There were, of course, both technological and institutional changes, but they occurred very slowly. There were slow changes in farming technologies that evolved over time. The new world provided new crops, the use of which spread gradually over the entire world. In their time, feudalism and its end, and slavery and its end, represented important institutional changes. The enclosure movement was another institutional change with profound consequences. Many of the changes in technology and institutions were precipitated by exogenous events, such as the Black Plague (see, e.g., Ruttan and Hayami 1984).

Clearly, the Enlightenment helped create the cognitive mindsets that were conducive to innovation and change. Joel Mokyr (2009) suggests that the reason the Industrial Revolution began in England, rather than somewhere else in Europe, has a lot to do with social mindsets, e.g., the belief in the possibility of progress and social norms of honest dealing among businessmen.

33. This is, of course, a simplification. Conniff (2011) writes that this image of Luddites was due to particularly skillful branding, and that in reality the Luddites were not against machines, but "confined their attacks to manufacturers who used machines in what they called 'a fraudulent and deceitful manner' to get around standard labor practices."

34. According to a recent Pew Poll, a third of Americans do not believe there is solid evidence the earth is warming, and nearly 60 percent do not think that warming is mostly because of human activity (Pew Research, 2012, "More Say There Is Solid Evidence of Global Warming," October 15, http://www.people-press.org/2012/10/15/more-say-there-is-solid-evidence-of-global-warming/, accessed February 26, 2013). And according to a Gallup poll, nearly 50 percent of Americans do not believe in human evolution (http://www.gallup.com/poll/155003/hold-creationist-view-human-origins.aspx,

accessed February 26, 2013). If it is difficult to change people's beliefs about matters on which there is such overwhelming scientific evidence, it should be obvious that beliefs about our social and economic system may persist, even in the face of considerable evidence to the contrary. (Beliefs about markets being efficient and stable provide but one instance. While there was a wealth of theory, empirical evidence, and historical experiences suggesting otherwise before the 2008 crisis, it is remarkable how that crisis left the beliefs of so many adherents of "market fundamentalism" essentially unshaken.)

35. The ideas in this and the following paragraphs represent joint work with Karla Hoff and are elaborated in Hoff and Stiglitz (2010, 2011).

36. But that doesn't fully explain why these ideas are adopted by some individuals and groups and rejected by others. Chapter 16 provides a partial explanation.

37. While there are some immediate and important policy implications of these observations, we are not able to pursue them further in this book.

38. These ideas are developed more extensively in Stiglitz (1995b) and Sah and Stiglitz (1987a, 1987b).

39. They are also examples of ideas that are hard to protect with patents, though in some cases, America's business-process patents attempt to do so.

40. We do not comment here on whether their empirical approach really does capture fully the set of related capabilities. Since their work (see also Hidalgo and Hausmann 2009), alternative approaches to characterizing the product space have been explored (see, e.g., Jarvis 2013; Pietronero, Cristelli, and Tacchella 2013). The effects of an improvement in one sector on other sectors depends not just on the similarity of those sectors, but on the institutional arrangements, e.g., providing scope for exploiting linkages. Thus, the fact that natural resource sectors have traditionally not been closely linked to other sectors may be partly a result of the absence of effective industrial policies and the exploitive relationships often evidenced in that sector.

41. See chapters 4 and 12 for further discussions of why geography matters.

42. As the previous paragraph explained, even the notion of the production function is questionable, because without further research and development, we simply may not be able to produce with technologies markedly different from those currently in use. But putting that qualification aside, the standard formulations have $Q = F(\mu K, \lambda L)$, where Q is output, K is capital input, L is labor input, μ is the level of capital-augmente technological progress, and λ is the level of labor-augmenting progress, assuming that, in effect, all technologies are affected in a similar way. If labor is more productive in a capital-intensive technology, it is similarly more productive in a labor-intensive technology.

43. In chapter 6, we develop a theory of endogenous technological progress, including an analysis of the factor bias of technical change. I can be shown that, under plausible conditions, the economy evolves toward a steady state

in which the output capital ratio is equal to the rate of growth divided by the savings rate.

44. With perfect knowledge and in the absence of learning spillovers, a defender of the efficiency of the market economy might argue that the initial situation could not have been an equilibrium: Firms should have realized that would they shift to the capital-intensive technology there would have been more learning, from which they would have benefited. But knowledge of the learning benefits associated with alternative technologies is at best limited, and hence undertaking the capital-intensive strategy would have been risky—even if firms were sufficiently forward looking. Moreover, if learning spillovers are important (as we argue that they are), then the economy may be trapped in the low-learning equilibrium even without risk aversion. Moreover, if future benefits are discounted enough, the benefit of shifting to the high-learning technology may appear to be less than the costs; it is "optimal" to stay in the low-learning technology.

45. Of course, with modern globalization, global capital producing firms in the developed countries may have an incentive to develop these more labor-intensive technologies. But it is natural that they have developed capacities for research/learning of a particular kind—that which saves labor, at the expense of more capital.

46. This section draws heavily upon Hoff and Stiglitz (2010, 2011).

47. In contrast, field experiments have become, for example, a bigger part of the practice and study of development economics and increasingly a part of the learning strategies of some big businesses.

48. There is now a large literature in behavioral economics (with origins in psychology) based on these ideas, including the role of framing and biases in perceptions (see Ariely 2008; Thaler and Sunstein 2008; Kahneman 2011).

49. See Kindleberger and Aliber (2005). The most recent example is, of course, the real estate bubble that led to the Great Recession of 2008. As Stiglitz (2010b) explains, it is hard to reconcile behavior observed there with any notion of rationality (see also Holt 2009).

50. These ideas will be discussed further briefly in chapter 16 See also Hoff and Stiglitz (2010).

51. It is only, however, one determinant of learning, as evidenced by beliefs in evolution. While there is a correlation between beliefs in evolution and education and income, the United States stands out as a country with beliefs in evolution that correspond to those of far poorer and less-educated societies. For example, a survey by the British Council and the market research company Ipsos MORI reports that about 33 percent of Americans "agree the scientific evidence for evolution exists." This is a lower percentage than Argentina, China, India, Mexico, or Russia. See "God or Darwin? The World in Evolution Beliefs," *Guardian*, July 1, 2009, http://www.guardian.co.uk/news/datablog/2009/jul/01/evolution.

52. Bénabou (2008b) and Bénabou and Tirole (2006) see individuals as having the ability to choose their preferences (beliefs) so as to maximize their (meta-) utility. Our emphasis, in contrast, is on the social construction of preferences—where "outside" influences play a central role. The individual does not choose their preferences (beliefs) in isolation.

53. Some of what we are saying here can be expressed in terms of standard Bayesian inference: individuals often hold strong prior beliefs, so strong that new information has little impact on posteriors. The literature on confirmatory bias suggests that priors may be held with far greater conviction than can be justified.

54. This is what Hoff and Stiglitz (2010) refer to as "uber-ideologies." Gramsci argued that "The claim presented as an essential postulate of historical materialism, that every fluctuation of politics and ideology can be presented and expounded as an immediate expression of the [economic] structure, must be contested in theory as primitive infantilism . . ." (1971: 407).

55. As Hoff and Stiglitz (2011) note, prior to the seventeenth century, while slavery existed, it was not associated with race. Indeed, they suggest that the construct of race and racial differentiation may have evolved in part to reconcile Enlightenment beliefs in the equality of all men with the economic interests in slavery.

56. In this sense, our analysis is similar to that of Akerlof and Kranton (2010), who focus on identity and how it can be shaped.

57. As we emphasize below, the rewards do not have to be pecuniary. Even when societies pay lip service to learning, they often punish those who question received authority.

58. These beliefs are held in spite of overwhelming evidence to the contrary. For instance, the bipartisan National Commission on the Causes of the Financial and Economic Crisis in the United States, 2011, agreed, with one dissent, that government efforts to encourage housing among the poor were not responsible for the crisis. Stiglitz (2010b) presents further evidence: Not even the default rates on CRA lending (lending directed at poor communities) was higher than that on other lending. Another example is provided by the electricity shortages that developed in the early years of this century in California. Believers in free markets were quick to blame government regulations, particularly those associated with the environment. The real culprit, it turned out, was Enron's manipulation of the electricity market. When the market was re-regualated to prevent such manipulation, the shortage miraculously disappeared.

59. Many years ago, Tibor Scitovsky (see, e.g., Scitovsky 1986) described the drivers of human behavior—including the quest for excitement. See also Bénabou and Tirole (2003).

60. See, in particular, the important work by Hoff (1997). Later work has elaborated on her ideas (see, e.g., Hausmann and Rodrik 2003). Experiments are an important part of the learning strategies of some firms. Hal Varian (2011), chief economist at Google, reports in a letter to the *Economist*, "Last year at Google the search team ran about 6,000 experiments and implemented around 500 improvements based on those experiments. The ad side of the business had about the same number of experiments and changes. Any time you use Google, you are in many treatment and control groups. The learning from those experiments is fed back into production and the system continuously improves."

61. For an elaboration of this argument, see Emran and Stiglitz (2009).

62. Interestingly, the price system typically doesn't even work in the context of firms interacting with each other, simply because it is too difficult to value each individual patent. Often firms create patent pools, agreements to allow each other to make use of certain patents. (Such patent pools can often serve as effective barriers to entry, making it more difficult for firms that are not part of the agreement to enter the market.)

63. The parties to the contract obviously view these provisions in this way. But contract provisions which may be in the private interests of the contracting parties may not be socially desirable (see Greenwald and Stiglitz 1986).

64. However, the analysis below will show that markets can be so inefficient in allocating resources that sometimes growth can be increased even without a sacrifice in the short run.

65. That is, choosing a point on the production possibilities schedule where indifference curves are not tangent.

66. We note again, though, that our approach has questioned the relevance of the standard formulation of the production possibilities curve.

67. Some individuals may have an ability to learn quite generally, while others have developed more focused capacities. A well-structured learning society would recognize these differences.

68. The analysis of this section is based on Sah and Stiglitz (1989b) and Stiglitz (1995a).

69. There can be competitive effects going the other way, which we ignore for ease of exposition.

70. It should be obvious, given our emphasis throughout the book on externalities, that we do not believe that unfettered markets lead to efficient (let alone "fair") outcomes. It is even possible that welfare in the low-innovation economy might be higher than in the high-innovation equilibrium.

71. Sah and Stiglitz (1989b) provide a more elaborate model showing the existence of multiple equilibria.

4. Creating a Learning Firm and a Learning Environment

1. That is, it is hard to write good incentive-compatible innovation contracts. For instance, when a firm fails to produce a promised innovation, it is difficult to establish whether it was because of lack of effort or because of the intrinsic difficulty of the task. Cost-plus contracts, or other contracts designed to share the risk of the unknown costs required to make an innovation, have their own problems (see, e.g., Nalebuff and Stiglitz 1983a).

2. An alleged major disadvantage of firms is that transactions within firms are typically not mediated by prices, with all of the benefits that accrue from the use of a price system. But if the benefits of using prices exceeded the costs, firms presumably could use prices to guide internal resource allocations, and some enterprises do so, at least to some extent..

3. For instance, Sah and Stiglitz (1985, 1986) show that the hierarchical decision making which often characterizes large corporations leads to a greater likelihood of rejecting good projects but a smaller likelihood of accepting bad projects. But they go on to show how committees, "polyarchies," and more complex decision-making structures (e.g., polyarchies of hierarchies) can lead to improved decision making with fewer bad projects accepted and more good projects (see Sah and Stiglitz 1988a, 1988b). Large organizations may similarly encounter problems in choosing successor management teams. Sah and Stiglitz (1991) analyze the problem and show how it may be addressed.

4. For a discussion of convergence in productivity across industrial firms, see Rodrik 2013. His results stand in contrast to those presented in chapter 2.

5. As we noted earlier, it is these learning benefits that help explain an economy's industrial structure—the boundaries of what goes on inside firms. In general, the diseconomies of scale and scope (related, for instance, to oversight) are greater in agriculture than in industry. In the case of modern high-tech agriculture, there are increased benefits of learning, and that will affect the optimal size of establishments.

6. For a brief discussion of Xerox, see Wessel (2012).

7. The importance of these factors has clear implications for the conduct of macroeconomic policy, which we discuss later in this book.

8. This is consistent with earlier results on the inefficiency of competitive markets with labor mobility (see Greenwald and Stiglitz 1988; Arnott and Stiglitz 1985).

9. Exploitation by money lenders in the rural sector led to the development of rural cooperatives, e.g., in the United States and in Scandinavia.

10. Some learning, as we noted earlier, also gets at least partly embodied in capital goods.

11. In a model presented in chapter 11, the pace of learning in the industrial sector is related to the gap between the state of knowledge of the developing country and the developed country—there is some knowledge spillover across borders.

12. There are exceptions, including the increase in productivity in the U.S. recession that began in 2008. While there are several explanations of this distinctive aspect of the downturn, one is the increasingly short-sighted behavior of firms which ignores the long-run costs of firing or laying off trained workers. In that case, it will still be true that there will be long-run adverse effects of the downturn on productivity. In the Great Depression productivity growth also appears to have been quite high, in part due to important investments made by government (including in transportation; Field 2011).

13. This is, of course, consistent with standard results on unit roots (see Dickey and Fuller 1979; Phillips and Perron 1988).

14. The previous discussion explained why long-lived stable firms provided an environment that was more conducive to learning.

15. For a more extensive discussion, see Stiglitz (2002a).

16. This can be put slightly differently: With capital (debt and equity rationing), the shadow price of capital often increases dramatically in recessions (see Greenwald, Stiglitz, and Weiss 1984; Greenwald and Stiglitz 2003).

17. To identify the effects of the reduced cash flow on firm investment, including investment in R & D, they focus on two situations where changes in cash flow or net worth might be uncorrelated, or negatively correlated, with future expectations. The first study focused on the automobile industry in the United States, particularly in the aftermath of the oil price shocks. Each of these shocks had strongly adverse effects on sales of American automobiles, particularly since they were not as fuel efficient as foreign cars. On the other hand, assuming that American firms could acquire the technological know-how to construct fuel-efficient cars, these oil price shocks should have increased the level of expenditures on R & D. For the unexpected changes in factor prices meant that, while the industry had gone far along the learning curve for large cars, they were still at the beginning of the learning curve for fuel-efficient cars. But the decrease in cash flow had an immediate and direct negative effect on those R & D expenditures, and those firms that were hit the hardest reduced their expenditures the most. Our econometric study corrected for the effect of future sales expectations, and even taking this into account, the effect of cash flow changes on R & D expenditures was significant.

A second study focused on the airline industry in the aftermath of deregulation, which increased competition, lowered prices, and adversely affected cash flows. But the increased output meant that the return to reducing the cost per passenger mile was increased. The evidence was consistent with a dominant role played by cash constraints: The rate of productivity increases declined after deregulation, and those airlines whose cash positions were more adversely affected had the most marked effect on their rate of productivity increase.

Other studies have corroborated these findings. Hall (1992), based on earlier work (Hall 1990, 1991), shows in a large panel of U.S. manufacturing firms during the 1980s that firms that took on more debt subsequently reduced both investment and R & D. In the approximately 250 firms that increased their debt by at least one-half the book value of the capital stock during one year, the decreased R & D expenditures were large enough to account for a reduction in private industrial R & D spending in the United States of 2.5 percent, about one billion 1982 dollars.

18. These effects may be in evidence even in somewhat milder downturns (see Greenwald and Stiglitz 2003; Filippettia and Archibugia 2010; OECD 2009).

19. See chapter 14 below for an elaboration of these arguments and references.

20. Note, however, the complicated second-best nature of these problems: With more mobility, firms will invest less in training, and therefore the benefit of mobility will be reduced.

21. See, in particular, Arnott and Stiglitz (1985) and Greenwald and Stiglitz (1988). Arnott and Stiglitz focus on the case where there are turnover costs with costly search. Firms can affect the quit rate by raising wages. In the simplest model, where all workers and firms are identical, in the social optimum, there would be no labor turnover (except that caused by the death of a worker). But the market equilibrium will, in general, be characterized by a wage dispersion. There is excessive labor turnover (relative to the efficient level), as workers who are unfortunate enough to be hired by low-wage firms seek higher-wage firms. They also examine a model in which firms differ in nonpecuniary attributes, individuals only learn about these attributes by working at a firm, and as a result some level of labor turnover is socially desirable. Workers, in their mobility decision, do not pay sufficient attention to the costs that their mobility decisions impose on firms; and firms do not pay any attention to the costs that their actions to reduce mobility impose on other firms (e.g., if one firm raises wages, it reduces quits at the given firm, but may increase search at other firms.) In more complicated models, hiring and quitting decisions can impose externalities through impacts on the quality of labor (see Arnott, Hosios, and Stiglitz 1988).

5. Market Structure, Welfare, and Learning

1. In *Verizon v. Trinko*, the Supreme Court referred to collusion as the "supreme evil" of antitrust. Verizon Communications Inc. v. Law Offices of Curtis V. Trinko, LLP (02-682) 540 U.S. 398 (2004) 305 F.3d 89.

2. This discussion draws heavily upon Stiglitz (2010c).

3. The imperfections of capital markets go deeper: To get a loan, the innovator has to describe to the creditor his project; but the innovator worries that should he do that, the creditor may be able to steal his idea, or build on his idea to create a still better product. Thus, the struggle to appropriate returns from an idea runs into conflict with the necessity to get funding from others (whom one may not be able to trust).

4. It should be remembered too that the antitrust movement of the progressive era focused as much on the political consequences of trusts—the concentration of power—as on the economic consequences, which got fully explicated only with the development of the modern theory of monopoly.

5. As we noted in the previous chapter, Schumpeter even thought (incorrectly in our view) that recessions could have salutary consequences.

6. That is, of course, now changed. The large increases in inequality over the past quarter century mean that even significant increases in average incomes may not be accompanied by reductions in poverty (see Stiglitz 2012b).

7. This was the objective of Dasgupta and Stiglitz's two 1980 papers.

8. If we had assumed a constant elasticity demand curve, the first-order condition could have been written

$$p = c/(1 - 1/\eta), \tag{1'}$$

where η = the elasticity of demand. The assumption of linearity greatly simplifies the analysis, but the qualitative results are more general.

9. χ corresponds to what, in our later models, we identify as the learning elasticity, h.

10. If we had assumed a constant elasticity demand curve, the first-order condition would have been (using the symmetry conditions):

$$p = c/(1 - 2/\eta). \tag{3'}$$

11. This holds so long as $d\ln \{\chi\, c(a - c)/I\}/d\ln I < 0$, a sufficient condition for which is that $\chi' \leq 0$ and $c < a/2$. so long as $\chi' \leq 0$.

12. If $\chi\, (a - 2c)/(a - c) + 1 < 0$ and $\chi \geq 0$, then $I_i > I_m$.

13. It is straightforward from the above equation to derive sufficient conditions under which this is true.

14. The analysis of this chapter is not quite complete. In a multiperiod model, both the monopolist and the duopolist need to solve a multiperiod maximization problem, taking into account the lower costs associated with investments in R & D today on future production costs in all future periods. As we noted in Chapter 4 more-durable firms are likely to have in effect lower discount rates and therefore value future cost reductions more. This may further strengthen the advantages of monopoly.

15. In that case, with no spillovers, if $C_i^d = C^m$, there would be the same level of innovation and the same costs. The question is, at that level of output, is the marginal revenue of the Cournot duopolist less (or greater) than the marginal cost? For if it is less, then the duopolists will contract production, and that will mean that innovation will be lower. Marginal revenue at $C_i^d = C^m$ will be less than marginal cost if $p(2C^m) < c/(1 - 2/\eta)$, or equivalently if $p(2C)/p(C) < (1 - 1/\eta)/(1 - 2/\eta)$. Using second-order approximations, we can show that provided the elasticity of demand is large enough, the above condition will be satisfied.

16. And follow from an observation made by Arrow (1962b) in his classic paper.

17. Similar results hold for a large innovation, where if the firm is the only one to succeed, it lowers the price below c to the monopoly price (given c^*).

18. There is a little of the flavor of Sutton's *Sunk Costs and Market Structure* (1991) here. In Sutton's story, concentration levels are bounded from below in certain industries even as demand in those industries grows—tougher ex post price competition and the presence of fixed costs limit entry ex ante. Here the intuition is that as market demand grows, output of the incumbent grows. This increased learning lowers marginal costs, toughening ex post potential competition.

19. The optimal level of innovation, given the actual level of output, will be smaller with monopoly than with competition.

20. Capital market imperfections help explain why firms are risk averse. With risk aversion, firms may also undertake less innovation (see Greenwald and Stiglitz 1993, 2003). Nalebuff and Stiglitz (1983a) explain why risk-averse managers may undertake excessively correlated research strategies.

21. There may also exist asymmetric and mixed strategy equilibria.

22. An early attempt, using a rather different approach from that of this book, is Dasgupta and Stiglitz (1980a).

23. This section is based on joint work with Partha Dasgupta (1988a). Since Arrow's (1962a) original paper on learning by doing, there has developed a large literature on market structure and learning (see, for instance, Spence 1981).

24. This analysis provides a critique of Spence (1981), who provides the equations describing the market dynamics but does not detail their implications.

With product differentiation and diseconomies of scale and scope, equilibria in which multiple firms coexist are more stable and robust.

25. And eventually, Google's Chrome. In some ways, this experience is partially consistent with Schumpeter's view: While Microsoft has remained the dominant PC operating system now for more than three decades, its dominance in the browser market was much more short-lived.

26. See, e.g., Baumol (1982); Baumol, Panzar, and Willig (1982); and Martin (2000). The implication was that the "contestable equilibrium" was the same as a constrained Pareto optimum, where lump sum taxes and subsidies (or, more broadly, cross-sector subsidies) were not feasible and where each enterprise had to at least break even. But even if lump sum taxes and subsidies are not available, government interventions, even if restricted to commodity taxes and subsidies, are still desirable (see Sappington and Stiglitz 1987).

27. Similar results can arise even in the absence of irrationality. If each potential researcher draws randomly from a sample indicating the likelihood of success (the cost of achieving success), then those who get the most favorable draw will undertake the project. (This will be true even though they realize that it is likely that they have enjoyed a more favorable draw than others. The recognition that this is the case will lead them to have a higher threshold before undertaking the project. The reasoning here is parallel to that of the winners' curse in auctions.)

28. The distortions associated with monopolies in the context of imperfect information are more extensive, as they attempt to engage in price discrimination, extracting as much of the consumer surplus as they can (see Stiglitz 1977; Stiglitz 2009, intro. to part 2).

29. Recall the discussion of Chapter 4.

30. See, e.g., Dasgupta and Stiglitz (1980, 1988a); Fudenberg, Gilbert, Tirole, and Stiglitz (1983); Stiglitz (1987). These are not just theoretical niceties describing what possibly might happen: Microsoft took actions to discourage and suppress potential rivals, so as to maintain its dominant position. Their predatory behavior lowered the returns that these innovative rivals obtained on their inventive activities, serving notice on other potential rivals that Microsoft was able and willing to engage in activities to discourage entry—even if they were flagrant violations of competition laws, and even if they entailed significant short term losses in profits. In doing so, almost surely the pace of innovation was lowered both from what it would have been in the absence of this anticompetitive behavior and from the socially optimal level.

31. The literature suggesting an inverted U-shaped relationship between competition and innovation has to be treated with caution, in light of our perspective that market structure is *endogenous*. There may be common factors leading to both more competition and more innovation (e.g., a larger and more diversified opportunity set, drawing on a larger variety of skill sets).

Appendix C of the next chapter discusses briefly some of this literature on Schumpeterian competition. Most of this literature does not address many of the issues which have been the focus of this and the next chapter.

32. Chapter 15 explores a number of implications concerning the design of the patent system. The analysis of appendix C to the next chapter suggests that "utility patents," which allow the patenting of small innovations, by encouraging competition for "small" innovative steps may adversely affect the overall pace of innovation.

33. In particular, in models with monopolistic competition. See Dixit and Stiglitz (1977), Stiglitz (1986b, 1989). Dixit and Stiglitz do show that there is a "benchmark" case in which markets balance average costs and product variety perfectly. But the presumption is that that is not the case.

34. See, e.g., Dasgupta and Stiglitz (1980); Fudenberg, Gilbert, Tirole, and Stiglitz (1983).

6. The Welfare Economics of Schumpeterian Competition

1. See Greenwald and Stiglitz (1986), who develop the concept of *constrained efficiency*, i.e., taking into account the existing differences in information and the costs of acquiring and producing information. Beginning in the late 1960s, Stiglitz had explored the nature of the inefficiencies which arise when there is imperfect information and incomplete risk markets. Stiglitz (1975b) showed that there could exist Pareto inferior equilibria, and Newbery and Stiglitz (1982) showed that trade restrictions could make everyone in all countries better off. Stiglitz (1972, 1982) showed that stock market equilibria were in general not (constrained) Pareto efficient—Diamond's (1967) earlier result suggesting that they were rested on the special assumption that there was only one commodity, no bankruptcy, and highly restricted specifications of risk. Our 1986 paper in a sense provided a general formulation that embraced these and other earlier studies. (Arnott, Greenwald, and Stiglitz 1994 provides an alternative general formulation. See also Stiglitz 2009.) We extended our generic 1986 results to search and other models in 1988.

2. This was one of the central points made in Stiglitz's 1974 lecture before the Association of University Teachers of Economics in Manchester, U.K. (Stiglitz 1975a). In November 1978, he elaborated on the problems arising from the public-good nature of knowledge in a lecture to an InterAmerican Development Bank – CEPAL meeting in Buenos Aires (published later as Stiglitz 1987b). Knowledge is a special kind of public good—a global public good, the benefits of which could accrue to anyone in the world. After developing the concept of international public goods in an address to a UN meeting in Vienna (Stiglitz 1995b), Stiglitz (1999) applied that concept to knowledge.

3. For references on the topics of international public goods and knowledge as a public good, see the previous note.

4. As we commented earlier, and we elaborate on later in this chapter and elsewhere in the book, this is true so long as there are not other market failures. Pervasive rent seeking in some innovation sectors may lead to excessive expenditures on some forms of research.

5. One should, perhaps, not put too much emphasis on the fact that these individuals did not appropriate the full benefits of their innovations. There is little evidence that they would have worked any harder with fuller appropriability. Discussions among economists focus on economic incentives; these may be far from the most important determinants of learning and innovation, as we noted in chapter 3.

6. This result provides a telling criticism of aggregate endogenous growth models that have assumed competition. Only the limiting case of perfect spillovers is consistent with full competition, but then there will be little incentive for engaging in R & D or investing in learning (Romer 1994; Stiglitz 1990). Romer's use of Dixit and Stiglitz (1977) preferences provides a simple parameterization within which one can incorporate long-run dynamics in a model with imperfect competition. As Dixit and Stiglitz note, however, that utility function has some very special properties, and one should be careful about using that utility function, especially for making welfare assessments, e.g., on the optimality of the number of firms (diversity) in the market equilibrium. Alternative specifications can give markedly different results. See, e.g., Stiglitz (1986b).

7. Chapter 3 provided an extensive discussion of the nature of these spillovers.

8. If there are spillovers across sectors (products), but spillovers external to the firm are not full, there is a natural multiproduct monopoly (under our assumptions of linear technology) as a result of these natural economies of scope. These economies of scope and scale and offsetting diseconomies of scope and scale (e.g., arising from limits of the span of control and the benefits of managerial specialization) help define the boundaries of firms.

9. Given the lower level of production, however, the level of investment in learning/R & D may be optimal. When we say that there is less learning under monopoly, we mean *less learning than there would be in a first-best situation where the level of output was optimal and the level of learning reflected that higher level of output*. Later in this book, we will show that the level of learning is less than it would be in the second-best situations where there is government intervention, through subsidies, *even when there are costs to raising the taxes required to finance those subsidies*. Much of this chapter, however, focuses on the simpler question: Is the level of innovation higher with monopoly or competition?

10. Optimal learning may involve producing at a loss, necessitating borrowing (see Dasgupta and Stiglitz 1988).

11. This is an explanation of the high observed average returns to investment in technology (see Council of Economic Advisers 1995).

12. For a more extended discussion of these issues, see Stiglitz (2006, 2008, 2013).

13. This is, of course, a more general point, applicable as well to the entry of firms in monopolistically competitive markets. An entrant captures a fraction of the consumer surplus generated by its new product, but some of the entrant's profits are, in effect, profits diverted from other firms. Whether entry is socially desirable or not depends on the relative magnitude of these two effects. In some special cases, the market equilibrium may be efficient, but more generally, it is not (see, e.g., Dixit and Stiglitz 1977; Stiglitz 1986b).

14. More precisely, $S(n^* + 1)/(n^* + 1) < I$, and $S(n^*)/n^* \geq I$. In other words, profits would be negative with additional entry and are nonnegative at n^*.

15. See the discussion in chapter 15. Boyle (2003, 2008) refers to the patenting of knowledge that was previously in the public domain as the enclosure of the commons.

16. Strikes and wars represent similar inefficient breakdowns in bargaining (Farrell 1987). See also Shapiro (2010) for a discussion of holdup in the context of patents.

17. These problems are exacerbated by the fact that the "boundaries" of knowledge are often hard to define precisely. This and the more general problem of the patent thicket are discussed more extensively in chapter 15.

18. These problems can be exacerbated by other deficiencies in the market. Compensation schemes that reward individuals on the basis of relative performance encourage "herding" behavior, where individuals do what others are doing (see Nalebuff and Stiglitz 1983a).

19. In chapter 15, we describe in greater detail the problems that arise in the context of what has been called the patent thicket.

20. The discussion of this section borrows from Dasgupta and Stiglitz (1988a).

21. Inappropriately designed intellectual property regimes can actually inhibit innovation. (See the discussion in Chapter 15.)

22. Greenwald and Kahn (2009) have shown that most of the decrease in manufacturing employment, at least prior to 2000, was a result of improvements in technology (rather than globalization).

There is a large literature supporting the view that innovation in the United States has been "skill-biased." See, e.g., Greiner, Rubart, and Semmler (2003); Goldin and Katz (2008); Autor and Dorn (2013); Autor, Levy, and Murnane (2003); Autor, Katz, and Kearney (2008).

23. Volcker's 2009 comments were widely reported in the news media. See, for example, Pedro da Costa and Kristina Cooke, 2009, "Crisis May Be Worse than Depression, Volcker Says," , Reuters, February 20. http://uk.reuters.com/

article/2009/02/20/usa-economy-volcker-idUKN2029103720090220 (accessed February 27, 2013).

24. For a more extensive discussion, see Stiglitz (2010b).

25. This analysis builds on Stiglitz (2006b), which itself builds off a large literature on factor-biased induced innovation, going back to Ahmad (1966), Drandakis and Phelps (1966), Fellner (1961), Kennedy (1964), and Samuelson (1965), with antecedents in the literature in economic history (e.g., Salter 1966; Habakkuk 1962).

26. Similar results obtain in a more dynamic, multiperiod model.

27. The share of labor is simply a function of λ, if K, L, and the unemployment rate are all fixed. In the standard models, the unemployment rate is zero. In the discussion below, we allow the unemployment rate to be endogenous.

28. The Shapiro-Stiglitz (1984) model is set in an infinite-period context. It is easy to set our choice of technique within such a context.

29. See J. Hicks (1932), for a discussion of a typology of innovation.

30. There are other interpretations, discussed briefly below. It seems, for instance, that at times wages did not fully adjust and that at times, as a result, firms had difficulty hiring workers. This will result in the shadow wage exceeding the market wage.

31. We also note that the dynamics can be markedly different from those of the standard Solow model, where convergence to equilibrium is monotonic. As we show in the appendix, convergence is oscillatory. We note, however, that the smooth convergence to the steady state in the Solow model is a function of its extreme simplifying assumptions. Other slight modifications (vintage capital, savings depending on the distribution of income) can also lead to more complicated dynamics. See, e.g., Akerlof and Stiglitz (1969); Cass and Stiglitz (1969); or Stiglitz (1967).

32. This is consistent with the evidence on the stagnation of median wages in the United States over a span of more than forty years and a decline in wages of unskilled workers (e.g., workers with only a high school education).

33. For a more extensive discussion of the issues raised, see Stiglitz (2010b).

34. For a more extensive discussion of these ideas, see Stiglitz (1975a, 1994c, 2010a).

35. We noted in chapter 5 that the firms that went bankrupt in Korea were not on average less productive than those that did not.

36. Even more so in countries, such as the United States, where those with money have disproportionate weight in the political process.

37. In the standard competitive model, where each firm faces a horizontal supply curve of labor of each type, these effects are not likely to rise. But in practice, labor mobility is imperfect. Firms are engaged in a bargaining process with their workers. The nature of technology—which they can shape—affects this bargaining process. Note that this analysis does not require that firms

coordinate their actions, to increase their bargaining power vis-à-vis workers (though under some circumstances they may in fact do so.) Rather, so long as there is imperfect mobility of workers, it pays each firm to take actions which increase its bargaining power vis-à-vis its workers.

38. See Braverman and Stiglitz (1986) for an analysis of these issues in the context of an agricultural economy.

39. In perfectly competitive labor markets, any nonpecuniary cost would lead to a demand for higher wages and thus would be taken into account by the firm, but this is not so in imperfectly competitive markets.

Moreover, in a world with uncertainty and imperfect information, management may come to believe that technologies that save on labor are profitable. There may be an "equilibrium fiction" in which the evidence, as they see it, confirms those beliefs (Hoff and Stiglitz 2010). This is especially so in managerial capitalism (with agency costs which enable managers to exercise considerable discretion for their own benefit), where managers may value their own time and trouble more than would be the case in an efficient market economy.

Interestingly, such beliefs will, in fact, serve the interests of the managerial/capitalist "class" as a whole, leading to outcomes that are consistent with what they might have wanted to do collusively, though they had no mechanism by which to do so.

40. There is, in this sense, a kind of increasing returns to scale. The more innovators think about how to improve labor efficiency, the better at it they get. This suggests that the innovation frontier, rather than being concave, may in fact be (at least in part) convex.

41. This is one of the points raised by Phelps (2013).

42. We should perhaps more accurately say that markets *never* exist in a vacuum. Society has to set the rules and regulations that govern them, e.g., what kinds of contracts can be enforced, and how they are to be enforced. Thus, the notion that there are "unfettered markets" is a chimera, an idea that is often used by those who are trying to shape markets in a particular way (*as if* there was a "right way" by which markets *should* be organized)—often in ways that are in their own interests.

43. More accurately, they result in less R & D or less learning than would occur in the first-best situation; given the lower output associated with monopoly, conditional on the monopoly power persisting, the optimal degree of investment in R & D is lower.

44. East Asia did this as a central part of its development strategy (see Stiglitz 1996; World Bank 1993).

45. We should emphasize, however, the difficulties of ascertaining well-being, highlighted by the work of the Commission on the Measurement of Economic Performance and Social Progress (Stiglitz, Sen, and Fitoussi 2010).

For instance, while for most individuals improvements in life sciences have increased overall health, these gains have to be offset against increases in insecurity and decreases in the quality of the environment.

46. It is straightforward to show that $\sigma = -f'(f - Kf')/ff''$.

47. Equation (A.19) can be thought of as derived from an efficiency-wage model, where the efficiency wage is a function of the unemployment rate and the minimum wage, and the minimum wage rises with productivity. The wage an individual receives is $W = wa = G(U)W_{min}$.

48. Stiglitz (2006b) shows that the equilibrium is, in general, stable.

49. By contrast, in the text we noted the possibility of "learning to learn," implying that the process of skill-biased technological change may feed upon itself.

50. See, e.g., Dasgupta and Stiglitz (1980a, 1980b, 1988a); Fudenberg, Gilbert, Tirole, and Stiglitz (1983); Gilbert and Newbery (1982); Stiglitz (1987a); Greenwald and Stiglitz (forthcoming).

51. Stiglitz (2013b) describes how firms contribute to and take out of the pool of knowledge, affecting the innovation opportunity set. Dosi and Stiglitz (forthcoming) review the empirical literature and argue that the opportunity set is the most important determinant of the level of innovation. Successors thus benefit from this knowledge.

52. A similar argument applies in the case of product innovation.

53. Aghion and Howitt identify a similar effect, which they attribute to monopoly power. But the effect can be strong even when monopoly power is limited, e.g., because there is a sequence of rapid innovations, the effect of which is to lower consumer prices.

54. In the discussion below, we delineate carefully the effects of competition in innovation from those arising from competition in production. Schumpeter (implicitly) identified two sets of effects, that on the *marginal* returns to investment and that on the *ability* to invest. In a world with imperfect capital markets, there may be heavy reliance on internal finance, especially for R & D, which cannot be collateralized. We focus on the former effect, leaving to a later occasion an analysis of the latter.

55. In their work, and in much of the literature, a Poisson process is assumed. This is convenient for modeling steady states; but such processes have very special properties.

56. So too, the aggregative approach taken by Aghion and Howitt leaves unaddressed key issues about the sectoral direction of resource allocation and R & D, e.g., between industrial sectors and agricultural/craft sectors (the subject of Greenwald and Stiglitz forthcoming). Again, because of space limitations, we do not explore these issues here.

57. In Aghion and Howitt, there are a separate set of research firms who own the patents. In practice, most research is done by incumbent producing firms

because of the importance of the knowledge that is acquired in the process of production and the imperfect transferability of such tacit knowledge. This knowledge not only increases productivity directly (learning-by-doing) but also enhances research capacities. But even if this were not so, firms engaged in prior research on a product have a knowledge advantage over entrants, so there should be some tendency for perpetuation of monopoly power. As we have emphasized, knowledge spillovers are always imperfect.

58. For an early formulation of innovation with stochastic entry, see Futia 1980. Even with stochastic outcomes, in the absence of diseconomies of scope or differential knowledge on the part of potential entrants, any project that was worth undertaking for an entrant would be worth undertaking by the incumbent (see Dasgupta and Stiglitz 1980b; Sah and Stiglitz 1987).

59. With potential follow-on effects for subsequent innovation.

60. See, e.g., Aghion et al. (2005) and the references cited there.

61. We will say a little bit about a third aspect, the riskiness of the research strategy, and virtually nothing about a fourth, the extent of correlation of a given firm's research strategy with that of others. However, in the analysis, particularly in section 1, we show the importance of these.

62. Some of the more recent literature on Schumpeterian competition follows in this tradition. See, e.g., the excellent survey paper by Aghion, Akcigit, and Howitt (2013) and the papers cited there.

63. We can use (A.31) to derive an equivalent expression:

$$I = \phi'^{-1}\{-1/[c_0 Q(c_0)]\}.$$

64. Such nonconvexities arise naturally in the economics of information and knowledge. See Radner and Stiglitz (1984).

65. In this equation, the elasticity of demand is valuated at the point where $p = c_0$. At this point, we are not assuming constant elasticity demand functions.

66. This just highlights the fact that economies where R & D and learning are important are rife with convexities.

67. We should also note that the demand functions may be shifted from the earlier analysis as a result of income effects, the absence of profits from the exercise of monopoly power, and the imposition of lump sum taxes.

68. Not only are the two hypotheses questionable, the result on the efficiency of equilibrium is not general. In a market with multiple commodities, which the government can tax and subsidize differently, the contestability equilibrium is not efficient.

69. Highlighting the observation made earlier: if limitations on research are provided by access to capital, and if access to capital is affected by next period's profits, then there may be more investment in R & D under Cournot, even though marginal returns are lower.

70. Gross profits of the Cournot entrant (denoted R_C) are (using (A.45a)) $c_1(\alpha^2/\eta)Q_C/(1 - \alpha/\eta)$. Profits under Bertrand are $(c_0 - c_1)Q_B$. At $c_1 = c_0$, $R_C > R_B = 0$. At the boundary point between a small and large innovation, given by (A.47), $\alpha = 1$ and $R_B = R_C$. Using the facts that $Q_C > Q_B$, $Q_{1C} = \partial R_C/\partial c_1 < \partial R_B/\partial c_1 = Q_B$, it is clear that for all small innovations, $R_C > R_B$.

71. At Q_i equal to that of the myopic monopolist, Q_m, Marginal revenue = $p + p'Q_m < p(Q_m) + p'(Q_m)Q_m = c_1$.

72. Assume c_1 remains the same. Then

$$Q_1 = (a + c_0 - 2c_1)/3b < (a - c_1)/2b = Q_m$$

if $a + c_1 - 2c_0 > 0$, i.e., from (A.50b), if $Q_0 > 0$. Obviously, a higher Q leads to a lower c_1, leading in turn to a still higher Q.

73. $R = (p - c_1)Q = (a - c_1)Q - bQ^2$, which is maximized at $Q = (a - c_1)/2b$.

74. Cournot is $4/9$ that of Bertrand, for small innovations; myopic monopoly is $\frac{1}{2}$ that of Bertrand.

75. From the indirect utility function, $V_p = V_Y Q_1$, $dp/dc_1 = 1/3$ in Cournot equilibrium.

76. Most of the literature has taken the first approach, though some (such as Dasgupta and Stiglitz 1980a) have taken the second. In practice, there are often multiple entrants.

77. In contrast to the discussion of sections 8 and 9, we assume that there is no way that a potential entrant can, by allocating more resources to the speed of innovation as opposed to the depth of the innovation, increase the likelihood that it will be first. This is obviously a special case, but this assumption greatly simplifies the analysis. One way of thinking about the R & D process is in terms of a stochastic process as described in the next section. There is a small variance in the time of arrival, and the marginal costs of reducing the mean time of arrival are very large.

78. One can easily specify a game form for which this occurs.

79. This is the solution, provided the level of innovation is small. Alternatively, I^* is the solution to

$$I^* = c_0[1 - \phi(I^*)]Q[c_0(1 - \phi(I^*)/(1 - 1/\eta)]/(\eta - 1).$$

80. This follows from the assumption that $\phi'' > 0$. In the more general case, e.g., that depicted in figure 6.6b, there can exist more than one point at which the revenue and cost curves cross. So too in the case of large innovations, because both the revenue and cost curves are convex. The contestability equilibrium is that associated with the highest level of innovation, for a firm undertaking that level of investment would undercut potential rivals.

81. As c_1^1 diminishes, the slope of the revenue curve gets steeper. It is thus possible that there is more than one value of c_1^1 for which the revenue curve and cost curves have the same slope.

82. If $-c_1''^1(a - 2c_1^1 + c_1^2) + 2(c_1'^1)^2 > 0$, there is a unique value of c_1^1 corresponding to any value of c_1^2 in (A.69). Even if the above condition is not satisfied, there is always a value of I_1 that maximizes the first firm's profits, given I_2. Because of the nonconvexities, the reaction functions may not be as simple as depicted in the figure.

83. Which depends in turn on the elasticity of $\phi'(I_1)$.

84. For simplicity, we are assuming all firms have the same innovation function and the incumbent departs. Similar results hold if he does not.

85. More accurately, because n must be an integer, n^e is the largest value of n such that $\prod^i \geq 0$.

86. Recall our earlier caveat that these results depend on the likelihood of success being independent. If the different firms are engaged in identical research strategies, presumably the results would be highly correlated and ΔP would be zero or small.

87. Similarly, if firms are risk averse.

88. That was the central message of Dasgupta and Stiglitz (1980a).

89. For $n > n_{max}$, the value of profits in the symmetric equilibrium (where all firms engage in research) is negative.

90. In practice, there are likely to be large knowledge differentials, so that the cost of innovation is lower for some firms than for others. In this case, n_{max} is such that the expected profits of the next firm to enter (given the optimal response of all the other firms) is negative.

91. Except, as noted, in the case of a large innovation, where the innovator lowers the price below the marginal cost of production of the incumbent.

92. This is the essential insight of the "persistence" theorem (Dasgupta and Stiglitz 1980a). For a small innovation, the incumbent's optimal price may be above c_0 (its marginal cost the previous period), which would be the price confronting an entrant.

93. Entry can also occur because of the "irrational exuberance" of innovators—who may have more confidence in their own research project than it deserves. Thus, some of the dynamism of capitalism may be attributed to irrational expectations (see Knight 1921).

94. Note that, in general, the acceleration of research (in this model, the "sinking" of research expenditures) is not efficient, i.e., the threat of entry may actually lead to higher costs. It is even possible that it leads to a lower level of innovation.

95. This is highlighted by Dixit and Stiglitz (1977), who show that with the Dixit-Stiglitz utility function, the market for entry is "constrained Pareto efficient." The result is not general.

96. In moving to the analysis of a long-run maximization problem, it is convenient to change to constant-elasticity demand curves, which allow for the analysis of steady-state behavior.

97. While this assumption has become conventional in the literature, it is questionable. A bigger innovation today may draw down the pool of available ideas, and thus further improvements may be more difficult.

98. We do the calculations for the harder case of large innovations. The calculations for small innovations are similar. (See section 2.)

99. That is, the myopic monopolist sets $2\pi_1/2I_1 = 0$. From (A.88), since $2v_1/2I_1 > 0$, the non-myopic monopolist increases I relative to the myopic monopolist.

100. It follows from (A.88) that the magnitude of the deviation in I, between the myopic and non-myopic monopolist is increasing in δ.

101. For large innovations, the analysis is identical to that of the previous subsection, since at the price chosen by the monopolist, it does not pay for competitors (with the old technology) to produce.

102. Thus, the one-period output is smaller with the persistent monopolist, but the cost saving from more innovation relates to the (PDV) of all future outputs. With a small discount factor, that number will be very large.

103. In this formulation, we have assumed that there is no spillover of knowledge across sectors. It is easy to generalize the results to cases where there is some knowledge spillover.

104. This formulation assumes that the fruits of the research done this period become immediately available. A more plausible assumption is that there is a one-period lag. Nothing hinges on this assumption.

105. We assume that innovative activity each period builds on the benchmark of inherited knowledge, i.e., that an investment in innovation of I^t at time t leads to a percentage reduction in costs of $\phi(I^t)$, regardless of the level of previous innovation. This assumption greatly simplifies the analysis, but the qualitative results would be similar so long as research investments at time t don't fully dissipate opportunities in subsequent periods. At the other extreme, we could consider a case where the marginal cost of production at time $t + 2$ is a function only of total two-period investment: $c_{t+2} = c_t \Psi(I_{t+1} + I_{t+2})$, as opposed to the model investigated here, where $c_{t+2} = c_t \phi(I_{t+1}) \phi(I_{t+2})$. Appendix D investigates a case where innovators at time t deplete the "knowledge pool," making further innovation more difficult until the knowledge pool has been replenished by basic research. The model of section 3 considers a similar situation, where faster innovation at time t makes innovation the next period more difficult.

106. It should be obvious that we require that $\delta H^a < 1$; otherwise, the PDV of utility becomes infinite, and the problem is not well-defined. We assume that the above condition is satisfied at all (relevant) values of I.

107. It is clear that there is a unique solution to (A.96) for $\delta = 0$ (and by continuity, δ near zero), so long as $h' \leq 0$. But if δ is large, the left-hand side of (20) may be increasing in I, even if $h' \leq 0$, since $d[\delta H^a/(1 - \delta H^a)]/d(\ln I) = \delta h H^a/(1 - \delta H^a)^2 > 0$.

108. We can think of all the investment being made up front, with the research maturing in T years, or, alternatively, that there is a steady flow of research. A flow of "i" for a period of T years has a (PDV) cost of $I = i(1 - e^{-rT})/r$. If a flow of i yields an innovation at time T, that is equivalent to a PDV of $I = i(T)(1 - e^{-rT})/r$ yielding an innovation at T.

109. If as T goes to zero, the required investment increases sufficiently, entry deterrence is still possible. And in that case, it is always desirable for the incumbent to deter the entrant. We assume that the entrant assumes that it will be the dominant firm for a period that does not increase (or increase too rapidly) as T decreases.

110. How much investment the incumbent must make depends, obviously, on the information structure. If the incumbent can observe instantaneously what rivals are doing, then it need not invest ahead of time as much as it would if there were long lags in observation.

111. These are, obviously, extreme assumptions—highlighting the sensitivity of results to particular assumptions concerning the innovation process.

112. We model this as if the firm invests a flow for a period T, for a total PDV of investment of I, after which it receives a flow of profits $Q(1 - 1/H)$ for a period of T (until the next innovation arrives) of investment.

113. In fact, the entrant takes the interval over which it makes profits as given and maximizes

$$\lambda(1 - \lambda^*)Q(1)[1 - 1/H(I, T)]/r - I$$

with respect to T.

114. That is, $\{I^e, T^e\}$ do not in general maximize either social welfare or $H(I, T)/T$.

115. The analysis by Dasgupta and Stiglitz (1980a) is predicated on that assumption.

116. These knowledge spillovers are the focus of this book. Here, *intertemporal* knowledge spillovers have played a central role in our analysis.

117. In some cases, this is almost the explicit objective of R & D activity, e.g., in the case of "me-too" innovations in the pharmaceutical industry. Thus, while this appendix focuses on the overall pace of innovation, we should emphasize that the market has distorted incentives—excessive incentives for innovations which appropriate part of the rents of previous successful innovators and too few incentives for fundamental innovations. This appendix, exploring the intertemporal linkages and externalities associated with innovative processes,

has delineated the large number of forms that they can take, with different implications for the nature of distortions in the innovative process. While a persistent monopolist "internalizes" these externalities, and thus is not subject to these distortions, we have suggested that it faces an alternative set of incentive problems, for all—most importantly, potentially deficient incentives to innovate. But even with a sequence of monopolists, incentives are attenuated relative to a "first-best" since even the sequence of monopolists do not capture the consumer surplus generated over the long-term by their innovative activity.

In Appendix D, we show that similarly to other common-source problems, unbridled competition does not lead to the maximum production (of innovations, of fish, etc.). The analogy that has emerged in this appendix is even stronger. Just as in fisheries there is a danger from overfishing premature fish and not letting the stock of fish mature to the level where the steady-state flow of fish would be maximized, here too there is a tendency to capture (patent) ideas at too young a stage, impeding the subsequent development that would be associated with a faster rate of overall innovation.

118. As we noted, this is more generally true in the theory of imperfect and monopolistic competition.

119. And it is assumed that the incumbent firm cannot undertake some of the research projects that entrants can undertake, e.g., because of diseconomies of scope. If it can, it can be shown that any project that would be worthwhile for an entrant to undertake would be undertaken by the incumbent.

120. Dosi and Stiglitz (2014) argue that these opportunities may be the most important determinant of the pace of innovation.

121. These ideas are developed more fully in Appendix D.

122. This appendix is inspired in part by joint work with Giovanini Dosi, who, surveying the empirical evidence on innovation, has argued that the available set of opportunities plays a more important role in determining the pace of innovation than intellectual property rights (see Dosi and Stiglitz 2014). This appendix shows the endogenous determination of the opportunity set.

123. See, e.g., Bessen and Meurer (2008). That said, it should not be surprising that there have been a large number of attempts at finding correlations between some measure of the strength of a country's intellectual property regime and economic growth, or some variable purportedly related to economic growth, such as inward-bound foreign direct investment. As most scholars engaged in this research have recognized, these studies are bedeviled by a large number of econometric problems, e.g., of identification. With global harmonization, there is a dearth of natural experiments. Even when such experiments exist, long lags and the influence of a multiplicity of other factors affecting innovation and growth make it difficult to establish definitive, or even convincing, results.

Historical studies suggest a multiplicity of influences on the level of innovation: Several European countries with weak intellectual property rights had flourishing innovative sectors—more flourishing than others with stronger intellectual property rights (Chang 2001, 2002). See also David (1993, 2002).

More recent critiques of IPR regimes have focused on "flaws" in the IPR regime, arising from the patent thicket, the bias for excessive patenting (as opposed to the incentives for fighting patents), holdups, incentives for evergreening, etc. Whether it is possible to adequately "correct" these flaws, so that the net effect on the pace of innovation (as opposed to the level of investment in R & D, taking into account the distortions associated with these flaws) of the IPR regime is positive remains contentious. It is clear, however, that the relationship between IPR and innovation depends on fundamental rules of the IPR regime, governing what can be patented, the breadth and standards of patenting, how patents are enforced, and so forth.

More narrowly focused studies have identified areas where particular patents have had adverse effects on follow-on research. In particular, evidence presented in the Myriad BRAC gene patent litigation detailed adverse effects both on the development of tests and further research. (See *Association for Molecular Pathology v. Myriad Genetics*, 569 U.S. 12-398 [2013]; Huang and Murray 2008; Williams 2013).

The discussion of this appendix abstracts from the details of the patent system, which are discussed at length extensively in the large literature on intellectual property. So too, we ignore the details of the patent system which affect the welfare effects, e.g., the consequences of IPR regimes for access to lifesaving medicines.

The state of the current debate around IPR is surveyed by the contributions to the Winter 2013 *Journal of Economic Perspectives* symposium (Boldrin and Levine; Moser; Hagiu and Yoffie; and Graham and Vishnubhakat).

124. Dasgupta and David (1994) also argue for the importance of other nonpecuniary motivations for research. See also David (2004a, 2004b).

125. See Dosi and Stiglitz (2013) and the references cited there.

126. To use Boyle's (2003) evocative phrase. See also Heller (1998); Heller and Eisenberg (1998).

127. We should emphasize the importance of the word *design*. There are many details to the IPR system, such as the breadth of the patent, which affect the extent to which knowledge is added to or "subtracted" from the pool. Knowledge that is not available for others to use is, in effect, subtracted from the pool. Broad patents subtract more from the available knowledge pool than more narrowly defined patents. Matters are, of course, far more complicated than this simple arithmetic analogy would suggest. Knowledge that can be

used, but at a price, is in a sense "partially" available, and even knowledge that cannot be used directly can trigger research. By the same token, some, perhaps much, of the investment in R & D in a poorly designed IPR regime is devoted to inventing around a patent or to increasing the rents that can be extracted out of a patent (e.g., by evergreening). In such circumstances, even if tighter IPR leads to more investment in R & D, it may not lead to faster real innovations, i.e., an increased pace of increases in standards of living.

128. P_{min} is defined by the lowest value of P for which $H(P) = 0$.

129. This would obviously not be the case if the number of firms is very small (say $n = 1$ or 2). In this simple formulation, the price of fish, p, is given exogenously.

130. It is easy to generalize (A.114) to include situations where there is imperfect competition among the firms (i.e., we generalize pQ to a more general revenue function R). The model is consistent with alternative interpretations of how additional investments in fishing fleets affect the marginal catch. For our purposes, these details are irrelevant.

131. The full welfare calculation is more complicated, because of the effects of externalities, even if markets are competitive. Ignoring the effect on P and the cross-firm externality associated with the increase in fishing costs for each firm, the marginal value of resources used by each firm is then equal to the marginal costs, and the value of the benefits of the marginal firm equals its marginal costs. The fact that the cross-firm externality effect (at fixed P) is negative implies that if the pool effect is small (P is only slightly greater than $\hat{P}$), it is still desirable to tax entry.

132. Matters are, of course, more complicated than this discussion might suggest. In the long term, the innovation may be "enabling," even if it takes away economic opportunities in the short term, because it provides the knowledge base on which further innovations can eventually be built. See, e.g., the various contributions to the Winter 2013 symposium on patents in the *Journal of Economic Perspectives*.

133. Notice that this formulation explicitly rejects the view that there is a fixed stock of knowledge to be discovered. If that were the case, then it is possible that a large value of "discovered" knowledge would diminish the set of knowledge to be discovered, and it is possible that $H_P < 0$, or even more, that $H_{PK} < 0$, i.e., the marginal return to research investments diminishes as the size of the knowledge pool increases. This could result in a figure looking more like that depicted earlier for fishing stocks.

134. All that the analysis below requires is that dH/dP not increase too much, for then there may not be a stable equilibrium pool of knowledge.

135. This is consistent with general results showing a fundamental nonconvexity in the value of information (see Radner and Stiglitz 1984).

136. We can think of I as the pace of, say, labor-augmenting technological change. For purposes of this analysis, however, we do not have to be specific about how we parameterize the level of innovation.

137. Throughout this section, we hold n constant.

138. Implicitly differentiating (A.116).

139. In the next section, we shall show how these results can easily be generalized.

140. We are explicitly assuming that knowledge is *not* industry specific.

141. This formulation allows us to avoid the more complicated intertemporal maximization problem that would arise if each firm's current innovation level depended not only on the current pool of publicly available knowledge, but on a pool of privately available knowledge. Qualitative results for this more general problem would, however, be similar to those described here.

142. $d(\ln I)/d\xi = [d(\ln H)/dP]dP/d\xi - d[\ln \gamma(\xi)]/d\xi < 0.$

143. These results can be seen directly in figure 6.14a, where, while the effects on P^* are unambiguously negative, those on i^* are indeterminate.

144. Notice that this formulation is consistent with there being many firms in each industry. The profits of any firm are a function of its own innovations and those of others in the industry.

145. More precisely, $dI/dn = H_P(\partial I/\partial n)_{|P}/[H_P(K, P) - \gamma(\xi)(I_i Z_P + I_P)].$

146. By analogy, in the first section, more fishing firms, *given a stock of fish*, will discourage investment by each of the fishing firms, as the marginal return to investment (at a given level of i and P) is reduced. In the context of innovation, see Aghion and Howitt (1992, 1998); Stiglitz (2013a, 2013b) and discussions elsewhere in this book.

147. But the analysis shows equally that if more competition should lead to lower innovation *at a fixed P*, then it will lead to more innovation in equilibrium. And that may well be the case. It is possible that more competition (large n) so lowers the marginal return to investments in R & D at any given level of research of others (and P), that investment by each firm is diminished enough that the depletion of the knowledge pool is actually reduced as competition increases.

148. There is a huge literature on the subject, some of which suggests an inverted U-shaped relationship, some of which suggests that innovation may decline monotonically with n. The empirical literature is bedeviled with the problems noted in earlier footnotes, and even the theoretical literature does not always separate clearly the effects of entry *given* a particular opportunity set, versus the effects with an endogenous opportunity set. The literature in which prior innovation affects returns to current investments in R & D typically emphasizes the benefits that arise from the increase in the "baseline" knowledge, from which current research efforts depart, rather than the

negative effects of the drawdown in the knowledge pool that has been the focus of this analysis. See, e.g., Aghion and Howitt (1992, 1998); Aghion et al. (2005); Aghion, Akcigit, and Howitt (2013); and Stiglitz (2013a, 2013b).

149. Thus, an increase in n, especially beyond a certain critical level, may lead to lower I, keeping P fixed, and thus to a higher level of innovation—taking into account the effect of entry on the size of the opportunity set (P).

150. There is, by now, a large literature discussing these and other similar reforms to the intellectual property regime. For a brief review, see below chap. 15.

151. As advocated, for instance, by Lewis and Reichman (2005).

7. Learning in a Closed Economy—the Basic Model

1. We reiterate that while we couch the results in this part of the book in terms of learning that results from doing, there are analogous results when firms make explicit investments in R & D.

2. Here, as elsewhere in the book, we use the terms *manufacturing* and *agriculture* in a quite broad way. *Manufacturing* includes other activities that typically occur within cities, including services like telecommunications and large-scale retail. *Agriculture* includes activities that are geographically dispersed and that occur in small production units, like crafts.

3. We are also assuming time-separable utility functions and utility functions which are separable in goods and leisure. Nothing essential depends on these assumptions.

4. The assumption that the spillovers are *perfect* is, of course, a polar case. In subsequent chapters, we will loosen this assumption. None of the qualitative results depends on this assumption.

5. $\psi(0) < 1$ implies that learning (cost reductions) occurs even in the absence of production. For simplicity, in much of the discussion below, we assume $\psi(0) = 1$.

6. In the next chapter, we will analyze the more general case where the labor supply is variable.

7. It should be emphasized, however, that the variables on the right-hand side of (21a) may themselves be functions of the taxes and subsidies and that there may be multiple values of t_M satisfying (21). For instance, higher subsidies for the industrial sector will normally be associated with a higher value of second-period output, and h too can depend on the level of industrial output.

8. Alternatively, we can write $\beta_M = \{d(\ln C_M)/d[\ln(p_M/p_A)]\}\{d[\ln(p_M/p_A)]/d(\ln \tau_M)\}$, where $d[\ln p_M/p_A)]/d(\ln \tau_M)$ can be calculated in a straightforward way, given in the next footnote. Similarly for β_A.

9. Relative consumption, C_M/C_A, is just a function of relative prices $p = (1 - \tau_M)/(1 + t_A)$: $C_M/C_A = Q[(1-\tau_I)/(1 + t_A)]$. Since $\tau_M C_M = t_A C_A$, $p = (1 - \tau_M)/(1 + \tau_M Q(p))$, which gives p as a function of τ_M. The elasticity of substitution, σ, is defined as $d[\ln (C_M/C_A)]/d\{\ln[(1-\tau_M)/(1 + t_A)]\}$, where $dt_A/d\tau_M = (C_M/C_A) + \tau_M[d(C_M/C_A)/d\tau_M]$. Thus, $d[\ln(C_M/C_A)]/d(\ln \tau_M) = \sigma\, d(\ln p)/d(\ln \tau_M)$.

10. The analysis is somewhat more complicated than (25) suggests, because the terms in (25) are not themselves constant and may, in fact, depend on the tax rate.

11. We ignore here any effects on labor supply.

12. In the figure, U_m^t is the tth-period utility under monopoly, U_c^t, under competition. While U_m^t is slightly less than U_c^t, U_m^{t+1} is much greater than U_c^{t+1}.

13. ν is itself an endogenous variable, depending on the magnitude of learning, ψ, the learning elasticity, h, the discount factor, and properties of the demand function. For instance, if there is a high level of learning, ν will tend to be large; if there is a high elasticity of learning, ν will be smaller than it otherwise would have been.

14. There are two other situations that deserve brief mention. The first is where there are not full spillovers, but competition is maintained within the learning sector as a result of diseconomies of scale. To take the extreme case, assume there were no within-sector learning spillovers but only cross-sector learning spillovers. Then each competitive firm would take full account of the benefits of its learning to itself—just as the monopolist would. In that case, the only distortion in the competitive equilibrium arises from the cross-sector externality. As long as there are spillovers, production in the learning sector will be suboptimal, and a first-period consumption subsidy would be desirable. The other case of interest is that where there is imperfect competition in both sectors. If the degree of monopoly is roughly the same, then both will raise prices relative to marginal costs, but relative prices will be unaffected. Hence, monopoly power won't distort (relative) production of the two goods; it will result in internalization of the within-sector externality, but not of the cross-sector externality. The results are much as discussed in the previous paragraph. Of course, the reduction in real wages not only has distributional effects, but will also affect labor supply, and thus learning. Some of these issues are discussed more extensively in the next chapter.

8. A Two-Period, N-Good Model with Endogenous Labor Supply

1. This is not an innocuous assumption but is done to simplify what is already a fairly complex analysis. Without separability, government may wish

to induce more consumption of the learning good(s) by exploiting complementarities and substitutability between these goods and consumption of various other goods at later dates.

2. H is the output per unit input; the function ψ introduced in the previous chapter is the input per unit output. Clearly $H = 1/\psi$.

3. While this is precisely true in the case of logarithmic utility functions discussed below, in the more general case, the analysis is somewhat more complicated because of the endogeneity of ξ_k, as discussed below.

4. Under normal circumstances, growth (an increase in H, productivity) will lead to an increase in consumption; but matters are slightly more complicated, as first-period consumption is subsidized because of the benefit of learning. If H_0, the increase in productivity with no subsidies, is large relative to δh_k (the value of the learning benefits), then $C_k^{t+1} > C_k^t$.

5. Recall that in terms of our previous notation, Ψ is the special case of H where there are no spillovers.

6. $U_i^t - v^{t\prime} = -\tau^* v^\prime = -\delta U_i^{t+1} G^\prime(L_i^t) L^{t+1}$.

7. These formulae provide a characterization of the equilibrium, but it is important to note that, in general, the elasticities can themselves depend on taxes and subsidies.

8. With full spillovers, the learning function is $G = G(L^t/n, L^t/n, \ldots)$ for all sectors. An increase in L^t thus increases learning by G_i. Denoting by G^* the function

$$G(L^t/n, L^t/n, \ldots), \text{ with } G^{*\prime} = G_i, \text{ we can write the first-order}$$
condition with full spillovers as

$$\Sigma \, U_i^t/n - v^{t\prime} = U_i^t - v^{t\prime} = -\delta \Sigma \, U_i^{t+1} \, G^{*\prime}(L_i^t) L^{t+1}/n = -\delta U_i^{t+1} \Psi^{\prime *}(L^t) L^{t+1}.$$

Substituting G^* for $G\Psi$, we obtain exactly the same results, though with a slightly different interpretation. It is likely, because of learning spillovers, that normally $G^{*\prime}$ would be greater than it would be, implying a higher level of subsidy.

9. Since, in the first period (omitting the superscript t), $\Sigma\, p_i C_i = L + \Sigma\, \tau_i C_i$, at $\tau = 0$, $\Sigma\, dC_i/d\tau = dL/d\tau > 0$. Both the income and substitution effects lead to an increased labor supply.

10. We make use of the fact that $V_{pi} = -V_I C_i$.

11. As we have noted before, one must take care in interpreting this and other optimal tax/subsidy formulas in this book, because the variables on the right-hand side are typically not constants but functions of the subsidy rate itself. Still, they provide insights into the determinants of the appropriate subsidies for optimally designed subsidies.

12. With a positive wage elasticity, ζ_j is normally greater than unity. If there is zero labor elasticity and a logarithmic utility function, then $\zeta_j = 1$ for all j. If a sector has elasticity of demand less than unity, ζ for that sector is less than unity.

For an explicit derivation of the scale parameter in the case of the symmetric model, see the discussion below in section 4.

13. Obviously, converse results hold if the demand elasticity is less than unity.

14. In this case of symmetry, $\rho = \delta V_I^{t+1}/V_I^t$.

15. That is, $(n - 1)h_{ij} >> h_{ii}$.

16. The techniques used in this section can be used to evaluate the scale parameter as a function of the tax rate in the nonsymmetric cases as well.

17. ε_{Lw} in turn can be related to underlying properties of the utility functions. In the case of separable utility functions, $\varepsilon_{Lw} = (1 - 1/\eta)/(\nu + 1/\eta)$, where η is the (absolute value of the) elasticity of marginal utility of consumption and ν is the elasticity of the marginal disutility of labor.

18. It is worth noting that in the absence of the strong assumptions of separability, consumption the first period may depend on prices (taxes) the second period. This obviously complicates the calculations considerably.

19. Both of these are total derivatives, taking into account the direct effect of the change in τ and the indirect effect on the tax in the next period.

20. Again, since β^t and β^{t+1} are functions of the tax/subsidy rate, a fuller analysis requires expressing the optimal tax/subsidy in terms of underlying parameters, as in the earlier analysis.

9. Learning with Monopolistic Competition

1. In particular, the value of ζ_i (the relative scale parameter) is sensitive to the elasticity of demand, the amount of learning in this sector, the elasticity of labor supply, what happens in other sectors, and so on. As we have noted, $p_i^t = (1 - \delta\zeta_i h_i)/(1 - 1/\acute{\eta}_i)$. On the other hand, $p_i^{t+1} = 1/[H^i(1 - 1/\acute{\eta}_i)]$. If $H^i = 1/(1 - \delta\zeta_i h_i)$, the price would be the same both periods. The smaller the elasticity of demand, the higher the markup, so the larger the sensitivity of price to any differences between H^i and $1/(1 - \delta\zeta_i h_i)$.

2. More formally, we can use the techniques used in chapter 8 to calculate an approximation to ζ^m. Equations (2) and (3) allow us to write ζ^m as a function of h. For small h:

$$\zeta^m(h) = \zeta^m(0)[1 + [d(\ln \zeta^m)/d(\ln L^t)]\varepsilon_{Lw}\delta\zeta^m h].$$

Similarly, $\zeta^m(0) = 1 + \varepsilon_{Lw}H_0$. Hence,

$$\zeta^m(h) = (1 + \varepsilon_{Lw}H_0)[1 + d(\ln \zeta^m)/d(\ln L^t)]\varepsilon_{Lw} \, \delta\zeta^m h$$

$$=(1 + \varepsilon_{Lw}H_0)/[1 + (1 + \varepsilon_{Lw}H_0)(h\varepsilon_{Lw} - 1)\delta h\varepsilon_{Lw}],$$

which for small h can be approximated by

$$(1 + \varepsilon_{Lw}H_0)/[1 + (1 - \varepsilon_{Lw}^2 H_0\delta h)].$$

ζ^m is greater than unity and increases with the elasticity of labor supply and the level and elasticity of learning.

3. For instance, in the absence of learning, by setting $\kappa_i(1 - \tau_i) = 1$, or $\tau_i = 1 - 1/\kappa_i = 1/\acute{\eta}_i$, we can correct the monopoly distortion.

4. Equations (A.1) and (A.2) can be derived explicitly from equations (2) and (3) in the text. It turns out simpler if we describe the equilibrium in terms of labor inputs each period rather than consumption levels.

$$p_i^t(L_i^t) = [1 - \delta(L_i^{t+1}/L_i^t)h_i](1 - 1/\acute{\eta}_i),$$

or

$$L_i^{t+1} = [1 - (1 - 1/\acute{\eta}_i)p_i^t(L_i^t)][L_i^t/(h_i\delta)]. \qquad (A.5)$$

Equation (A.5) is a simple equation giving second-period labor input as a function of first-period labor input, where demand and technology elasticities may not be constant and may depend on first-period consumption (labor input). Equations (2) and (3) were the first-order conditions for the monopolist maximizing output (input), *given the output of all other firms*. This is the monopolistically competitive equilibrium. The demand elasticity, $\acute{\eta}_i$, is thus the partial elasticity—taking the output of other firms as given, how much the firm's price would have to change if it wished to increase sales by 1 percent. In the symmetric case, however, we can reinterpret (5) as a general equilibrium equation. In other words, we can drop the subscript i, and let $p^t(L/n)$ be the price level that would elicit the labor supply L, i.e., that solves (in the case of separable utility functions)

$$u_i'(L/n) = pv'(L). \qquad (A.6)$$

Note that $d(\ln p)/d(\ln L)$ is no longer the inverse of the (partial) elasticity of demand, but is given by

$$d(\ln p)/d(\ln L) = 1/\{d(\ln u')/d[\ln (L/n)] - d(\ln v')/d(\ln L)\}. \qquad (A.7)$$

We can then write

$$d(\ln L^{t+1})/d(\ln L^t) = 1 + d(\ln h_i)/d(\ln L_i)$$

$$- \gamma^t [d(\ln p^t)/d(\ln L^t) + d(\ln \acute{\eta}_i^t)/d(\ln L_i^t)]/(\eta - 1), \qquad (A.8)$$

where

$$\gamma = (1 - 1/\acute{\eta}_i)p_i^t(L_i^t)/[1 - (1 - 1/\acute{\eta}_i)p_i^t(L_i^t)]. \qquad (A.9)$$

Similarly, we can rewrite (A.3) to generate an equation giving second-period output (input) as a function of first-period input.

$$p_i^{t+1}(L_i^{t+1}H) = H/(1 - 1/\acute{\eta}_i) \qquad (A.10)$$

Again, we now focus on the symmetric equilibrium, with $L_i^{t+1} = L^t/n$. Totally differentiating (A.10), we obtain

$$\frac{d(\ln L^{(t+1)})}{(d \ln L^t)} = \frac{h(\eta' - 1)}{1 + \frac{\eta'}{\eta' - 1}\left(\frac{d \ln \eta'}{d \ln L^{t+1}}\right)}. \qquad (A.11)$$

Equations (A.5) and (A.10) define the equilibrium. It should be clear that they can take on quite complicated shapes, since h, $\acute{\eta}_i$, $d(\ln u')/d[\ln (L/n)]$, and $d(\ln v')/d(\ln L)$ can vary with the level of consumption and labor inputs.

It is clear that there can then exist multiple equilibria.

10. Long-Term Growth and Innovation

1. And typically, asymptotic labor supply goes to either its upper or lower bound.

2. Obviously, in the more general case, there is a transition to the steady state.

3. It is worth noting that the standard theory of monopoly requires a demand elasticity that is greater than unity.

4. $u^{t+n} = U_0 + ng$.

$$\Sigma\, ng\delta^n = \Sigma\, g\delta^n + \delta\, \Sigma\, g\delta^n + \delta^2\, \Sigma\, g\delta^n \ldots = g\, \Sigma\, \delta^n/(1 - \delta) = g/(1 - \delta)^2.$$

5. $\alpha_M/\upsilon_M - (1 - \alpha_M)/(1 - \upsilon_M) + (\alpha_M/\upsilon_M)h/(1 - \delta) = 0$, or

$$\alpha_M(1 - \upsilon_M)[1 + h/(1 - \delta)] = \upsilon_M(1 - \alpha_M), \text{ or}$$

$$\upsilon_M[1 + \alpha_M h/(1 - \delta)] = \alpha_M[1 + h/(1 - \delta)].$$

6. For convenience, we switch to continuous time. Analogous results hold in the discrete time version.

7. The full intertemporal maximization problem is somewhat more complicated and can be analyzed using standard techniques.

8. The simplest form is $\hat{H} = 1$ for $E < E^*$; that is, there is no learning.

9. As we noted earlier, Arrow's original model focused on learning through investment. But with the capital output ratio fixed, cumulative investment grows with output.

10. Long-run steady states require asymptotically constant elasticities.

11. The Infant-Economy Argument for Protection: Trade Policy in a Learning Environment

1. Indeed, in some circles, opposition to free trade would be grounds for taking away one's certification as an economist.

2. Actually, the circumstances in which free trade is welfare enhancing are more restricted than is justified by this widespread presumption. For instance, when there are imperfect risk markets, free trade can actually make all individuals worse off (see Newbery and Stiglitz 1982). For a broader discussion of these issues, see Charlton and Stiglitz (2006, 2012).

3. It is worth noting that in popular discussions, it is often argued that openness leads to more learning and that there are learning benefits associated with trade. While this may be true, this positive learning effect needs to be offset against the effects associated with the structure of production. For reasons set forth in earlier chapters, we believe that the latter effects predominate. For a contrasting view, see Grossman and Helpman (1991), who, however, essentially entirely ignore the effects upon which we focus.

4. There is a long history of the infant-industry argument for protection, dating at least back to the mid-nineteenth-century work of List (1841). For a more extensive discussion, see Chang (2002, 2003); Charlton and Stiglitz (2005); and Stiglitz (2006a). The discussion here borrows heavily from Dasgupta and Stiglitz (1988a).

5. Recall that we are using these terms as metaphors. *Agriculture* includes small-scale rural nonagricultural and craft activities. *Industry* may even include industrial agriculture.

6. As discussed at greater length in chapter 5 and formalized in earlier chapters in part 2.

7. Stiglitz and Weiss (1981) explain why there may be credit rationing with imperfect and asymmetric information.

8. In the case of East Asia, governments used rule-based systems, providing more finance to those firms that had demonstrated prowess in exporting, and especially in areas where there were significant potential technological spillovers.

9. A bank's granting of a loan, in this case, is little different from a government's decision about which researcher to support—except that in the latter case, the government can simultaneously evaluate different research applications, while the bank can only guess at what other researchers are receiving funding. Moreover, the government can assess the marginal social return associated with each project, while the private lender has to judge the expected (private) return of this particular project, i.e., the (average) probability of success times the profits that the firm will get if successful. As explained in earlier chapters, in the case of innovation, expected private returns are not closely aligned with (expected) marginal social returns. With government financing, projects get funded so long as expected marginal social returns are positive. With private financing, projects get funded so long as the bank's expected return is positive. In both cases, those with more learning potential get more access to funds. But the cutoff and the mix of projects can be markedly different. In particular, the government can take into account learning externalities.

10. One might argue that since patent protection is time limited (though firms have found clever ways of extending the effective life of patents), so too should protection be time limited. The analysis presented below shows that this may not be correct.

11. What is essential in this example is the unitary elasticity of substitution. There are problems in modeling long-term economic growth with nonunitary elasticity of substitution and differential rates of growth of productivity. With an elasticity of substitution less than unity, the high-productivity growth sector's share of global gross domestic product shrinks to zero; while with an elasticity of substitution greater than unity, it expands to unity. Both limits are uninteresting. At the same time, it is unsatisfactory simply to assume a unitary elasticity of substitution. A finite-period model of the kind presented below avoids this modeling dilemma.

12. As we noted in chapter 5, the existence of profits may not suffice to attract actual entry. Entrants care about what the market will look like after entry, and they may believe that after entry, competition would be sufficiently keen that they would make a loss. The incumbent can take entry-deterring actions which reinforce such beliefs. The incumbent can, in particular, undertake sufficient learning that it preempts entry of rivals.

13. It should be clear that in a more competitive marketplace, the sum of profits should be lower.

14. With constraints (and costs) associated with levying taxes, especially in developing countries, protectionism (a hidden tax) may seem preferable. But this lack of transparency is an important argument against protectionism.

15. Taxpayers in the country bear the costs of the infant-industry subsidy to help create an effective competitor. Government must judge whether such subsidies are worthwhile by assessing the value of the future profits it can glean from the eventual profits of the entrant plus the value of the consumer surplus that accrues to their citizens, ignoring the benefits to citizens of other countries. (If the monopolized good is an input into production, there can be further benefits from competition: higher profits to the firms that use the good as an input, higher consumer welfare from the lower prices on consumer goods that may result, higher tax revenues to the government. Such benefits are themselves global public goods, since all producers anywhere benefit. But there are likely to be localized benefits as well, and not just from knowledge spillovers; there can be, for instance, beneficial design interactions between the user and producer of the intermediate products.)

16. See chapters 3, 4, and 12 for a discussion for why geography matters for spillovers.

17. The only assumption that differs from that of earlier chapters is that concerning spillovers over space. We assume that there are perfect spillovers within a country, but no spillovers across borders. Obviously, this is a limiting case, and the more general case can be analyzed as in chapter 8.

18. Alternatively, it was argued that if it eventually should develop a comparative advantage in manufacturing, there was no point to anticipating the change. The critical assumption was that technology was exogenous.

19. As we noted in chapter 1, there are difficult problems in ascertaining a country's dynamic comparative advantage.

20. In the previous chapter, for simplicity, we normalized our units so that (in the first period) $Z = 1$ for both goods.

21. In a two-period model, nothing depends on this parameterization. In a longer-run model, we want there to be a steady state rate of growth. As the economy grows, if productivity growth depends on scale, then the rate of growth will increase.

22. It is easier to accommodate cases where η is greater than or equal to one.

23. We can use the framework of the previous chapters to give a precise calculation of U_0^a/U^f by using the indirect utility function, $U_0^a/U^f = V(p^L)/V(p^D)$.

24. That is, under our assumptions, using the notation of the previous footnote, p^L and p^D are fixed, and all that happens over time is that the scale of the economy changes.

25. As we noted earlier, the assumption of a fixed labor supply is, however, not innocuous.

26. $U^{t+1} = U^t + \ln(1 + g)$, and, using the same techniques employed earlier,

$$W = \Sigma\, U^0\{(1 + t[\ln(1 + g)]\}\delta^t,$$

from which (4) follows directly.

If U is not logarithmic but exhibits constant elasticity with respect to the scale of consumption (as before), with a fixed elasticity of marginal utility, there is a parallel analysis.

27. If at $\pi = 0$, $\partial U^*/\partial(\ln \pi) + g'\pi/[(1 - \delta)(1 + g)] < 0$, then there can be a corner solution at $\pi = 0$; and if at $\pi = 1$, $\partial U^*/\partial(\ln \pi) + g'\pi/[(1 - \delta)(1 + g)] > 0$, there can be a corner solution at $\pi = 1$. In particular, this means that if $g'(0)/\{(1 - \delta)[1 + g(0)]\} < 1 - k$, then $\pi = 0$.

28. So long as $g'' < 0$ and $g' > 0$, there is a unique solution to (7).

29. k is a measure of the difference in comparative advantage; κ is a measure of the difference in absolute advantage in the industrial sector.

30. Generalizing the results to the case where it is a trivial matter.

31. It would be an easy matter to generalize this to the case where the lagging country is nonnegligible in size and continues to import some industrial goods. We would then need an additional equation to solve simultaneously for π^{L*} and π^{D*}.

32. That is, along the first-order condition $W_\pi = 0$, $d\pi/d\kappa = -W_{\pi\kappa}/W_{\pi\pi}$. The denominator is always negative, so that the sign of $d\pi/d\kappa$ is the same as that of $W_{\pi\kappa}$, and the sign of $W_{\pi\kappa}$ is the same as that of $(f_{\pi\kappa}/f_\pi) - [f_\kappa/(1 + f)]$. We expect that an increase in κ reduces growth (when there is less catching up, there is less growth, at a given level of π), and that an increase in κ also reduces the marginal benefit of increasing π. In effect, we assume that the marginal effect dominates.

33. Notice the similarity between this result and the simple model in the appendix of chapter 2, where the backward firm never fully caught up.

34. Moreover, as we noted in an earlier footnote, even in the "normal" case, the result that the curve giving the optimal value of π as a function of κ is downward sloping depended on our assumption concerning the sign of $(f_{\pi\kappa}/f_\pi) - [f_\kappa/(1 + f)]$.

35. Assuming that the constraint (21) is binding.

36. See the discussion of dynamics with learning gaps earlier in this chapter.

37. See Korinek and Servén (2010). Other instruments, such as investment subsidies/tax credits and interest rates, are also relevant. For a discussion of the use of exchange rates (and changes in exchange rate) in the context of the East Asia miracle, see Stiglitz (1996).

38. Using the indirect utility function, it is easy to show that the effect of a change in the exchange rate depends on the magnitude of net exports or imports.

39. Though one should note there is some evidence of convergence within manufacturing. See Rodrik (2013).

40. But see Greenwald and Stiglitz (2010a, 2010b); and Stiglitz (2006a).

41. However, the same qualification exists as in note 39 (see Rodrik 2013).

41. An analysis of the full global general equilibrium effects of such policies, if pursued by enough developing countries to have systemic effects, is beyond the scope of this book.

12. The Role of Industrial and Trade Policy in Creating a Learning Society

1. For a survey, see, e.g., Acemoglu and Robinson (2012). For earlier discussions, see the 2001 World Development Report (World Bank 2001), Stiglitz (2000b), North (2005), and the references cited there.

2. For a broader discussion, see Stiglitz 2012b.

3. See Stiglitz (1998c), which describes development as a "transformation" into a society which recognizes that change is possible and that learns how to effect such.

4. See Stiglitz (2002), which lays out some of the reasons that matters turned out so differently from the way that the advocates of structural adjustment had anticipated.

5. We should be somewhat more careful. Williamson (1990) articulated the Washington Consensus in the context of the policies that were pushed in Latin America, and Africa's structural adjustment policies began well before his formulation of these ideas. But the underlying beliefs about economics and economic policy, which Williamson put so clearly, had long dominated development thinking in the international economic institutions, and the ideas were applied not just in Latin America. Williamson actually distanced himself from some of the ideas that subsequently get identified with the Washington Consensus. He was, for instance, always cautious about capital market liberalization, and capital market liberalization was *not* part of the set of policies he identified as the Washington Consensus (see Stiglitz 2008c; Williamson 2008; as well as other papers in Serra and Stiglitz 2008). For further discussion of the Washington Consensus, see Stiglitz (1998a, 1999c, 2002a).

6. In chapter 14 we will explain why even this prescription may have been misguided, at least from our learning perspective; what matters is *real* stability, as much or even more than *price* stability, and the excessive focus on the latter may have undermined the former (see Stiglitz et al. 2006).

7. It is, perhaps, worth noting that what is viewed as corruption in one society may not be viewed in that way by others. Many outsiders look at the American system of large campaign contributions and revolving doors,

which seems to "buy" favorable legislation, as a form of corruption, even if there isn't money stuffed into brown paper envelopes for the politicians themselves.

8. Dixit (2012) has argued that firms from developing countries may have a knowledge advantage in dealing with governments of other developing countries.

9. See chapters 3 and 4 for more extensive discussions of why geography matters and why learning (and learning policies) that may be relevant in one locale may be less so in others.

10. Herbert Simon emphasized that if there are differences in the performance of public and private enterprises, the differences could not be explained just by differences in incentives, since in both, typically, most individuals work for others and have to be incentivized (see, e.g., Simon 1991). "This examination of authority and organizational identification should help explain how organizations can be highly productive even though the relation between their goals and the material rewards received by employees, if it exists at all, is extremely indirect and tenuous. In particular, it helps explain why careful comparative studies have generally found it hard to identify systematic differences in productivity and efficiency between profit-making, nonprofit, and publicly controlled organizations" (Simon 1991, 39).

11. Rashid (2011, 2012) and Detragiache, Tressel, and Gupta (2008) provide data and an empirical analysis strongly supporting this conclusion. Greenwald and Stiglitz (2003) present the general theory.

12. See, e.g., Shapiro and Stiglitz (1984); Stiglitz (2002b); and the references cited there.

13. Episodic periods of labor scarcity, where firms cannot easily fill vacancies, may provide further impetus for highly risk-averse firms to focus on saving labor. See, e.g., the historical discussion of Salter (1960) and the literature to which it gave rise, including Kennedy (1964); Fellner (1961); Atkinson and Stiglitz (1969); Ahmad (1966); Stiglitz (2006b); Samuelson (1965); and Drandakis and Phelps (1966). For a recent discussion, see Acemoglu (2010), who shows how labor scarcity can encourage innovation if the technology is "strongly labor saving."

14. It is difficult to track inequality because of data limitations. The *Africa Progress Report* states that 24 countries in Africa have Gini coefficients in excess of 42, the level in China. It also points out that in a number of cases, recent growth has not been matched by falling poverty—which they attribute to inequality: "In many countries, the pattern of economic growth is reinforcing these inequalities" (Africa Progress Panel 2012, 16).

15. See, e.g., Newbery and Stiglitz (1982), who show that free trade can make everyone worse off (that is, it can be Pareto inferior) when there are imperfect risk markets, because it increases risk.

16. There is a long-standing theoretical presumption that this would be so for advanced countries (Stolper and Samuelson 1941), but there is also evidence that this is so even for developing countries (see Stiglitz 2006a). With trade liberalization often associated with an increase in unemployment, it is not surprising that there are adverse distributional consequences: Those at the bottom are most likely to be laid off, and higher unemployment puts downward pressure on wages (see Furman and Stiglitz 1999). The adverse effects of trade liberalization were often exacerbated by simultaneous measures liberalizing financial and capital markets, which contributed to economic volatility (see, e.g., Stiglitz 2008a, 2010e, 2012a). For further discussions of the possible adverse effects of liberalization on inequality, see World Bank (2005); and Topalova (2010).

17. See, e.g., Rodriguez and Rodrik (2001). Wacziarg and Welch (2003) found that roughly half of the countries in their survey experienced zero or even negative changes in growth post-liberalization.

18. A few econometric studies (cross-country regressions) have been particularly influential (see, e.g., Dollar 1992; Sachs and Warner 1995). But while these authors were careful to qualify their results, others have not been.

19. See Charlton and Stiglitz (2006, 2013). They note that sub-Saharan Africa's share of world exports decreased from 3.9 percent in 1980 to 1.9 percent in 2006, and the least-developed countries did even worse, with their average share falling from .06 percent to .02 percent over the period. Part of the explanation, as they point out, is that there are other nontariff barriers to trade, including supply constraints and infrastructure deficiencies, providing the rationale for "aid for trade."

20. See, in particular, Chang (2002, 2003). Moreover, developing countries that have reduced their tariffs have not been able to make up for the resulting shortage of revenues, e.g., through value-added taxes.

21. And indeed, with constraints on taxation (or subsidies), differential taxation of traded goods (as compared to domestically produced goods) is in general desirable (Dasgupta and Stiglitz 1971, 1974, 2000; Emran and Stiglitz 2005). These results are consistent with those that show that certain types of liberalization (e.g., of intermediate goods and capital goods) may have beneficial effects (see Estevadeordal and Taylor 2008). The effects of liberalization may depend too on the economy's situation and structure: When there already is a high level of unemployment, liberalization may have adverse effects, even if it has more positive effects in other circumstances (see Charlton and Stiglitz 2005).

22. See the brief discussion in chapter 4 above and the more extensive discussion in chapter 14 below.

23. Where tariffs are much higher on produced goods than on raw materials (see, e.g., Charlton and Stiglitz 2005).

24. Recall our discussion in chapter 3 on the observed distance in product space between the production of different commodities, with mining and

hydrocarbons being more distant from other commodities (see, e.g., Hidalgo et al. 2007).

25. Irwin and Kroszner (1999) outline the conversion of the Republican Party away from its long-time support for industrialization behind high tariff walls, beginning in the 1940s.

26. Of course, trade interventions have sometimes not worked out well. (They have been used as protectionist tools by special interests, rather than to redirect society's resources toward creating a learning society.) But the history of successful interventions suggests that failure is not inevitable. And hopefully, countries will learn from the failures (and successes) of the past, so that the returns from future interventions will presumably be greater than those from past interventions.

27. In chapter 2, we noted similarly that the existence of large unexploited potential productivity was confirmed by special historical circumstances where there was a sudden need to increase output.

28. Moreover, the circumstances confronting Latin America in the 1960s and East Asia in the 1980s and 1990s were markedly different. It is not obvious that an export growth strategy would have worked in the 1960s.

29. See Rodrik and Subramanian (2005) for the case of India. Rodrik (2001) shows that growth relative to all developing countries actually increased from 1975 to the 1980s, even though import duties increased.

30. As we noted earlier, U.S. public investments in research have had enormously high returns (Stiglitz and Wallsten 1999; Council of Economic Advisers 1995).

31. See the references cited earlier in this chapter.

32. The returns on U.S. government investments in technology and science are even higher than those of the private sector (which in turn are far higher than private sector returns elsewhere; see Council of Economic Advisers 1995).

33. Though some conservatives do argue, on this basis, that there should be a return to the gold standard, and that there should be no role for discretionary monetary policy. However, since the failure of monetarism, these extreme positions have garnered little support among economists.

13. Financial Policy and Creating a Learning Society

1. The existence of these externalities provides the rationale for financial sector regulation, and the failure to adequately take into account these externalities provides an important part of the explanation of the 2008 and other financial crises (see Stiglitz 2010b).

2. At the center of lending activities are issues of information: assessing credit worthiness and monitoring fund usage. Markets characterized by imperfect and asymmetric information—features which are central to financial

markets—are inherently characterized by externalities, resulting in market allocations not being (constrained) Pareto efficient (Greenwald and Stiglitz 1986). There are, in fact, a number of distinct categories of externalities, besides those associated with the macro-instability upon which the next chapter focuses. Actions (investments) affect credit constraints, self-selection constraints, incentive compatibility constraints, and price distributions.

3. By the Riegle-Neal Interstate Banking and Branching Efficiency Act of 1994.

4. They may also have learned bad risk management practice or a variety of other bad practices that have come to light in the aftermath of the financial crisis.

5. See also Beck, Demirgüç-Kunt, and Martinez Peria (2010). We note that there are some empirical studies that claim the opposite (see Clarke, Cull, Martinez Peria, and Sanchez 2006).

6. Because of differential information, there is likely to be more subjective risk associated with a project in the developing country than in the home country, so the expected return required to induce a loan will have to be correspondingly greater. Matters may be even worse: The foreign lender may know that in competing for domestic borrowers, it faces a winner's curse. If there are local lenders with better information, the foreign lender only succeeds in "winning" if it offers a loan at too low of an interest rate—at an interest rate below the rate at which the (better) informed domestic lender is willing to lend.

7. Even borrowers will care about their lender's life expectancy. Lending is informationally intensive; borrowers develop a relationship with the lender, which makes the market for loans particularly imperfect. If a lender goes into bankruptcy in a downturn, borrowers are especially likely to find it difficult to find an alternative source of funds (see Jaffee and Stiglitz 1990; Greenwald and Stiglitz 2003).

8. The fact is that backing any country's banking system is its government; credit default swap spreads for banks and for the sovereigns of those banks are highly correlated (IMF 2012a). Argentina and the events of the global financial crisis of 2008 showed that depositor beliefs are not always fully rational: Governments did not always come to the rescue in the way hoped.

9. Iceland provides an interesting case, because depositors in the U.K. and the Netherlands evidently felt that their assets were secure, though any "rational" analysis would have made clear the severe limitations in this small country's ability to protect them. The governments of the Netherlands and the U.K. put enormous pressure on Iceland, but in the end, largely failed.

10. A result that is particular startling, given the destruction of the war and the impediments posed to trade.

11. While the United States did not fully create "national banking" until the 1990s, the country's national banking system was created in 1863, with the

National Currency Act, which created a system of regulation for nationally chartered banks (the Office of the Comptroller of the Currency, under the U.S. Department of Treasury). These newly established nationally chartered banks were able to attract funds from outside the state, and though funds didn't flow as freely as they might have with banks that could operate freely across state boundaries, funds flowed more freely than in the previous regime.

12. More recently, some foreign banks have engaged in extensive consumer lending, taking advantage of their "learning" about how to better exploit uninformed consumers, replacing in some cases even more exploitative local money lenders.

13. Thus, *financial market liberalization* refers to opening up a country's markets to foreign financial institutions and the deregulation of financial markets more generally, while *capital market liberalization* focuses on the movement of capital itself into and out of a country. Discussions of capital market liberalization usually focus on short-term capital flows (bank lending, portfolio investments) rather than foreign direct investment.

14. See, e.g., Prasad et al. (2003) and Kose et al. (2006). For these authors, the fact that volatility did not decrease in many of the countries which became more financially integrated into the global economy was a puzzle. As Stiglitz (2008a) pointed out, in models with imperfect and asymmetric information (endogenous capital market imperfections), pro-cyclical capital flows could easily be explained. More generally, in models with finite-lived individuals, capital market liberalization could lead to more volatility of consumption. (The standard models assumed infinitely lived individuals.)

15. See, e.g., Stiglitz (2000a, 2002a, 2006a, 2008a); Stiglitz et al. (2006, 2008); and the references cited there.

16. Thailand provides an example. There is an important distinction between short-run flows, the major effect of which may be an increase in the exchange rate, thus discouraging export sectors, and foreign direct investment, which *may* go into sectors associated with more learning and learning externalities.

17. See Stiglitz (2002) for a fuller discussion of the East Asia crisis and its impact on the structure of these economies.

18. It is worth noting that in Arrow's (1962a) original analysis of learning by doing, learning was related not to output, but to investment.

19. Earlier discussions also noted other impediments to financing research. The borrower had to disclose enough information to make the lender willing to provide money, but then the lender could "steal" the idea, appropriating the returns for himself.

20. For a fuller discussion, see Stiglitz (2010c).

21. This section borrows heavily from Greenwald and Stiglitz (2003); Hellman, Murdock, and Stiglitz (1996, 1997, 1998, 2000, 2002); Honohan

and Stiglitz (2001); Murdock and Stiglitz (1993); and Stiglitz and Uy (1996).

22. Part of the reason is that information (like knowledge more generally) is a public good. If capital markets were really informationally efficient, as its advocates claim, there would be no incentive to gather information. Everyone would try to be a free rider on the investments in information of others. While securitization may lead to improved risk diversification, it had adverse effects on incentives for assessing credit worthiness and monitoring, and these effects played out disastrously. For the general theory, see Grossman and Stiglitz (1976, 1980). For a discussion of the problems posed by securitization, and an explanation why the contention that it improves risk diversification may be incorrect, see Stiglitz (1992, 2010b).

23. Financial restraint needs to be distinguished from financial repression, which typically entailed large negative real interest rates. One of the standard arguments against financial restraint was that the lower (real) interest rates associated with it led to less savings; but interestingly, the East Asian countries all had very high savings rate. This may be partly because the interest elasticity of savings may be very low, but it also may be partly because government policies enhanced both the safety and convenience of financial savings.

24. The lower lending rates in turn helped increase firm equity, enabling them to engage in more risky investment (see Greenwald and Stiglitz 1993).

25. Moreover, it has also been more widely recognized that private banks also engage in "connected" lending, and, especially when the private bank looms large in the economy, taxpayers wind up picking up the tab. The distinction, in this sense, between public and private institutions is somewhat blurred. Monitoring public institutions may, in fact, be easier than monitoring private institutions.

26. We are suggesting, in other words, the creation of Arrow-Debreu securities related to the macro-state of the economy. Though it should be relatively easy to create these risk products, neither government nor the private sector has done so.

Governments and international organizations have, however, created instruments designed to eliminate, or at least reduce, risks associated with expropriation.

27. Moreover, there are limits to the interest rate that banks can charge in the initial period, because of adverse selection and incentive effects, described by Stiglitz and Weiss (1981).

28. This argument is quite apart from the question of the role that small firms play in generating new ideas.

29. As the prime minister of one developing country argued, this was the most important example of a taking by one country of another country's intellectual property (see Stiglitz 2006a).

14. Macroeconomic and Investment
Policies for a Learning Society

1. As we noted in chapter 4, there are exceptions, including the increase in productivity in the 2008 U.S. recession. In footnote 12 of chapter 4, we discussed alternative explanations. Note, however, that while the above analysis suggests that typically, foreign investors are more sensitive to adverse signals, domestic investors have access to inside information. Thus, there will be some cases where that inside information indicates to them to leave before there is an adverse public signal to which foreign investors react. In the Tequila crisis of 1994/1995, it appears that Mexicans attempted to take their money out of the country first (see Lederman et al. 2003).

2. There are, of course, other explanations. For example, they have greater incentives to become tax havens, because the loss in domestic revenues from increased tax avoidance is more than offset by the increase in foreign revenues.

3. Since weaknesses in the local banking system would not be highly correlated with weaknesses in the large international banks.

4. An exception occurs if banks become so undercapitalized that they "gamble on resurrection."

5. Moreover, as we noted above and in chapter 4, learning benefits from having a stable environment.

6. This is the case in most developing countries. Some critics have suggested that a low exchange rate exposes a country to more inflation. Two responses are in order: First, that would only be the case if the central bank did not take offsetting actions. When the economy is already at full employment, the exchange rate affects the composition of output, and it may still be the case that it shifts it toward the learning sectors. Second, inflation is affected not by the level of the exchange rate (which affects relative prices), but by changes in the exchange rate.

7. As we noted earlier, there are still costs of such an intervention—the opportunity cost of forgone consumption or investment. As we showed, the learning benefits may well exceed these opportunity costs.

8. See chapter 13 for a discussion of some of the adverse learning consequences of such policies.

9. In some cases, learning can be related to the choice of technology by the firm, and government policies can affect such choices.

10. Some investment treaties provide foreign investors greater protections than they do domestic firms (see, e.g., Stiglitz 2006a, 2008e).

11. We omit the inclusion of public goods the second period. It would complicate the analysis, without adding any insights into the particular questions at hand.

12. In this simplified formulation, because there is no second-period production of public goods, learning-by-doing in the production of public goods is not relevant. In a more general model, it would be.

13. We have made use of the standard results: $-V_{pi}^t/V_I^t = C_i^t = L_i^t$.

14. Moreover, individuals who are absorbed with ensuring their basic survival have less ability to learn. Good systems of social protection thus enhance individuals' learning capacities.

15. Intellectual Property

1. For a slightly longer discussion, see Stiglitz (2006a). (Stiglitz was the member of the Council of Economic Advisers responsible for innovation and intellectual property at the time the Uruguay Round was being discussed within the Clinton Administration.)

2. Conditional on the level of production, however, the level of expenditure on innovation may be optimal, as we noted earlier.

3. For a broader discussion of this issue, including empirical evidence, see Dosi, Marengo, and Pasquali (2006); and Dosi and Stiglitz (forthcoming).

4. We should reiterate our cautionary note: More competition does not necessarily lead to more innovation. As we noted in chapters 5 and 6, however, especially because of agency problems (managerial capitalism), a monopoly may have little to spur it into innovation. This effect may dominate in markets with only one or two firms.

5. Moreover, as we noted earlier in the volume, monopoly innovators fail to take into account any consumer surplus that results from large innovations — or the consumer surplus that accrues from higher levels of innovation.

6. With perfect information, presumably the owner of intellectual property could act as a perfectly discriminating monopolist and extract from potential users the surplus associated with the use of knowledge — so that there would be no distortion. But information is imperfect, and owners of intellectual property are far from perfectly discriminating monopolists. (For a discussion of imperfect information and monopoly distortion, see Stiglitz [1977].)

7. For a more extensive discussion of this point and related issues, see Mowery et al. (2001); David (2004a, 2004b); and Dosi and Stiglitz (forthcoming).

8. He in fact used his patent to try to organize an automobile cartel. Had the patent not been challenged by Henry Ford, who wanted to create a low-priced car, the development of the automobile would have been greatly impeded. For a discussion of this and other problems with the patent system, see Stiglitz, 2006a.

9. For an early discussion of the importance of the scope of the patent, see Merges and Nelson (1994).

10. There is now a large literature on this subject. See, e.g., Farrell and Shapiro (2008); Lemley and Shapiro (2007); and Shapiro (2001, 2010).

11. For a discussion of this story, see, e.g., Crouch (1989). Fighting their patent claims may also have diverted the attention of the Wright brothers from making further development in their own design, contributing to the United States falling behind Europe in the development of the airplane. The irony is that it appears that the critical insight concerning the control of the airplane had been patented decades earlier, in 1868, by British inventor Matthew Piers Watt Boulton. Had the patent examiners known of this earlier patent, they might not have granted the Wright brothers their patent. The limitations of the U.S. patent system may be further highlighted by the fact that the Wright brothers' original patent application in 1903 was rejected. It was only when they reapplied, using a patent attorney, that they were granted the patent.

12. Michael Heller and his coauthors have provided other examples of how patents can deter innovation, invoking the term *anticommons*. See Heller (1998, 2008); and Heller and Eisenberg (1998).

13. It used to be the case that once granted a patent, the owner could exclude others from using that intellectual property *until the patent was overturned*. This has become a source of special concern, given the large number of bad patents— patents which should not have been issued, some of which are eventually overturned. Those who have such patents could impose extortionary demands on those who wish to make use of their patents. These patent owners can even insist that those to whom they grant license not sue—eliminating a major source of challenge to patents.

14. *eBay Inc. v. MercExchange, L.L.C.*, 547 U.S. 388 (2006). Case documents can be found at http://www.supremecourt.gov/opinions/05pdf/05–130.pdf. (Accessed January 15, 2013.)

15. The court decision went some way to creating what intellectual property lawyers like Reichmann had long called for, a "liability system," under which those who use another's intellectual property have to pay compensation, but the owner of the intellectual property cannot exclude someone from using the property.

16. In 2012, a small company named X2Y sued Intel, Apple, and HP to exclude from the American market all of Intel's advanced microprocessors, all of Apple's computers (which employ these microprocessors), and those HP computers that do so. The claim was that these microprocessors infringed, in their "packaging," on an X2Y patent. X2Y had offered to sell this and a bundle of other patents for a few million dollars. Intel viewed it as a holdup and refused. The cost to Intel, Apple, and HP—let alone to the U.S. economy—of the exclusion would have been the order of billions of dollars. The law providing for the exclusion had a narrow exception—the exclusion order was not to

be issued if it was against the public interest. But the International Trade Court (ITC) had so narrowly defined the exception that it had been used only four times in forty years. The irony, of course, was that a law designed to protect American firms against foreign firms who violated the intellectual property rights of Americans was being used by a small American firm that had spent a miniscule amount on research—and far more on lawyers—to hold up some of America's leading IT companies, who were spending billions on research. Those who argued against the exclusion order contended not only that exclusion would have a large negative effect on the economy in the short run, but also that it would be counterproductive, disincentivizing research.

17. In practice, there is usually some value to a me-too innovation—for instance, there may be some patients for whom the side-effects are less—but still, the social return to such innovations is very limited and less than the private returns.

18. See chapter 6 for a formal model demonstrating this.

19. There is a large literature on the subject. For a review, see, e.g., Gallini (2002).

20. For instance, in the case of "orphan drugs," the life of the patent was extended, because it was thought that the benefits from greater incentives to innovate exceeded the costs. A still better way of creating incentives for such innovation, however, could have been provided through the prize system.

21. In April 2010, the U.S. District Court for the Southern District of New York invalidated patents on a pair of genes linked to breast and ovarian cancer held by Myriad. But in July 2011, the Court of Appeals for the Federal Circuit overturned this decision (Pollack 2011). In 2013, the Supreme Court supported the District Court decision that one could not obtain a patent for isolating a naturally occurring gene. *Association for Molecular Pathology v. Myriad Genetics,* 569 U.S. 12-398 (2013)

22. See Brunswick, 36 Fed. Cl. at 207; cited in Love (2004, 13).

23. Differences in politics—including the influence of the pharmaceutical and entertainment industries—may, however, be the predominant explanation of the differences.

24. *United States v. W. Elec. Co.,* 1956 Trade Cas. (CCH) ¶ 68,246, at 71,139 (D.N.J. 1956).

25. Earlier, we noted the airplane patent pool that helped resolve conflicting claims and that allowed progress to go forward on further developing the airplane.

26. Under a U.S. law called the Tunney Act (Antitrust Procedures and Penalties Act, 15 U.S.C. §16), members of the public have an opportunity to comment on a proposed settlement of a civil antitrust suit before it is accepted by a court. At the time of the proposed Microsoft settlement, I filed an affidavit together with Jason Furman (later the deputy head of the U.S. National

Economic Council and chairman of the Council of Economic Advisers under President Obama) explaining why limiting the length of the patent would be a preferable way to address the anticompetitive abuses.

27. The discussion of this section is adapted from Stiglitz (2008b); Stiglitz (2013a); and Dosi and Stiglitz (forthcoming. It draws heavily upon Freeman (1987); Lundvall (2010); and Nelson (2004).

28. The general theory of prizes is set forth in Nalebuff and Stiglitz (1983a, 1983b). Subsequently, there has developed a large literature on the use of prizes as an incentive system (including Love and Hubbard 2007; Davis and Davis 2004; and the papers cited there). Also, a bill has been introduced into the U.S. Senate to use prizes as a way of incentivizing medical research. And in 2012 the WHO Consultative Expert Working Group on Research and Development: Financing and Coordination (CEWG), linked with its Commission on Intellectual Property Rights, Innovation and Public Health (set up by WHO in 2003 to look at the relationship between intellectual property, innovation, and public health), recommended establishing a prize system, as well as other measures to make medical research more "open." The CEWG also recommended creating patent pools and putting research outputs that address the health needs of developing countries into the public domain or making them available through open licensing.

29. For a recent discussion, see Kremer and Williams (2010). For an earlier discussion, see Stiglitz (2006a) and the references cited in earlier footnotes.

30. The Royal Agricultural Society in England also provided prizes. Brunt, Lerner, and Nicholas (2011) show that these prizes provided effective inducements to research.

31. Some of the benefits from using competitive markets to disseminate the knowledge can be obtained if the government buys out patents, i.e., giving the patent holder what the monopoly profits would have been (see Kremer 1998).

32. This chapter is devoted to IPR and its impact on creating a learning society. There are also questions associated with producing knowledge, e.g., whether knowledge production is best carried on in public, private for-profit, or nonprofit institutions. The issues of production and finance largely can be separated. Production can be undertaken privately or publicly; finance can be undertaken privately or publicly. At one extreme are government research laboratories—publicly financed research that is also publicly "produced." The IPR system is often described as the polar opposite, a private-sector solution combining private funding and private finance. But this description is misleading in two respects that we have already noted: First, much of the innovation is based on basic research that is publicly funded and often publicly produced or at least produced by not-for-profit entities, such as universities. And second, in the case of both health and defense, even the seemingly "private" funding under

an IPR regime is really public funding, since all defense expenditures are from the public purse and since the government provides most of the funding for health care expenditures in most countries. Even in the most market-oriented country, the United States, much of the funding comes from government: The National Institutes of Health represent publicly financed and publicly produced research; and government spending on health care, both through its program for poor people, Medicaid, and its program for elderly people, Medicare, represents a large share of total health care spending.

33. We say "excessive" because it may in fact be optimal to have several independent, parallel research efforts.

34. The evidence is that capital markets do not fully spread risks faced by firms, because of imperfections of information. See, e.g., Greenwald and Stiglitz (1990), who discuss the effect of information imperfections on firm behavior and argue that informational problems in the capital market cause firms to act in a risk-averse manner. (See also Stiglitz, 1982c). There is also considerable empirical evidence that markets do not efficiently distribute risk; i.e., firms act in a risk-averse manner, even when risks are uncorrelated with the market (see, e.g., Stiglitz 1982b).

35. For broader discussions of these issues, see Cimoli et al. (2013); Lewis and Reichman (2005); Nelson (2004); and Odagiri et al. (2010).

36. In this sense, as we have repeatedly noted, knowledge is a public good. Indeed, it is a *global* public good (see Stiglitz 1999a).

37. There were two critical ideas in the resolution. It recognized that intellectual property "is not an end in itself" (statement by Brazil on September 30, 2004, before the WIPO General Assembly at the introduction of the proposal for a development agenda), and it reiterated WIPO's mission to "promote creative intellectual activity" and "the transfer of technology to developing countries." The new development agenda calls for ascertaining how different intellectual property regimes affect developing countries.

38. Statement by Brazil on September 30, 2004, before the WIPO General Assembly at the introduction of the proposal for a development agenda.

39. See, e.g., Stiglitz (2006a). Indeed, it was not even clear that the IPR regime that was foisted on the world through TRIPS was well designed for the United States, as we suggested in the beginning of the chapter. It reflected the interests of the entertainment and pharmaceutical industries, and not of the scientific community.

40. For instance, in granting pharmaceutical patents, developing countries should reserve the right to grant a compulsory license for any lifesaving or life-extending drug. To be exempt from this provision, the patent applicant would have to state that the patent does not cover any such medicinal use; and if subsequently such a use were established, the government would have the right to issue a compulsory license, limited, of course, to sales for such usages.

In the context of trade agreements, see Charlton and Stiglitz (2012) and Ismail (2007) for a discussion of the "right to development."

41. See also Odagiri et al. (2010) and the various chapters of Cimoli et al. (2013).

16. Social Transformation and the Creation of a Learning Society

1. As we also noted in chapter 3, in some quarters and in some countries, it appears that the notion that policies ought to be based on the principles of the Enlightenment has to be constantly relitigated.

2. For instance, a classic experiment in psychology by Bruner and Potter (1964) suggests that preconceived ideas serve as unconscious filters of sensory impressions.

3. *Confirmatory bias* is the tendency to search for, interpret, and remember information in a way that supports one's initial beliefs. For a survey, see Rabin and Schrag (1999).

4. On the other hand, it provides a more disciplined approach to the formation of beliefs than that based on "animal spirits," which suggests that any set of beliefs is possible.

5. In this sense, our analysis goes beyond standard behavioral economics, which has used insights from psychology to modify economists' traditional reliance on hypotheses concerning individual rationality.

6. Of course, sociologists have long recognized the importance of social constructions (see, e.g., Douglas 1986), but they have not focused on modeling "equilibrium," where there is some correspondence between beliefs and perceptions and what the individuals observe.

Some economic historians have also emphasized ideas similar to those articulated here (see, e.g., North 2005).

7. Standard theory treats the categories as if they were objectively determined. Standard rational expectations theory assumes that individuals use all the relevant information, updating prior beliefs through a Bayesian process. There are no biases.

This approach is also markedly different from the very interesting models of Piketty (1995); Bénabou (2008a, 2008b); and Bénabou and Tirole (2002), who assume that individuals *strategically* choose the probability that they will remember certain signals.

8. There are an infinite number of possible correlations between observables. Individuals have to choose which among these they study. They do not gather information about many of these possible correlations because the way

we see the world suggests that they are irrelevant. If we came to believe that they were relevant, they possibly would be. This is called preconfirmatory bias. Fryer and Jackson (2008) analyze bias that emerges from categorization. See also Loury (2002).

9. Again, there is a large literature in both psychology and economics consistent with this hypothesis. Smith et al. (2008) showed that invoking in experimental subjects the feeling that they have little power impairs their performance in complex cognitive tasks. Steele (2010) provides a survey of the literature demonstrating that cuing an identity associated with a stereo-type, or cuing a condition that could confirm a negative stereotype, shifts an individual's performance in the direction of the stereotype. See also Hoff and Pandey (2011); and Afridi, Li, and Ren (2011). Experiments summarized by Compte and Postlewaite (2004) demonstrate that psychological states can affect performance. Among the earliest examples are the efficiency wage theories in economics, which noted that perceptions of unfairness can affect morale, which can in turn affect performance (see Stiglitz 1974; and Akerlof and Yellen 1986).

10. Efficiency wage theory (referred to in an earlier footnote) provided early examples of this. Perceptions of fairness can affect morale, morale can affect behavior, and this can explain the persistence of dysfunctional inequality.

11. The possibility of multiple equilibria of this sort is enhanced once it is recognized (as in chapter 11) that a more dynamic society enhances the returns associated with innovative skills and attributes, while in a less dynamic society the relative returns of bureaucrats may be higher. A high-learning society creates an ecology which is self-supporting.

12. See in particular the report of the National Commission on the Causes of the Financial and Economic Crisis in the United States (2011).

13. The complexity of the issues is illustrated by vicissitudes in attitudes toward government policies to restimulate the economy. In the aftermath of the collapse of Lehman Brothers, there was a moment in which all the world adhered to Keynesian ideas. But within two years, there was a shift toward "Hooverite" fiscal austerity policies—even though the empirical (scientific) evidence that such policies would lead to slower growth with disappointing results on deficit reduction had actually mounted in the interim.

14. But it is not as if those who believe in that institution—or even the smaller group that benefits from it—got together and figured out a set of beliefs that would accomplish what they sought. As we have noted, the theory we have presented is incomplete, in that it does not adequately explain when beliefs change and when they do not. But we believe it is a step forward to break out of the mold of rational expectations, in which the variables described above play no role.

15. Even the way we perceive institutions is affected by the prisms through which we look at the world, by our ideology. At one time, some economists suggested that institutions have a simple role in society—to fill in the "holes" in markets, to remedy market failures (see North 1973). Arnott and Stiglitz (1991); and Hoff and Sen (2006), as well as others, showed that nonmarket institutions purportedly resolving a market failure (like incomplete insurance markets) could, in this sense, be dysfunctional—they could lead to Pareto inferior outcomes.

More recent literature has highlighted the role of institutions in preserving inequalities—in the context of repeated games, equilibria in which one group is exploited by others may be sustained (see, among others, Dasgupta 2005; and Mookherjee and Ray 2003).

16. In the United States, those wanting to insulate the Fed from scrutiny as it provided massive subsidies to certain banks opposed Fed transparency (see Stiglitz 2010b).

17. The ideas in this paragraph are developed more fully in Stiglitz (2012b).

18. We are deeply indebted to Tim Besley for discussions on the ideas in this section (see Besley and Torsten 2009, 2010, forthcoming; and Besley, Persson, and Sturm 2010). Hoff and Stiglitz (2004a, 2004b, 2007) modeled the political economy of transition from communism to a market economy, employing analogous ideas. See also Acemoglu and Robinson (2000).

17. Concluding Remarks

1. See Stiglitz (2011) and the references cited there.

2. As we noted earlier, there can be some knife-edge circumstances, where firms begin in precisely identical situations, and remain so. But these are highly unstable. Any perturbation that leads one firm to have any advantage over others will have cumulative effects, until that firm becomes dominant.

3. We emphasized in earlier chapters that the market is *constrained* Pareto inefficient—even taking into account the costs of gathering information or removing information asymmetries.

20. Commentary: The Case for Industrial Policy

1. Aghion is also the author of a leading textbook in that area, *Endogenous Growth Theory* with Peter Howitt, and coeditor of the *Handbook of Economic Growth* with Steve Durlauf.

2. The choice by governments as different from one another as those of Germany, the U.K., the United States, or France, to protect the automobile

industries located on their territories, illustrates that point. The policy mix of providing credit support for the refinancing of automobile conglomerates, the "cash for clunkers" programs to speed up the renewal of domestic car fleets, R & D supports to accelerate the conversion of the car fleet to electric vehicles, the support given to first- and second-order subcontractors, the implementation of foreign aid policies whereby recipient domestic industries can also operate in the countries that provide the foreign aid, all this shows the extent to which countries which experience a crisis can mobilize the instruments available to them in order to avoid the collapse of a sector which is decisive for economic activity.

Afterword: Rethinking Industrial Policy

1. Thus, Frankel and Romer (1999) and Wacziarg (2001) point to a positive effect of trade liberalization on growth. In particular, Wacziarg showed that increasing trade restrictions by one standard deviation would reduce productivity growth by 0.264 percent annually. Similarly, Keller (2002, 2004) showed that 70 percent of international R & D spillovers are due to cross-country trade flows. More recently Aghion et al. (2008) pointed to large growth-enhancing effects of the trade liberalization and delicensing reforms introduced in India in the early 1990s, particularly in more advanced sectors or in Indian states with more flexible labor market regulations. And several studies summarized in Aghion and Griffith (2006) point to a positive effect of liberalizing product market competition and entry on innovation and productivity growth by incumbent firms, particularly those that are more advanced in their sector.

2. See also Young (1991).

3. However, Harrison (1994) questions these findings.

4. More specifically, relatedness between products i and j is measured by:

$$\phi_{i,j} = \min\{P(x_i/x_j), P(x_j/x_i)\},$$

where $P(x_i/x_j)$ is the probability that a country export (enough of) good i conditional upon exporting (enough of) good j.

References

Abernathy, William J., and Kim B. Clark. 1985. "Innovation: Mapping the winds of creative destruction," *Research Policy*, 14 (1): 3–22.

Acemoglu, Daron. 2010. "When Does Labor Scarcity Encourage Innovation?" *Journal of Political Economy* 118 (6): 1037–1078.

Acemoglu, Daron, and James Robinson. 2012. *Why Nations Fail*. New York: Random House.

——. 2000. "Why Did the West Extend the Franchise? Democracy, Inequality and Growth in Historical Perspective." *Quarterly Journal of Economics* 115 (4): 1167–1199.

Acemoglu, Daron, Philippe Aghion, L. Bursztyn, and D. Hemous. 2009. "The Environment and Directed Technical Change." NBER Working Paper 15451. http://www.nber.org/papers/w15451.

Acemoglu, Daron, Philippe Aghion, and Fabrizio Zilibotti. 2006. "Distance to Frontier, Selection and Economic Growth." *Journal of the European Economic Association* 4 (1): 37–74.

Acemoglu, Daron, James Robinson, and Thierry Verdier. 2012. "Can't We All Be More Like Scandinavians?" MIT Working Paper, March 2012. http://economics.mit.edu/files/8086.

Africa Progress Panel. 2012. *Africa Progress Report: Jobs, Justice and Equity*. Available online: http://www.africaprogresspanel.org/publications/policy-papers/africa-progress-report-2012/ (accessed February 27, 2013).

Afridi, Farzana, Sherry Xin Li, and Yufei Ren. 2011. "Social Identity and Inequality: The Impact of China's Hukou System." Manuscript, University of Texas at Dallas. http://ideas.repec.org/p/cde/cdewps/190.html.

Aghion, Philippe. 1999. "Development Banking." *Journal of Development Economics* 58: 83–100.

Aghion, Philippe, and Peter Howitt. 1998. *Endogenous Growth Theory*. Cambridge: Massachusetts Institute of Technology Press.

——. 1992. "A Model of Growth through Creative Destruction," *Econometrica*, 60 (2): 323–351.

Aghion, Philippe, Peter Howitt, and and Susanne Prantl. 2013. "Patent Rights, Product Market Reforms, and Innovation," February, Harvard University working paper.

Aghion, Philippe, Ufuk Akcigit, and Peter Howitt. 2013. "What Do We Learn from Schumpeterian Growth Theory?" NBER Working Paper 18824.

Aghion, Philippe, Nick Bloom, Richard Blundell, Rachel Griffith, and Peter Howitt. 2005. "Competition and Innovation: An Inverted U Relationship." *Quarterly Journal of Economics* 120 (2): 701–728.

Aghion, Philippe, Robin Burgess, Stephen Redding, and Fabrizio Zilibotti. 2008. "The Unequal Effects of Liberalization: Evidence from Dismantling the License Raj in India." *American Economic Review* 98 (4): 1397–1412.

Aghion, Philippe, Mathias Dewatripont, L. Du, A. Harrison, and P. Legros. 2012. "Industrial Policy and Competition." Manuscript, Harvard University. http://scholar.harvard.edu/files/aghion/files/industrial_policy_and_competition.pdf.

Aghion, Philippe, David Hemous, and Enisse Kharroubi. 2009. "Cyclical Budgetary Policy, Credit Constraints, and Industry Growth." working paper Harvard University. http://scholar.harvard.edu/aghion/publications/credit-constraints-cyclical-fiscal-policy-and-industry-growth.

Ahmad, Syed 1966. "On the Theory of Induced Invention." *Economic Journal* 76: 344–357.

Aizenman, Joshua, and Yothin Jinjarak. 2009. "Globalisation and Developing Countries—a Shrinking Tax Base?" *Journal of Development Studies* 45 (5): 653–671.

Akerlof, George. 1970. "The Market for 'Lemons': Qualitative Uncertainty and the Market Mechanism," *Quarterly Journal of Economics,* 89: 488–500.

Akerlof, George A., and R. E. Kranton. 2010. *Identity Economics: How Our Identity Shapes Our Work, Wages and Well-Being*. Princeton, N.J.: Princeton University Press.

Akerlof, George A., and Joseph E. Stiglitz. 1969. "Capital, Wages and Structural Unemployment." *Economic Journal* 79 (314): 269–281.

Akerlof, George A., and Janet L. Yellen. 1990. "The Fair Wage-Effort Hypothesis and Unemployment." *Quarterly Journal of Economics* 105 (2): 255–283.

——. 1986. *Efficiency Wage Models of the Labor Market*. Cambridge: Cambridge University Press.

Alchian, Armen. 1963. "Reliability of Progress Curves in Airframe Production." *Econometrica* 31: 679–693.

Alloy, Lauren B. and Lyn Y. Abramson 1979. "Judgment of Contingency in Depressed and Nondepressed Students: Sadder but Wiser?" *Journal of Experimental Psychology: General* 108 (4): 441–485.

Aoki, Masahiko. 1970. "A Note on Marshallian Process under Increasing Returns." *Quarterly Journal of Economics* 84 (1): 100–112.

Argote, Linda, and Dennis Epple. 1990. "Learning Curves in Manufacturing." *Science* 247: 920–924.

Argote, Linda, Sara L. Beckman, Dennis Epple. 1990. "The Persistence and Transfer of Learning in Industrial Settings." *Management Science* 36 (2): 140–154.

Ariely, Dan. 2008. *Predictably Irrational: The Hidden Forces That Shape Our Decisions*. Rev. and expanded ed. New York: Harper Collins.

Arnott, Richard, and Joseph E. Stiglitz. 1991. "Moral Hazard and Nonmarket Institutions: Dysfunctional Crowding Out or Peer Monitoring?" *American Economic Review* 81 (1): 179–190.

——. 1985. "Labor Turnover, Wage Structure & Moral Hazard: The Inefficiency of Competitive Markets." *Journal of Labor Economics* 3 (4): 434–462. Reprinted in *Selected Works of Joseph E. Stiglitz*, vol. 2, *Information and Economic Analysis: Applications to Capital, Labor, and Product Markets*, 581–600. Oxford: Oxford University Press, 2013.

Arnott, Richard, Bruce Greenwald, and Joseph E. Stiglitz. 1994. "Information and Economic Efficiency." *Information Economics and Policy* 6 (1): 77–88.

Arnott, Richard, A. Hosios, and Joseph E. Stiglitz. 1988. "Implicit Contracts, Labor Mobility and Unemployment." *American Economic Review* 78 (5): 1046–1066.

Arrow, Kenneth J. 1965. *Aspects on the Theory of Risk-Bearing*. Helsinki: Yrjö Jahnssonin Säätiö.

——. 1962a. "The Economic Implications of Learning by Doing." *Review of Economic Studies* 29: 155–173.

——. 1962b. "Economic Welfare and the Allocation of Resources for Invention." In *The Rate and Direction of Inventive Activity: Economic and Social Factors*, ed. R. Nelson, National Bureau of Economic Research (NBER). Princeton, N.J.: Princeton University Press.

——. 1951a. "An Extension of the Basic Theorems of Classical Welfare Economics." In *Proceedings of the Second Berkeley Symposium on Mathematical Statistics and Probability*, ed. J. Neyman, 507–532. Berkeley: University of California Press.

——. 1951b. *Social Choice and Individual Values*. New York: Wiley.

Arrow, Kenneth J., and F. Debreu. 1954. "Existence of an Equilibrium for a Competitive Economy." *Econometrica* 22: 265–290.

Arrow, Kenneth J., W. R. Cline, K-G. Maler, M. Munasinghe, R. Squitieri, and Joseph E. Stiglitz. 1996. "Intertemporal Equity, Discounting, and Economic Efficiency." Chapter 4 in *Climate Change 1995: Economic and Social Dimensions of Climate Change*, ed. J. Bruce, H. Lee, and E. Haites, 21–51. Cambridge: Cambridge University Press.

Arvis, Jean-François. 2013. "How Many Dimensions Do We Trade In? Products Space Geometry and Latent Comparative Advantage." World Bank Policy Research Working Paper 6478, available online at http://elibrary.world-bank.org/doi/pdf/10.1596/1813-9450-6478 (accessed December 5, 2013).

Asher, Harold. 1956. "Cost-Quantity Relationships in the Airframe Industry." Paper no. R-291, RAND Corp., Santa Monica, Calif.

Atkinson, Anthony B., and Joseph E. Stiglitz. 1980. *Lectures on Public Economics*, McGraw-Hill, New York.

Atkinson, Anthony B., and Joseph E. Stiglitz. 1969. "A New View of Technological Change." *Economic Journal* 79 (315): 573–578.

Autor, David H., and David Dorn. 2013. "The Growth of Low Skill Service Jobs and the Polarization of the U.S. Labor Market." *American Economic Review* 103 (5): 1553–1597.

Autor, David H., Lawrence F. Katz, and Melissa S. Kearney. 2008. "Trends in U.S. Wage Inequality: Revising the Revisionists." *Review of Economics and Statistics* 90 (2): 300–323.

——. 2006. "The Polarization of the U.S. Labor Market." *American Economic Review* 96 (2): 189–194.

Autor, David H., Frank Levy, and Richard J. Murnane. 2003. "The Skill Content of Recent Technological Change: An Empirical Investigation." *Quarterly Journal of Economics* 118 (4): 1279–1333.

Azvolinsky, Anna. 2012. "Lack of BRCA Testing Approval Creates Snag for Cancer Trials." *Nature Medicine* 18 (1310). doi:10.1038/nm0912-1310a. Published online September 7, 2012.

Baily, Martin Neil, and Robert M. Solow. 2001. "International Productivity Comparisons Built from the Firm Level." *Journal of Economic Perspectives* 15 (3): 151–172.

Baily, Martin Neil, Charles Hulten, David Campbell, Timothy Bresnahan, and Richard E. Caves. 1992. "Productivity Dynamics in Manufacturing Plants." *Brookings Papers on Economic Activity: Microeconomics*, 187–267.

Baldwin, R. 1969. "The Case Against Infant-Industry Tariff Protection." *Journal of Political Economy* 77 (3): 295–305.

Barrios, Salvador, and Eric Strobl. 2004. "Learning by Doing and Spillovers: Evidence from Firm-Level Panel Data." *Review of Industrial Organization* 25 (2): 175–203.

Barth, Erling, Karl O. Moene and Fredrik Willumsen. 2013. "The Scandinavian Model: an Interpretation," working paper, May 29.

Baumol, William J. 1982. "Contestable Markets: An Uprising in the Theory of Industry Structure." *American Economic Review* 72 (March): 1–15.

Baumol, William J., John C. Panzar, and Robert D. Willig. 1982. *Contestable Markets and the Theory of Industry Structure*. New York: Harcourt, Brace and Jovanovich.

Bayraktar, Nihal, and Yan Wang. 2004. "Foreign Bank Entry, Performance of Domestic Banks and Sequence of Financial Liberalization." Policy Research Working Paper Series 3416, World Bank, Washington, D.C.

Beck, Thorsten, and Asli Demirgüç-Kunt. 2006. "Small and Medium-Size Enterprises: Access to Finance as a Growth Constraint." *Journal of Banking and Finance* 30: 2931–2943.

Beck, Thorsten, Asli Demirgüç-Kunt, and Ross Levine. 2000. "A New Database on Financial Development and Structure." *World Bank Economic Review* 14: 597–605.

Beck, Thorsten, Asli Demirgüç-Kunt. and Vojislav Maksimovic. 2008. "Financing Patterns Around the World: Are Small Firms Different?" *Journal of Financial Economics* 89: 467–487.

Beck, Thorsten, Asli Demirgüç-Kunt, and Maria Soledad Martinez Peria. 2010. "Foreign Banks and Small and Medium Enterprises: Are They Really Estranged?" http://www.voxeu.org/index.php?q=node/4828.

Bénabou, Roland. 2008a. "Groupthink: Collective Delusions in Organizations and Markets." Manuscript, Princeton University, Princeton, N.J.

——. 2008b. "Ideology." *Journal of the European Economic Association* 6 (2–3): 321–352.

Bénabou, Roland, and Jean Tirole. 2009. "Over My Dead Body: Bargaining and the Price of Dignity." In *Papers and Proceedings of the One Hundred Twenty-First Meeting of the American Economic Association, American Economic Review* 99 (2): 459–465.

——. 2006. "Incentives and Prosocial Behavior." *American Economic Review* 96 (5): 1652–1678.

——. 2003, "Intrinsic and Extrinsic Motivation." *Review of Economic Studies* 70 (3): 489–520.

——. 2002. "Self-Confidence and Personal Motivation." *Quarterly Journal of Economics* 117: 871–915.

Berg, Andrew, and Jonathan Ostry. 2011. "Inequality and Unsustainable Growth: Two Sides of the Same Coin?" IMF Staff Discussion Note No. 11/08, April, International Monetary Fund.

Bértola, Luis, and José Antonio Ocampo. 2012. "Learning from Latin America: Debt Crises, Debt Rescues and When and Why They Work." Institute for the Studies of the Americas Working Paper, Institute for the Study of the Americas.http://americas.sas.ac.uk/sites/default/files/files/filestore-documents/events/Papers/Bertola_and_Ocampo_paper.pdf.

Besanko, David, Ulrich Doraszelski, Yaroslav Kryukov, and Mark Satterthwaite. 2010. "Learning-by-Doing, Organizational Forgetting, and Industry Dynamics." *Econometrica* 78: 453–508.

Besley, Tim, and Torsten Persson. 2011. "The Logic of Political Violence." *Quarterly Journal of Economics* 126 (3): 1411–1445.

——. 2010. "State Capacity, Conflict and Development." *Econometrica* 78 (1): 1–34.

——. 2009. "The Origins of State Capacity: Property Rights, Taxation and Politics." *American Economic Review* 99 (4): 1218–1244.

Besley, Tim, Torsten Persson, and Daniel M. Sturm. 2010. "Political Competition, Policy and Growth: Theory and Evidence from the United States." *Review of Economic Studies* 77 (4): 1329–1352.

Bessen, James, and Michael J. Meurer. 2008. *Patent Failure: How Judges, Bureaucrats, and Lawyers Put Innovators at Risk*, Princeton, N.J.: Princeton University Press.

Bittlingmayer, George. 1988. "Property Rights, Progress, and the Aircraft Patent Agreement." *Journal of Law and Economics* 31 (1): 227–248.

Blitzer, C., P. Dasgupta, and Joseph E. Stiglitz. 1981. "Project Appraisal and Foreign Exchange Constraints." *Economic Journal* 91 (361): 58–74.

Boldrin, Michele, and David K. Levine. 2013. "The Case against Patents," *Journal of Economic Perspectives*, 27 (1): 3–22.

Boyle, James. 2008. *The Public Domain: Enclosing the Commons of the Mind*. New Haven, Conn.: Yale University Press.

——. 2003. "The Second Enclosure Movement and the Construction of the Public Domain." *Law and Contemporary Problems* 66 (33): 33–74.

Brandt, Loren, Johannes Van Biesebroeck, and Yifan Zhang. 2012. "Creative Accounting or Creative Destruction? Firm-Level Productivity Growth in Chinese Manufacturing." *Journal of Development Economics* 97 (2): 339–351.

Braverman, A., and Joseph E. Stiglitz. 1986. "Landlords, Tenants and Technological Innovations." *Journal of Development Economics* 23 (2): 313–332.

Bruce, James P., Hoesung Lee, and Erik F. Haites, eds. 1996. *Climate Change 1995: Economic and Social Dimensions of Climate Change*. Cambridge: Cambridge University Press.

Bruner, J., and M. C. Potter. 1964. "Interference in Visual Recognition." *Science* 144 (3617): 424–425.

Brunt, Liam, Josh Lerner, and Tom Nicholas. 2011. "Inducement Prizes and Innovation." NHH Dept. of Economics Discussion Paper No. 25/2011, December 1. http://ssrn.com/abstract=1972290; or http://dx.doi.org/10.2139/ssrn.1972290.

Cabral, Luis, and Michael Riordan. 1994. "The Learning Curve, Market Dominance, and Predatory Pricing." *Econometrica* 62: 1115–1140.

Cass, David., and Joseph E. Stiglitz. 1969. "The Implications of Alternative Saving and Expectations Hypotheses for Choices of Technique and Patterns of Growth." *Journal of Political Economy* 77 (4), Part 2: 586–627.

Chang, Ha Joon. 2003. "Kicking Away the Ladder: Infant Industry Promotion in Historical Perspective." *Oxford Development Studies* 31 (1): 21–32.

——. 2002. *Kicking Away the Ladder—Development Strategy in Historical Perspective*. London: Anthem Press.

——. 2001. "Intellectual Property Rights and Economic Development: Historical lessons and emerging issues," *Journal of Human Development and Capabilities*, 2 (2): 287–309.

Charlton, Andrew, and Joseph E. Stiglitz. 2012. "The Right to Trade: A Report for the Commonwealth Secretariat on Aid for Trade." London: Commonwealth Secretariat, August.

——. 2006. "Aid for Trade: A Report for the Commonwealth Secretariat." London: Commonwealth Secretariat. Published in *International Journal of Development Issues* 5 (2): 1–41; abridged version in *Swiss Review of International Economic Relations* 61 (2): 2006.

——. 2005. *Fair Trade for All*. New York: Oxford University Press.

Cimoli, Mario, Giovanni Dosi, Keith E. Maskus, Ruth L. Okediji, Jerome H. Reichman, and Joseph E. Stiglitz, eds. 2014. *Intellectual Property Rights and Development*. Oxford: Oxford University Press,.

Cimoli, Mario, Giovanni Dosi, and Joseph E. Stiglitz, eds. 2009. *Industrial Policy and Development: The Political Economy of Capabilities Accumulation*. New York: Oxford University Press.

Clarke, George, Robert Cull, Maria Soledad Martinez Peria, and Susana M. Sanchez. 2005. "Bank Lending to Small Businesses in Latin America: Does Bank Origin Matter?" *Journal of Money, Credit and Banking*, 37 (1): 83–118.

Coase, R. 1937. "The Nature of the Firm." *Economica* 4 (16): 386–405.

Commission on Growth and Development. 2008. "The Growth Report: Strategies for Sustained growth and Inclusive Development," The International Bank for reconstruction and Development/The World Bank, Washington D.C. Available at http://web.worldbank.org/WBSITE/EXTERNAL/EXTABOUTUS/ORGANIZATION/EXTPREMNET/0,,contentMDK:23225680~pagePK:64159605~piPK:64157667~theSitePK:489961,00.html (accessed 12 Nov 2013).

Compte, Oliver, and Andrew Postlewaite. 2004. "Confidence-Enhanced Performance." *American Economic Review* 94 (5): 1535–1557.

Conniff, R. 2011 "King Ludd's War: in Luddite Protests, Which Began 200 Years Ago This Month, Technology Wasn't Really the Enemy." *Smithsonian Magazine* 41 (11): 82.

Corlett, W. J., and D. C. Hague. 1953. "Complementarity and the Excess Burden of Taxation," *Review of Economic Studies* 21: 21–30.

Council of Economic Advisers. 1995. "Supporting Research and Development to Promote Economic Growth: The Federal Government's Role." White Paper, October. http://clinton1.nara.gov/White_House/EOP/CEA/econ/html/econ-top.html.

Crouch, Tom D. 1989. *The Bishop's Boys: A Life of Wilbur and Orville Wright.* New York: Norton.

Dasgupta, Partha S. 2005. "Economics of Social Capital." *Economic Record* 81 (S1): S2–S21.

——. 2001. *Human Well-Being and the Natural Environment.* New York: Oxford University Press.

——. 1993. *An Inquiry into Well-Being and Destitution.* New York: Oxford University Press.

——. 1969. "On the Concept of Optimum Population." *Review of Economic Studies* 36 (107): 295–318.

Dasgupta, Partha and Paul David. 1994. "Toward a new economics of science," *Research Policy*, 23(5): 487–521.

Dasgupta, Partha S., and Geoffrey M. Heal. 1979. *Economic Theory and Exhaustible Resources.* Cambridge: Cambridge University Press.

——. 1974. "The Optimal Depletion of Exhaustible Resources." *Review of Economic Studies* 41, *Symposium on the Economics of Exhaustible Resources*, 3–28. Edinburgh, Scotland: Longman Group.

Dasgupta, Partha S., and Joseph E. Stiglitz. 2000. "Formal and Informal Institutions," in *Social Capital: A Multifaceted Perspective*, ed. P. Dasgupta and I. Serageldin, 59–68. Washington, D.C.: World Bank.

——. 1988a. "Learning by Doing, Market Structure, and Industrial and Trade Policies." *Oxford Economic Papers* 40 (2): 246–268.

——. 1988b. "Potential Competition, Actual Competition and Economic Welfare." *European Economic Review* 32 (May): 569–577.

——. 1982. "Market Structure and Resource Depletion: A Contribution to the Theory of Intertemporal Monopolistic Competition." *Journal of Economic Theory* 28 (1): 128–164.

——. 1981a. "Entry, Innovation, Exit: Toward a Dynamic Theory of Oligopolistic Industrial Structure." *European Economic Review* 15 (2): 137–158.

——. 1981b. "Market Structure and Resource Extraction Under Uncertainty." *Scandinavian Economic Journal* 83: 318–333.

——. 1981c. "Resource Depletion Under Technological Uncertainty." *Econometrica* 49 (1): 85–104.

——. 1980a. "Industrial Structure and the Nature of Innovative Activity." *Economic Journal* 90 (358): 266–293.

——. 1980b. "Uncertainty, Market Structure and the Speed of R&D." *Bell Journal of Economics* 11 (1): 1–28.

——. 1977. "Tariffs Versus Quotas As Revenue Raising Devices Under Uncertainty." *American Economic Review* 67 (5): 975–981.

——. 1974. "Benefit-Cost Analysis and Trade Policies." *Journal of Political Economy* 82 (1): 1–33.

——. 1972. "On Optimal Taxation and Public Production." *Review of Economic Studies* 39 (1): 87–103.

——. 1971. "Differential Taxation, Public Goods, and Economic Efficiency." *Review of Economic Studies* 38 (2): 151–174.

Dasgupta, Partha S., Richard Gilbert, and Joseph E. Stiglitz. 1983. "Strategic Considerations in Invention and Innovation: The Case of Natural Resources." *Econometrica* 51 (5): 1430–1448.

——. 1982. "Invention and Innovation Under Alternative Market Structures: The Case of Natural Resources." *Review of Economic Studies* 49 (4): 567–582.

——. 1981. "Energy Resources and Research and Development." In *Erschopfbare Ressourcen*, ed. Horst Siebert, 108: 85–108. Berlin: Duncker and Humbolt.

Dasgupta, Partha S., Geoffrey M. Heal, and Joseph E. Stiglitz. 1980. "The Taxation of Exhaustible Resources." In *Public Policy and the Tax System*, ed. G. A. Hughes and G. M. Heal, 150–172. London: George Allen and Unwin.

Dasgupta, Partha S., Geoffrey M. Heal, Joseph E. Stiglitz, Richard Gilbert, and David Newbery. 1977. *An Economic Analysis of the Conservation of Depletable Natural Resources*. Prepared for the Federal Energy Administration, May.

David, Paul A. 2004a. "From Keeping Nature's Secrets to the Institutionalization of Open Science." In *Collaborative Ownership and the Digital Economy (CODE)*, ed. R. A. Ghosh, 85–106. Cambridge, Mass.: MIT Press.

——. 2004b. "Understanding the Emergence of 'Open Science' Institutions: Functionalist Economics in Historical Context." *Industrial and Corporate Change* 13: 571–589.

——. 2002, "Does the New Economy Need All the Old IPR Institutions? Digital Information Goods and Access to Knowledge for Economic Development," Presented at Wider Conference on the New Economy in Development, Helsinki.

——. 1993, "Intellectual Property Institutions and the Panda' Thumb: Patents, Copyrights, and Trade Secrets in Economic Theory and History," in *Global Dimensions of Intellectual Property Rights in Science*, ed. M.B. Wallerstein, M.E. Mogee and R.A. Schoen, 19–62. Washington, D.C.: National Academies Press.

——. 1975. *Technical Choice Innovation and Economic Growth: Essays on American and British Experience in the Nineteenth Century*. London: Cambridge University Press.

Davis, Lee, and Jerome Davis. 2004. "How Effective Are Prizes as Incentives to Innovation? Evidence from Three 20th Century Contests." Paper presented at the DRUID Summer Conference, May 7.

Debreu, G. 1959. *The Theory of Value*. New Haven, Conn.: Yale University Press.

——. 1952. "Market Equilibrium." *Proceedings of the National Academy of Sciences* 42 (1956): 876–878.

De la Fuente, Angel, and Rafael Doménech. 2006. "Human Capital in Growth Regressions: How Much Difference Does Data Quality Make?" *Journal of the European Economic Association* 4 (1): 1–36.

Delli Gatti, Domenico, Mauro Gallegati, Bruce Greenwald, Alberto Russo, and Joseph E. Stiglitz. 2013. "Sectoral Imbalances and Long Run Crises." in *The Global Macro Economy and Finance*, ed. Franklin Allen, Masahiko Aoki, Jean-Paul Fitoussi, Nobuhiro Kiyotaki, Richard Gordon, and Joseph E. Stiglitz, 61–97. IEA Conference Volume No. 150-III, Houndmills, UK and New York: Palgrave.

———. 2012. "Mobility Constraints, Productivity Trends, and Extended Crises." *Journal of Economic Behavior & Organization* 83 (3): 375–393.

Denison, Edward F. 1962. *The Sources of Economic Growth in the United States and the Alternatives Before Us.* New York: Committee for Economic Development.

Detragiache, Enrica, Thierry Tressel, and Poonam Gupta. 2008. "Foreign Banks in Poor Countries: Theory and Evidence." *Journal of Finance* 63 (5): 2123–2160.

Diamond, P. 1967. "The Role of a Stock Market in a General Equilibrium Model with Technological Uncertainty." *American Economic Review* 57: 753–776.

Diamond, Peter A., and James Mirrlees. 1971a. "Optimal Taxation and Public Production I: Production Efficiency." *American Economic Review* 61: 8–27.

———. 1971b. "Optimal Taxation and Public Production II: Tax Rules." *American Economic Review* 61: 261–278.

Dick, Andrew R. 1991. "Learning by Doing and Dumping in the Semiconductor Industry." *Journal of Law and Economics* 34 (1): 133–159.

Dixit, A. 2012. "Corruption: Supply-Side and Demand-Side Solutions." Text for Silver Jubilee Lecture at the Indira Gandhi Institute for Development Research, February.

Dixit, A., and Joseph E. Stiglitz. 1977. "Monopolistic Competition and Optimum Product Diversity." *American Economic Review* 67 (3): 297–308.

Dollar, D. 1992. "Outward-oriented developing economies really do grow more rapidly: Evidence from 95 LDCs, 1976–85." *Economic Development and Cultural Change* 523–544.

Dosi, Giovanni, and Joseph E. Stiglitz. 2014. "The Role of Intellectual Property Rights in the Development Process, with Some Lessons from Developed Countries: An Introduction." In *Intellectual Property Rights and Development*, ed. M. Cimoli, G. Dosi, K. Maskus, R. Okediji, J. Reichman, and Joseph Stiglitz. Oxford: Oxford University Press.

Dosi Giovanni, L. Marengo, and C. Pasquali. 2006. "How Much Should Society Fuel the Greed of Innovators? On the Relations Between

Appropriability, Opportunities and Rates of Innovation." *Research Policy* 35 (8): 1110–1121.

Dosi, Giovanni, Richard Nelson, Christopher Freeman, Luc Soete, and Gerald Silverberg, eds. 1988. *Technical Change and Economic Theory*. London: Pinter.

Douglas, Mary. 1986. *How Institutions Think*. Syracuse, N.Y.: Syracuse University Press.

Drandakis, Emmanuel, and Edmund S. Phelps. 1966. "A Model of Induced Invention, Growth, and Distribution." *Economic Journal* 76 (December): 832–840.

Dwyer, Douglas. 1998. "Technology Locks, Creative Destruction, and Nonconvergence in Productivity Levels." *Review of Economic Dynamics* 1 (2): 430–473.

Edgeworth, Francis Y. 1925. *Papers Relating to Political Economy*, vol. 3. London: Macmillan.

Elborgh-Woytek, Katrin, Jean-Jacques Hallaert, Hans P. Lankes, Azim Sadikov, and Dustin Smith. 2006. "Fiscal Implications of Multilateral Tariff Cuts." IMF Working Paper WP/06/203, Washington, D.C.

Ellerman, David, and Joseph E. Stiglitz. 2001. "Not Poles Apart: 'Whither Reform?' and 'Whence Reform?'" *Journal of Policy Reform* 4 (4): 325–338.

——. 2000. "New Bridges Across the Chasm: Macro- and Micro-Strategies for Russia and Other Transitional Economies." In *Zagreb International Review of Economics and Business* 3 (1): 41–72.

Emran, Shahe, and Joseph E. Stiglitz. 2009. "Financial Liberalization, Financial Restraint, and Entrepreneurial Development." Institute for International Economic Policy Working Paper Series, Elliott School of International Affairs, The George Washington University, January.

——. 2005. "On Selective Indirect Tax Reform in Developing Countries." *Journal of Public Economics*, April, 599–623.

Estevadeordal, Antoni, and Alan Taylor. 2008. "Is the Washington Consensus Dead? Growth, Openness, and the Great Liberalization, 1970s–2000s." NBER Working Paper 14264.

Farrell, Joseph. 1987. "Information and the Coase Theorem." *Journal of Economic Perspectives* 1: 113–129.

——. 1986. "How Effective Is Potential Competition?" *Economics Letters* 20: 67–70.

Farrell, Joseph, and Carl Shapiro. 2008. "How Strong Are Weak Patents?" *American Economic Review* 98 (4): 1347–1369.

——. 1988. "Dynamic Competition With Switching Costs." *RAND Journal of Economics* 19 (1): 123–137.

Fellner, William. 1961. "Two Propositions in the Theory of Induced Innovations." *Economic Journal* 71 (282): 305–308.

Field, Alexander J. 2011. *A Great Leap Forward: 1930s Depression and Economic Growth*. New Haven, Conn.: Yale University Press.

Filippettia, Andrea, and Daniele Archibugia. 2010. "Innovation in Times of Crisis: National Systems of Innovation, Structure, and Demand." *Research Policy* 40 (2): 179–192.

Fink, Carsten, and Keith E. Maskus, eds. 2005. *Intellectual Property and Development*. Oxford: Oxford University Press.

Fleisher, Belton, Haizheng Li, and Min Qiang Zhao. 2010. "Human Capital, Economic Growth, and Regional Inequality in China." *Journal of Development Economics* 92 (2): 215–231.

Florida, Richard. 2002. *The Rise of the Creative Class: And How It's Transforming Work, Leisure, Community and Everyday Life*. New York: Perseus.

Foster, Lucia, John. C. Haltiwanger, and C. J. Krizan. 2001. "Aggregate Productivity Growth. Lessons from Microeconomic Evidence." Chap. 8 in *New Developments in Productivity Analysis*, 303–372. Cambridge, Mass.: National Bureau of Economic Research.

Frankel, Jeffrey A., and David Romer. 1999. "Does Trade Cause Growth?" *American Economic Review* 89: 379–399.

Freeman, Christopher. 1995. "The National System of Innovation in Historical Perspective", *Cambridge Journal of Economics*, 19: 5–24.

——. 1987. *Technology Policy and Economic Performance: Lessons from Japan*. London, New York: Pinter.

Friedland, Roger, and Robert R. Alford. 1991. "Bringing Society Back In: Symbols, Practices, and Institutional Contradictions." In *The New Institutionalism in Organizational Analysis*, ed. Walter W. Powell and Paul J. DiMaggio, 232–263. Chicago: University of Chicago Press.

Fryer, Roland, and Matthew O. Jackson. 2008. "A Categorical Model of Cognition and Biased Decision Making." *The B.E. Journal of Theoretical Economics* 8 (1), Article 6.

Fudenberg, Drew, and Jean Tirole. 1982. "Learning-by-Doing and Market Performance." CERAS D.P.8, Ecole Nationale des Ponts et Chaussees.

——. 1983. "Learning-by-Doing and Market Performance," *Bell Journal*, 14 (2): 522–530.

Fudenberg, Drew, Rirchard Gilbert, Jean Tirole, and Joseph E. Stiglitz. 1983. "Preemption, Leapfrogging and Competition in Patent Races." *European Economic Review* 22 (June): 3–32.

Furman, J., and Joseph E. Stiglitz. 1999. "Economic Consequences of Income Inequality." In *Symposium Proceedings, 1998: Income Inequality: Issues and Policy Options*, 221–263. Symposium held by Federal Reserve Bank of Kansas City, Jackson Hole, Wyoming.

——. 1998. "Economic Crises: Evidence and Insights from East Asia." *Brookings Papers on Economic Activity*, no. 2, 1–114. Presented at Brookings Panel on Economic Activity, Washington, D.C., September 3, 1998.

Futia, Carl A. 1980. "Schumpeterian Competition," *The Quarterly Journal of Economics* 94 (4): 675–695.

Gallini, Nancy T. 2002. "The Economics of Patents: Lessons from Recent U.S. Patent Reform." *Journal of Economic Perspectives* 16: 131–154.

Gertner, Jon. 2012. *The Idea Factory: Bell Labs and the Great Age of American Innovation*. New York: Penguin.

Ghemawat, Pankaj, and A. Michael Spence. 1985. "Learning Curve Spillovers and Market Performance." *Quarterly Journal of Economics* 100: 839–852.

Gilbert, Richard J., and David M. Newbery. 1982. "Preemptive Patenting and the Persistence of Monopoly." *American Economic Review* 72 (3): 514–526.

Goldin, Claudia, and Lawrence Katz. 2008. *The Race Between Education and Technology*. Cambridge, Mass.: Harvard University Press.

Goozner, Merrill. 2010. "Ruling on BRCA Gene Patents Could Have Limited Impact." *Journal of the National Cancer Institute* 102 (11): 754–757.

Gordon, R. 2012. "Is U.S. Economic Growth Over? Faltering Innovation Confronts the Six Headwinds." NBER Working Paper 18315, August.

Graham, Stuart, and Saurabh Vishnubhakat. 2013. "Of Smart Phone Wars and Software Patents." *Journal of Economic Perspectives* 27(1): 67–86.

Gramsci, Antonio. 1971. *Selections from the Prison Notebooks of Antonio Gramsci*, ed. and trans. Quintin Hoare and Geoffrey Nowell Smith. New York: International.

Grandstrand, Ove. 2005. "Innovation and Intellectual Property Rights." In *The Oxford Handbook of Innovation*, ed. I. Fagerberg, D. Mowery, and R. Nelson, 266–290. Oxford: Oxford University Press.

Greenwald, Bruce, and Judd Kahn. 2009. *Globalization: n. The Irrational Fear That Someone in China Will Take Your Job*. Hoboken, N. J.: John Wiley.

Greenwald, Bruce C. and Joseph E. Stiglitz. 2014a. "Industrial Policies, the Creation of a Learning Society, and Economic Development," in *The Industrial Policy Revolution I: The Role of Government Beyond Ideology*, ed. Joseph E. Stiglitz and Justin Yifu Lin, 43–71. New York: Palgrave Macmillan.

——. 2014b. "Learning and Industrial Policy: Implications for Africa," in *The Industrial Policy Revolution II: Africa in the 21st Century*, ed. Joseph E. Stiglitz, Justin Yifu Lin, and Ebrahim Patel, 25–29. New York: Palgrave Macmillan.

——. 2010a. "A Modest Proposal for International Monetary Reform." In *Time for a Visible Hand: Lessons from the 2008 World Financial Crisis*, ed. S. Griffith-Jones, J. A. Ocampo, and Joseph E. Stiglitz, 314–344. Initiative for Policy Dialogue Series. Oxford: Oxford University Press.

——. 2010b. "Towards a New Global Reserves System." *Journal of Globalization and Development* 1 (2), Article 10. A different version of the paper, with the same title, appears in *The Future Global Reserve System: An Asian Perspective*, ed. J. D. Sachs, M. Kawai, J.-W. Lee, and W. T. Woo, Asian Development Bank, June.

——. 2006. "Helping Infant Economies Grow: Foundations of Trade Policies for Developing Countries." *American Economic Review: AEA Papers and Proceedings* 96 (2): 141–146.

——. 2003. *Towards a New Paradigm in Monetary Economics.* Cambridge, UK: Cambridge University Press.

——. 1993. "Financial Market Imperfections and Business Cycles." *Quarterly Journal of Economics* 108 (1): 77–114. Reprinted in *Selected Works of Joseph E. Stiglitz*, vol. 1, *Information and Economic Analysis*, 617–648. Oxford: Oxford University Press, 2009.

——. 1990. "Asymmetric Information and the New Theory of the Firm: Financial Constraints and Risk Behavior." *American Economic Review* 80 (2): 160–165. Also NBER Working Paper 3359.

——. 1988. "Pareto Inefficiency of Market Economies: Search and Efficiency Wage Models." *American Economic Review* 78 (2): 351–355.

——. 1986. "Externalities in Economies with Imperfect Information and Incomplete Markets." *Quarterly Journal of Economics* 1 (2): 229–264.

Greenwald, Bruce C., Alec Levinson, and Joseph E. Stiglitz. 1993. "Capital Market Imperfections and Regional Economic Development," in *Finance and Development: Issues and Experience*, ed. Alberto Giovannini, 65–93. Cambridge: Cambridge University Press.

Greenwald, B., M. Salinger, and J. E. Stiglitz. 1990. "Imperfect Capital Markets and Productivity Growth." Paper presented at NBER Conference in Vail, Colo., April 1990, revised March 1991 and April 1992.

Greenwald, Bruce C., Joseph E. Stiglitz, and Andrew Weiss. 1984. "Informational Imperfections in the Capital Markets and Macroeconomic Fluctuations." *American Economic Review* 74 (2): 194–199.

Greif, Avner, and David Laitin. 2007. "A Theory of Endogenous Institutional Change." *American Political Science Review* 98 (4): 633–652.

Greiner, Alfred, Jens Rubart, and Willi Semmler. 2003. "Economic Growth, Skill-Biased Technical Change and Wage Inequality: A Model and Estimations for the U.S. and Europe." New School working paper. http://www.newschool.edu/nssr/cem/papers/wp/labor/wineq.pdf.

Griliches, Zvi, and Dale W. Jorgenson. 1967. "The Explanation of Productivity Change." *Review of Economic Studies* 34 (3): 249–283.

——. 1966. "Sources of Measured Productivity Change: Capital Input." *American Economic Review* 56 (2): 50–61.

Grossman, G., and E. Helpman. 1991. *Innovation and Growth in the Global Economy.* Cambridge, Mass.: MIT Press.

Grossman, S., and Joseph E. Stiglitz. 1980. "On the Impossibility of Informationally Efficient Markets." *American Economic Review* 70 (3): 393–408.

——. 1976. "Information and Competitive Price Systems." *American Economic Review* 66 (2): 246–253.

Gruber, Harald. 1998. "Learning by Doing and Spillovers: Further Evidence for the Semiconductor Industry." *Review of Industrial Organization* 13 (6): 697–711.

Habakkuk, H. J. 1962. *American and British Technology in the Nineteenth Century*. London: Cambridge University Press.

Hagiu, Andrei, and David B. Yoffie. 2013. "The New Patent Intermediaries: Platforms, Defensive Aggregators, and Super-Aggregators." *Journal of Economic Perspectives*, 27(1): 45–66.

Hahn, Frank. 1966. "Equilibrium Dynamics with Heterogeneous Capital Goods." *Quarterly Journal of Economics* 80: 633–646.

Hall, Bronwyn H. 1992. "Investment and Research and Development at the Firm Level: Does the Source of Financing Matter?" Working Paper, University of California, Berkeley.

——. 1991. "Corporate Restructuring and Investment Horizons." In *Capital Choices: Changing the Way America Invests in Industry*, ed. Michael Porter. Cambridge, Mass.: Harvard University Press.

——. 1990. "The Impact of Corporate Restructuring on Industrial Research and Development." *Brookings Papers on Economic Activity*, 85–136.

Hall, Robert E., and Dale W. Jorgenson. 1967. "Tax Policy and Investment Behavior." *American Economic Review* 57 (June): 391–414.

Harberger, Arnold C. "Monopoly and Resource Allocation." *The American Economic Review*, 1954, *44* (Papers and Proceedings of the Sixty-sixth Annual Meeting of the American Economic Association):7787.

——. 1971. "On Measuring the Social Opportunity Cost of Labour." *International Labor Review* 103 (6): 559–579.

Hausmann, Ricardo, and Bailey Klinger. 2007. "The Structure of the Product Space and the Evolution of Comparative Advantage." CID Working Paper No. 146. Center for International Development at Harvard University, April 2007. Available at http://www.hks.harvard.edu/var/ezp_site/stor-age/fckeditor/file/pdfs/centers-programs/centers/cid/publications/faculty/wp/146.pdf (accessed December 5, 2013).

Hausmann, Ricardo, and Dani Rodrik. 2003. "Economic Development As Self-Discovery." *Journal of Development Economics* 72 (2): 603–633.

Hausmann, Ricardo, Jason Hwang, and Dani Rodrik. 2007. "What You Export Matters." *Journal of Economic Growth* 12 (1): 1–25.

Hayek, Friedrich A. 1945. "The Use of Knowledge in Society." *American Economic Review* 35 (4): 519–530.

Heilbroner, Robert L. 1980. *The Worldly Philosophers*. 5th ed. New York: Simon and Schuster.

Helleiner, Gerald K. 1994. *Trade Policy and Industrialization in Turbulent Times*. New York: Routledge.

Heller, Michael. 1998. "The Tragedy of the Anticommons: A Concise Introduction and Lexicon." *Harvard Law Review* 76 (1): 6–25.

——. 2008. *The Gridlock Economy: How Too Much Ownership Wrecks Markets, Stops Innovation, and Costs Lives*. New York: Basic Books.

Heller, Michael A., and Rebecca S. Eisenberg. 1998. "Can Patents Deter Innovation? The Anti-Commons in Biomedical Research." *Science* 280: 698–701.

Hellman, Thomas, Kevin Murdock, and Joseph E. Stiglitz. 2002. "Franchise Value and the Dynamics of Financial Liberalization." In *Designing Financial Systems in Transition Economies: Strategies for Reform in Central and Eastern Europe*, ed. Anna Meyendorff and Anjan Thakor, 111–127. Cambridge, Mass.: MIT Press.

——. 2000. "Liberalization, Moral Hazard in Banking and Prudential Regulation: Are Capital Requirements Enough?" *American Economic Review* 90 (1): 147–165. Also published in *Industrial Organization and Regulation* 3 (17), August 2000.

——. 1998. "Financial Restraint and the Market Enhancing View." In *The Institutional Foundations of East Asian Economic Development*, ed. Y. Hayami and M. Aoki, 255–284. London: MacMillan.

——. 1997. "Financial Restraint: Toward a New Paradigm." In *The Role of Government in East Asian Economic Development*, ed. M. Aoki, H. Kim, and M. Okuna-Fujiwara, 163–207. Oxford: Clarendon Press.

——. 1996. "Deposit Mobilisation Through Financial Restraint." In *Financial Development and Economic Growth*, ed. N. Hermes and R. Lensink, 219–246. New York: Routledge.

Helpman, Elhanan, and Paul Krugman. 1991. *Innovation and Growth in the Global Economy*. Cambridge, Mass.: MIT Press.

Henry, Claude, and Joseph E. Stiglitz. 2010. "Intellectual Property, Dissemination of Innovation, and Sustainable Development." *Global Policy* 1 (1): 237–251.

Hertel, G., M. Krishnan, and S. Slaughter. 2003. "Motivation in Open Source Projects: An Internet based Survey of Contributors to the Linux Kernel", *Research Policy*, 32(7): 1159–1177.

Hertel, Guido, Sven Niedner, and Stefanie Herrmann. 2003. "Motivation in Open Source Projects: An Internet based Survey of Contributors to the Linux Kernel." *Research Policy*, 32 (7): 1159–1177.

Hicks, John R. 1935. "Annual Survey of Economic Theory: The Theory of Monopoly." *Econometrica* 3 (1): 1–20.

——. 1932. *Theory of Wages*. London: Macmillan; New York: St. Martin's.

Hidalgo, César A., and Ricardo Hausmann. 2009. "The Building Blocks of Economic Complexity." *Proceedings of the National Academy of Sciences of the United States of America*, 106 (26), 10570–5. doi:10.1073/pnas.0900943106.

Hidalgo, César A., Bailey Klinger, Albert-László Barabási, and Ricardo Hausmann. 2007. "The Product Space Conditions the Development of Nations." *Science* 317 (5837, July): 482–487.

Hirsch, Werner. 1952. "Manufacturing Progress Functions." *Review of Economics and Statistics* 34: 143–155.

Hirschman, Albert O. 1982. "The Rise and Decline of Development Economics." In *The Theory and Experience of Economic Development*, ed. M. Gersovitz and W. A. Lewis, 372–390. London: Allen and Unwin.

——. 1958. *The Strategy of Economic Development*. New Haven, Conn.: Yale University Press.

Hoff, Karla. 1997. "Bayesian Learning in an Infant Industry Model." *Journal of International Economics* 43 (3–4): 409–436.

Hoff, Karla, and Priyanka Pandey. 2011. "Names Can Hurt You (by Cueing Your Response to Incentives): Experimental Evidence on Identity and Development." Manuscript, World Bank.

——. 2006. "Discrimination, Social Identity, and Durable Inequalities." *American Economic Review, Papers and Proceedings* 96: 206–211.

——. 2005. "Opportunity Is Not Everything: How Belief Systems and Mistrust Shape Responses to Economic Incentives." *Economics of Transition* 13 (2), Special issue on *Institutions and Economic Performance*: 445–472.

Hoff, Karla. and Arijit Sen. 2006. "The Kin System as a Poverty Trap?" In *Poverty Traps*, ed. Samuel Bowles, Steven Durlauf, and Karla Hoff, 95–115. Princeton, N.J.: Princeton University Press.

Hoff, Karla, and Joseph E. Stiglitz. 2011. "The Role of Cognitive Frames in Societal Rigidity and Change." World Bank. http://www.econ.yale.edu/ seminars/develop/tdw11/hoff-110404a.pdf.

——. 2010. "Equilibrium Fictions: A Cognitive Approach to Societal Rigidity." *American Economic Review* 100 (2, May): 141–146. Extended version available as Policy Research Working Paper 5219, World Bank Development Research Group, February 2010. http://www-wds.worldbank.org/external/ default/WDSContentServer/IW3P/IB/2010/02/26/000158349_2010022608 3837/Rendered/PDF/WPS5219.pdf.

——. 2007. "Exiting a Lawless State." *Economic Journal* 118 (531): 1474–1497.

——. 2004a. "After the Big Bang? Obstacles to the Emergence of the Rule of Law in Post-Communist Societies." *American Economic Review* 94 (3): 753–763.

——. 2004b. "The Transition Process in Post-Communist Societies: Towards a Political Economy of Property Rights." In *Toward Pro-Poor Policies: Aid, Institutions and Globalization*, ed. B. Tungodden, N. Stern, and I. Kolstad, 231–245. New York: World Bank/Oxford University Press.

——. 2001. "Modern Economic Theory and Development." In *Frontiers of Development Economics: The Future in Perspective*, ed. G. Meier and Joseph Stiglitz, 389–459. Oxford: Oxford University Press.

Hollander, Samuel. 1965. *The Sources of Increased Efficiency: A Study of Du Pont Rayon Plants*. Cambridge, Mass.: MIT Press.

Holt, Jeff. 2009. "A Summary of the Primary Causes of the Housing Bubble and the Resulting Credit Crisis: A Non-Technical Paper." *Journal of Business Inquiry* 8 (1): 120–129.

Honohan, Patrick, and Joseph E. Stiglitz. 2001. "Robust Financial Restraint." In *Financial Liberalization: How Far, How Fast?* ed. G. Caprio, P. Honohan, and Joseph Stiglitz, 31–63. Cambridge, UK: Cambridge University Press.

Hsieh, Chang-Tai, and Peter J. Klenow. 2009. "Misallocation and Manufacturing TFP in China and India" *Quarterly Journal of Economics* 124 (4): 1403–1448.

Huang, Kenneth G. and Fiona E. Murray. 2008 "Does patent strategy shape the long-run supply of public knowledge? Evidence from human genetics," *Academy of Management Journal* 52(6): 1193–1221.

Humphreys, Macartan, Jeffrey D. Sachs, and Joseph E. Stiglitz, eds. 2007. *Escaping the Resource Curse*. New York: Columbia University Press.

IMF. 2012a. "Sovereigns, Banks, and Emerging Markets: Detailed Analysis and Policies." *Global Financial Stability Report*, Chapter 2. http://www.imf.org/external/pubs/ft/gfsr/2012/01/pdf/c2.pdf.

IMF. 2012b. "The Liberalization and Management of Capital Flows: An Institutional View." Online publication of the International Monetary Fund. http://www.imf.org/external/np/pp/eng/2012/111412.pdf.

Irwin, Douglas A., and Randall S. Kroszner. 1999. "Interests, Institutions, and Ideology in Securing Policy Change: The Republican Conversion to Trade Liberalization after Smoot-Hawley." *Journal of Law and Economics* 42 (2, October): 643–674.

Ismail, Faizel. 2007. "Mainstreaming Development in the WTO: Developing Countries in the Doha Round," report of CUTS International, available online at http://library.fes.de/pdf-files/bueros/genf/04888.pdf (accessed November 25, 2013).

Jaffe, Adam, and Josh Lerner. 2004. *Innovation and Its Discontents*. Princeton, N. J.: Princeton University Press.

Jaffe, Adam, Josh Lerner, and Scott Stern, eds. Year? Annual. *Innovation Policy and the Economy*. Cambridge, Mass.: MIT Press for National Bureau of Economic Research.

Jaffee, Dwight, and Joseph E. Stiglitz. 1990. "Credit Rationing." In *Handbook of Monetary Economics*, ed. B. Friedman and F. Hahn, 837–888. Amsterdam: Elsevier Science Publishers.

Janeway, William. 2012. *Doing Capitalism in the Innovation Economy,* Cambridge University Press

Jarmin, Ron S. 1994. "Learning by Doing and Competition in the Early Rayon Industry." *RAND Journal of Economics* 25 (3): 441–454.

Jayadev, Arjun, and Joseph E. Stiglitz. 2010. "Medicine for Tomorrow: Some Alternative Proposals to Promote Socially Beneficial Research and Development in Pharmaceuticals." *Journal of Generic Medicines* 7 (3): 217–226.

——. 2009. "Two Ideas to Increase Innovation and Reduce Pharmaceutical Costs and Prices." *Health Affairs* 28 (1): w165–w168.

Johnson, Simon, and James Kwak. 2010. *13 Bankers: The Wall Street Takeover and the Next Financial Meltdown* New York: Vintage.

Jourdan, P. 2014. "Towards a Resource-Based African Industrialisation Strategy." *The Industrial Policy Revolution II: Africa in the 21st Century*, ed. Joseph E. Stiglitz, Justin Yifu Lin, and Ebrahim Patel, 364–386. New York: Palgrave Macmillan.

Jovanovic, Boyan, and Saul Lach. 1989. "Entry, Exit, and Diffusion with Learning by Doing." *American Economic Review* 79 (4): 690–699.

Kahneman, Daniel. 2011. *Thinking, Fast and Slow*. New York: Farrar, Straus and Giroux.

Kaldor, Nicholas. 1961, "Capital Accumulation and Economic Growth." In *The Theory of Capital*, ed. F. A. Lutz and D. C. Hague, International Economic Association Conference. London: Macmillan; New York: St. Martin's.

——. 1957. "A Model of Economic Growth." *Economic Journal* 67:591–624.

——. 1934. "The Equilibrium of the Firm." *Economic Journal* 44 (173): 60–76.

Kaldor, Nicholas, and James A. Mirrlees. 1962. "A New Model of Economic Growth." *Review of Economic Studies* 29 (June): 174–192.

Kamien, Mort and Nancy Schwartz. 1975. "Market Structure and Innovation: A Survey," *Journal of Economic Literature*, 13(1): 1–37.

——. 1972. "Timing of Innovation and Rivalry," *Econometrica*, 40 (1): 43–60.

Kanbur, R. 1979. "Impatience, Information, and Risk Taking in a General Equilibrium Model of Occupational Choice." *Review of Economic Studies* 46 (4): 707–718.

Karl, Terry Lynn. 1997. *The Paradox of Plenty: Oil Booms and Petro-States*. Berkeley, California: University of California Press.

Keller, Wolfgang. 2004. "International Technology Diffusion." *Journal of Economic Literature* 42: 752–782.

——. 2002. "Technology Diffusion and the World Distribution of Income: The Role of Geography, Language, and Trade." University of Texas, unpublished.

Kennedy, Charles. 1964. "Induced Bias in Innovation and the Theory of Distribution." *Economic Journal* 74 (September): 541–547.

Keynes, John Maynard. 1930. "Economic Possibilities for Our Grandchildren." In *Essays in Persuasion*. New York: W. W. Norton, 1963, 358–373.

Khan, Mushtaq H. 2014. "Technology Policies and Learning with Imperfect Governance." in *The Industrial Policy Revolution II: Africa in the 21st Century*, ed. Joseph E. Stiglitz, Justin Yifu Lin, and Ebrahim Patel, 243–280. New York: Palgrave Macmillan.

———. 2012. "Governance and Growth: History, Ideology and Methods of Proof," in *Good Growth and Governance in Africa: Rethinking Development Strategies*, ed. Akbar Noman, Kwesi Botchwey, Howard Stein, and Joseph E. Stiglitz. 51–79. New York: Oxford University Press.

Kihlstrom, Richard E., and Jean Jacques Laffont. 1979. "A General Equilibrium Entrepreneurial Theory of Firm Formation Based on Risk Aversion." *Journal of Political Economy* 87: 719–848.

Kindleberger, Charles P., and Robert Aliber. 2005. *Manias, Panics, and Crashes: A History of Financial Crises*, 5th ed. New York: Wiley Investment Classics.

Klenow, Peter J., and Andrés Rodríguez-Clare. 1997. "The Neoclassical Revival in Growth Economics: Has It Gone Too Far?" In *NBER Macroeconomics Annual 1997*, vol. 12, ed. Ben S. Bernanke and Julio J. Rotemberg, 73–103. Cambridge, Mass.: MIT Press.

Knight, Frank. 1921. *Risk, Uncertainty, and Profit*. Boston: Houghton Mifflin.

Korinek, Anton, and Luis Servén. 2010. "Undervaluation Through Foreign Reserve Accumulation: Static Losses, Dynamic Gains." Policy Research Working Paper 5250, World Bank, Washington, D.C.

Kose, M. Ayhan, Eswar Prasad, Kenneth Rogoff, and Shang-Jin Wei. 2006. "Financial Globalization: A Reappraisal." IMF Working Papers, WP/06/189.

Kremer, Michael. 1998. "Patent Buy-outs: A Mechanism for Encouraging Innovation." *Quarterly Journal of Economics*, (November): 1137–1167.

Kremer, Michael, and H. Williams. 2010. "Incentivizing Innovation: Adding to the Tool Kit." In *Innovation Policy and the Economy*, ed. J. Lerner and S. M. Stern, 1–17. Cambridge, Mass.: MIT Press for the National Bureau of Economic Research.

Krueger, Anne O., and Baran Tuncer. 1982. "An Empirical Test of the Infant Industry Argument." *American Economic Review* 72: 1142–1152.

Krugman, Paul. 1981. "Trade, accumulation and uneven development," *Journal of Development Economics* 8 (2): 149–161.

———. 1979. "Increasing Returns, Monopolistic Competition, and International Trade." *Journal of International Economics* 9 (4): 469–479.

Leahy, Dermot, and J. Peter Neary. 1999. "Learning by Doing, Precommitment and Infant-Industry Promotion." *Review of Economic Studies* 66 (2): 447–474.

Lederman, Daniel, Ana María Menéndez, Guillermo Perry, and Joseph Stiglitz. 2003. "Mexican Investment After the Tequila Crisis: Basic Economics, 'Confidence' Effects or Market Imperfections?" *Journal of International Money and Finance* 22: 131–151.

Leibenstein, Harvey. 1966. "Allocative Efficiency vs. X-Efficiency." *American Economic Review* 56 (3): 392–415.

Lemley, Mark A., and Carl Shapiro. 2007. "Patent Holdup and Royalty Stacking." *Texas Law Review* 85(7): 2163–2173.

Lerner, Josh and Jean Tirole. 2002. "Some Simple Economics of Open Source." *Journal of Industrial Economics*, 2002, 50(2): 197–234.

Levhari, David. 1967. "Further Implications of Learning by Doing." *Review of Economic Studies* 33: 31–38.

——. 1966. "Extensions of Arrow's Learning by Doing." *Review of Economic Studies* 33 (2): 31–38.

Levin, Richard C. 1978. "Technical Change, Barriers to Entry, and Market Structure." *Economica* 45 (180): 347–362.

Levin, Richard C., Alvin K. Klevorick, Richard. R. Nelson and Sidney Winter. 1987. "Appropriating the Returns from Industrial R & D," *Brookings Papers on Economic Activity*, 1987 (3): 783–831.

Lewis, Tracy, and Jerome H. Reichman. 2005. "Using Liability Rules to Stimulate Local Innovation in Developing Countries: Application to Traditional Knowledge." In *International Public Goods and Transfer of Technology under a Globalized Intellectual Property Regime*, ed. K. Maskus and J. Reichman, 337–366. Cambridge University Press.

Lieberman, Marvin B. 1987. "The Learning Curve, Diffusion, and Competitive Strategy." *Strategic Management Journal* 8 (5): 441–452.

——. 1984. "The Learning Curve and Pricing in the Chemical Processing Industries." *RAND Journal of Economics* 15: 213–228.

Lin, Justin Y. 2012. *New Structural Economics: A Framework for Rethinking Development and Policy*. Washington, D.C.: World Bank.

——. 2010. "New Structural Economics: A Framework for Rethinking Development." Policy Research Working Paper 5197.

Lin, Justin Y., and Célestin Monga. Forthcoming. "Comparative Advantage: The Silver Bullet of Industrial Policy." In the proceedings of the International Economic Association's Washington roundtable on industrial policy.

Lin, Justin Y., Fang Cai, and Zhou Li. 2003. *The China Miracle: Development Strategy and Economic Reform*. Sha Tin, N.T., Hong Kong: Chinese University Press for the Hong Kong Centre for Economic Research and the International Center for Economic Growth. Lin paper is in the IEA Washington volume.

Lipsey, R. G., and Kelvin Lancaster. 1956–1957. "The General Theory of Second Best." *Review of Economic Studies* 24 (1): 11–32.

List, Friedrich. 1841. *Das nationale System der politischen Oekonomie*. Stuttgart: J. G. Cotta.

Loury, Glenn C. 2002. *The Anatomy of Racial Inequality*. Cambridge, Mass.: Harvard University Press.

——. 1979. "Market Structure and Innovation," *Quarterly Journal of Economics*, 93: 395–410.

Love, James. 2004. "Compensation Guidelines for non-Voluntary use of a Patent on Medical Technologies," Working Paper, September 7.

Love, James, and T. Hubbard. 2007. "The Big Idea: Prizes to Stimulate R & D for New Medicines." *Chicago-Kent Law Review.* 1519–1554.

Lucas, Robert E. Jr. 1993. "Making a Miracle," *Econometrica* 61 (2): 251–272.

———, 1990. "Why Doesn't Capital Flow from Rich to Poor Countries?" *American Economic Review* 80 (2): 92–96.

———. 1988. "On the Mechanics of Economic Development." *Journal of Monetary Economics* 22: 3–42.

Lundvall, Bengt-Åke, ed. 2010. *National Systems of Innovation: Toward a Theory of Innovation and Interactive Learning.* London: Anthem.

Maddison, A. 2001. *The World Economy: A Millennial Perspective.* Paris: Development Centre of the Organisation for Economic Co-operation and Development.

Malerba, Franco. 1992. "Learning by Firms and Incremental Technical Change." *Economic Journal* 102 (413): 845–859.

Malhotra, Kamal, et al. 2003. *Making Global Trade Work for People.* London: Earthscan.

Mansfield, Edwin. 1967. *Econometric Studies of Industrial Research and Technological Innovation,* New York: Norton.

Martin, Stephan. 2000. "The Theory of Contestable Markets." Working paper, Purdue University. http://www.krannert.purdue.edu/faculty/smartin/aie2/contestbk.pdf.

Matsuyama, Kiminori. 1992. "Agricultural productivity, comparative advantage, and economic growth," *Journal of Economic Theory* 58(2): 317–334.

Mazzucato, Mariana. 2013. *The Entrepreneurial State: Debunking Public vs. Private Sector Myths.* London: Anthem.

McCall, Morgan W. Jr. 2004. "Leadership Development Through Experience." *Academy of Management Executive* 18 (3): 127–130.

Meade, James E. 1955. *Trade and Welfare.* London: Oxford University Press.

Merges, R., and R. Nelson. 1994. "On Limiting or Encouraging Rivalry in Technical Progress: The Effects of Patent Scope Decisions." *Journal of Economic Behavior and Organization* 25: 1–24.

Merton, Robert. 1973. *The Sociology of Science: Theoretical and Empirical Investigations.* Chicago: University of Chicago Press.

Mian, Atif. 2006. "Distance Constraints: The Limits of Foreign Lending in Poor Economies." *Journal of Finance* 61 (3): 1465–1505.

Mokyr, Joel. 2009. *The Enlightened Economy: An Economic History of Britain, 1700–1850.* New Haven, Conn.: Yale University Press.

Mookherjee, Dilip, and Debraj Ray. 2003. "Persistent Inequality." *Review of Economic Studies* 70: 369–393.

Moretti, Enrico 2011. "Local Labor Markets." In *Handbook of Labor Economics,* ed. O. Ashenfelter and D. E. Card. Amsterdam: Elsevier, volume 4, part B, pp. 1237–1313.

Moser, Petra. 2013. "Patents and Innovation: Evidence from Economic History." *Journal of Economic Perspectives* 27 (1): 23–44.

Mowery, David C., Richard R. Nelson, Bhaven N. Sampat, and Arvids A. Ziedonis. 2001. "The Growth of Patenting and Licensing by U.S. Universities: An Assessment of the Effects of the Bayh–Dole Act of 1980." *Research Policy* 30 (1): 99–119.

Murdock, K., and Joseph E. Stiglitz. 1993. "The Effect of Financial Repression in an Economy with Positive Real Interest Rates: Theory and Evidence." Working paper, August.

Murphy, Kevin M., Andrei Shleifer, and Robert W. Vishny. 1989. "Industrialization and the Big Push." *Journal of Political Economy* 97 (5): 1003–1026.

Myrdal, Gunnar. 1968. *Asian Drama: An Inquiry into the Poverty of Nations.* New York: Twentieth Century Fund.

Nakamura, Maso, Sadao Sakakibara, and Roger Schroeder. 1998. "The Adoption of Just-in-Time Manufacturing Methods at US- and Japanese-Owned Plants: Some Empirical Evidence." *IEEE Transactions on Engineering Management* 45 (3): 230–240.

Nalebuff, Barry J., and Joseph E. Stiglitz. 1983a. "Information, Competition and Markets." *American Economic Review* 73 (2, May): 278–284. Reprinted in *Selected Works of Joseph E. Stiglitz,* vol. 1, *Information and Economic Analysis,* 400–408. Oxford: Oxford University Press, 2009.

——. 1983b. "Prizes and Incentives: Toward a General Theory of Compensation and Competition." *Bell Journal* 14 (1, Spring): 21–43. Reprinted in *Selected Works of Joseph E. Stiglitz,* vol. 2, *Information and Economic Analysis: Applications to Capital, Labor, and Product Markets,* 407–431. Oxford: Oxford University Press, 2013.

National Commission on the Causes of the Financial and Economic Crisis in the United States. 2011. *The Financial Crisis Inquiry Report of the Bipartisan National Commission on the Causes of the Financial and Economic Crisis in the United States.* http://www.gpo.gov/fdsys/pkg/GPO-FCIC/pdf/GPO-FCIC.pdf.

Nelson, Richard R. 2004. "The Challenge of Building an Effective Innovation System for Catch-up." *Oxford Development Studies* 32 (3): 365–374.

Nelson, Richard R., and Edmund S. Phelps. 1965. "Investment in Humans, Technological Diffusion and Economic Growth." Discussion Paper 189, Cowles Foundation, Yale University, New Haven, Conn.

Nelson, R. R., and Sidney G. Winter. 1993. "In Search of Useful Theory of Innovation." *Research Policy* 22 (2): 108.

——. 1982. *An Evolutionary Theory of Economic Change.* Cambridge: Belknap Press of Harvard University Press.

——. 1977. "Forces Generating and Limiting Concentration under Schumpeterian Competition," *Bell Journal* 9 (2): 524–548.

Newbery, David, and Joseph E. Stiglitz. 1982. "The Choice of Techniques and the Optimality of Market Equilibrium with Rational Expectations." *Journal of Political Economy* 90 (2): 223–246.

Noman, Akbar, and Joseph E. Stiglitz. 2012a. "African Development Prospects and Possibilities." In *The Oxford Companion to the Economics of Africa*, ed. E. Aryeetey et al., 33–40. Oxford: Oxford University Press.

——. 2012b. "Introduction and Overview." *Good Growth and Governance for Africa: Rethinking Development Strategies*, ed. A. Noman, K. Botchwey, H. Stein, and Joseph E. Stiglitz. New York: Oxford University Press.

——. 2012c. "Strategies for African Development." In *Good Growth and Global Governance in Africa*, ed. A. Noman, K. Botchwey, H. Stein, and Joseph E. Stiglitz, 3–47. New York: Oxford University Press.

Noman, Akbar, K. Botchwey, H. Stein, and Joseph E. Stiglitz, eds. 2012. *Good Growth and Governance for Africa: Rethinking Development Strategies*. New York: Oxford University Press.

Nordhaus, William D. 1969a. "An Economic Theory of Technological Change." *American Economic Association Papers and Proceedings* 59 (May): 18–28.

——. 1969b. *Invention, Growth and Welfare: A Theoretical Treatment of Technological Change*. Cambridge, Mass.: MIT Press.

North, Douglass C. 2005. *Understanding the Process of Economic Change*. Princeton, N.J.: Princeton University Press.

North, Douglass C. 1991. "Institutions." Journal of Economic Perspectives 5 (1): 97–112.

——. 1971. "Institutional Change and Economic Growth," Journal of Economic History 31 (1): 118–125.

North, Douglass, and Robert Thomas. 1973. *The Rise of the Western World*. Cambridge: Cambridge University Press.

Nunn, Nathan, and Daniel Trefler. 2010. "The Structure of Tariffs and Long-Term Growth."*American Economic Journal: Macroeconomics* 2(4): 158–194.

Obstfeld, Maurice, and Kenneth Rogoff, 2000. "The Six Major Puzzles in International Macroeconomics: Is There a Common Cause?" In *NBER Macroeconomics Annual 2000*, ed. B. S. Bernanke and K. Rogoff, 339–390. Cambridge Mass.: MIT Press.

Odagiri Hiroyuki, Akira Goto, Atsushi Sunami, and Richard R. Nelson, eds. 2010. *Intellectual Property Rights, Development, and Catch Up: An International Comparative Study*. Oxford: Oxford University Press.

OECD. 2009. "Policy Responses to the Economic Crisis: Investing in Innovation for Long-Term Growth." June. Report published online at http://www.oecd.org/science/inno/42983414.pdf.

——. 2011. *OECD Factbook*. Data available online via Google Public Data explorer, http://www.google.com/publicdata/directory.

Patel, Pari and K. Pavitt. 1994. "The Nature and Economic Importance of National Innovation Systems", *STI Review* 14, OECD, Paris.

Pecchi, Lorenzo, and Gustavo Piga, eds. 2008. *Revisiting Keynes: Economic Possibilities for Our Grandchildren*. Cambridge, Mass.: MIT Press.

Perleman, Michael. 2002. *Steal This Idea: Intellectual Property and the Corporate Confiscation of Creativity*. New York: Palgrave.

Phelps, Edmund S. 2013. *Mass Flourishing: How Grassroots Innovation Created Jobs, Challenge, and Change*. Princeton, N.J.: Princeton University Press.

Pietronero, Luciano, Matthieu Cristelli, and Andrea Tacchella. 2013. "New Metrics for Economic Complexity: Measuring the Intangible Growth Potential of Countries." Paper presented at the Plenary Conference of the Institute for New Economic Thinking, Hong Kong, April 4–7.

Piketty, Thomas. 1995. "Social Mobility and Redistributive Politics." *Quarterly Journal of Economics* 110: 551–583.

Pollack, Andrew. 2011. "Ruling Upholds Gene Patent in Cancer Test." *New York Times*, July 29. http://www.nytimes.com/2011/07/30/business/gene-patent-in-cancer-test-upheld-by-appeals-panel.html.

Porter, Michael E. 1990. *The Competitive Advantage of Nations*. New York: Free Press. (Republished with a new introduction, 1998.)

Prasad, Eswar, Kenneth Rogoff, Shang-Jin Wei, and M. Ayhan Kose. 2003. "The Effects of Financial Globalization on Developing Countries: Some Empirical Evidence." IMF Occasional Paper no. 220. Washington, D.C.: International Monetary Fund.

Rabin, Matthew, and Joel L. Schrag. 1999. "First Impressions Matter: A Model of Confirmatory Bias." *Quarterly Journal of Economics* (February): 37–82.

Radner, Roy, and Joseph E. Stiglitz. 1984. "A Nonconcavity in the Value of Information." In *Bayesian Models in Economic Theory*, ed. Marcel Boyer and Richard Kihlstrom, 33–52. Amsterdam: Elsevier Science Publications. Reprinted in *Selected Works of Joseph E. Stiglitz*, vol. 1, *Information and Economic Analysis*, 537–554. Oxford: Oxford University Press, 2009.

Rajan, Raghuram, and Luigi Zingales. 1998. "Financial Dependence and Growth." *American Economic Review* 88:559–586.

Rashid, Hamid. 2012. "Foreign Banks, Competition for Deposits and Terms and Availability of Credit in Developing Countries." Working Paper.

——. 2011. "Credit to Private Sector, Interest Spread and Volatility in Credit-Flows: Do Bank Ownership and Deposits Matter?" DESA Working Paper No. 105, ST/ESA/2011/DWP/105, May. http://www.un.org/esa/desa/papers/2011/wp105_2011.pdf.

Reinganum, Jennifer F., 1982a, "A Dynamic Game of R & D: Patent Protection and Competitive Behavior," *Econometrica*, 50 (3): 671–688.

——. 1982b. "Patent Races with a Sequence of Innovations," Working Paper, Cal Tech.

——. 1981, "Dynamic Games of Innovation," *Journal of Economic Theory* 25 (1): 21–41.

Rodriguez, Francisco, and Dani Rodrik. 2001. "Trade Policy and Economic Growth: A Skeptic's Guide to the Cross-National Evidence." In *NBER Macroeconomics Annual 2000*, vol. 15, ed. Ben S. Bernanke and Kenneth Rogoff, 261–338. Cambridge, Mass.: MIT Press.

Rodrik, Dani. 2013. "Unconditional Convergence in Manufacturing." *Quarterly Journal of Economics* 128 (1): 165–204.

——. 2010. "Diagnostics Before Prescription." *Journal of Economic Perspectives* 24 (3, Summer): 33–44.

——. 2001. "The Global Governance of Trade: As If Development Really Mattered." Background paper for the Trade and Sustainable Human Development Project, United Nations Development Programme, New York.

Rodrik, Dani, and Arvind Subramanian. 2005. "From Hindu Growth to Productivity Surge: The Mystery of the Indian Growth Transition." *IMF Staff Papers* 52, no. 2.P.

Romer, Paul. 1994. "The Origins of Endogenous Growth." *Journal of Economic Perspectives* 8 (1): 3–22.

——. 1990. "Endogenous Technological Change." *Journal of Political Economy* 98: S71–S102.

——. 1986. "Increasing Returns and Long-Run Growth." *Journal of Political Economy* 94 (5, October): 1002–1037.

Rothschild, Michael, and Joseph E. Stiglitz. 1976. "Equilibrium in Competitive Insurance Markets: An Essay on the Economics of Imperfect Information." *Quarterly Journal of Economics* 90 (4, November): 629–649.

Ruttan, Vernon W., and Yujiro Hayami. 1984. "Toward a Theory of Induced Institutional Innovation." *Journal of Development Studies* 20 (4): 203–223.

Sachs, Jeffrey D. and Andrew Warner. 1995. "Economic Reform and the Process of Global Integration," Brookings Papers on Economic Activity, Economic Studies Program, The Brookings Institution, vol. 26 (1, 25th A): 1–118.

Sah, Raj Kumar, and Joseph E. Stiglitz. 1991. "The Quality of Managers in Centralized Versus Decentralized Organizations." *Quarterly Journal of Economics* 106 (1, February): 289–325.

——. 1989a. "Sources of Technological Divergence Between Developed and Less Developed Countries." In *Debt, Stabilizations and Development: Essays in Memory of Carlos Diaz-Alejandro*, ed. G. Calvo, 423–446. Oxford: Basil Blackwell.

——. 1989b. "Technological Learning, Social Learning and Technological Change." In *The Balance Between Industry and Agriculture in Economic Development*, ed. S. Chakravarty, 285–298. London: Macmillan.

——. 1988a. "Committees, Hierarchies and Polyarchies." *Economic Journal* 98 (391, June): 451–470.

——. 1988b. "Qualitative Properties of Profit-Maximizing *K*-out-of-*N* Systems Subject to Two Kinds of Failure." *IEEE Transactions on Reliability* 37 (5, December): 515–520.

——. 1987a. "The Invariance of Market Innovation to the Number of Firms." *RAND Journal of Economics* 18 (1, Spring): 98–108.

——. 1987b. "Price Scissors and the Structure of the Economy", *Quarterly Journal of Economics*, 102: 109–134.

——. 1986. "The Architecture of Economic Systems: Hierarchies and Polyarchies." *American Economic Review* 76 (4, September): 716–727.

——. 1985. "Human Fallibility and Economic Organization." *American Economic Review* 75 (2, May) 1985): 292–296. Reprinted in *Selected Works of Joseph E. Stiglitz*, vol. 1, *Information and Economic Analysis*, 409–416. Oxford: Oxford University Press, 2009.

Salter, W. E. G. 1966. *Productivity and Technical Change*, 2nd ed. Cambridge: Cambridge University Press.

Samuelson, Paul A. 1965. "A Theory of Induced Innovation along Kennedy-Weizsacker Lines." *Review of Economics and Statistics* 33:133–146.

——. 1954. "The Pure Theory of Public Expenditure." *Review of Economics and Statistics* 36: 387–389.

——. 1948. "International Trade and the Equalisation of Factor Prices." *Economic Journal* 58 (230, June): 163–184.

——. 1938. "Welfare Economics and International Trade." *American Economic Review* 28: 261–66.

Sappington, David, and Joseph E. Stiglitz. 1987. "Information and Regulation." In *Public Regulation*, ed. E. Bailey, 3–43. London: MIT Press.

Scherer, Frederic M. 1970. *Industrial Market Structure and Economic Performance*, Chicago: Rand McNally.

Schmookler, Jacob, 1962. "Economic Sources of Innovative Activity," *Journal of Economic History* 22: 1–20.

Schumpeter, Joseph A. 1951 [1934]. "*Depressions: Can We Learn from Past Experience?*" In *Essays of J. A. Schumpeter*, ed. R. V. Clemence, 108–117. Cambridge, Mass.: Addison-Wesley.

——. 1943. *Capitalism, Socialism and Democracy*. New York: Harper.

——. 1912. *Theorie der Wirtschaflichen Entwicklung*. Leipzig: Duncker and Humbolt. Translated in 1934 as *The Theory of Economic Development: An Inquiry into Profits, Capital, Credit, Interest and the Business Cycle*.

Schwoon, Malte. 2008. "Learning by Doing, Learning Spillovers and the Diffusion of Fuel Cell Vehicles." *Simulation Modelling Practice and Theory* 16 (9): 1463–1476.

Scitovsky, Tibor. 1986. *Human Desire and Economic Satisfaction: Essays on the Frontiers of Economics*. New York: New York University Press.

Scotchmer, Suzanne. 2004. *Innovation and Incentives*. Cambridge, Mass.: MIT Press.

Serra, Narcís, and Joseph E. Stiglitz, eds. 2008. *The Washington Consensus Reconsidered: Towards a New Global Governance*. New York: Oxford University Press.

Shapiro, Carl. 2010. "Injunctions, Hold-Up, and Patent Royalties." *American Law and Economics Review* 12 (2): 280–313.

——. 2007. "Patent Reform: Aligning Reward and Contribution." Working Paper 13141, National Bureau of Economic Research, Cambridge, Mass. http://papers.nber.org/papers/w13141.

——. 2001. "Navigating the Patent Thicket: Cross Licenses, Patent Pools, and Standard Setting." In *Innovation Policy and the Economy*, ed. Adam Jaffe, Josh Lerner, and Scott Stern, 119–150. Cambridge, Mass.: MIT Press.

Shapiro, Carl, and Joseph E. Stiglitz. 1984. "Equilibrium Unemployment as a Worker Discipline Device." *American Economic Review* 74 (3): 433–444.

Shell, Karl. 1966. "Toward a Theory of Inventive Activity and Capital Accumulation." *American Economic Association Papers and Proceedings* 56: 62–68.

——, ed. 1967. *Essays on the Theory of Optimal Economic Growth*. Cambridge, Mass.: MIT Press.

Shell, Karl, and Joseph E. Stiglitz. 1967. "Allocation of Investment in a Dynamic Economy." *Quarterly Journal of Economics* 81 (November): 592–609.

Sheshinski, E. 1967a. "Optimal Accumulation with Learning by Doing." In *Essays on the Theory of Optimal Economic Growth*, ed. Karl Shell. Cambridge, Mass.: MIT Press, 31–52.

——. 1967b. "Tests of the Learning-by-Doing Hypothesis." *Review of Economics and Statistics* 49: 568–578.

Simon, Herbert A. 1991. "Organizations and Markets." *Journal of Economic Perspectives* 5 (2): 25–44.

Skeath, Susan. 1997. *Learning from "Learning by Doing": Lessons for Economic Growth*. Palo Alto, Calif.: Stanford University Press.

——. 1995. "A Role for Trade Policy? Markets with Informational Barriers to Entry." *International Trade Journal* 9 (2): 247–271.

——. 1993. "Strategic Product Choice and Equilibrium Traps for Less Developed Countries." *Journal of International Trade and Economic Development* 2 (1): 1–26.

——. 1988. "Learning, Price Effects and Income Growth." Working Paper, Princeton University, Princeton, N.J.

Smith, Pamela, Nils B. Jostmann, Adam D. Galinsky, and Wilco W. van Dijk. 2008. "Lacking Power Impairs Executive Functions." *Psychological Science* 19 (5): 441–447.

Solow, Robert M. 1970. *Growth Theory—An Exposition*. Oxford: Oxford University Press.

——. 1962a. "Substitution and Fixed Proportions in the Theory of Capital." *Review of Economic Studies* 24 (June): 207–218.

——. 1962b. "Technical Progress, Capital Formation, and Economic Growth." In *Papers and Proceedings of the Seventy-Fourth Annual Meeting of the American Economic Association*, *American Economic Review* 52 (2): 76–86.

——. 1960. "Investment and Technical Progress." In *Mathematical Methods in the Social Sciences, 1959: Proceedings of the First Stanford Symposium*, ed. K. J. Arrow, S. Karlin, and P. Suppes, 89–104. Stanford, Calif.: Stanford University Press.

——. 1957. "Technical Change and the Aggregate Production Function." *Review of Economics and Statistics* 39 (3): 312–320.

——. 1956. "A Contribution to the Theory of Economic Growth." *Quarterly Journal of Economics* 70: 65–94.

Solow, Robert M., J. Tobin, M. E. Yarri, and C. C. von Weizacker. 1966. "Neo-Classical Growth with Fixed Factor Proportions." *Review of Economic Studies* 33 (April): 79–116.

Spence, A. Michael. 1983. "Contestable Markets and the Theory of Industry Structure: A Review Article." *Journal of Economic Literature* 21 (3, September): 981–990.

——. 1981. "The Learning Curve and Competition." *Bell Journal of Economics* 12 (1): 49–70.

——. 1973. "Job Market Signaling," *Quarterly Journal of Economics* 87 (3): 355–374.

Steele, Claude M. 2010. *Whistling Vivaldi and Other Clues to How Stereotypes Affect Us*. New York: Norton.

Stiglitz, Joseph E. 2013a. "Institutional Design for China's Innovation System: Implications for Intellectual Property Rights." In *Law and Economic Development with Chinese Characteristics: Institutions for the 21st Century*, ed. D. Kennedy and Joseph E. Stiglitz. New York: Oxford University Press.

——. 2013b. "Intellectual Property Rights, the Pool of Knowledge, and Innovation." Columbia University working paper.

——. 2012a. "Contagion, Liberalization, and the Optimal Structure of Globalization." *Journal of Globalization and Development* 1 (2), article 2, 45 pages.

——. 2012b. *The Price of Inequality: How Today's Divided Society Endangers Our Future*. New York: W. W. Norton.

——. 2012c. "Rebuttal Testimony of Dr. Joseph Stiglitz on Behalf of Respondents Responding to Direct Testimony of Dr. Stern." In the Matter of Certain Microprocessors, Components Thereof, and Products Containing Same, United States International Trade Commission, Investigation No. 337-TA-781.

——. 2012d. "Direct Testimony of Joseph E. Stiglitz on Behalf of Respondents." In the Matter of Certain Microprocessors, Components Thereof, and Products Containing Same, United States International Trade Commission, Investigation No. 337-TA-781.

——. 2011. "Macroeconomic Fluctuations, Inequality, and Human Development." *Journal of Human Development and Capabilities* 13 (1): 31–58.

——. 2010a. "Evolutionary Theory and the Current Economic Crisis." Presented at the American Economic Association annual meeting, January 2010. http://www2.gsb.columbia.edu/faculty/jstiglitz/download/papers/2010_Evolutionary_Theory.pdf.

——. 2010b. *Freefall: America, Free Markets, and the Sinking of the World Economy.* New York: W. W. Norton.

——. 2010c. Introduction to *Capitalism, Socialism and Democracy* by Joseph A. Schumpeter, ix–xiv. London: Rutledge.

——. 2010d. "Learning, Growth, and Development: A Lecture in Honor of Sir Partha Dasgupta." Presented at the World Bank's Annual Bank Conference on Development Economics 2010: Development Challenges in a Post-Crisis World. Published in French as "Apprentissage, croissance et développement: conférence en l'honneur de Sir Partha Dasgupta," in *Revue D'Économie du Développement*, no. 4, December 2011, 19–86.

——. 2010e. "Risk and Global Economic Architecture: Why Full Financial Integration May Be Undesirable." *American Economic Review* 100 (2, May): 388–392.

——. 2010f. "A Social Democratic Agenda for a More Dynamic Indian Economy: Creating an Innovative and Learning Society." The 2010 Jawaharlal Nehru Memorial Lecture, New Delhi, November 18, available at http://www2.gsb.columbia.edu/faculty/jstiglitz/download/speeches/2010.11.18.Social.Democratic.Agenda.India.pdf (accessed December 5, 2013).

_____2010g. "Development-Oriented Tax Policy." In *Taxation in Developing Countries*, ed. R. H. Gordon, 11–36. New York: Columbia University Press.

——. 2009. "Information and Economic Analysis." In *Selected Works of Joseph E. Stiglitz*, vol. 1, *Information and Economic Analysis*, 29–52. Oxford: Oxford University Press.

——. 2008a. "Capital Market Liberalization, Globalization, and the IMF." In *Capital Market Liberalization and Development*, ed. Joseph E. Stiglitz and J. A. Ocampo, 76–100. New York: Oxford University Press. (Earlier version published as "Capital-Market Liberalization, Globalization and the IMF," *Oxford Review of Economic Policy* 20 (1, Spring 2004): 57–71.)

——. 2008b. "The Economic Foundations of Intellectual Property." *Duke Law Journal* 57 (6, April): 1693–1724. Sixth annual Frey Lecture in Intellectual Property, Duke University, February 16, 2007.

——. 2008c. "Is There a Post-Washington Consensus Consensus?" In *The Washington Consensus Reconsidered: Towards a New Global Governance*, ed. Narcis Serra and Joseph E. Stiglitz, 41–56. New York: Oxford University Press.

——. 2008d. "Toward a General Theory of Consumerism: Reflections on Keynes' *Economic Possibilities for Our Grandchildren*." In *Revisiting Keynes: Economic Possibilities for Our Grandchildren*, ed. G. Piga and L. Pecchi, 41–87. Cambridge, Mass.: MIT Press.

——. 2008e. "Regulating Multinational Corporations: Towards Principles of Cross-Border Legal Frameworks in a Globalized World Balancing Rights with Responsibilities," *American University International Law Review*, 23(3): 451–558, Grotius Lecture presented at the 101st Annual Meeting of the American Society for International Law, Washington, D.C., March 28, 2007.

——. 2006a. *Making Globalization Work*. New York: Norton.

——. 2006b. "Samuelson and the Factor Bias of Technological Change." In *Samuelsonian Economics and the Twenty-First Century*, ed. M. Szenberg, L. Ramrattan, and A. Gottesman, 235–251. New York: Oxford University Press.

——. 2004. "Towards a Pro-Development and Balanced Intellectual Property Regime." Keynote address presented at the Ministerial Conference on Intellectual Property for Least Developed Countries, World Intellectual Property Organization (WIPO), Seoul, October 25.

——. 2003. *Roaring Nineties*. New York: Norton.

——. 2002a. *Globalization and Its Discontents*. New York: Norton.

——. 2002b. "Information and the Change in the Paradigm in Economics." Abbreviated version of Nobel lecture. *American Economic Review* 92 (3, June): 460–501.

——. 2001a. "Democratic Development as the Fruits of Labor." Chapter 9 in *The Rebel Within*, ed. Ha-Joon Chang, 279–315. London: Wimbledon Publishing. (Originally the keynote address at the Industrial Relations Research Association, Boston, January 2000.) Shortened version: *Perspectives on Work* 4 (1): 31–38.

——. 2001b. "Participation and Development: Perspectives from the Comprehensive Development Paradigm." In *Democracy, Market Economics & Development: An Asian Perspective*, ed. Farrukh Iqbal and Jong-Il You, 49–72. Washington, D.C.: World Bank. Also Chapter 7 in *The Rebel Within*, ed. Ha-Joon Chang, 220–249. London: Wimbledon.

——. 2001c. "Challenges in the Analysis of the Role of Institutions in Economic Development." In *Villa Borsig Workshop Series 2000: The Institutional Foundations of a Market Economy*, ed. Gudrun Kochendorfer-Lucius and Boris Pleskovic, 15–28. German Foundation for International Development (DSE).

———. 2000a. "Capital Market Liberalization, Economic Growth, and Instability." In *World Development* 28 (6): 1075–1086.

———. 2000b. "Formal and Informal Institutions." In *Social Capital: A Multifaceted Perspective*, ed. P. Dasgupta and I. Serageldin, 59–68. Washington, D.C.: World Bank.

———. 2000c. "Whither Reform? Ten Years of Transition." In *Annual World Bank Conference on Economic Development*, ed. B. Pleskovic and Joseph E. Stiglitz, 27–56. Washington, D.C.: World Bank.

———. 1999a. "Knowledge as a Global Public Good." In *Global Public Goods: International Cooperation in the 21st Century*, ed. Inge Kaul, Isabelle Grunberg, and Marc A. Stern, United Nations Development Programme, 308–325. New York: Oxford University Press.

———. 1999b. "Knowledge for Development: Economic Science, Economic Policy, and Economic Advice." In *Annual World Bank Conference on Development Economics*, ed. B. Pleskovic and Joseph Stiglitz, 9–58. Washington, D.C.: World Bank.

———. 1999c. "More Instruments and Broader Goals: Moving Toward the Post-Washington Consensus." In *Development Issues in the 21st Century*, ed. G. Kochendorfer-Lucius and B. Pleskovic, 11–39. Berlin: German Foundation for International Development. Also Chapter 1 in *The Rebel Within*, ed. Ha-Joon Chang, 17–56. London: Wimbledon, 2001. Also in *WIDER Perspectives on Global Development*, ed. United Nations University—World Institute for Development Economics Research, 16–48. Houndmills, UK: Palgrave MacMillan, 2005. (Originally presented as the 1998 WIDER Annual Lecture, Helsinki, January 1998; also keynote address at Villa Borsig Winter Workshop, February 1998.)

———. 1999d. "Taxation, Public Policy and The Dynamics of Unemployment." *International Tax and Public Finance* 6: 239–262. (Paper presented to the Institute of International Finance, Cordoba, Argentina, August 24, 1998.)

———. 1998a. "An Agenda for Development in the Twenty-First Century." In *Annual World Bank Conference on Development Economics 1997*, ed. Joseph E. Stiglitz and B. Pleskovic, 17–31. Washington, D.C.: World Bank.

———. 1998b. "Pareto Efficient Taxation and Expenditure Policies, With Applications to the Taxation of Capital, Public Investment, and Externalities." Presented at conference in honor of Agnar Sandmo, Bergen, January.

———. 1998c. "Towards a New Paradigm for Development: Strategies, Policies and Processes." Ninth Raul Prebisch Lecture delivered at the Palais des Nations, Geneva, October 19, UNCTAD. Published as chapter 2 in *The Rebel Within*, ed. Ha-Joon Chang, 57–93. London: Wimbledon Publishing, 2001.

———. 1996. "Some Lessons from the East Asian Miracle." *World Bank Research Observer* 11 (2, August): 151–177.

———. 1995a. "Social Absorption Capability and Innovation." In *Social Capability and Long-Term Economic Growth*, ed. Bon Ho Koo and D. H. Perkins, 48–81. New York: St. Martin's.

———. 1995b. "The Theory of International Public Goods and the Architecture of International Organizations." Background Paper No. 7, Third Meeting, High Level Group on Development Strategy and Management of the Market Economy, United Nations University—World Institute for Development Economics Research, Helsinki, Finland, July 8–10.

———. 1994a. "Economic Growth Revisited." *Industrial and Corporate Change* 3 (1): 65–110.

———. 1994b. "Endogenous Growth and Cycles." In *Innovation in Technology, Industries, and Institutions,* ed. Y. Shionoya and M. Perlman, 121–156. Ann Arbor: University of Michigan Press,.

———. 1994c. *Whither Socialism?* Cambridge, Mass.: MIT Press.

———. 1992. "Banks Versus Markets as Mechanisms for Allocating and Coordinating Investment." In *The Economics of Cooperation: East Asian Development and the Case for Pro-Market Intervention*, ed. J. A. Roumasset and S. Barr, 15–38. Boulder, Colo.: Westview. (Presented at Investment Coordination in the Pacific Century: Lessons from Theory and Practice Conference, University of Hawaii, January 1990.) Reprinted in *Selected Works of Joseph E. Stiglitz*, vol. 2, *Information and Economic Analysis: Applications to Capital, Labor, and Product Markets*, 258–272. Oxford: Oxford University Press, 2013.

———. 1990. "Comments: Some Retrospective Views on Growth Theory." In *Growth, Productivity, Unemployment: Essays to Celebrate Bob Solow's Birthday*, ed. Peter Diamond. Cambridge, Mass.: MIT Press.

———. 1989. "Monopolistic Competition and the Capital Market." In *The Economics of Imperfect Competition and Employment—Joan Robinson and Beyond*, ed. G. Feiwel, 485–507. New York: New York University Press; also published in *The Monopolistic Competition Revolution in Retrospect*, ed. S. Brakman and B. Heijdra, 49–67. Cambridge, UK: Cambridge University Press, 2004.

———. 1988. Economic Organization, Information, and Development." In *Handbook of Development Economics*, ed. H. Chenery and T. N. Srinivasan, 185–201. Amsterdam: Elsevier Science.

———. 1987a. "Learning to Learn, Localized Learning and Technological Progress." In *Economic Policy and Technological Performance*, ed. P. Dasgupta and P. Stoneman, 125–153. Cambridge, UK: Cambridge University Press.

———. 1987b. "On the Microeconomics of Technical Progress." In *Technology Generation in Latin American Manufacturing Industries*, ed. Jorge M. Katz, 56–77. London: Macmillan. (Originally presented to IDB-CEPAL Meetings, Buenos Aires, November 1978.)

——. 1987c. "Technological Change, Sunk Costs, and Competition." *Brookings Papers on Economic Activity* 3: 883–947.

——. 1986a. "Theory of Competition, Incentives and Risk." In *New Developments in the Analysis of Market Structure*, ed. Joseph E. Stiglitz and F. Mathewson, 399–449. Cambridge, Mass.: MIT Press.

——. 1986b. "Toward a More General Theory of Monopolistic Competition." In *Prices, Competition, & Equilibrium*, ed. M. Peston and R. Quandt, 22–69. Oxford: Philip Allan/Barnes & Noble Books.

——. 1982a. "The Inefficiency of the Stock Market Equilibrium." *Review of Economic Studies* 49 (2, April): 241–261.

——. 1982b."Ownership, Control and Efficient Markets: Some Paradoxes in the Theory of Capital Markets." In *Economic Regulation: Essays in Honor of James R. Nelson,* ed. Kenneth D. Boyer and William G. Shepherd, 311–341. Michigan State University Press. Reprinted in *The Selected Works of Joseph E. Stiglitz, Volume II: Information and Economic Analysis: Applications to Capital, Labor, and Product Markets*, Oxford: Oxford University Press, 2013, 99–114.

——. 1982c. "Information and Capital Markets." In *Financial Economics: Essays in Honor of Paul Cootner*, ed. William F. Sharpe and Cathryn Cootner, 118–158. New Jersey: Prentice Hall. Also NBER Working Paper 678. Reprinted in *The Selected Works of Joseph E. Stiglitz, Volume II: Information and Economic Analysis: Applications to Capital, Labor, and Product Markets*, Oxford: Oxford University Press, 2013, pp. 55–84.

——. 1981. "Potential Competition May Reduce Welfare." *American Economic Review* 71 (2, May): 184–189.

——. 1977. Monopoly, Non-Linear Pricing and Imperfect Information: The Insurance Market." *Review of Economic Studies* 44 (3, October): 407–430.

——. 1975a. "Information and Economic Analysis." In *Current Economic Problems: Proceedings of the Association of University Teachers of Economics, Manchester, 1974*, ed. J. M. Parkin and A. R. Nobay, 27–52. Cambridge, UK: Cambridge University Press.

——. 1975b. "The Theory of Screening, Education and the Distribution of Income." *American Economic Review* 65 (3, June): 283–300. Reprinted in *Selected Works of Joseph E. Stiglitz, Volume I: Information and Economic Analysis*, Oxford: Oxford University Press, 2009, 99–121.

——. 1974a. "Theories of Discrimination and Economic Policy." In *Patterns of Racial Discrimination*, ed. G. von Furstenberg et al., 5–26. Lexington, Mass.: D. C. Heath/Lexington.

——. 1974b. "Alternative Theories of Wage Determination and Unemployment in L.D.C.'s: The Labor Turnover Model," *Quarterly Journal of Economics*, 88 (2): 194–227. Subsequently published in *Development Economics, 1*, ed. D. Lal, 288–321 Elgar, 1992. Reprinted in *The Selected Works of Joseph E. Stiglitz,*

Volume II: Information and Economic Analysis: Applications to Capital, Labor, and Product Markets, Oxford: Oxford University Press, 2013, 461–487.

——. 1972. "On the Optimality of the Stock Market Allocation of Investment." *Quarterly Journal of Economics* 86 (1, February); 25–60. (Presented to the Far Eastern Meetings of the Econometric Society, June 1970, Tokyo, Japan.)

——. 1967. "A Two-Sector, Two Class Model of Economic Growth." *Review of Economic Studies* 34 (April): 227–238.

Stiglitz, Joseph E., and José Antonio Ocampo. 2008. ed. *Capital Market Liberalization and Development*. New York: Oxford University Press.

Stiglitz, Joseph E., and M. Uy. 1996. "Financial Markets, Public Policy, and the East Asian Miracle." *World Bank Research Observer* 11 (2, August): 249–276.

Stiglitz, Joseph E., and Hirofumi Uzawa, eds. 1969. *Readings in the Modern Theory of Economic Growth*. Cambridge, Mass.: MIT Press.

Stiglitz, Joseph E., and Scott J. Wallsten. 1999. "Public-Private Technology Partnerships: Promises and Pitfalls." *American Behavioral Scientist* 43 (1, September): 52–74. Also published in *Public-Private Policy Partnerships*, ed. P. Rosenau, 37–59. Cambridge, Mass.: MIT Press, 2000.

Stiglitz, Joseph E., and Andrew Weiss. 1981. "Credit Rationing in Markets with Imperfect Information." *American Economic Review* 71 (3, June): 393–410.

Stiglitz, Joseph E., José Antonio Ocampo, Shari Spiegel, Ricardo Ffrench-Davis, and Deepak Nayyar, eds. 2006. *Stability with Growth: Macroeconomics, Liberalization, and Development*. The Initiative for Policy Dialogue Series. Oxford: Oxford University Press.

Stiglitz, Joseph E., Amartya Sen, and Jean-Paul Fitoussi. 2010. *Mismeasuring Our Lives: Why GDP Doesn't Add Up*. New York: New Press. 2008 report available at http://www.stiglitz-sen-fitoussi.fr/en/index.htm.

Stiglitz, Joseph E. and Scott J. Wallsten. 1999. "Public-Private Technology Partnerships: Promises and Pitfalls," *American Behavioral Scientist*, 43(1): 52–74. Also published in *Public-Private Policy Partnerships*, P. Rosenau (ed.), Cambridge, MA: MIT Press, 2000, pp. 37–59.

Stokey, Nancy 1986. "Dynamics of Industry Wide Learning," W. P. Heller, R. M Starr, and David Starrett, Eds., *Economic Equilibrium Analysis: Essays in Honor of Kenneth Arrow*, Vol. II., Cambridge University Press.

Stolper, Wolfgang F., and Paul A. Samuelson. 1941. "Protection and Real Wages." *Review of Economic Studies* 9 (1): 58–73.

Sunstein, Cass. 2001. *Republic.com*. Princeton, N.J.: Princeton University Press.

Sutton, John. 1991. *Sunk Costs and Market Structure: Price Competition, Advertising, and the Evolution of Concentration*. Cambridge, Mass.: MIT Press.

Thaler, Richard H., and Cass R. Sunstein. 2008. *Nudge: Improving Decisions About Health, Wealth, and Happiness*. New York: Penguin.

t'Hoen, Ellen F.M. 2003. "TRIPS, Pharmaceutical Patents and Access to Essential Medicines: Seattle, Doha and Beyond." in *Economics of AIDS and Access to HIV Care in Developing Countries: Issues and Challenges*, ed. J. P. Moatti, B.Coriat, Y. Souteyrand, et al., 39–67. Paris: ANRS.

Thompson, Peter. 2010. "Learning by Doing." Chapter 10 in *Handbook of the Economics of Innovation*, ed. Bronwyn H. Hall and Nathan Rosenberg, 1: 429–476. Amsterdam: North-Holland.

Topalova, Petia. 2010. "Factor Immobility and Regional Impacts of Trade Liberalization: Evidence on Poverty from India." *American Economic Journal: Applied Economics* 2 (4): 1–41.

United Nations Development Programme (UNDP). 2003. *Making Global Trade Work for People*. See Malhotra.

Uzawa, Hirofumi. 1968. "The Penrose Effect and Optimum Growth." *Economic Studies Quarterly* 19: 1–14.

——. 1965. "Optimum Technical Change in an Aggregate Model of Economic Growth." *International Economic Review* 6 (1): 18–31.

Varian, Hal. 2011. "Federalism Offers Opportunities for Casual Experimentation." *Economist*. April 27. http://www.economist.com/node/21256696.

Violante, Giovanni. No date. "Skill-Based Technical Change." Working paper. New York University. http://www.econ.nyu.edu/user/violante/Books/sbtc_january16.pdf.

Wacziarg, Romain. 2001. "Measuring the Dynamic Gains from Trade." *World Bank Economic Review* 15: 393–429.

Wacziarg, Romain, and Karen Horn Welch. 2003. "Trade Liberalization and Growth: New Evidence." NBER Working Paper 10152. National Bureau of Economic Research, Cambridge, Mass.

Walters, Carl J., and C. S. Holling. 1990. "Large-Scale Management Experiments and Learning by Doing." *Ecology* 71 (6): 2060–2068.

Weber, Steven. 2005. *The Success of Open Source*. Cambridge, Mass.: Harvard University Press.

Weinberg, Bruce A. 2006. "A Model of Overconfidence." Manuscript, Ohio State University, May.

Wessel, Maxwell. 2012. "Big Companies Can't Innovate Halfway." Blog of the *Harvard Business Review*, October 4. http://blogs.hbr.org/cs/2012/10/big_companies_cant_innovate_halfway.html.

Williams, Heidi L. 2013. "Intellectual Property Rights and Innovation: Evidence from the Human Genome." *Journal of Political Economy* 121 (1): 1–27.

Williamson, John. 2008. "A Short History of the Washington Consensus." in *The Washington Consensus Reconsidered: Towards a New Global Governance*, ed. Narcis Serra and Joseph E. Stiglitz, 41–56. New York: Oxford University Press.

———. 1993 "Democracy and the 'Washington consensus.'" *World Development* 21 (8, August): 1329–1336. http://www.sciencedirect.com/science/article/pii/0305750X9390046C.

———. 1990. "What Washington Means by Policy Reform." In *Latin American Adjustments: How Much Has Happened?*, ed. J. Williamson. Washington, D.C.: Institute for International Economics.

Winter, Sidney G. 1993. "Patents and Welfare." *Industrial and Corporate Change* 2 (2): 211–231.

World Bank. 2005. *World Development Report 2005: A Better Investment Climate for Everyone*. New York: World Bank and Oxford University Press.

———. 2001. *World Development Report 2000–2001: Attacking Poverty*. New York: World Bank and Oxford University Press.

———. 1999. *World Development Report 1998–99: Knowledge for Development*. New York: Oxford University Press.

———. 1993. *The East Asian Miracle: Economic Growth and Public Policy*. World Bank Policy Research Report. Oxford: Oxford University Press.

Yeyati, Eduardo Levy, and Alejandro Micco. 2007. "Concentration and Foreign Penetration in Latin American Banking Sectors: Impact on Competition and Risk." *Journal of Banking & Finance*, Elsevier, 31 (6, June): 1633–1647.

Young, Alwyn. 2003. "Gold into Base Metals: Productivity Growth in the People's Republic of China During the Reform Period." *Journal of Political Economy* 111 (6): 1220–1261.

———. 1993. "Invention and Bounded Learning by Doing." *Journal of Political Economy* 101: 443–472.

———. 1991. "Learning by Doing and the Dynamic Effects of International Trade." *Quarterly Journal of Economics* 106: 369–406.

Zhu, X. 2012. "Understanding China's Growth: Past, Present, and Future." *Journal of Economic Perspectives* 26 (4, Fall): 103–124.

Zimmerman, M. B. 1982. "Learning Effects and the Commercialization of New Energy Technologies: The Case of Nuclear Power." *Bell Journal of Economics* 13: 297–310.

Notes on Contributors

PHILIPPE AGHION   Philippe Aghion is the Robert C. Waggoner Professor of Economics at Harvard University, having held previous appointments at University College London, Nuffield College, Oxford, European Bank for Reconstruction and Development (London), Centre Nationale de la Recherches Scientifique, and the Massachusetts Institute of Technology. His main research work is on economic growth and on contract theory. He is a fellow of the American Academy of Arts and Sciences and a fellow of the Econometric Society and recipient of the John von Neumann Award. He is coeditor of the *Review of Economics and Statistics*. He published with Peter Howitt the book *Endogenous Growth Theory* (MIT Press).

KENNETH J. ARROW   Kenneth J. Arrow is a Nobel Laureate in Economic Sciences and Professor Emeritus at Stanford University. He was awarded the Nobel Prize in 1972 "for pioneering contributions to general economic equilibrium theory and welfare theory." Arrow began his graduate study in economics and statistics at Columbia University. He has held positions on the Cowles Commission for Research in Economics and at the University of Chicago, Harvard University, and Stanford University. His research, apart from social choice theory, has focused on general economic equilibrium. The profound transformation of the general equilibrium theory is marked by his groundbreaking work. He helped open new productive paths for research in this area and, in so doing, has made fundamental contributions to the renewal of the theory. Kenneth Arrow earned his Ph.D. at Columbia University.

BRUCE C. GREENWALD   Professor Bruce C. Greenwald holds the Robert Heilbrunn Professorship of Finance and Asset Management at Columbia Business School and is the academic director of the Heilbrunn Center for Graham & Dodd Investing. Described by the *New York Times* as "a guru to Wall Street's gurus," Greenwald is an authority on value investing with additional expertise in productivity and the economics of information. Greenwald has been recognized for his outstanding teaching abilities. He has been the recipient of numerous awards, including the Columbia University Presidential Teaching Award, which honors the best of Columbia's teachers for maintaining the university's long-standing reputation for educational excellence.

ROBERT SOLOW   Robert Solow is Professor Emeritus at Massachusetts Institute of Technology. He was awarded the 1987 Nobel Memorial Prize in economics for contributing to what is still the standard method of analyzing the mechanics of economic growth and for exhibiting the importance of research and technological innovation in improving economic productivity. In 1961, he received the John Bates Clark Award, given to the best economists under age 40. Mr. Solow also served on the staff of President John F. Kennedy's Council of Economic Advisors and was president of the American Economic Association in 1979. In 2000, he was awarded the National Medal of Science. Since 2000, Solow has been a Foundation Fellow at the Russell Sage Foundation.

JOSEPH E. STIGLITZ   Joseph E. Stiglitz received his Ph.D. from MIT in 1967, became a full professor at Yale in 1970, and in 1979 was awarded the John Bates Clark Award. He has taught at Princeton, Stanford, and MIT and was the Drummond Professor and a fellow of All Souls College, Oxford. He is now University Professor at Columbia University in New York and cochair of Columbia University's Committee on Global Thought. He is also the founder and copresident of the Initiative for Policy Dialogue at Columbia. In 2001, he was awarded the Nobel Prize in economics for his analyses of markets with asymmetric information, and he was a lead author of the 1995 *Report of the Intergovernmental Panel on Climate Change*, which shared the 2007 Nobel Peace Prize. In 2011, *Time* named Stiglitz one of the 100 most influential people in the world.

MICHAEL WOODFORD   Michael Woodford is the John Bates Clark Professor of Political Economy at Columbia University. His first academic appointment was at Columbia in 1984, after which he held positions at the University of Chicago and Princeton University, before returning to Columbia in 2004. He received his A.B. from the University of Chicago, his J.D. from Yale Law School, and his Ph.D. in Economics from the Massachusetts Institute of Technology. He has been a MacArthur Fellow and a Guggenheim Fellow and is a Fellow of the American Academy of Arts and Sciences, as well as a Fellow of the Econometric Society, a Research Associate of the National Bureau of Economic Research, and a Research Fellow of the Centre for Economic Policy Research.

Index

Baily, Klinger, 35
Baltic countries, 30–32, *31*;
    convergence to high performance
    level, 33–34
Bayh-Dole Act, 54, 433, 439
Bayraktar, Nihal, 403
belief systems and social constructs,
    460–63; beliefs versus reality,
    62; biased perceptions, 70–71;
    capitalism and selective framing
    of evidence, 71; cognitive frames,
    61–62, 72–74; *The Entrepreneurial
    State: Debunking Public vs. Private
    Sector Myths*, 445; equilibrium
    fiction, 71, 73, 75, 471, 481;
    invisible hand notion, 18–19;
    mindsets, 9, 48, 57, 61–63, 73, 457–
    59, 472; persisting beliefs, 465–66
benefit tax, 450
Berners-Lee, Timothy, 136
Bertrand equilibria, 195–96, 234, 236;
    asymmetric Bertrand equilibria
    and nonexclusivity, 200–202, *201*;
    Cournot competition compared
    to, 191–96; distinct features of,
    191; marginal return to increased
    investment in R & D, *208*, 208–9,
    209; multiple potential entrants:
    contestability, 198–200, *199*;
    stochastic research and, 207–10,
    208, *209*; symmetric equilibrium,
    198
Bertrand price-competition model,
    103, 110–12, 116, 119
best practices: catching up to, 38–39;
    cross-border knowledge flows, 93;
    failing to learn, 32; gap between
    average and, 18, 44, 81–82; gap
    between productivity and, 29–30,
    80; microscopic perspectives, 34;
    model farms, 54; productivity
    growth total versus hours paid, *39*

biased perceptions, 70–71
BlackBerry, 435
Bloom, Nicholas, 506
BNDES. *See* Brazilian Development
    Bank
Boyle, James, 433
BRAC genes, 145
Brazil, 500; development banks, 395;
    industrial policies and, 390–91;
    infant aircraft industry, 502–3;
    sugar-based ethanol development,
    388
Brazilian Development Bank
    (BNDES), 395
Britain: aggressive protection and
    subsidies, 389; factor endowments
    in, 24; financial market
    liberalization example, 403–4;
    terms of trade, 4. *See also* United
    Kingdom
broad tariff protection, 4–5, 500–501
bureaucracy, innovation and,
    84–85, *85*
Burns, Arthur, 504

Canada, *39*
capital: 2008 global financial
    crisis, 42, 96, 151, 372, 405, 418,
    491, 495; access, 401; controls,
    405; Frontier moved out by
    investing in, 40–43, 92; improved
    allocation of, 42; for R & D,
    79, 408
capitalism: aftermath of 2008 crisis,
    42, 96, 151, 372, 405, 418, 491,
    495; capital flows: failure of
    standard theory, 407–15; China's
    state-directed, 389; crony, and
    corruption, 375; innovation as
    heart of, 57, 101; managerial,
    478; recessions and depressions,
    40; Schumpeter's optimistic

First Annual Arrow Lecture,
485–87
fixed labor supply, no lump sum
taxation, two sectors, 324–26
Florida, 404–5
follow-on innovation, 432–33, 451
Ford, Henry, 82
foreign banks' advantage, 404;
restrictions on, 412
foreign direct investment (FDI),
40–41, 66, 420, 477; Africa's,
422; China's, 507; government
subsidies to promote, 423; Japan
and, 421; Korea's, 421; Malaysia
and, 423
France: Colbertist policy, 509; G_7
countries productivity growth
comparison, *39*; opposing
government intervention, 510
Frankel, Jeffrey A., 493
free trade: equilibrium, *339*, 342;
financial market liberalization,
402–5, 407, 414–17, 475, 477;
knowledge as free good, 507;
learning and, 54–55; in learning
economy, 54–55; possibilities
curve, *339*, 342; Schumpeter on,
101–2; utility value and autarky,
340, 340–41, 345; Washington
Consensus, 23, 80, 374–75, 402,
405, 481, 493, 509–10. *See also*
liberalization; trade policies
the Frontier, 40–43, 92
funds diversion, 405–6

G_7 countries, 37–38; productivity
growth comparison, *39*
Gates Foundation, 447
GDP. *See* gross domestic product
geographic and cultural localization,
65–66
Georgia, 404–5

Germany: factor endowments, 24;
G_7 countries productivity growth
comparison, *39*; industrialization
strategy, 27; manufacturing value
chain, 495; opposing government
intervention, 510
global environment: 2008 global
financial crisis, 42, 96, 151, 372,
405, 418, 491, 495; clean versus
dirty technologies, 517–21;
imbalances in production, 361–62,
501–2; learning economy benefits,
61; McKinsey Global Institute,
501–2; modern science on climate
change, 62; societal learning about
new products, 49; WCED, 442
GNP. *See* gross national product
Google, 71
government intervention, 4–5, 9,
98–99, 481; aggressive protection
and subsidies, 389, 511; arguments
for, 42–43; banking and financial
policy, 404–5; Brazil's aircraft
industry, 502–3; Brazil's ethanol
industry, 388; carbon tax, 517–21;
in catching-up countries, 333–34,
509–21; clean innovation subsidy,
517–21; climate change, 495,
517–21; closed economy, 265, 476;
countercyclicality and, 520–21; to
create learning economy, 87, 479;
to create learning society, 404,
476; criticisms of, 489, 511–12;
delayed intervention impacting
consumption, *518*; development
banks, 395, 411, 412; economy
during World War II, 37–38;
encouragement of learning sector,
272; evidence-based general theory
of growth and employment,
160–61; in financial policy, 404,
476; -funded research, 444–45;